RISK AND

INSURANCE

Mark R. Greene

Professor of Insurance and
Head, Department of Marketing
and
Industrial Management
University of Oregon

SOUTH-WESTERN PUBLISHING CO.

CINCINNATI 27   NEW ROCHELLE, N. Y.

CHICAGO 44   BURLINGAME, CALIF.

DALLAS 2

F30

Preface

Writing in the area of risk and insurance is a hazardous task for several good reasons. Not the least of these reasons lies in the implied promise of the author to render simple that which is not so simple, to be reasonably complete in an area that is changing rapidly, and to offer something new in a field whose major outlines have in the past been well established. A casual observer might justifiably be suspicious of an author attempting to create certainty out of uncertainty when his very subject material deals extensively with risk and the difficulties in handling it.

Nevertheless, the author has attempted in this book to accomplish three main goals. First, in recognizing that one book in insurance is the maximum number that most college students will ever study, the author has tried to cover the basic ideas, problems, and principles found in *all* types of modern-day insurance and other methods of handling risk. The basic problems caused by risk in our world have been emphasized first, before posing solutions. Thus, Chapter 14 deals entirely with the liability risk, while Chapter 15 treats liability insurance as one of the solutions to the problems of negligence liability. Again, Chapter 19, treats the problems of the destruction of human life values, while Chapters 20 through 24 consider life and health insurance as solutions to the problems. In this way the author hopes that those who are first undertaking a study of risk and insurance will come away with an understanding of what problems there are which insurance can help meet and thus will see why a nation such as ours is devoting such a large portion of its resources to risk reduction and loss-spreading activities. It is hoped that the student will obtain some help in solving his own personal problems of risk management, as well as develop an appreciation of risk and insurance in society.

The second goal in writing this book is to present in considerable detail some of the fundamental unifying elements of risk and insurance. In areas with so many diverse features, some attempt at unification is almost a necessity. To illustrate, all of Chapter 2 is devoted to a consideration of utility, probability, and the law of large numbers and their application to insurance and risk management. It is hoped that an understanding of Chapter 2 will help the student obtain a much more sophisticated perspective over such complex problems as rate-making, underwriting, and financial regulation than would be possible without such treatment. Another example of this unification is in Chapters 8 and 9, which are devoted to common legal elements of contracts, a study of which should permit the student to make more rapid progress in understanding any insurance policy than would otherwise be possible.

Third, the author has tried to stimulate further thought about the problems of risk and insurance through somewhat varied questions at the end of each chapter. It should be recognized that one book cannot (and perhaps should not) contain "all the answers" but rather should be a stimulus in encouraging the student to advance his knowledge of the subject. Many of these questions are not answered in the text but can usually be used to illustrate principles developed in the book or as additional examples of problems or policies in insurance.

The book is divided into six parts, as follows:
Part I   The Nature of Risk and Risk Bearing
Part II   The Insurance Institution
Part III   Fundamentals of Insurance Contracts
Part IV Major Property and Liability Insurance Contracts
Part V   Life and Health Insurance
Part VI Government Regulation of Insurance

The organization seems logical to the author, but individual teachers may find other orders of subject matter to their liking.

Exceedingly little use has been made of the device to present insurance by means of reprinting contractual provisions. It is felt that space can better be used to explain, interpret, and analyze than to describe too much policy language. Reference to standard policy forms is often a useful supplementary method of teaching risk and insurance, however, and kits of policies are available to interested teachers. In cooperation with the American Risk and Insurance Association, an organization of those interested in higher education for risk and insurance subjects, policy kits have been prepared and are available in quantity free for classroom use in college by writing to one or both of the following: (1) American Mutual Insurance Alliance, 20 North Wacker Drive, Chicago 6, Illinois, (2) The Insurance Information Institute, 60 John Street, New York 38, New York.

There are many who should be thanked for their kind assistance and inspiration to the author in the preparation of this book. Only a few can be specifically named here. I would like to express my gratitude particularly to Dr. John S. Bickley, the University of Texas, and Dr. Howard C. Launstein, Marquette University, for their constructive criticisms in reading the manuscript. I owe a debt of thanks to Dr. Robert I. Mehr, who taught me my first formal college course in insurance, and to Dr. John S. Bickley, who taught me my last formal college course in insurance, for their inspiration and for their patience with an obstinate pupil. I would also like to thank my students, both graduate and undergraduate, whose searching questions have prompted a more orderly treatment of risk and insurance than would otherwise have been possible.

Mark R. Greene

Eugene, Oregon
May, 1962

Contents

PART II   THE INSURANCE INSTITUTION

PART III   FUNDAMENTALS OF INSURANCE CONTRACTS

**PART IV   MAJOR PROPERTY AND LIABILITY INSURANCE
CONTRACTS**

Concepts in

Risk and Insurance

WHY STUDY RISK?

It has been aptly said, "The only thing certain in life, with the exception of death and taxes, is uncertainty." When a person gets married, goes into business, decides to attend college, buys a home, or does innumerable other things that affect his life in any important way, he is naturally somewhat apprehensive over the outcome. He is uncertain as to how this particular action will turn out, but he always hopes for the best. He has usually considered the various alternatives and made up his mind only after weighing the advantages and disadvantages of each course of action. We say that this individual is facing the uncertainties of the future, that is, the different kinds of *risks*. Usually he is happier after making a decision that he is almost certain is correct. He likes the oft heard advice, "Be sure you're right, then go ahead." Conversely, he usually dislikes decisions that he has to make "in the dark," those with more risk attached.

As an illustration, consider the various uncertainties that enter into the purchase of a home. The family breadwinner must make the decision whether or not to buy a certain home in the environment of uncertainties such as:

1. Is the level of my income high enough and certain enough to enable me to make the payments for 20 years?
2. Will my health permit me to continue to work for 20 years?
3. How can I protect the investment for my family's benefit in case I should die before the loan is repaid?
4. How can I protect my investment in case of fire, flood, windstorm, or other peril?
5. Is it possible that my investment will lose value through neighborhood deterioration, or because of a job transfer and consequent forced sale of the property?
6. Would it be better to rent rather than to buy, and use my funds for other purposes? If so, what risks characterize the alternative uses of my funds?
7. In order to have exactly the type of house I want, should I take the risk of building a home rather than buying?

Oftentimes, if the potential home buyer cannot find satisfactory answers to these and other questions, he may decide that "the risks are too great" and fail to purchase a home. Indeed, the subject of risk is of great importance to an "economic man." Risk has an element of distastefulness (economists would call it disutility) that make him want to eliminate it. The more completely he can avoid risk, the better.

Because people usually try to avoid all the uncertainties they can, the subject of risk and its wise management has received important consideration by social scientists for many years. They have tried to identify what types of risks there are, just what is meant by risk and other related terms, and how to avoid or to handle risk in some satisfactory manner. Insurance is one of the chief methods that has been used to handle risk, but it is a subject of much complexity and consequent misunderstanding. Much of this misunderstanding stems from the failure of its users to appreciate the basic nature of risk and the relationship of insurance to other methods used to handle risk. In other words, before we can handle risk successfully, we must know precisely what it is with which we are dealing. This inquiry leads into a consideration of other terms, such as probability, the law of large numbers, peril, and hazard. These concepts of risk and insurance are discussed below.

THE NATURE OF RISK

Although the term *risk* is used in many ways in this book, *risk* is defined as the *uncertainty* as to the occurrence of an economic loss. The economic loss may take many forms, such as the loss of property by physical perils such as fire, tornado, or explosion. It may take the form of premature death of a key man in a business enterprise, or of a family breadwinner. It may result from a lawsuit to recover damages for some negligent act. Whatever its form, the risk of economic loss is something most people wish to avoid. Hence, it becomes especially important to have a clear understanding of its nature.

THE DEGREE OF RISK

What is meant by a "high degree" of risk, or a "low degree" of risk? It is not proper to state that risk is high when it is very likely, or almost certain, that a loss will occur. For in this case, there is little uncertainty about the occurrence of the loss, and actually the degree of risk is quite low. Conversely, if it is nearly impossible for a loss to occur, its chances being one in a million, it is improper to say risk is low; for one never knows whether or not the loss will happen to *him*.

For example, assume that Jack Smith goes into his basement one morning and smells smoke. His house is on fire. He realizes suddenly that he has not purchased fire insurance, so right after phoning the fire department he phones his insurance agent and says, "Cover me." The agent says, "Sorry, Jack, we can't insure a burning building." Did the agent refuse because the risk was too high? Not at all. In this case, there is no risk at all, for there is no uncertainty as to loss. The loss has already occurred. Furthermore, there is very little risk that more damage will occur before the firemen arrive. The agent cannot bind his insurer in such a situation. As obvious as this example may seem, there are many similar cases each year where individuals seek insurance on an event that is almost certain to cause loss. They have failed to distinguish between an event that is subject to risk and an event that is *probable*.

RISK DISTINGUISHED FROM PROBABILITY

It is necessary to distinguish carefully between risk and probability. Many elementary mistakes in risk management occur because of failure to recognize the difference between these two concepts. As will be developed in Chapter 2, *probability* refers to the long-run chance of occurrence of some event. Insurers are particularly interested in the probability, or chance, of loss, or more accurately, the probability that some peril will occur and cause a loss to one of a group of insured objects. An insured, on the other hand, is more interested in the risk, or uncertainty, as to whether the loss will happen to him individually. In other words, the insurer is most closely concerned with probability, and the insured, more closely concerned with risk. Actually, probability has little meaning if applied to the chance of occurrence of a single event. It has meaning only when applied to the chance of occurrence of a *large number* of events.

Risk, as differentiated from probability, is the uncertainty that a given event, one of many possible events, will or will not occur. This uncertainty can be measured by statistical means which will be elaborated and explained further in Chapter 2. Briefly, the degree of risk associated with an event is a measure of the degree to which this event will occur in a manner different from what is predicted. It may be, for example, that there are 1,000,000 persons age 25 in a certain economy and it is predicted from past experience that 3,000 of them will die in a given time period. The probability of loss is thus .003. An individual may be interested in the risk that he will be among the 3,000 who are supposed to die. An insurer who has 10,000 persons covered under life insurance contracts may be interested in the risk that some number, *other* than the probable number, namely 30, will die within the given time period. Clearly, the probability of death is the same, no matter from whose viewpoint one is speaking. The risk, however, is quite different for the insurer and the insured.

The reason that the risk is different is understood, almost intuitively, by recognizing that the "law of large numbers" is operating in the case of the insurer, but not in the case of the individual insured. The *law of large numbers,* a basic law of mathematics, says that as the number of exposure units increases, the more certain it is that actual loss experience will equal probable loss experience. Hence, the risk diminishes as the number of exposure units increases. The individual seldom has a sufficient number of exposure units to reduce his risk significantly through the operation of the law of large numbers. He may join with other individuals, however, and obtain this advantage. Basically the insurance mechanism is the device through which such a grouping task can be effectively accomplished.

THE BURDEN OF RISK

To some, the idea of risk bearing and risk assumption is tantalizing, an element which makes life more interesting. What these individuals have in mind mostly is the uncertainty of making a profit or a gain, and not the uncertainty of incurring disastrous losses. In this book, we will be dealing with the latter type of uncertainty. Recognizing that risk assumption carries with it the possibility of losses as well as gains, most individuals constantly seek ways of avoiding the former in as efficient a manner as possible, without destroying the possibility of gain.

How does risk create an economic burden? It does so in several ways. In the first place, risk necessitates the setting aside of a reserve fund to meet losses if and when they do occur. Such a reserve fund, if it were not used for this purpose, could be employed in other ways, presumably at greater advantage than its use as a demand deposit in a bank, or as an investment at low interest rates in a form readily convertible into cash.

Secondly, the existence of risk not only raises the cost to society of certain services, but may also deprive society altogether of services "too risky" to warrant the investment of savings. There is, in general, a shortage of "risk capital" in all nations, with most investors preferring greater or lesser degrees of safety. This attitude was epitomized by a saying attributed to Mark Twain, who commented that he was more interested in the return *of* his money than he was in the return *on* his money. In other words, because there are various degrees of risk attaching to business enterprise, the riskier the venture, the greater the return that must be promised to investors; hence, the more costly that particular service is to society. And if risk is too great, the service may be withdrawn altogether.

Two examples will illustrate the burden of risk. For several hundred years in the early history of the United States, the western part of the nation was left unsettled, in spite of the existence of great natural resources and potential wealth. Risk was high, and physical hardships for settlers were routine. It was not until railroads were built and law enforcement established that risk was reduced sufficiently to encourage large-scale settlement. A current example of the burden of risk is found in experimentation with peacetime uses of atomic energy. Even the largest corporations, before making substantial investments in this field, have demanded protection against what might be ruinous liability suits resulting from atomic accident.

An additional burden of risk is the lowered feeling of well-being and mental unrest that accompanies risk. One of the greatest human drives is to achieve security. A feeling of security seems necessary before most people can work efficiently and perform creative achievements. As long as a society is forced to spend a major share of its energies fighting its enemies or struggling against the elements for survival, it is classed as a relatively primitive society. The same generalization applies to an individual. This perhaps explains why men struggle hard to achieve an advanced civilization and to cultivate a secure atmosphere in which creativity can be expressed and wherein relative abundance can be established.

RISK DISTINGUISHED FROM HAZARD AND PERIL

Many persons commonly employ the terms "risky," "hazardous," and "perilous" synonymously. For clarity in thinking, however, the meaning of these words should be carefully distinguished.

A *peril* may be defined as a contingency which may cause a loss, and a *hazard* is that condition which makes the occurrence of the peril more likely. Both of these terms are more closely related to probability than they are to risk. For example, one of the perils that can cause loss to an auto is collision. A condition that makes the occurrence of collisions more likely is an icy street. The icy street is the hazard and the collision is the peril. In winter, the *probability* of collisions is higher owing to the existence of icy streets. In such a situation, the *risk* of loss is no higher or lower, since we have defined risk as the uncertainty that underlying probability will "work out" in practice. Thus, if an insurance firm predicts higher collision losses in a northern area than in a southern area (if it estimates higher probability of loss), and it has a large enough number of automobiles insured in the northern area, normally the actual number of losses will equal what was predicted. The risk, as such, is no different than it might be in a southern area where probability of such loss is much lower.

TYPES OF HAZARDS DISTINGUISHED

In the paragraph above, a hazard was defined as a condition that makes the occurrence of a peril more likely. This definition might also be expanded to include conditions that make the loss more severe, once the peril has occurred and has caused a loss. What are the various types of hazards which not only increase the probability of loss, but also increase the severity of loss, once it occurs? Although there have been many classifications used, there seem to be only three basic types of hazards: 1) physical, 2) moral, and 3) morale.

1) Physical hazard

A *physical* hazard is a condition stemming from the physical characteristics of an object that increases the probability and severity of loss from given perils. Physical hazards include such phenomena as the existence of dry forests (hazard to fire), earth faults (hazard to earthquakes), and icebergs (hazard to ocean shipping). Such hazards may or may not be within the control of man. Many hazards to fire, for example, can be controlled, such as by placing restrictions upon building camp fires in forests during the dry season. Some hazards, however, cannot be controlled—little can be done to prevent or to control ocean storms.

2) Moral hazard

A *moral* hazard stems from the mental attitude of the insured. Because of indifference to loss or owing to an outright desire for the loss to occur, the individual either brings about his own loss or intentionally does nothing to prevent its occurrence or to alleviate its severity even if he could do so.

Moral hazards are typified by individuals with known records of dishonesty or indifference. Such hazards may exist in situations where excessive amounts of fire insurance are requested on "white elephant" properties, properties no longer profitable and where an incentive might exist to "sell the building to the fire insurance company." Every underwriter knows that fire losses are more frequent in depression periods, for example. During the depression of the 1930's, life insurers had such a substantial rise in the frequency of claims for disability income that the coverage had to be withdrawn almost completely. This action resulted from excessive coverage granted during a period of high incomes. When incomes fell, apparently many insureds felt they were worth more disabled than whole and so caused their own disabilities.

3) Morale hazard

Even though an individual does not *consciously* want a loss, nevertheless there may be a *subconscious* desire for a loss with the result that losses tend to be higher among a group with this mental attitude. The *morale* hazard includes such hazards as the mental attitude that characterizes an accident-prone person. This type of individual does not appear to cause deliberately the accidents that frequently happen to him, but the psychologist would probably diagnose the cause of excessive and repeated accidents as a subconscious mental desire to gain attention.

The morale hazard also includes a situation, which insurers are trained to recognize almost instinctively, where those who are in a position to have a loss and who need protection against it, tend to be the only ones in a larger group who apply for protection. Thus, those in the low areas of flood zones may be the only applicants for flood insurance. Among applicants for group health insurance, there is a tendency for those in good health to be outnumbered by those who have bad medical histories, and hence will be ultimately causing a majority of the claims under the policy. Insurers refer to such a situation as *adverse selection* and, of course, take all sorts of precautions against it. Without such precautions, the loss tends to become certain, and hence uninsurable, as will be discussed shortly.

PURE RISK VERSUS SPECULATIVE RISK

A distinction has been made between pure risk and speculative risk which further clarifies the nature of risk.[1] In *pure risk,* there is uncertainty as to whether the destruction of an object will occur; a pure risk can only produce loss, should the peril occur. Examples of pure risk include the uncertainty of loss of one's property by fire, flood, windstorm, or other peril, or the uncertainty of total disability caused by accident or illness. In *speculative risk* there is uncertainty about an event under consideration that could produce either a profit or a loss, such as a business venture or a gambling transaction. The distinction is significant because usually the pure risk is insurable, while the speculative risk is normally handled by methods other than insurance. This brings us to the subject of the various ways of handling risk.

WAYS OF HANDLING RISK

One individual cannot reduce his risk alone, unless he controls a large enough number of exposure units. Obviously it is impossible for most people to meet this condition. After all, we have but one life. Most people own no more than one house; and even if two or three autos are owned, this is an insufficient number to allow the law of large numbers to "work."

The question arises then, "What alternatives are there for handling risk?" For convenience, the ways of handling risk may be grouped under the following four headings:

1) Assuming the risk.
2) Combining the objects subject to risk into a large enough group to enable accurate prediction of the loss. This method includes the insurance mechanism.
3) Transferring or shifting the risk to another individual.
4) Utilizing loss-prevention activities.

1) Assuming the risk

This method (also called noninsurance) is perhaps the most widely used of all ways to handle risk. Most people go through life assuming a wide variety of risks, perhaps not realizing they are even doing so. The limitation of funds usually prevents one from using other methods except for those risks where the severity of loss, should it occur, is very burdensome.

---

[1] Albert H. Mowbray and Ralph H. Blanchard, *Insurance* (5th ed.; New York: McGraw-Hill Book Company, Inc., 1961), p. 6.

Laying aside a fund in a bank to meet some possible loss is not "self-insurance," but is really assumption of risk. Many persons erroneously believe that they have used "insurance" in such a case. Insurance, however, is not possible unless a large enough number of exposure units can be grouped, and most individuals cannot meet this requirement by themselves. An example will make it clear why the setting aside of a "rainy day" fund is not insurance. If a person saves $1,000 in the bank to pay for a hospital bill, he has no way of knowing whether or not this fund is adequate. A single period of hospitalization could easily exhaust his savings, and a second period of hospitalization might occur before the savings could be restored. Thus, he has not actually reduced the risk of loss of savings due to an illness requiring hospitalization. However, a properly drawn insurance plan, in which the risk of loss is effectively transferred to another, will take care of any number of hospitalizations.

2) Combining the objects subject to risk

The method of combination is the system of handling risk that usually involves the use of large numbers. As pointed out previously, when sufficiently large numbers are grouped, the actual loss experience over a period of time will closely approximate the probable loss experience. To the extent that this is true, risk has been greatly reduced or even eliminated for all concerned.

One of the clearest illustrations of the combination method of reducing risk is found in the practices of early Chinese merchants. These merchants took periodic trips inland to gather merchantable products for sale on the coast. In traveling down the Yangtze River, the merchants would gather above the rapids and redistribute their cargoes so that each boat had a small portion of the other merchants' cargo aboard. Thus, if one boat were lost in the rapids, no one merchant would have suffered a total loss. This simple cooperative scheme saved many traders from ruin, and increased the profits of all.

Commercial insurance companies utilize the combination method as the basis of their insuring operations. These companies simply persuade a large number of individuals, known as *insureds* or *assureds,* to pool their individual risks in a large group, and in that manner reduce or eliminate their risks. The insurance company has little if any risk in a pure sense of the word. The risk simply disappears because risk is defined as the uncertainty of loss surrounding an *individual* object. When all of the individual objects are pooled into one group, the risk is no longer present, providing certain other requirements (to be discussed in Chapter 3) are met. This process may be compared to an alliance of a group of nations to ward off the danger of attack. Individually, each nation may have substantial risk, but in a group the risk to each one is greatly reduced.

A commercial insurer is not the only social or economic institution which can employ the combination method of handling risk. Large business organizations frequently have a sufficiently large group of insurable objects so that they can accurately predict loss experience. For example, a firm may make a study of automobile collision losses to determine for a given period of time just what losses may be expected from a large fleet of autos owned by the concern. From these data the firm makes careful estimates of the funds needed to meet these losses and lays aside funds for this purpose. It does this with relative certainty that, within narrow limits, the fund so set up will actually equal the losses to be suffered. This method of handling risk has been termed *self-insurance* and is to be distinguished from the practice of laying aside a "rainy day" fund to meet some emergency with no assurance that the fund will be adequate if the emergency should occur and cause a loss. This latter plan has been called *noninsurance* and is actually assumption of the risk.[2] Self-insurance is treated in considerable detail in Chapter 4.

The method of combination also has been used to meet various types of *uninsurable* risks,[3] such as the risk of losing one's markets due to product obsolescence, or by actions of competitors. The wave of business mergers in recent years has been attributed in part to the desire to reduce such market risk.[4] Thus, two or more firms may combine into one for the purpose of securing a more diversified product line, so that in the event the sale of one product is unprofitable, another might compensate for it. The uncertainty of loss from one unprofitable line is thus reduced.

3) Transferring or shifting the risk

In the *transfer* or *shifting* method, one individual pays another to assume a risk that the transferor desires to escape. The risk bearer agrees to assume the risk for a price. The risk of loss is often the same to the

---

[2] M. R. Greene, "Risk Management," *Best's Insurance News, Fire and Casualty Edition* (July, 1955), p. 116.
[3] See Chapter 3 for a discussion of these risks.
[4] Federal Trade Commission, *Report of Corporate Mergers and Acquisitions* (May, 1955), pp. 103–143.

transferee as it was to the transferor. The risk bearer (transferee), however, may have superior knowledge concerning the probability of loss, and thus may be in a better financial position to assume the risk than the transferor. Nevertheless, the risk still exists.

It is easy to confuse the transfer method of handling risk with the combination method. The essential difference between the two lies in the fact that in the transfer method, the risk is not necessarily reduced or eliminated; whereas in the combination method, the risk is actually greatly reduced or perhaps almost completely eliminated.

Examples of risk transfer are found in many phases of business activity. A furniture retailer may not wish to stock large quantities of furniture for fear that prices may fall before he can dispose of his stock, or that the stock will be unsalable due to style changes. He therefore buys only limited quantities of goods at a time, thus forcing a wholesaler to carry sufficient inventories to meet his demands. The wholesaler in this case is the bearer of risk of loss due to price changes. The risk of loss is not necessarily reduced to the wholesaler. Such risk of loss must be charged for ultimately in the form of higher prices than would prevail if the retailer bought in large quantities. The wholesaler may attempt in turn to shift the risk backward to the manufacturer.

Insurance companies themselves often operate as transferees of risk, rather than utilize the combination method, simply because it is impossible to obtain a sufficiently large number of exposure units in order to allow the law of large numbers to operate. If Lloyd's of London accepts an insurance contract covering the loss to the hands of a famous pianist, they are acting in the capacity of risk transferees, not as agents to pool the risks of large numbers of pianists. In commercial insurance operations, it is often difficult to tell just where the combination method ends and the transfer method begins, for there are many instances in which an insurance concern has an insufficient number of exposure units to obtain extremely accurate predictions of loss experience. To the extent that the loss cannot be predicted accurately, the insurance company owners act as transferees. Again, the risk is not necessarily reduced.

4) Utilizing loss-prevention activities

It is sometimes erroneously believed that loss prevention is "good insurance." However, while loss-prevention activities normally produce reductions of *probable* losses and alleviate the severity of these losses, they do not affect the degree of risk. For example, the work of the National Safety Council has been beneficial in reducing the probability of accidental deaths on the highways. Medical research and public health measures have reduced the probability of death and sickness from disease. These activities, however, have no direct effect on *risk* in the sense we have defined it. The risk of loss is the uncertainty that in a given time period, actual losses will equal probable losses. Even though probable losses are reduced, or increased, as the case may be, risk may yet be present since there is still the *possibility* that there may be substantial deviations from underlying probability.

However, risk of loss is eliminated if loss-prevention activities reduce the probability of loss to zero. One may eliminate the risk of having an auto accident by eliminating the *possibility* of exposure; that is, by never riding in a car or venturing upon a street where autos travel. If a sure-fire vaccine against arthritis were discovered and universally applied, there would be no risk of becoming ill from this source because the vaccine would have reduced to zero the probability of having the disease. Thus, risk may be eliminated by first eliminating the possibility of loss.

SUMMARY

1. Risk is the uncertainty as to the occurrence of an economic loss.
2. Probability is the long-run chance that out of a given number of possibilities, a certain number of specific events will occur.
3. Risk and probability should be distinguished from hazard and peril, terms often used synonymously. A peril is an event that causes a loss, while a hazard is a condition that makes the occurrence of a peril more likely or increases the likelihood of loss once a peril occurs.
4. Risk is measured in terms of the degree of variation that actual events bear to probable events.
5. The larger the number of exposures, the smaller is the variation that actual events bear to probable events; that is, the smaller the risk. The law of large numbers states that for a very large number of exposures we can predict within very narrow limits the actual number of occurrences of an event that we wish to identify.
6. Since risk imposes an economic burden on society and upon individuals alike, it becomes important that ways of handling risk in a scientific manner be developed.
7. Risk may be handled in at least four different ways: by assumption, by combination, by transfer, and by loss-prevention activities. Insurance is primarily an example of the combination method, but insurance companies utilize the transfer method and loss-prevention activities as well.

QUESTIONS FOR REVIEW AND DISCUSSION

1. Is it ever possible that a condition which could be a hazard in one case is a peril in another case? Give some example.

2. Is there any point in studying risk management as a science when the state of our knowledge of future events will always remain uncertain? Why?

3. What words, if any, should be substituted for *risk* or *risky* in the following statements to make them accurate? Why?
   (a) When boys play with fire in a dry forest, a high degree of *risk* is present.
   (b) An icy highway is a *risky* factor in driving safety.
   (c) To underwrite this *risk* (building) is dangerous.
   (d) Flood is a *risk* we won't take.
   (e) You don't have a large enough group of people to enable us to reduce the *risk* sufficiently to handle this on a group basis.

4. A certain investor took great pleasure in "playing the stock market," especially in highly speculative issues. He expressed the feeling that it was the risk he took which gave him the most fun.
   (a) Do you think this feeling is genuine?
   (b) Would you suggest an alternative explanation for the pleasure that many take in gambling?

5. What type of hazard is illustrated in each of the following situations?
   (a) An "accident-prone" driver.
   (b) A known embezzler applying for a job as cashier.
   (c) The owner of several lumber mills that have burned over the years precisely when lumber prices declined sharply.
   (d) A teen-age driver.
   (e) A tinder-dry forest.
   (f) A retail liquor dealer in a poor neighborhood.
   (g) A northern shipping route in winter.

6. (a) Differentiate between pure risk and speculative risk. Why is such a distinction important? Explain.
   (b) In what way is insurance related, if at all, to speculative risk?

7. (a) Distinguish between assuming the risk and self-insuring the risk.
   (b) In what basic way are these two concepts different?

8. What economic institutions other than insurance companies have used the combination method of handling risk? Explain.

9. In what sense is a business merger a risk-handling device? Explain.

10. It has been said that our defense expenditures are actually "insurance" premiums against the peril of war. Is this true? Why? If not, how would you classify such costs? Explain.

Probability, Risk,

and Insurance

Questions such as the following are often asked by students of risk and insurance:

What right does an insurance company have to assume that, just because it had a certain pattern of losses in the past, it will have a similar pattern in the future?

In determining the probability of loss in a certain group, what mathematical assumptions are made? Are they valid? Can they be applied universally?

What limitations, if any, are there in applying the "law of large numbers?"

How many exposure units must an insurer have to obtain "relatively accurate" predictions as to the losses in an insured group?

How does one measure the risk that the insurer assumes?

How can one justify paying more for insurance than is indicated by calculating the "mathematical expectation" of loss?

In order to answer some of the questions posed above, a fairly refined treatment of some basic concepts in probability, risk, and insurance is necessary. Probability theory is intimately related to many underwriting, rate making, and legal principles in insurance. A working knowledge of probability is essential if one is to obtain more than a superficial understanding of insurance and risk management. Accordingly, this chapter presents a few of the basic concepts underlying probability without attempting a rigorous mathematical development of the subject. A discussion of the role of utility analysis and its relationship to probability analysis as applied to the problem of insurance buying is also included.

PROBABILITY

Laymen are apt to define probability in a very simple manner such as "the chance of occurrence of an event" or the "long-run chance of occurrence." Intuitively, most people understand that a "probable" event is one which is "most likely" to occur. However, such definitions are not very useful in analyzing and solving a scientific problem because they are too vague. Before we can employ probability in a useful manner, a more refined definition is necessary. Certain terms must be introduced and explained. Only in this way can major errors be avoided in using probability theory as a tool of risk management.

Definition

Our definition of probability begins with the concept of a sample space and an event. Imagine a set, S, of possible events or outcomes of a given description. Such a set might consist of a listing of the number of collisions of all automobiles registered in a certain state during a given year. We refer to this set as the *sample space* of the events in which we are interested. Other sample spaces might consist of all the deaths among individuals aged 21 in the United States, or the sinkings of all ships of a certain description while traveling on the North Atlantic route.

Next, consider a smaller segment of the total set, which we may call E, a *subset* of S. In the case of automobile insurance, such a subset might describe the number of collisions involving all high-priced automobiles—those costing $4,000 or more when new. The total set S describes the number of collisions among all automobiles in a certain state in a given time period. We wish to know what the probability is that there will be a collision of a car priced higher than $4,000. To determine the probability, we shall assign a number called a *weight* to each individual event in the set S. This weight might be assigned according to some empirical evidence concerning our past knowledge of the likelihood of loss among automobiles, such as the region in which the automobile is driven or the type of driver. Let the expression $W(S)$ be the sum of all weights in the set S, and $W(E)$ represent the sum of all weights in the subset E. Then the probability p that a high-priced auto will be involved in a collision would be represented by the expression

$$p(E) = \frac{W(E)}{W(S)}$$

If it is presumed that all the simple events in the set S are equally likely, this formula may be reduced to a simple ratio of the number of outcomes in the subset E to the total number of outcomes in the set S, or simply,

$$p(E) = \frac{E}{S}$$

Alternatively, we can express the probability q, that there will be no loss to a high-priced automobile, as

$$q(E) = \frac{S - E}{S}$$

To illustrate, assume that set S consists of 10,000 automobiles, 9,000 of which cost under \$4,000, and 1,000 of which cost \$4,000 or more when new. Assign a weight of one to all cars under \$4,000 in value and a weight of two to all cars over \$4,000 in value. The probability that there will be a collision to a high-priced automobile, is by our definition:

$$p(E) = \frac{W(E)}{W(S)}$$
$$= \frac{2 \times 1,000}{(2 \times 1,000) + (1 \times 9,000)}$$
$$= \frac{2,000}{11,000} = \frac{2}{11}$$

If all events received equal weight,

$$p(E) = \frac{E}{S} \qquad\qquad q(E) = \frac{S - E}{S}$$
$$= \frac{1,000}{10,000} = \frac{1}{10} \qquad = \frac{10,000 - 1,000}{10,000} = \frac{9,000}{10,000} = \frac{9}{10}$$

Thus, there is a $\frac{2}{11}$ probability that there will be a loss to a high-priced car (and a corresponding probability of $\frac{9}{11}$ that there will be no such loss) when different weights are applied to different types of events contained in the set. If equal weights are assigned to all events in the set, or sample space, the probability of loss to a high-priced car turns out to be $\frac{1}{10}$ (and the probability of no such loss is therefore $\frac{9}{10}$). The significance of weights is illustrated by these examples. It is through changing of weights that the insurance underwriter can accurately reflect his evaluation of the probability of occurrence of the various events in which he is interested.

Description of events

The preceding definition of probability involves the assumption that some one of the events in the set S is bound to occur. Furthermore, it is assumed that the events are described in such a way as to be *mutually exclusive*, which means that both events cannot happen at once. For example, the events "loss to a high-priced car" and "loss to any car" are not mutually exclusive since any car may also include a high-priced car. The two events could happen simultaneously. The quantity expressed as $W(E)$ in the formula on page 16 refers to events which are mutually exclusive of one another.

As another example, consider the probability of death. The event "a person dies" and "a person lives" are mutually exclusive and they exhaust all possibilities. A person either lives or dies; he cannot do both at once. Assuming equal likelihood of events, it is proper to state that the probability of death can be expressed as a simple fraction of the number of people dying during a given time period out of some total number living at the beginning of the period. For example, if there are 100,000 people living at the beginning of the year and 2,000 die, the probability of death for that group would be 2 per cent and the probability of survival is therefore 98 per cent. On the other hand, if we were told that out of 100,000 people, 2,000 catch the flu and 5,000 catch colds, we cannot say that 7 per cent catch *either* a cold *or* the flu because the events are not mutually exclusive. It is possible (and very likely) that there are people who catch a cold *and* also catch the flu. Unless we know this number, we cannot determine the total probability of catching either a cold or the flu. This leads us to the following basic rule, referred to as the *additive rule:*

> The total probability of occurrence of two or more mutually exclusive events is the sum of the respective probabilities of the separate events.

If the events are not mutually exclusive, other methods of defining the probabilities must be formulated.

As an example of the additive rule, assume that there is a well-mixed deck of playing cards, and we wish to calculate the probability of drawing either an ace or a king on a single draw. Since there are four aces and four kings, the probability of drawing an ace would be $4/52$ or $1/13$, and the probability of drawing a king would also be $1/13$. We are assuming that it is just as likely to draw an ace or a king as any other card, since the deck is well mixed. Under the additive rule the total probability of drawing either an ace or a king is, therefore, $2/13$. We know that it is impossible to draw a card marked ace-king, since there is no such card in the set. The event "draw a card which is an ace" is mutually exclusive with the event "draw a card which is not an ace." We must have one event or the other, and never both, on a single draw. As another example in coin tossing, the event "flip a head" is mutually exclusive with the event "flip a tail." The probability of flipping either a head or a tail is ½ + ½, or 1. It is assumed that it is impossible for any other event to occur, such as "flip and the coin stands on end." Therefore, the sum of the probabilities of each separate event in a set is always one, as shown below.

Positive weights

It is assumed in probability theory that all assignments of weights to individual events in a set will be positive. Since probability is expressed as a ratio of events in a subset to events in the total set, it can be seen that the probabilities of all events when added together must equal one. If an event is certain to happen, its probability will be one; if the event cannot happen, its probability is zero. It follows that the sum of p, the probability that an event will occur, and q, the probability that it will not occur, equals one.

In summary, we may say that there are three axioms upon which the definition of probability is built. These are:

1. Probability is a number between 0 and 1 that is assigned to an event.
2. The sum of the probabilities assigned to a set of mutually exclusive and collectively exhaustive events must equal 1.
3. The probability of an event which is composed of a group of mutually exclusive events in a set is the sum of the individual probabilities.

Probability is approximate

Only in rare instances can it be said that probability is known absolutely. For example, in drawing balls from an urn containing six red balls and four white balls mixed at random, it can be said that the probability of drawing a white ball is .4.

$$p(\text{white ball}) = \frac{W(E)}{W(S)} = \frac{E}{S} = \frac{4}{10} = .4$$

In real life such precision is seldom possible, however, because it is difficult to determine precisely just how many lives will be lost out of a group, what percentage of autos will be wrecked in a given year, or what proportion of total employees will steal. What is done is to observe how many lives are lost out of a sufficiently large group, how many cars are wrecked, and how many employees steal. These losses are then expressed as a percentage of the total number of exposure units in order to obtain an *empirical* estimate of probability.

From an empirical standpoint, probability may be looked upon as the long-run frequency of events, expressed as a percentage. If an event happens w times out of a possible number of cases, n, the empirical probability may be expressed as the fraction w/n. It should be recognized, however, that this fraction represents historical data. Its use in predicting future events is necessarily limited to an approximation unless the past exactly repeats itself, which is a most unlikely situation. It should also be recognized that because the probability is, say, $3/4$ that a given event will happen, this does not imply that we can expect the event to happen exactly three out of four times in a small number of cases. If n is small, there may be large variations from the probable number of events. It is only as n approaches infinity that the fraction w/n can express the empirical probability with precision. This observation, termed the law of large numbers, is further discussed below.

Independent events

A concept of great importance in probability and in its application to insurance is that of *independent events*. Two events are said to be independent when the outcome of one event in a group of possible events does not affect our assessment of the probability of the next event. For example, flipping a coin and obtaining a head should not affect our assessment of the probability of securing heads on the next flip. Even if we have obtained 10 heads in a row, our assessment of the outcome of the next flip should not change since there is nothing to persuade us that the probability of heads on the next flip is any different from the probability on prior flips—that is, it is still 50 per cent. The coin "has no memory" and is not impelled to "make up for past results."

An example of events which are *not* independent is that of drawing balls from an urn without replacing each ball after each draw. Thus, if there are five white balls and five red balls in an urn, the probability of drawing a white ball on the first draw is $5/10$. If a white ball is drawn but not replaced, the probability of drawing a white ball on the second draw is now $4/9$. The result on the first draw affected our assessment of the probability on the second draw.

An example in insurance in which exposures will not produce independent losses would be the case of insuring a group of employees against illness, after it has been determined that two or three employees have contacted typhoid. The fact that typhoid is spreading affects our assessment of the probability of further losses. The losses are certainly not independent of one another in this case.

Independent trials

Just as two or more events in a given set may be independent of one another, the outcomes of a succession of experiments may be considered independent of one another. In such a case the sample space is defined in terms of successive *trials*, and the outcomes are the various results that can occur in such trials. For example, consider a coin-flipping experiment in which we flip two coins twice. The sample space may be defined as Heads, Heads; Heads, Tails; Tails, Heads; Tails, Tails. Thus, there are four possible "events" in these two trials. We may assign a probability of ¼ to each event. If we are interested in the event of all outcomes in which heads appear, the probability we would assign to this event would be ¾.

Randomness

Events are said to occur at random when equal probabilities are assigned to each event in the sample space. If we are just as likely to draw one ball from an urn as any other ball, we may say that our selection is random. If the balls were marked in some way or were not mixed thoroughly, the trials might not be random since perhaps the balls on top would have different characteristics than the balls at the bottom.

If an insurance company agreed to insure everyone who passed by a certain street corner, would it have a random selection from a set comprising all the people in that city? Decidedly not, since during the daytime, men and children would probably not be properly represented and those who were unemployed might be "overrepresented." There is *not* an equal probability that *any* person may be selected. Similarly, if an insurance company is considering applications for life insurance that are given voluntarily without prior solicitation, can it consider that these applications constitute a random selection from a set comprising the insurable population? No, because those who have a tendency to be in poor health would be more likely to apply than those who are in good health.

Randomness and independence of events
—their significance in insurance

Randomness and independence of events are of crucial importance in insurance. Underwriters make every attempt to classify exposure units into groups in which the losses may be considered independent random events. In this way a uniform charge to each member of the group can be easily justified, since each member knows that the loss is just as likely to happen to him as to any other. If the probability of loss to himself were less than to the others, an insured would be unwilling to pay the same premium as all the rest.

Another result of randomness in insured groups is that a loss is just as likely as not to be suffered twice by the same insured. If a person is struck by an automobile this month and if automobile accidents are randomly distributed, the person has the same chance of being struck again next month as he had this month. Thus, it may be false reasoning to assume that if one has suffered a loss, it will not be "his turn again" for a long time.

Compound probability

If two or more independent events may happen simultaneously or in sequence, the probability that all events will occur is the product of their separate probabilities.

To illustrate, suppose we wish to know the probability of obtaining two heads in a row in a coin-flipping experiment. Since the events are assumed to be independent, the joint probability is $\frac{1}{2} \times \frac{1}{2} = \frac{1}{4}$. Similarly, if the probability of "A" living to age 65 is $\frac{3}{4}$ and the probability of his wife living to age 65 is $\frac{4}{5}$, the probability of *both* "A" and his wife living to age 65 is $\frac{3}{4} \times \frac{4}{5} = \frac{3}{5}$, always assuming independence.

The events "living to age 65" and "not living to 65" are mutually exclusive.[1] We can observe that the probability of "A" *not* living to 65 is $1 - \frac{3}{4}$, or $\frac{1}{4}$; similarly, for "A's" wife the probability of *not* living to 65 is $1 - \frac{4}{5}$, or $\frac{1}{5}$. Therefore, the separate compound probabilities should be additive, as indeed they are, as demonstrated below:

Event	*Probability*
Both "A" and wife live to 65	$\frac{3}{4} \times \frac{4}{5} = \frac{12}{20}$
"A" lives to 65, wife does not	$\frac{3}{4} \times \frac{1}{5} = \frac{3}{20}$
"A" does not live to 65, wife does	$\frac{1}{4} \times \frac{4}{5} = \frac{4}{20}$
Neither "A" nor wife lives to 65	$\frac{1}{4} \times \frac{1}{5} = \frac{1}{20}$
	$\frac{20}{20} = 1$

There are four possible events, each pair of which is mutually exclusive. One and only one of these four events is possible. The total probability is therefore one.

The application of compound probability in insurance may be seen in a contract known as the joint and last survivorship annuity. In this contract an insurer writes an annuity on two lives, usually a husband

---

[1] If the events are not mutually exclusive, other rules of probability are available to aid in the task of assigning probability values to the events.

and wife, and promises to pay an income to the two individuals as long as either one is alive. Thus, the probability of survival of two lives jointly becomes important.

Repeated events

If we know the probability is p that an event will happen in a single trial, then the probability that the event will *not* happen can be stated by the equation $q = 1 - p$. We can calculate the probability that the event will happen r times in n independent trials by means of the binomial formula.[2] The binomial formula uses the rules of compound events and the additive property of mutually exclusive events discussed on page 21.

It is of importance in insurance to estimate the probability of certain numbers of losses in an insured group. If there are 10,000 automobiles being insured, the binomial formula (or other approximating formulas) may be used to calculate the chance of 10 losses, 100 losses, 200 losses, or any other number of losses, providing we know both p and q. Similarly, if there are 10 exposure units, such as houses, and we know from past experience that the separate probability of loss of any one house by fire each year is .01, reference to a binomial table tells us that the probability is:

.37 that the number of houses that burn will be none
.37 "   "   "   "   "   "   "   "   " one
.19 "   "   "   "   "   "   "   "   " two
.06 "   "   "   "   "   "   "   "   " three
.01 "   "   "   "   "   "   "   "   " four or more

Total 1.00

The above schedule is a sample of a *probability,* or a *frequency distribution,* in this case, a theoretical probability distribution known as the *binomial distribution.* It is only one of the many types of probability distributions used in insurance, but one of the most important. In order to use the binomial formula, it is assumed that the following conditions are met:

    1. There are two possible events, or outcomes, which are mutually exclusive.

---

[2] The binomial formula is: Probability of r "successes" in n trials equals $\dfrac{n!}{r!(n-r)!} p^r q^{n-r}$.

The expression $n!$ is read "n factorial." The word factorial refers to a successive multiplication of the numbers $n, n-1, n-2 \ldots 0!$. Thus, 4! means $4 \times 3 \times 2 \times 1$, or 24. 0! is conventionally defined to be 1. Tables of binomial probabilities are generally available for obtaining the values in the above formula for small values of n (150 or less). For larger values of n, other formulas, such as the Poisson or normal density functions, are used as an approximation.

2. The probability of each event is known, or can be estimated.
3. Since each event is independent of all other events, the probability of each event does not change from trial to trial, but is constant throughout the entire process. Because the probability of occurrence is known, and since there are only two events, we also automatically know the probability that the event will *not* occur (one minus the probability that it will occur).

It can be seen that if a series of repeated events follows the Bernoulli process [3] (that is, meets the above conditions), the insurer will have a powerful tool for predicting the frequency of losses. Even when all the conditions above are not met perfectly, the binomial theorem is extremely useful in making educated guesses as to the frequency of losses. For example, in insurance the true probability of loss is never known *exactly,* since even for large numbers of exposure units, there will be some variation. Yet, a mathematical model can be of great help to the insurer in making estimates that otherwise would have to be made without much guidance.

Expected value

The *expected value* of an event is determined by preparing a schedule of possible outcomes and by weighting each outcome by its probability. The results are then added and a quantity known as the expected value of the event is obtained.

In the preceding example relating to house fires, assume that the average dollar loss per fire is $1,000. The insurer might reason as follows: since there is a .37 chance of one loss, the expected value or cost of this loss is $370. If the loss occurs, the insurer must pay $1,000; but the insurer is not at all positive that the loss will occur. Therefore, the insurer assigns a probability to the loss should it occur, and the result is that he weighs the probability of one loss and evaluates it at $370. Similarly, the expected cost of two losses is .19 × $2,000, or $380; three losses, .06 × $3,000, or $180, etc. Such calculations are used in making estimates of total losses and provisions are made for charging each insured an appropriate premium. In the binomial distribution, the total of all the expected losses is the number of trials, or events, times the expected long-run frequency (.01 in the above example) times the money outlay per loss. If there are 10 houses, each fire in which causes an average loss of $1,000, theoretically, the total expected cost of the losses is 10 × .01 × $1,000, or $100. Of course, if the insurer had only

---

[3] The events in the binomial process are called Bernoulli trials, after Jacob Bernoulli, who was one of the first mathematicians to formalize this theorem.

10 houses, he could not be at all sure that $100 is the proper premium, because of insufficient exposure. In addition, the insurer would have to make an adjustment for his costs of doing business. These problems are considered in detail in Chapter 26.

Expected value enters into our daily life in many significant ways. For example, suppose a contractor is asked to build a house. If all goes well and no unusual conditions arise, he figures that he will earn $1,000 profit on the contract with a probability of .9. There is, however, a .1 probability that he may spend an unplanned amount such as $1,000 on extra excavation costs if soil conditions are poor. Thus, the expected value of the contract is $900 — $100, or $800 as shown in the following table.

EXPECTED VALUE OF CONTRACT

PROBABILITY	OUTCOME	EXPECTED VALUE
.9	+$1,000	+$900
.1	−$1,000	−$100
1.0		$800

The contractor may consider the opportunity of building this house along with several other opportunities for the employment of his capital. Other things being equal, the contractor will probably accept the proposition that offers the highest expected value. He might also be willing to pay up to $100 as a sort of insurance premium to someone to assume the risk of loss in case soil conditions are poor. In this way the contractor may feel that he can plan with greater certainty.

Expected value considerations must often be modified in making a decision because a decision maker may not want to run *any* probability of a very large loss, even though he may also have a probability of gain large enough to offset it. For example, the contractor may not be willing to accept the contract under any conditions if there is a .90 probability of making $10,000, but a .1 probability of losing $20,000, even though the expected value of the contract is $9,000 — $2,000, or $7,000. This may be true because he could not afford a $20,000 loss if it should occur.[4] The analytical tool necessary to treat this problem is the concept of *utility,* which is discussed later in this chapter.

---

[4] See Robert Schlaifer, *Probability and Statistics for Business Decisions* (New York: McGraw-Hill Book Company, Inc., 1959), Chapter 2 for a discussion of the concept of expected value and utility in decision making. In addition, Samuel Goldberg, *Probability: An Introduction* (New York: Prentice-Hall, Inc., 1960), Chapter 5 has an excellent discussion of the binomial distribution and its applications, including decision-making under uncertainty.

RISKS OF THE INSURER

Under the somewhat unrealistic conditions imposed by the binomial distribution, the probability of having *exactly* one house burn in a consideration of only 100 houses is .37. There is a probability of .26 that two or more houses will burn. This is true even though the long-run probability (mathematical expectation) of loss is exactly one house. Thus, we can begin to see why an insurer must be concerned primarily with large numbers of exposures. With only a few exposures, the insurer cannot be at all certain that he will realize, in practice, his mathematical expectation of loss. His risk may be defined as the uncertainty attached to the proposition that actual losses equal probable losses.

While consideration of the binomial model is an interesting, theoretical tool in explaining some basic results in risk and insurance, in the real world the assumptions of this system do not usually hold, or hold only imperfectly. For example, in the real world, we do not know in advance what the true *p,* probability of loss, is; but we must estimate it. This estimate involves statistical errors. Not only are there risks introduced by these errors, for a given time period, but the insurer is also faced with the problem that the underlying probability is constantly shifting. It may be .01 in one time period, .005 in another time period, and .015 in another time period. Calculations of the estimated probability are invariably made for a past time period; but the insurance contract must cover a future period, and there are frequent changes, such as changing legal conditions, inflation, and changed attitudes toward loss, which must be judged individually.

In the real world, the insurer cannot be certain that losses are indeed independent events. The probability of loss in a binomial distribution is assumed to remain constant for each trial. However, in a group of insured exposure units, the probability may change after one or two losses have been experienced because loss-prevention measures may be introduced, or people may become more careful than they were before the loss.

Another reason why the assumptions of the binomial model do not usually hold in the real world is that there may not be a sufficient number in an insured group so that the mathematical expectation of loss will be realized with the required degree of certainty.

All of the various ways in which the underlying assumptions of probability estimates may not be realized in practice may be said to constitute the *risks of the insurer*. It is sometimes argued that the insurer has no risk since he can combine sufficient numbers of exposure units to make losses nearly perfectly predictable. This is a gross oversimplification of the real situation, as the previous discussion has indicated. In fact, one of the basic reasons why insurance is a science is the necessity of devoting great study to the ways in which the insurer's risks may be met successfully in practice. Many tools of analysis from other disciplines are used to help reduce the insurer's risks. For example, in life insurance, a medical analysis of the physical condition of the applicants for insurance helps ensure that those accepted are, as nearly as can be determined, homogeneous in nature, and not subject to nonrandom influences which would distort the loss experience on which premiums are based. Many important concepts from mathematics are used in reducing the insurer's risk. As we have seen, the theoretical binomial distribution and other distributions, such as the Poisson and the normal, are used. Some of the implications of the normal distribution are explored below.

The law of large numbers

One of the risks of the insurer is that he does not know in advance what the true probability of loss is. He must estimate this true probability by experimentation, the results of which are never exact and involve certain degrees of uncertainty. The law of large numbers is of vital significance in analyzing this problem, because it tells the insurer that he can obtain as precise an answer as he deems necessary by increasing the number of "observations" indefinitely.[5]

The law of large numbers tells us that if we do not know the underlying probability of occurrence of certain events, we can estimate it more and more precisely by increasing the number of our observations in a sampling process. The average value of a very large number of observations will approximate very closely the true average of the population from which the observations were taken. To illustrate, assume that we do not know how many people age 25 will die in a given year (that is, the probability of death at age 25) but that we are trying to estimate the number. We observe a group of 500 persons age 25 during one year and none of them die. The next year we observe another group of 500 25-year olds and this time two die. In the third year we observe another similar group and one dies. If this experiment is repeated a very large number of times, we may note that although there are fluctuations from

---

[5] The law of large numbers is generally attributed to Jacob Bernoulli, *Ars Conjectandi,* 1713.

group to group, on the average one in 500 dies. Empirically, we are justified (given independence of the events) in assuming that the probability of death of *all* persons age 25 is $\frac{1}{500}$, or .2 per cent.

The foundation of insurance rests upon the law of large numbers. The insurer, in effect, obtains a very large number of observations by virtue of the fact that, in the above case, mortality records of millions of people at different ages are available for analysis. These records are summarized in mortality tables, and are available for use by life insurers. The insurer usually has a very large number of random samples, and knows that he has a fairly accurate measure of the underlying probability of loss.

Number of exposures required for a given accuracy

A question of considerable interest, both to the commercial insurer and the would-be self-insurer, is how large an exposure (that is, how many individual exposure units) is necessary before a given degree of accuracy can be achieved in obtaining an actual loss frequency that is sufficiently close to the expected loss frequency. It is well enough to say that as the number of exposure units becomes indefinitely large, the actual loss frequency will equal the expected true loss frequency; but it is never possible for a single insurer, whether he is a commercial insurer or a self-insurer, to group together an "indefinitely" large number of exposures. Undoubtedly many individuals are under the mistaken assumption that they are in a position to self-insure if they have under their own control, say, 10 automobiles. These persons think that certainly it would be unusual for more than one or two automobiles to be lost in a given time period, or that no more than one damage suit would befall them. That this position is a dangerous one will be illustrated shortly.

The question arises, how much error is introduced when the insured group is not sufficiently large? More precisely, an insurer might wish to ask, "How many exposure units must be grouped together so that I can be 95 per cent sure that the number of actual losses will differ from expected losses by no more than five per cent?" It is assumed that the expected losses for a very large population of exposures are known, or can be estimated from industry-wide data, or can be determined subjectively. Essentially, the insurer wishes to know how stable his own loss experience will be. Certain mathematical and statistical laws help provide an answer to this question. While the assumptions required by these laws may not always hold in the real world, they enable the insurer to make an approximation which will be of considerable help to him in making a sound decision. The required assumption is that the losses occur in the manner assumed by the binomial theorem. In other words, each loss occurs independently of each other loss, and the probability of loss is constant from occurrence to occurrence. Stated in mathematical terms, the losses are to be viewed as Bernoulli trials.

Normal distribution

It can be shown that if losses behave in the manner assumed, they will be distributed approximately normally.[6] What is meant by being "distributed approximately normally"? Figure 2–1 illustrates graphically the general shape of a normal, or bell-shaped, distribution. In a normal distribution the frequency of occurrence of the measured events is distributed symmetrically in the general shape of a bell about the mean value.[7] In Figure 2–1 the frequency of occurrence, or probability of loss, is shown on the vertical axis, and the number of losses appears on the horizontal axis. If there are 100 exposure units, each of which has a probability of occurrence of loss of .30, the mean number of losses is 30. The probability that exactly 30 losses will occur is .09; that exactly 26 losses will occur is .06; that exactly 25 losses will occur is .05; etc. Summing all the probabilities in this manner will result in a total probability of one, since the events are mutually exclusive and collectively exhaustive and independent. Note that the number of losses on the graph starts with 20, since the probability that less than 20 losses will occur, when the expected number of losses is 30, is very small, actually, .0089. Similarly, the number of losses ends around 40, since it is very unlikely, with probability .0125, that more losses than this number will occur. In theory, it is possible to have 100 losses out of the total number of 100 exposure units, and so the vertical bars would never reach the horizontal axis. The bars would be so close to it after the limits shown, however, that for all practical purposes the probability of having a loss of less than 20 or more than 40 can be ignored.

The significance of the fact that losses are normally distributed is that we can calculate within known tolerances, the probability that losses will fall within a certain range of their mean number. This will be explained by an example. Before the example is given, however, we must review what is meant by a statistical measure of dispersion known as *standard deviation*.

---

[6] For a mathematical proof of this, see E. Parzen, *Modern Probability Theory and Its Applications* (New York: John Wiley, 1960), pp. 239–245.

[7] There are other distributions which fit this description too. The precise meaning of a normal curve must be given by a somewhat complex mathematical formula. To avoid explaining this formula, an explanation is given in terms of the binomial, which, as has been noted, is closely approximated by the normal curve.

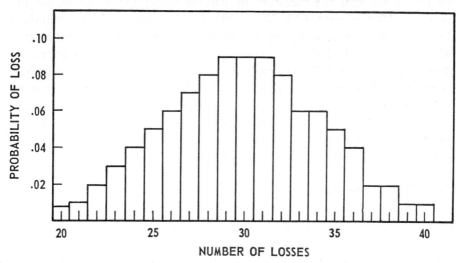

Figure 2–1

OCCURRENCE OF 30 LOSSES, BINOMIALLY DISTRIBUTED, WITH PROBABILITY .30, OUT OF 100 EXPOSURE UNITS

Standard deviation

Standard deviation is a number which measures how close a group of individual measurements are to their average value. For example, if a group of 10 trees is such that individual tree heights range from 6 to 100 feet, but the average tree height is 50 feet, we would find that the dispersion of individual tree heights is rather great. The trees range in height from 6 to 100 feet and to say that the "average height of the trees is 50 feet" is not very descriptive of the height of these trees. For example, in comparing the above group of trees with another group of 10 trees, which range in height from 45 to 55 feet, but whose average height is 50 feet, one naturally seeks a way to state precisely just how the two groups differ. The concept of standard deviation is probably the most important statistical tool used to accomplish this purpose. By comparing the standard deviation of the heights of the two groups of trees, one can indicate precisely how much variation in height occurs. It is possible to state, for example, that the height of three fourths of all the trees falls within one standard deviation of the mean height in one group, and that only 10 per cent of the trees fall within one standard deviation of the mean height of the other group. With such a statement, we have a much more accurate description of the average height of the two groups of trees than would be true if we simply compared the average height of the two groups.

Standard deviation is thus a gauge of the dispersion of measurements about the mean. If, for example, the standard deviation is 20 feet, we might say that the "scatter" of heights about the mean is, on the average, 40 per cent $(20/50 = .40)$ in the range of one standard deviation, 80 per cent in the range of two standard deviations, etc.[8] When standard deviation is expressed as a per cent of the mean, as above, statisticians call the result the *coefficient of variation,* which is one way to characterize the concept of mathematical risk to the insurer. If losses from a group of exposure units have a low coefficient of variation, there is less risk associated with this group of exposures than with another group with a high coefficient of variation, since the insurer can say with greater certainty just what his financial outlay is likely to be.

Confidence intervals

What conclusions can be drawn if the losses are normally distributed? In the normal curve it can be demonstrated that roughly 68 per cent of all losses will fall within a range of one standard deviation from their mean number; approximately 95 per cent will fall within two standard deviations of the mean; and about 99 per cent will fall within three standard deviations of the mean. If we know the standard deviation of a distribution, we are able to make *confidence interval* statements. For example, we can say with 68 per cent confidence (or probability) that our events will fall within one standard deviation of the mean, with 95 per cent probability that our events will fall within two standard deviations of the mean, etc.

Figure 2–1 illustrates a binomial distribution, which although similar in shape to a normal distribution, is not actually a normal distribution.[9] However, since the normal distribution is a good approximation of the binomial distribution, we can employ the principles which apply to the normal distribution to illustrate the nature of confidence interval statements. In Figure 2–1 the expected number of losses out of an in-

---

[8] To obtain the standard deviation of a group of measurements, first find the average value by adding the values of all individual items and dividing by the total number of items. Each individual value is then subtracted from this average and the resulting figure is squared. These squared differences are added and the result is divided by the number of items. We then have the mean of the squared deviations, which is known as the variance. The square root of the variance is the standard deviation. *Example:* Find the standard deviation of five numbers, 0, 1, 2, 3, 4. *Solution:* Mean is 2. Sum of squared deviations from mean is 10. Average of squared deviations is 2, the variance. Standard deviation is 1.414 (the square root of 2).

[9] A normal distribution is continuous in nature, while the binomial distribution is defined in such a way that each trial must be counted separately as an integer, and is called a discrete distribution. It is for this reason that the range of standard deviations must be expressed in whole numbers.

sured group of 100 units is 30. The standard deviation is approximately 4.6 losses.[10] Thus, the probability is .68 that the actual number of losses will be within the range of about 26–34 (approximately one standard deviation range); .95 that the actual number of losses will be in the range 21–39 (approximately a two standard deviation range); and .99 that the actual number of losses will be in the range 16–44. Due to rounding, these figures are only approximate.

With only 100 exposures and with a probability of .30, the insurer cannot be too sure just how his losses will turn out. He expects 30, but he cannot be more than 95 per cent confident that his loss experience will be even within the range of roughly 21–39, a coefficient of variation of 30 per cent. This is a rather wide dispersion and might not satisfy the insurer's standards of accuracy. He may be satisfied with a 95 per cent confidence interval, but he may want this interval to be somewhat narrower than that stated above.

A simple mathematical formula is available which will enable the insurer to estimate the number of exposures required for a given degree of accuracy. Unless mathematical tools such as the one given below are used with great caution and are interpreted by experienced persons, wrong conclusions may often be reached. The formula is given only as an illustration of how such tools can be of help in guiding an insurer to reduce his risk. The formula is based on the assumption that losses in an insured population are distributed normally.[11] The formula is concerned only with the occurrence of a loss, and not with an evaluation of the *size* of the loss, which is an entirely different problem beyond the scope of this book. The formula is based on the knowledge that the normal distribution is an approximation of the binomial distribution, and that known percentages of losses will fall within one, two, three, or more standard deviations from the mean. The formula [12] is

$$N = \frac{s^2}{4e^2}$$

---

[10] Actually the standard deviation is 4.58, obtained by a mathematical shortcut. The mean loss, or expected loss, in the binomial distribution is given by the quantity np (number of trials times the long-run probability), or in this case, $(100)\,(.30)$, or 30. The standard deviation of a binomial distribution is secured from the formula: $\sqrt{np(1-p)}$, or in this case, $\sqrt{(100)(.30)(.70)} = 4.58$.

[11] Of course, there is no guarantee that losses will necessarily be distributed normally. Statistical tests can establish the existence or nonexistence of a normal distribution of past loss histories, on which assumptions can be made concerning a given future expectation for a loss experience. If the tests of a binomial distribution are met, however, losses will be approximately normally distributed.

[12] See E. Parzen, *op. cit.*, pp. 228–232, for the mathematical derivation of a similar formula.

Where: *N* is the number of exposure units sufficient for a given degree of accuracy.

e is the degree of accuracy required, expressed as a ratio of actual losses to the total number in the sample.

s is the number of standard deviations of the distribution. The value of *s* tells us with what level of confidence we can state our results. Thus, if *s* is one, we know with 68 per cent confidence that losses will be as predicted by the formula; if *s* is two, we have 95 per cent confidence, etc.

As an example, suppose in the above case, where our probability of loss is .30 (not an unusual probability in certain areas for collision of automobiles) we want to be 95 per cent certain that the actual loss ratio (number of losses divided by total number of insured units) will not differ from the expected loss ratio of .30 by more than two percentage points, that is, .02. In other words, we want to know how many units there must be in our insured group in order to be 95 per cent certain that the number of losses out of each 100 units will fall in the range 28–32. Substitution in the formula, $\dfrac{s^2}{4e^2}$, yields $\dfrac{2^2}{4(.02)^2}$, or 2,500 exposure units. The value of *s* is 2 in this case because of our requirement of a 95 per cent confidence interval statement—we know that 95 per cent of all losses will fall within a range of two standard deviations of the mean.

As another example, suppose we are satisfied with an accuracy of .05 for the value of *e*. In this case, the formula yields $2^2/4(.05)^2$, or 400 exposure units. If we are satisfied with an accuracy of .10, we would need only $2^2/4(.10)^2$, or 100 exposure units. If we wished to be "99 per cent sure" that our loss frequency will not differ from the expected loss frequency by more than .02, we would need $3^2/4(.02)^2$, or 5,625 exposure units.

In the above illustration, the probability of loss was very large. In many fields of insurance it is somewhat unusual to experience such large probabilities. It is much more common for the probability of loss to be about five per cent or less. If the probability of loss is only five per cent, the insurer will undoubtedly wish to insist on a higher standard of accuracy than was true in the preceding case. Thus, .03 might be satisfactory when the expected loss ratio is .30, because a deviation of .03 from a mean of .30 represents only a 10 per cent error (.03/.30 = .10). If the basic probability is only .05, however, an error of .03 in the above formula becomes a deviation of *60 per cent* away from the expected loss (.03/.05 = .60). Hence, the insurer may say that if the expected loss is .05, his standard of accuracy will be .005, or 10 per cent away from the expected loss. Substitution of .005 for *e* in the above formula yields, at a 95 per cent confidence level, $2^2/4(.005)^2$, or 40,000 exposure units as the minimum number necessary.

In life insurance it is interesting to observe that at a young age, such as 20, the probability of loss is less than .002. If a life insurer is to be 95 per cent confident that its actual number of deaths among all insured lives, age 20, is to be within .0002 (again, a 10 per cent standard of accuracy) of its expected death rate, it must insure $2^2/4(.0002)^2$ lives, or an astounding 25 million lives. Such a figure would be an impossible goal, since there are not that many persons at age 20 presently living in the United States. Obviously the above formula cannot be used slavishly, but merely as a guide to indicate the degree of insurer risk at various levels of insured groups. Various methods are used to reduce insurer risk when it is difficult or impossible to group a sufficient number of exposures. One way is to combine the classes of exposures so as to produce a broader base on which to calculate losses. Another way is to transfer an unwanted class of exposures to others through reinsurance, which is discussed in Chapter 7.

Credibility tables

The use of a mathematical model in determining the number of exposure units needed to achieve a given degree of loss stability is important in preparing credibility tables. *Credibility tables* indicate the degree of reliability that a rate maker can ascribe to loss experience on existing exposure units. For example, if a rate maker is to raise or lower an insurance rate, based on higher or lower loss ratios which he observes in the past year among his insured group, an important question which must be answered is, "Is this insured group large enough to produce a credible rate?" Mathematical and statistical techniques based on the same principles which underlie the formula used above are very useful in this regard (See Chapter 26).

Risks of the individual

The basic risk to an individual is the uncertainty which exists as to whether the loss will happen to *him*. He may know that the *probability* of loss is small, but he has no way of knowing where or on whom the "lightning may strike." If the *possibility* of a serious loss exists, even though its *probability* is small, the individual will generally seek some way of avoiding this possibility.

From the preceding discussion, it was seen that rarely will a private individual have a sufficient number of exposure units to achieve a high degree of accuracy in his statistical predictions as to loss. We may say that for the individual, risk is very high indeed. Hence, to avoid this risk he may seek insurance or use other methods of risk avoidance. Of course, an individual may not really care whether a loss occurs to him or not, since the amount of money involved may be very small in relation to his existing wealth. He may be unwilling to buy insurance against the occurrence of a small loss, such as fire insurance on a woodshed, even if the coverage is very inexpensive. Yet he may be willing to buy insurance on a new automobile, even if the mathematical expectation of loss is less than the premium he must pay, simply because he is unwilling to expose to loss an investment which is relatively large when compared with his total wealth.

For example, suppose that there is a two per cent probability that collision will completely destroy a person's automobile. The owner of a $1,000 auto may realize that the expected value of the loss is .02 × $1,000, or $20. Yet he may find that collision insurance would cost $40, because the insurer must charge enough to pay for all expected losses plus the costs of doing business. Should the owner insure? If a $1,000 auto represents a large portion of this person's total wealth, he likely will insure. If, however, the person is wealthy and has several other vehicles more valuable than this one, he may not insure. This situation suggests a very important fundamental principle of insurance. *Due to the element of risk, an individual may be willing to pay more to avoid a loss than the true expected value of this loss.* In fact, if it were not for this phenomenon, insurance could not exist. The insurer must always charge more for his service than the expected value of the loss. If an individual acted solely according to the criterion of expected loss, he might never buy insurance, assuming, of course, that he knows the expected value of the loss. In many cases, however, he will not know the expected value of the loss. Nevertheless, as will be developed below, risk is a burden on society and individuals are willing to pay money to avoid it.

Utility

Another way of studying the problem of risks to an individual is through the concept of utility, particularly marginal utility. *Marginal utility* refers to the subjective value to the consumer of the last unit of a commodity purchased. It is presumed that the value of each additional unit of a good has less value to the consumer (although the price is the same) than the unit of a good immediately preceding it. As more and more goods are purchased, a point is reached where the price of the article will not be worth its cost to the user. Thus, the consumer will buy no more goods at that price.

Use of the marginal utility concept in insurance is believed to have been first suggested formally by Daniel Bernoulli in a famous article written in 1738.[13] Bernoulli argued that each additional dollar of income received by an individual is worth less and less to him, in the same manner that additional units of a commodity are worth less and less to their user. Thus, a given dollar of income to a rich man is less valuable *to him* than the same income would be to a poor man. It follows that the *loss* of a dollar by a rich man is less serious than the loss of this same dollar would be to a poor man. Thus, the rich man's expected loss from an uncertain venture has less utility—is less serious—than the same expected loss from the same venture to a poor man. Therefore, the poor man will have a greater reason to insure against this loss than the rich man. If there are two gamblers of equal initial wealth who enter into a game with an equal probability of winning, the winner will "win" less than the loser will "lose" because the winner will obtain less utility from his new wealth than the loser has sacrificed.[14]

Bernoulli used an example of marine insurance to illustrate his point. In this example a Petersburg merchant has purchased commodities in Amsterdam which he could sell for 10,000 rubles if he had them in Petersburg. He therefore orders them to be shipped to Petersburg by sea, but is in doubt as to the wisdom of purchasing insurance. The probability of loss by sea perils is five per cent of the selling price, but the cheapest insurance he can obtain costs eight per cent, or 800 rubles. The insurance premium exceeds the expected value of the loss

---

[13] Daniel Bernoulli, "Exposition of a New Theory on the Measurement of Risk" (translated by Louise Sommer), *Econometrica*, Vol. XXII, No. 1 (January, 1954), pp. 23–36.

[14] The great classical economist, Alfred Marshall, reflects the opinion that gambling cannot be justified under marginal utility theory because the expected happiness derived from the winnings is always less than the unhappiness from losing, even in a fair game, *i.e.*, where the cost of entering into the game corresponds directly to the probability of winning.

The converse of this argument is ". . . A theoretically fair insurance against risks is always an economic gain. But, of course, every insurance office, after calculating what is a theoretically fair premium, has to charge in addition to it enough to pay profits on its own capital, and to cover its own expenses of working. . . . The question whether it is advisable to pay the premium which insurance offices practically do charge, is one that must be decided for each case on its own merits." Alfred Marshall, *Principles of Economics* (New York, MacMillan & Co., 1898), p. 210 n. Thus, Marshall indirectly refers to the willingness of individuals to pay more for insurance to avoid risk than the expected value of a loss. The amount they are willing to pay for insurance, then, depends on the loss of utility to the individual occasioned by the possibility of loss.

by 300 rubles (800 − 500 = 300). Bernoulli poses the question as to how much wealth the merchant must have before it is sensible for him to abstain from insuring the goods. Using a formula, he develops the answer—5,043 rubles of wealth. The formula rests on the argument that the utility resulting from a small increase in wealth is inversely proportionate to the quantity of goods previously possessed.[15] The conclusion that if the merchant has more wealth than 5,043 rubles he can afford not to buy insurance may not be satisfactory to all persons. This is the same as saying that a saving of $800 in insurance premiums is worth a possible loss of $10,000, one whose probability is five per cent, if the person has wealth of $5,000 or more. While Bernoulli's formula may not express adequately the utility curve of many individuals, it illustrates the fundamental truth that utility enters into decision-making with respect to insurance in an important way. We all recognize intuitively that we would be reluctant to purchase insurance on some trivial risk, such as the risk of losing a cheap fountain pen; but if the pen were encrusted with diamonds and represented 90 per cent of our wealth, we would surely seek to insure it against all insurable perils.[16]

Measuring utility

The question arises as to how utility analysis can be practically employed to study buying decisions in insurance. First, a way must be found to measure the utility of each buyer—that is, his attitude toward

---

[15] Specifically, the expected value of a risky venture is the geometric mean of the product of the possible gains and the possible losses. In Bernoulli's words, "Any gain must be added to the fortune previously possessed, then this sum must be raised to the power given by the number of possible ways in which the gain may be obtained; these terms should then be multiplied together. Then of this product a root must be extracted, the degree of which is given by the number of all possible cases, and finally the value of the initial possessions must be subtracted therefrom; what then remains indicates the value of the risky proposition in question." In the case of the merchant there are 95 ships which get through and 5 which are lost. If x represents the merchant's present fortune, $x + 10,000$ represents the wealth of the merchant if the ships get through. The expected value, using the above instructions, is $\sqrt[100]{(x + 10,000)^{95}x^5}$ (the 100th root of the product of the possible gains and the possible losses). The merchant's total fortune, with insurance, after paying the insurance premium of 800 rubles, is $(x + 9,200)$. Equating these two quantities and solving for x yields 5,043 rubles, the required initial fortune in order to justify taking the risk. In a similar way the insurer must have a fortune of 14,243 rubles to justify taking the merchant's risk for a premium of 800 rubles.

[16] John von Neumann and Oskar Morgenstern, in their classic book *Theory of Games and Economic Behavior* (Princeton University Press, 1944) developed some of the methods by which utility values could be assigned specific numbers. For an excellent summary and readable explanation of these methods, see Robert Schlaifer, *op. cit.,* Chapter 2. Also see Milton Friedman and L. J. Savage, "The Utility Analysis of Choices Involving Risk," *Journal of Political Economy,* Vol. LVI (1948), pp. 279–304 and reprinted in *Readings in Price Theory,* American Economic Association (Richard D. Irwin, Inc., Homewood, Illinois, 1952), pp. 57–96. The authors develop an interesting model purporting to explain why a low-income person might be willing both to purchase insurance *and* to gamble at the same time.

risk. For example, we have stated that a large loss is considered more serious than a small loss, but how do we determine how much more serious? Friedman and Savage have outlined a method for determining this value.[17] Essentially, this method involves determination of the point at which an individual is indifferent between two alternatives, a certain sum of money on one hand and an uncertain, but larger sum of money on the other. The method may be outlined as follows:

1. Select any two amounts, say $500 and $1,000, and assign an arbitrary value of utility of 0 and 1 respectively.
2. Select any intermediate amount, say $600. Find the utility of this $600 income.
3. Ask the individual if he would be indifferent between a certain income of $600 or a pth probability of $500 and a qth probability of $1,000. Find the value of p so that he would be indifferent. For example, see if the person would be indifferent between $600 and a $\frac{1}{10}$ chance at $500 and a $\frac{9}{10}$ chance at $1,000 (if he says he would prefer the latter, reduce the odds). Say the value of p turns out to be $\frac{2}{5}$. This means that he is indifferent between a certain income of $600 and a $\frac{2}{5}$ chance of $500 and a $\frac{3}{5}$ chance at $1.000. The actuarial value of the chance is $200 plus $600, or $800. But he would just as soon have a certain amount of $600 than an uncertain amount of $800. This is because of his particular set of values and outlook on uncertainty.
4. The value of the utility, because of our arbitrary initial assignments, is .6, arrived at as follows:
   $$U (600) = \tfrac{2}{5} U (500) + \tfrac{3}{5} U (1,000)$$
   $$U (600) = \tfrac{2}{5} (0) + \tfrac{3}{5} (1) = .6$$
   Where U ($) = a person's utility assignment to a given sum of money
5. Repeat the experiment for every value between $500 and $1,000.
6. To get utilities for values outside the range of $500–$1000, proceed as follows: Offer the consumer a chance p, of $500 and a chance, q, of say $10.000 and a certainty of $1,000, varying p until the consumer is indifferent between the two. Say p is $\frac{4}{5}$. This means that the consumer is indifferent between the certain amount of $1,000 and an uncertain amount of $400 ($\frac{4}{5} \times$ $500) plus $2,000 ($\frac{1}{5} \times $10,000) or $2,400.
   A utility of 1 has been assigned to an amount of $1,000 and 0 to $500; so,
   $$\tfrac{4}{5} U (500) + \tfrac{1}{5} U (10,000) = U (1,000)$$
   $$\tfrac{4}{5} (0) + \tfrac{1}{5} U (10,000) = 1$$
   $$\tfrac{1}{5} U (10,000) = 1$$
   $$U (10,000) = 5$$

---

[17] *Loc. cit.*

Graphically, the continuous values might appear as:

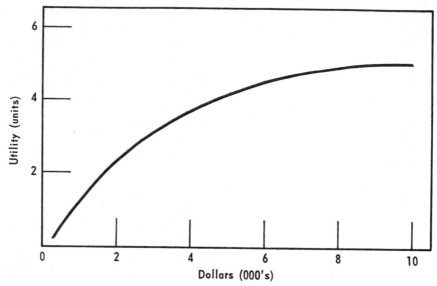

If an individual were "linear" in money, his utility curve in the above chart would be represented by a straight line instead of a curved line. However, it is believed that relatively few individuals have such an outlook on risk, for this would mean that a person would be completely indifferent between a certain amount of money such as $1,000 and a .01 chance of receiving $100,000. Few persons would pay $1,000 for a one per cent chance of winning $100,000. If the above argument is true, utility analysis must be taken into consideration in any decision involving risk, such as insurance.

To illustrate in a specific way the application of utility to an insurance buying decision, assume that Smith's outlook on risk has been measured by the above process and can be summarized as follows:

POSSIBLE MONETARY OUTCOME IF FIRE OCCURS	UTILITY POINTS ASSIGNED
− $50,000	− 2,000
− 10,000	− 300
− 5,000	− 60
− 1,000	− 10
− 500	− 3
0	0
+ 500	+ 3

Apparently Smith is not an extremely rich man because a serious loss of $50,000 means far more to him that a loss of more modest proportions, such as $10,000. A loss of $50,000 would mean a loss of utility to him of 2,000 points, whereas a loss of $10,000, one fifth as much as before, means a loss of only 300 points, 15 per cent of the utility loss of $50,000. Similarly, a loss of only $500 means a loss of utility of only 3 points. A loss of $500 is 5 per cent of the loss of $10,-000. The loss of utility assigned to $500, 3 points, is only 1 per cent of the utility loss of the 300 points which were assigned to $10,000.

Now suppose that, for a premium of $1,000, Smith can insure against a loss of $50,000, whose probability of occurrence is .01. Smith knows that the probability of loss is only one per cent and that therefore the long run likelihood of loss, if he were exposed to this loss for very many years, would likely cost him, on the average, $500. Should he purchase the insurance? According to Smith's utility curve, a loss of $50,000 means a loss of 2,000 utility points. In the long run he could expect to lose one per cent of these, or 20 points. In other words, the mathematical expectation of utility loss is 20 points. However, the utility points that he assigns to a premium outlay of $1,000 is only 10 points. Accordingly, he should certainly purchase insurance. *He should in fact purchase insurance on all risks until the expected utility of the premium outlay equals the expected utility of the loss.* This rule can be illustrated in the table below:

(1) Monetary Outcome if Fire Occurs	(2) Utility Points Assigned	(3) Proba- bility of Occur- rence	(4) Expected Value of Utility Lost by Fire (2) × (3)	(5) Insurance Premium		(6) Loss in Utility Points by Paying Premiums [from (2)]
				(As a per cent)	In dollars	
− $50,000	− 2,000	.01	− 20	2	$1,000	− 10
− $10,000	− 300	.05	− 15	10	1,000	− 10
− 1,000	− 10	.10	− 1	20	200	− 1
− 500	− 3	.20	− .6	40	200	− 1
− 200	− 1	.30	− .3	60	120	− .6

According to the above table, Smith should insure losses in the amounts above $1,000, but not below $1,000. Below $1,000, the insurance premium is "too high" since the utility loss by paying premiums exceeds the expected value of the utility loss of fire. For example, Smith is asked to pay $200 for insuring against a loss of $500 whose probability of occurrence is .2. The loss of utility by paying this amount is a certain amount, namely, one point. The expected value of the utility loss by fire, however, is only .6 points. This result occurs because the insurer is assumed to charge premiums at a rate which is twice the expected value of the loss in order to cover its operating expenses. At the same time it will be observed that Smith is more nearly "linear in money" as the possible loss approaches zero.

SUMMARY

1. The basic theorems of probability are of great importance in insurance, especially in rate-making, financial management, and contractual provision formulation. They are of crucial importance in protecting the solvency of the insurer by enabling more accurate predictions of losses, especially when empirical data are scanty and "educated guesses" must be made as to the course of future events. They give guidance to the underwriter in determining what constitutes an adequate number of exposure units in order to achieve financial stability. Probability theory is also an important guide to the would-be self-insurer in assessing the nature of his risk.

2. Probability is defined as the long-run frequency of certain events expressed as a percentage of the total number of possible events in a sample space, each of which has been assigned some number called a weight to reflect its relative importance in the total. Probability is a number between 0 and 1 assigned to an event.

3. When events in a sample space are defined to be mutually exclusive, the total probability of occurrence of two or more events is the sum of the respective probabilities of the separate events. This is called the additive rule in probability. The sum of such probabilities cannot exceed 1, and cannot be less than 0.

4. An important assumption in insurable events is that the events are independent and random. Independence means that knowing the probability of one event does not affect the assessment of probability of the next event in a sample space. Randomness means that each event in a sample space is just as likely to occur as any other event. Insurers try to classify exposure units in such a way that occurrence of losses will be independent and random.

5. If two or more independent events may happen simultaneously or in sequence, the probability that all events will occur is the product of their separate probabilities. Known as the rule of compound probability, this statement underlies the more complicated methods of determining the probability of occurrence of a given number of events out of a larger number of events in the sample space, a device most useful to the insurer who is interested in the probability of occurrence of more than one loss.

6. The concept of expected value is basic to probability calculations. Expected value of an event or a series of events is calculated by preparing a schedule of possible outcomes, multiplying each outcome by its probability, and summing.

7. The chief risks of the *insurer* are: (a) the uncertainties involved in estimating the probability of an event, (b) the uncertainties involved in determining that the events to be insured are independent and random, or that they conform to other mathematical assumptions, and (c) the fact that the insurer may not have a sufficient number of exposures to predict losses with a required degree of certainty. The coefficient of variation is one way to characterize the risk of the insurer in obtaining a sufficient number of exposure units for mathematical accuracy.

8. The chief risk of the *insured* is the uncertainty attached to whether or not a given loss will occur to him individually. Since this risk is generally very large due to the inability of the average insured to obtain a sufficient number of exposure units to obtain accurate predictions as to occurrence of losses, ways are sought to reduce risk through insurance and other means. It is not the probability of loss which causes difficulty, but rather the *uncertainty* as to whether an individual will be among those who are expected to suffer loss. Losses which are certain can be prepared for in advance by those affected. It is the uncertain loss which requires refined methods of handling.

9. The concept of utility is an important tool in explaining the economic growth of the insurance mechanism as a way of handling risk. Without the idea of utility, it would be difficult to explain why anyone would buy insurance against a loss of $10,000, whose "expected value" (10,000 x the probability of occurrence) is .001 of $10,000, or $10. The answer lies in the fact that to most people the potential loss of $10,000 is so great that they are willing to pay far more than $10 to avoid the possibility of losing this much.

QUESTIONS FOR REVIEW AND DISCUSSION

1. "A" is in a card game of poker and on the first round one ace has been dealt to "A" and one ace to another player.
   (a) What is the probability of "A" drawing a matching ace?
   (b) What is the risk that he will do so? Explain.

2. A jar contains 1.000 marbles—300 red, 300 white, and 400 blue.
   (a) If the marbles are mixed and drawn at random, what is the probability of drawing a blue marble in 10 tries? in 100 separate drawings of 10 marbles each?
   (b) What is the risk in each case? Explain.

3. In spinning a roulette wheel, it is said that "the wheel has no memory." This means that if there are one half black numbers and one half red numbers on a wheel, each color alternated, each color has an equal chance of coming up each spin.
   (a) What is the probability of getting a red number after 10 black numbers in 10 successive spins? after five successive spins have been black?
   (b) How do you account for the fact that the same color might appear 10 times in succession? Discuss.

4. A common misunderstanding of the law of large numbers or the law of averages is that the longer one goes without an accident, the more likely it is that "his turn" is coming up. Why is this a misunderstanding of the law of large numbers?

5. A man flips a coin 100 times and obtains 35 heads. He reasons that if he flips the coin another 100 times he will get about 65 heads to "make up" for his failure to get 50 heads during the first 100 flips. Accordingly, he flips the coin another 100 times but obtains only 40 heads. He reasons that since he was "off" by 15 heads on the first set of flips, and is now "off" by 25 from the expected 100, the law of averages is letting him down. Do you agree with him? Why?

6. A student decides to gamble on a game of cards in a casino with a probability of winning one in four. He reasons that he has a better chance of winning if he plays a long time than if he plays a short time, on the grounds that he can make up for his losses by betting more heavily after a series of losses. Advise him.

7. A famous French mathematician D'Alembert argued the following: flip two coins twice. There is a possibility of getting 0, 1, or 2 heads, each with equal probability. Therefore, the probability of getting one head is ⅓ and not ½ as commonly believed. What important element in the analysis of probability did D'Alembert ignore?

8. An insurer is asked to insure under a group policy the lives of the passengers on a large ship, but refuses on the grounds that the events are not distributed randomly. Explain the insurer's attitude. Is it logical?

9. An underwriter argues that if the probability of a house burning by fire is .02 and the probability of its being damaged by windstorm is .03, the probability that it will be damaged by either fire *or* windstorm is .05. Is this true? Why?

10. An insurer is asked to write a contract covering two automobiles in a family. There is a one in ten probability that the father will have an accident and a one in five probability that the son will have an accident.
    (a) What is the probability that both will have an accident?
    (b) What assumptions underly your answer?

11. John says that his ideal girl is one with the following characteristics: she must be blonde, have brown eyes, her father must have gone to Harvard, and she must have a master's degree in mathematics. If the probabilities of these qualities are, respectively, .3, .1, .01, and .001, what is the probability that John will meet a girl who will eventually lead him to the altar?

12. From Figure 2–1, page 29,
    (a) Indicate the probability that *exactly* 30 losses will occur; 40 losses will occur.
    (b) Verify that if one takes each number of losses from 20 to 40 and multiplies each by its separate probability of occurrence, the result is 30.
    (c) What is another name for the result that out of 100 exposure units, 30 losses are "most probable"?

13. In Figure 2–1, page 29, verify that approximately 68 per cent of the losses fall within a range of 26–34 (one standard deviation of the mean) and 95 per cent of the losses fall within a range of 22–38 (two standard deviations of the mean).

14. (a) Calculate the standard deviation of the following five numbers: 11, 8, 4, 7, and 10.
    (b) Find the coefficient of variation.
    (c) In what sense is the coefficient of variation a measure of the risk of the insurer? Explain.

15. An insurance company actuary makes the following statements: "If our losses are distributed normally, we can be 99 per cent certain that losses will fall within three standard deviations of the mean." What type of a statement is this, and of what value is it in insurance?

16. A large industrial concern owns 1,500 automobiles which are scattered throughout the United States and used by its salesmen. From past data the firm's insurance manager knows that 15 per cent of these autos are involved in a collision each year, with an average loss of $400. In the past, commercial insurance has been carried. The question is now being raised as to the feasibility of self-insurance, but the insurance manager questions its advisability on the ground that variations of losses in a given year could cause an unusual amount of profit fluctuation in certain territories. He would be willing to self-insure, however, if it could be demonstrated that there is only a one per cent probability that the actual loss frequency would vary from the expected loss frequency by more than three per cent.
    (a) Does the firm have a sufficient number of automobiles to guarantee the result asked for by the insurance manager, assuming that the firm's automobile collisions are normally distributed? Show all calculations.
    (b) Answer (a) on the basis that the firm is satisfied with an accuracy of .06.
    (c) Find the degree of accuracy, in loss frequency, which 1,500 automobiles will produce under the assumptions of a two standard-deviation confidence interval and a normal distribution of losses.
    (d) How much dispersion from the expected loss frequency would be represented by this degree of accuracy?

17. A firm is considering the advisability of self-insuring bodily injury liability. In this field, the firm's expected loss frequency is only .04; but the severity of losses, once they occur, is such that the average amount of claim is $10,000. The firm is insistent that before self-insurance can be attempted it must be true that there is a 95 per cent probability that the actual loss frequency will not differ from the expected losses by more than .004. How many automobiles must the firm have in order to self-insure its bodily injury liability risk?

18. (a) Is it generally true, in your opinion, that a wealthy individual can afford not to insure more often than a poor person?
    (b) What theoretical argument would support this position? Explain.

19. You are given an opportunity to purchase a ticket on a horse whose probability of winning $20 is 50 per cent.

    (a) How much would you pay for the ticket? How much would you pay if the winning ticket (whose probability of payoff is still 50 per cent) paid $10? $1,000? $10,000? $1,000,000? In each case, assume it is your own money you are paying, and that you have this amount of money plus a 10 per cent margin in your bank account.

    (b) What has this experiment to do with risk?

20. The text states that "If an individual acted solely according to the criterion of expected loss, he might never buy insurance." Why is this true?

21. In a famous work, A. H. Willett stated: "The fundamental facts of human nature on which the doctrine of risk is based are that in economic affairs uncertainty is in general a disagreeable state of mind, and that the disagreeableness increases as the uncertainty increases. This means more than that every man prefers a certain gain to a probable one of the same amount. . . . It means that every man . . . prefers a certain return of five per cent to an uncertain return which may be nothing or may be the two limits. This general statement is subject to numerous qualifications . . . other things being equal, the man with a large fortune will be less unwilling to expose a definite sum to a given risk than one with little wealth." Interpret this statement in terms of expected value. Do you agree with it? Why?

22. A. H. Willett stated: "It must be noticed also that the statement that risk or uncertainty entails a burden upon society by no means implies that society would necessarily be better off if all risk were avoided . . . The fact that capital can obtain the extra reward necessary to induce it to enter a hazardous employment shows that society values so highly the product of industry that it prefers to bear the extra expense rather than content itself with the products of safe investments. . . ."

    (a) To what extent, if any, does insurance encourage investment in hazardous enterprises through reduction of risk?

    (b) How is investment in hazardous enterprises of benefit to society?

23. "Uncertainty is a form of disutility that no one will voluntarily incur unless something is to be gained by so doing." Do you agree? Explain.

24. T. N. Carver, the economist, stated: "The risk to the entrepreneur is less than to those whom he relieves of it. . . . This is due to no actuarial principle, as in the case of the insurance company, but to the superior foresight and skill in avoiding loss. His real net income is, therefore, properly called risk-taker's rent, and is due, not to the risks which he assumes, but to the risks which he does not assume . . . his net income, or profit, arises from the fact that he is able to reduce his own risk below that which others would have to carry."

    (a) By what "actuarial" principle does the insurer reduce his risk below that of the insured? Explain.

    (b) Why does this principle apparently not apply to the general entrepreneur?

How Insurance

Handles Risk

The questions arise, "Of the various methods of handling risk, how does insurance rank? How is it used most successfully? Is it a "cure-all" or does it have some limitations?" For example, it is often heard that insurance is nothing better than a gamble. Is this true? What are the types of risks that are uninsurable? Is insurance a "racket" or does it play an important part in our economic life? What social and economic values are attributed to insurance? Are there any social and economic costs to society because of insurance? These and other questions are explored within this chapter.

INSURANCE DEFINED

Insurance may be defined in two major contexts: (1) as an economic or social institution designed to perform certain functions, and (2) as a legal contract between two parties. A definition that relies exclusively on either of these contexts is undesirable because each has something to offer to the person seeking a comprehensive definition. The advantages of the first, the functional definition, are that it is descriptive of the basic way in which insurance reduces risk—by combining a sufficient number of exposure units to make the loss predictable. Such a definition, however, does not appear to contemplate an insurance agreement where no risk *reduction* takes place. As noted in Chapter 1, many contracts of insurance exist where the insurer takes on a risk as a transferee and where there is no actual reduction of the risk in society as a whole. The risk is merely taken off the shoulders of one party and placed on the shoulders of a second party, for a consideration.

On the other hand, a strictly legal definition of insurance does not describe the subject in a sufficiently broad way to include those insurance arrangements that are not effected by a private legal contract, as in the case of social security and unemployment insurance. What is needed is a definition that combines both approaches. The following definition is offered as a basis for this discussion.

Insurance is an economic institution that reduces risk both to society and to individuals by combining under one management a large group of objects so situated that the aggregate losses to which society is subject become predictable within narrow limits. Insurance is usually effected by, and can be said to include, all legal contracts under which the insurer, for consideration, promises to reimburse the insured for any loss suffered during the term of the agreement.

This definition stresses how the main economic function performed by insurance, namely risk reduction, is accomplished by society and the individual. The emphasis on the word "usually" is made because not all insurance is effected by means of a legal contract. Thus, this definition is broad enough to contemplate various types of social insurance. Furthermore, this definition will include an insurance agreement in which there is no particular reliance on the "law of large numbers" as a means of predicting a loss because the definition contemplates an arrangement under which a risk is simply transferred by means of a legal contract.

REQUISITES OF INSURABLE RISKS

Unfortunately, not all risks are insurable. While insurance relies upon the law of large numbers as a basis for its economical operation, there are many situations that can cause loss where the law of large numbers does not operate satisfactorily. In other situations it may operate reasonably well under most instances, and in still other cases the law works almost ideally. There are many degrees of insurability in between these extremes.

A few illustrations will make this clearer. The peacetime use of atomic energy is still in its infancy. Insurers as a class are usually unwilling to cover this type of peril except under rigidly controlled conditions. The reason is, of course, that there has been no opportunity to collect statistics over a sufficient length of time on losses resulting from this peril so that insurers can accurately predict the probable loss experience. At present, the uncertainty of loss from atomic energy is insurable only when the insurer can inspect carefully the conditions under which a given insured is using a nuclear reactor and then only if rigid standards of safety are maintained. Even then, each insurer will impose conservative limits of liability.

In the field of life insurance, on the other hand, insurers have gathered reliable statistics over many years and have developed tables of mortality that have proved reliable as estimates of probable loss. Furthermore, life insurance is well accepted—it is relatively easy for the insurer to obtain a large group of exposure units. Here the law of large numbers works so well that for all practical purposes the life insurance company is able to eliminate its risk.

We can classify the requisites of insurable risks under two general headings: (1) those requirements that usually must be met from the standpoint of the insurer, and (2) those requirements that are usually necessary from the standpoint of the insured.

These requirements, as presented below, are not necessarily complete. For example, legal requirements, such as insurable interest, which are presented in Part III, are not discussed below. The requisites listed are intended to be suggestive of the type of underwriting standards usually looked upon as basic to the acceptance or rejection of risks as submitted to the insurer. These requirements should not be considered absolute, as iron rules, but rather as guides. In practice, for example, it is not at all uncommon for an insurer to accept a risk even though some of the following requirements are not met, providing the premium to be earned is great enough to compensate the insurer for his risk.

Requisites from the standpoint of the insurer

From the standpoint of the insurer, there are several requisites of insurable risks that must be met:

1) The number of objects must be of sufficient number and quality to allow a reasonably close calculation of probable loss.

2) The loss, should it occur, must be accidental and unintentional in nature.

3) The loss, when it occurs, must be capable of being determined and measured.

4) The loss should not be subject to the catastrophic hazard.

1) Objects to be of sufficient number and quality. The number of objects must be of sufficient number and quality to allow a reasonably close calculation of the probable loss. The probable loss must be subject to advance estimation. If only a few objects are covered, the insurer is subject to the same uncertainties of random experience as the insured. The quality of the objects to be insured must be homogeneous so that reliable statistics of loss can be formulated. Thus, it would be improper to group commercial buildings with private residences for purposes of fire insurance since the hazards facing these classes of buildings are entirely different. Furthermore, the physical and social environment of the group should be roughly similar so that no unusual factors are present that would cause losses to one part of the group and not to the other part. Thus, buildings located in a hurricane zone must not be grouped with buildings not found in such a zone.

2) Loss to be accidental and unintentional. There must be some uncertainty surrounding the loss. Otherwise, there would be no risk. If the risk or uncertainty has already been eliminated, insurance serves no purpose since the main function of insurance is to reduce risk. Thus, if a person is dying from an incurable disease which will cause his death within a given time, there is little uncertainty or risk concerning the payment of loss; insurance would not be feasible. Theoretically, the insurer could issue a policy, but the premium would have to be large enough to cover both the expected loss and the insurer's cost of doing business. The cost of such a policy would probably seem prohibitive to the insured.

Because of the requirement that the loss be accidental, insurers normally exclude in all policies any loss caused intentionally by the insured. If the insured knew that the insurer would pay such losses, a moral hazard would be introduced, and there would be a tendency for losses and premiums to rise. If premiums become exceedingly high, so few would purchase insurance that the insurer would no longer have sufficiently large numbers of exposure units to be able to obtain a reliable estimate of future loss. Thus, the first requirement of an insurable risk would not be met.

It has been said that insurance is one commodity that must be purchased "before it is needed." Once the fire starts, it is too late to buy fire insurance. While this statement illustrates the requirement that the loss must not be certain to happen, it ignores a basic truth about insurance. This truth is that insurance is not purchased, as such, to recover losses, but is a method of eliminating the uncertainty that exists for each individual as to whether or not the loss will happen to him. Looked upon in this light, insurance performs its chief function during the period *before* any loss. The insured has the satisfaction and security of knowing that should he be the one to have the loss, he will be reimbursed. Yet he hopes that he will not "need" the insurance. Insurance has been defined as the distribution of losses of the unfortunate few among the fortunate many. Each insured hopes that he will be among the "fortunate many," for seldom does the insurance policy fully compensate the "unfortunate few" for *all* of their losses. Even if one's house burns and he is fully insured, he often cannot recover in full for the lost use of his house, the additional expenses of providing temporary living arrangements elsewhere, the inconvenience, the depreciation, and, perhaps, the lost income resulting from the fire. Only the uninformed, or perhaps the dishonest, secretly hope for the loss to occur so they can "get something out of their insurance."

3) *Loss to be determinable and measurable.* The loss must be definite in time and place. It may seem unnecessary to add this requirement since most losses are easily recognized and most are capable of being measured with reasonable accuracy. It is a real problem to insurers, however, to be able even to recognize certain losses, let alone to measure them. For example, in health insurance, the insurer may agree to pay the insured a monthly income if "he should become so totally disabled as to be unable to perform the duties of his occupation." The question arises, however, as to who will determine whether or not the insured meets this condition. Often it is necessary to take the insured's word that he is unable to work. Thus, it may be possible for a dishonest person to feign illness in order to recover under his policy. If this happens, the second requirement, that the loss be unintentional, is not met.

Even if it is clear that a loss has occurred, it may not be so easy to measure it. For example, what is the loss from "pain and suffering," or of an auto accident victim? Often only a jury can decide. What is the loss of cargo on a sunken ship? It often takes a staff of adjusters many months or even years to decide. Suffice to say that, before he can safely assume the burden of risk, the insurer must set up procedures to determine if the loss has actually occurred, and if so, how much it is.

4) *Loss not to be subject to catastrophic hazard.* Conditions should not be such that all or most of the objects in the group might suffer loss at the same time and possibly from the same peril. Such simultaneous disaster to insured objects can be illustrated by reference to large fires, floods, and hurricanes that have swept major geographical areas in the past. The history of fire insurance reveals that hardly a major American city has escaped a catastrophic fire sometime in its history. In certain areas hurricanes sometimes flatten entire cities within a matter of minutes. If an insurer is unlucky enough to have on its books a great deal of property situated in such an area, it obviously suffers a loss that was not contemplated when the rates were formulated. Most insurers avoid this risk by ample dispersion of insured objects.

Requisites from the standpoint of the insured

From the standpoint of the insured, the two main requisites of insurable risks are:

1) The potential loss must be severe enough to warrant the protection.

2) The probability of loss should not be too high.

1) Potential loss must warrant protection. It would seem apparent that most individuals do not normally try to insure some minor contingency, the loss from which they can well afford to bear. There are many instances, however, among individuals who fail to recognize the severity of a potential loss. For example, it is not uncommon to discover that a person has insured against collision an automobile valued at $350, and at the same time carries little or no insurance against the loss of his life, whose value to his dependents may be worth $100,000 or more.

What is a serious loss to one person may not be serious to another. In general, a person will seek protection against those losses that he cannot comfortably absorb out of his current income or savings. A basic principle of insurance buying, however, is that the most economical use of insurance premiums is first against the serious loss and then against the less serious losses, and not *vice versa*.

2) Probability of loss not to be too high. It may seem contradictory to urge that one of the insured's requirements is that he should not protect himself against a highly probable loss. The point to remember, however, is that the more probable the loss is, the more certain it is to occur. The more certain it is, the greater the premium will be. A time is ultimately reached when the loss becomes so certain that either the insurer withdraws the protection or the cost of the premium becomes prohibitive, or both.

The basic purpose of insurance is to protect against the improbable loss. It has been estimated that if the chance of loss is greater than 50 per cent, the insurer finds it impossible to offer the protection because the premium becomes too great to be "worth it" to the insured. The contract becomes one of "trading dollars" with the insurer, but on an unfavorable basis to the insured, since the insurer must collect more money than he pays out to policyholders in order to cover the cost of doing business.

TYPES OF RISKS FACING THE INDIVIDUAL

It is now pertinent to raise the issue of which risks fall into the category of insurable risks and which do not. The following outline is suggestive of each type:

I. Insurable Risks

    A. Property risks—the uncertainty surrounding the occurrence of loss to property from perils that cause:
        1. Direct loss of the property.
        2. Loss of property indirectly.

    B. Personal risks—the uncertainty surrounding the occurrence of loss of life or income due to:
        1. Premature death.
        2. Physical disability.
        3. Old age.
        4. Unemployment.

    C. Legal liability risks—the uncertainty surrounding the occurrence of loss due to negligent behavior of third parties arising out of:
        1. The use of automobiles.
        2. The occupancy of buildings.
        3. Employment.
        4. The manufacture of products.
        5. Professional misconduct.

II. Uninsurable Risks

    A. Market risks—factors that may result in loss to property or income, such as:
        1. Price changes, seasonal or cyclical.
        2. Consumer indifference.
        3. Style changes.
        4. Competition offered by a better product.

    B. Political risks—uncertainty surrounding the occurrence of:
        1. Overthrow of the government, or war.
        2. Restrictions imposed on free trade.
        3. Unreasonable or punitive taxation.
        4. Restrictions on free exchange of currencies.

    C. Production risks—uncertainties surrounding occurrence of:
        1. Failure of machinery to function economically.
        2. Strikes or other labor troubles.
        3. Failure to solve technical problems.
        4. Exhaustion of raw material resources.

The several types of insurable risks which face the individual will be thoroughly discussed in Parts IV and V of this text.

Reference to the preceding list will illustrate why most of the uninsurable risks mentioned fall into that category. Let us use market risks as the first example. Take the case of a manufacturer who wishes to insure that the price of his product will not fall more than 10 per cent during the policy year. Such a risk is subject to the catastrophic loss, since simultaneous loss from this source is possible to all of the firm's products in a depression. Further, the losses are not subject to advance calculation since, in an ever-changing, free, competitive market such as ours, past experience is an inadequate guide to the future. Hence, the insurer would have no realistic basis for computing his premium. Furthermore, in times of rising prices, few would be interested in the coverage; and in times of falling prices, no insurer could afford to take on the risk. The insurer could get no "spread of risks" over which to average out good years with bad years. Again, if such insurance were offered, there would be a tendency for each person to increase his output since the possession of a price guarantee would in all probability drive the price downward, thus bringing about the very contingency against which the manufacturer was insured!

Political risks are also beyond the control of the insured for the most part, since losses from this source cannot be estimated accurately nor measured. For example, many "war risks" are such that one cannot measure the degree to which many types of losses stem from a war or from some other peril. Also, this peril often brings about catastrophic losses. Again, since no two wars are alike and their courses cannot be predicted, there is no way of scientifically calculating a premium.[1]

To the extent that risks are uninsurable, the management of a business firm, or an individual, will employ one or more of the other methods of handling risk discussed on page 8. This subject is explored more thoroughly in Chapter 4.

INSURANCE AND GAMBLING

It is common to confuse insurance with gambling, for to many, it is often difficult to see clearly why insurance is not gambling. Even legal authorities have not always made a clear distinction between the two,[2]

---

[1] The student should ask himself the extent to which each of the types of risks in the outline is insurable, applying the criteria presented in this chapter.

[2] For example, in E. R. Dillavou and C. G. Howard, *Principles of Business Law* (Sixth ed.; New York: Prentice-Hall, Inc., 1957), p. 800, it is stated: "Since insurance *partakes somewhat of the nature of a gambling contract,* to avoid the evil effects that might develop from wagers concerning the life or property of others, the courts require the insured to have an insurable interest in the person or property insured by him." (Italics supplied by author.)

classifying both insurance and gambling contracts under the category of *aleatory* contracts. In such contracts it is possible for one party to give up a great deal more than he receives in the transaction. Aleatory contracts are contrasted with another group called *commutative* contracts, under which each party gives up approximately equal value in exchange for the promises or acts of the other. Insurance may appear to be a contract under which there is a possibility for the insurance company to pay to a given party a great deal more than it has received in premiums; but this does not mean that insurance is thereby a gambling contract. In fact, from an economic standpoint, gambling and insurance are exact opposites.

Gambling creates a new risk where none existed before, whereas insurance is a method of eliminating or greatly reducing (to one party anyway) an already existing risk. This may be illustrated as follows: John said to Jack, "I'll bet you $5,000 to $50 that Dick's house will not catch fire within one year." If Jack takes the bet, a new risk has been created for each person. If the house burns, Jack wins $5,000; but if it does not burn, he loses $50. Before the gamble, neither party had any risk of losing any money from this source, nor, of course, of gaining any. After the gamble, each party becomes subject to a new risk of losing money.

Contrast the preceding incident with the situation in which Dick goes to the fire insurance company and insures his house for $5,000 and the insurer charges a premium of $50. Dick had the risk of having his house destroyed by fire before he entered into the insurance transaction. He has an *insurable interest* in his house. Afterward he has eliminated the risk of loss from this source in return for a premium of $50. He has exchanged a large *uncertain* loss for a small, but *certain,* loss, namely, the premium.

INSURANCE AND SPECULATION

Speculation is a transaction under which one party, for a consideration, agrees to assume certain risks, usually in connection with a business venture. A good example of speculation is found in the practice known as *hedging*. In hedging, a flour miller, for example, may have purchased grain to grind into flour. He realizes, however, that before the grinding can be completed, the price of grain, and consequently that of flour, may have changed, causing him either profit or loss. The miller prefers to avoid the price risk and to concentrate on his main business operation—

flour milling. Therefore, after buying the grain, the miller enters into an equal and opposite transaction in the grain futures market whereby a speculator, in effect, assumes the price risk.[3]

What is the distinction between speculation and insurance? The central purpose of the two types of transactions is very similar, but the actual contracts do not bear any obvious similarity. A speculator is a transferee of risk, and the transferor is usually a businessman wishing to pass on a price risk to someone more willing and able to bear it than himself. Such a businessman then is using the transfer method of handling risk. Normally the risk is a type that insurers are unwilling to handle because it fails to meet the tests of insurability—the risk is unpredictable or is subject to the catastrophic loss. Perhaps the main difference between insurance and speculation lies in the type of risks that each is designed to handle, and in the resulting differences in contractual arrangements. The main similarity lies in the central purpose behind each transaction.

Let us follow the hedging example through to illustrate these similarities and differences. The futures contract is one to buy or to sell grain (or some other commodity) at a given price and at a given time in the future. The futures contract does not follow the form of an insurance contract, under which one party promises to reimburse another for a loss. Yet the purpose of the futures contract, from the viewpoint of the hedger, is a reimbursement for loss, if any, arising from falling grain prices in the future. The miller has a risk and he is shifting it to the speculator by this means.

The speculator's purpose is to agree to take the price risks in the hope of making a net profit out of the sum total of his transactions. In other words, the speculator hopes to "guess right" about price trends a majority of the time. His position is similar to a commercial insurer who accepts risk as a transferee without the benefit of having a large number of exposure units over which to spread his operations. He may be compared to an underwriter from Lloyd's who agrees to pay a given sum if, for example, rain causes a loss to the promoters of a public event.

In summary, from a legal viewpoint, the purpose of the insurance contract and the speculative contract is to transfer risk. The type of contractural arrangement used in each case is entirely different because

---

[3] No attempt will be made here to explain in detail just how the hedging operation is effected. For a complete explanation, see T. N. Beckman, H. H. Maynard, and W. R. Davidson, *Principles of Marketing* (6th ed.; New York: The Ronald Press Company, 1957), Ch. 28.

Several other examples of speculation might have been given. Much of the stock market trading serves speculative purposes. In fact, almost any business situation in which a price risk is involved serves as a potential market for the speculator.

of the nature of the risk to be handled. Neither of the contracts is a gambling contract because no new risk is created that did not exist before. In most cases, however, insurance transactions have the benefit of the law of large numbers and thus can greatly reduce the risks involved. In speculation, however, the risk is seldom eliminated, but is borne by another person who is presumably better able to handle it.

INSURANCE AND BONDING

A *bond* is a legal instrument whereby one party (the *surety*) agrees to reimburse another party (the *obligee*) should this person suffer loss because of some failure by the person bonded (the *principal* or *obligor*). Thus, if a contractor furnishes a bond to the owner of a building, the surety will reimburse the owner if the contractor fails to perform his duties as agreed upon and thereby causes a loss to the owner.

A bond may sound like a contract of insurance, but there are some important differences to be considered:

1. The bonding contract involves three primary parties, while the insurance contract normally involves only two.
2. In bonding, if the principal defaults and the surety makes good to the obligee, the surety enjoys the legal right to attempt to collect for its loss from the principal. In insurance, the insurer does not have the right to recover losses from the insured, for this would defeat the purpose of the contract.
3. In bonding, the surety sees as its basic function the lending of its credit, for a premium. It "expects no losses," and reserves the legal right to collect from the defaulting principal. The insurance contract is set up with the presumption that there will be losses, and is viewed by its managers as a device to spread these losses among the insured group.
4. The nature of the risk is different. Usually a bond guarantees the honesty of an individual, as well as his capacity and ability to perform. These are matters within the control of the individual. The insurance contract, ideally, covers losses outside his control.
5. Finally, in insurance, the contract is usually cancellable by either party, and nonpayment of premium or breach of warranty by the insured is a good defense of the insurer in avoiding its liability. In a bond, however, the surety is often liable on the bond to the beneficiary regardless of whether the premium has been paid, and regardless of breach of warranty or fraud on the part of the principal. In addition, the bond oftentimes cannot be canceled until it has been determined that all the obligations of the principal have been fulfilled.

SOCIAL AND ECONOMIC VALUES OF INSURANCE

It has been implied in the foregoing discussion that to distinguish between insurable and uninsurable risk serves a useful purpose. This purpose is that insurance has peculiar advantages as a device to handle risk and so ought to be extended as far as possible, in order to bring about the greatest economic advantage to a given society. In order to establish the validity of this point, some of the social and economic values of insurance are listed below:

1) The amount of accumulated reserve funds needed to meet possible losses is reduced.

2) Cash reserves that insurers accumulate are freed for investment purposes, thus bringing about a better allocation of economic resources and increasing production.

3) Since the supply of investable funds is greater than would be true without insurance, capital is available at a lower cost than would otherwise be true.

4) The entrepreneur with adequate insurance coverage is a better credit risk.

5) Insurers actively engage in loss-prevention activities.

6) Insurance contributes to business and social stability and peace of mind by protecting business firms and the family bread-winner.

1) Reduction of accumulated reserve funds

Perhaps the greatest social value, and indeed the central economic function, of insurance is to obtain the advantages that flow from reduction of risk. As noted in Chapter 1, one of the chief economic burdens of risk is the necessity of accumulating reserve funds to meet possible losses. One of the great advantages of the insurance mechanism is that it greatly reduces the total of such reserves which are required for a given economy. Since the insurer can predict losses in advance, it needs to accumulate only enough funds to meet these losses and to cover expenses. If each individual had to set aside such funds, he would need an amount far greater than the insurance company because the individual, not knowing precisely how much would be required, would tend to be conservative. For example, in most localities, a $15,000 residence can be insured against fire and perhaps other physical perils for as little as $50 a year. If insurance were not available, the individual would probably feel he had to accumulate funds at a much more rapid rate than $50 a year.

2) Freeing of cash reserves for investment purposes

Another aspect of the same advantage described above is the fact that the cash reserves which insurers accumulate are made available for investment. Insurers as a group, and life insurance firms in particular, have become among the largest and most important institutions to collect and distribute the nation's savings. Table 3–1 is a statistical compilation of the annual sources of long-term capital funds used by business for the period 1952–1960. Prior to 1957, life insurance companies, supplying about 20 per cent of total national needs, were the largest single source of such funds. Since 1957, life insurance companies have ranked among the three leading sources, providing approximately 20 per cent of the funds needed in 1960. When it is realized that without a regular plan of savings, as is involved in an insurance contract, probably much of this saving would either not be made at all, or would not be available in such a way as to be cheaply transferred to corporate users, the real contribution of insurance may be more fully appreciated.

The result of the insurance mechanism, then, is to free for investment purposes funds that would otherwise be unavailable for that purpose. Thus, the insurance mechanism encourages new investment. For example, if an individual knows that his family will be protected by life insurance in the event of his premature death, he may be more willing to invest his savings in a long-desired project, such as a business venture, without feeling that he is robbing his family of their basic income security. In this way a better allocation of economic resources is achieved than would otherwise be possible.

3) Availability of investment capital at lower cost

Since the supply of investible funds is greater than would be true without insurance, capital is available at lower cost than would otherwise be true. Other things being equal, this brings about a higher standard of living since increased investment itself will raise production and cause lower prices than would otherwise be the case. Insurance has another influence in this regard. Because it is an efficient device to reduce risk, investors may be willing to enter fields they would otherwise reject as too risky. Thus, society benefits by increased services and new products, which are the hallmarks of increased living standards.

4) Entrepreneur becomes better credit risk

Another advantage of insurance lies in the importance of insurance to credit. Insurance has been called the basis of our credit system. It

Table 3–1
MAJOR SOURCES OF LONG-TERM CAPITAL FUNDS IN THE UNITED STATES, 1952–1960

(BILLIONS OF DOLLARS)

Source	1952	1953	1954	1955	1956	1957	1958	1959	1960*
Life insurance companies	5.2	5.1	5.6	5.6	5.9	5.1	4.7	5.1	5.3
Savings and loan associations	2.8	3.6	4.1	5.3	4.3	4.3	5.6	7.5	6.8
Individuals and others †	3.4	3.5	2.1	4.7	4.7	6.1	4.8	4.1	1.7
Commercial banks	1.9	1.6	3.3	2.3	1.5	1.8	4.7	2.7	1.3
Mutual savings banks	2.1	2.0	2.5	2.2	2.4	2.1	2.8	1.7	2.1
Corporate pensions funds	1.5	1.5	1.9	1.6	2.4	2.7	2.7	2.8	3.5
Federal agencies	.9	.1	.2	.5	.8	1.5	.5	2.4	1.5
State retirement fund	.5	.6	.8	.9	1.1	1.3	1.5	1.4	1.7
Property-casualty companies	.8	1.1	1.1	1.0	.9	1.0	.9	1.3	1.5
Investment companies	.5	.4	.4	.6	.9	1.0	1.3	1.3	1.1
Total	19.6	19.5	22.0	24.7	24.9	26.9	29.5	30.3	26.5

* Estimated.
† Includes nonfinancial corporations.
Source: Compiled by the economics department of Bankers Trust Company from various sources, reported in *The Investment Outlook* for 1961 (New York: Bankers Trust Company, 16 Wall Street, 1961) Table 2.

follows logically that if insurance reduces the risk of loss from certain sources, it should mean that an entrepreneur is a better credit risk if he carries adequate insurance. One of the earliest known instances of the use of insurance was in connection with credit. This took the form of what was known as a *bottomry contract,* used by the early Romans and Greeks. The bottomry contract provided that if a trader borrowed money to finance a cargo to be sold in a distant port, and an ocean peril caused the vessel to be lost, the money lender would forgive the debt which had been incurred. Naturally, the interest rate charged for the loan was somewhat higher than it would have been without this guarantee, the difference amounting to the premium for insurance.

Today it would be difficult or impossible to borrow money for many business purposes, or for the purchase of a home, without insurance protection that meets the requirements of the lender. One of the most significant things done to restore the confidence of people in banks following their mass closure in 1933, was the establishment of the Federal Deposit Insurance Corporation to insure deposits. Also during the 1930's federal insurance on home loans laid the foundation for a great expansion of long-term credit for home ownership, credit that was not generally available prior to that time.

5) Loss-prevention activities

Another social and economic value of insurance lies in its loss-prevention activities. While it is not the main function of insurance to reduce loss, but merely to spread losses among members of the insured group, nevertheless insurers are vitally interested in keeping losses at a minimum. Insurers know that if no effort is made in this regard, losses would have a tendency to rise, since it is human nature to relax vigilance when it is known that the loss will be fully paid by the insurer in any case. If the probability of loss rises, premiums must also keep pace; and it is likely that fewer and fewer would be able to afford the insurance. Thus, eventually the offer of insurance would be withdrawn for want of sufficient volume of business. Furthermore, in any given year, a rise in loss payments reduces the profit to the insurer, and so loss prevention provides a direct avenue of increased profit.

Insurers have, in many respects, done a remarkable job of loss prevention and of stimulating an atmosphere in which other loss-prevention organizations can work effectively. While space does not permit a complete analysis of this subject, a few examples will be given. Insurers have for many years sponsored a body known as Underwriters Laboratories, which tests new products for physical hazards that may lead to fire. The very existence of such an organization has undoubtedly had great effect in encouraging safer manufacturing standards. Again, in calculating rates for fire insurance, credit is given for measures taken that will reduce fire loss to buildings, and that encourage good fire departments, better building codes, and community activity toward fire prevention.

Safety on the highways has long been of great concern to the automobile insurance business. Through such organizations as the National Safety Council, the possibility of loss from motor vehicle accidents has been drawn continually to the attention of the motorist. Pressure for better highways and for safer automobiles has been maintained. As a result, since the middle 1930's the annual number of automobile deaths has not risen for over 20 years, in spite of a rise of over 50 per cent in the number of vehicles on the highways and the vastly increased number of miles driven.

6) Contribution to business and social stability

A final advantage of insurance lies in its contribution to business and social stability. Adequately protected, a business need not face the grim prospect of liquidation following an insured loss. A family need not break up following the death of the breadwinner, or following his permanent and total disability. An unemployed worker usually has a small income to tide him over until he can find another job. A business venture can be continued without interruption even though a key man or the sole proprietor dies. A family need not lose its life savings following a bank failure. Old-age dependency can be avoided. Loss of a firm's assets by theft can be reimbursed. Whole cities ruined by a hurricane can be rebuilt from the proceeds of insurance.

SOCIAL AND ECONOMIC COSTS OF INSURANCE

No institution can operate without certain costs. These costs are listed below in order that an impartial view of the insurance institution, as a social device, can be obtained:

1) Cost of operating the insurance business.
2) Cost of losses that are intentionally caused.
3) Cost of losses that are exaggerated.

1) Cost of operating the insurance business

The main social cost of insurance lies in the use of economic resources, mainly labor, to operate the insurance business. The annual overhead of property insurers accounts for about 40 per cent of their earned premiums. In 1956, a group of 357 property and liability insurance companies spent about 36 per cent of their premium income to cover expenses and showed no statutory underwriting profit,[4] for this year happened to be one of unusually heavy loss payments. In a more normal year, perhaps the property and liability insurance business would show about 5 per cent of earned premiums as profit, and would expect losses to run between 50 and 60 per cent of earned premiums; the remainder would be used for the expenses of doing business. The point is that the advantages of insurance are not obtained for nothing. They should be weighed against the cost of obtaining the service.

2) Cost of losses that are intentionally caused

A second social cost of insurance is attributed to the fact that if it were not for insurance, certain losses would not occur. What is referred to are those losses that are caused intentionally by people in order to collect on their policies. While there are no reliable estimates as to the extent of such losses, it is possible that they are only an extremely small fraction of the total loss payments. Insurers are well aware of this hazard and, as we shall later see, take numerous steps to keep it at a minimum, both in underwriting the risk and in effecting loss adjustments.

3) Cost of losses that are exaggerated

Separate from the above costs, and yet related to them, is another social cost of insurance—the tendency to exaggerate the extent of damage that results from purely unintentional loss occurrences where the loss is insured. There are good studies to illustrate this point. For example, one survey noted a definite indication that loss payments to families insured for accident and sickness claims tend to be higher than the reported losses of uninsured families.[5] This probably is true because part of the extent of loss is within the control of the insured. In other words, once the accident or sickness has occurred, an individual may decide to undergo more expensive medical treatment; or the physician may prescribe it, if it is known that the insurer will "foot" most or all of the bill.

---

[4] *Best's Fire and Casualty Aggregates and Averages* (1957), p. 12.
[5] O. W. Anderson and J. J. Feldman, *Family Medical Costs and Voluntary Health Insurance: A Nationwide Survey* (New York: McGraw-Hill Book Company, Inc., 1956).

Another illustration of added costs due to exaggerated losses is seen in the field of legal liability insurance. It is a recognized fact that juries tend to be more generous with an injured plaintiff in a negligence case if it is realized that a liability insurer will be paying whatever judgment is handed down.[6] Another example is found in automobile insurance covering physical damage to the auto. Where it is known that an insurance company is involved, there seems to be an unmistakable tendency for repairmen to exaggerate the extent of loss, sometimes in collusion with dishonest insureds.

In weighing the social costs and the social values of insurance, it appears that the advantages far exceed the disadvantages. If this were not true, in a free market system such as ours, insurance would not be utilized to the extent that it is. No one forces businessmen and individuals to buy insurance. They do so because of the great economic services attained thereby. These services cost something, of course; but, like most expenses, insurance premiums are looked upon as essential to the successful operation of a business. To enable the reader to understand the extent of insurance growth and utilization, this chapter will conclude with a brief treatment of the size of the industry.

THE GROWTH OF INSURANCE

The insurance industry has enjoyed one of the more enviable records of long-term growth of any financial institution. From humble beginnings, it has developed into one of the major industries of the United States, and is regarded as essential to a highly developed industrial nation. In the period 1900 to 1945, the assets of life insurance companies, for example, increased approximately 57-fold, while assets of all banks in the United States increased about 15-fold.[7] This relative gain in the rate of growth has not been maintained in recent years, as shown in Table 3–2, where insurance firms' assets are compared with the major financial institutions. Table 3–2 indicates the size, as measured by assets, of major financial institutions in this country in 1941 and 1960.

---

[6] As a matter of fact, an organization of attorneys has been formed for the purpose of devising ways and means of securing larger judgments for injured plaintiffs. Without the existence of almost universal liability insurance covering auto accidents in particular, it is doubtful if such an organization would have been formed.

[7] Calculated from statistical tables given in *Life Insurance Fact Book*, 1958, and *Historical Statistics of the United States 1789–1945* (U. S. Bureau of the Census, Washington, D. C. 1949), p. 262. These data for banks do not correspond precisely with the data given in Table 3–2, since the former are derived from data from the Comptroller of the Currency, which treats branches as separate banks.

Table 3–2

TOTAL ASSETS OF MAJOR FINANCIAL INSTITUTIONS IN THE UNITED STATES, 1941 AND 1960

(BILLIONS OF DOLLARS)

Institution	1941	1960	Per Cent Increase
Commercial banks...............................	$50.7	$199.5	294
Mutual savings banks.............................	10.4	39.1	276
Property and liability (casualty) insurance companies...	5.4	30.1	458
Life insurance companies..........................	32.7	119.8	268
Savings and loan associations......................	6.0	71.5	1,080

Source: Federal Reserve Bulletin, June, 1958, pp. 667–677; and Best's Fire and Casualty Aggregates and Averages, 1957, p. 1.

In 1960, the total assets of all types of commercial insurance firms were 72 per cent of the assets of all commercial banks. In 1941, the proportion was 75 per cent. Thus, it is seen that insurers are comparable to banks in size. While life insurance companies are growing at a slightly slower rate than commercial banks, property and liability companies have a rate of growth approximately half again as much as commercial banks. Finally, even though savings and loan associations have been growing at a tremendously rapid rate, averaging over 50 per cent each year, they are still 60 per cent of the size of life insurance companies alone.

Each year insurance companies collect staggering sums as premium income. In 1960, life insurance companies collected $17.4 billion, while property and liability insurance companies collected $15.0 billion.[8] These amounts, which do not include investment income, represented over 7 per cent of the national income for that year. This percentage remained fairly constant at 7 per cent in the United States in the period 1945 to the late 1950's.

Literally millions of individuals own policies of insurance. A survey covering the year 1960, for example, revealed that 65 per cent of the population, 118 million persons, owned some form of life insurance.[9] Similar findings have been found in the field of health insurance. Estimates compiled annually by the Health Insurance Council reveal that in the United States in 1959 over 128 million people owned some type of health insurance coverage.[10]

---

[8] *Life Insurance Fact Book,* 1961, p. 52, and *Best's Fire and Casualty Aggregates and Averages* (1961), p. 1.

[9] *Life Insurance Fact Book,* 1961, p. 7.

[10] Health Insurance Council, *Source Book of Health Insurance Data* (1960), p. 11.

SUMMARY

1. Insurance is an economic institution that reduces risk both to society and to individuals by combining under one management a large group of objects so situated that the aggregate losses to which society is subject become predictable within narrow limits. Insurance is usually effected by, and can be said to include, all legal contracts under which the insurer, for consideration, promises to reimburse the insured for any loss suffered during the term of the agreement.

2. From the standpoint of the insurer, the requisites of insurable risks are four: (a) There must be a sufficient number of homogeneous exposure units to allow a reasonably close calculation of probable future losses; (b) The loss must be accidental and unintentional in nature; (c) The loss must be capable of being determined and measured; and (d) The exposure units must not be subject to simultaneous destruction.

3. From the viewpoint of the insured, the main requirements of insurability are: (a) The loss must be severe enough to warrant protection; and (b) The probability of loss should not be so high as to command a prohibitive premium when compared with the possible size of the loss.

4. Risks facing individuals may be classified into insurable and uninsurable risks. Uninsurable risks include market, political, and production risks.

5. The essential difference between insurance and gambling is that insurance transfers, eliminates, or reduces existing risk, while gambling creates new risk.

6. The main distinction between insurance and speculation is that speculation deals usually with business risk, which is not insurable, but is transferred from one party to another. In insurance, the risk concerns an insurable fortuitous event and employs the combination method to reduce it.

7. Insurance differs from bonding in many particulars. In general, bonding is a method of transferring risk, while insurance reduces risk through combination. The types of loss covered in bonding contracts are often much more comprehensive in nature than in insurance. For example, the loss is often within the control of the principal.

8. There are many social and economic values of insurance, but perhaps the greatest value lies in the many benefits flowing from the reduction of risk in society. The benefits of insurance are achieved at the expense of certain social costs, the chief one of which is the cost of the economic resources used to operate the insurance business.

QUESTIONS FOR REVIEW AND DISCUSSION

1. A writer on insurance states, "An adequate explanation of insurance must include either the building up of a fund or the transference of risk, but not both." Is this statement in conflict with the position taken in this text? Explain.

2. Why do private insurers generally not insure against flood peril? strikes? style changes? depreciation? unemployment? Discuss.

3. If a department store guarantees its merchandise against mechanical failure within a period of five years, does the guaranty constitute insurance? Discuss.

4. In this chapter, the growth of insurance companies was compared with the growth of banks. Different factors, however, have operated in each case, which might explain the early rapid growth of insurance assets, and the slowing down which was noted later. One of these facts would certainly be the nature of risks faced by each type of institution. Explain and contrast these risks, indicating how they might have accounted for the different rates of growth of the two institutions.

5. In a study of surety rate making, it was pointed out that bonding companies have a substantial number of losses each year from defaulting principals. It seems clear that the premiums charged must provide for such losses. Is this in conflict with the statement in the text that bonding companies expect no losses? Explain.

6. "D," a wealthy investor, feels that the market is such that the price of certain securities he owns will fall in the near future. He therefore sells these securities to "A," who is of the opinion that these securities will not fall in price. Who is the speculator, "D" or "A," or both? Is such a transaction gambling? Explain.

7. A firm warrants that certain parts in its used automobiles are in good running order and will function properly for a period of one year. If the parts fail, the warranty pays for the replacement. The state insurance department attempted to impose its regulations on this firm because "the company is warranting the mechanical reliability of the mechanical features of the auto and this amounts to insuring the buyer against any defects in those parts." The firm's representatives claimed, on the other hand, that it was only warranting the fact that its inspectors had inspected a particular auto. How would you decide whether this is a proper example of insurance or not? What is your decision? Explain.

8. (a) Give two current examples of each of the following types of risks: (1) market, (2) political, and (3) production.
   (b) Under what conditions, if any, would it be possible to issue commercial insurance on these risks? Explain.

9. It has been argued that if it were possible to insure against all risks there would be no justification for our free system of competitive enterprise, one of the fundamental tenets of which is that profits are a reward for risk-taking. If risk-taking were eliminated, so would be profits. To what extent, in your opinion, is there a danger that the extension of private insurance will threaten our system of free enterprise? Discuss.

10. Suggest some possible ways by which the social costs of insurance can be reduced.

11. Two farmers agree that if either one of their barns were to burn down, the other farmer would help rebuild it. Is this an insurance arrangement? Why, or why not?

12. It is common to hear a person say that he is "insurance poor," and yet one seldom hears the complaint that one is "savings poor." Is there any justification for either of these complaints? Discuss.

13. A text on industrial organization and management contains the statement: "Insurance should be the last resort, not the first, in meeting business risks. Insurance increases the current cost of doing business and thus narrows the profit margin and makes the product more vulnerable to competition." Evaluate, indicating what elements of truth, as well as misconceptions, underlie this statement.

14. A recent article reported as follows: "Large underwriting losses, estimated as high as $25 million, have been reported for insurers, who during the past year have underwritten financing operations of feed companies in the production of broiler and fryer chickens." The insurance plan was a contract agreeing to reimburse a feed company for losses resulting from advances to broiler growers at a premium of about one cent a chick. The insurer would pay 80% of any loss that the feed company sustained in broiler financing operations. Thus, if a bird costing 60 cents to produce sold for 50 cents, the insurer paid eight cents of the ten cent loss.

    The production of broilers and fryers is financed mainly by feed companies, which advance the feed and sometimes furnish the chicks to growers. The feed companies receive reimbursement nine weeks later when the birds go to market.

    The broiler growers were enthusiastic, but the result of the plan was disastrous. Underwriters quit writing the coverage on brooder houses, with no liability extending beyond the nine-week brood period ending in late November.

(a) What are the essential requirements of an insurable peril? Explain each briefly.

(b) Which of these requirements appear to be violated in the insurance plan described above? In your answer give an indication of the probable reason for the failure of the plan and the cause of the huge underwriting losses.

Insurance and

4

Risk Management

There are few areas of greater importance to business than the management of business "risks." In this sense, risk management is the function of executive direction over all phases of the business enterprise that affect the ultimate profit of the firm. Such a concept of risk management, however, is too general to be of great value for our purposes. A more workable definition contemplates that *risk management* is that set of executive functions which deals with insurable risks, and devises the best methods of handling them. The *risk manager,* in other words, is the executive responsible for seeing that the profit of the firm is not destroyed by the occurrence of some peril that is usually outside the direct control of the business enterprise. He is dealing with pure risk, not speculative risk.[1] Risk management is sometimes called insurance management, but the two are not the same. *Insurance management* deals only with the administration of the firm's insurance program, while risk management covers all the various methods of handling risk, as outlined in Chapter 1.

The term risk manager has been viewed in three different ways by various individuals. First, in the broadest sense, the risk manager has been seen as the general entrepreneur who assumes all risks of loss of his capital, controls the enterprise, and receives profit or suffers loss. As such, he is in charge of all risks, both insurable and uninsurable. Second, in the *narrow* sense, the risk manager is seen as an insurance manager, or a buyer, who does nothing but supervise the firm's purchase of insurance policies; he makes recommendations as to what risks will be insured and on what basis. Third, between these two extremes, we find the term risk manager frequently applied to the individual whose functions [2] are much broader than those of an insurance buyer, but con-

---

[1] For a distinction between these two concepts, see page 8.

[2] As one writer explained the functions of a risk manager, "He should not try to deal, nor should he be expected to deal, with loss arising from an executive's mistake, from the inadequacy of a research laboratory, from the failure of a product to perform as intended, or from the incompetence of salesmen." H. P. Stellwagen, "A Rational Basis for Buying Insurance," Insurance Series No. 102 (New York: American Management Association, 1954), p. 4.

siderably narrower than those of the entrepreneur himself. It is in this sense that the risk manager will be dealt with in this chapter.[3]

THE DEVELOPMENT OF RISK MANAGEMENT

At one time business enterprises paid little careful attention to the problem of handling pure risks. Insurance policies were purchased on a haphazard basis, with considerable overlapping and duplicated coverage on one hand, and complete gaps in coverage of important exposures on the other. Little control over the cost of losses and insurance premiums was exercised. Many risks were assumed when they should have been insured and *vice versa*. It was gradually realized that greater attention to this aspect of business management would reap great dividends. Instead of having insurance decisions handled by a busy executive whose primary responsibility lay in another area, management began to assign this responsibility first as a part-time job to such officers as the treasurer, and later as a full-time position to an individual specifically trained for this purpose.

As the full scope of responsibility for risk management was realized, an insurance department was established, with several people employed. At first, the department manager was known usually as simply "the insurance buyer." Later, his title began to be changed to "insurance manager" or "risk manager." Naturally many different titles, including the term "insurance buyer," are still used, but the tendency is to reflect in the title the broader nature of the manager's duties and responsibilities. Assistants to the "insurance manager," as he is typically called today, often include specialists in various branches of insurance, law, statistics, and personnel relations.

Risk managers are now organized into associations, of which the main one is the American Society of Insurance Management, with over 600 member firms.[4] The insurance division of the American Management Association, is also very active in the field of risk management, holding workshop seminars for its members and conducting at least two conferences each year. Its publications form an important part of the basic literature of risk management.

---

[3] The writer wishes to acknowledge the work of the Insurance Division of the American Management Association, whose publications on insurance management were drawn upon for illustration of risk management problems in this chapter.

[4] The ASIM publishes a national magazine entitled *The National Insurance Buyer*, and is dedicated to the task of advancing the profession of risk management.

PROBLEMS FACING THE RISK MANAGER

A consideration of the problems faced by the risk manager in a business enterprise can give an appreciation of the various reasons for the rise of this new executive function into a position of importance in the organizational structure. The environment in which a modern business operates, particularly the large corporation, is far more complex than it was even thirty years ago. The nature of this complexity can be seen in such things as the more complicated relationships that exist between the corporation and the government, in the ever-changing competitive markets, and in the world-wide scope of many business enterprises with its attendant risks. In such environment, the problem of insurable risk becomes more complex and its analysis more important.

Today, not only are the hazards facing business many sided, but the losses which stem from various perils are also more serious than they were before 1930. Illustrative of this is the fact that many industrial enterprises are highly integrated. The interruption of one link in a chain of many corporate units can cause a string of losses in other links of the chain. Furthermore, productive machinery is much more complicated and expensive than formerly when labor was used to a much greater extent. An automatic factory may have supplanted several smaller plants, thus increasing the degree of concentration of values in one location. Specialized engineering skill may be necessary to analyze the risk involved in such a factory. General management can no longer be expected to keep close watch on the many technical phases of operations. Hence, a specialist is employed for this purpose.

The following examples illustrate the specific problems facing the risk manager in the environment of a modern corporate enterprise.[5]

Problem 1: The risk manager learns that his company has entered into a sales agreement under which $10 million of new plant facilities will be required to fill the needs of a new customer. These needs are sufficiently specialized so that the production cannot be sold to anyone else. What new exposures are created that might require attention by the risk manager?

Problem 2: The risk manager learns that the research department of his company is getting a supply of radioactive material. What are the implications of this move and what steps should be taken by the risk manager?

---

[5] Real-life situations adapted from A. J. Ingley, "Managing Corporate Risks, Risk Analysis," Insurance Series No. 112 (New York: American Management Association), p. 5.

Problem 3: The firm is buying out another company with four plants which produce a type of product entirely different from that of the acquiring firm. One week is allowed to set up necessary insurance coverage. What procedures must be followed to be sure that coverage is properly secured?

RESPONSIBILITIES AND FUNCTIONS OF THE RISK MANAGER

The above problems are merely suggestive of the work of the risk manager, and it remains to set forth a more formal statement of his responsibilities and functions.

The risk manager has certain general responsibilities. He is held responsible for the adequacy of the firm's insurance program, and for helping to formulate and administer the firm's policy regarding insurance matters. It is his responsibility to see that the firm's profits are not lost because of some peril, the occurrence of which could have been insured against, or otherwise adequately handled. The insurance manager is expected to keep abreast of developments in the insurance field and to obtain coverage at the lowest cost compatible with other factors such as the safety of the insurer and the quality of its service. It is his responsibility to see that attention is paid to loss-prevention activities. He sees that the firm meets all contractual agreements in its insurance policies, and he negotiates settlement of insured losses. He is expected to make recommendations to higher management on all aspects of risk management, such as what to insure and what not to insure. He keeps records of losses and expenses to guide him in making sound recommendations and as a guide to scientific decision-making.

The specific functions of the risk manager, in carrying out these responsibilities, may be set forth as follows:

1) To recognize the various exposures to loss. In other words, the risk manager must first of all be aware of the possibility of each type of loss. This is a fundamental duty that must precede all other functions.

2) To estimate the frequency and size of loss; that is, to estimate the probability of loss from various sources.

3) To decide the best and most economical method of handling the risk of loss, whether it be by assumption, self-insurance, reduction of hazards, transfer, commercial insurance, or some combination of these methods.

4) To administer the various programs of risk management, including the tasks of constant re-evaluation of the programs, record keeping, and the like.

1) Recognizing exposures to loss

To recognize the various exposures to loss is the most difficult and complex task of all those facing the risk manager. A modern business enterprise of substantial size offers almost limitless opportunities for loss, and the insurance manager is expected to make an evaluation of all of them. Of course, he must be intimately familiar with all phases of the business operation in order to accomplish this task. He must be aware of all new plans for plant expansion and for entering into new business operations. He must work closely with top management and with all heads of departments in order to get a clear insight into these features. He must travel extensively if the business is decentralized geographically. He must recognize that there are many types of losses other than those caused directly by physical perils. Examples are losses from legal liability, from lost profits and fixed charges, from dishonesty of employees, from liability assumed under contract, and from union agreements.

To aid in recognizing the various types of exposures to loss, many risk managers set up formal flow charts, which reflect the many facets of the flow of men and materials within the physical plant layout. Reports from each department or division concerning the nature of any loss, no matter how trivial, are used as a guide by the risk manager in recognizing potential sources of major loss. The risk manager should be a person of great imagination who travels about his firm's plant and constantly attempts to imagine how a loss might occur, in order that a problem can be recognized and consequently met with as little difficulty as possible. For example, the risk manager might observe that while a fire hydrant is close to the plant, there is a possibility of it being blocked off by heavy traffic, or perhaps by a freight train. In case of fire, there might be a total loss due to the absence of effective water supply. Or, the risk manager might observe a weakness in internal accounting procedure whereby exposure to fidelity losses is created. In one case, a risk manager correctly diagnosed that the real loss from fire would not be in the destruction of the firm's ice house, but in the cost of removal of 5,000 tons of solid ice contained within the house. Thus, insurance was purchased to cover the cost of this removal at so much per ton.

2) Estimating the probability of loss

Once the exposure is recognized, the next step is to estimate the size and frequency of the loss. There are countless losses that may happen, but no particular problem would arise if they did. Other losses, however, could bankrupt the firm if they should occur. The risk manager first studies the records of past losses within the firm, if any, and then consults the loss experience of other firms or perhaps that of a commercial insurer.

He must keep constant surveillance over values of real estate and other property and see that up-to-date appraisals are on hand in order that the severity of loss resulting from the occurrence of a given peril can be accurately estimated. In one firm, a study was made of fire loss in ice houses that were located on leased property with spur-track facilities and that were widely scattered geographically. The maximum original value of each house was $1,500. Since the losses suffered over a period of fifteen years were almost nothing, the firm realized that the probability of loss from fire was not serious and decided to self-insure that particular risk. The risk manager, however, may not be able to obtain accurate estimates of certain possible losses. A good example lies in the difficulty of estimating the size of a lawsuit due to the negligence of some company employee. In such cases the manager must use his best judgment.

Sometimes rather ingenious methods are devised to estimate the possibility of loss. One formula was developed by a risk manager to measure the exposure to dishonesty losses within a firm. This formula involved the calculation of an index made up of three elements—the cash, inventory, and gross sales. For example, for small firms, the amount of dishonesty insurance required was 20 per cent of cash, 5 per cent of inventory, and 10 per cent of the annual gross sales. This system was developed after an accountant who had only $1,500 of cash at his disposal at any one time was able to steal $187,000 over a period of years.[6]

3) Handling the risk of loss

Once the probability of loss has been estimated, the risk manager is in a good position to decide the best method of handling the risk. It is obvious that if the loss would cause no real hardship to the firm, even if it should occur, the risk of loss could well be assumed.

If it is determined that the probability of loss is high, it is likely that insurance would be an expensive proposition. In such a case, the risk manager must determine whether to insure in whole or in part, or to self-insure. On this point a great deal of controversy exists. Before this controversy is analyzed, it should be observed that, as noted in Chapter 1, there is a difference between insurance, self-insurance, and

---

[6] George A. Conner, "Yardstick of Dishonesty Exposure," *The National Insurance Buyer,* Vol. III, No. 6 (November, 1956), p. 42.

risk assumption. *Insurance* refers to the use of a commercial insurer who may be able to reduce the risk greatly by combining a large number of other similar exposure units, or who, for a premium, may accept the risk as a transferee. By *self-insurance,* we refer to a situation, described below, where the individual firm meets certain requirements, and then performs essentially all the functions that are usually performed by the commercial insurer. *Risk assumption,* or *noninsurance,* means that the firm does nothing about the risk, but expects to bear any losses out of current working capital and to charge them off to current expense. It is important that the conditions appropriate to each method be understood by the risk manager.

Assumption.   Many exposures to loss are so inconsequential that they may properly be ignored. For example, the risk manager may feel that the risk of collision loss to old vehicles is such that it should be entirely assumed. Or he may assume the first $100 of loss to each vehicle. Such perils as pilferage, breakage of tools or windows, or robbery of vending machines are often assumed because the firm can easily absorb the occasional loss from these sources.

In addition to assuming certain losses, many firms also assume responsibility for certain services necessary to the insurance device. In group health insurance, for example, the firm may handle the claims of employees for illness and accidents. It may see that proper loss forms are filled out, physicians' statements are received in satisfactory form, and other papers are filed in support of the claim. Often the insured can perform such functions more economically than the insurer, and will receive an allowance for it in the premium.

Self-insurance.   What are the requirements that should be met before a firm can properly self-insure? Self-insurance will not usually be attempted unless the loss, should it occur, is severe enough to cause financial embarrassment to the insured. In other words, some method other than assumption of the risk is indicated, and the firm is deciding between one of the other methods of risk management. The following conditions are suggestive of the type of situations where self-insurance is possible and feasible:

1. The firm has a sufficient number of objects so situated that they are not subject to simultaneous destruction. The objects are also reasonably homogeneous in nature and value so that calculations as to probable losses will be accurate within a narrow range. If these conditions are present, the firm will be able to predict accurately the size of fund necessary to meet the risk involved.

2. Management is willing to set aside a fund to meet the large and unusual losses. Until the fund is built up, normally a program of outside commercial insurance must be maintained. As the size of the self-insurance fund increases, the amount of outside insurance can be reduced and finally eliminated. It is not satisfactory to have merely a "book" reserve for this purpose, since such a balance sheet transaction would not provide the cash if the loss were to occur. The fund must be actually set aside from operating assets and invested in securities that can be readily convertible into cash should the need arise. If a firm feels that a separate fund is not required, that it can meet any losses out of working capital, then it is not using self-insurance, but is simply assuming the risk, or using noninsurance.

3. The firm must have accurate records, or have access to satisfactory statistics, to enable it to make good estimates of the expected loss. Otherwise, it is guessing at the size of the necessary fund and has not successfully handled the risk of loss. To increase the accuracy of the calculations, it is wise to use data over as long a period as possible, not merely the last five or ten years. If outside data are used, it is necessary to exercise extreme caution to see that the data employed are applicable to the firm's own experience.

4. The general financial condition of the firm should be satisfactory. There is a tendency for businessmen who are in financial difficulties to believe that self-insurance is a good way to save on insurance. While it is often true that the firm can save money by self-insuring, this is possible only when all of the preceding conditions are met. If a firm is in financial straits, it is unlikely that the necessary fund will be set aside or that, if it is set aside, it will be of sufficient size to meet the risk. If the manager of the firm cannot afford insurance premiums, it is even more unlikely that he can afford the loss should it occur, or that he can "afford" to set aside a self-insurance fund.[7]

5. The self-insurance plan requires careful administration and planning. Someone has to be in charge of investing the self-insurance fund, paying claims, inspecting exposures, preventing losses, keeping necessary records, and performing the many other duties connected with any insurance program. If the necessary specialized executive talent is not available, if the business cannot appreciate the necessity of paying continuing attention to all the details of carry-through, self-insurance will not be a satisfactory solution.

---

[7] There is an old story to illustrate the conservative approach to this problem. A young man rising in the financial world approached J. P. Morgan for advice. Wishing to impress him about his financial status, the young man asked how much it cost to own a yacht, whereupon the elder Morgan replied, "If you are worried about the cost of owning a yacht, you can't afford to own one." So it is with self-insurance. If the risk manager is in doubt, he should probably avoid self-insurance.

Reasons for use of self-insurance. The central reason for the use of self-insurance is to save money. In general insurance lines, the insurer's expenses may range between 40 and 50 per cent of the premium dollar. It is not realized by some that a substantial part of this, perhaps 10 or 15 per cent, is for the benefit of the insured, directly or indirectly. Such expenses include those for the prevention of losses, for providing certain services to the insured, for reserve funds held for future losses, and for ultimate return to the insured either in loss payments, dividends, or both. Even then, the firm may conclude that the services can be provided more cheaply by itself. For example, one firm claimed that, as a result of self-insurance, the annual savings of collision insurance on a fleet of passenger cars and trucks averaged about $12,000.[8]

Other reasons for self-insurance include dissatisfaction with the services of the commercial insurer, difficulties in securing favorable rate classifications, and difficulties in securing outside insurance.

Why self-insurance is not generally used. In spite of the advantages of self-insurance, most firms continue to employ the services of the commercial insurer for one or more of the following reasons.

1. The firm may decide that even though in the long run self-insurance could result in monetary savings, there are advantages in stabilizing insurance costs and in making this cost predictable each year. The insurance premium constitutes a regular deduction for tax purposes, and also enables management to stabilize profits. Under the self-insurance plan, profits may be higher one year, but drop considerably in the years in which losses occur. If one of these losses occurs in a year which has been generally unprofitable, not only are losses exaggerated that year, but a tax deduction could also be lost due to the limited time within which losses of one year can be "carried forward" or "carried back" as an offset to profits in other years.

2. A firm may simply wish to avoid the details involved in managing what may amount to a miniature insurance company within its organization. Management may feel that to do so would amount to fragmentation of executive talent and would constitute a diversion from the central business with which it is concerned.

3. The firm may want an outside, disinterested party to settle claims. In the field of credit insurance, for example, oftentimes the insurer can render better, more efficient collection service than the insured. In workmen's compensation where personal bias may influence a claim, there are distinct advantages to hav-

---

[8] A. G. Westcott, "Risk Insurance," Insurance Series No. 112 (New York: American Management Association, 1956), p. 13.

ing a third party, rather than the firm itself, deal with an injured employee.

4. The firm may want the inspection service of a commercial insurer. Let us say that a firm has steam boilers in which any loss from explosion can be virtually prevented by careful and regular inspections. However, such inspections require a person with a specialized training. It might be uneconomical for the firm to hire a full-time inspector, and an outside inspector may not be available. If, on the other hand, the firm employs the services of a commercial insurer, the insurer will furnish inspection along with the insurance policy at a reasonable cost. Even if the firm maintains an inspection department, it may wish an outside inspection as a check on its own.

5. For reasons relating to its personnel, a firm may desire outside insurance in some lines, even though self-insurance is possible. For the dishonesty peril, the fact that the employee is bonded may itself be a deterrent to wrongdoing. Also, in case of robbery, an employee may feel that he does not have to risk his life to save company property if it is insured in any event. As observed above, in workmen's compensation, better employee relations can be maintained if the outside insurer handles the claims. Any disagreements will usually be lodged in the form of complaints against the insurer rather than the firm.

Hazard reduction. Regardless of whether self-insurance is used or commercial insurance is purchased, the risk manager is vitally interested in loss-prevention activities. It is indisputable that ideally the best way to handle risk is to eliminate the possibility of loss where possible. While complete achievement of this goal is seldom possible, nevertheless, any degree to which it is achieved results in substantial savings to the insured, not only in lowered insurance premiums, but also in a smoother, more efficient conduct of the business.

Many risk managers are in direct charge of their company's accident-prevention program. Among their varied duties are:

1. Keeping accurate records of all accidents by number, type, cause, and total damage incurred.
2. Maintaining plant safety-inspection programs.
3. Devising ways and means to prevent recurrence of accidents.
4. Keeping top management "accident conscious."
5. Seeing that proper credits are obtained in the insurance premium for loss-prevention measures.
6. Minimizing losses by proper salvage techniques and other action at the time of a loss.
7. Working with company engineers and architects in planning new construction so as to secure the maximum safety and to

secure important insurance premium credits when the structure is completed and in use.

An example of what hazard-reduction activities can achieve is provided in a case drawn from aviation manufacture. A plane that was nearly finished caught fire on the assembly line. While a major catastrophe was avoided by quick action of a sprinkler system, still one life was lost, personal injuries were suffered, and property damage amounted to $500,000. Investigation showed that the fire was caused when a short circuit in the electrical system ignited gasoline that was used for testing the fuel system. The testing fuel had become mixed with a "low-flash" highly flammable fuel. As a result, a new testing fuel with a "high-flash" point was adopted and control procedures were tightened. Later on, a nonflammable gas that was nonhazardous and which gave substantial production advantages, was developed.[9] It is doubtful that anything would have been done about this accident if the firm had not had an individual—an insurance manager—to take action to see that the firm profited from past mistakes.

Transfer of risk. Handling the risk by the transfer method is an important device that has not been neglected by insurance managers. Transfers of risk may be grouped under two classifications: (1) those involving transfer to an insurance company, and (2) those involving transfer to parties other than an insurance company. The former type is treated later in this chapter as part of managing the insurance program. We shall now be concerned with the latter type.

An interesting example of the transfer method to parties other than insurance companies is found in the use of lease plans. An individual firm may not have a sufficiently large number of automobiles to justify self-insurance. Therefore it may decide that the administrative problems of ownership of vehicles, including the insurance details, can be advantageously transferred to a firm specializing in this business. Accordingly, the firm leases all its autos and thus avoids the problem of auto insurance by transferring the ownership risk to the leasing firm. The firm may lease many other types of property (examples range from floor carpeting to entire buildings) for substantially similar reasons—that of transfer of the ownership risk to specialists. The lessors, of course, may use commercial insurance; but as far as the lessee is concerned, he has handled the risk by transfer.

---

[9] George H. Connerat, "Risk Abatement," Insurance Series No. 112 (New York: American Management Association, 1956), p. 10.

Another example of the transfer device is to delay taking responsibility for goods during the period of their transportation. A trader may have his choice of terms of sale, under which he can have the seller assume all risks of loss until the goods arrive at the buyer's warehouse. In this way the buyer has transferred his risk to the seller and has avoided an insurance problem. A similar illustration of transfer lies in the common practice of subcontracting. The transferor engages a subcontractor to manufacture certain supplies, assuming all risks therefor. Thus, the transferor is enabled to escape the responsibility of providing for the risk of loss attendant upon making the goods himself.

Commercial insurance.   Commercial insurance is probably the most important and frequently used method of handling risk that is employed by the risk manager. Much of the analysis of risk management organization, policies, and principles which follows is related to the commercial insurance phase of his work. Once the risk manager has analyzed his exposures; determined the probability of loss; taken all loss-preventive measures; and decided what risks not to insure, what to transfer, and what to self-insure, he must then set up an economical and efficient program of commercial insurance for the remaining risks.

Managing the insurance program involves the following steps, each of which will be briefly elaborated:

1) Deciding which forms of coverage are best suited to the firm's needs.
2) Selecting agents, brokers, and insurers.
3) Negotiating for coverage.
4) Analyzing and selecting methods of reducing insurance costs.
5) Seeing that the terms of insurance contracts are complied with.
6) Handling loss settlements and negotiations with adjustors.
7) Designing and maintaining adequate records of insurance coverage and other data necessary to a sound program of insurance.

1) Deciding upon the form of coverage.   Deciding which forms of insurance are best suited to the firm's needs presents one of the most valuable areas of creativity in which the insurance manager can make a contribution. Oftentimes entirely new contract forms, many of which have become standard offerings of the insurance companies, are initiated by the insurance manager. There are literally hundreds of choices available to the risk manager, who must make a selection, usually with guidance from established agents, brokers, or insurers, to meet his firm's particular needs. Each program of insurance should be tailored specifically, since no two situations are exactly alike. For a specific illustration of this problem, reference is made to Chapter 11, wherein two major forms of business interruption insurance are explained.

Once the contracts are in force, it is the duty of the insurance manager to verify that the contracts actually state what was intended. Various exclusions, warranties, and conditions must be studied and any necessary changes effected; and management must be advised of the limitations of protection. Rates, premiums, dividends, or discounts must be checked to verify their accuracy. The insurance manager submits any necessary data required under the terms of the insurance contracts. For example, many forms of coverage are subject to an audit at the end of the year, and require submission of final data on payrolls, sales, and the like, so that the proper premium can be determined.

2) Selecting agents, brokers, and insurers.   Insurance is normally purchased through established agents or brokers, who are independent businessmen that provide a necessary liaison between the seller and the buyer. Wise selection of these representatives can make a great deal of difference in the work of the insurance manager, for it is from these individuals that he obtains up-to-date information, expert advice, and skilled aid in negotiation with insurers. The insurance manager cannot hope to be an expert in all lines of insurance. He usually needs the help of the agent or the broker in handling the many phases of his work with commercial insurance. Since there are great differences in the quality of services of various agents and brokers, the insurance manager must exercise great care in their selection.

It is sometimes argued that having both a capable agent or a broker *and* the insurance manager is not necessary, since the work of one duplicates that of the other. While this may be true to some extent, in a great majority of cases there are not sufficient areas of duplication to warrant this conclusion. As we have seen, the job of the risk manager is much broader than simply negotiating for insurance. Furthermore, the typical insurance agent or broker serves hundreds of customers and cannot give specialized attention to the needs of all. Normally the agent cannot afford to service in a detailed manner more than a few of his largest customers. It is no more logical to assume that either party should be abolished than to assume that a department store buyer is not needed simply because there are ample wholesale or manufacturer's salesmen available to advise the store on its needs.

3) Negotiating for coverage. Negotiating for coverage oftentimes is a complicated matter that requires great ingenuity on the part of the insurance manager. The firm may have specialized needs that are not readily available in the insurance "market." [10] Lengthy and complex bargaining sessions may be necessary in order to place the coverage in a satisfactory manner and at a mutually agreeable price. Oftentimes it is the insurance manager (frequently with help from his agent or broker) who obtains valuable concessions from insurers in the matter of satisfactory renewal of policies. The task is complicated by the fact that many times it is necessary to cover a given exposure by dealing with a dozen or more separate insurers, each of which takes a fraction of the total risk. Securing uniform coverage of a fire exposure of perhaps one hundred million dollars, not an uncommon exposure among large corporations, is not the simplest of tasks, when several insurers are involved.

4) Analyzing and selecting methods of reducing insurance costs. Insurance costs can be reduced in many ways, and the insurance manager must analyze each method with a view of obtaining coverage at the lowest cost compatible with safety and service considerations.

Judicious selection of *deductibles* can be a great cost saver. While deductibles are of many types, essentially they all have one purpose— to control costs and to effect a more efficient method of handling the risk by commercial insurance. Usually the purpose of a deductible is to eliminate from the coverage small losses that are almost certain to occur and, hence, are very expensive to insure. For example, an automobile insurer may quote a premium of $65 a year for $50 deductible collision insurance on a $3,000 automobile, and $35 a year for $100 deductible collision on the same auto. By taking the $100 deductible insurance, the insured saves $30 a year, and gives up $50 of coverage for each accident. Assuming the insured has one accident during the year, the effective rate on this extra $50 of coverage is 60 per cent. This may be compared to the rate of 1.2 per cent ($35 ÷ $2,900) that applies to the whole policy. The insurance on the extra $50 is extremely costly!

Use of certain contractual provisions can also greatly reduce insurance costs. For example, agreements to employ certain loss-preven-

---

[10] The *insurance market* refers to the supply side of the insurance service—the sphere in which price-making forces operate between the insurance seller and the insurance buyer. When it is asked "How is the market for fire insurance?" what is meant is, "Under what terms or conditions is fire insurance available from various sellers?"

tion methods, agreements to maintain in force sufficient coverage to equal a stated percentage of total exposed values, and agreements to assume certain administrative responsibilities will all reduce the cost of insurance if these provisions are properly analyzed and applied. As another example, writing a fire insurance contract to exclude from coverage the foundation of a building will reduce premiums without lessening the quality of coverage.

Some insurance costs can be lowered by buying "in quantity," and by negotiating a contract to cover a period longer than one year. Insurance costs can be reduced by a wise selection of insurers who operate more efficiently than others through such methods as: the use of mechanical accounting equipment, careful selection of insureds, more economical distribution methods, and more astute investment policies. Of course, the insurance manager must take care not to select a low-cost insurer that saves money by refusing to pay proper claims, that gives poor service, or that saves money by failing to set up adequate emergency reserves.

As outlined in a preceding section, insurance costs may be lowered by the use of self-insurance or noninsurance for certain risks. Self-insurance need not cover the whole amount of the loss, but only a specified portion. It is not uncommon for some insurance managers to recommend that the firm self-insure, say, the first million dollars of loss, and purchase commercial coverage on the remainder. In this way the economies of self-insurance, if any, can be realized without assuming a risk of catastrophic proportions.

5) Complying with the terms of the contract.   The entire purpose of insurance can be defeated if the firm, knowingly or unknowingly, violates the terms of the contract and thus is unable to collect when a loss occurs. It is the job of the insurance manager to know his contracts thoroughly so that the terms can be complied with, both before, at the time of, and after the loss occurs. For example, he must see that necessary permits are granted for extrahazardous operations which might otherwise suspend coverage under the fire insurance policy. He must see that proper methods are followed to do all that is possible to reduce the size of loss once the insured peril occurs. Otherwise, the firm may lose its coverage. As an illustration, a large corporation once had to pay a substantial liability judgment because it had failed to notify the insurer of the accident until almost a year had passed. The terms of the policy in this case had called for immediate notification of any loss.

6) Handling loss settlements and negotiations. An important and specialized task of the insurance manager is to handle the negotiations for all loss settlements. Oftentimes the amount of the loss is not easily determinable. If recent appraisals are not available on the value of a building now totally destroyed, it may take considerable discussion to agree on a settlement. The insurance manager may have to do much research to establish the value, say, of an ocean marine loss, or of a fire loss in a warehouse of goods for which adequate records have not been maintained. The insurance manager normally fills out proof-of-loss forms for employees making claims under group disability policies and sometimes he is required to "go to bat" when cases are questioned. The risk manager is the one to decide whether a claim will be filed under the policies, that is, to recognize an insured loss. The terms of many policies are sufficiently complex so that recoverable losses are easily overlooked. This is particularly true under the "all-risk" forms, wherein any loss that is not specifically excluded is covered.

7) Designing and maintaining adequate insurance records. The design and maintenance of proper insurance records is itself a specialized task that may require substantial time and effort on the part of the insurance manager. Typical of the records that will be kept are:

1. Insurance policy premiums and loss recoveries, termination dates by type of contract.
2. List of all automobiles owned, their description and value.
3. Automobile collision losses.
4. Automobile property damage and bodily injury liability cases.
5. List, description, and appraisals of all real property.
6. List, description, and appraisals of major classes of personal property.
7. Number, type, and loss from industrial accidents.
8. Payroll summary for workmen's compensation insurance.
9. Status of workmen's compensation claims.
10. Fire loss reports, including data on cause and amount of loss.

The reasons for maintaining these and other records include the following: (1) to enable the insurance manager to effect proper renewals of insurance coverage and avoid lapsing of coverage; (2) to furnish the basis for studies of self-insurance, noninsurance, and insurance proposals; (3) to provide material for reports to management concerning the operation of the insurance department; (4) to help control future losses and to enable the risk manager to analyze the cost of losses; (5) to provide data necessary for an advantageous settlement of insured loss claims; and (6) to enable the accounting department to allocate insurance costs among the various divisions or locations. This list is not meant to be comprehensive, but only suggestive of the many purposes served by adequate records.

4) Administering the risk management program

On the preceding pages have been outlined the first three of the four major functions of risk management—recognizing the exposures, estimating the probability of loss, and deciding upon the best method of handling the risk. The final function of risk management is that of administering the program. We shall consider three phases of the administration:

1) Policy formulation.
2) Organization.
3) Administrative tools.

1) Policy formulation. A *business policy* is defined as a plan, procedure, or rule of action followed for the purpose of securing consistent action over a period of time. Presumably, administrative policies are studied carefully before being put into effect and thus have a distinct advantage over *ad hoc* decisions made on the spur of the moment. It is likely that a policy, once established, remains unchanged as long as the same conditions which gave rise to it continue to exist. An insurance management policy, then, becomes a rule or a course of action that will be followed unless there are good reasons to change it, or to make exceptions in a given case. A policy usually is general in nature and allows for discretion in interpreting how the policy is to be carried out.

The advantage of having definite policies to guide insurance management is that once the rule is adopted, executives do not have to take time to restudy recurring problems before making decisions. Furthermore, as implied above, inconsistent behavior is avoided. All agents and insurers, all parties affected under the contract, receive equal treatment so long as their situations are similar.

Some examples of insurance management policies adopted by one company, a large chemical corporation, are:

1. It is the policy of this company to assume (as a charge against reserves, profits, or surplus) losses resulting from risks considered as not significant in relation to the cash position of the corporation.

2. It is the policy of this company to purchase insurance for risks not assumed.

3. It is the policy of this company to eliminate, or improve, as far as practicable, the conditions and practices which cause insurable losses.[11]

A statement of insurance management policy for a drug manufacturer is: [12]

It is our policy to assume the risks of property damage, legal liability, and dishonesty in all cases where the exposure is so small or dispersed that a loss would not significantly affect our operations or financial position, and to insure these risks as far as practicable whenever the occurrence of a loss would be significant.

It will be observed that these statements of policy are expressed in general terms, and constitute *major* policies for insurance management. A firm may have hundreds of *minor* policies, dealing with mechanical details of handling insurance records, purchasing procedures, and the like.

Policies should be based on sound principles. A *principle* differs from a policy in the following way: A principle states a general truth about a given subject area and is not subject to rapid alteration, whereas a policy may be changed overnight by executive decision. A principle may be defined as a general truth or law, a settled law or rule of conduct. As such, a principle applies until the basic facts upon which it is based change their character. A policy, on the other hand, may be contrary to sound principles and oftentimes it is, as will be illustrated below.

Formulating sound policies in insurance management requires an understanding of basic insurance principles, an understanding that this textbook seeks to supply. Some illustrations of insurance principles will be given here to clarify the preceding discussion. The principles selected are those which underlie the statements of policy given above.

Principle of insurable risk. A basic principle of insurance, the *principle of insurable risk,* was discussed in Chapter 3. This principle involves the conditions under which a risk can be economically insured; namely, that the events to be insured must be of sufficient number, must be homogeneous in character, must be subject to accidental loss that can be measured, must cause economic hardship to the insured, and must not be such that the probability of loss is extremely

---

[11] C. Z. Greenley, "Responsibility for Risk Management," Insurance Series No. 111 (New York: American Management Association, 1956), p. 23.
[12] James C. Cristy, "Responsibility for Risk Management," Insurance Series No. 111 (New York: American Management Association, 1956), p. 21.

high. The principle states that if any of the preceding conditions are not met, the risk is not economically insurable. It is obvious that the policies stated above are dependent on this principle. If these policies are adhered to, the firm can expect that its insurance management is being conducted in the most economical way possible. For example, the buyer who is guided by the principle of insurable risk will not insure losses that he himself can easily afford to assume.

The large loss principle.   The *large loss principle*—a corollary to the principle described above—states that the greatest economy in insurance buying can be achieved by placing coverage first on those perils which can cause crippling losses, and second, on other perils. The firm will pay for small losses out of current working capital, that is, assume these risks, and will be able to collect large losses from the insurer. While this seems to be an elementary proposition, it is surprising how often firms have a policy of "insuring everything." Usually such firms are the first to complain about being "insurance poor," as indeed they probably are. Sometimes the reverse is true, and the firm has a policy of insuring nothing but those risks which are absolutely required by law to be insured. By assuming large risks whether they can afford to do so or not, such firms are taking unnecessary and unjustified liberties with stockholders' funds. For example, a few years ago a stock brokerage firm in Canada declared bankruptcy after an embezzlement loss of $600,000 in negotiable stocks and bonds was discovered. The money had been taken in small amounts over a period of years. Failure to insure such losses is very common; yet it seems inexcusable when insurance is available at relatively low cost.

Principle of hazard reduction.   Another basic principle of insurance, the *principle of hazard reduction,* states that other things being equal, reducing the hazard is in general an effective and desirable method of reducing insurance costs. It seems undeniable that to prevent the loss in the first place, if possible, is better than running a risk. Hence, a formal policy of reducing or eliminating all causes of loss, insofar as practicable, is based on sound principle. The truth of this principle may be further illustrated by reference to the discussion in Chapter 1 under the heading, "Ways of Handling Risk."

An example of a policy not conforming to sound insurance principles is illustrated by one which stated that the commercial insurance for the firm should not be let out for bid from year to year. The firm felt that in the long run a risk manager should look at protection first, and cost next, and that to jump from insurer to insurer each year is not conducive to the best relationship with the insurer. However, it was noted earlier that one of the duties of the insurance manager is to obtain insurance at the lowest cost *compatible* with safety and service features. If the insurance manager can obtain a comparable contract at significantly lower cost from a new insurer that is just as safe and offers comparable service, it might be difficult to justify retention of the "regular" insurer. Competition is often keen in insurance business. To ignore differences in cost among insurers seems to run counter to a basic economic principle that, other things being equal, consumers will maximize their utility under a competitive system which favors the lowest cost producer selling at the lowest price.[13]

2) *Organization.* How should the insurance department, as it is commonly called, be organized? Where should it fit in the corporate structure? The answer to these questions lies in discovering what responsibilities and duties are placed on the risk manager, and then arranging his work so that he will have the authority to carry out these duties. It does little good to inform the risk manager that he has the responsibility for insurance management throughout the corporation, and then give him authority over only one phase of the work, or confine his authority to one plant to the exclusion of others.

Authority and responsibility. Authority means the right to make decisions over the actions of others. In the usual business organization, authority is delegated to various officers according to the particular responsibilities that they have. If these responsibilities are broad in scope, authority should also be broad. It is highly desirable that an officer have the right to make any decisions about the work of anyone who is in a position to help the officer perform his duties. It is not necessary that the officer have authority over all the activities of people with whom he works, but only over those activities that relate to this officer's particular function.

Typically, the risk manager reports to the treasurer of the organization. Sometimes it is not recognized that the risk manager has duties that affect many divisions within the organization. The risk manager must have access to information that will enable him to ascertain new exposures, such as when the business merges with another, takes on a new contract involving legal risks, or acquires new property. He should

---

[13] For an interesting discussion of this topic, see W. B. Whitney, "Competition in Insurance, Problem or Asset?" Insurance Series No. 117 (New York: American Management Association, 1957), pp. 10–13.

be given authority to acquire this information at all levels in the organization. He should have authority to negotiate final insurance arrangements with commercial insurers, and to hire and to fire his own immediate assistants. If the risk manager lacks such authority, his work is handicapped and he may find himself in the unenviable position of having the responsibility for all the duties that risk management involves but being unable to discharge these duties because of inability to require the cooperation of others within the organization.

Communication.   One of the chief organization jobs of the risk manager is to establish efficient methods of communication. Arrangements must be made for communication between various departments such as accounting, manufacturing, legal, and sales, so that necessary information can be made available to the risk manager, statistical tabulation jobs accomplished, and safety inspection reports made. Since the risk manager in a large firm cannot be expected to be an expert in all phases of the company's operations, he may need a staff of special assistants to aid him. A risk manager might employ an individual with an actuarial background, a pension consultant, or a statistician, as well as file clerks and secretaries.

Importance of centralized risk management.   In a corporation in which management is decentralized, there are cogent reasons for centralizing certain functions in order to achieve uniformity and the greatest efficiency. Authority for risk and insurance management should definitely be centralized for at least three reasons: (1) to avoid duplication and overlapping of coverage with its resulting wastes; (2) to secure the economies of blanket policies, broader forms, and quantity discounts in insurance purchases; and (3) to secure the services of a full-time, specially trained insurance department that is equipped to handle all insurance questions. To do otherwise is to fragment efforts to such a degree that no effective insurance management is possible.

When the business is large and far-flung, a carefully laid-out plan of organization is even more essential than it is in a small integrated business enterprise. The insurance manager must establish contacts with operating managers, set up machinery to process claims, devise cost allocation methods, and communicate with insurance and government officials in the various areas where the firm's operations are conducted. He must travel extensively and, of course, secure the willing cooperation of all the many executives upon whom he relies for information.

One firm handled the problem of an organization with decentralized management by means of a committee system. At each plant, key executives were chosen to constitute a committee through which all questions relating to insurance could be channeled to and from the risk manager. Any information required at the plant level could be easily developed through this committee and transmitted to the insurance manager. In this way, the sympathy and support of general management for insurance problems was achieved.

3) *Adminstrative tools.* Of the many administrative devices available to the risk manager, two will be discussed here; (1) the manual, and (2) the survey.

The manual. A *manual* serves as an operating guide and as a statement of the firm's policies and procedures in regard to any one phase of management. An insurance manual usually contains formalized statements of policy, procedure, responsibility, and authority relating to the insurance department; listings of major types of insurance in force; steps to be taken in the event of loss; and perhaps a compilation of facts about insurance exposures, number of employees, buildings and autos and their values, etc.

The purpose of insurance manuals is to gather in one accessible place an understandable guide to all insurance matters. Perhaps in no other way, for example, can the provisions of policies be known and consistently followed by all concerned. A manual often serves as an instruction book as well as a reference guide.

The objectives of an insurance manual include the following: [14]

1. To outline insurable risks to which the corporation is exposed.
2. To state the corporation's policy on the control of insurable risk.
3. To define the responsibility for executing corporate policy.
4. To record the measures taken to carry out corporate policy.
5. To outline the activities needed for good insurance management.

Too much detail in a manual is undesirable. Furthermore, the manual should be so arranged that revisions can be made easily. The manual should be specifically directed at a given objective, and must be usable in the sense that it helps someone perform his job more satisfactorily. A manual can be a valuable tool for any firm, and it should be considered indispensable for the large corporation with an insurance department of substantial size.

The survey. The *survey* is essentially a tool that is employed by the risk manager to obtain an accurate measure and analysis of the

---

[14] James C. Cristy, "Manuals for Insurance Administration" Insurance Series No. 102, (New York: American Management Association, 1954), p. 20.

various exposures to loss to which a firm is subjected. Survey procedure involves the development of facts which are necessary for a complete analysis of insurable perils. Normally a prepared check list of every facet of the business enterprise is followed so that important facts will not be omitted and so that all the necessary information in underwriting the risk will be easily available.

For example, in analyzing the exposure to public liability claims, a survey should uncover answers to the following questions: [15]

1. What products are manufactured, prepared, or assembled?
2. What products made by others bear the label of the firm?
3. What guarantee of products is issued?
4. What is the volume of work contracted by the firm for others?
5. What products are installed, serviced, removed, or demonstrated by the firm?
6. What is the volume of work done under contract by others for the firm? Are certificates of insurance required?
7. Is there any new construction contemplated or in progress?
8. What liability is assumed by the firm under lease agreements for real estate? for equipment?
9. Does the firm sponsor athletic teams, stock car races, or use any other unusual forms of advertising?
10. Does the firm use boats? If so, are they owned or hired?
11. Does the firm sponsor a display booth?
12. Does the firm operate an airport?
13. Does the firm maintain an infirmary for employees, or provide any other type of professional services for employees?
14. What is the record of all bodily injuries and property damage premiums and losses during the past five years (type, number, cost)?

Securing answers to these questions can help uncover exposures to liability claims that otherwise might never have occurred to the risk manager. The check list serves as a reminder of each type of exposure and also provides data that will be needed when the risk is commercially insured. Accurate information will usually simplify the placing of insurance, and enable it to be purchased on more favorable terms than if the underwriter has to make guesses about the extent of hazards in the firm.

A good survey has the advantage of preventing overlapping of coverages as well as duplication of insurance. It brings to light facts which might reduce, as well as increase, premiums. It is an indispensable tool of good risk management.

---

[15] The student should ask himself what possible exposure would be uncovered by each answer to these questions.

SUMMARY

1. Risk management is the function of executive direction over insurable risks and of devising the best methods of handling such risks. While risk management has been developed most highly as a separate management science in large business enterprises because of increasingly complex problems surrounding the management of these firms, the risk management function should be recognized in all business enterprises as a vital part of administration.

2. The risk manager has certain specific duties: to recognize various exposures to loss, to estimate the frequency and size of these losses, to choose and to implement the best of the various alternative methods of handling the risk, and to administer such programs as loss prevention, record keeping, and reevaluation of exposures to loss.

3. One of the most important duties of the risk manager—supervising the insurance program—has many facets, and the job is such that the specialized and concentrated attention by a full-time executive is usually justified. Use of such an officer, however, does not eliminate the need for the services of an agent or a broker.

4. There are several important ways in which a risk manager can effect savings in insurance costs without destroying the effectiveness of an insurance program. These methods include greater use of deductibles, use of certain contractual provisions, loss-prevention programs, and in some cases, self-insurance. Each of these methods must be used with great care in order to be effective.

5. To be effective, the risk management program must be properly organized, must have realistic policies based on sound insurance principles, and should make use of certain administrative tools such as insurance manuals and surveys.

QUESTIONS FOR REVIEW AND DISCUSSION

1. How does risk management differ from insurance management? Explain.

2. Explain each of the three views that has been taken of the job of the risk manager.

3. With the advent of peacetime usage of atomic energy, the demand for liability insurance has exceeded the supply. The Atomic Energy Act of 1954 requires that private users must hold the government not liable for any claim to life and property resulting from the operation of a licensed reactor. Hence, the demand for private insurance has been great.

   (a) What problems might the use of atomic energy create for the risk manager?

   (b) Would risk from the use of atomic energy be a possible subject for self-insurance? Discuss, with reference to the requirements for self-insurance.

   (c) What type of damage might be expected to stem from accidents with nuclear reactors?

4. Some countries (Mexico, for example) do not permit foreign investors to purchase insurance outside their boundaries. Other countries have exchange restrictions so that their currencies cannot be converted into dollars with which to buy insurance from American companies. What problems might such situations create for the risk manager of an American firm with a foreign operation?

5. A risk manager for a large concern read of an experiment whereby a group of "problem" drivers showed striking improvement in driving efficiency, and lowered accident rates after they had been given a daily dose of 150,000 units of Vitamin A for a certain period. A similar group who had not taken the vitamin showed no improvement over the same period.
   (a) What has this experiment to do with the job of the risk manager?
   (b) What should the risk manager do, if anything, after reading this article?

6. Studies of accident prevention reveal that for every accident there are dozens of "near misses" which could have caused losses, but did not. What do these studies suggest regarding the duties of a risk manager in keeping accident records?

7. The loss records of a group of insurance companies revealed that in 15 of 21 cases, the lost profits and charges resulting from fire exceeded the direct loss of property by fire. In total, the direct fire loss was $380,904, while the loss of profits and charges resulting from shut downs were $2,-654,256. What do these facts reveal about the importance of recognizing exposures to loss?

8. Why is it recommended that the insurance manager "have access" to the top executives of all major divisions of a business enterprise? Discuss.

9. Define and distinguish between the concepts of *policy* and *principle*.

10. A newly appointed insurance manager of a large concern found that his company was carrying insurance on films, projectors, and cameras although the largest single off-premises exposure did not exceed $600. Advertising exhibits off premises were being insured although the most expensive exhibit could be replaced for $2,500. The company also insured some rental houses located on industrial land. Rental income was unimportant, and everyone agreed that the houses would not be replaced even if they were destroyed. Was the company policy based on sound insurance management principles? Why or why not?

11. Is it necessary to have both a full-time insurance manager *and* an insurance broker or an agent, or are their services overlapping? Discuss.

12. Discuss the pros and cons of using the same insurer year after year regardless of lower insurance costs available elsewhere.

13. Why might self-insurance be undesirable even if savings in direct insurance costs could be demonstrated?

14. A business firm is considering the addition of a new building structure to its present plant and requests its risk manager to prepare such information as he can which will be of value to management in deciding which

type of structure to build. The risk manager is presented with the following building types now being considered:

(1) Combustible: Combustible exterior walls and roof (including skeleton metal on wood framing).

(2) Hollow block: Exterior walls of unlisted hollow concrete units, not less than 8″ thick, with main loads carried by pilasters of same materials.

(3) All metal: Exterior walls and roof of all-metal construction, with no combustible supporting members, nailing strips, etc.

An excerpt from the report turned in by the risk manager is given below:

RISK UNDER FULL PROTECTION

TYPE OF BUILDING	NOT SPRINKLERED		SPRINKLERED	
	BUILDING COST	INSURANCE COST	BUILDING COST	INSURANCE COST (ANNUAL)
(1) Combustible.......	$53,130	$5,090	$58,740	$925
(2) Hollow block......	$56,430	$1,925	$62,280	$630
(3) All-metal..........	$59,730	$1,330	$65,340	$560

COMPARISONS

	"NS"—NOT SPRINKLERED "AS"—SPRINKLERED	ADDITIONAL COST OF (B) OVER COST OF (A)	ANNUAL PREMIUM SAVINGS
Comparing (A)	*with (B)*		
1. NS Combustible	AS Combustible	$ 5,610	$4,165
2. "	NS Hollow block	3,300	3,165
3. "	AS Hollow block	9,150	4,460
4. "	NS All-metal	6,600	3,760
5. "	AS All-metal	12,210	4,530
6. AS Combustible	AS Hollow block	3,540	295
7. "	AS All-metal	6,600	365
8. NS Hollow Block	AS Hollow block	5,850	1,295
9. "	AS Combustible	2,310	1,000
10. "	NS All-metal	3,300	595
11. "	AS All-metal	8,910	1,365
12. AS Hollow Block	AS All-metal	3,060	70
13. NS All-Metal	AS Combustible	(Cr., $990)	405
14. "	AS Hollow block	2,550	700
15. "	AS All-metal	5,610	770

(a) Interpret the report of the risk manager to the management.

(b) What type of building would you recommend if you had no information as to the purpose of the building? Prepare a list of reasons to support your recommendations in terms you think that the management will comprehend.

(c) What additional comparisons might the risk manager have made to make the report more intelligible?

Types of Insurers and

(5) Their Marketing Systems

When one buys aspirin or fresh bananas he seldom inquires into the nature of the social or economic institutions that were responsible for making these products available to him, nor is there any compelling reason for him to do so. When one buys the services of a lawyer or a doctor, however, he is usually as interested in the qualifications of the person consulted as he is in the services needed, and rightly so, for the two factors cannot be separated. When one buys insurance, should he have a knowledge of the nature of the social institutions that provide the service? The position taken in this and the next two chapters is that he should. The nature of the insurer and the type of distribution system employed by it influence greatly both the cost and quality of the insurance service received. If the buyer is to entrust the security of his income and property to an insurer, he should certainly take a close look at the basic characteristics of that insurer.

CONDITIONS FAVORING THE GROWTH OF INSURANCE

Insurance institutions are shaped by the nature of the economic and social environment in which they grow and mature. There are at least three basic conditions necessary before the institution of private insurance can flourish:

1) The economic system must be a free system.
2) Society should be highly developed and industrialized.
3) Legal relationships should be well organized, known to all, and fairly enforced.

1) The need for a free system

Insurance does not grow under conditions in which the risk element is absent. Although insurance exists to some extent in countries where the tools of production are owned by the government and where basic economic decisions are made by some central authority, it never assumes great importance as a separate economic device to reduce risk. The government in such countries assumes most of the risks and in a sense acts as one great insurance company.

2) The need for a highly developed, industrialized society

The institution of insurance does not flourish in an economy that is primarily agricultural, or industrially undeveloped. This is true not because risks are entirely absent, but because they are not developed to the degree necessary to support a highly organized system of institutions to handle them. In an agricultural society, individuals have a tendency to be relatively independent, to be willing to assume many more risks than is true in more industrialized societies. Furthermore, people in agricultural societies are not as dependent on money as such, as is true in the more advanced economies. A large part of a farmer's needs may be supplied at home, and thus there would be little trade. A peril that destroys one crop would probably not leave the farmer entirely without food supply, because other crops, or help from neighbors, would supply his needs. If a building burns, perhaps neighbors cooperate voluntarily to restore it or to replace it and no dollar remuneration is felt to be necessary.

By contrast, in a highly developed, industrialized society, productive workers are dependent on money income. Their jobs are usually specialized so that the occurrence of some peril which interrupts their income, or destroys accumulated property, is often a serious economic blow. Help from neighbors is usually impossible to obtain in the degree that it might have been available in early times, for individuals cannot take off from their jobs at will. In the highly developed, industrialized society, standards of living are derived from trading the results of one's labor for the results of others' labor. This exchange involves the shipment of goods long distances, which gives rise to many risks not faced in a nonmanufacturing environment. Consequently, in industrial societies, methods to meet risks must be correspondingly highly developed, and insurance tends to flourish.

3) The need for well-organized legal relationships

Insurance as an institution flourishes best within a society in which legal relationships are well organized, known to all, and fairly enforced. An impartial system of justice is an absolute essential to a sound program of insurance, for the insurance device must usually be effected by means of a legally enforceable contract. Where political influence, frequent wars or revolutions, or dishonesty of the people upset the judicial system or law enforcement, insurance cannot flourish. While no complete "proof" of the above statement can be given, uncertainties are not predictable as accidental occurrences. Even if they were, it seems intuitively clear that if the insurer could never be sure that its legal rights would be enforced under its contracts, it could not afford to continue in business. As a further example, a war might result in such damage to the monetary system of an economy that an insurance company could not meet its obligations. In Japan, for example, the effect of World War II on the life insurance companies in that country caused their entire reorganization.[1]

As we have seen, insurance has grown tremendously in the United States, where a minimum of adverse circumstances has existed. In general, the United States has been characterized by great political stability, fair law enforcement, and a high degree of honesty among its people. Furthermore, it has become rapidly industrialized under a system of free competitive enterprise. All the conditions necessary for the rapid growth of insurance have existed. An understanding of these conditions is helpful in explaining why insurance has not grown rapidly in certain nations such as the Soviet Union, India, China, some European countries, and most South American nations.

THE FIELD OF INSURANCE

Classified by type of coverage, the field of insurance is usually broken down into two areas: personal and property.

Personal coverages

Personal coverages are those relating directly to the individual. In personal coverage lines, the risk is the possibility that some peril may interrupt the income that is earned by an individual. There are four such perils: death, accidents and sicknesses, unemployment, and old age. Insurance is written on each. Private insurers tend to specialize in the first two coverages, and governmental insurers tend to specialize in the latter two. Governmental insurers, however, offer certain insurance on all of these perils, while private carriers do not offer insurance against unemployment, and provide for old age only to a limited extent through the savings features of life insurance and annuity policies.

---

[1] M. Suetaka, "Post-War Trend of Life Insurance in Japan," *Journal of the Chartered Life Underwriters* (September, 1950, and June, 1951).

Property coverages

Property coverages are directed against perils that may destroy property. Property insurance is distinguished from personal insurance in that personal insurance covers perils that may prevent one from earning money with which to accumulate property in the future, while property insurance covers property that is already accumulated. Property insurance is used here in the broad sense to include fire, marine, liability, casualty, and surety insurance. Sometimes property insurance is referred to as *general insurance,* while personal insurance is called *life and health insurance.* These terms are used loosely, however, and are not so comprehensive as the other names.

Private and public insurance

Insurance institutions in this country have taken two basic forms of ownership: private and public (also called governmental or social insurance).

Private insurance consists of all types of coverage written by privately organized groups, whether they consist of associations of individuals, stockholders, policyholders, or some combination of these. *Public insurance* includes all types of coverage written or sponsored by governmental bodies—federal, state, and local.

Voluntary and involuntary coverages

Private and public insurance may be further classified into two subgroups: voluntary and involuntary insurance coverages. A great majority of governmental insurance is *involuntary;* that is, it is required by law that the insurance be purchased by certain groups and under certain conditions. Most private insurance, however, is *voluntary,* although the purchase of certain types of insurance is required by law, for example, automobile liability insurance in New York, North Carolina, and Massachusetts, and workmen's compensation insurance in some states.

Chart 5–1 presents the major classifications of insurance with the major types of coverage under each classification. In interpreting the chart, it should be observed that the types of coverage under each heading are meant to be suggestive of each type and not a comprehensive listing, which would take too much space, and make the chart too complicated to be useful. In addition, governmental insurance includes coverage offered by both state and federal agencies, and includes areas in which some governmental body merely sponsors or guarantees the coverage that is actually offered by a private agency (such as savings

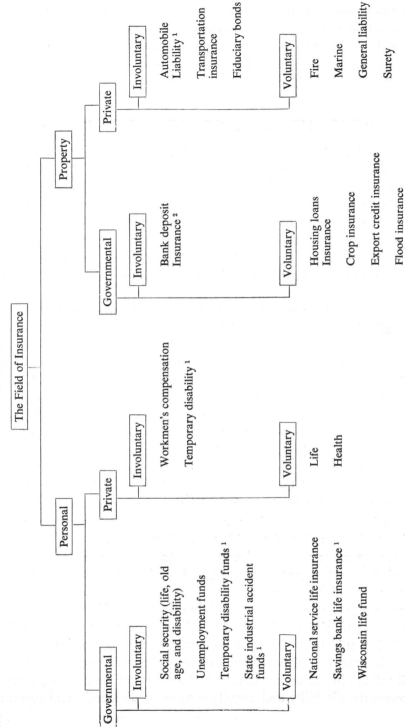

Chart 5–1

The Field of Insurance

Personal

Governmental

Involuntary
- Social security (life, old age, and disability)
- Unemployment funds
- Temporary disability funds [1]
- State industrial accident funds [1]

Voluntary
- National service life insurance
- Savings bank life insurance [1]
- Wisconsin life fund

Private

Involuntary
- Workmen's compensation
- Temporary disability [1]

Voluntary
- Life
- Health

Property

Governmental

Involuntary
- Bank deposit Insurance [2]

Voluntary
- Housing loans Insurance
- Crop insurance
- Export credit insurance
- Flood insurance

Private

Involuntary
- Automobile Liability [1]
- Transportation insurance
- Fiduciary bonds

Voluntary
- Fire
- Marine
- General liability
- Surety

[1] Applicable in only a few states.
[2] Bank deposit insurance required only in certain types of banks.

bank life insurance). Involuntary private insurance includes those offerings required to be purchased under certain conditions in some states.

This text will be devoted mostly to the field of private insurance, although some attention will be given to the major types of governmentally sponsored insurance.

IMPORTANCE OF MAJOR LINES OF INSURANCE

In order to give some concept of the relative importance of the major lines of insurance, Table 5–1 has been prepared, showing the estimated premiums received in 1960 by each type of insurer.

Table 5–1 reveals that, measured by premium income, the total of personal insurance is over three fourths of the total income of private and governmental insurers, while property insurance accounts for approximately the remaining one fourth. These data are only approximate, because no attempt has been made to include every conceivable type of insurance. For instance, only one example of property insurance issued by governmental insurers has been included. Comprehensive data are not available, but it is estimated that the aggregate amount of such insurance written by these insurers is small. Again, the table omits data from many of the miscellaneous governmental insurance operations in the field of personal insurance, since these are insignificant in size.

It may be seen that the income from life insurance is only slightly larger than the income from property insurance among private insurers. For all insurers, however, the total of personal insurance business is over three times the level of property insurance, measured by premium income. As we will see later, there are sound reasons for this emphasis, for the greatest potential loss facing an individual is the loss of his income from the occurrence of given perils. The great emphasis on personal insurance by governmental insurers accounts for the preponderance of total premiums collected on this type of coverage.

It may come as a surprise to some to observe the size of governmental personal insurance programs in relation to the total of all private personal insurance programs. The data quoted for governmental insurers do not include amounts paid under state welfare and retirement programs, and civil service employees' retirement programs, which, if included, would bring the total for governmental insurers considerably above the total for private plans. In terms of benefit payments, the total of all private life insurance payments, including death benefits, matured endowments, disability and annuity payments, dividends, and surrender values, in 1960, was $7.5 billion, less than the amounts paid out under the federal old-age and survivor's program alone! [2]

Table 5–1

ESTIMATED PREMIUM INCOME IN MAJOR CLASSES OF INSURANCE, 1960
(BILLIONS OF DOLLARS)

Private insurers

Personal insurance
Life insurance and annuity premium income [1]		$13.3
Health insurance: [2]		
Group contracts	$2.9	
Individual contracts	1.8	
Blue Cross—Blue Shield	2.8	
Workmen's compensation	1.4	8.9
Total private personal		$22.2

Property insurance
Total property-liability insurance premium income [3]	11.5
Total private insurers	$33.7

Governmental insurers

Personal insurance
Net social security tax contribution [4]	$ 9.3
Unemployment insurance [5]	2.2
National service life and U. S. government life insurance premium income [6]	.52
Railroad retirement taxes [7]	.60
Total government personal	$12.62

Property insurance
Receipts of Federal Crop Insurance Corporation [8]	$ .02
Total governmental insurers	$12.64
Grand total—private and governmental insurers	$46.34

Sources:
[1] *Life Insurance Fact Book, 1961,* p. 54.
[2] Health Insurance Association of America. Workmen's compensation premiums were taken from *Best's Insurance Reports,* 1961, and are composed of $476 million written by mutual insurers plus $942 million written by stock insurers.
[3] *Best's Insurance Reports,* 1961. Data exclude workmen's compensation and private health insurance premiums.
[4] *Budget of the United States Government, 1962* (United States Bureau of the Budget, 1961) p. 972.
[5] *Ibid.* p. 973.
[6] *Ibid.* p. 941.
[7] *Ibid.* p. 937. Data exclude receipt of funds from the Social Security Administration.
[8] *Ibid.* p. 335.

Table 5–2 provides some indication of the relative size of the various types of property insurance. Automobile insurance of various kinds accounts for 47.3 per cent of the total property insurance premiums collected by stock insurers. Fire, extended coverage, and allied fire lines are second in importance, aggregating 30.6 per cent of the total. The remaining 22.1 per cent is accounted for by all other types of property insurance. The great importance of automobile insurance in the field of

---

[2] Derived from *Life Insurance Fact Book, 1961,* p. 47.

property coverages is, of course, explained by the tremendous expansion of auto traffic, accompanied by steadily rising loss and premium payments.

Table 5–2

RELATIVE IMPORTANCE OF TYPES OF PROPERTY INSURANCE WRITTEN BY STOCK INSURERS, 1960

Type of Property Insurance	Premiums Written (Millions of Dollars)	Per Cent of Total
Fire.	$1,387	16.0
Extended coverage.	480	5.5
Allied fire lines.	122	1.4
Multiple peril policies.	668	7.7
Total fire and allied lines.	$2,657	30.6
Automobile bodily injury liability.	$1,873	21.6
Automobile property damage liability.	784	9.1
Automobile physical damage.	1,440	16.6
Total automobile.	$4,097	47.3
Miscellaneous bodily injury liability.	$ 610	7.0
Miscellaneous property damage liability.	147	1.7
Ocean marine.	213	2.5
Inland marine.	346	4.0
Fidelity and surety.	300	3.5
Glass.	42	.5
Burglary and theft.	106	1.2
Boiler and machinery.	63	.7
All other.	85	1.0
Total.	$1,912	22.1
Grand total.	$8,666	100.0

Source: Derived from *Best's Fire and Casualty Aggregates and Averages*, 1961, pp. 26–27.

TYPES OF PRIVATE INSURERS

Private insurers are generally classified according to ownership arrangements. There are four distinct types: 1) stock companies, 2) mutual companies, 3) reciprocals, and 4) Lloyds associations.

1) Stock companies

A *stock company* is a corporation organized as a profit-making venture in the field of insurance. For those companies organized in the United States, a minimum amount of capital and surplus is prescribed by state law to serve as a fund for the payment of losses and for the protection of policyholders' funds paid in as advance premiums. Stock companies, like all insurers, are organized with authority to conduct certain types of insurance business; and under the so-called multiple-line laws of most states, stock companies can be chartered to deal in all types of insurance, with the exception of life and health insurance. Even this limitation is not imposed in some states.

Stock companies in property insurance normally conduct their operations through the independent agency system, explained on page 115. They usually, but not always, operate by setting a fixed rate through rate-making organizations, with the approval of the insurance commissioner of any state in which they are admitted to do business. Some stock companies pay dividends to policyholders on certain types of insurance. Stock companies never issue what are called *assessable* policies, wherein the insured can be assessed an additional premium if the company's loss experience is excessive. The stockholders are expected to bear any risk of losses, and they also reap any profits from the enterprise.

2) Mutual companies

Mutual companies are organized under the insurance code of each state as nonprofit corporations owned by policyholders. There are no stockholders. There are no profits as such, since any excess income is either returnable to the policyholder-owners as dividends or is used to reduce premiums. The company is managed by a board of directors elected by policyholders. The bylaws of a mutual may provide for additional assessments to policyholders in the event that funds are insufficient to meet losses and expenses. In most mutuals, however, assessments are not permitted once the company reaches a certain size. Only in very small mutuals are assessments usually provided for. Even then, the assessment is usually limited to one additional annual premium.

There are many types of mutual organizations operating under different laws and with different types of businesses. In any given state it is necessary to examine the insurance code in order to determine the precise nature of the mutual.

Class mutual.   Some organizations, known as *class mutuals,* operate only in a given type or class of insurance, such as farm property, lumber mills, factories, and hardware risks.

Farm mutual.   Where farm property is insured, the group is known as a *farm mutual,* and may be organized under a separate section in the insurance code. Such mutuals insure a large proportion of farm property in some states, primarily because of the specialized nature of the risks. Many farm mutuals operate on the assessment plan, and, in some cases, the assessments are unlimited; each policyholder binds himself for a pro rata share of all losses and expenses of the company.

Factory mutual. A type of class mutual specializing in insuring factories is known as a *factory mutual.* These organizations have been noted for the emphasis that they place on loss-prevention activities. Each member must meet high standards of safety before he is accepted into the group. A large advance deposit premium, more than sufficient to meet expected losses, is required; any unneeded portion is returned to the policyholder at the end of the year. The factory mutual generally does not solicit small risks due to the relatively high cost of inspections, engineering services, surveys, and consultations, which are provided by the organization with a view toward preventing the loss before it occurs.

General writing mutual. Perhaps the most commonly known mutual in property insurance is the general writing mutual. The *general writing mutual* is one that accepts many different types of insureds; it is not a specialist writing in a certain class. General writing mutuals require an advance premium calculated on about the same basis as that of a stock insurer. In contrast to specialized mutuals, general writing mutuals operate in several states or even internationally. Where an advance premium is required, they usually set the premium to equal that of the stock insurer and contemplate a dividend or a rate reduction if experience warrants it. Many mutuals insist on relatively high underwriting standards, taking only the best risks in order that a dividend will more likely be paid. Some general writing mutuals reduce the initial rate below the stock company level, however, and do not plan on paying any dividends. Some mutuals are both *participating* and *deviating;* that is, they plan to cut the initial rate somewhat below stock company levels, and in addition to pay a dividend, if warranted.

Fraternal carrier. In the life insurance field, a type of mutual insurer known as a *fraternal,* deserves mention. A fraternal carrier is authorized to do business under a special section of the insurance code providing certain requirements are met. A fraternal is defined as a nonprofit corporation, society, order, or voluntary association, without capital stock, organized and carried on solely for the benefit of its members and their beneficiaries. Fraternals have a lodge system with a ritualistic form of operation and a representative form of government, which provides for the payment of benefits in accordance with definite provisions in the law. A fraternal offers only life and disability insurance contracts. As a charitable and benevolent institution, it is usually exempt from taxation.

Originally fraternals started out as pure assessment companies, charging no advance premium and assessing each member periodically for losses payable under the rules of the society. This proved to be unsound and most fraternals now operate on a full legal reserve basis, similar to other life insurers. An interesting difference exists between the life insurance contract issued by a fraternal and that issued by other life insurers in that the rules of the society are an implied part of the contract even though they are not attached to it. In some states a fraternal is required to include a provision in the bylaws declaring that if contributions of the members are insufficient to pay all matured death and disability claims in full and to provide for the creation and maintenance of the funds required by law, additional increased or extra rates of contribution shall be collected from the members to meet such deficiencies. Thus, it is possible for the holder of a fraternal life insurance policy to be subject to additional premiums or assessments, even though the society operates on a legal reserve basis.

Fraternal organizations underwrite only a small part of the total life insurance in force. At the close of 1957, they had $11.8 billion of life insurance outstanding, or two and one-half per cent of the total life insurance in force. Fraternals have not enjoyed the rate of growth that is characteristic of the industry. Since 1940 the amount of total ordinary life insurance in force has tripled, while the amount of fraternal insurance has doubled in the same period.

3) Reciprocals

A *reciprocal,* or *interinsurance exchange* as it is sometimes called, differs from a mutual, not in basic concept, but in the form of legal control and in the capital requirements. In basic concept, both mutuals and reciprocals are formed with the purpose of making the insurance contract available to policyholders "at cost"; that is, there are no profits as such and no stockholders to compensate. In both cases, the policyholders own the company.

In the legal control and capital requirements of reciprocals and mutuals, however, basic differences arise. In a reciprocal, the owner-policyholders appoint an individual or a corporation known as an *attorney-in-fact* to operate the company. In a mutual, the policyholders elect a board of directors to manage the company. A mutual is incorporated with a stated amount of capital, whereas a reciprocal is unincorporated with no capital as such. Sometimes state laws require that a reciprocal furnish a contingent fund in the form of a deposit with the insurance commissioner for the benefit of the subscribers. Otherwise, the reciprocal organization has no capital other than the advance premiums deposited by the owners.

A reciprocal is fairly easily formed. The state law may provide, for example, that when a group of individuals, known as subscribers, approach the commissioner of insurance with evidence that they have applications for coverage of at least 2,500 automobiles, or 200 applications for workmen's compensation insurance on at least $3 million of payroll, the exchange, through its attorney-in-fact, may be authorized to commence business, providing other requirements are met. The other requirements may include a minimum deposit, a statement of the type of insurance to be offered, a copy of the agreement between the subscribers and the attorney-in-fact, and other similar information.

A reciprocal agreement provides that each subscriber shall have an individual account. To this account are credited any advance premiums and any share of investment earnings that might be attributed to it. The account is charged with its pro rata share of the year's expenses and losses. Any excess belongs to the subscriber and when he leaves the group, he is paid the balance. If there are losses, his liability is limited to the amount in his account plus any assessment provided for in the agreement. This assessment liability is at least one additional annual premium. The liability of the subscribers is thus several, not joint, as in a general partnership.

In some states the law provides for limitation of the assessment liability of a reciprocal if the organization maintains an undivided surplus. Thus, if the surplus reaches a given size, say $300,000, policies may be issued without any assessment liability. In such an organization it is difficult to see any real difference between it and a mutual.

In a reciprocal each subscriber is also an insurer. The subscriber applies for coverage on a house, for example, in the amount of $10,000. In so doing, he agrees to insure other houses of the subscribers and is liable for losses in the proportion that $10,000 bears to the total fire insurance written in the exchange. Thus, if the exchange has $1 million in fire insurance outstanding, the individual with the $10,000 house is liable for one per cent of all losses, subject to the limitations of his assessment liability.

The attorney-in-fact is not an insurer, but only a manager. He has almost unlimited power over the operation of the business; and in times past, this power has been abused, with consequent failure of the reciprocal. Since the commissions of the attorney-in-fact depend only upon the volume of business, some attorneys have accepted business without regard for its quality. This has brought numerous losses in some cases.

Oftentime the attorney's authority is controlled by an advisory committee of subscribers who are given the power to prevent abuses and even to remove the attorney under certain conditions. The concentration of power in the attorney, the limited capital and danger of insolvency, and the contingent liability of subscribers are among the prices paid by subscribers for any savings in insurance costs that might result from joining a reciprocal.

4) Lloyds associations

A *Lloyds association* is an organization of individuals joined together to underwrite risks on a cooperative basis. The most important distinguishing characteristic of a Lloyds association is that each person assumes risks in his own name and does not bind the organization for his obligations. Each underwriter [3] is individually liable for losses on which he has assumed risks to the fullest extent of his personal assets, unless he has caused his liability to be limited.

Lloyds associations are similar to reciprocals since in both of these organizations the individual underwriter is an insurer. In Lloyds, however, the individual underwriter may not always be an *insured,* as he always is in a reciprocal. In other words, a Lloyds association is a proprietary organization bent on profit, and the underwriter member is always an individual insurer. A reciprocal is composed of individuals seeking ways to obtain insurance at "cost," and its members are both insurers and insureds at the same time.

Lloyds associations are of two types: 1) London Lloyd's and 2) American Lloyds.

1) London Lloyd's. The Lloyd's of London are among the best-known insurers in the world and are in fact one of the earliest known types of insuring operations. It is said to have started as early as 1688 in London, England, as an informal group of merchants taking marine risks while drinking coffee at Lloyd's Coffee House. Their operations are world-wide and they operate extensively in the United States largely in what is known as a *surplus line* market. This market consists of risks that domestic insurers have rejected for one reason or another. Lloyd's business is sold through registered brokers who are given the authority

---

[3] The term "underwriter" is said to have originated with Lloyds. The method of assuming risk is for each member to write his name *under* the total amount of any one insurance application that its member wants to take. Thus, if a member assumes $1 million of a $10 million marine venture, he signs his name on the application for $1 million and thereby assumes $1 million of liability. He thereby becomes known as an *underwriter*.

to represent them in this country. In no state except Illinois and Kentucky are Lloyd's of London admitted to do business on any basis except as surplus line insurers.

There are about 3,600 members of Lloyd's of London who operate through groups known as *syndicates*, each with a manager who acts as a general agent to bind the individual underwriter on various risks offered him. The Lloyd's corporation, it should be stressed, is not liable to the policyholder on risks assumed by its members. Nevertheless, the corporation sets up rigid standards of membership, and there has never been a reported instance in which the Lloyd's organization has defaulted on any obligation. There are a number of contingent funds created to back up the promises of the underwriters in event one becomes insolvent.[4]

2) *American Lloyds.* American Lloyds are authorized in most states under the insurance laws of the state. Typically the law provides that only certain types of insurance, such as fire, ocean marine, inland transportation, and automobile insurance, may be written by Lloyds groups. The law further states that some minimum number of underwriters, such as 25, is necessary in order to start an association, each member of which must have an individual net worth of a certain amount, such as $20,000. As a protection for policyholders, some laws provide for a minimum deposit, such as the same amount deposited by insurance corporations authorized to transact business in similar lines of insurance. The law commonly indicates that the underwriters may not expose themselves to loss in any one risk of an amount in excess of a stated proportion of the cash and invested assets, unless proper reinsurance is effected.

American Lloyds do not enjoy the reputation for financial solvency that is attributed to London Lloyd's. In the past it has been common for members of American Lloyds associations to limit their individual liabilities, and otherwise protect themselves against catastrophic claims. Reserves have been inadequate and failures are not uncommon. Some states, such as New York, prohibit the formation of new associations of Lloyds.

Relative importance of private insurers

The relative importance of the four types of private insurers, in terms of premium volume, is presented in Table 5–3.

---

[4] Examples are the central guarantee fund of several million pounds held by the corporation, a trust fund deposited in New York for the benefit of American policyholders, underwriting deposits made by individual underwriters, and reserves held by underwriting agents. For a complete statement of the security provisions required by Lloyd's of London, see *Best's Insurance Guide with Key Ratings,* issued annually.

Table 5–3

**PREMIUM VOLUME OF MAJOR TYPES OF PROPERTY LIABILITY
INSURERS, 1931 AND 1960**

Insurer	Premiums Written (Millions of Dollars)		Per Cent of Total	
	1931	1960	1931	1960
Stock companies.............	$1,531	$10,527	84	70.3
Mutual companies............	261	3,899	14	26.0
Reciprocals.................	37	523	2	3.5
Lloyds associations..........	2	23	...	.2
Totals.................	$1,831	$14,972	100	100.0

Source: *Best's Fire and Casualty Aggregates and Averages, 1961,* p. 1.

During the period 1931–1960, stock insurers suffered a declining share of total property insurance premium volume, while mutuals increased their share by about 80 per cent. Seventy per cent of the property insurance, however, is still written by stock insurers. Reciprocals and Lloyds associations, while enjoying great relative growth, still have only a small portion of the total volume.

In the field of life insurance, mutual companies are predominant. In 1957, mutual companies held 63 per cent of all life insurance in force. Stock companies and miscellaneous types of life insurers held the balance. In 1950, the mutual companies enjoyed 70 per cent, and the stock companies, 30 per cent, of the life insurance in force. It thus appears that in life insurance the mutuals are losing relative to stock insurers, and that in property insurance, the reverse is true.

In each type of insurance—property and life—the minority type of insurer is gaining, but for different reasons. One of the major reasons for the growth of stock insurers in the life insurance field is the greater relative growth in *numbers* of stock companies. Stock insurers constituted 89 per cent of the total of 1,439 companies in the United States in June of 1960. A majority of the stock insurers are small concerns that were formed in the 1950's. Most of them have been organized in the west south-central region of the United States, particularly in Texas, Louisiana, and Arizona. These three states alone had 535 life insurers in 1960, or one third of all insurers. Other leading states were Illinois, with 58; and Indiana and South Carolina, each with 54. These data include life insurers of both types operating in 1960.[5] Other reasons for the great expansion of stock insurers include the ease with which life

---

[5] Most of these insurers are stock companies. Data are taken from the *Life Insurance Fact Book, 1961* (New York: Institute of Life Insurance, 1961), pp. 98–99.

insurance companies may be formed in these states, certain tax advantages available to life insurers in reporting investment income, and generous supplies of capital seeking outlets for investment.

On the other hand, the mutual companies in property insurance have grown more rapidly than stock insurers primarily because the mutuals have tended to specialize in the types of insurance (particularly automobile coverages) for which the markets have been growing most rapidly. Furthermore, mutuals have used cost-cutting methods that have made the product available at generally lower rates than those offered by stock insurers.

In summary, the data show that in the field of property insurance, stock companies are most significant, while in life insurance, mutual companies predominate. In both fields, the dominant type of insurer has been losing its relative share of the total market.

CHANNELS OF DISTRIBUTION IN INSURANCE

Channels of distribution in insurance can best be understood by reviewing the familiar channels used in the marketing of tangible goods. A *channel of distribution* for a tangible commodity is the path taken by the *title* to the goods in the movement from producer to consumer. Usually, but not always, the actual physical commodity moves along the same path as the title. The important thing to remember about a channel of distribution is that it refers to the changes in *ownership* of the goods as they are distributed to consumers. The most efficient ways to accomplish this distribution is a subject of constant study in marketing because of the substantial cost involved in the distribution of goods, as opposed to their manufacturing costs. Studies reveal, for example, that on the average, it costs between 50 and 60 per cent of the consumer's dollar to market tangible commodities. The cost of distribution of insurance likewise is very substantial, as is shown later, and warrants careful analysis.

The type of channel taken by any given commodity is determined, in a free enterprise system, by whichever method is most efficient, least costly, and most likely to maximize the long-run objectives of the manufacturer. This ordinarily means that the consumer pays the lowest possible cost for the final product.

A typical channel of distribution for hardware products, for example, is from manufacturer to wholesaler, to retailer, to consumer. This would be termed a *long* or *indirect* channel, with at least two middlemen taking title to the goods. The wholesaler and the retailer are independent businessmen, taking the risks of their operations, making an investment in inventories, having complete ownership of the commodity, and disposing of it in any way calculated to maximize profits or to minimize losses. In the distribution of some types of goods, furniture, for example, the wholesaler is often circumvented and the goods move directly from manufacturer to retailer to consumer. A few goods are transferred without the aid of independent middlemen and go into consumer hands directly from the manufacturer, who is often represented by door-to-door salesmen. This type of operation is termed a *direct* channel.

In the field of insurance, there are many different arrangements that may be made for the distribution of the insurance contract. These arrangements are comparable to the channels taken by physical goods. For example, life insurance generally takes a short, direct channel, while property insurance normally uses a long, indirect channel with one or more independent middlemen involved. In some fields of property insurance, notably automobile coverage, increasing emphasis has been placed in recent years upon the use of more direct channels. Some of the reasons for these developments will be explained below.

Direct distribution

In the field of life insurance, the distribution channel is usually direct. A salesman called an agent or underwriter contacts the ultimate consumer and reports directly to the insurer, or to an intermediary, commonly called a *general agent,* who in turn reports to the insurer. The authority of the underwriter or agent is limited; he cannot be called an independent middleman, since he is actually an employee working under contract under the guidance and supervision of the insurer or his authorized representative.

A general agent, in life insurance, is an individual employed usually at a state or county level to hire, train, and supervise the agents under him. The general agent sometimes collects premiums and remits them to the home office of the insurer. Usually the general agent represents only one insurer, and works on a salary and commission plan, or sometimes on commission only. The general agent is not an independent middleman in the sense that a typical wholesaler is, for the general agent does not exercise final control over the issuance and the terms of the contract. He cannot normally bind his company in putting a contract in force. He exercises no control over the amount of the premium. He has no investment in "inventory." He does not "own" any business he writes, and has no legal right to exercise any control over policyholders once he leaves the employment of his company.

The system of direct distribution has grown up in life insurance because of several basic factors:

1) The need of the insurer to maintain close control over the policy "product."
2) The need of the insurer to exercise great control over sales promotion and competition.
3) The infrequent purchase of life insurance.
4) The ability of the agent to make a better living through specialization.

1) Need for close control over "product." The insurer needs to maintain close control over the policy "product" because of its complicated nature, its long duration, and because of the fiduciary relationship required between the insurer and the insured. A direct channel is appropriate where such close control is desired.

2) Need for control over sales promotion and competition. Life insurance is very competitive. The policies of the many companies competing for business are similar in nature. Hence, extra promotion and competition on the basis of superior salesmanship of agents often represent the difference between rapid and mediocre rates of growth of a life insurer. The insurer can exercise much greater control over these factors by employing a direct channel of distribution.

3) Infrequent purchase of life insurance. There are no compelling reasons for life insurance to be offered as one of the many contracts available from a given agent, as is true in property insurance. A buyer usually purchases life insurance infrequently, has infrequent need for claims service, and has little day-to-day contact with the agent regarding endorsements to policies, requests for information, and the like. This is not to imply that the life insurance agent renders no service once the contract has been put in force. He stands ready as the major local person who represents his company to the insured, answers questions, and writes letters to the insurer on behalf of the insured. But this service is not so demanding of his time that a large business operation would be required to provide it. His time is best spent in securing new sales for his company.

4) Better living through specialization. The life insurance agent has usually found it possible to make a better living by specializing in his field than by taking on as many different kinds of insurance as he can. Insurance is a complex subject. Fitting life insurance to an individual's particular needs partakes of a professional service supplied by the agent. Advanced knowledge of his subject is required to render the quality of sales service usually expected of him. He generally does not become an expert in all lines of insurance, but, rather, concentrates in one area. Because the agent usually finds that one company offers all the types of life insurance necessary for his clients' needs, and because he wishes to avoid the necessity of becoming familiar with the rate manuals and procedures of many companies, the agent usually represents one company only.[6] This situation calls for a direct channel of distribution, for each life insurer can usually distribute its contracts in sufficient volume in a given area at the lowest cost by hiring representatives to cover the area. There is no need for hiring any other middleman to handle the product.

Indirect distribution (American Agency System)

The channel of distribution for a majority of property insurance lines is indirect. A system of middlemen, comparable to the wholesaler-retailer system in tangible-goods marketing, is used. This system has been termed the *American Agency System.*

In property insurance, the middleman most comparable to the wholesaler is called the *general agent,* while the retailer is called the *local agent.* These terms are not to be confused with those that are applied in the field of life insurance.

General agent. In property insurance, the general agent usually has a great deal of authority over the distribution of the insurance contract. While he does not "take title" in the same sense that a wholesaler would take title to the inventory that he purchases from a manufacturer, nevertheless, the general agent has the incidents of ownership that accomplish almost the same purpose as would be accomplished by outright ownership. For example, the general agent can vary the terms of the contract in individual instances; he has considerable authority to negotiate the price of the contract, where this is permitted under state laws governing rates; and he has authority over the terms of distribution agreements with local agents. His dealings with the insurer are almost in the nature of banking. His contract calls for producing business on the general terms agreed upon and at a given commission rate. He has almost complete control over the business he writes and looks upon his

---

[6] There is a definite tendency for more and more successful agents to "broker" business through other life insurers and also to branch out into nonlife lines. However, accurate information on the extent to which this has taken place is not available.

insurer as a source to pay losses, to be responsible for policyholders' funds, to meet the requirements of insurance commissioners, to effect reinsurance agreements, and the like. The general agent, like a wholesaler, usually represents more than one company.

Local agent. The local agent, likewise, is an independent middleman in the property insurance business. Known as the "retailer," he deals with the final consumer of insurance. The local agent may represent from ten to twenty separate insurers in his office. He has authority to bind these insurers on most of the contracts that he writes. In most cases the local agent is supplied with forms, and has the authority to write a policy in his office and deliver it to the insured. The local agent "owns" the business he writes. That is, he has the legal right of access to customer files and to solicit the renewal of policies. The insurer does not have the right to give this renewal information to another agent. If the insurer cancels the agency contract of the local agent, usually the local agent will renew the policies of this insurer with a new insurer, and there is little that the old insurer can do about it. The agent works on a commission basis. He has the responsibility of collecting premiums and after retaining his commission, remits the balance to the general agent or to the insurer directly.

The branch office system. Oftentimes a given insurer will not use a general agent, but will work directly through local agents, or set up a branch office to deal with local agents. This plan is known as the *branch office system.* It corresponds to a manufacturer's sales branch in the tangible-goods field. This system gives the insurer more control over the distribution of its contracts than is provided when a general agent is employed.

It is significant to note that while the general agent may be replaced, his *functions* are merely transferred to the branch office, perhaps at lower cost. The branch office performs the same general duties performed by the general agent. Of course, only one company, instead of several, is represented in a branch office, and consequently greater specialized attention to the problems of one insurer is possible than is true in a general agency. This same objective is also achieved through the fact that the branch office manager is salaried and, hence, greater supervision of his activities is possible than is true under the general agency.

Direct writing. As noted before, in some lines of property insurance, independent middlemen have been dispensed with and the contract is marketed directly from the insurer to the insured, with or without an intermediary. Small amounts of insurance are sold directly by mail and no agent of any kind is employed; all negotiations are made between the insurance company and the consumer. In most cases, however, the insurer employs a representative to handle its business, to solicit prospects, to take care of paper work, and, in general, to serve as the insurer's direct contact with the insured. Insurers who employ this type of distribution are called *direct writers*. They include some of the largest automobile insurers in the business.[7] Direct writers have their greatest volume in the field of automobile insurance, but are expanding into other lines, such as residential fire insurance. In general, direct writers have been able to sell insurance at lower cost to the final consumer and this, plus a vigorous advertising campaign, has contributed greatly to their success.[8] The lower cost has been achieved largely by stricter underwriting and by paying smaller allowances to the agent for the production and servicing of business. For example, a total of 30 stock companies classified as "participating and deviating" (offering either lower rates or offering dividends, or both) paid direct commissions of 19.14 per cent of the premiums written in 1956. These companies employ independent agents. The leading direct writers, on the other hand, showed direct commission expenses ranging from four to nine per cent of the premiums written.[9]

An explanation of the growth of companies employing direct channels of distribution may be found in some observations about the nature of consumer buying habits in insurance and in other fields. As noted earlier, channels of distribution tend to be fixed in a free enterprise system according to whether or not they are as efficient as alternative methods. In the tangible-goods field, the postwar experience has noted the growth of discount houses that generally concentrate in the sale of so-called shopping goods, which command a relatively high price, are subject to infrequent purchase, and are substantially standardized in nature. These houses take a considerably lower markup on such goods than is traditional and still make enough profit to justify their existence. They generally offer the consumer little or no credit, or other services that are typically offered by competitors, and they save money in other ways.

---

[7] Examples are State Farm Mutual, Allstate, Nationwide Mutual, Liberty Mutual, and Farmers Insurance Group.

[8] A survey of newspaper advertising in 1956, conducted by the American Newspapers Publishers Association, revealed that property liability insurance companies spent $3,205,327 in 900 daily newspapers in 660 cities, of which 74% was spent by direct writers, 22% by companies using independent agents, and 4% by the National Board of Fire Underwriters.

[9] Derived from *Best's Fire and Casualty Aggregates and Averages, 1957.*

In the sale of automobile insurance, a situation similar to that of the discount house exists. The product consists of a fairly standardized policy issued once or twice a year, costing a substantial sum of money and requiring little service except when a claim arises. The traditional allowance to the independent agent is about 20 per cent of the premium dollar. This allowance is granted year after year, even though the agent may do little to earn it after the business is first procured. With the tremendous growth in the number of autos in the United States, a mass market in this field became possible; and some insurers saw an opportunity to capture a large amount of it by devising more efficient methods of business development. Accordingly, innovations such as continuous policies, lower agents' commissions, direct billing from the insurer to the consumer, and specialized adjusting offices to handle claims were instituted. These innovators were rewarded with a great relative growth. For example, in 1960, four large direct writers collected about 19 per cent of all the automobile insurance premium volume, compared to a negligible amount during the previous ten years.[10]

Is the American Agency System doomed?　Naturally those insurers and their agents committed to the traditionally long channel of distribution have become concerned over the future of their business, for the inroads of the direct writers are unmistakably clear. Opinion has been expressed that the agency system is doomed, that it will only be a matter of time until the direct writers "take over" completely, and that the independent agent will pass from the competitive scene. Before such a radical view is taken, however, it is well to examine the fundamental economic basis of the independent agency system.

Advantages of the agency system for the consumer.　The agency system grew because it was needed to distribute the product of insurance efficiently. The agency system is an efficient way for the consumer, particularly the business consumer, to buy insurance. Such an individual might be spending $10,000 a year on 100 or more different insurance policies. To place this volume of business among many insurers by direct negotiation would be a time-consuming and unrewarding task. To keep track of the many involved details and to keep abreast of the technical knowledge needed to place this business intelligently would be nearly impossible without assistance. The point can be further under-

---

[10] Derived from *Best's Fire and Casualty Aggregates and Averages, 1961.* The insurers are State Farm Mutual, Allstate, Nationwide Mutual, and Liberty Mutual, which wrote a total volume of $1.158 billion in premiums in 1960, compared to a total industry volume of approximately $6 billion.

stood by comparing the consumer's problem in buying insurance with the purchasing problems of a food retailer. Such a retailer may stock up to 6,000 separate items. If he were forced to deal directly with the manufacturers' representatives in securing these goods, he would not have time to conduct his business because of the necessity of talking to a continuous stream of manufacturers' salesmen.

The independent agent, who represents many companies and receives a constant flow of information from his insurers, can efficiently supply professional assistance to his customers. The consumer receives valuable aid from his agent when a loss occurs. The agent helps the insured file proofs of loss and intervenes in his behalf if a controversy occurs. The agent might be instrumental in helping the insured obtain coverage on risks that might otherwise be turned down by an insurer. Finally, the independent agent helps the insured plan a well-rounded, integrated program of insurance.

Advantages of the agency system for the insurer.   The agency system evolved also because it is economical for the insurer. Most insurers would find it uneconomical and undesirable to attempt to place a single agent or perhaps two agents in a given territory, as is done by a life insurer, with the expectation that these agents would represent only this insurer for all the business which the insurer hopes to develop in the territory. There are several reasons why this is true.

First, the financial capacity of many insurers is such that they cannot accept all the business offered them from one geographical or industrial location for fear of undue concentration of risks. An insurer would thus turn down business offered it, its agents would lose commissions, and in addition, the consumer would have to "shop around" in order to obtain coverage. Matters are greatly simplified if the agent represents several insurers and can thus obtain markets for all the business he develops.

Second, even if the insurer accepted all business offered it, there is doubt that a typical agent could obtain sufficient business in the usual geographical area within which he operates to justify his salary, if he were salaried, or to enable him to earn a suitable living through commissions which are currently allowed on the sale of property insurance. The typical policy premium in property lines is smaller and the commission is smaller than is true in life insurance. In addition, competitive factors are such that the total potential volume of business in a community is limited in amount and is divided among at least as many insurers as is true in life insurance.

Third, when an insurer enters a given territory, certain minimum services to the consumer must be offered—claims must be handled, premiums collected, credit extended, and questions of policyholders answered. The insurer is expected to take care of the myriad of details that it could not do directly. Moreover, the insurer could not afford to perform these functions through a salaried representative until the volume of business in a specific area had grown sufficiently large to justify the expense. This is usually not possible, except perhaps in metropolitan areas. Even where the volume of business does increase sufficiently, the insurer is not likely to wish to jeopardize the goodwill of policyholders and agents by switching to a direct-writing system.

Outlook for the agency system and direct writing. Direct writing has tended to grow in areas where there is a mass market for a standardized product that requires little continuous service. Since these conditions do not exist in all areas of insurance, particularly in the industrial market, it is extremely doubtful that direct writers will capture all the market. It is perhaps true that the basic nature of a typical agency contract will be altered to reflect the changed conditions brought on by direct writing. For example, insurers might take over some of the services now performed by agents, and reduce commission rates accordingly. This has already been done in some areas. It seems unlikely, however, that the independent agency system will be replaced by direct writing unless the property insurance business should become much more greatly concentrated than it is now and unless other basic conditions, now appearing quite unlikely, should come about.

As one authority stated: [11]

> The agency companies are under pressure to cut costs, the direct writers are under pressure to give more service. The end result will probably be, not the demise of either one of the competing marketing systems, but the improvement of each.

SUMMARY

1. A free enterprise system of economics; a highly developed, industrialized society; and a well-organized, honest, legal system, are among the prerequisites to a flourishing insurance institution.
2. There are two predominant legal forms taken by insurers: stock companies and mutual companies. Property insurance is dominated by stock companies, while life insurance is dominated by mutuals. In both lines of insurance, however, the minority forms of insurers are gaining. Lloyds

---

[11] Chester M. Kellogg, "Present Insurance Outlook," an address before the conference of Mutual Casualty Companies, Lake Delton, Wisconsin (June 6, 1956).

and reciprocals, as types of insurers, do a negligible portion of the total insurance business in the United States.

3. As measured by premiums collected, personal insurance (coverages involving the risk of loss of a person's income) is over three times as large as property insurance (coverages involving the risk of loss of a person's property). Governmental insurers account for about one fourth of the total insurance premiums collected, with privately organized insurers receiving the remaining three fourths.

4. In general, there are two basic methods of distributing the insurance service. The first method—direct distribution—used in life insurance predominantly, involves the use of semi-independent representatives whose authority is limited. The second method—indirect distribution or the "American Agency System"—following the pattern of distributing tangible consumer goods, involves the use of middlemen who operate independent businesses.

5. While the direct writing method of distribution is gaining in prominence in lines where standardized contracts and large-scale sales are possible, the traditional American Agency System continues to predominate the insurance distribution scene because of certain basic advantages which it enjoys. Undoubtedly the two systems will exist side by side in the foreseeable future.

QUESTIONS FOR REVIEW AND DISCUSSION

1. Why does insurance flourish better in an industrialized economy rather than in an agricultural economy? What other conditions seem to be necessary for a healthy growth of insurance? Discuss the reasons, in each case.

2. Benjamin Franklin organized an early fire insurance company called the "Philadelphia Contributionship for Insuring Houses from Loss by Fire." At first it was felt that people would voluntarily join the group, but this proved erroneous. Vigorous solicitation proved necessary. What conditions for the rapid growth of insurance were lacking in Franklin's time?

3. (a) What are the two major types of insurance? Explain the basic logic behind the classification of insurance used in this chapter.
   (b) Which type of insurance is most important from the standpoint of premium income? What reasons would you suggest for the relationship observed?

4. To many, fire insurance is the most important type of all property insurance. This was true before 1940. Is it still true today? Explain.

5. The mutual insurer has been called "communistic" in concept because there are no stockholders. Mutual advocates counter this charge with the statement that gain is the motive of the organizers of both stock and mutual companies. Evaluate these arguments.

6. (a) Do mutuals provide for assessments?
   (b) What advantages and disadvantages are there to the policyholder in being subject to assessments?

7. What motive prompted the formation of factory mutuals?

8. Why do not factory mutuals solicit small risks?

9. What problem exists in fraternals with regard to offering a policy at a fixed premium? Explain.

10. (a) What dangers exist in the reciprocal form of organization?
    (b) What advantage is there in the reciprocal form for the policyholder?

11. In both reciprocals and Lloyds associations, individuals are the underwriters. What significant differences exist between individuals in the two forms of organization?

12. Lloyd's of London operate largely in the surplus line market. Explain what is meant by "surplus line."

13. Lloyd's of London have a distinguished record of financial stability over many years, a record not shared by American Lloyds. Explain the probable reasons for this.

14. What trends characterize the respective market share of stocks and mutuals in property and in life insurance? Can you suggest any reasons for these trends?

15. To what extent are the channels of distribution in insurance comparable to those in the marketing of tangible goods? Explain.

16. Why should one study the channels of distribution for tangible goods? for insurance? Explain.

17. Explain the differences between a general agent in property insurance and in life insurance.

18. Why is direct writing typical in life insurance, but the exception in property insurance?

19. Does the American Agency System involve a long channel or a short channel of distribution? Is this system doomed because of the action by direct writers? Discuss.

20. What services to the buyers are rendered by the insurance retailer?

21. (a) Is the insurance retailer as important to an individual consumer as he is to the large industrial buyer? Explain why or why not.
    (b) Is the situation the same for the retailer in the tangible-goods field?

22. What services does the insurance retailer render the insurance company?

CHAPTER 6

Selecting

an Insurer

The preceding chapter has dealt with the various forms of legal organization for insurers and has considered the different systems of distribution used by them. The question now arises, how does one go about deciding which type of insurer and which type of distribution system is best?

Perhaps the first reaction in approaching the problem of selecting an insurer is simply to ignore it. This is probably the most common behavior. It is rationalized on the grounds that either there are no important differences in insurers from the viewpoint of the buyer, or that if differences do exist, it is not worth the time, expense, and trouble to make an intelligent analysis of the differences. This type of thinking can be an expensive and sometimes dangerous procedure. As will be explained, not all insurers are alike in matters of insurance costs, financial strength, and the quantity and quality of services. The financial importance of insurance expenses becomes apparent when it is recalled that expenditures for various kinds of insurance in 1960 totaled more than $46 billion (Table 5–1). This was slightly more than 11 per cent of the $412 billion of national income in that year. Significant savings through a scientific selection of insurers are possible. Paying no attention to the problem at all may result in purchase of insurance from an insolvent insurer.

The problem of an intelligent selection of insurers is complicated by the claims and the counterclaims of different types of companies offering insurance. For example, there appears to be a longstanding argument between stock and mutual insurers as to the advantages of each. Each type of insurer claims superiority over the other. Mutuals, for example, have argued that since they have no stockholders, they can operate at lower costs than other types of insurers, because there are no profit allowances in their premium structures. Some mutuals also argue that they have more efficient management, and that they are more inclined than stock companies to look after the interests of policyholders. Stock companies, on the other hand, hold that the capital contributions by stockholders give greater financial strength to their type of organization. Furthermore, stock companies say that since the stockholders take the risk, they absorb losses as well as profits. This benefits the policyholder, who is assured of a fixed premium, not subject to assessment, and of a fixed contract that cannot be changed in any manner, which is not true in the case of mutuals.

It is felt that while these arguments raise certain questions that should be examined, no final resolution of the controversy can be made, even if volumes of analysis were devoted to it. Rather, this chapter will attempt to offer certain guides to be used in approaching the problem of insurer selection.

SELECTION OF PROPERTY INSURERS

From the viewpoint of the buyer, there are three main factors to consider in selecting an insurer:

1) Cost of the coverage.
2) Financial solvency and stability of the insurer.
3) Quantity and quality of service offered, both by the insurer directly and through the agency system it uses.

In making comparisons on these points, extreme care should be exercised. An insurer that offers a premium lower than that of another insurer may be making up for it by reducing the amount of service, perhaps at the expense of financial strength. Hence, all three factors must be studied before any conclusions are reached.

Before proceeding to make any comparisons of cost, financial strength, or service, the first step in making an intelligent selection of an insurer is to find a group of insurers who are willing to offer comparable contracts to the applicant on terms that are satisfactory. Not all companies offer every insurance facility or every type of insurance contract.[1] If there are only one or two available insurers, the problem is considerably simplified. Furthermore, some insurers refuse, even for an additional premium, to delete or to add certain features that the insured may desire. This may further narrow the field of choice. Finally, contrary to the understanding of most laymen, some insurers may not be interested in accepting the insured's application at the rate that they are allowed to charge, because the insured may not meet minimum underwriting standards or because the particular class of business is not profitable to

---

[1] For example, there are only two insurers in the United States that at present offer credit insurance, the type of coverage against failure of debtors to pay their obligations.

the underwriter. Thus, drivers under a certain age may not be considered a profitable class of risk and are rejected by some companies.

1) Cost of the coverage

It is not a simple matter to compare the cost of insurance contracts or to determine which type of insurer is the least expensive. The initial premium paid may not be comparable among various companies because of significant differences in the terms of the contract. When the contract terms are standardized, premium comparisons may not be valid because of differences in the services offered by various insurers. Even if all these factors were held constant, innumerable other considerations would make a precise comparison impossible. For example, one insurer might offer the lowest premium in the first year in an attempt to "buy" business, in the same manner as a retailer advertises a loss leader in order to attract people into his store. Then, in later years, after the policyholder is a customer, the premium may be raised, certain services eliminated, loss claims settled on a niggardly basis, contractual provisions restricted upon renewal, or other methods used to make the business more profitable. Of course, the insured could change insurers whenever this happened, but he would have to make a continuing study of his coverage and of the many complex factors affecting cost in order to know which insurer to select. It is doubtful that many insureds can effectively accomplish such a task.

Some attempts have been made to select the lowest cost insurer or to eliminate high-cost insurers from consideration on the basis of aggregate loss and expense ratios. Other things being equal, it is reasoned that the company with the lowest loss and expense ratios is the most efficient and, in the long run, will be the most satisfactory. To illustrate this type of reasoning, the following analysis of data for stock and mutual insurers is presented. As mentioned earlier, a long-term argument between these two types of insurers has existed regarding the relative merits of each, with particular attention being paid to the cost factor.

Reference to Table 6–1 reveals a comparison of loss, expense, and profit ratios for stock and mutual insurers for certain major lines of insurance. The *loss ratio* is the percentage that losses incurred in a given year bear to the premiums earned in a given line of insurance during that year. The percentage of the premium dollar paid out in losses is the indicated measure of care with which the insurer underwrites his business. The lower this percentage, presumably the "better off" each policyholder is, for in the last analysis, insurance is a device for spreading losses among the members of a group; and the lower the loss experience,

Table 6–1

UNDERWRITING EXPERIENCE OF STOCK AND MUTUAL INSURERS DOING BUSINESS IN NEW YORK STATE BY SELECTED LINES, 1953–1959

Type of Insurance	Losses Incurred As % of Premiums Earned		Expenses Incurred As % of Premiums Earned		Net Underwriting Gain	
	Stock	Mutual	Stock	Mutual	Stock	Mutual
Fire insurance						
1953	45.5	34.6	46.9	37.0	7.6	28.4
1954	44.2	36.4	47.4	38.2	8.4	25.4
1955	46.2	37.5	47.9	39.1	5.9	23.4
1956	51.7	40.7	49.0	39.1	− .7	20.2
1957	51.7	42.2	49.7	38.5	− 1.4	19.3
1958	51.6	40.8	49.4	39.0	− 1.0	20.2
1959	50.7	44.2	48.7	38.4	.6	17.4
Homeowners' multiple peril						
1956	51.6	39.3	62.9	65.1	−14.5	− 4.4
1957	52.2	41.2	54.1	52.2	− 6.3	6.6
1958	50.5	39.9	51.4	46.6	− 1.9	13.5
1959	45.7	36.9	50.2	46.1	4.1	17.0
Group accident and health						
1953	78.0	76.9	13.3	15.2	8.7	7.9
1954	76.8	74.9	18.7	15.8	4.5	9.3
1955	78.9	81.0	17.6	14.6	3.5	4.4
1956	81.0	83.3	16.8	16.2	2.2	.5
1957	83.9	88.2	15.5	16.2	.6	− 4.4
1958	82.8	83.9	15.5	15.9	1.7	.2
1959	82.3	83.6	15.7	15.8	2.0	.6
Automobile bodily injury liability						
1953	54.5	56.9	43.0	37.7	2.5	5.4
1954	54.0	54.3	42.7	38.8	3.3	6.9
1955	58.7	59.4	43.8	40.3	− 2.5	.3
1956	65.4	60.9	44.8	40.5	−10.2	− 1.4
1957	70.7	62.7	45.5	41.8	−16.2	− 4.5
1958	66.9	64.3	44.5	40.4	−11.4	− 4.7
1959	63.0	64.1	43.2	38.7	− 6.2	− 2.8
Automobile collision						
1953	45.6	43.9	43.6	34.7	10.8	21.4
1954	39.9	36.0	43.6	34.2	16.5	29.8
1955	44.1	39.3	44.6	36.1	11.3	24.6
1956	52.9	46.6	45.5	36.2	1.6	17.2
1957	57.0	50.8	46.0	36.6	− 3.0	12.6
1958	51.4	45.9	44.7	35.3	3.9	18.8
1959	49.8	47.1	42.8	34.3	7.4	18.6

Source: *1957 Loss and Expense Ratios* (New York: New York Insurance Department, 1958) and *1959 Loss and Expense Ratios* (New York: New York Insurance Department, 1960). Data are based on the country-wide experience of all insurers admitted to do business in New York, except insurers with a premium volume of less than $10,000 in the line of business presented. Incurred losses are based upon the case estimate reserves and exclude allocated claim expense. Figures are on a net basis after reinsurance. Expenses do not include federal income tax; the net gain is gain before federal income tax, but after state and local taxes. Data for mutuals do not include factory mutuals

the "cheaper" the coverage each member obtains for himself. *Expenses* in this table include general overhead, loss adjustment expense, acquisition costs, and state and local taxes. On the expense side, presumably the insurer with the lowest ratio of expenses to premiums earned is the most efficient from the insured's point of view, for the insurer has been able to conduct its business at the least cost to the policyholder. *Net underwriting gain* summarizes the financial results of an insurer's operations, giving the analyst a convenient method of comparing the final underwriting results of several companies. Net underwriting gain is the difference between 100 per cent and the sum of the loss and expense ratios.

Loss ratios.   How valid are the assumptions stated above? Let us consider loss ratios first. In Table 6–1, it appears that in fire insurance, homeowners' multiple peril insurance, and automobile collision insurance, mutual companies have experienced considerably lower loss ratios than stock insurers for the period shown. This has resulted in a larger underwriting gain for mutuals in the fields of fire insurance and automobile collision insurance. In mutuals, this gain is presumably distributed to the policyholders, resulting in their obtaining insurance at a lower cost than would be possible from stock insurers in the same lines over the same period.

Unfortunately it cannot be concluded that this type of analysis is valid unless all other factors related to insurance costs are compared and found to be the same. Perhaps the most obvious possible explanation for the lower loss ratios experienced by mutuals is the difference in the type of risks insured. Possibly the class of risks insured has been consistenly better in the mutual insurers. This fact alone could explain the better underwriting "profit" in mutuals, but for an insured who does not meet the high underwriting standards of mutuals, this factor could also mean that coverage would be denied. In other words, for this type of insured, the "lowest cost" type of coverage might not be available.

Another explanation for the lower loss ratios of mutuals might be that mutual insurers have been less liberal than stock insurers in loss settlements, or have failed to set aside as liberal safety reserves for future losses. Each of these factors would have lowered the loss ratio, but would not normally be a favorable factor for the insured. Another explanation might be traced to the method of keeping the statistics. The data in Table 6–1 are "calendar year" statistics, not "policy year" statistics. In other words, the losses may have resulted from policies issued in a prior year, but the premiums earned include money collected primarily in the current year. Thus, the ratio in a given year might be misleading as a guide to which insurer offers coverage at the "lowest cost." This factor thus necessitates that for any meaningful comparison, several years' data should be considered.

The lower loss ratios in fire, homeowners' multiple peril, and automobile collision policies were not repeated in the fields of group accident and health and automobile bodily injury liability insurance for the mutual insurers. In the latter two fields, there appears to be a tendency for mutuals to experience slightly larger loss ratios than is true for stock insurers, with only a few exceptions in certain years. What would account for this? One probable explanation is that mutuals could be charging lower initial premiums than stock insurers. For example, let us say that two insurers had identical losses of $50 each, and that in one case the initial premium was $80 and in the other case the initial premium was $100. The first insurer would reveal a loss ratio of 62.5 per cent, while the second insurer would have a loss ratio of 50 per cent. Yet, one should not conclude from this comparison that either carrier is the "cheaper." It is generally true that in property and liability insurance, mutual carriers offer "deviated" rates below those of stock insurers. Thus, one might expect that, other things being equal, the mutuals would show higher loss ratios because of this factor alone.

In summary, it is seen that extreme care must be taken when attempting to determine the relative cost of an insurer by comparison of loss ratios. On the basis of published industry figures, however, mutuals appear to have lower loss ratios than stock insurers.

Expense ratios. Reference to Table 6–1 shows that mutual insurers generally have lower expense ratios than stock insurers, with the greatest differentials existing in fire and in automobile collision insurance. Practically all of these differentials can be traced to lower acquisition costs, since the mutuals pay around 15 per cent for commissions and brokerage allowances for fire insurance business and about 10 per cent for automobile collision business. This compares to approximately 25 per cent and 20 per cent respectively for stock insurers. Differences in other expense items are not nearly so great for the two types of insurers.[2] It should be remembered that the lower expense ratios are made more significant by the fact that the initial premium charged by mutuals is often lower than that for stock insurers.

Mutual insurers are in the position of not only charging a lower initial rate, but also of conducting their business at a generally lower overhead expressed as a percentage of that rate. This, together with lower loss ratios, has resulted in a higher net underwriting gain for

---

[2] *Ibid.*

mutuals. Table 6–1 reveals that for all types of insurance, other than group accident and health, mutuals obtained either a higher underwriting gain or a lower underwriting loss than stock insurers. In five of the seven years' data presented for the group accident and health insurance, mutuals failed to obtain a higher underwriting gain (or a lower underwriting loss) than did stock insurers.

In interpreting these results, it should be recalled that the other major factors, financial strength and quality of services rendered, should also be given careful consideration. These factors are discussed below. In other words, before selecting an insurer on the basis of lower costs, one should seek to determine the basic reasons for the lower costs, and then decide if any of these reasons is detrimental to him.

2) Financial solvency and stability of the insurer

To obtain insurance at a lower cost at the expense of financial strength in an insurer is obviously foolish. The main item of interest to one in the purchase of insurance is a guarantee of compensation for a covered loss. If bad financial policies, inadequate premiums, or poor underwriting standards endanger the fund that is set aside for losses, a person may find that he has carried insurance for many years to no avail. The loss occurs, but the insurer is bankrupt. This is poor solace for the doubtful advantage of having obtained a lower initial premium!

It is often assumed that because of the fairly rigorous system of state regulation over insurance, financial solvency of the insurer is more or less guaranteed and that the average policyholder has little to fear. While this assumption is no doubt justified in a great majority of cases, there have been and will continue to be failures, with consequent losses to policyholders, particularly in certain states.[3] Thus, the matter of financial solvency assumes paramount importance in the problem of selecting an insurer.

Financial statement analysis. Analysis of the financial solidity of an insurer follows the same basic principles common to that type of study of any corporate entity. Conventional financial statement analysis applies, but certain adjustments, to be explained presently, are necessary in order to fit technical insurance concepts into conventional financial analytical molds.

---

[3] According to the *Wall Street Journal,* between the period 1939 and 1955, nearly 140 insurance companies failed in Texas, more than all other states combined in the same period. Between 1956 and 1957, 51 more companies failed and more are anticipated. Texas has about a third of all insurers chartered in the United States, four times as many as second ranking New York. Not all companies fail with losses to policyholders, of course, because other insurers take over the business. *Wall Street Journal* (May 2, 1957), p. 20.

In any corporate balance sheet, the analyst who seeks a guide to financial solvency usually directs his first attention to the amount of debt shown in relation to the net worth of the enterprise. Too much debt indicates a possible inability to pay interest and repayment of principal in times of stress, with resulting bankruptcy. Thus, the *net worth to debt ratio* is a common tool of financial statement analysis. Such a ratio is usually calculated over a period of years in order to discover any adverse trends, and it is usually compared with that of other concerns with similar characteristics in order to discover any substantial deviation from "average."

For insurance companies, the net worth to debt ratio is probably the most significant single ratio employed. It is also one of the most widely used ratios. On insurance company balance sheets, the term "net worth" is called "policyholders' surplus," and the "debt" becomes the sum of various miscellaneous liabilities. The largest single item of "debt" on a fire insurer's balance sheet, for example, is called the "unearned premium reserve." One authority, Roger Kenney, insists that for satisfactory strength, the ratio of policyholders' surplus to the unearned premium reserve should be at least 1:1, unless extenuating circumstances exist that would permit a lower ratio.[4] The 1:1 ratio means a margin of safety of 100 per cent of the unearned premium reserve.

What light does such a ratio throw upon the financial stability of fire insurers? How do fire insurers measure up to this 1:1 ratio criterion? The rationale behind such a ratio is as follows: The unearned premium reserve on an insurance company's balance sheet refers to its liability to policyholders for premiums collected in advance. In fire insurance it is common to collect as many as three or five years' premiums in advance, and the liability to policyholders for these funds is the most important single obligation that the fire insurer commonly has. It is out of such funds that the company pays fire losses and bears its overhead expense. If policies are canceled, advance premium payments must be returned.[5] Thus, in fire insurance, the unearned premium reserve is the most accurate single measure of total demands on the insurer's assets.

Of course, funds representing the unearned premium reserve are conservatively invested by the insurer. However, a margin of safety is desirable in case the assets, which are represented primarily by stocks

---

[4] Roger Kenney, *Fundamentals of Fire and Casualty Insurance Strength* (Dedham, Massachusetts: Kenney Insurance Studies, 1957), p. 37.

[5] If the insurer cancels the policy, such refunds are made pro rata; if the insured cancels, the refunds are made short rata. See Chapter 10.

and bonds, should decline in value. The company's surplus represents assets that provide this margin of safety. Policyholders' surplus includes reinvested earnings and funds contributed by the owners. It is the net worth of the insurer. If an insurer has the 1:1 ratio that Kenney feels is desirable, it will have $2 in assets for every dollar of liability in the unearned premium reserve; that is, for every $2 in assets, $1 is contributed by stockholders and $1 by policyholders. Kenney feels that this margin might be reduced somewhat if in the normal course of events, there is evidence based on past records that the company will suffer no unusual losses from its business during the time that the advance premium payments are being earned; that its assets are not invested to a large extent in risky securities; that a parent company would assume any unusual liabilities; that management of the insurer is of high caliber; and that expenses have been low.[6]

Table 6–2

COMMON BALANCE SHEETS OF STOCK AND MUTUAL INSURERS WRITING FIRE AND ALLIED LINES, 1960

	767 Stock Companies	375 Mutual Companies
Assets		
Bonds.......................................	47.4%	68.9%
Common stock............................	33.5	14.2
Preferred stocks..........................	3.0	2.3
Other.......................................	16.1	14.6
	100.0%	100.0%
Liabilities and surplus		
Loss reserves..............................	23.9%	34.0%
Unearned premium reserve.................	28.8	25.3
Miscellaneous............................	5.6	8.3
Total liabilities.........................	58.3	67.6
Policyholders' surplus *....................	41.7	32.4
	100.0%	100.0%

* Policyholders' surplus consists of paid-up capital, surplus, and voluntary reserves in stock companies. In mutuals, it includes only the latter two items, since there is no capital stock. In the place of capital stock, mutual companies show on annual statements the item "guarantee fund."
Source: *Best's Fire and Casualty Aggregates and Averages, 1961.*

Table 6–2 presents common balance sheet summaries for 767 stock companies and 375 mutual companies writing in the field of fire and allied lines. It can be observed that stock insurers more than meet the

---

[6] Kenney, *op. cit.*, pp. 37–43.

Kenney 1:1 ratio, since there is a ratio of policyholders' surplus to un-earned premium reserve of about 1.4:1. For mutuals, the ratio, 1.3:1, is slightly less than that of stock insurers. Thus, while the financial position of both types of insurers seems quite safe, based on data for one year, the stock carriers appear to have a slightly greater margin of safety for policyholders than do mutuals. Mutuals, on the other hand, have a greater proportion of assets invested in bonds than do stock insurers (a favorable factor for financial strength). It cannot be concluded that either stocks or mutuals, as a group, are financially weak. Stock com-panies, however, may be in a position to withstand longer periods of adversity than mutuals.

Where the unearned premium reserve does not constitute a great majority of the liabilities of an insurer, comparisons should be made between policyholders' surplus and total liabilities. However, the total liabilities are likely to be less comparable because of the lack of account-ing uniformity employed by insurers in calculating the various items making up total liabilities.

In liability insurance, the ratio of policyholders' surplus to un-earned premiums would not be an appropriate measure of financial strength. For these insurers unearned premium reserves are usually small because in liability insurance, policies are usually for a one-year term or less. Hence, there are smaller amounts of funds collected in advance. The most significant liability item is the reserve for losses. It is appropriate, therefore, to compare the policyholders' surplus with the reserve for losses. Kenney has suggested no particularly desirable ratio between these two factors because loss reserves are subject to great flexi-bility and to a lack of uniformity between different insurers. He suggests, instead, that the potential liability be measured by new premium volume, and that the appropriate ratio between premium volume in liability insurance and policyholders' surplus not exceed 2:1. In other words, a lia-bility insurer should not normally accept more than two dollars of pre-miums for every dollar of surplus, if it is to maintain high standards of financial solidity.

Are these standards maintained by the industry? In 1956, the com-bined financial statements for 57 standard rate stock insurers operating in casualty and surety lines revealed that these insurers earned $1.35 of premiums for every dollar of policyholders' surplus. A group of eight comparable mutual insurers, on the other hand, earned $3.30 of pre-miums for every dollar of policyholders' surplus. It would appear that these mutuals are not meeting the standards, and are assuming more potential liability than is safe, while stock insurers are not writing as much business as their surplus would allow. However, examination of the individual financial statements of large, highly rated mutual casualty insurers reveals repeated instances where the company writes several dollars of premiums for each dollar of surplus.[7] It seems apparent that other measures of financial strength must be considered. A single ratio or even a set of ratios will not tell the whole story.

Best's ratings.   One approach to the problem of how to consider all the relevant factors in judging the financial strength of an insurer is illustrated by the financial ratings given by Best.[8] The ratings attempt to measure five factors that affect the financial stability of an insurer:

1. Underwriting results.
2. Economy of management.
3. Adequacy of reserves for undischarged liabilities of all kinds.
4. Adequacy of policyholders' surplus to absorb unusual shocks.
5. Soundness of investments.

Best's ratings would consider, for example, that even though a given insurer had a high ratio of policyholders' surplus to unearned premium reserves, careless underwriting, extravagant management practices, or unsound investment policies that resulted in asset losses could, within a short time, completely offset its good surplus position.

The ratings are of two types. The first type includes those that assess the general reliability of the insurer from the viewpoint of the policyholders. These ratings are "A+" or "A" (excellent), "B+" (very good), "B" (good), "C+" (fairly good), and "C" (fair), and are applied to all types of insurers on which information can be obtained. If inadequate information is available, the ratings are omitted. The second type of rating reflects the size of "free" resources, that is, net worth. There are 15 such ratings, ranging from AAAAA for insurers with $25 million of net worth or more, down to CC, for insurers with $250,000 of net worth or less.[9]

An analysis of the ratings presented in Table 6–3 reveals that the "A+" or "A," and "B+" ratings constitute a great majority of all policyholder ratings assigned, and that only in a minority of cases are lower ratings used. It seems fair to conclude that these ratings may

---

[7] *Ibid.,* p. 253.

[8] See *Best's Insurance Reports,* or a summary of various types of financial data found in *Best's Insurance Guide with Key Ratings.* Each of these annual publications covers over 1,100 property-liability insurance carriers in the United States. Fairly complete financial information about any carrier is available.

[9] The net worth figures in Best's include an estimate of equities in unearned premium reserves and loss reserves, as well as paid-in capital and surplus, and surplus reserves of various types. See Chapter 27 for a detailed explanation of these reserves and equities. See Appendix A for a statement of the methods used in compiling Best's ratings.

Table 6–3

POLICYHOLDER RATINGS ASSIGNED BY BEST TO STOCK, MUTUAL, AND RECIPROCAL INSURERS WRITING PROPERTY AND LIABILITY INSURANCE, 1954 AND 1960

Rating	Stock Companies 1954 Number	1954 Per Cent of Total	1960 Number	1960 Per Cent of Total	Mutual Companies 1954 Number	1954 Per Cent of Total	1960 Number	1960 Per Cent of Total	Reciprocals 1954 Number	1954 Per Cent of Total	1960 Number	1960 Per Cent of Total
A or A + (excellent)	482	65.0	512	67.4	277	75.0	286	79.2	42	61.7	37	59.7
B + (very good)	55	7.6	61	8.0	38	10.3	25	6.9	2	2.9	3	4.8
B (good)	21	2.8	17	2.2	16	4.2	17	4.7	5	7.3	5	8.1
C + (fairly good)	2	.2	6	.8	4	1.0	9	2.5	2	2.9	1	1.6
C (fair)	4	.6	2	.3	3	.8	4	1.2	1	1.5	…	…
Not rated	175	23.8	162	21.3	32	8.7	20	5.5	16	23.7	16	25.8
Total	739	100.0	760	100.0	370	100.0	361	100.0	68	100.0	62	100.0

Source: *Calculated from Best's Insurance Guide with Key Ratings, 1955 and 1961.* Ratings are omitted for the following reasons: necessary information was refused or furnished too late for use; the company disputes the application of the rating system, or disputes the construction of items appearing in annual statement; or where the company has less than four years' operating experience available.

serve adequately as a guide to which companies, presumably those with lower ratings, should be investigated more closely if insurance is to be carried with them. The great majority of all insurers meet Best's high standards of financial safety. The public has further protection in that it is the duty of the insurance commissioner in most states to examine each insurer for financial solvency at least once every three years.

It is interesting to observe from Table 6–3 that mutual insurers have attained a higher proportion of A or A+ ratings than either stock or reciprocal insurers, and furthermore, this proportion increased over the period 1954–1960. A smaller percentage of mutual companies received no ratings than either of the other two types of insurers. About the same relative number of stocks, mutuals, and reciprocals received B+ and B ratings. There were so few companies receiving C+ and C ratings that it is not possible to make valid financial comparisons. However, it appears that mutuals as a group are at least as safe as, if not safer than, stock companies in spite of the superior ratios of policy-holders' surplus to liabilities previously noted for stock insurers. Reciprocals as a group had the poorest showing, rating-wise, with over one fourth of the total number being not rated, and only about 60 per cent receiving A or A+ ratings.

In summary, it may be stated that there are no simple methods that can be used to determine the financial strength of an insurer. In cases where the unearned premium reserve is the major item of liability on the insurer's balance sheet, some notion of the relative standing of insurers can be obtained by comparing the ratio of policyholders' surplus to the unearned premium reserve. In many cases, particularly among insurers writing both fire and liability lines, the unearned premium reserve may be the largest single liability; but there are other substantial liabilities, such as loss reserves. In these cases, the best comparison to make is between policyholders' surplus and total liabilities. A comparison of policyholders' surplus and premium volume does not appear to be a particularly valid measure of the safety of an insurer, and can be used as no more than a guide to further investigation, in cases where the ratio exceeds 2:1 by substantial margins. Best's ratings are useful for the purpose of obtaining over-all comparisons of financial stability among different insurers, but these ratings appear to be most useful as a device to isolate notably weak carriers for possible further investigation.

On the basis of the published ratios employed, it appears that, in general, stock companies have higher margins of safety in policyholders' surplus than mutuals, and write less volume of business in proportion to policyholders' surplus than do mutuals. However, an analysis of Best's policyholder ratings gives mutuals the edge in financial strength. It may be concluded that no single test of financial strength should be relied upon in evaluating a given insurer, but that several tests over a period of years should be employed. These tests should include a consideration of the margin of safety for policyholders, underwriting losses and expenses, adequacy of liability reserves, and the soundness of investments.

3) Quantity and quality of service offered

In the last analysis, the element of service is perhaps the deciding factor in the selection of an insurer. Given comparable contracts and equivalent degrees of financial strength, the applicant for insurance is faced essentially with the question, "Do the insurers competing for my business offer coverage at lower cost, and if so, what in the way of service, if anything, is given up in obtaining this lower cost?" As we have seen in the field of property insurance, mutuals, as a group, tend to have lower ratios of expense and loss than stock companies. Of course, this does not necessarily apply to *all* mutuals and to *all* stock companies. Nevertheless, the question of service is a vital one in determining whether any saving in insurance cost is actually a net saving or merely a symptom of the fact that certain functions are not being performed by an insurer who offers coverage at lower premiums.

It has been seen that the main factor accounting for the lower expense of mutuals is the smaller amount of commissions paid to agents. The question then becomes, "Are agents' services being lost by dealing with mutuals, and if so, is the loss of these services worth the savings involved, if any, in dealing with mutuals?"

Proponents of stock property insurance companies direct considerable attention to the superior services that are rendered the insured when dealing with an independent agent, services sometimes not available when dealing with mutuals. These services, it is claimed, are more than worth the higher expense allowances involved in dealing with stock insurers. Such services include having the agent "go to bat" for the insured when claims occur on which there is some question of coverage, having an expert available to answer questions and to offer professional counsel on all matters relating to insurance, receiving short-term credit for insurance expenses, and enjoying the economy of dealing with one business establishment for all insurance needs.

Mutual advocates, on the other hand, stress that the cost-cutting features made possible by the direct-writing system do not necessarily mean any loss of service, as is often claimed by independent agents. They point out, for example, that the insured loses nothing by having one continuous policy rather than a new policy each year. This practice, followed generally by the independent agent, has resulted in a substantial needless expense caused by the return of policies that must be canceled by the agent, with the result that sometimes free insurance is provided for a limited period. Other cost-cutting techniques, such as streamlined adjustment procedures and direct billing from the insurer's home office rather than from the agent, have reduced expenses at no loss of real service to the policyholder. Mutuals clinch these arguments by reference to market surveys which show that in most cases consumers feel they are not getting any particular personal service from agents and that they are not often consulted, even at renewal time, about their insurance.

Mutual advocates claim that in many cases all the advantages of dealing with independent agents are also possible with mutuals because many independent agents represent both types of insurers. The mutuals stress that even though a given company may not be in a position to service all the needs of the insured, the savings involved in dealing with mutuals are well worth the inconvenience of dealing with more than one outlet for insurance needs.

Proponents of mutuals argue further that since many mutuals are small and organized by interested groups with loss prevention as a basic part of their program, losses are kept at a minimum, with consequent savings to members. Furthermore, professional service to aid the member in reducing his losses is not usually available to the same degree from independent agents. Mutuals also claim that the independent agent is too concerned with large accounts, and spreads his services too thinly to be of much benefit to the small account.

Stock companies deny most of the arguments presented by mutuals. Nevertheless, recognizing the validity of some of the arguments, they have taken steps to counter the advantages of mutuals and the system of direct writing. For example, stock companies have formed subsidiary companies that have adopted some of the same cost-reducing methods used by mutuals, such as continuous policies and direct billing. In the lines of insurance where competition is greatest, stock companies have reduced commissions to agents by substantial amounts. They have also developed "package" policies that involve a substantially greater premium, with the hope that one of the results would be to provide agents with greater incentive to service the small account. Finally, they have sponsored advertising campaigns designed to promote the advantages to be obtained by dealing with independent agents.

It may be concluded that while the independent agency system does not appear to be doomed (see the discussion on page 114), competition from mutual insurers in certain lines has resulted in changes in the marketing and administrative systems of stock insurers. The future will no doubt see further changes. The matter of agency service is one of the most significant factors in the selection of an insurer, and in many cases it is the deciding factor. It would appear that the independent agency system is still the most economical system of insurance distribution for most industrial accounts, but that, for many personal accounts, it is being challenged strongly by both stock and mutual direct writers. In a free society it is desirable that active competition should operate to bring insurance services to different consumers in the most economical manner possible.

SELECTION OF LIFE INSURERS

Few thoughtful savers would invest in a business or in the stock of a corporation without a careful investigation beforehand. Comparisons would be made among companies of the same type, and their achievements over a period of years would be analyzed. The advice of established independent brokers would be sought, and in the case of large investments, perhaps an individual study of a corporation, including visits to the plant and interviews with management, would be made. Yet, in buying life insurance, which for many constitutes their only major lifetime savings plan, it is doubtful if in the majority of cases any investigation or analysis takes place. Sizable investments are made over a period of years on the doubtful assumption that "all life insurance companies are alike, so why worry." Apparently the word of the agent that "my company is very sound," is all that is needed to persuade the buyer of the financial worth of the insurer represented.

Study of financial data

Even a cursory examination of financial data readily available reveals sizable differences in results, both in underwriting and in investment experience, of life insurance companies. It seems logical that the buyer should exercise as much care in selecting a life insurer as he does in buying property liability insurance, or in the purchase of a house or a business. The job of analysis is not easy, however, and it is necessary to exercise considerable care and judgment in any meaningful study.

A study of which is the "best" life insurer often revolves around deciding between two or three companies whose policies are currently being considered for purchase. It would not be feasible for any but the largest purchasers to make a comprehensive analysis of the 1,500 life insurance companies writing business in the United States today. In the selection process, the same general principles that have been discussed in connection with property and liability insurers, can be applied but with certain differences in emphasis.

Comparison of contracts

To be certain that one is making a valid comparison between two insurers, one must be sure that the contract desired is the same in each case. It is the problem of determining whether or not the contracts are identical that is probably the most difficult one in the field of life insurance. This problem is less complex in property liability insurance because, generally, policy standardization has proceeded to a greater extent in that field, and the contracts are of much shorter duration. Furthermore, it is less costly to shift from one insurer to another in property liability insurance than it is in life insurance. This is true because the first year's acquisition cost in a life insurance policy is heavy, usually exceeding the annual premium. Taking out a life insurance policy one year and dropping it the next is an expensive procedure. This makes a careful selection of the life insurer all the more important. Once it has been determined that the contracts are identical, the factors of cost, financial strength of the insurer, and matters of service can be considered in order to arrive at some decision regarding the "best insurer." There are so many complex particulars to be examined in the life insurance contract, however, that the process of determining comparability is no easy task.

It is not possible at this point to delve into all the various provisions of the life contract; but to illustrate the point, consider the problem of comparing two policies, alike in premium and in many other major respects. One policy contains a provision that pays the insured $10 a month for life per each $1,000 of insurance in the event of total and permanent disability, and the other pays only $5 for the same coverage. It might appear that the policy promising $10 a month is to be preferred. Closer examination reveals, however, that the company paying $5 indemnity for permanent and total disability issues a policy, at no extra cost, that contains a clause under which the insurer forgives all future premium payments in case the insured becomes totally and permanently disabled. The other company makes an added charge for such an endorsement. Now the decision is not so clear cut as to which company's contract is better. When it is realized that there are dozens of such points of difference to be resolved, one can appreciate the extent of the problem of obtaining valid contract comparisons.

Cost. Comparing the cost of life insurance offered by different insurers is a difficult task that is complicated by the many contractual differences previously mentioned that exist among the various insurers. Policies generally run for many years and the contract that may be the least expensive in the short run may be the costliest in the long run. In addition, there are also significant differences in the quality of services rendered by agents of different companies. These differences do not imply that the task is hopeless, only that extreme care must be taken in obtaining a valid comparison.

If it is determined that two contracts are sufficiently alike to warrant a comparison of cost, the next step is to compare the gross premiums charged. At this point there is an adjustment that must be made, depending upon whether either of the insurers is offering a participating rate or a nonparticipating rate. The term *participating* refers to the common practice of making an overcharge in the premium with the idea of returning a "dividend" to the policyholder. Both stock and mutual insurers write participating policies, but the practice is much more common with mutuals. Stock insurers generally offer a *nonparticipating* rate; that is, a rate lower than the participating rate, but at a fixed level. The purpose of the higher participating rate is to provide a margin for contingencies. The insurer in life insurance generally guarantees for life the initial rate charged. Thus, if costs rise, he has no opportunity to increase the premium. By means of charging a higher initial rate than actually required, the insurer can protect himself so that if insurance costs rise, the costs can be passed on to the individuals involved through smaller dividends. If insurance costs fall, these same individuals can enjoy larger dividends. In the case of stock insurers writing nonparticipating insurance, it is expected that if insurance costs rise, stockholders will bear any losses, while if insurance costs fall, they will receive the resulting profits.

What are the elements of "cost" in life insurance? There are three: 1) mortality, 2) interest, and 3) overhead, or loading, as it is called. The insurer with the lowest rate of mortality experience, with the highest rate of interest earned on policyholders' funds over a period of years, and with the lowest cost of doing business will be the "lowest cost" insurer, *other things being equal.* Unfortunately, it is seldom possible to hold other factors constant.

1) Mortality. The element of mortality in the cost of life insurance refers to the death rate among policyholders. Since all companies base their life insurance premiums on the same mortality "table," one might expect no differences to arise from this source of cost. It is possible, however, for one insurer to be more restrictive in its underwriting than another and thus experience a lower rate of mortality. Unfortunately, since published figures on mortality experience are not generally available, the average person cannot easily obtain comparisons on this point. It is sometimes possible to obtain information directly from the insurer's actuary about a particular company's mortality rate in a given year compared to the mortality rate assumed in the established mortality table. Since death benefits are of great importance in the company's total outlay, differences in mortality rates can be very significant in judging cost.

2) Interest. Best compiles and publishes figures for the net interest earned by recommended life insurance companies. Among 263 companies in 1959, interest earnings after federal income taxes ranged from a low of 1.85 per cent to a high of 5.97 per cent.[10] The industry average for that year was 3.96 per cent before taxes. Interest after taxes was not reported but would probably be around 3.5 per cent. Again, these figures should be interpreted carefully. To illustrate, the factor of interest is of utmost importance to the applicant for a life insurance policy, such as an endowment, that contains a large element of dollar savings. On the other hand, interest is of less importance to the applicant for contracts with no savings element, such as term insurance.

Another consideration lies in the major reasons for a higher interest return among certain insurers. The insurer that earned 5.97 per cent had 41 per cent of its funds invested in mortgages and 21 per cent in real estate, which is permitted in the state in which it is chartered to do business. This would appear to be unconservative to many analysts, who would conclude that the higher interest return may have been secured at the expense of safety of investments. The insurer earning only 1.85 per cent interest return, on the other hand, had 82 per cent of its assets invested in cash and government bonds. The probable reason for this pattern of investment is that the company wrote largely term and group life insurance, which have little or no investment element. Thus, this firm had relatively little need for long-term investment or for emphasizing a larger interest return. The matter of interest return would be of relatively little importance to this firm's major customers. It can be seen that even

---

[10] *Best's Chart of Recommended Life Insurance Companies, 1960* (New York: Alfred M. Best Company, 1960).

among "recommended" companies there are substantial differences in the factors of interest earnings and expenses of doing business.

3) Overhead or Loading. Best calculates annually the overhead per $1,000 of insurance coverage for about 250 "recommended" life insurance companies. For the year 1959 the overhead expenses ran from a low of $1.53 per $1,000 of insurance written to a high of $7.61.[11] However, the company with the lowest overhead happened to be the Wisconsin Life Fund, whose policies are available only to residents of Wisconsin. The Fund pays no agent's commissions and probably receives certain subsidies, either directly or indirectly, from the state of Wisconsin. The company with the highest ratio of expenses per $1,000 of insurance written might have concentrated in a type of insurance business where expenses of underwriting or of selling are relatively high. Nevertheless, in the selection of an insurer, there are important differences in overhead that should not be overlooked.

Some of the differences in expense can be accounted for by differences in distribution efficiency. Some insurers spend substantial sums for the scientific selection, training, and supervision of their agency force. Others spend very little. It is logical that, in the long run, the insurer which has the most efficient agency plant can secure business at the lowest cost. For example, higher commissions are needed to attract agents and brokers who receive no training or other aid. Turnover among such agents and brokers is higher, thus necessitating greater hiring costs. Normally the expenses of the firm with the greatest volume of business will be lower than those of firms with relatively small volumes. This is true because the fixed costs can be spread over a larger volume. This factor favors the large insurer. Expenses of insurers employing no agents should be expected to be lower than those of companies with large agency plants. However, there are relatively few life insurers who operate without agents, for reasons that will be presented in Chapter 20.

Dividend comparisons. To aid the prospective policyholder in estimating the cost of his life insurance, mutual companies usually publish scales of estimated dividends, based on past performance with respect to the three elements of cost discussed above. The total dividends for say, twenty years, are subtracted from the total premiums to be paid in, and the difference is represented as the "cost" of the insurance policy. Sometimes the agent subtracts from this figure the cash value of the

[11] *Ibid.*

policy and represents any difference to be the final "net cost." For example, the published dividends, premiums, and cash values of an ordinary life policy issued at age 25 for one large mutual insurer are as follows:

Total of 20 years' premiums. $427.09
Total of 20 years' dividends 89.59
   Net   payments. $337.50
Cash value in 20 years. 328.00
Twenty-year net cost (per $1,000 of coverage). . . . .$ 9.50

A calculation such as that given above may lead the buyer to believe that his insurance has been provided at little or no "net cost," and that therefore comparisons of cost are of little importance. This, of course, is an incorrect assumption. The insurer has no secret gold mine or oil well out of which to pay for insurance service. Insurance is provided by contributions of the insured group and by interest earnings on the funds that are pooled. The low "net-cost" figure given above is made possible by the fact that the policyholder has given up interest earnings which would have been possible if the money had not been paid in as premiums. What has happened is that the insurance company has taken the policyholders' funds, earned interest on them, and that interest has been almost sufficient to pay for the insurance service and death claims.

Companies are careful to point out that dividend estimates are only educated guesses about what future dividends will be if current experience, conditions, and principles of dividend distribution are the same in the future as they were in the past. There is the likelihood, however, that the applicant will rely upon these figures as the best possible estimates. It is very misleading, of course, to rely on such estimates and calculations as a basis for comparing the net cost of life insurance among various insurers. For example, one company could easily show superior performance by being more liberal in its estimates of future dividends than another company. Yet the underlying factors affecting dividends, mortality, interest, and loading, could be identical, and the "more liberal" company would have to lower its dividends below those promised. It might turn out that the underlying cost factors would actually favor the company promising the least in the way of future dividends. No one can accurately forecast all the different factors involved, particularly for a period as long as twenty years. It is commonly assumed, for example, that long-run trends in mortality rates are downward and that long-run trends in overhead expenses are about constant. The net effect of these two trends could reduce the cost of insurance. Yet a slight reduction in the interest earnings of a given insurer could easily wipe out any savings shown in the other two factors.

In summary, although there are substantial differences in costs among insurers, there is no precise way in which one can determine the "lowest cost" insurer in life insurance. About all that can be done as an initial guide is to determine which insurer appears to have the lowest expense ratio and the highest average rate of interest return on investments. If possible, a further investigation of mortality experience would be valuable. Net-cost comparisons can be very misleading and should probably be either completely avoided, or interpreted with extreme care because of the inherent difficulties of forecasting cost results. Finally, cost should not be considered in isolation, since the elements of financial strength must also be carefully weighed in the selection of a life insurer.

Financial strength. In life insurance there are several factors that are unique in assessing the financial strength of an insurer, as compared with the same problem in property liability insurance. First, the types of investments made in life insurance are much more closely regulated and restricted than in property liability insurance because of the long-term nature of the contract and because of the greater relative size of unearned premium reserves. The unearned premium reserve, which in life insurance is called the *policy reserve,* is necessarily large because usually the policyholder combines savings with insurance. The policy reserves are held in trust for policyholders and the law does not permit any speculation with these reserves. Therefore, practically all the investments made by life insurers are in the form of bonds and mortgages.

Second, the size of the policyholders' surplus in life insurance is usually a small fraction of total assets, far less than in the case of the typical property insurer. For example, in the Metropolitan Life Insurance Company, the largest financial corporation in the world, the ratio of policyholders' surplus to total assets is less than six per cent. This small ratio does not mean financial weakness, however, as long as the assets (for the most part, policy reserves) are safely invested.

A third factor in assessing the relative financial strength of a life insurer lies in the method of calculating the policy reserve. As will be seen in a later chapter, there are several legal methods of calculating the policy reserve, some of which are more conservative than others. The method used depends on the relative ease with which the company can finance new business. Stronger companies can use accumulated funds to finance new business and thus can employ a somewhat more conservative method of estimating policy reserve requirements. Weaker companies, in effect, use a method that results in lower policy reserve requirements, thus freeing funds to acquire new business. The net effect of using different methods of calculating policy reserves does not necessarily mean that a company is financially unsafe, but that in relation to another insurer, it may provide lower margins of safety. In property insurance there is generally only one pattern of legal rules governing the calculation of the unearned premium reserve. In other words, in selecting a life insurer one must consider not only the *size* of the policy reserve, but also the *method* by which it is calculated. In selecting a property insurer, however, only the *size* of the unearned premium reserve, when compared to policyholders' surplus, is significant.

Bearing in mind these differences, one can retain a proper perspective in assessing the financial strength of life insurers as compared with property insurers. In life insurance, probably the two most important elements of financial strength are: 1) the safety of the investments and 2) the relative size of policyholders' surplus, which includes all types of reserves for contingencies as well as any contributed capital of the owners.

1) Safety of the investments. Investment data for life insurers are reported by several rating agencies that gather information from the annual statements furnished by each insurer to the commissioner of insurance in each state in which the insurer operates. The information is public and any analyst can obtain it directly by inquiring at the state insurance commissioner's office.

The record of investment safety in the life insurance industry is one of the best of all industries in the United States. For example, during the depression period from 1929 to 1939, only 19 life insurance companies, representing about five per cent of all companies then operating, retired with initial losses to policyholders of $1 million or more. The initial losses totaled $130 million, fifty per cent of which was later recovered as other companies took over the retired insurers' business. In the same period, 12,000 banks were reported to have failed, with loss to depositors of $3 billion.[12] The final losses to policyholders of life insurers were approximately .2 per cent of the average assets of the companies then operating. It seems fair to state that this record of safety has reduced the risk of loss to policyholders as close to zero as is feasible for any type of saving under modern conditions.

---

[12] A. M. Best, "Rating in the Financial Structure of Insurance Companies," *Administrative Problems in Corporate Insurance Buying,* Insurance Series No. 96 (New York: American Management Association, 1952), p. 8.

There are at least three basic reasons why life insurance investment has achieved such an enviable record. First, as indicated before, the assets of life insurers are composed of bonds and mortgages that constitute a first claim on the assets of their issuers for both principal and interest. Second, the bonds and mortgages are long term in nature and are purchased so that maturities are staggered over a period of time. Thus, it is unlikely that any one life insurance company would have a large amount of its investments maturing at any one time, such as in a general depression or under other conditions that would make it likely that any sizable percentage of its investments would be in default. Even in case of default of certain investments, most life insurers have enjoyed a stable rate of growth, so that the current premium income has been sufficient to pay all current outlay required under maturing policies. Third, at least once every three years, the insurance commissioner in each state is required to make an inspection of each company operating in his state. This inspection includes a judgment as to the safety of assets and adequacy of reserves. In addition, submission of annual financial statements is required. Each state requires minimum standards of safety when an asset is purchased, and in many cases the state regulates what types of bonds and mortgages may be purchased.[13] During the financial panic of the early 1930's when the prices of all securities had fallen drastically in value, many life insurers were threatened with technical insolvency under the methods of valuation then employed. Through special action of regulatory authorities, however, life insurers were permitted to value certain assets at original cost rather than market price and this prevented any such financial embarrassment.

2) Relative size of policyholders' surplus. The adequacy of reserves may be studied for life insurers in the same manner as for property liability insurers. The ratio of policyholders' surplus to total assets may be compared with the average for the industry, and any existing trends determined. Opinions of rating agencies such as Best or Dunne can be considered.[14] Correspondence with the insurance commissioner may also be fruitful, particularly in cases where there is some doubt about a given insurer.

Service. The element of service in the selection of a life insurer has two aspects: 1) the amount of service to be obtained from the agent,

---

[13] The student should study the insurance code in his state to determine what regulations apply to the investment policies of life insurers.

[14] See *Best's Life Insurance Reports*, published annually, or *Dunne's International Insurance Reports*, published annually.

and 2) the amount of service to be obtained from the home office of the insurer. The element of service in life insurance is fully as important as in property liability insurance, although it is not often recognized as such.

1) Service from the agent. The agent can act merely as an order taker, or he can develop and maintain over the years a comprehensive plan of insurance designed to meet the unique needs of his client. The agent can personally write letters on behalf of his customer, take care of details such as beneficiary changes, and handle premium collections, as a convenience to his client, or he can ignore demands for aid or refer the client to the home office for answers. The agent can sell a policy that comes closest to meeting the real needs of the client, or he can sell the policy that nets him the greatest commission, regardless of whether it is appropriate.

No matter what quality of service is obtained, the premium is the same, so it behooves the insurance buyer to examine carefully how much in the way of service he can expect of his agent. The variations in service can spell the difference between a satisfactory insurance arrangement and one that fails to accomplish for the insured many things which are possible, but which oftentimes the insured does not know of at all. In judging the degree and quality of service that may be received from an agent, one can get some indication by the methods employed in selling the coverage; evidence of professional accomplishment, such as possession of the C.L.U. designation; [15] length of time the agent has been in the business; and references from outside impartial sources.

2) Service from the home office. Service from the home office of the insurer is very important. The life insurance policy often is a long-term contract involving thirty or forty years of premium payments, and twenty or more additional years of annuity payments either to the insured or to his beneficiaries. The dispatch with which these payments is handled is vital to the success of the insurance plan. Insurance companies often pride themselves on paying death claims of thousands of dollars within hours after the proof of loss has been submitted. Because agents come and go, the service of the insurer as a continuing influence over the years is of greater importance than it would be if the insured could deal with one agent indefinitely.

---

[15] C. L. U. stands for Chartered Life Underwriter. This designation is given by the American College of Life Underwriters, Philadelphia, Pennsylvania, after the full-time life insurance agent has passed a series of five comprehensive examinations in life insurance and related fields.

The quality and quantity of service rendered by the home office of the insurer is also reflected in the willingness to handle settlement options on a flexible basis. For example, if the insured has left the policy proceeds to a trustee for the benefit of his widow, will the insurance company allow the trustee to elect one of the various settlement options that normally can be elected only by a direct beneficiary? A survey of 120 insurers reveals that less than half will allow such a procedure.[16] Or, suppose that the primary beneficiary dies while receiving the policy proceeds on a lifetime income basis with a certain number of guaranteed payments. Will the insurer hold at interest the value of the remaining payments due for a secondary beneficiary, such as a minor, until the secondary beneficiary claims the money? This could be a valuable service because the interest guarantees may be liberal and the safe management of the money is assured. Yet, of the 120 companies surveyed, 48 do not offer such a service.[17]

SUMMARY

1. Since not all companies writing insurance are alike in such matters as price of the product, financial strength, and quantity and quality of services offered, the prudent insurance buyer will make an analysis of the particular insurer before entrusting it with his financial security.

2. The first step in the intelligent selection of an insurer is to make sure that each insurer to be analyzed offers a comparable insurance contract. The factors of the cost of insurance, the financial strength and stability, and the quantity and quality of services offered are all interrelated. The final selection of the insurer should be withheld until all factors have been studied.

3. Some notion concerning the cost of the insurance service may be obtained by an examination of the ratio of losses and expenses to premiums earned for individual insurers.

4. Examination of published underwriting experience of stock and mutual insurers reveals that mutuals tend to have lower loss ratios and lower expense ratios than stock insurers. This conclusion applies to groups of companies only and one cannot be certain that this is true of any or of all individual insurers.

5. The financial strength of an insurer may be judged by the ratio of policyholders' surplus to liabilities, by Best's ratings, by the adequacy of reserves for contingencies, by the soundness of investments, and by the trends in loss and expense ratios. The tests should be compared for several continuous years. No conclusions can be drawn as to whether or not stocks or mutuals are financially "stronger."

---

[16] *Settlement Options* (New York: Flitcraft, Inc., 1955), p. 72. This publication answers 36 similar questions about settlement options for the 120 insurers.

[17] *Ibid.*, p. 50.

6. Quantity and quality of service rendered, economy, and convenience in the administration of one's insurance program are important factors in the selection of an insurer. For most industrial consumers, insurers using the independent agency system are perhaps best situated to meet the service needs of the buyer. Direct writing companies, on the other hand, have offered insurance at lower cost for those not requiring as much service as others.

7. The sound selection of a life insurer involves the same general pattern of analysis as is true in selecting a property liability insurer. Special care should be taken to see that the contracts being considered are identical, that misleading dividend comparisons are avoided, and that the interest earnings on the assets are considered. The personal service rendered by an agent differs widely in life insurance and is a significant factor in the selection of a particular insurer. Willingness of the home office to render aid in fitting life insurance to the individual needs of the buyer is also an important factor.

QUESTIONS FOR REVIEW AND DISCUSSION

1. John Jones has a brother-in-law, Jim Smith, in the insurance business. Jones feels that nothing can be lost by giving all his life insurance business to Smith. Make a list of specific reasons why this might not be the best procedure.

2. Is there anything inherent in the legal organization of an insurer that would tend to make a given type of insurer superior over another type in: (a) management, (b) cost, (c) financial strength? Discuss.

3. Oftentimes the problem of selecting an insurer is solved by the fact that a diligent search is necessary in order to find a company that will accept the buyer's application. Explain why this might be true.

4. "A" argues that the insurer with a high loss ratio is actually more desirable than one with a low loss ratio because a high loss ratio is the best evidence that management is returning to the policyholder group a larger proportion of the premium dollar than the company with a low loss ratio. Criticize this argument.

5. Explain the terms
   (a) Loss ratio.
   (b) Expense ratio.
   (c) Net underwriting gain.

6. Why is it true that the loss ratio of an insurer writing at a lower premium than another may be larger even though actual losses are identical? What significance does this have in the analysis of mutual company figures?

7. Consult a service such as *Best's Insurance Reports* to obtain a list of insurers that have discontinued business in the previous year. Develop a classification of the reasons for discontinuance. What light does this investigation throw on the problem of financial strength of insurance companies?

8. "The most significant single ratio that tests the financial strength of an insurer is the ratio of policyholders' surplus to total liabilities." Explain the logic behind such a ratio.

9. What is the justification for using the unearned premium reserve as an estimate of total liabilities in applying the ratio mentioned in Question 8 to fire insurers? Explain.

10. Explain why a 1:1 ratio of policyholders' surplus to total liabilities means $2 of assets behind each $1 of liabilities.

11. Under what conditions should an analyst be satisfied with a ratio lower than 1:1 for a fire insurance company?

12. Why is the 1:1 ratio for fire insurance companies not appropriate for insurers writing primarily liability and other miscellaneous casualty lines? Explain.

13. The ratio of premium volume to policyholders' surplus has shown stock companies to be "safer" than mutual companies. Yet, there are large and reliable mutuals who do not meet the figure suggested as a maximum safe ratio. What criticisms of this ratio as a measure of financial strength could be advanced?

14. What advantages and disadvantages are inherent in the use of Best's ratings as a measure of the financial strength of insurers?

15. (a) In evaluating the cost of insurance, why must a consideration of the service of the agency force be given equal or even greater weight than the service of the insurer itself?
    (b) What differences exist in the factor of service in life insurance as compared with property liability insurance?

16. (a) Discuss the arguments of stocks and mutals relating to the degree of service rendered by each.
    (b) Is the service rendered by an insurer dependent upon its legal form of organization? Explain.

17. (a) In life insurance, what is the advantage of a nonparticipating rate?
    (b) Of a participating rate?
    (c) Which do you prefer? Why?

18. What are the three elements of cost in life insurance? For each element, indicate how possible future trends might affect the cost of life insurance.

19. What dangers exist in selecting a life insurer on the basis of "net-cost" illustrations?

20. In what ways does the analysis of the financial strength of a life insurer differ from that of a property insurer?

21. From a copy of *Best's Life Chart* select five "low-cost" and five "high-cost" companies on the basis of expense ratios and rates of interest earned. Look up each company in *Best's Life Reports* and try to arrive at a logical explanation why each company is classed as "high cost" or "low cost."

22. Why has the life insurance industry achieved such a good record of financial strength over the years?

CHAPTER 7

Functions and

⑦ Organization of Insurers

One of the most difficult and challenging problems faced by business generally lies in the area of organization. The insurance industry is certainly no exception to this statement. Since World War II the insurance industry has been undergoing a basic change in its internal organizational structure, a change which it has been argued by some, has raised more problems than it has solved. To understand the reason for these changes it is necessary to see just what it is that an insurance company does, why it does it, and what alternatives there are in the way functions may be performed. These and other issues are discussed within this chapter.

FUNCTIONS OF INSURERS

The functions performed by any insurer necessarily depend on the type of business it writes, the degree to which it has shifted certain duties to others, the financial resources available, the size of the insurer, the type of organization used, and other factors. Nevertheless, it is possible to describe the usual functions that are carried out, and it should be remembered that the specific nature and extent of each function varies somewhat from insurer to insurer. These functions are normally, but not always, the responsibility of definite departments or divisions within the firm.

The chief activities that are carried on by insurers are:

1) Production (selling).
2) Underwriting (selection of risks).
3) Rate-making and statistical control.
4) Managing claims.
5) Investing and financing.
6) Accounting and other record keeping.
7) Providing certain miscellaneous services, such as legal aid, marketing research, engineering services, and personnel management.

1) Production

One of the most vital functions of an insurance firm is to secure a sufficient number of applicants for insurance to enable the company to operate. This function, usually called *production* in an insurance company, corresponds to the sales function in an industrial firm. The term production is a proper one for insurance because the act of selling an insurance policy *is* production in its true sense. Insurance is an intangible item and does not exist until a policy is sold.

As we have seen, most insurers operate under an agency system whose job is to perform the production function. An agency system is usually necessary for a commercial insurer because without vigorous selling activities it would be difficult, if not impossible, to secure the necessary volume of business to allow the law of large numbers to operate successfully. Furthermore, without sufficient business volume, the overhead per policy would likely be very great, thus necessitating a premium that would be too high to justify the purchase of a policy by any but the prospect in greatest need of protection. This type of prospect is not considered desirable by the insurer, who views insurance as the spreading of losses among *all* individuals exposed to loss and not among just those most likely to suffer losses.

The production department of any insurer supervises the relationships with agents in the field. In firms, such as direct writers, where a high degree of control over field activities is achieved, the production department recruits, trains, and supervises the agents or salesmen. Its responsibility runs deeper than this, however. Many insurers support marketing research departments whose job is to assist the production department in the planning of marketing activities, such as determining market potentials, designing and supervising advertising, conducting surveys to ascertain consumer attitudes toward the company's services, and forecasting sales volume.[1]

In firms using independent agents as the primary channel of distribution, the extensive use of facilitating services in the production of business is not common. "Special" agents are used to explain company policies and to serve as the chief point of contact between the home office and the field forces. The chief job of selling is left to the independent agency force, and the production department has the responsibility of selecting the agents, putting them under contract, and exercising general control over the manner in which the business is produced.

---

[1] A study of these activities among insurers was made by the author and was reported in "Marketing Research As an Aid to Insurance Management, *Journal of Insurance* (December, 1957).

2) Underwriting

Underwriting insurance has to do with all the activities necessary to select risks offered to the insurer in such a manner that general company objectives are fulfilled.

The objective of underwriting. The main objective of underwriting is to see that the applicants accepted will have a loss experience similar to that assumed when the rates were formulated. To this end, certain standards of selection relating to physical and moral hazards are set up when rates are calculated, and the underwriter must see that these standards are observed when a risk is accepted. For example, it may have been decided that a company will accept no fire exposures situated in agricultural areas, or will take no one for life insurance who has had tuberculosis within a period of five years.

The underwriter, in reviewing an application for fire insurance where a building is located at the edge of an agricultural area, or in reviewing an application for life insurance in which the individual had tuberculosis four and one-half years ago, asks himself the question: "Can I make an exception for these applications, or must I reject them because they do not come within the technical limitations of my instructions?" In answering these questions, the underwriter visualizes what would happen to the company's loss experience if a very large number of identical risks were to be accepted. If the aggregate experience would be very unfavorable, he will probably reject the applications.

In sound underwriting, it is recognized that while profitable business is an important objective, it is a mistake to accept only business in which it is extremely certain that no losses will occur. To do so would no doubt make the job of the producer more difficult, if not impossible, and would mean too low a volume of business to support operations. As in many things, a happy medium must be sought between the extremes of very safe and very hazardous exposures on which to write insurance.

Services that aid the underwriter. The underwriter has the aid of many services in carrying out his work. In life insurance he is assisted by medical reports from the physician who made the examination of the applicant, by statements made by the applicant himself, by information from the agent, by an independent report (called an inspection report) on the applicant prepared by an outside agency created for that purpose, as well as by advice from his company's own medical adviser. In fire and liability insurance (as well as life insurance), the underwriter has the services of reinsurance facilities (to be discussed later), mapping departments to report on the degree of concentration of exposures in any one area, and credit departments to report on the financial standing of applicants.

Company procedures that aid the underwriter. In carrying out his work, the underwriter is also guided by fairly definite company procedures regarding the various physical and moral hazards that affect the probability of loss in given lines of business. In fire insurance, for example, a great deal of assistance is given by the rules that set up definite classes of buildings, with definite characteristics, such as types of construction, type of occupancy, degree of protection by city services, and exposure to various physical hazards. Unless there is something unusual about the structure or its occupancy, there is very little problem of selection because most of the important underwriting decisions have already been made. In assessing the moral hazard, however, serious problems may arise for which few rules have been promulgated. One rule that is widely observed is that if a serious moral hazard is known to exist, the business is rejected outright and no attempt is made to accept it at higher than normal rates, or to impose other restrictions. The difficulty lies in judging whether or not a moral hazard actually exists. Judgment of the underwriter is of paramount importance to the general success of any insurance company, and in the matter of assessing the moral hazard, the quality of his judgment is put to one of its severest tests.

Policy writing. Part of the work of the underwriting department may be most concisely described as *policy writing.* In property and liability insurance, the agent frequently issues the policy to the customer, filling out forms provided him by the company. For this reason, the agent is often termed an "underwriter." A check upon his work to determine the accuracy of rates charged, whether or not a prohibited risk has been taken, and other matters is done by the *examining* section in the home office of the insurer. In life insurance, the policy is usually written in a special department, whose main task is to issue written contracts in accordance with instructions from the underwriting department and, since most policies are long term in nature, to keep a register of them for future reference.

Conflict between production and underwriting. Because the underwriting department has often turned down business that has been previously sold by an agent, an apparent conflict of interest has arisen between these two areas. The problem is similar to that which exists between credit and sales in other firms, with a "good sale" ruined because credit is not approved. The "conflict" is, of course, only apparent. Neither the agent nor the underwriter will profit long by "too strict" or "too loose" underwriting. Too strict underwriting will tend to choke off acceptable business and may create unnecessary expenses involved in canceling business already bound by the agent. Too loose underwriting may involve losses of such substantial size that the company may be forced to withdraw entirely from a given line, to the detriment of the agent.

3) Rate-making and statistical control

Closely allied to the function of underwriting is that of *rate-making,* a function which is extremely technical in most lines of insurance. The details of rate-making will be discussed in Chapter 26.

Rate-making. In general, rate-making involves first the selection of classes of exposure units on which to collect statistics regarding the probability of loss. In life insurance this particular task is relatively uncomplicated since the major task is to estimate mortality rates according to age and sex, and, in some cases, by occupational groups. In other fields, such as fire and workmen's compensation, very elaborate classifications are necessary. In the latter field, for example, several hundred classes of industries are distinguished and a rate is promulgated for each class.

Once the appropriate classes have been set up, the problem becomes one of developing reliable data for each class over a sufficiently long period of time. Converting the data thus accumulated into a useful form for the purpose of developing a final premium becomes the next step. This involves incorporating estimates of the cost of doing business into the premium structure on an equitable basis. The rate-making function involves estimation of the cost of including certain policy benefits, or of changing policy provisions or underwriting rules, as well as the cost of writing business on which no data whatsoever have been accumulated.

Actuarial services. The rate-maker must have considerable skill in solving the various mathematical problems that face the insurer, a class of problems described as *actuarial.* It is through actuarial services that estimates can be made of the real meaning of data collected by the company from inside and outside sources. For example, if losses begin to rise in a certain class of business, does this mean that the rates will have to be restudied and revised upward, and if so, by how much? Or are such losses evidence of a mere random experience for which no significant conclusions can be drawn? What are the necessary sizes of the various reserves that must be provided? What results can be expected in losses and premiums if a new underwriting policy is followed, if a different accounting method or loss table is used, if there is a change in the investment earnings of the company? Solutions to these and many other questions are usually sought from the actuary. In life insurance, the actuary is of especial importance due to the practice of accumulating and distributing policyholders' funds over extended periods of time.

Statistical control. By its very nature, statistical control is vital to the success of insurance management. Not only are valid statistics required by tax and regulatory authorities, but, as will be seen, these data are essential to various rate-making organizations. The compilation of industry-wide statistics is necessary, in order that actuarially sound rates can be made. Few industries rely on such statistics to the extent that the insurance industry does. The insurance industry has been a leader among those utilizing advanced electronic data processing computers to perform the many tasks required of accounting and statistical departments.

4) Managing claims

Settling losses under insurance contracts and adjusting any differences that arise between the company and the policyholder describe the function of *claims management*. Claims management is often accomplished in the field through independent adjusters who are employed to negotiate certain types of settlements on the spot. Such adjusters usually have considerable legal training. The claims department of an insurer will have the responsibility of ascertaining the validity of written proofs of loss, investigating the scene of the loss, estimating the amount of the loss, interpreting and applying the terms of the policy in loss situations, and finally approving payment of the claim. These functions are more extensive in property liability insurance than in life insurance because of the higher frequency of losses, the predominance of partial losses, and the uncertainty of the amount of loss in individual cases.

The felicitous management of claim settlements is of paramount importance to the success of an insurer. Niggardly claims settlement brings with it public ill will, which may take years to overcome.[2] Oftentimes, negotiations with the claims department is the only direct contact

---

[2] As was stated by one authority: "There is nothing quite so private as public relations. The insurance profession must handle each loss with every person in a satisfactory way. Public relations is the stone stalagmite and personal experience is the drop of water that builds the stone."

that the insurance buyer has with the insurer. A bad impression received on that occasion may result in loss of business, court action, regulatory censure, or even suspension of the right to carry on business in the jurisdiction involved. On the other hand, an overly liberal claims settlement policy may ultimately result in higher rate levels and loss of business through lower premiums charged by competitors.

5) Investing and financing

When an insurance policy is written, the premium is generally paid in advance for periods varying from six months to five or more years. This advance payment of premiums gives rise to funds held for policyholders by the insurer, funds that must be invested in some manner. Every insurance company has such funds, as well as funds representing paid-in capital, accumulated surplus, and various types of reserves. Selecting and supervising the appropriate investment medium for these assets is the function of the *investment department*. The investment income is a vital factor to the success of any insurer. In life insurance, solvency of the insurer depends on earning a minimum guaranteed return on assets. In property and liability insurance, investment income has accounted for a very substantial portion of total profits and has served to offset frequent underwriting losses.

Since the manner in which insurance moneys are invested is the subject of somewhat intricate governmental regulation, the investment manager must be familiar with all the laws of the various states in which his company operates. Investments must also be selected with due regard to the financial policies of the insurer. Property insurers typically have a combined capital and surplus ranging between 30 and 50 per cent of total assets (see Table 6–2 on page 127), and funds equivalent to this may be invested in common and preferred stocks. The extent to which this is done depends upon the class of business written and upon the need for liquidity. Life insurers, on the other hand, have few of their assets invested in common and preferred stocks, primarily because the nature of the life insurance obligation dictates that guaranteed amounts be repaid to policyholders.[3] To accomplish this, bonds and mortgages are usually selected as the major investment medium. Large insurers have separate departments for major classes of investments, such as for real estate loans, policy loans, and city mortgages.

---

[3] Life insurers as a group had only four per cent of their total assets invested in common and preferred stocks as of 1959. State laws impose definite restrictions on the extent to which life insurers may invest in these stocks.

Financing refers to the planning and control of all activities that are related to the supplying of funds to the firm. Normally in insurance, few outside funds have to be raised since most of the normal financing requirements are met by reinvested profits. However, problems such as determination of dividend policies, meeting state solvency requirements, and handling the occasional negotiations for both long- and short-term capital sources fall within the province of the chief financial officer, who is often in charge of investments as well.

6) Accounting

The accounting function for insurance management has essentially the same purpose as accounting for the operating results of any firm, namely, to record, classify, and interpret financial data in such a way as to guide management in its various policies.

7) Miscellaneous functions

Various functions such as legal aid, marketing research, engineering services, and personnel work, are often performed for an insurer by individuals or firms outside the company, or by a specialized department set up within the company.

Legal aid. The function of the legal adviser is to assist others in the company to perform their tasks. Underwriters receive aid in the preparation of policy contracts and endorsements so that the company's intention will be phrased in correct legal terminology. In the administration of claims, particularly in disputed claims, legal aid is important and if court action is required, the legal staff must represent the company.

Legal aid is required in drawing up agency contracts, in investigating bond indentures and real estate titles, in preparing reports to the insurance commissioner, and in advising on insurance legislation. Hardly any phase of an insurer's many activities can be effectively performed without competent legal advice. Most large insurers have their own legal departments. Others use outside counsel only. All companies use outside counsel on occasion.

Marketing research. Reference has already been made to the role of marketing research in assisting the production department. As yet, marketing research is not usually performed within the firm, except in the case of very large companies. When carried on, the marketing research typically involves only selected types of research, such as testing and developing effective advertising. The role of such research can be a vital factor in the long-run success of any insurer. The success that direct-writing insurers have had in winning markets away from those insurers using the indirect channel of distribution has increased the interest of the latter in marketing research.

The role of marketing research is to narrow the area within which executive judgment must operate; that is, to make for more scientific decision-making than is possible by merely playing hunches. Marketing research can assist management in many ways, and its usefulness is not confined to production alone. For example, one firm conducted psychological surveys among a sample of policyholders to determine what basic motivations existed that affected their behavior toward the insurer. Results of this and other research led the company to establish a program of policyholder participation in company decision-making.

Engineering services. Engineering services are utilized, particularly in the field of property insurance, as valuable aids to rate-making and underwriting. It is the function of the engineer to advise with respect to the conditions—that is, hazards—which make losses more likely. His services in loss-prevention and salvage operations are extremely important to the insurance mechanism.

Information concerning the physical characteristics of exposed property is necessary for intelligent underwriting. Rate-making classifications are usually developed on the basis of physical characteristics, and rate charges and credits are made on this basis. For example, the engineer provides information that will help answer the question, "How long will fireproof glass resist breaking when subjected to the heat of a burning building?" If a building has such glass, the underwriter is in a much better position to assess its importance than he would be without such information. Again, the engineer may provide answers to the following questions: "How much money will it cost to restore a burned building to its former condition? Is it economically feasible to raise this sunken ship? For safety, in the event of an explosion, how far should an oil tank be placed from a building? Do seat belts really prevent or reduce injury in automobile accidents?" The usefulness of such information to the insurer is readily apparent.

Personnel management. Personnel management normally includes selection and discharge of employees, keeping employment records, supervision of training and educational programs, administration of recreational and fringe benefit programs, and other similar functions. Most large companies and many small ones have separate personnel departments. Regardless of the size of the firm, personnel management is an essential function. Insurance, particularly life insurance, has experienced a somewhat more rapid turnover of employees than other industries. The need for giving increased attention to the problem of turnover and discovering the causes of this condition have increased the scope and importance of personnel management among insurance companies.

ORGANIZATION OF INSURERS

The functions performed in most insurance companies have been described. The matter under present consideration is that of deciding the best methods of organizing the concern in order that these functions may be performed most efficiently. Two major types of organization—internal and external—will be discussed. *Internal organization* may be defined as the manner in which the work and the individuals who perform it are arranged within the business firm. Good organization implies that each individual knows what his relationship is to all others; that is, what the lines of authority and responsibility are. *External organization* refers to the relationships with groups outside the firm that aid in accomplishing the firm's objectives.

Internal organization

There are four distinct patterns of interrelationships or authority, few of which are used exclusively in any one business organization. These organizational patterns are 1) line, 2) functional, 3) line and staff, and 4) committee.

1) Line organization. A *line organization,* exemplified by that type of organization used predominantly by the military, is one in which each person in authority has complete control over how another person below him will perform his job. Thus, each person has only one superior.

The chief advantages of the line organization are its simplicity, the ease with which each person in the organization can see the lines of authority, and the speed with which decisions can be made. In a large firm, however, a pure line organization tends to become unwieldy. The tasks to be performed often become too complex for the line manager to supervise, and communications downward in the chain of command tend to break down. For these reasons the line organization is seldom used exclusively in modern business, but is combined with other forms of organization.

2) Functional organization. A *functional organization* is one in which each person in authority has control only over certain aspects of another person's duties. Thus, each person has several superiors with each one controlling different phases of the job. Like the line organization, a functional organization is seldom seen in its pure form. Certain difficulties arise when one person reports to more than one superior. Also, it is seldom possible to break down into separate and distinct segments the task to be performed. To the extent that functions overlap, the worker may discover that one superior tells him to do one thing, and another superior tells him to do another. As a result, there is a tendency for conflict of authority and no final supervision over the whole task.

3) Line-and-staff organization. To overcome the disadvantages of a pure line, or a pure functional, type of organization, management has devised countless modifications or combinations of authority. One very widely used combination is the *line-and-staff organization.* In this type of organization one person is in authority over the entire task to be performed, but he has at his disposal staff assistants who study certain problems and make recommendations to the line officer as to what should be done. The staff assistant cannot order anyone to do anything, nor can he tell anyone how a task is to be performed. The staff assistant makes recommendations which the line officer can adopt or reject as he sees fit. In this way the "chain of command" is preserved; each person still has only one superior, but the line officer has the benefit of expert advice and presumably can more effectively perform his tasks in a large, complex organization.

One of the problems with the line-and-staff organization is that the staff officer sometimes forgets that his authority is limited to that of giving advice. He may attempt to see that his recommendations are carried out by giving orders without actually having authority to do so. One of the fundamental rules of organization is that responsibility and authority should move hand in hand. That is, if one has the responsibility to see that certain things are done, he must also have authority to carry out his work, and this usually means exercising line authority over another's work. The staff officer may view his task as that of seeing that his recommendations carry weight, and yet, because of his limited authority, he may find that his recommendations are not being put into effect. Therefore, there is a tendency for the staff officer to ursurp the authority of a line officer. Only through very careful planning of organization can such a tendency be overcome.

4) Committee. The problem referred to above has, in part, led to the development of a type of organization in which staff experts are given authority to see that their voices are heard and can carry weight. This organizational form is known as the committee. The committee organization is used extensively in the field of insurance because so many decisions affect all phases of the operation.

In committee organization, the authority stems from a committee, usually composed of executives who are themselves heads of certain departments within the organization. For example, let us suppose that an unauthorized agent sends in an application for a large amount of fire insurance on a type of exposure in which the firm is inexperienced, and the underwriter immediately observes that acceptance of the risk would mean a departure from established policy. If the risk is accepted, what rate will be charged? What are the legal implications of accepting business from an unauthorized agent? Does the company have facilities to service claims from this type of business if losses should occur? Does the company have the financial capacity to underwrite such a risk? Will established agents object if the company alters its channel of distribution? It is obvious that consultation with other executives of the company may be desirable before a decision is made. Hence, a committee meeting is held and the matter is decided by the assembled group. Examples of various committees that may be organized are the finance committee, the executive committee, and the underwriting committee.

Chart 7–1 shows an organizational pattern of a large property liability insurer. It is to be noted that the authority stems basically from the stockholders (or from policyholders in a mutual company), although their control over the company is usually indirect. Normally, all the stockholders do is elect the board of directors, which actively manages the firm. The board, in turn, elects the major officers and gives them authority to operate the company, subject to the will of the board. Each department head, in turn, has line authority over the members of his department. As discussed previously, some departments are created to serve others in a staff capacity. The vice-presidents of agencies, underwriting, and administration together form an administrative board to which all other major officers of the company report, except the vice-president of finance who reports directly to the president. In this way the advantages of committee organization are realized.

Territorial organization. The type of organization used by a given insurer and the types of departments created depend upon the particular problems it faces. The most common basis is a centralized management

Chart 7–1

**ORGANIZATION CHART OF LARGE STOCK INSURANCE GROUP,
HANDLING ALL LINES**

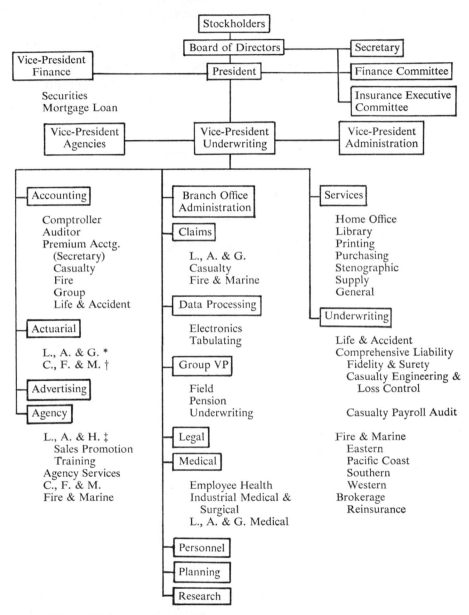

* Life, Accident, and Group
† Casualty, Fire, and Marine
‡ Life, Accident, and Health

with departments organized on a functional basis, as illustrated in Chart 7–1. However, other bases, such as territorial, are commonly used, often concurrently with the functional type. The insurer in Chart 7–1, for example, recognizes territorial organization in its underwriting of fire and marine lines.

An insurer may create branch offices for certain major geographical regions. Many insurers organized in the eastern part of the United States have established branch offices on the West Coast. Certain functions, such as investment and finance, legal, actuarial, and general accounting, are often carried out by the main home office; while other functions, such as underwriting, claims, rate-making, and production are decentralized in each of the branches. Decentralization is a general practice when the size of distant markets increases to the point that it is more efficient to make certain decisions at a local level rather than to refer everything to a central home office. An example of such a decision might be the underwriting of certain risks where frequent contact with the insured is necessary. Dealing from afar might be unwieldy, inefficient, and ultimately cause a loss of the business.

Product organization. In some insurance operations, particularly among multiple-line insurers, the problems arising from differing classes of insurance are so technical and specialized that it is inefficient to have all types of business handled by the same staff. Accordingly the business may be organized according to product divisions. For example, as illustrated by Chart 7–1, the insurer may divide the underwriting function by line of business, in this case, life and accident, comprehensive liability, and fire and marine.

In a life insurance company, it is common to find separate divisions handling group life insurance, group disability insurance, industrial life insurance, and group pensions. Within each group, major functions such as underwriting, accounting, claims, production, and policyholder service may be performed, with other functions being carried on by the home office.

In property and liability insurance, particularly in multiple-line companies, separate divisions are commonly created for the major types of insurance, such as fire, inland marine, bonding, liability, automobile, and workmen's compensation. Again, each division will perform certain major operating functions and use the centralized facilities of the insurer for the service functions, such as actuarial, investment, legal, and general accounting. The degree of autonomy of product divisions varies with each firm, with some divisions being almost completely self-sufficient, and others being highly dependent on the centralized administration for service and for various aspects of decision-making.

Group organization. Insurance in the United States developed early along essentially specialized lines. It was felt by most organizers that the technical problems of underwriting insurance were such that they could be handled best by having each company concentrate on a given type of coverage. In this manner, each peril could be studied separately and more rapid progress in developing suitable methods of insuring could be developed than if the efforts of the company were spread out over all kinds of perils. Furthermore, it was believed that it would be easier for the states to determine more accurately the financial ability of the insurer to assume the risks that it intended to insure if its operations dealt with a single peril. Accordingly, most state laws were drawn up giving insurers authority to write only specific types of coverage, such as fire and allied lines, liability, bonds, and life insurance. Reserve requirements in each state generally differed, depending on what type of insurance was underwritten. Usually there were three types of companies—property, casualty, and life—whose underwriting authority was limited to specific kinds of insurance.

The early growth of group organization. In a system where a company is authorized to write only certain lines of insurance, several problems become apparent. A fire insurer might have built up an organization of agents that handled its business. The agents, however, might wish to sell all kinds of insurance. This necessitated the use of several different insurers. It was natural that the fire insurer would find it desirable to seek authority to broaden its offerings to include whatever its agents demanded. Since it could not offer all types of insurance itself, oftentimes it allied itself with a casualty insurer whose underwriting authority included the type of insurance needed. This alliance was usually accomplished by the formation of a "group" of companies with centralized management and common ownership. It was the motive of obtaining wider agency representation and of securing diversification of business that led to the initiation of group operations. The first such consolidation was in 1898, when control of Mechanics and Traders Insurance Company was purchased by National Fire of Hartford. With the great growth of casualty insurance, more companies entered into group operations until, in 1929, 357 firms were operating as members of about 90 separate groups.

This somewhat arbitrary device to obtain some of the advantages of large-scale operations in insurance management began to decline in importance with the depression period that began in the early 1930's. Hard times forced the industry into a retrenchment period characterized by consolidations and retirements. During World War II, shortages of personnel and other wartime restrictions were among the influences that prevented the group organization from regaining its former pre-eminence. In 1947, the National Association of Insurance Commissioners, an association of insurance regulatory authorities, approved a recommendation to sponsor what became known as multiple-line legislation, which eliminated the statutory limitations that gave rise to group organization. Multiple-line laws, which have been adopted in every state, now permit insurers to write different classes of insurance within a single firm. Thus, it has been suggested that group-type management will cease to grow and may gradually be abandoned by the industry.

Today's importance of group organization. In spite of the advent of multiple-line powers, group organization in insurance management has continued to grow in importance. Table 7–1 shows the extent of this growth as measured by the number of groups operating, and the number of companies involved from 1952 to 1957.

Table 7–1

GROUPS OF COMPANIES IN THE UNITED STATES, 1952–1957

Year	Number of Groups	Number of Companies
1952............	115	350
1953............	120	355
1954............	120	360
1955............	122	369
1956............	123	362
1957............	128	367

Source: *Best's Insurance Reports, 1958.* Data after the year 1957 have not been reported.

Table 7–2 shows the leading groups and their premium volume in 1960. In 1957 there were 365 fire and casualty companies and two life insurance companies operating in groups, representing an estimated 90 per cent of all insurance business.[4]

Reasons for the continuing importance of group organization. There are several probable explanations for the continued importance of the group-type organization, even though the original reason for its

---

[4] *Best's Insurance Reports—Fire and Casualty, 1958.*

Table 7–2

**NET PREMIUMS WRITTEN BY LEADING GROUPS
OF INSURERS, 1960**

Group of Insurers	Million of Dollars
Stock Company Groups	
Travelers..............................	$869
Aetna Life.............................	748
America Fore Loyalty...................	551
Hartford..............................	516
Allstate...............................	502
Continental National...................	389
Insurance Company of North America.....	384
U.S.F. & G............................	301
Royal Globe...........................	275
Home.................................	263
The Fund.............................	261
American Insurance.....................	184
Employers Group.......................	182
General Motors........................	175
St. Paul F. & M.......................	173
Aetna Fire............................	162
General of America....................	154
Great American........................	143
Crum & Forster.......................	141
Maryland Casualty.....................	137
Mutual and Reciprocal Groups	
State Farm............................	$506
Liberty Mutual........................	390
Nationwide...........................	257
Kemper...............................	225
Farmers Insurance.....................	185
Employers Mutual.....................	146
Hardware Mutual......................	104
American Mutual Liability..............	96
Northwestern Mutual...................	60
Michigan Mutual......................	53

Source: *Best's Insurance Reports, 1961,* p. ix.

formation no longer exists. First, there appear to be no compelling reasons to suggest that consolidation would necessarily be more efficient from a management viewpoint than the present system. In fact, the problems facing multiple-line operations are such that the evidence seems just the opposite. Except for certain functions, such as investment operations, general accounting, and top policy making, which can be performed more efficiently on a consolidated basis, it is likely that decentralized and separated managements are more satisfactory. Underwriting, for example, is still a relatively specialized task and often requires years of training before competency is achieved. In companies attempting to combine into one policy many types of coverage, underwriting problems have been difficult to solve because of the shortage of individuals competent to analyze more than one type of coverage. Certainly, to undertake an entirely new type of organization is expensive; and unless there is a strong likelihood of greater efficiency from it, reorganization would not be indicated.

Second, the present type of organization is particularly adaptable to experimentation with new underwriting techniques. In meeting the competition of direct-writing organizations, for example, many stock companies have formed subsidiary companies to try such innovations as continuous policy forms, direct billing, and new policy combinations. If successful, such experiments may be extended. If unsuccessful, they can be dropped with little adverse influence or ill will that might otherwise reflect on the parent company.

Third, present companies are decentralized geographically in many cases, and it would be difficult to consolidate effectively several companies organized in different states. Many such concerns have been advertised for years, and consolidation might mean the loss of this investment and the goodwill that it represents. Manpower might be lost, and training capable replacements would be an expensive procedure.

Finally, there has been a trend for property insurance companies to enter the life insurance field. Multiple-line laws in most states, however, do not permit consolidated firms to sell life insurance along with other types. A separate organization is necessary. This requirement fits into the established pattern of group-type organization.

Multiple-line organization.   Companies commonly described as *multiple-line* are those firms that underwrite many types of property and liability insurance within the administrative framework of a single organization. Only rarely may such companies handle life insurance directly, but must do so through a separate company.[5] The multiple-line type of organization is urged as a method of permitting the simplification of insurance contracts. It is felt by most insurance authorities, for example, that requiring a separate policy for every type of coverage is an inefficient technique and quite unnecessary. Why not combine, say, fire, windstorm, automobile, residence liability, residence burglary, and a

---

[5] In Oregon, insurance companies have had multiple-line powers since 1917, and may be authorized to write all types of insurance including life. However, only one insurer, The Insurance Company of Oregon, has actually taken advantage of this authority and handles all types of coverage.

personal property floater into one "package policy" designed for the homeowner, who would be able to have just one company, one policy, and one agent for most of his insurance needs? If this were possible, it is argued, the agent would have a much larger commission from personal lines and would be able to service each customer more satisfactorily than if he had only a small portion of the customer's total business. Furthermore, the customer would be able to purchase many coverages he might not buy individually, thus enabling the insurer to obtain a wider spread of risks.

A disadvantage of the system of compartmentalization of insurance lines lies in the inflexibility that it introduces into the insurance business. An insurer can write only the lines in which it is specifically authorized. Thus, if a new type of insurance protection is needed, special authority must be sought in the state legislature before the coverage can be offered. For example, at one time in New York, malpractice insurance on physicians and insurance covering damage to property caused by falling aircraft or motor vehicles were not permitted. However, multiple-line powers solve such an enigma. As noted previously, all states have now passed multiple-line legislation.

As can be seen from the preceding discussion of group organization, the insurance industry has moved slowly in altering its basic organization form to accommodate the new multiple-line powers. It is not surprising that a type of organization that grew up over the last one hundred years, one to which the industry has adjusted, will not give way over night to a new concept. Multiple-line powers have created new problems for which solutions will be developed only gradually. Reference has already been made to the lack of trained manpower, particularly in underwriting. The lack of a body of statistical data on which to base rates for new policy combinations is another roadblock that will be overcome only as time permits the accumulation of data. New merchandising methods to accommodate the changed concept of insurance packages must be developed in such a way that existing agents can be used effectively and compensated fairly. Since a package policy involves new selling techniques and requires a substantial increase in the average premium charged per policy, devices such as premium financing and training tools for agency personnel must be developed by the industry. Finally, new methods of regulating multiple-line companies must be developed. Basic questions such as what should be the reserve requirements for the new package policies; how often should multiple-line companies be examined; how should rates that are fair, adequate, and not excessive be developed; and what new license requirements should be imposed for insurance agents—are examples of issues that must be resolved in the regulatory sphere.

All-line organization. *All-line organization* refers to that type of arrangement by which an insurer may write literally "all lines" of insurance under one administrative charter. In 1960 there were thirteen states in which this is permitted by state law.[6] However, many insurers, through company fleets, write all lines and for all practical purposes seem to enjoy the same advantages as insurers who offer such coverages under one administrative framework. One of the great problems in effecting full all-line underwriting is the securing of agency personnel trained to handle literally every type of insurance. Insurance is usually considered too complex a subject for all types of agents to be competent in any area in which they choose to write business. Another problem is that of finances. It takes a considerable investment in time and money for an insurer and its agency plant to enter the life insurance business, whether this is done through merger or whether the life insurance business is started from "scratch." Nevertheless, all-lines underwriting seems to be gaining favor among insurers. In many property and liability agencies at the local level, a "life man" has been employed to handle the increasingly important source of business to the agency—the life and health insurance premium.

External organization

A great deal of the organization in insurance has to do with group cooperation. This cooperation is accomplished through associations of various kinds designed for very definite purposes. Many vital tasks in insurance could not be accomplished without such cooperation. Only a few of the many associations can be described here, for a complete listing of all of them would fill a volume.[7]

Rate-making organizations. Rate-making organizations are of high-ranking importance. Even though it might appear that such groups would be in violation of antimonopoly laws, most states specifically authorize rate-making groups. This type of cooperation is essential because many companies do not have a sufficiently large volume of busi-

---

[6] Alabama, Alaska, Connecticut, Delaware. Georgia, Maine, Mississippi, North Dakota, Oregon, Rhode Island, South Carolina, Tennessee, and Wisconsin. See Hugh Harbison, "Legal Environment for All Lines Insurance," in *All Lines Insurance,* Dan McGill, Editor (Homewood, Illinois, Richard D. Irwin, Inc., 1960) p. 23.

[7] This is literally true. *The Insurance Almanac,* published annually, contains the names and descriptions of hundreds of types of insurance organizations.

ness in certain lines to enable them to develop rates that are statistically sound. When the experience of many companies is pooled, however, as is done by a rate-making organization, there is a large enough body of data to permit scientific rate calculation. The rate-making organization is usually supported financially by member companies, but in some states the government owns and operates the agency. This is common in the field of workmen's compensation insurance. State regulation has general jurisdiction over insurance rating practices to see that the rate-making association does not dispense rates that are excessive or discriminatory among different classes of insureds. Rate-making cooperation is common in fire, automobile, bonding, inland marine, and workmen's compensation insurance. In life insurance, while there are no rate-making bodies as such, a similar result is achieved by the universal adoption of certain standard mortality tables that are used by all insurers.

The influence of rate-making cooperation goes beyond the mere setting of fairly uniform rates. If companies are to charge similar rates, it follows that most of them must also plan fairly similar amounts for losses and expenses. In order to achieve this result, policy provisions must be quite uniform, or the cooperating insurers would not experience loss ratios that were uniform. Thus, rate-making bodies have worked toward uniform policy provisions and standard policies in general. This has had a far-reaching influence on the insurance business and has enabled an orderly development of the coverage. As will be seen, the standardization of policies is widespread. Another influence in some lines of insurance has been the control exercised by rate-making bodies over allowances for agency commissions and other expenses. This has controlled, at least partially, competitive bidding for agents' services and has kept the production cost of insurance at a reasonable level in most lines of insurance.

Loss-prevention groups.   Another important cooperative organization in insurance has been in the field of loss prevention. The importance of this subject has already been discussed in Chapter 3. One of the best known of such organizations is the National Board of Fire Underwriters, an association of stock fire insurance companies dedicated to fire prevention. Underwriters Laboratories, originally formed through the cooperation of fire underwriters for the purpose of testing combustibility of various materials at the World's Fair in Chicago in 1893, has grown in influence and scope of activity until today its seal of approval is famous. This seal is looked for by most buyers of products such as electrical applicances, building materials, and fireproof containers, where the factor of fire safety is of importance. In liability insurance, the National Safety Council has had similar influence.

Reinsurance organizations. Reinsurance is largely accomplished through cooperative activity among insurers and is one of the vital types of external organization that serves the essential needs of underwriters. Reference to the use of reinsurance as an underwriting tool has been made earlier, and this chapter concludes with a discussion of this significant activity.

Reinsurance may be defined as the shifting by a primary insurer, called the *ceding company*, of a part of the risk it assumes to another company, called the *reinsurer*.

Uses and advantages of reinsurance. One may wonder why an insurer that has gone to all the expense and difficulty of securing business would voluntarily transfer some of it to a third party. There are several reasons for this, the main one being that the primary insurer is often asked to assume liability for loss in excess of the amount that its financial capacity would permit. Instead of accepting only a portion of the risk and thus causing inconvenience and even the ill will of its customer, the company accepts all the risk, knowing that it can pass on to the reinsurer the part that it does not care to bear. The policyholder is thus spared the necessity of negotiating with many companies and can place his insurance with little of the delay that such a procedure would involve. Using a single policy with a single premium also simplifies insurance management procedures. The policy coverage is not only more uniform and easier to comprehend, but the added guaranty of the reinsurer also makes it that much safer.

From the viewpoint of the insurer, reinsurance not only distributes the risk, but it also has other uses and advantages. Stabilized profits and loss ratios are an important advantage in the use of reinsurance. It is true that oftentimes good business must be shared with others, but in return some bad business is also shared. In the long run, it is usually considered more desirable to have a somewhat lower but stable level of profits and underwriting losses than it is to have a higher, but unstable level. This is not to imply that reinsurance arrangements necessarily reduce average profit levels, but they do iron out fluctuations that would normally occur. Furthermore, reinsurance does not always mean the loss of premium volume, for one of the results of reinsurance is the procurement of new business. As a member of a group of ceding companies organized to share mutual risks, one ceding company must usually accept the business of other insurers. Some companies obtain a significant portion of their total premium volume in this manner, and others engage exclusively in the reinsurance business.

Reinsurance is also used to allow for a reduction in the level of unearned premium reserve requirements. For new small companies especially, one of the limiting factors in the rate of growth is the legal requirement that the company set aside premiums received as reserves for policyholders. Since no allowance is made in these requirements for expenses incurred, the insurer must pay for producers' commissions and for other expenses out of surplus. As the premiums are earned over the life of the policy, these amounts are restored to surplus. In the meantime, however, the insurer may not be able to finance all the business it is offered. Through reinsurance, the firm can accept all the business it can obtain from its agency force and then pass on to the reinsurer part of the liability for risk, and with it the reserve requirement.[8]

Finally, reinsurance may be used to retire from business or to terminate the underwriting on a given type of insurance. If a firm wishes to liquidate its business, it could conceivably cancel all its policies that are subject to cancellation and return the unearned premiums to the policyholder. However, this would be quite unusual in actual practice because of the necessity of sacrificing the profit that would normally be earned on such business. It would probably be impossible to recover in full the amount of expense that had been incurred in putting the business on the books. Through reinsurance, however, the liabilities for existing insurance can be transferred and the policyholders' coverage remains undisturbed. If an insurer desires to retire its life insurance business and to cease underwriting this line, it may do so through reinsurance. Since the life insurance policy is noncancellable, the policyholder has the right to continue his protection as he desires. If it were not for reinsurance, the insurer would find it difficult, if not impossible, to achieve its objective of relieving itself from the obligation of seeing that the insured's coverage is continued.

Types of reinsurance agreements.   Organization for reinsurance is found in many different forms, from individual contractual arrangements with reinsurers to various types of "pools" whereby a number of primary insurers agree to accept certain types of insurance on some prearranged basis.

---

[8] For a full discussion of this topic, see Chapter 27.

INFORMAL FACULTATIVE AGREEMENT. The simplest type of reinsurance is known as an *informal facultative* agreement. Under this arrangement a primary insurer, in considering the acceptance of a certain risk, "shops" around for reinsurance on it, attempting to negotiate coverage specifically on this particular contract. A life insurer, for example, may receive an application for $1 million of life insurance on a single life. Not wishing to reject this business, but still unwilling to accept the entire coverage, the primary insurer communicates full details on this application to another insurer with whom it has done business in the past. The other insurer may agree to assume, let us say, all loss above $100,000 on this contract for a certain percentage of the premium. The primary insurer then puts the contract in force. The reinsurance agreement does not affect the insured in any way. Informal facultative reinsurance is usually satisfactory when reinsurance is of an unusual nature or when it is negotiated only occasionally. Such an arrangement becomes cumbersome and unsatisfactory, however, if reinsurance agreements must be negotiated regularly.

FORMAL FACULTATIVE AGREEMENTS. Occasionally an insurer will have an agreement whereby the reinsurer is bound to take certain types of risks if offered by the ceding company, but the decision of whether or not to reinsure remains with the ceding company. Such an arrangement may be called a *formal facultative* contract, and is used where the ceding company is often bound on certain types of risks by its agents before it has an opportunity to examine the application. If the exposure is such that reinsurance is not needed or desired, the ceding company may retain the entire liability. In other cases it will submit the business to the reinsurer, who is bound to take it. Such reinsurance agreements are often unsatisfactory for the reinsurer because of the tendency for the ceding company to keep better business for itself and pass on the more questionable lines to the reinsurer.

AUTOMATIC OR OBLIGATORY AGREEMENT. To protect all parties concerned from such a tendency as described above, to speed up the transaction, and to eliminate the expense and uncertainties of individual negotiation, reinsurance may be provided whereby the ceding company is required to cede certain amounts of business, and the reinsurer is required to accept them. Such an agreement is described as *automatic* or *obligatory*. There are several types of such agreements, called *treaties,* because oftentimes each member to the agreement accepts reinsurance from the other. The amount that the ceding company keeps for its own account is known as its *net retention,* and the amount ceded to others is known as the *cession.*

Excess line or first surplus treaty. Under an *excess line,* or *first surplus,* treaty, the ceding company decides what its net retention will be for each class of business. The larger its net retention, the more the other members of the treaty will be willing to accept. Thus, if the ceding company will retain $10,000 on each dwelling fire exposure, the agreement may call for cession of up to "five lines" or $50,000 for reinsurance. The primary insurer could then take a fire risk of $60,000. On the other hand, if the ceding company is willing to retain only $5,000 on a residential fire exposure, it may have only four lines acceptable for reinsurance, and could not take more than $25,000 of fire insurance on a single residence.

First surplus treaties call for the primary insurer to bear all losses up to the amount of its net retention, and the reinsurers to share any balance. Sometimes a second surplus, or even a third surplus, treaty is arranged to take over business that is beyond the limits set by the first surplus treaty. The surplus treaty is probably the most common type of reinsurance in use today.

Reinsurance pool or exchange. An extension of the treaty idea, differing from it only in form, is the *reinsurance pool* or *exchange.* Pools are usually formed to provide reinsurance in given classes of business, such as cotton, lumber, or oil, where hazards are of a special nature and where the mutual use of engineering or inspection facilities provides an economy for participating members. Each member of the pool agrees t place all described business it obtains into the pool, but it shares some agreed proportion, such as 10 or 16.67 per cent, of the total premiums and losses. This type of treaty is referred to as a *quota share* or *pro rata* type of agreement. Quota share treaties are especially suitable for new small firms whose underwriting capacity is limited, and who would be unable to get started without such an arrangement because of their inability to meet the drain on surplus imposed by unearned premium reserve requirements.

Excess of loss treaty. It is not uncommon for a primary insurer to find that, while it is willing to accept up to $10,000 on each exposure insured in a given class, it is unable to stand an accumulation of losses that exceeds $50,000. Under the excess line, or first surplus treaty, the primary insurer is liable for all amounts up to $10,000, and even if it suffered ten losses each in the amount of $10,000, it would not collect anything from the reinsurers. To impose a limit on losses, a type of treaty known as *excess of loss* has been developed whereby the reinsurer agrees to be liable for all losses exceeding a certain amount on a given class of business during a specific period. Normally, such treaties are used when there is a danger of catastrophic losses. Such a contract is simple to administer because the reinsurers are liable only after the ceding company has actually suffered the agreed amount of loss. Since the probability of large losses is small, premiums for this reinsurance are likewise small.

Spread of loss treaty. A variation of the excess of loss type of reinsurance is the *spread of loss* treaty under which the primary insurer decides what loss ratio it is prepared to stand on a given kind of insurance, and agrees with a reinsurer to bear any losses that would raise the loss ratio above the agreed level over a period of, say, five years. Thus, the ceding company has "spread" its losses over a reasonable time period and, in effect, has guaranteed an underwriting margin through reinsurance. In this way, an unusually high loss ratio in a poor underwriting year is averaged in with other years, and the reinsurer is obligated to pay only when the five-year loss ratio exceeds the stipulated amount.

There are many variations of reinsurance agreements under which the losses of the primary insurer are limited. The main advantages of such agreements are: (1) underwriting profits are more or less directly controlled; and (2) the agreements are simpler to administer than other types of reinsurance because it is not necessary to render continuing reports to the reinsurer (called *bordereau*) nor to keep books on each reinsurer's share of total risks assumed. The disadvantages include: (1) while underwriting profits are set at a minimum, the premium for reinsurance is set in such a way that profits of the ceding company are limited and any benefits from good underwriting experience must be shared heavily with the reinsurer; and (2) underwriting is said to become careless because the ceding company personnel know that losses are limited through reinsurance, and forget that ultimately the ceding company must pay for loose underwriting in the form of higher reinsurance premiums.

SUMMARY

1. The major functions of an insurer are: (a) production (selling), (b) underwriting, (c) rate-making and statistical control, (d) claims manage-

ment, (e) investing and financing, (f) accounting, and (g) miscellaneous functions, such as legal aid, marketing research, engineering services, and personnel management. These functions are performed both by the home office and by the agency staff in the field.

2. Underwriting is the task of selecting subjects for insurance in such a way that the assumptions underlying the rate structure are realized in practice. It is the underwriting, claims handling, and rate-making tasks which are most nearly exclusive functions of insurance. The other functions, while they are necessary to carry out these basic tasks, are not exclusively insurance functions, since they are common to most business enterprises.

3. There are two general types of organization in insurance: internal and external. Internal organization refers to the way in which an individual insurer or its subsidiaries, if any, carry out their tasks. External organization refers to the work done through cooperative groups such as rate-making, safety, or engineering associations.

4. Two central plans for internal organization may be identified: (a) single-line organization and (b) multiple-line organization. The former plan describes the pattern of organization typically used by insurers that write only specific lines of insurance. such as fire or life. This plan has led to what is known as group operations, or company fleets, whereby insurers merge into units under centralized control for the purpose of offering a more complete and diversified insurance service than is possible for each company operating separately. Multiple-line organization, on the other hand, describes the plan of operation used by insurers that are authorized to write several lines of insurance within the framework of a single administrative entity. Multiple-line organization has become legally possible in the United States only since World War II.

5. Because single-line organization and its related group type of operation have evolved over many years in the United States, it is doubtful that it will be suddenly replaced by the multiple-line organization, which has created many basic changes and problems for insurers. Rather, it is likely that the two systems will coexist for an indefinite period.

6. Other distinguishable internal organizational concepts are product and territorial organization. In general, as an insurer grows, it is more likely to use some form of territorial decentralization and for very large insurers, this is accompanied by decentralized product divisions.

7. The insurance industry is characterized by a more extensive use of cooperative groups and associations than is true of almost any other industry. Most of these associations are formed because it has been found that it is more economical to pool resources for carrying out tasks which

are mutually needed than to perform them individually. Indeed, some tasks, such as rate-making, loss prevention, and reinsurance, can be performed in no other way.

8. Reinsurance is an important example of one task that is accomplished by external organization. The uses of reinsurance include distribution of risk, stabilization of profits, reduction of legal reserve requirements, and facilitation of retirement from business. The major types of reinsurance are informal facultative, formal facultative, and automatic, the latter type being the most widely used.

QUESTIONS FOR REVIEW AND DISCUSSION

1. Mr. Dudley M. Pruitt, president of the Casualty Actuarial Society, told the Society recently, "We have left it to the underwriter to judge the risk. . . . It is our duty to discover and display relationships, and it is in a clear and easy reading of these relationships that the underwriter may expect to substitute scientific assurance for hunch and hope."
   (a) What sort of relationships does the author of this statement have in mind?
   (b) Does the underwriter typically operate more by "hunch and hope" in life insurance or in liability insurance? Why?

2. A speaker at an insurance convention once argued that the disadvantage of competition between agency companies and direct writers did not lie in the expense differential, but in rating methods. He said, in part: "Few companies, and certainly no bureau, keep records of auto premiums by class and losses by classification. . . . The rates applied by classes in auto insurance are formula figures arrived at by a social philosophy rather than by the realistic approach used by the direct writer."
   Do you think these statements are true? Are they in conformity with sound principles of rate-making? Discuss.

3. In a study by the New York Insurance Department of 350 insurers which had ceased business in that state, the overwhelmingly major reason for financial difficulty lay in inadequate underwriting. Explain the connection between inadequate underwriting and the financial difficulty referred to.

4. (a) Explain what is meant by the "conflict between underwriting and production" in insurance.
   (b) Do you agree that such a conflict is real, or is it only apparent?

5. It is stated in the text that there are two major classifications of organization in insurance. Name and describe each type.

6. (a) What basic legal problem gave rise to group organization?
   (b) Now that this legal hurdle has been largely eliminated, will group organization disappear? Why or why not?

7. What major problems are inherent in the multiple-line type of organization?

8. When 1959 automobiles were introduced, it was found that, on the average, windshields had 16 square feet of glass as compared with 11 square feet in the latest prior models. Accordingly, additional rates of $3 for each 1959 auto insured for full coverage comprehensive and $1 for each car with $50 deductible comprehensive were prescribed by the National Automobile Underwriters Association.
   (a) Why is it necessary or desirable for the Association to prescribe the rate increase rather than have each individual insurer calculate its own?
   (b) What officer in the insurance company would be most closely concerned with this problem?
   (c) What other departments of an insurer might be affected by the increased rate? Explain.

9. Do not rate-making organizations carry on what amounts to price fixing, and is this not in violation of the Sherman Antitrust Act? Discuss.

10. It has been stated that action through groups is often more effective than action by individuals. Recently a number of insurers reduced their production allowances in the rate calculation for certain types of insurance. The reduction, which resulted in a cut in commission rates to agents, was strongly opposed by agents, who took legal action through their association, the League of Independent Insurance Producers, to prevent this reduction. It was charged that the insurers acted in concert to restrain trade in violation of the Sherman Antitrust Act.
    Suggest possible reasons for the desirability of action at the group level rather than action by individual agents in such a problem.

11. (a) Which function has been of greater importance with most insurers— investing or financing? Why?
    (b) Are there any important differences in the functions of investing and financing among life insurers as opposed to property and liability insurers? Explain.

12. The policyholder is said to be injured if claims management is either too liberal or too strict. Explain.

13. Bring to class a report of an article illustrating the application of marketing research in insurance. Do you think this function is likely to increase or to decrease in importance in the future? Explain.

14. It is stated that the facultative reinsurance agreement is the simplest of all kinds of reinsurance. Explain, giving in your answer a definition of reinsurance.

15. A certain insurer is willing and able to assume all the risks on residential fire offered to it in a certain city. However, it fears a catastrophic-type loss in case of a forest fire, which could destroy the whole city. Suggest an appropriate type of reinsurance agreement that would solve this problem.

16. (a) Explain what is meant by a first surplus treaty and give an illustration of its application.
    (b) How does such an agreement differ from quota share reinsurance?

17. In 1882 a general agent of the Phoenix Insurance Company of Hartford, Connecticut, wrote the following letter to a policyholder in Kansas requesting windstorm insurance:

"Dear Madam:
    In reply to your esteemed favor of the 23rd instant, we beg to say that windstorms being entirely foreign to the business of fire insurance in which we are engaged, we have nothing to do thereof. Neither do we suppose that any other respectable fire company does, but only such companies that must resort to some ludicrous method or worse in order to get any business. One would hardly expect to find ready made horseshoes for sale in a millinery store yet such a commodity would have as fitting a place in such a stock as windstorms would have in the business of fire insurance. Now do we not speak the truth?
    P.S. If against wind, why not also against rain, hail, crushing by snow, accidents caused by faulty construction of buildings, etc., etc., etc. The proposition is too absurd for any strictly legitimate fire insurance company to consider for a moment."

Contrast the underwriting philosophy expressed in the above letter with that existing today. What is illustrated concerning the organizational problems of changing to a multiple-line basis?

Legal Principles

Underlying Insurance Contracts

Insurance is effected by legal agreements known as contracts or policies. A contract, contrary to many impressions, cannot be complete in itself, but must be interpreted in light of the legal and social environment of the society in which it is made. This chapter is concerned with the specific legal doctrines which underlie the insurance contract and are vital to its understanding.

PRINCIPLE OF INSURABLE INTEREST

A fundamental legal principle underlying all insurance contracts is the principle of *insurable interest*. Under this principle an insured must demonstrate a financial loss to himself or be unable to collect amounts due him when the insured peril occurs. Insurable interest is always a legal requirement, because to hold otherwise would mean that an insured could collect when he had no personal loss. This would establish a moral hazard and would be deemed contrary to public policy. The doctrine of insurable interest is also necessary to prevent insurance from becoming a gambling contract.[1] In life insurance an important reason for requiring insurable interest is to prevent murder.

Insurance follows the person and not the property. Thus, insurance is said to be *personal*. A policy can be written covering a certain piece of property and an individual may be named as the one who would suffer a financial loss if the peril were to occur and cause damage. However, if at the time of the loss the individual named no longer had an interest in the property, there would be no liability under the policy. For example, suppose that "A" insures his automobile. Later he sells his car to "B" and shortly thereafter the auto is destroyed. Since "A" has no further financial interest in the car, he cannot collect under

---

[1] See page 52 for a discussion of the difference between insurance and gambling.

177

the policy. "B" has no protection under the policy since he is not named as an insured or as having any interest in the auto at the time the policy was written.

What constitutes insurable interest?

In most instances it is simple to demonstrate a financial loss when the insured property is destroyed. If the insured is the legal owner of the property which has a value that has been diminished by the occurrence of an insured peril, he can demonstrate that a financial loss has occurred to him. However, in many cases a loss occurs when an individual is not a legal owner. In other words, ownership is not the only evidence of insurable interest. For instance, "C" leases a building under a long-term lease whereby the lease may be canceled if a fire destroys a certain percentage of the value of the building. "C" has an insurable interest in the building because of the lease.

In addition to ownership, there are other rights under contract which are often sufficient to establish an insurable interest in property, the continued existence of which affects the contract and its value to the insured. Thus, the holder of a contract to receive oil royalties has an insurable interest in the oil property so that in the event of an insured peril, indemnity can be collected, the amount of the indemnity being measured by the reduction in royalty resulting from the insured peril.[2] Likewise, legal liability growing out of contracts establishes insurable interest in property. For example, a garage keeper has an insurable interest in the stored automobiles for which he has assumed liability for destruction by fire.

A *secured* creditor, such as a mortgagee, has an insurable interest in the property on which he has lent money. A building contractor has an insurable interest in property on which he has worked, because he has a mechanic's lien. In each of the two cases, loss of the building would endanger the ability of the individuals to collect amounts due them. However, a *general* creditor—one without specific liens on the property—is not regarded as having a sufficiently great property right to give him an insurable interest in it. In most states, however, if he reduces his debt to a judgment, he then has an insurable interest in the debtor's property. A businessman has an insurable interest in the profits he expects to earn from the use of property and in the expenses incurred in managing that property.

---

[2] See *National Filtering Oil Co.* v. *Citizens Insurance Co.* 106 N.W. 535 (1887).

In life insurance, an insurable interest is always presumed to exist for a person who voluntarily insures his own life. It is well said that an individual's loss, upon his death, is inestimable. He may procure life insurance and may make anyone his beneficiary regardless of whether the beneficiary has an insurable interest in his life. It may be argued that a person does not personally suffer loss upon his own death or that, at least, he does not live to claim any indemnity for this loss. Nevertheless, the courts have taken the attitude of not questioning insurable interest when a person insures his own life, so long as it is not done to evade antigambling laws.

Sometimes parties will attempt to avoid the insurable interest requirements in life insurance and try to use the contract as a wagering agreement. Courts will usually set aside such contracts, however. For example, two individuals met in a saloon and after a short acquaintance, one agreed to insure his life and then assign the policy to the other if the first would reimburse him for the premium. The insured person died and the insurer refused to pay when the facts surrounding the application became known. The court upheld the insurer's refusal to pay on the grounds that the transaction was conceived to use the life insurance policy as a means of effecting a wager. The intention was to avoid the requirement of insurable interest by having the *cestui que vie* (person whose life is insured) take out the policy with the sole purpose of transferring it to another who had no insurable interest.

When one takes out life insurance on another's life, he must have an insurable interest in that person's life. Thus, a corporation or other business firm may insure the life of a key man because his death would cause financial loss to the firm. A wife may insure the life of her husband because his continued existence is valuable to her and she would suffer a financial loss upon his death. The same statement may apply to almost anyone who is dependent on an individual. A father may insure the life of a minor child, but a brother may not ordinarily insure the life of his sister. In the latter case there would not usually be a financial loss to the brother upon the death of his sister, but in the former case the father would suffer financial loss upon the death of his child. A creditor has an insurable interest in the life of a debtor because the death of the debtor would subject the creditor to possible loss.

When the insurable interest must exist

In property and liability insurance it is very common to effect coverage on property in which the insured does not have an insurable interest at the time the policy is written, but in which he expects to have such an interest in the future. Thus, a building contractor insures a building in the course of construction for its full completed value. At the time the policy is written he obviously has no interest in the completed building because it does not yet exist. However, the insurance is issued and is effective so long as the contractor actually has an interest *when* and if a loss occurs. Likewise, in marine insurance a shipper often obtains coverage on cargo he has not yet purchased in the anticipation of buying cargo for a return trip. As a result, the courts generally hold that in property insurance, insurable interest need exist only at the time of the loss and not at the inception of the policy.

On the other hand, in life insurance it is the general rule that insurable interest *must* be in existence at the inception of the policy, but is not necessary at the time of the loss. This follows because life insurance is not a contract of indemnity (explained below), while property liability insurance is. Also, the courts view life insurance as an investment contract. To illustrate, assume that a wife who owns a life insurance policy on her husband later obtains a divorce. If she continues to maintain the insurance by paying the premiums, she may collect upon the subsequent death of her former husband, even though she is remarried and suffers no particular financial loss upon his death. It is sufficient that she had an insurable interest when the policy was first issued. In a similar way, a corporation may retain in full force a life insurance policy on an employee who is no longer with the firm. A creditor may retain the policy on a life of a debtor who has repaid his obligation. In other words, in life insurance the general rule is that a continuing insurable interest is not necessary.[3]

PRINCIPLE OF INDEMNITY

The principle of indemnity states that a person may not *collect* more than his actual cash loss in the event of damage caused by an insured peril. Thus, while a person may have purchased coverage in excess of the value of the property, he cannot make a profit by collecting more than his actual loss if the property is destroyed. Many insurance practices result from this important principle. In general, only contracts in property and liability insurance are subjected to this doc-

---

[3] In Texas the rule pertaining to a continuing insurable interest has been modified by statute so that this statement is not strictly true in that state.

trine, although there are exceptions in some states where statutes have modified its application. Life insurance and most health insurance policies are not contracts of indemnity.

The principle of indemnity is closely related to insurable interest. The problem in insurable interest is to determine whether or not any loss is suffered by a person insured, whereas in indemnity the problem is to obtain a measure of that loss. In the basic fire insurance contract, the measure of "actual cash loss" is the current replacement cost of destroyed property less an allowance for estimated depreciation. In liability insurance, the final measure of loss is determined by reference to a court action concerning the amount of legal liability of the insured for negligence. In any event, the purpose served by the principle of indemnity is to place the insured in the same position, no better or no worse, than he was before the loss.

One of the important results of the principle of indemnity is the typical inclusion of clauses in insurance contracts regarding other insurance. The purpose of such clauses is to prevent the insured from taking out duplicating policies with different insurers in the expectation of recovering more than his actual loss. Typically, such clauses provide that all policies covering the same risk will share pro rata in the loss. Thus, by operation of this type of clause, if Jones carries $4,000 fire insurance in Company "A" and $6,000 in Company "B," the two insurers will divide a $1,000 fire loss, 40 per cent and 60 per cent, respectively.

As noted above, there are some exceptions to the application of the principle of indemnity in property insurance. In about half of the states, *valued policy* laws have been passed whereby the insurer must pay the entire face amount of the policy in the event of total loss of the insured object.[4] Ocean marine and some inland marine contracts are "valued," and it is assumed that the insured will take out insurance equal to the full value of the object. Finally, it is becoming increasingly common to permit the sale of what is known as "replacement" insurance, contracts under which there is no deduction for depreciation in the settlement of losses on depreciable property. Exceptions to the principle of indemnity will probably continue until it is felt that they begin to constitute a moral hazard, giving the insured an incentive to destroy his own property in the hopes of making a "gain."

---

[4] Since most losses are partial and not total, valued policy laws have relatively little actual effect in insurance. They apply usually only to real estate. Rather than appraise every piece of real estate, most insurers probably find it less expensive to pay an occasional total loss that has been insured for an amount in excess of its actual value.

PRINCIPLE OF SUBROGATION

The principle of subrogation grows out of the principle of indemnity. Under the principle of subrogation, one who has indemnified another's loss is entitled to recovery from liable third parties, if any, who are responsible. Thus, if "D" negligently causes damage to "E's" property, "E's" insurance company will indemnify "E" to the extent of its liability for "E's" loss and then have the right to proceed against "D" for any amounts it has paid out under "E's" policy. One of the important reasons for subrogation is to reinforce the principle of indemnity; that is, to prevent the insured from collecting more than his actual cash loss. If "E's" insurer did not have the right of subrogation, it would be possible for "E" himself to recover from his policy and then recover again in a legal action against "D." In this way "E" would collect twice. It would be possible for "E" to "arrange an accident" with "D," collect twice, and split the profit with "D." A moral hazard would exist and the contract would tend to become an instrument of fraud.

Another reason for subrogation is to hold rates below what they would otherwise be. In some lines of insurance, particularly liability, recoveries from negligent parties through subrogation are substantial. While no specific provision for subrogation recoveries is made in the rate structure, the rates would have to be higher if such recoveries were not permitted. A final reason for subrogation is that the burden of loss is more nearly placed on the shoulders of those responsible. Negligence should not escape penalty because of the insurance mechanism.

Subrogation does not exist in lines where the principle of indemnity does not apply, such as life insurance and health insurance. Also, subrogation does not give the insurance company the right to collect against the insured, even if the insured is negligent. Thus, if "E" negligently, but accidentally, burns down his own house while thawing out a frozen water pipe with a blowtorch, he can collect under his fire policy; but the insurer cannot proceed against him for compensation. Otherwise, there would be little value in having insurance.

It is not uncommon for an insurer to waive rights of subrogation under certain circumstances where, by so doing, there is no violation of the principle of indemnity. Suppose, for example, that a manufacturer has agreed to hold a railroad not liable for losses arising out of the maintenance of a spur track that the railroad has placed on the manufacturer's property. In effect, the manufacturer has assumed legal liability that would otherwise be the responsibility of the railroad. Now assume that a spark from one of the railroad's engines sets fire to the manufacturer's building and the railroad is found to be negligent, and hence legally liable for the ensuing damage. The insurer will pay the loss, but under its rights of subrogation will proceed against the railroad. However, the manufacturer has previously agreed to assume all losses arising out of the existence of the spur track. Therefore, any amount collected becomes the ultimate liability of the manufacturer because of the "hold harmless" agreement. If this were not the case, the manufacturer would have been in the position of collecting for his loss from the insurer but returning it to the railroad because of the hold harmless agreement. Therefore, the insurer will waive the subrogation clause in the fire contract because to enforce it would mean that its insured would not be compensated at all.

If an insured acts in such a way as to destroy or reduce the value of the insurer's right of subrogation, he violates the provisions of most subrogation clauses and forfeits his rights under the policy. For instance, suppose "F" collides with "G" in an automobile accident. "F" is flustered and embarrassed and he tells "G" that "Nobody is really to blame; let's just settle with our insurance companies and let it go at that." Unfortunately, there are witnesses to this statement. It is later determined that "G" is palpably negligent and had it not been for "F's" statement, "F's" insurer would have been able to subrogate against "G" for amounts paid to "F." The insurer may deny liability to "F."

Subrogation rights of the insurer cannot be avoided by a settlement between the primary parties after the insurer has paid under the policy. In such a case the insurer is entitled to reimbursement from the insured who has received any payment from the negligent party.

The insurer is entitled to subrogation only after the insured has been fully indemnified. If the insured has borne part of the loss himself through the application of deductibles, inadequate coverage, or because of legal costs involved in collection against third party claims, the insurer may claim recovery only after these costs have been repaid. For example, assume that "H's" house, valued at $10,000 and insured for $7,000 is totally destroyed through the negligence of "I." "H" sues "I," but is able to collect only $5,000. "H" also collects $7,000 from his insurance company. The insurer enjoys subrogation only after "H" has been fully indemnified. Therefore, the insurer is entitled only to $2,000 and not the full $5,000 that was recovered from "I." [5]

---

[5] There are occasional exceptions to this rule when the contract so provides. In credit insurance, for example, the insurer and the insured would share the amounts collected from negligent third parties in the proportion that each party's loss bore to the total loss.

PRINCIPLE OF UTMOST GOOD FAITH

Insurance is said to be a contract of *uberrimae fidei* or *utmost good faith*. In effect, this principle imposes a higher standard of honesty on parties to an insurance agreement than is imposed in ordinary commercial contracts. The principle of utmost good faith has greatly affected insurance practices and casts a greatly different light on the interpretation of insurance agreements than many persons often suppose, as will be seen. The application of this principle may best be explained in connection with a discussion of representations, concealments, and warranties.

Representations

A *representation* is a statement made by an applicant for insurance before the contract is effected. Although the representation need not be in writing, it is usually embodied in a written application. An example of representation in life insurance would be "Yes" or "No" to a question as to whether or not the applicant had ever been treated for any physical condition by a doctor within the previous five years. If a representation is relied upon by the insurer in entering into the contract, and if it proves to be false at the time it is made or becomes false before the contract is made, there is said to exist a legal grounds for the insurer to avoid the contract.

Avoiding the contract does not follow unless the misrepresentation is *material* to the risk. That is, if the true facts had been known, the contract either would not have been issued at all or would have been issued on different terms. If the misrepresentation is inconsequential, its falsity will not affect the contract. However, a misrepresentation of a material fact makes the contract *voidable* at the option of the insurer. The insurer may decide to affirm the contract or to avoid it. Failure to cancel a contract after first learning about the falsity of a material misrepresentation may operate to defeat the insurer's rights to cancel at a later time, under the doctrines of waiver or estoppel (explained on page 196).

It is generally held that even an innocent misrepresentation of a material fact is no defense to the insured if the insurer elects to avoid the contract. The applicant for insurance speaks at his own risk and if he makes an innocent mistake about a "fact" he believes to be true, he is held for his carelessness. Thus, let us say that "A" in applying for insurance on his automobile states that there is no driver under age 25 in his family. However, it turns out that his 16-year-old son has been driving the family car without his father's knowledge. Lack of this knowledge is no defense when the insurance company refuses to pay a subsequent claim on the grounds of material misrepresentation. It is not necessary for the insurer to demonstrate that a loss occurred arising out of the misrepresentation in order to exert its right to avoid the contract.[6] Thus, in the above case, let us assume that "A" has the accident himself and then it is learned for the first time that he has a 16-year-old son driving. Since this situation is contrary to that which "A" had previously stated, the insurer may usually legally refuse payment. However, if the court holds that a statement given in the application was one of opinion, rather than fact, and it turns out that the opinion was wrong, it is necessary for the insurer to demonstrate bad faith or fraudulent intent on the part of the insured in order to avoid the contract.[7] For example, let us say that an applicant is asked, "Have you ever had cancer?" and the applicant says "No." Later it develops that the applicant actually had cancer. The court might well find that the insured was not told the true state of his health and was under the impression that he had some other ailment. If the question had been phrased "Have you ever been told you had cancer?" a "yes" or "no" answer would be clearly one of fact, not opinion. An honest opinion should not be grounds for recision.

Concealments

A *concealment* has been defined as "Silence when obligated to speak." A concealment has approximately the same legal effect as a misrepresentation of a material fact. It is the failure of an applicant to reveal a fact that is material to the risk. Because insurance is a contract of utmost good faith, the applicant is required to exercise a higher standard of honesty than might prevail in an ordinary commercial transaction. It is not enough that he answer truthfully all questions asked him by the insurer before the contract is effected. He must also volunteer facts that he believes to be material, even if he knows that to reveal them might result in rejection of the application, or the payment of a higher premium.

For example, if "A" is buying a used car on an "as is" basis, he has an opportunity to try it out, drive it around, and even have an independent mechanic inspect it. If the used-car salesman knows that

---

[6] In some states, Missouri, for example, there are exceptions to this statement. In these states, the loss must find its present cause in the fact misrepresented before the insurer may deny liability.

[7] See E. W. Patterson, *Essentials of Insurance Law* (2nd ed.; New York: McGraw-Hill Book Company, Inc., 1957), pp. 382–396, for an interesting discussion of this point.

the car has been driven 200,000 miles and the speedometer has been set back to read 60,000 miles, is he obligated to reveal this information? Custom and a knowledge of the tendencies in used-car salesmanship must dictate a negative answer to this question in the minds of most people. The two parties are more or less on an equal basis and at arm's length. Each has an opportunity to protect himself against the nondisclosures of the other.

In insurance, however, the applicant is often in a position to know material facts about the risk that the insurer does not. To allow concealment of these facts would not be fair to the insurer. After all, the insurer does not ask questions such as "Is your building now on fire?" or "Is your car now wrecked?" The most relentless opponent of an insurer's defense suit would not argue that if an insured obtained coverage under such circumstances, he would be exercising even an elementary standard of fairness.

The important, often crucial, question about concealments lies in whether or not the applicant knew the fact withheld to be material. The tests of a concealment are: (1) Did the insured know of a certain fact? (2) Was this fact material? and (3) Was the insurer ignorant of this fact? The test of materiality is especially difficult because often the applicant is not an insurance expert and is not expected to know the full significance of every fact that might be of vital concern to the insurer. The final determination of materiality is the same as it is in the law of representation; namely, would the contract be issued on the same terms if the concealed fact had been known? There are two rules determining the standard of care required of the applicant: one, the stricter, applies to ocean marine risks; the other applies to insurance on land risks.

Ocean marine risks. In marine insurance, as it developed in early England, ships were often insured after they had set sail. Thus, there was no way for the insurer to inspect the ship. Usually the shipper had a better knowledge of the actual conditions of the risk than did the underwriter. Furthermore, since insurance was necessary to the expanding overseas trade in England, there was a desire to do everything possible to nurture the growth of this significant activity. Accordingly, very strict rules governing disclosures were adopted. Lord Mansfield, sometimes called the father of English insurance law, writing in 1776,[8] held that even innocent concealments could void the contract: [9]

---

[8] The student may recognize this date as that during which Adam Smith published his famous *Wealth of Nations,* in which the philosophy of individual responsibility was so ably propounded and applied to business generally.

[9] Patterson, *op. cit.,* p. 450, quoting *Carter* v. *Boehm,* 3 Burr. 1905, 1909 (1776).

Although the suppression should happen through mistake, without any fraudulent intention; yet still the underwriter is deceived, and the policy is void; because the risk run is really different from the risk understood and intended to be run, at the time of the agreement.

Following this philosophy is the British Marine Insurance Act of 1906, which holds that as a test of concealment in marine insurance, the assured is deemed to know every fact or circumstance which, in the ordinary course of business ought to be known by him, and failing to reveal it, thereby is guilty of concealment. This philosophy is recognized by American courts.

Land risks.   In land risks, the United States courts have been unwilling to apply the same standards of *uberrimae fidei* as they have in ocean marine risks. English courts, however, generally apply the same standards to all risks. In land risks, insurance companies generally inspect the properties they insure, or have an opportunity to do so. Thus, they do not rely so heavily on the accuracy of statements by the insured, who oftentimes does not have a good knowledge of the various facts about the risk and their significance to the insurer. Decisions have been rendered in the United States whereby failure to disclose the fact of a recent fire of incendiary origin by an unknown party, or of the use of kerosene lamps in the picking room of a cotton factory, did not constitute concealments. In general, the nonmarine, or land, rule is that a policy cannot be avoided unless there is fraudulent intent to conceal material facts. Thus, in nonmarine risks, a fourth test of concealment is added to the three mentioned on page 186. This test is: Does the insured *know* that the insurer does *not* know of a material fact? Under this test, intentional withholding of material facts with intent to deceive constitutes fraud. Assume that "H" learns that his wife "W" is going to "end it all" in the family auto by driving over a cliff. "H" immediately obtains collision insurance on the vehicle without telling all he knows. As a result, "H" is guilty of a concealment and the insurer may avoid the contract. Here "H" knows about a material fact; the insurer does not know of it; and "H" *knows* the insurer is ignorant of it. Furthermore, "H" has no right to assume that the insurer should know of it.

In life insurance, cases of concealment are not common because of the reluctance of courts to enforce the doctrine strictly and because of the general use of a very long list of questions in the application concerning the applicant's background. An applicant's failure to disclose the fact that he had been threatened with murder and was carrying a gun for protection, was held not to be a concealment.[10] Likewise, in a famous case, a bank teller who had been stealing money from the bank, failed (rather understandably) to disclose this fact when he applied for life insurance. He later died from a brain congestion brought on when his thefts were discovered. The court refused to consider this a concealment.[11]

In determining which facts must be disclosed, if known, it has been held that facts of general knowledge, or facts known by the insurer already, need not be "disclosed." There is also the inference from past cases, though not a final determination, that the insurer cannot defend on the grounds of concealment those facts that are embarrassing or self-disgracing to the applicant, such as the failure of the bank teller in the case above to reveal his occupation as an *embezzling* bank teller.

Warranties

A *warranty* is a clause in an insurance contract holding that before the insurer is liable, a certain fact, condition, or circumstance affecting the risk must exist. For example, in marine insurance the contract may provide "warranted free of capture or seizure." This statement means that if the ship is involved in a war skirmish, the insurance is void. Or a bank may be insured on condition that a certain burglar alarm system be installed and maintained. Such a clause is condition precedent and acts as a warranty.

A representation made by an insured, if incorporated into and made a part of the contract, is turned into a warranty. A warranty creates a condition of the contract, and any breach of warranty, *even if immaterial,* will void the contract. This is the central distinction between a warranty and a representation. A misrepresentation does not void the insurance unless it is material to the risk, while under common law any breach of warranty, even if held to be minor, voids the contract. The courts have been somewhat reluctant to enforce this rigid dictum, and in many jurisdictions the rule has been relaxed either by statute or by court decision.

Warranties may be express or implied. *Express* warranties are those stated in the contract, while *implied* warranties are not found in the contract, but are assumed by the parties to the contract. Implied warranties are found only in ocean marine insurance. For example, a shipper purchases insurance under the implied condition that the ship is

---

[10] *New York Life* v. *Bacalis,* 94 F. 2d 200 (C.A. Fla. 1938).
[11] *Penn Mutual Life Insurance Co.* v. *Mechanics Savings Bank and Trust Co.* 72 Fed. 413, 435 (C.C.A. 6, 1896).

seaworthy, that the voyage is legal, and that there shall be no deviation from the intended course. Unless these conditions have been waived by the insurer (legality cannot be waived), they are binding upon the shipper.

A warranty may be promissory or affirmative. A *promissory* warranty describes a condition, fact, or circumstance to which the insured agrees to be held during the life of the contract. An *affirmative* warranty is one that must exist only at the time the contract is first put into effect. For example, an insured may warrant that his ship left port under convoy—affirmative warranty—and may warrant that it will continue to sail under convoy—promissory warranty.

INSURANCE AS A LEGAL CONTRACT

A *contract* is an agreement embodying a set of promises that are enforceable at law, or for breach of which the law provides a remedy. These promises must have been made under certain conditions before they can be enforced by law. In general, there are four such conditions, or requirements, which may be stated as follows:

1) The agreement must be legal; it must not be against public policy or be otherwise illegal.
2) The parties must have legal capacity to contract.
3) There must be evidence of agreement of the parties to the promises. In general this is shown by an *offer* by one party and *acceptance* of that offer by the other.
4) The promises must be supported by some consideration, which may take the form of money, or by some action by the parties that would not have been required had it not been for the agreement.

Insurance contracts must meet these essential requirements. The peculiar problems involved in applying the requirements to insurance are discussed below.

1) Legality

As indicated before, to be legal the insurance contract must not violate the requirement of insurable interest, nor may the contract protect and encourage illegal ventures, such as rum-running or narcotics trade. Obtaining insurance on life or property without an insurable interest would violate antiwagering statutes and would lead to arbitrary and intentional destruction of the subject matter. In early England, it was not uncommon to allow private individuals to take out insurance on the lives of public figures, such as the king. The premiums for such contracts would vary daily, depending on reports from the sick bed. Such a policy would be unthinkable today.

2) Capacity

Parties to the policy of insurance must have legal capacity to contract. While capacity is seldom questioned in insurance, there have been instances where a minor has exercised his legal right to rescind his agreement (before reaching the age of majority) and to recover the full cost of his premium without any adjustment for the value of insurance protection received.[12] This follows, because a minor is a legal infant and does not have the power to make binding contracts except for necessary items of support actually furnished him. The courts have not yet come to the point of interpreting insurance to be a necessary item in the support of an infant. Several states, however, have passed statutes granting a minor who has reached a certain age (14½ years in New York) the power to make binding contracts of insurance.

Other parties who have no legal capacity to contract are: (1) insane persons—those who do not have the ability to understand the nature of the agreement into which they enter; (2) intoxicated persons; and (3) corporations that act outside the scope of their authority as defined in their charters, bylaws, or articles of incorporation.

3) Offer and acceptance

In insurance the agreement is effected by one party making an offer and by the other party accepting that offer. Until there has been both an offer *and* an acceptance, there is no contract. To be valid, an offer must be communicated effectively to the offeree. An offer can be withdrawn at any time before it is accepted. Therefore, it becomes important to determine, in many cases, what constitutes a legal offer. If "A" goes to his agent to purchase insurance and the agent fills out an application that "A" signs, has the agent made an offer which "A" accepts by signing the application? If so, the insurance is in force. If not, when is the contract in effect? The answers to these questions are vital in determining when coverage attaches and can often spell the difference between collecting and not collecting for a loss.

It is the general rule in insurance that it is the *applicant,* not the agent, who makes the offer. The agent merely solicits an offer. *When*

---

[12] See *New Hampshire Mutual Fire Insurance Co.* v. *Noyes,* 32 N.H.345. It should be added that if a minor does not rescind the contract immediately upon reaching the age of majority, he is thereafter bound by it.

the contract goes into effect depends upon the authority of the agent to act for his principal in a given case. In property and liability insurance, it is the custom to give the local agent authority to accept offers of most lines of insurance "on the spot." If the insurer wishes to escape from its agreement, it usually may cancel the policy upon prescribed notice. In life insurance, the agent generally does not have authority to accept the applicant's offer for insurance. The insurer reserves this right, and the policy is not bound until the insurer has passed on the application. If the insurer wishes to alter the terms of the proposed contract, it may do so and this is construed as making a counter offer to the applicant, who may accept or reject as he sees fit.

A legal offer by an applicant for life insurance must be supported by a tender of the first annual premium. Usually, the agent gives the insured a *conditional receipt,* which provides that acceptance takes place when the insurability of the applicant has been determined. Thus, let us say that "B" applies for life insurance, tenders an annual premium with the application, passes his medical examination, and then is run over and killed by a truck, all before the insurer is even aware that an application has been made for insurance. "B's" beneficiaries may collect under the policy if it is determined that "B" was actually insurable at the time of his application and had made no false statements in his application.

If the applicant for life insurance does not pay his first annual premium in advance, he has not made a valid offer. In this case, the insurer's agent transmits the application to the home office, where it is acted upon and questions of insurability are determined. The insurer sends the policy back to the agent for delivery and the agent is instructed to deliver the policy only if the insured is still in good health. This constitutes, on the part of the insurer, an offer that may be accepted by paying the annual premium at the time of delivery.

In summary, the offer in insurance can be made in either of two ways: (1) by filling out an application and rendering other considerations required of the applicant, and (2) by offering a completed policy to the applicant. Normally, the offer is effected by means of the first method, but occasionally, and especially in life insurance, the second method is used, depending upon the power of the agent in the circumstances.

4) Consideration

All contracts that are legally enforceable must be supported by a consideration, and insurance is no exception. A *consideration* has been defined as a legal detriment, or more simply, as the act or promise that is bargained for. The insured's consideration is made up of his monetary payment plus his agreement to abide by the conditions of the insurance contract. The insurer's consideration is his promise to pay indemnity upon the occurrence of certain perils, to defend the insured in legal actions, or to perform other matters, such as inspection or collection services, as the contract may specify.

Oral contracts of insurance

While most insurance contracts are written, oral agreements of insurance are very common and the courts will enforce them. Often an oral agreement for insurance is made and a written notation, called a *binder,* is issued as evidence of the oral contract until the full written policy is issued. If it were not for binders, it might be difficult to prove that an oral contract ever existed. Even if there were witnesses, it would be difficult to obtain an accurate statement of just what the agreement was. Also, in many cases the insurer's agent is found to lack authority to bind contracts orally. Some states have passed statutes requiring certain types of contracts, such as life or fire, to be in writing, and sometimes the provisions of the insurer's charter will not allow oral contracts. Therefore, oral contracts are to be discouraged wherever possible.

Parole evidence rule

Under the *parole evidence rule* when an oral contract is reduced to writing, the written contract is to be construed as the entire agreement; and oral testimony to change it is inadmissible except under certain circumstances. Therefore, oral agreements that do not find themselves expressed accurately in the written contract are not enforceable, and it is dangerous for the insured to rely on them.

Effect of mistakes

When an honest mistake is made in a written contract of insurance, it can be reformed if there is proof of a mutual mistake or a mistake on one side that is known to be a mistake by the other party, and where no mention was made of it at the time the agreement was made. A mistake in the sense used here does not mean an error in judgment by one party, but refers to a situation where it can be shown that the actual agreement made was not the one stated in the contract. If "A" believes himself to be the owner of certain property, and insures that property, he cannot later demand all of his premium back solely because he found out that, in fact, he was not the owner of the property. This was a mistake in judgment or an erroneous supposition, and the courts will not relieve this kind of mistake.

As an example of mistakes found in life insurance policies, an insured paid up his policy and through a mistake by the insurer, the endorsement stated that the value of the paid-up contract was $5,495.-26, including interest. Actually the proper value was $1,994.65. The insured sued for the larger amount, and the court held that an honest mistake had been made by the company and that it was "inconceivable that a successful businessman would think that a policy which on his death paid $2,765 would at any time acquire a surrender value of $5,495.26!" [13] In another case the insurer issued a $1,000 life policy and by an error of one of its clerks included an option at the end of 20 years to receive an annuity of $1,051 rather than $10.51. The mistake was discovered 18 years later. When the insurer tried to correct the error, the insured refused payment of the smaller amount. In a legal decision, the court held that the mistake was a mutual one, the error of the insurer being in misplacing a decimal point, and the error of the insured being in either not noticing the error, or if he noticed it, in failing to say anything, an action amounting to fraud.[14] These decisions also illustrate the fact that insurance is a contract of *uberrimae fidei,* of utmost good faith on both sides, as discussed previously.

Contract of adhesion

The insurance contract is said to be a contract of *adhesion,* which means that any ambiguities or uncertainties in the wording of the agreement will be construed against the draftsman—the insurer. The insurer has the advantage in drawing up the terms of the contract to suit its particular purposes, and, in general, the insured has no opportunity to bargain over conditions, stipulations, exclusions, and the like. Therefore, the courts place the insurance company under a legal duty to be explicit and to make its meaning absolutely clear to all parties.

For example, if the contract states that it covers all cars owned by the insured and there is no definition of what is meant by "cars," the court may construe cars to mean everything from farm wagons to trucks. Accordingly, the insurer normally excludes certain types of vehicles from its policy so as to make its intentions clear. In interpreting the agreement, the courts will generally consider the entire contract as a

---

[13] *Flax* v. *Prudential Life Ins. Co.,* 3 Life Cases (2) 105, Fed.Supp. (1956).

[14] *Metropolitan Life Ins. Co.* v. *Henriksen,* 126 N.E. (2nd) 736 (Ill. App. Court—1955).

whole, rather than just one part of it. In the absence of doubt as to meaning, the courts will enforce the contract as it is written. It is no excuse that the insured does not understand or has not read the policy. He is bound by its terms, regardless.

LEGAL POWERS OF INSURANCE AGENTS

Reference has been made frequently to the significance of the agent in insurance contracts. The powers of insurance agents to vary the terms of the contract, to put the insurance in force, to deal with the insured, to handle settlements, and to perform many other affairs are of vital importance to a sound knowledge of insurance. An insurance corporation, after all, is a legal entity only, and it *must* function through agents of various kinds.

An *agent* is a person given power to act for his principal. Under the doctrine of *respondiat superior,* a *principal* is bound by the acts of his authorized agents. The power of a given insurance agent cannot be determined easily by reference to whether he is called a "general," a "special," or a "local" agent. The reason for this is that there is little uniformity in insurance terminology and, as has been seen, a general agent in property insurance has far different powers and functions from the general agent in life insurance.[15] Furthermore, the sense in which insurance practitioners use the terms for various types of agents may not be comparable to the sense in which attorneys view the terms.

For example, the law recognizes two major classes of agents: *general* and *special*. A *general* agent is a person authorized to conduct all of his principal's business of a given kind in a particular place. He is the company itself, legally speaking, in that capacity. As such, he can add or detract from a printed form, waive the terms of contracts, accept or reject risks, change rates, and do almost everything the company itself could do. In life insurance, the general agent has few or none of these powers, but in property insurance he often has at least some of these powers.

In the legal sense, an agent does not necessarily have to be a person serving in the channel of distribution for insurance, but may be any representative of the insurance corporation, such as the treasurer or the chief underwriter, who is given certain authority. He may fall in the classification of a *special* agent, a person who has authority to perform only a specific act or function and has no general powers. If anything

---
[15] See Chapter 4.

occurs that is outside the scope of his authority, he must obtain special power to handle it. If he handles matters outside the scope of his authority, he may or may not bind his principal for his acts, depending on certain circumstances, described below.

Source of authority

The basic source of authority for all insurance agents (using the word agent in its broad sense) comes from stockholders or policyholders and is formulated by the charter, bylaws, and custom. The agent in the channel of distribution for insurance is of greatest concern to us at this point, however, and the discussion will be confined to him. There are three distinct sources of authority for the agent: 1) from the agency agreement, 2) by ratification, and 3) by estoppel.

1) Agency agreement. The first source of authority, the agency agreement, is by far the most common. Agents generally obtain their authority to write insurance directly from the principal by an instrument known as an *agency agreement*. This agreement sets forth the specific duties, rights, and obligations of both parties. Unfortunately, the agreement is oftentimes inadequate as a complete instrument and the agent may do something which his principal did not intend him to do. This situation gives rise to other methods by which an agent is said to receive authority.

2) Ratification. An agent can also obtain authority by a process known as *ratification*. That is, an individual may perform some act concerning another person without any authority at all, and this act may be assented to at a later time by the person involved. Thus "A" writes an insurance policy covering "B's" house against loss by fire. "A" is not authorized to do this by any insurer. However, he later persuades insurer "C" to accept this risk, and thus becomes "C's" agent by ratification.

3) Agency by estoppel. A third way in which an agent can obtain authority is through a process known as *agency by estoppel. Estoppel* is a legal doctrine under which a person may be required to do something, or to refrain from doing something, that is inconsistent with his previous behavior. Suppose in the example above, insurer "C" continues to allow "A" to sell insurance even though "A" does not have an agency agreement with "C." Every time "A" sends in a policy, "C" accepts it. Gradually "A" becomes known as "C's" local agent in the community and no attempt is made to inform the public differently. To the public, "A" has the power to bind "C" to fire insurance contracts as is the custom with other local agents. Now, "A" writes coverage on "D's" house and before the policy is ratified by "C," the house burns. May "C" deny liability on the grounds that "A" had no authority to write the policy in the first place? It is very probable that the courts would say that because "C" had led the public to believe that "A" had authority to bind it, to allow "C" to escape payment would work a hardship on an innocent party, and the law would provide a remedy. "C" is *estopped* from denying liability, and "A" has become an agent by estoppel.

In summary, one can obtain the authority of an agent either expressly or by implication. One can have actual authority, but if he does not have actual authority but does have *apparent* authority, he may still bind his principal. His authority includes customary powers and all the powers necessary to carry out his job. Secret limitations on his authority that are not customary will not be effective as to innocent third parties. Courts have often extended an agent's authority beyond his actual authority because of these principles. For example, a company denied its liability under a policy of life insurance on the grounds of false statements in the application. It was shown that the agent had taken the responsibility of answering the questions for the insured, and that the agent had answered incorrectly even though the correct information was given him. The court held that knowledge of the agent is knowledge of the company and that to deny liability would be inequitable. The insurer had to pay.[16] Of course, if the insured knew of the wrong answers recorded by the agent, the insured would be guilty of fraud and could not collect. Most courts refuse to hold that when the applicant signs the application, he warrants the truth of everything in the application.

Estoppel v. waiver

A *waiver* is the voluntary relinquishing of a known right. Estoppel prevents one from asserting a right because of prior conduct that is inconsistent with such an assertion. The two legal doctrines are vital in an understanding of the law of agency. Often they are not clearly distinguished, even in court actions, and sometimes are used interchangeably. The two doctrines are of interest primarily in understanding how the acts of insurance agents may or may not be binding upon insurers. To illustrate, in a case involving an accidental death policy, a lower court dismissed the suit on the evidence that proofs of loss were

---

[16] *Atlas Life Insurance Co.* v. *Eastman,* 320 Pac. (2) 397. (Okla. 1957).

not filed as required under the policy. A higher court found that the company's agent had told the insured that it would do no good to file a proof of loss because there was no liability for payment for accidental death. The court decided that such an action amounted to a *waiver* of the requirement to file a proof of loss.[17] Had it not been for the doctrine of waiver, the beneficiary would have had no chance of collecting on this policy.

Estoppel operates when there has been no voluntary relinquishing of a known right. Estoppel operates to defeat a "right" which a person, technically speaking, possesses. When the enforcement of this right would work an unfair hardship on an innocent party who has been led to rely on certain conduct or actions of another person, the courts will deny the right under the doctrine of estoppel. Waiver and estoppel situations oftentimes arise when the policy is first put into force. Let us say that an agent writes a fire insurance policy with the full knowledge that some condition in the policy is breached at the time it is issued. For example, the insured might be engaged in a type of business that the insurer has instructed its agents not to write and has excluded in the policy. The agent issues the policy anyway, and there is a loss before the insurer has had an opportunity to cancel the contract. Most courts would say that action by the agent in writing a policy known to be invalid at its inception constituted a waiver of the breached condition, and the insurer would be estopped from denying liability.

In an attempt to protect themselves from actions of agents in waiving policy conditions, insurers sometimes insert a *nonwaiver clause* in the contract, which indicates that the agent has no power to waive any policy condition without the written consent of the insurer. For example, the standard fire insurance policy (1943 New York Standard Fire Policy) states:

> No permission affecting this insurance shall exist, or waiver of any provision be valid, unless granted herein or expressed in writing added hereto.

However, some courts have held that the agent can waive this clause along with any other; other courts have upheld it. Most courts agree that such a clause, at most, constitutes a warning as to the limited authority of local agents.

Often waivers by agents occur during the term of the policy. Suppose an agent learns of some breach of warranty and does nothing to warn the insured of this breach. Does failure to cancel the policy estop

[17] *Keel* v. *Independent L. & A. Insurance Co.* 99 So. (2) 225—(Fla. 1957).

the insurer from denying liability at a subsequent time? Clearly no estoppel would be permitted unless there was good evidence that the insured actually relied on certain actions of the agent.[18] Mere silence does not give permission to breach the contract. But if the insured asked the agent to obtain an endorsement permitting some condition that would violate a policy provision (such as storing of gasoline supplies in an insured building) and the agent indicated he would take care of it and failed to do so before the loss, the courts would probably hold that a waiver existed. In this case the insurer would be estopped from denying liability under the contract.

In deciding whether actions by agents constitute waivers, courts will consider the degree of authority of the particular agent, the extent to which the insured relied on the conduct of the agent or the company in its actions regarding some breach of contract, and the seriousness of the breach of condition. For example, at the time of loss, the adjuster may investigate the claim and discover a breach of contract. There have been instances where continued action to settle the loss under such conditions has amounted to a waiver of the breach. Normally, if the insurer investigates facts at the time of loss, this is not construed as a waiver of a breach of condition; but if the adjuster requires the insured to do more than file a formal proof of loss, the insurer may find itself paying a claim that it otherwise could avoid due to violation of some policy conditions.

Agents v. brokers

In most areas of insurance, middlemen, known as brokers, operate. A *broker* is the legal agent of the *insured* and does not have the same powers as a local agent although he operates at the same level. A broker is employed by the individual seeking coverage to arrange insurance for him on the best possible terms. The broker has contacts with many insurers, but does not have an agency agreement with them. He is thus free to deal with any insurer that will accept the business he offers. The broker cannot bind any insurer orally to a risk because he has no prior arrangements such as would be described in an agency agreement. Thus, in dealing with a broker, one should not assume that he has coverage the moment he orders the insurance. One is covered only when the broker contacts an insurer that agrees to take the risk.

---

[18] An example of such action might be the acceptance of a renewal premium by an agent who knew of the violation of the policy condition.

SUMMARY

1. An understanding of legal principles is vital to a proper understanding of the insurance contract itself. There are several differences in the application of these legal principles to life insurance as opposed to general insurance.

2. Insurable interest is necessary for any insurance contract to be valid. The principles of indemnity and subrogation flow out of the principle of insurable interest. Both are necessary to reinforce the principle of insurable interest.

3. Because insurance is a contract of utmost good faith, breach of warranty or the making of a material misrepresentation on the part of the insured can void the coverage. A concealment has the same legal effect as a material misrepresentation.

4. Insurance is effected by means of a legal contract and must meet the general requirements of contracts. Thus, the insurance contract must not be against public policy, must be enacted by parties with legal capacity to contract, must be effected with a meeting of the minds of the parties, and must be supported by a consideration. Oral contracts of insurance may be valid, although they should usually be avoided whenever possible. Insurance is a contract of adhesion and any ambiguities are construed against the insurer.

5. Insurance is effected through agents who have varying degrees of authority, depending upon the custom in different lines of insurance and upon the doctrines of waiver and estoppel. Brokers are agents of the insured, not the insurer, and cannot bind coverage orally.

QUESTIONS FOR REVIEW AND DISCUSSION

1. E. W. Patterson, writing in *Essentials of Insurance Law,* states: "Subrogation is a windfall to the insurer. It plays no part in rate schedules (or only a minor one). . . . Even as to tort-feasors, it is arguable that since the insurer is paid to take the risk of negligent losses, it should not shift the loss to another."
   (a) Do you agree with this statement in whole or in part? Explain.
   (b) State the general arguments for including subrogation clauses in insurance contracts.

2. Suit was filed by an insured to change the wording of a paid-up life insurance policy (Alldredge v. Security Life and Trust Co. 92 So. (2) 26, Alabama, 1957). The insured claimed that the company's general agent signed an agreement which would entitle the insured to a paid-up $7,000 policy on the payment of only four annual premiums of $322.28 each. Neither the policy nor the application therefor referred to this written instrument.
   (a) Do you think the suit should be successful? Why or why not?
   (b) Upon what legal doctrines does your decision rest?

3. In National Indemnity v. Smith-Grandy, Inc. (150 Wash. 109), Smith-Grandy, an auto dealer, telephoned a general agent in Seattle to place coverage on a truck that was then in transit from Detroit to Seattle. The dealer was told that coverage would commence immediately, which was at 3:15 p.m., on June 7, 1955, the day of the conversation. But the written policy which was subsequently issued stated that the coverage was from 12:01 a.m., June 7, 1955, to June 7, 1956. It was learned later that at 2:15 p.m., the truck had been in an accident that resulted in a claim against Smith-Grandy for $200,000. The insurer refused to pay the claim because the accident occurred before 3:15 p.m. In a suit against the insurer, Smith-Grandy argued that the time stated in the written policy governed the effective time of coverage, but the insurer defended on the basis of the agent's testimony that the coverage was not placed until 3:15 p.m.

    (a) How should this case be decided?

    (b) Explain the legal doctrines involved in this case.

4. "B" is the employee of a small manufacturer. He applies for a fire insurance policy on the manufacturing plant where he works because if the building burns, he knows he will lose his job. The agent refuses to write the policy. Upon what grounds is this refusal probably based? Explain.

5. A movie producer has spent $1 million making a movie satirizing the life of a popular public figure. He applies for a life insurance policy on this individual in the amount of $1 million. Will the life insurer issue the policy? If so, why? If not, why not?

6. "X" borrows $1,000 from "Y," who demands that "X" allow him to take out a life insurance policy on "X's" life as security for the debt in case "X" dies. Later on the debt is repaid, but "Y" keeps the policy in force. Five years later, "X" dies. May "Y" collect? Why, or why not?

7. Under what conditions, if any, is it necessary to prove insurable interest on the part of a beneficiary in life insurance? Explain.

8. In Liberty National Life Insurance Co. v. Weldon (3 Life Cases (2) 669, Alabama, 1957), the insurer issued a life insurance policy on a two-year old girl. The applicant for the insurance was the child's aunt. The parents knew nothing about the insurance. Later on the aunt poisoned the child, was found guilty, and was executed. In your opinion was the requirement of insurable interest met in this case? Why?

9. "A" is thinking of purchasing a car. He takes out an insurance policy on the car and orders the car delivered to another city where he intends to take possession and to close the deal. Before he becomes the legal owner, the car is destroyed. In the meantime, the former owner has dropped his coverage on the car.

    (a) Who suffers the loss?

    (b) Is there any effective insurance covering this loss?

    (c) Would your answer be different if the car had been destroyed after "A" had taken title, bearing in mind that the insurance was placed *before* he had taken title?

10. Distinguish between the doctrine of insurable interest and the principle of indemnity.

11. "D" has a house valued at $15,000. He takes out insurance in two companies, each in the amount of $15,000. If the house is totally destroyed, can he collect in full from both companies? Why, or why not?

12. Suppose "D" purchases fire insurance that provides for the replacement of any loss without regard to depreciation. Is this provision in violation of the principle of indemnity? Explain.

13. "A" is killed in an auto accident in which "B" has been held to be negligent. "A's" life insurer pays $50,000 under "A's" life insurance policies. Does the insurer have the right to sue "B" for this amount? Why, or why not?

14. "T's" house, valued at $10,000, is burned for a total loss through "U's" negligence. "T" collects $6,000, the full face of his fire insurance policy. "T's" insurer sues "U" and collects $5,000. How is the $5,000 divided between "T" and the insurer? Explain.

15. In an application for life insurance, the applicant stated that he had no illness, that he went to a physician only twice a year for a check-up, and that he had no application for insurance pending with any other company. Shortly after the policy was issued, the insured died. The company denied liability when it was discovered that the insured had seen a doctor six times within ten weeks preceding his application. Furthermore, the insured had applied to another insurance company for $50,000 of life insurance at the same time as the current application.

    (a) May the insurer properly deny liability?

    (b) What legal doctrine of insurance is involved in this case?

    (c) What is the test of materiality in a representation?

16. Distinguish between a concealment and a misrepresentation.

17. (a) What two standards of care are imposed in determining whether or or not a concealment will void a policy?

    (b) Explain the reasons for these two standards of care.

18. An applicant for fire insurance failed to reveal that he had received various threats that, unless he paid a certain sum of money, his house would be burned. Do you think this would constitute a concealment? Why?

19. Differentiate between (a) warranty and representation; between (b) promissory warranty and affirmative warranty.

20. There was a plot to burn a house for fire insurance. Ten gallons of gasoline were poured over the floors. One of the plotters went into the house to retrieve some bed spreads, but something went wrong and the gasoline ignited before he could escape. In a suit to recover on the arsonist's life insurance, the insurer denied liability on the grounds that the whole thing was an illegal venture. (Taylor v. John Hancock Mutual Life Insurance Co. 132 N.E. (2) 579 (Ill. App. 1956). Do you think this defense is valid? Explain.

21. What is the connection between legality in an insurance contract and the requirement of insurable interest? Explain.

22. An applicant for life insurance in the amount of $6,500 did not submit his first premium with his application. The policy provided there would be no liability until a policy was issued and delivered during the lifetime and good health of the insured and upon payment of the full first premium. Two days after the application, the applicant passed his physical examination. However, the insurance company wrote its district manager that it would accept the policy only for a higher premium. In the meantime, the agent told the applicant that he had passed his physical, and collected the first annual premium. The company never issued the policy, for within 30 days after the original application, the applicant died of a heart attack. The estate of the insured sued on the grounds that the insurer's silence was implied acceptance of the risk, and it should be estopped from denying that a contract had been made. In your opinion, does the action of the agent and the silence of the insurer, pending an answer from the district manager, constitute sufficient evidence as to allow estoppel to be invoked? Discuss. (Hayes v. Durham Life Insurance Co., 96 S.E. (2) 109 (Va. 1957).

23. What two elements constitute the consideration in an insurance contract?

24. Are all oral contracts of insurance binding? Discuss.

25. (a) Under what conditions can a mistake be corrected in an insurance policy?
    (b) Do you think the insurer could have tried the case in Question 3 on the theory of correction of a mistake in the policy? Discuss.

26. Why is the principle of adhesion important in the interpretation of insurance contracts?

27. What is the doctrine of: (a) uberrimae fidei? (b) respondiat superior?

28. Distinguish between the powers of a general agent and those of a special agent.

29. By what three methods may one become an agent for another? Explain.

30. (a) Distinguish between the doctrines of waiver and estoppel.
    (b) Give an illustration of how each works.

Elements Common

to Most Insurance Contracts

There are many similarities in insurance contracts which can best be studied and analyzed at one time in order that duplication may be avoided when studying the various policies separately. For example, it will be seen that most contracts contain certain exclusions, such as for loss due to war, loss to property of an extremely fragile character, and loss due to the deliberate action of the named insured. Most property insurance contracts require the insured to notify the insurer of loss as soon as practicable, and usually require that the insured prove his loss. An understanding of these common elements greatly facilitates the understanding of insurance contracts generally, even when a given policy applies a different name to a certain type of provision or condition. The following analysis supplies an outline of the more significant provisions common to most insurance contracts.

THE INSURING AGREEMENT

One of the first things to look for in any contract is a statement of the essence of what is agreed upon between the parties. In insurance, this is found in the *insuring clause,* or *insuring agreement,* which normally states what it is that the *insurer* agrees to do, and the major conditions under which he agrees to do it. The insuring agreement normally starts out, "In consideration for the premiums herein paid and the conditions agreed to, the _____ Insurance Company hereby insures the above named person. . . ." The exact nature of what is promised is then set forth. As indicated in the preceding chapter, the insured promises only to pay his premium and to conform to the conditions of the policy. Conforming to the conditions is a part of his consideration, so technically the insured just agrees to pay a consideration. The most important, and in fact, the crucial part of the agreement is the statement of what the *insurer* promises. The specific nature of these promises is examined in Part IV.

NAMED PERIL V. ALL RISK

There are two general approaches used in framing insuring agreements. One, the traditional, is the named peril approach, and the other, which is being used more and more extensively, is the all-risk approach. The *named peril* agreement, as the name suggests, lists the perils that are proposed to be covered. Perils not named are, of course, not covered. The other type, *all risk,* states that it is the insurer's intention to cover all risks of loss to the described property *except* those perils specifically excluded.

The insuring agreement of a typical automobile insurance policy is illustrative of the named peril approach. The agreement may state:

> The company agrees with the insured . . . in consideration of the payment of the premium and in reliance upon the statements in the declarations and subject to the . . . terms of this policy . . . to pay. . . .

The policy then lists and describes the various perils against which coverage may be purchased under a particular form. Such perils are usually loss to the insured arising out of the ownership, maintenance, and use of the automobile, and include such losses as may result from negligent operation causing damage to others, loss from collision, loss from fire and theft, and loss from injuries to the insured and his passengers while riding in the car.

Typical of the all-risk approach is the insuring agreement of the personal property floater, which undertakes to insure "all risks of loss of, or damage to, property covered except as hereinafter provided." The policy then goes on to impose various limitations upon types of property covered (for example, automobiles, boats, and business property are excluded) and upon certain perils that are excluded (such as against loss resulting from war, wear and tear, mechanical breakdown, and breakage of fragile articles).

DEFINING THE INSURED

All policies of insurance name at least one person who is to receive the benefit of the coverage provided. He is referred to as the *named insured.* In addition, many contracts cover other individuals' insurable interest in the described property or cover them against losses outlined in the policy. These individuals are often called *additional interests* or *additional insureds* and they normally receive coverage somewhat less complete than that of the named insured.

For example, the family automobile policy covers not only the registered owner of the automobile, but in addition grants exactly the same coverage to the spouse if he or she is a resident of the same household. The policy also covers *any* other persons who are driving with the permission of either the named insured or his spouse, provided they are not driving the automobile in connection with any automobile business such as a service station, a garage, or a parking lot. Such additional insureds' coverage is limited and restricted in various ways. For example, the policy does not grant coverage to parties driving with permission of those who have been given permission to drive. Thus, if the named insured tells "A" he may drive the car and "A" in turn lends the car to "B," "B" has no insurance under the named insured's policy unless it can be shown that the named insured himself has given "B" definite permission to drive. Likewise, the coverage given to additional insureds when driving cars not owned by the named insured is less than that given to the named insured himself.

In a fire policy (New York Standard, 1943), likewise, the policy covers not only the named insured but also his legal representatives. Thus, if the named insured dies, the policy, by virtue of this provision, is effective in covering his estate until it is settled. In the comprehensive personal liability policy, the "insured" includes not only the named insured, but also his spouse and the relatives of either if they are living in the same household. In addition, the policy insures any employee of the insured who is operating certain farm equipment in the scope of his employment, any person under age 21 in the care of the insured, and any person or organization legally responsible for losses growing out of the use of animals or watercraft owned by an insured. Thus, if the named insured lends a horse to his neighbor and while the neighbor is riding, the horse breaks away and injures someone, the neighbor is covered under the named insured's liability policy.

THIRD PARTY COVERAGE

Many contracts of insurance may provide coverage on individuals who are not direct parties to the contract. Such persons are known as *third parties*. The rights of third parties are outlined in each contract and vary considerably.

In life insurance the beneficiary is a third party and has the right to receive the death proceeds of the policy, under conditions that are usually determined in advance by the named insured. The beneficiary can be changed at any time by the insured as long as he lives, unless he has formally given up this right—*i.e.*, has named the beneficiary irrevocably. The beneficiary's rights are thus contingent upon the death of the insured, unless the beneficiary has been named irrevocably. Similarly, a person such as a creditor, to whom a policy has been assigned, has certain rights as a third party to receive death proceeds and perhaps certain claims on the cash value of life insurance policies.

In the workmen's compensation insurance contract, the agreement is between two parties, an employer and an insurance company. The insurance company agrees to make such payments to employees as are required under the laws of the state relating to compensation of workmen who suffer job-connected injuries. The insurer's obligation is directly to the injured workman who is a third party under the contract. Depending on state law, the workman may bring legal action against the insurer for his benefits even though he was not a direct party to the agreement.

In medical payments insurance, coverage that is granted under automobile policies and under various liability policies is essentially a third party coverage. Under it, individuals who are not contracting parties are covered for injuries they may suffer under certain conditions, such as while riding in the automobile of the named insured or while on the property of the named insured. The insurer is obligated directly to the third parties, just as he is in workmen's compensation insurance.

In the field of property insurance, very often the third party is the one who has loaned money on property covered under the policy of the named insured. For example, in fire insurance, the lender is usually covered under what is known as the standard mortgagee clause; and in automobile insurance, under what is known as a loss payable clause. The lender is entitled to recover first if the property is damaged by a peril covered under the policy, with any excess going to the owner. The lender is entitled to advance notice in case the policy is about to be canceled for any reason, and he is usually permitted to pay the premium if the insured fails to do so. The lender's rights are not lost merely because the insured violates some provision of the policy and thereby loses his rights under the contract. Thus, if the insured uses his vehicle as a public livery, thereby suspending his coverage under the automobile policy, the lender is still entitled to the recovery of his interest in case the vehicle is destroyed. The insurer pays the lender, and through subrogation, as explained in Chapter 8, enjoys all the rights that the lender had against the insured. In this way the insured cannot benefit from payment to a third party when the insured was not entitled to payment on his own account.

EXCLUDED PERILS

Practically all contracts of insurance exclude from coverage certain perils, those factors causing losses. Normally a separate section, with all the excluded perils listed and described, appears in the contract. It is vital that the exclusions be noted and understood in order to understand satisfactorily the insurance contract. Providing for exclusions is the draftsman's way of describing and delimiting the insuring agreement in a way that is definite and unambiguous.

Perils are excluded for three different reasons:

1) Some perils are excluded because they are basically uninsurable.[1]
2) Others are excluded because it is intended to cover them elsewhere, such as in another type of policy.
3) Still others are excluded because it is intended to charge extra for them under an endorsement which may be added to the policy at the option of the insured.

1) Perils that are basically uninsurable

In all types of insurance it is very common to exclude loss arising out of war, warlike action, insurrection, and rebellion because losses from such sources cannot be predicted with any degree of reliability, and are often catastrophic in nature. Likewise, perils such as wear and tear, gradual deterioration, and moth and vermin are excluded because losses from this source are not accidental, and are in the nature of certainties and hence uninsurable. For a similar reason, losses to property resulting from deliberate action by the insured are excluded, such as arson, faulty workmanship, or voluntary increase of the hazard. In life insurance, suicide within two years (one year, in some policies) of the application is an excluded peril for the same reason.

2) Perils to be covered elsewhere

Some perils can be more easily covered in contracts that are specially designed for them. Thus, the personal automobile policy excludes losses arising out of business uses of the vehicle, and commercial automobile coverage excludes, under well-defined conditions, personal uses of the vehicle. The problems of insuring business and personal

---

[1] See Chapter 2 for a discussion of the requirements of insurable perils.

risks are entirely different and policies are designed for each purpose. The exclusion serves the purpose of eliminating duplicate coverage. A similar exclusion is found in fire insurance forms, liability contracts, and inland marine policies. Another example of this type of exclusion is in the exclusion of certain water damage and flood losses from fire forms. Such perils present special problems and must be insured separately.

3) Perils covered under endorsement at extra premium

The third type of exclusion may be illustrated by the provision in the standard fire policy that the policy shall not cover riot or explosion unless fire ensue, and in that event for loss by fire only. In subsequent endorsements the perils of riot and explosion are customarily added back into the policy at an extra premium. In this way those insureds who do not require additional coverage of certain perils may choose a more limited form of coverage.

EXCLUDED LOSSES

Most insurance contracts will contain provisions excluding certain types of *losses* even though the policy may cover the peril that causes these losses. For example, the fire policy covers direct loss by fire, but excludes *indirect* loss by fire. Thus, the policy will not cover loss of fixed charges or profits resulting from the fact that fire has caused an interruption in a business. Separate insurance is necessary for this protection. Neither does the policy cover losses caused by the operation of any law (such as building codes) requiring that a more expensive type of construction be used in replacing a building destroyed by fire.

Similarly, in health insurance, if the policy is designed to cover hospitalization expense due to the peril of illness, it will often exclude the cost of doctor bills that result from this same peril. In automobile insurance, loss due to the peril of collision will not include losses to the property of others from this peril. Such losses must be covered under separate agreements.

EXCLUDED PROPERTY

A contract of insurance may be written to cover certain perils and losses resulting from those perils, but it will be limited to certain types of property. For example, the fire policy excludes fire losses to money, deeds, bills, bullion, and manuscripts. Unless it is written to cover the contents, the fire policy on a building includes only integral parts of the building and excludes all contents. The automobile policy gives only very limited protection to personal property carried in the vehicle. The automobile policy also gives somewhat more limited protection to nonowned vehicles than it gives to owned vehicles of the insured. The liability policy usually excludes the property of others in the care, custody, and control of the insured.

EXCLUDED LOCATIONS

The policy may restrict its coverage to certain geographical locations. Relatively few property insurance contracts give complete worldwide protection. Fire insurance is usually restricted to property in set locations, with only a small part of the coverage, say 10 per cent of the face amount, applicable when some of the property is located elsewhere than on the chief premises of the insured. Automobile insurance is usually limited to cover the auto while it is in the United States, its possessions, or Canada. If the car is in Europe or Mexico, for example, coverage is suspended.

CLAUSES LIMITING AMOUNTS PAYABLE

In defining the coverage of an insurance contract, it is usually necessary for the insurer to limit the dollar amounts of recovery by including clauses such as deductibles, franchises, coinsurance arrangements, time limitations, dollar limits, and apportionment clauses. A policy may contain one or more of these clauses. The clauses serve many different purposes and it is not always possible to ascribe a single reason or even a group of reasons for the use of any one of them. In general, however, the clauses are used to reduce the costs of offering the insurance service; to prevent too many small, expensive-to-administer claims; to achieve a greater degree of fairness in the rate structure; and to place an upper limit on the insurer's obligation on any one policy. These purposes are aimed at converting the insuring agreement from a vague promise to indemnify into a definite, measurable contract which meets the requirements of insurable risks.

Deductibles

It is very common to stipulate that a definite dollar amount, say $50, will be borne by the insured before the insurer becomes liable for payment under the terms of the contract. For example, most people are familiar with the use of $50 and $100 deductibles in automobile collision insurance. More recently, $50 deductibles have been used in fire insurance contracts applying to all claims except those stemming from the occurrence of certain common perils, such as fire, lightning, explosion, and smoke. The purpose of these deductibles is to eliminate small claims. Small losses are expensive to pay, sometimes causing more administrative expense than the actual amount of the payment. It is to the insured's advantage that such deductibles be available, for oftentimes he is able to save considerable sums in his insurance cost by their use. For example, in automobile insurance the saving in the annual premium by the use of a $100 deductible for collision claims rather than a $50 deductible might amount to $35. This is the equivalent of saying that to reduce the deductible from $100 to $50 costs $35. The insured would be paying $35 a year for $50 of added coverage, an extremely high rate compared to that charged for the entire contract.

Franchises

A *franchise* is a deductible, expressed either as a percentage of value or as a dollar amount, under which there is no liability on the part of the insurer unless the loss exceeds the amount stated. Once the loss exceeds this amount, however, the insurer must pay the entire claim. Sometimes this franchise is termed "disappearing deductible," because the deductible has no effect once the total loss reaches the specified amount. In ocean marine insurance it is common to use a franchise agreement expressed as a percentage. Thus, the policy might provide that there shall be no loss payable on wheat unless the loss exceeds three per cent, except for losses caused by fire, sinking, stranding, or collision. But once the loss reaches this level, the insurer is responsible for 100 per cent of the claim.

There is more logic to the use of a franchise than a straight deductible if the sole purpose is to eliminate small claims. However, a straight deductible also eliminates many small claims which the insurer will never have to pay, and it eliminates a portion of large claims as well. In this way a straight deductible keeps down total loss payments. Likewise, the insured realizes that he will have to pay some part of each claim and thus has addititional incentive to minimize the frequency of his losses.

Coinsurance

The term coinsurance has at least two common meanings in insurance, one in the field of health insurance, and another in the field of fire insurance. In health insurance the coinsurance clause is simply a straight deductible, expressed as a percentage. Its purpose is to make the insured bear a given proportion, say 25 per cent, of every loss, because it has been found through experience that without such a control, the charges for doctors and other medical services tend to be greatly enlarged, thus increasing the premium to a prohibitive level. When the insured knows he must personally bear a substantial share of the loss, he is less inclined to be extravagant in this regard.

In fire insurance the coinsurance clause is a device to make the insured bear a portion of every loss *only when he is underinsured*. It thus becomes a device to prevent underinsurance. Underinsurance is looked upon as undesirable for two reasons. First, insurance companies are in business to restore their policyholders to the same position they were in before the loss. They obviously cannot accomplish this objective unless the insured is willing to protect the whole value of his property.

Second, it costs relatively more to insure the business of individuals who are underinsured than it does to handle the business of individuals who purchase insurance equal to the full value of the object—that is, those who take out "full insurance to value." This follows because most losses are partial, and the probability of partial losses is higher than the probability of total losses. Rates, as we have learned, depend on the probability of loss. Consequently, it follows that the *rate* charged for partial losses should be higher than the rate charged for total losses. No one knows whether his loss will be total or partial. Yet there is a tendency for the average person to assume that his loss will be partial and therefore he underinsures in order to save premium cost.

There are two possible contractual ways to combat underinsurance. In the first method as suggested above, the person who underinsures could be charged a higher rate than the person who takes out full insurance to value. In practice this procedure is difficult to administer because it involves the determination of what constitutes underinsurance in each case. Each building would have to be appraised by the insurer whenever the rate for the policy had to be determined in order to set the amount of insurance to be required. This procedure would be expensive and its cost would have to be reflected in higher premium charges. It might be difficult to persuade the average insured that he should bear this cost, especially since the actual frequency of fire losses is extremely low. However, this method is in fact used as noted below.

The second method of combating underinsurance, the one which has been generally adopted by the insurance industry, is the use of a coinsurance clause. The typical coinsurance clause pro rates any partial losses between the insurer and the insured in the proportion that the actual insurance carried bears to the amount required under the clause. Usually 80 or 90 per cent of the sound value [2] is the amount required. Thus, if there is a building with a $10,000 sound value written with a 90 per cent coinsurance clause, $9,000 of insurance is required. If the insured carries at least this amount, he collects in full for any partial loss. But if he carries half of this amount, or $4,500, he collects only half of any partial loss. If he carries $6,000, he collects two thirds of any partial loss. The amount collected in any case may be determined by the following formula:

$$\frac{\text{Amount of Insurance Carried}}{\text{Amount of Insurance Required}} \times \text{Loss} = \text{Recovery}$$

If the loss equals or exceeds the amount required under the clause (if the loss is nearly total), there is no particular penalty invoked by the coinsurance clause. Thus, if in the above case the loss were $9,000 at a time when the insured is carrying only $6,000 of insurance, substitution in the above formula yields the following: $\frac{\$6,000}{\$9,000} \times 9,000 = \$6,000$. The recovery is $6,000, the amount of insurance carried, and there is no particular penalty other than the fact that the insured did not carry sufficient insurance to cover his entire loss. In the above case, suppose the loss were $1,500. The recovery would be $1,000. Here the insured is carrying $6,000 of insurance, but recovers only $1,000 of a $1,500 fire loss.

By use of the coinsurance clause, the burden is placed upon the insured to keep the amount of his insurance equal to or above the amount required by the clause. Failing in this, he becomes a coinsurer and must bear part of any partial loss. In times of inflation, periodic reappraisals are necessary to see that sufficient insurance is being carried. It should be noted that coinsurance clauses in fire insurance are employed only on commercial buildings and equipment, and not on private dwellings. In some jurisdictions, the insured is permitted to

---

[2] Sound value means the actual cash value of the property; that is, the replacement cost less an allowance for depreciation.

omit the coinsurance clause by paying a higher rate, or conversely is allowed a substantial rate credit for using the coinsurance clause. In effect, this amounts to use of the method of rate adjustment to achieve equity in the rate structure instead of the use of coinsurance penalties.

Time limitations

Time is of the essence in most insurance policies. There are specified limits of time set forth, for example, during which the loss must be suffered, the insurer to be notified in event of loss, the claims to be paid, and the proof of loss to be submitted. We are now interested primarily in the time limits that affect the dollar amount of coverage. To illustrate, in health insurance contracts, and for that matter in nearly all contracts guaranteeing the payment of an income or periodic imdemnification for loss, there are often waiting periods before recovery begins. There are also time limitations that restrict the maximum period for which payments may be made. Thus, in a policy that pays the insured an income if he becomes permanently disabled, it is very common to provide that no income shall be payable during the first seven or thirty days of disability. Such a provision has the same purpose as a straight dollar deductible, namely, to eliminate small claims and to reduce the cost of coverage. In addition, the policy may provide that the income shall continue for one year, two years, ten years, or life, as the case may be. The insurer always specifies what time limit shall be imposed. This is necessary in order to meet the requirement that an insurable risk must be definite and measurable.

Time limitations are found in many kinds of insurance contracts other than health insurance. In business interruption insurance, the insurer promises to pay for profits and necessary continuing expenses lost as the result of an interruption of normal business operations due to the occurrence of a named peril. The payment necessarily depends primarily on the length of time the business was shut down as a result of the named peril. In life insurance the contract is often settled with the beneficiary by paying the proceeds in the form of an income, rather than in a lump sum. When this is done, the length of time the income is to continue is spelled out in the policy.

Dollar limits

Most insurance contracts provide for maximum dollar limits on recovery for given types of losses. In addition to the limits imposed by the face amount of the policy, there are two general types: specific limits and aggregate limits.

Specific dollar limits restrict payments to a maximum amount on any one definite item of property or from a named peril, as provided in the policy. *Aggregate* dollar limits restrict payments to some maximum amount on any one group of items of property. Thus, in the fire insurance "special" form, applicable to a dwelling, the policy has a specific limit of $250 on liability to plants, shrubs, and trees from any one loss. In addition, there is an aggregate limit which provides that no more than five per cent of the amount of insurance may apply to plants, trees, and shrubs in any one loss.

Another example of dollar limits is found in the manner in which insurers restrict their liability for losses resulting from bodily injury liability. Usually there is a specific limit of liability for damage to any one person, and there is an aggregate limit of liability applicable to loss in any one accident. Thus, if the limits of liability are expressed as "$10,000/$20,000 BI," it means that the company will be liable for no more than $10,000 to any person in a given accident, and in no case for more than $20,000 per accident in the event that more than one person files a claim for which the insured is liable.

Apportionment clauses

Practically all contracts of indemnity and many valued contracts contain *apportionment clauses* that limit the insurer's liability in case other insurance contracts also cover the loss.

For example, a contract may agree to pay the insured a certain income on a "valued basis" if he becomes permanently and totally disabled. It might stipulate, however, that in case the insured is collecting under other disability contracts as well, the indemnity will be reduced to the point that the insured will be prevented from collecting more than, say, three fourths, of his income prior to his disability. Sometimes the effect of the apportionment clauses is quite severe because one insurer may limit its liability to its proportion of all insurance covering the property regardless of whether the other insurance policies apply to a particular loss. As an example, suppose "A" has a building valued at $10,000 and he has fire policies in two companies, "X" and "Y," in the amount of $5,000 each. The policy in Company X is written to cover windstorm losses through the use of the extended coverage endorsement, and the policy in Company Y does not contain this endorsement. Company X's policy contains an apportionment clause. In case of a windstorm loss of $1,000, Company X pays only the proportion that its policy bears to all insurance on the property, or one half.

Thus, the insured collects $500 from Company X and nothing from Company Y because Company Y's policy did not insure against windstorm. The only solution to this problem is to make sure that all policies insuring the property are identical in their coverage.

The purpose of apportionment clauses, sometimes known as "pro rata liability," or distribution clauses, is to establish some procedure by which each insurer's liability may be determined when more than one policy covers the property. In the absence of such clauses, the insured might collect more than his actual cash loss, and a moral hazard could be created. In most property insurance lines, these clauses simply provide for an apportionment of coverage in the same proportion that the amount of each policy bears to the total insurance, as illustrated above. In other lines, such as automobile, the clause provides that with regard to certain losses, such as accidents involving a nonowned car or those involving medical payments claims, the policy will be "excess over any other applicable coverage." That is, the contract is to apply to losses only after the limits of liability of all applicable insurance contracts have been exhausted. In ocean marine insurance, it is the general rule that the limits of liability of the first policy to be written on a given exposure must be exhausted before subsequently issued contracts will have any liability. Other policies, such as the personal property floater, do not permit other insurance to be written on the described property. If it is found that other insurance has been written, this would act as breach of warranty and may void the coverage.

COMMON POLICY CONDITIONS

All contracts of insurance are written subject to certain conditions. Breach of these conditions is usually grounds for refusal to pay in the event of loss. Therefore, the condition should be read with care, even though in some cases the insurer does not insist upon complete or exact compliance. Most of the conditions have to do with loss settlements, actions required at the time of loss, valuation of property, cancellation of coverage, suits against the insurer, and other similar matters. The most important of these conditions will be discussed below.

Fraud

Even though it is unnecessary, many contracts state that misrepresentation or fraud will void the contract. This condition may be inserted in the contract as much to serve as a warning to the insured, as it is to state a condition that would be enforced by the courts even if the policy said nothing about it.

Notice of loss

Most contracts of insurance require the insured to give immediate written notice of any loss, if practicable. If it is not practicable to do so, the loss must be reported within a reasonable time. For example, if a forest fire destroys "A's" summer cabin that is situated in a remote area, "A" may not be able to reach outside communications for several days. If "A" made an attempt to notify the insurer as soon as he reasonably could, he would still be able to collect on his insurance policy. The purpose of this provision is to give the insurer a reasonable opportunity to inspect the loss before important evidence to support the claim and to establish the actual amount of damage is dissipated. As another example, if a person is injured in an accident he may be unable to give immediate notice of loss. However, his failure to notify the insurer promptly would not violate the notice of loss provision in his health insurance policy.

Proof of loss

The insured is given a certain period, usually 60 or 90 days, to render a formal proof of loss. It is not enough that the insurer be notified of the loss; it is necessary for the insured to prove the amount of the loss before he can collect. Usually the company adjuster or agent aids the insured in preparing the proof, but the burden is on the insured to accomplish the task. In this connection, the insured must submit to examination under oath as to the accuracy of his proof; must produce all books of account, bills, invoices, etc., that might help in establishing the loss; and must cooperate in any reasonable way to assist the insurer in verifying the proof.

In some cases, establishing the proof of loss is an extremely specialized and expensive task. In ocean marine insurance, for example, specialists known as *average adjusters* may spend years collecting all the proofs of loss resulting from a sunken ship and involving hundreds of cargo owners, in order that a final settlement can be made and the loss apportioned among the various insurers that are liable. In large fire losses, such as occured in the 1947 Texas City disaster, adjusters from all over the nation may spend months in the destroyed area reconciling all conflicts over claims for losses.

Appraisal

Most contracts of property insurance provide that if the two parties cannot agree on a loss settlement, each may select a competent and disinterested appraiser to determine the loss. An impartial umpire, selected and paid by each party, settles any remaining differences. Although this somewhat expensive procedure is not resorted to often, it must be complied with, however, before suit can be brought for recovery under the policy where the cause of the suit is failure to agree on the actual cash value of the loss.

Preservation of the property

Most contracts of property insurance contain provisions requiring the insured to do everything he can to minimize losses to his property when the insured peril occurs. In fire insurance the insured must protect the property from further damage. This means, for example, he must take all reasonable steps to cover up property that has been removed from the building to protect it from rain or exposure. Failing to do this, he may thereby relieve the insurer from any further liability for loss.

Ocean and inland marine policies contain a clause known as the *sue and labor clause,* which requires the insured to "sue, labor, and travel for, in and about the defense, safeguard, and recovery of the property insured hereunder." This may be interpreted to mean that the insured is required to hire salvors to protect a stranded ship from further loss, to hire guards to watch over a wrecked truck and its cargo, and to bring suit against a party liable for loss. The insurer agrees to be responsible for these expenses, in addition to paying the full limits of liability under the policy for loss. Thus, if the insured pays a salvage company $5,000 to save a stranded ship, but the effort fails and the ship becomes a total loss, the insurer will indemnify the insured for full value of his ship plus the $5,000 fee for salvage.

Cancellation

All contracts of insurance specify the conditions under which the policy may or may not be terminated. In general, life insurance and certain health insurance contracts may be terminated by the insured but not by the insurer except for a limited period named in the "contestable" clause. Property and liability contracts may be canceled by either party upon specified notice.

Property and liability insurance policies usually state that the insurer may elect to end its liability for losses after a five or ten days' notice. This gives the insured time to obtain coverage elsewhere so that he will not suffer any lapse of protection. In such cases the insurer is obligated to return any unearned premium on a pro rata basis. Thus, if the premium has been paid in advance for three years and the insurer cancels after one and one-half years have expired, it is obligated to return one half of the premium to the insured. However, if the insured cancels, the policy usually provides for what is known as a "short-rate" return of premium. In the above case the insured would get back only about 40 per cent of his premium instead of one-half. The reason for the difference in methods of refunding premiums lies in the fact that if the insured cancels before the end of the full term, the insurer should be entitled to some compensation for the extra cost involved in short-term policies. If the insurer cancels, however, the insured should not be penalized for the short-term coverage.

No reason need be given when either party elects to cancel such a contract as described above. The insurer in property and liability typically reserves the right to cancel because of the method of acquiring business. Historically, the local agent can bind the insurer to risks that lie within the scope of his authority. Oftentimes the agent may involve the insurer in risks that it wishes to avoid, or in which it already has a sizable concentration of exposure. The company may escape such obligations through the cancellation right, an underwriting practice known as *post selection*. Also, if the loss ratio on a given class of risks becomes larger than anticipated, or if a single exposure has an unreasonable number of claims, the insurer may cancel this unprofitable business. Thus, in automobile insurance it is common to cancel the coverage of an insured who proves to be accident prone, or where a distinct moral hazard is found to be present. These comments should not be interpreted to mean that insurance companies will cancel any policy on which a loss or two is reported. Insurance is written to cover losses and most insurers will not exercise their cancellation privilege unless the circumstances warrant it.

In life insurance and in certain other types of contracts, such as noncancelable income disability policies and credit insurance, there is no cancellation privilege given the insurer. If the insurer could cancel at will, the insured might be deprived of his coverage at the very moment he needed it most, because in these lines certain events that indicate the imminence of loss usually become apparent; thus the insurer would be warned of impending liability. For example, if life insurance could be terminated at the option of the insurer, the company could cancel the policy at the time the insured contracted a fatal illness, but before he died, thus escaping its liability for the ultimate death claim. Likewise in income disability policies, if the insured develops a heart attack, but is not disabled, the company might well cancel the coverage if it were permitted, because heart disabilities tend to recur and eventually become disabling. The insured could pay his premiums for many years and then lose his protection at the very time he needed it most. In credit insurance, the insurer agrees to compensate the insured for all losses stemming from the failure of unsecured creditors to pay their accounts. However, failure to pay an account usually stems from insolvency on the part of the creditor, a condition that can usually be predicted in advance by certain signs of financial weakness. The insurer is aware of these signs and could cancel the coverage whenever they appeared, thus defeating the purpose of the contract as far as the insured is concerned. Thus, the policy is not cancelable by the insurer.

Where a policy is not cancelable by the insurer but is subject to termination by the insured, there is no provision for return of premium as such to the insured. All premiums paid in are considered earned by the insurer. In life insurance, upon surrender of the policy, the insured is entitled to what are known as nonforfeiture values, which may have accumulated under his policy. These values originate from premium payments, but they are not identified as such in the policy; rather they form a pool of funds that in effect are excess premiums paid in and held for the insured as savings. This feature is discussed in greater detail in Chapter 21.

Assignment

An *assignment* is the transfer of the rights of one person to another, usually by means of a written document. In insurance it is common to allow the insured to assign his rights under the contract to another person. Usually such permission must be specifically granted. The person granting the right is called the *assignor* and the party to whom the right is granted is called the *assignee*. In life insurance the policy provides that if another person is to be given any rights under the contract, such as the right to receive death proceeds to the extent of a debt that existed between the assignor and the assignee, the insurance company must be notified. In the event of the death of the insured, such an assignment must be honored before any named beneficiary receives payment. This is very common when a lender requires protection before he will grant a loan to a borrower.

In fire insurance, oftentimes when a property is sold, it is desired to transfer the existing fire insurance policy to the new owner. This transfer ends the necessity of canceling the old policy, taking a short-rate return of premium, and placing a new policy in force. Permission of the insurer is required for such an assignment. In ocean marine insurance it is the usual practice to allow assignment of the coverage on cargo shipments without prior consent of the insurer. The assignment is accomplished by means of a document known as a *cargo certificate,* which may be endorsed somewhat in the same way as a negotiable instrument as the goods change hands in their journey from producer to final consumer.

The reason for requiring permission of the insurer before policy rights may be assigned is that insurance is a personal contract and one of utmost good faith, and the underwriting of it requires investigation into the personal characteristics of the insured. To allow assignments without consent of the insurer could impose obligations and risks that were never contemplated in the original contract.

SUMMARY

1. There are two general approaches used in framing insuring agreements—the named peril and the all-risk approaches. The tendency is to expand the use of all-risk contracts as time goes on.

2. It is common to cover many more than one individual as insureds under most insurance policies. These secondary interests normally do not receive as broad coverage as is given to the named insured. Policies also give certain privileges to persons known as third parties who are not direct parties to the contract. In fact, many insurance agreements are chiefly for the benefit of third parties.

3. All contracts of insurance contain exclusions of different kinds. There are excluded causes of loss, or excluded perils such as war, wear and tear, and intentional damage. There are often excluded losses and excluded property so that even if an insured peril occurs, not all the loss it may cause is covered. Most policies exclude or limit losses caused in certain locations, such as while the goods are away from a named location or while they are abroad.

4. An element common to insurance contracts is the practice of limiting amounts payable. Thus, there are various kinds of deductibles, franchises,

coinsurance arrangements, time limitations, named dollar limits of liability, and apportionment clauses. These clauses serve purposes other than merely keeping down the insurer's loss payments. They may encourage the insured to take out complete insurance to value or they may discourage him from this objective. They also serve to control the moral hazard and to define the insurer's obligation more precisely than would be possible without them, thus converting what might be an uninsurable risk into one that is insurable.

5. The major conditions of the insurance contract which follow fairly standard wording are fraud, notice and proof of loss, appraisal, preservation of the property at the time of loss, cancellation, and assignment. Each of these clauses has a different purpose which is intended to make the risk acceptable to the insurer.

QUESTIONS FOR REVIEW AND DISCUSSION

1. The insuring agreement of the personal property floater reads: "Perils insured. All risks of loss of or damage to property covered except as hereinafter provided." Should one assume from this that he has "all-risk" coverage for the property described? Explain.

2. John lends his car to Jim, who drives it to a nearby town where he has an accident that damages the front end. Later Jim lends the car to his friend Jack, who forthwith runs into a pedestrian and is sued for $5,000. Assuming John has complete automobile insurance coverage, which of the above accidents, if any, is covered? Why?

3. "A" has a comprehensive personal liability policy. His married son, "S," lives next door. A gardener who was to work on "A's" lawn made a mistake and started to work on "S's" lawn instead. "S" had been digging a trench for a waterpipe. The gardener stumbles over this half-covered trench and breaks his leg. He sues "S." Does "S" have coverage under "A's" comprehensive liability policy? Why?

4. "T" is the beneficiary under "X's" life insurance policy. "X" dies and it is discovered that "X" has named "Y" as a new beneficiary to replace "T." "T" sues the insurer, holding that as a third party he had certain rights that were violated. Assess "T's" position.

5. "D" is a worker employed at the plant of "Z." "D" is injured and is awarded a lifetime income of $137 per month from "Z's" workmen's compensation policy. Later, "Z" goes out of business. Ten years later "D's" payments suddenly stop. Does "D" have any rights to proceed against the insurance company, or must he sue "Z"? Explain.

6. Explain the major reasons for excluding certain perils from insurance contracts.

7. Differentiate between (a) excluded perils and (b) excluded losses, giving examples of each type.

8. An automobile policy excludes coverage from nonowned autos if they are furnished for the regular use of the named insured, but covers such cars if they are only occasionally used.
   (a) Explain the probable reason for this exclusion.
   (b) Is this exclusion sound from the standpoint of basic insurance principles? Why or why not?

9. The personal property floater excludes loss against breakage of eye glasses or glassware unless occasioned by certain named perils such as fire, theft, and lightning.
   (a) Why is such property excluded?
   (b) If you were designing a new policy, under what conditions would you cover such property? Discuss.

10. "A" is offered the choice of a major medical policy with a $100 deductible or with a $500 deductible. There are five members in his family and the deductible applies on a calendar year basis to each individual in the family. The cost of the policy with a $100 deductible is $200 a year while the cost of the policy written with a $500 deductible is $70 a year. Which policy should "A" take? Why? Defend your answer.

11. Explain the difference between a franchise clause and a straight deductible by use of an example.

12. A certain fire insurance policy is written with a 90 per cent coinsurance clause in the amount of $45,000. The actual replacement cost of the structure, less depreciation, is found to be $100,000.
   (a) What amount may be collected under this policy in the event of the following losses? (1) $1,000, (2) $5,000, (3) $50,000, (4) $80,-000, (5) $90,000. Explain your answer.
   (b) Does the clause reduce recovery below the amount insured in all of the above cases? Why?

13. Answer Question 12 (a) if the amount of insurance carried had been $60,000 instead of $45,000.

14. (a) Explain the reasoning behind the use of the coinsurance clause in Question 12.
    (b) Is there any other way in which to accomplish the purpose other than through the use of coinsurance? Explain.

15. A certain residential fire insurance form allows up to 10 per cent of the face amount of insurance to apply to losses described as "rental value," but in no case may the recovery exceed 1/12 of this amount in any one month.
    (a) If the policy is for $12,000 and the rental value of the property is $150 per month, how much can be collected if the insured is displaced from his house for two months?

(b) What type of dollar limits are illustrated in this case?

(c) What purpose is served by such limits?

16. The double indemnity provision in a life insurance policy provides that twice the face amount of the insurance will be paid for certain types of accidental death, providing death occurs within 90 days of the accident.

(a) What purpose is served by this type of time limitation?

(b) Is the time limitation in accord with sound insurance principles? Explain.

17. A certain type of health insurance policy providing an income in the event of permanent and total disability stipulates payments for two years in case of illness, but lifetime payments are provided if the disability is caused by accidental means.

(a) Account for the difference in the time limits noted.

(b) Are these limitations in accordance with sound insurance principles? Explain.

18. The standard fire insurance policy provides that "this company shall not be liable for a greater proportion of any loss than the amount hereby insured shall bear to the whole insurance covering the property against the peril involved, whether collectible or not." Would the principle of indemnity be violated if this clause were not included? Give an illustration.

19. Why is it unnecessary for a policy to state that fraud will void the contract?

20. While "A" is vacationing in Florida, his tool shed in Ohio burns and a neighbor notifies him that the shed was a complete loss. When "A" returns to Ohio ten days later, he notifies his insurance company of the fire and is surprised to find that the insurer denies liability. On what grounds does the insurance company's denial rest? Explain.

21. "Y's" house and its contents become a total fire loss, but "Y" has only a vague idea of what property actually was destroyed because he had no inventory of his household goods.

(a) How might "Y" go about establishing his loss?

(b) Is it likely he will be able to collect full indemnity, assuming he was fully insured? Why, or why not? Discuss.

22. What machinery is usually provided in an insurance contract to handle settlements of loss when the insurer and the insured disagree as to the amount of the claim? Explain.

23. Why are life insurance policies not cancelable by the insurer while fire insurance policies are?

24. Under what conditions may an assignment to a third party of an insurance contract be preferable to cancellation and subsequent rewrite in the name of the third party?

25. It is customary to give substantial allowances in the rate for the use of coinsurance clauses in fire insurance. Assume that a certain base rate is 1 per cent of value annually and that a reduction of 45 per cent in this rate is made for the use of a 90 per cent coinsurance clause.

   (a) How much insurance must be carried on a $10,000 building to avoid coinsurance penalties, and what would be the cost of this insurance annually?

   (b) If the insured does not have the coinsurance clause and therefore pays the full 1 per cent rate, how much insurance could he carry for the same net premium?

   (c) Explain the principle illustrated here about the use of coinsurance.

26. What precautions would you give to an insured who carries his fire insurance with a coinsurance clause if (a) he often has goods in his care on a consignment basis, and (b) his stock in trade fluctuates substantially during the year? Explain.

Fire Insurance

and Related Lines

While fire is one of man's most valuable servants, it has also proved to be one of his most destructive enemies. Each year in the United States it is estimated that more than 10,000 lives are lost in fires, and property valued at more than $1 billion is destroyed. Data on fire losses have been available since 1876, and since that year direct property fire losses have totaled about $40 billion. This sum represents an absolute loss to society because insurance serves primarily as a method to redistribute losses and not to prevent them.[1] This chapter concerns itself with the peril of fire, and with insurance techniques to reduce the risk of loss from this source and from other similar perils.

THE PERIL FIRE

Data collected by the National Fire Protection Association reveal that in 1957 in the United States there were approximately 844,000 building fires and over 1,180,000 fires not involving buildings, such as in aircraft, motor vehicles, forests, and ships. Table 10–1 reveals the incidence of fires by major class of occupancy and the resulting losses.

It will be observed that while building fires are less numerous than other fires, they do by far the greatest amount of damage. Residential fires are the most numerous type of building fires, and account for 29 per cent of the total fires, and 25.5 per cent of the total losses. Mercantile and manufacturing building fires tend to be severe, for while they constitute only about 6 per cent of the total fires, they do cause over 30 per cent of the total damage. It should be noted that, although the aggregate fire loss has been increasing steadily in the United States, total property exposed has increased tremendously and the rate of loss has actually declined to the point where best estimates place it at one third of the 1900 level.

---

[1] Some of these "losses" might not actually be true losses since it is undoubtedly true that society has benefited from the reconstruction of modern buildings to replace old, often dangerous, structures. The fire may have saved the cost of tearing down unsafe buildings and also speeded up progress in this area.

Table 10–1

FIRES AND FIRE LOSSES BY SELECTED OCCUPANCIES, 1957

Occupancy	No. of Fires *	Per Cent of Total	Total Losses †	Per Cent of Total
Public buildings............	16,000	.8	$ 76,932,000	6.0
Residential.................	587,100	29.0	326,630,000	25.5
Mercantile.................	71,000	3.6	185,926,000	14.5
Manufacturing.............	41,100	2.1	232,040,000	18.1
Miscellaneous..............	128,700	6.5	246,587,000	19.3
Other than building fires ‡...	1,181,600	58.0	211,811,000	16.6
Total.................	2,025,500	100.0	$1,279,926,000	100.0

* Based on 14 states.
† Based on 13 states.
‡ Motor vehicles, aircraft, rubbish, miscellaneous.
Source: Quarterly of the *National Fire Protection Association*, Vol. II, No. 2 (October, 1958).

Table 10–2

LEADING CAUSES OF FIRE, 1953–1958 *

Causes of Ignition	Claims		Property Loss	
	Number	Per Cent	In Dollars	Per Cent
Matches & smoking.....................	335,185	24.2%	$ 383,781,625	14.9%
Electricity & electrical equipment, except lightning & static....................	283,427	20.4	840,868,530	32.8
Lightning............................	167,844	12.1	147,233,888	5.7
Heat, flames, or sparks from sources other than defective heating units or welding torches............................	160,229	11.6	174,472,936	6.8
Defective heating units—all fuels combined.	137,783	9.9	278,799,262	10.9
Exposure............................	90,265	6.5	183,683,991	7.2
Defective or overheated chimneys, flues, etc..................................	51,228	3.7	86,665,354	3.4
Sparks from bonfires, rubbish, etc.........	42,268	3.0	61,003,898	2.4
Open lights...........................	30,714	2.2	26,710,913	1.0
Known but not otherwise classified........	30,465	2.2	74,619,295	2.9
Spontaneous ignition....................	24,884	1.8	101,498,809	4.0
Incendiarism, vandalism, etc..............	13,015	0.9	60,673,371	2.4
Welding torches.......................	7,982	0.6	95,812,674	3.7
Friction & friction sparks................	6,834	0.5	35,787,121	1.4
Backfire or hot exhaust from internal combustion engines.......................	3,035	0.2	6,252,390	0.2
Fireworks, firecrackers..................	1,813	0.1	2,662,763	0.1
Static electricity and static sparks.........	1,411	0.1	6,330,687	0.2
Total............................	1,388,382	100.0%	$2,566,857,507	100.0%

* Data are based on the number of reported fires where the cause is known, and do not represent the total number of fires or the total property loss in the United States for the period. It is estimated that the aggregate property loss in the United States during this period was approximately $5.7 billion.
Source: *Property Insurance Fact Book, 1960*, p. 4.

The causes of fire, as estimated by the National Board of Fire Underwriters, are given in Table 10–2, which covers the period 1953–1958. Smoking, use of matches, and misuse of electricity together cause a little over 44 per cent of all fires. The rate of fire loss per 1,000 population rises steadily as the size of city in which the fire occurs diminishes. In cities between 10,000 to 25,000 in population, there were nearly 6 building fires per 1,000 population in 1956, while the rate in cities of 1,000,000 and over was 3.5 fires per 1,000. As might be expected, fire loss is greatest in winter months.

A tragic factor about fires is the catastrophic damage of which they are capable. Many times in history entire cities have been virtually destroyed. In 1906, some 28,000 buildings were destroyed in the San Francisco fire; 17,430 buildings were lost in the Chicago fire of 1871; and in 1861, the entire city of Charleston, South Carolina, was destroyed by fire. The largest single building fire in history destroyed the General Motors plant at Livonia, Michigan, in 1953, an estimated $50 million loss. Even more tragic is the loss of life in some of these calamities. For example, 1,152 individuals lost their lives in the Peshtigo, Wisconsin, fire of 1871; 492 people died in the Cocoanut Grove Night Club fire in Boston in 1942; and countless children have died while trapped in school building fires.

Other perils, such as windstorms, tornadoes, and explosions, take their toll annually, both in lives and property. The tabulation in Table 10–3, compiled by the National Board of Fire Underwriters, illustrates the need for protection against the financial loss caused by these and other perils.

Table 10–3

A RECORD OF CATASTROPHES, 1958

Date	Place	Peril	Estimated Loss Payments *
February 24.........	California	Windstorm	$2,500,000
June 4..............	Wisconsin	Tornadoes and windstorm	2,500,000
June 7..............	Montana	Wind and hail	4,000,000
June 10.............	Kansas	Wind and hail	2,500,000
July 2..............	Montana	Wind and hail	4,000,000
September 27........	North Carolina	Hurricane	5,000,000

* Estimates are based on payments made prior to December 31, 1958. Data include only damage paid by insurers and do not include total damages.
Source: *Property Insurance Fact Book, 1960,* (National Board of Fire Underwriters), p. 23.

THE STANDARD FIRE POLICY

It appears that no matter what measures are taken to prevent fires, a certain amount of losses will occur. While theoretically all fire losses except a very small portion are preventable, modern industrial society has not yet organized itself in such a way that these losses are actually eliminated. Therefore, it becomes the primary function of the insurer to redistribute the burden over a large group in such a way that no one suffers a catastrophic loss from fire.

Before 1873, fire insurance contracts were unstandardized, meaning that they often contained different wording or wording which was mutually inconsistent when more than one policy was written on the same property. Such a system often involved not only omissions in coverage, but also produced conflicts which were not in the best interests of policyholders. Each insurer devised its own agreement and there was no attempt to integrate coverage in such a way as to provide uniform protection. For example, one insurer might include a provision in its policy that if another contract were written to cover the risk, the first policy would be void. The second contract covering the risk might contain the same provision and the insured would be without protection altogether when the loss occurred.

The uncertainties introduced by individualized contracts led the state of Massachusetts, in 1873, to establish a standard contract form. In 1880 this form became mandatory for all insurers doing business in the state. In 1887 New York followed suit, using a slightly different form. This form was then required in several other states and has become, with only slight modification, the standard of the industry. There was a revision in 1918 and again in 1943. The insuring agreement of the 1943 Standard Fire Policy is reproduced in Figure 10–1, and its major provisions are discussed below. It has been adopted and its use is mandatory in 49 states and the District of Columbia. New Hampshire still uses the New England form which differs from the New York form in several details that will not be explained here.

The insuring agreement

The insuring agreement of the standard fire policy, reproduced in Figure 10–1, is of basic importance to a sound understanding of the contract and deserves some specific comment and explanatory statements. It will be observed that the consideration for the contract consists of *both* a specified premium and an agreement to the provisions and stipulations which follow. Failure to pay the premium or to abide

IN CONSIDERATION OF THE PROVISIONS AND STIPULATIONS HEREIN OR ADDED HERETO AND OF the premium above specified, this Company, for the term of *years specified above* from *inception date shown above* At Noon (Standard Time) to *expiration date shown above* At Noon (Standard Time) at location of property involved, to an amount not exceeding the amount(s) above specified, does insure *the insured named above* and legal representatives, to the extent of the actual cash value of the property at the time of loss, but not exceeding the amount which it would cost to repair or replace the property with material of like kind and quality within a reasonable time after such loss, without allowance for any increased cost of repair or reconstruction by reason of any ordinance or law regulating construction or repair, and without compensation for loss resulting from interruption of business or manufacture, nor in any event for more than the interest of the insured, against all **DIRECT LOSS BY FIRE, LIGHTNING AND BY REMOVAL FROM PREMISES ENDANGERED BY THE PERILS INSURED AGAINST IN THIS POLICY, EXCEPT AS HEREINAFTER PROVIDED,** to the property described herein while located or contained as described in this policy, or pro rata for five days at each proper place to which any of the property shall necessarily be removed for preservation from the perils insured against in this policy, but not elsewhere.

Assignment of this policy shall not be valid except with the written consent of this Company.

This policy is made and accepted subject to the foregoing provisions and stipulations and those hereinafter stated, which are hereby made a part of this policy, together with such other provisions, stipulations and agreements as may be added hereto, as provided in this policy.

Figure 10–1

THE INSURING AGREEMENT OF THE STANDARD FIRE POLICY

by these provisions means a failure of the consideration, and hence a failure of the contract itself.

Policy term. Reference is made to noon standard time as being the time of inception and termination of the contract. This is intended to avoid disagreements that might arise over other time measurements, such as daylight saving time or solar time. If the fire commences during the policy period, all the damage caused by the fire is covered, even if part of the damage is done after the expiration of the policy. Thus, if a fire begins at 11:55 a.m. on the day the policy expires and most of the loss is caused after 12:00 noon, the policy pays the whole claim.

Actual cash value. The insuring agreement states that only the actual cash value of the property at the time of loss will be reimbursed, not to exceed the amount that it would cost to repair or to replace the property with material of like kind and quality. Some insureds might interpret this to mean that the insurer will restore all the burned property with material of like kind and quality. However, the insurer sets the replacement cost as a *maximum* reimbursement. *Actual cash value* is interpreted to mean replacement cost at the time of loss less any depreciation. Thus, if it costs $1,500 to rebuild a 40-year old roof that is almost worn out, the insurer normally will not rebuild the roof, but will make a cash settlement of an amount far less than this to allow for depreciation. As will be recalled from discussion in earlier chapters, fire insurance is a contract of indemnity and it is intended to put the insured in the same financial position with respect to damaged property as he was before the loss. The insured may buy coverage that will eliminate the deduction for depreciation, but this involves another type of insurance with an additional premium.[2]

In the case of buildings, factors such as obsolescence and a deteriorated neighborhood may be considered in arriving at the actual cash value. In a well-known case,[3] an old brewery was totally destroyed by fire. It had been insured for a substantial amount, but at the time of the fire was obsolete because the National Prohibition Act had made the brewing business illegal. The question was raised as to the amount of the recovery permitted under these circumstances, since the replacement cost less depreciation was substantially more than the building was worth as part of an illegal business. While no definite rule for measuring obsolescence was laid down, the decision established that obsolescence could be considered in reducing the recovery *below* the actual replacement cost less depreciation. In the case of personal property, replacement cost is the cost that would be incurred by the owner in obtaining comparable goods. This amount might be well above the original purchase price, if the trend of prices had been rising.

Interest of insured.   Recovery is limited to the extent of the legal financial interest of the insured in the property. This interest need not be sole ownership of the property, as was required in the 1918 form, nor must the interest be explained in the policy; but it must be proved at the time of any loss. Say that "A" and his brother "B" own a house jointly and "A" insures the house in his name and "B" is not named as an insured. In the event of loss, only "A" will recover and then only to the extent of his ownership, presumably one half of the value of the house. Thus, all interests should be named in the policy, or they cannot be paid in the event of loss.

---

[2] See page 241 for a discussion of replacement cost insurance.
[3] *McAnarney* v. *Newark Fire Insurance Co.,* 159 N. E. 902.

Direct loss. The words "direct loss by fire, lightning and by removal from premises. . . ." are of great importance. By *direct loss* is meant loss, the *proximate* cause of which is one or more of the three sources listed in the insuring agreement. No indirect loss, such as loss resulting from interruption of business or manufacture, is covered. Separate coverage is provided for this type of loss, and will be discussed in Chapter 11.

There have been many controversies in insurance over the meaning of the words "direct loss by fire." In the 1918 Standard Fire Policy, the peril lightning was not automatically covered and had to be added by endorsement to the basic contract. Many fires were caused by lightning and it became necessary to differentiate that part of the loss caused by lightning from that caused by fire, because the policy only covered direct loss by *fire*. Thus, if a building were struck by lightning, split in two, and then caught fire and burned to the ground, the policy would restore the value of a building that had been split in half, and not a whole building.

To avoid such difficulties, the 1943 Standard Fire Policy added lightning to the basic coverage, but the same problem still exists with regard to other physical perils (such as windstorm) for which protection may be added by endorsement. Suppose a building burns and leaves one wall standing. A week later this wall falls down during a windstorm and damages the insured's building that is situated next door. Is this a fire loss or a windstorm loss? It can be argued that if it had not been for the fire, the windstorm would not have had an opportunity to blow down the wall; therefore the fire is the proximate cause of loss. On the other hand, it might be argued that the wall might have stood indefinitely had it not been for the windstorm; therefore the windstorm was the proximate cause of loss. The doctrine of proximate cause says that a peril may be said to cause a loss if there is an unbroken chain of events leading from the peril to the ultimate loss. Adjusters and sometimes ultimately the courts have the responsibility of interpreting each case in the light of this doctrine in order to ascertain the real meaning of "direct loss by fire."

Sometimes the question is raised as to what constitutes fire. A *fire* may be defined as combustion in which oxidation takes place so rapidly that a flame or a glow is produced. Rust, is a form of oxidation, but of course is not a fire. Scorching or heat is not fire. Furthermore, the fire must be *hostile;* that is, it must be of such a character that it is outside its normal confines. Fires intentionally kindled in a stove are not covered in the policy, nor are articles accidentally thrown into the stove. Such fires are said to be *friendly*. However, once the fire escapes its confines and is in an area not intended, it becomes hostile and all loss resulting directly from it is covered. Direct loss by fire also includes such losses as damage from water or chemicals used to fight the fire, and broken windows or holes chopped in the roof by firemen, since these are often an inevitable result of the fire itself.

Location. The insuring agreement makes it clear that the coverage applies only while the insured property is at a location specified in the declarations, unless a fire threatens and the goods are moved away to a safe place for the sake of preserving them from destruction. The danger of fire varies greatly depending on the location of the property, and the insurers wish to restrict their coverage to areas that they have had an opportunity to inspect and approve. However, permission is granted to remove the goods to another place for a limited time, set at five days, for safety sake. Extensions of this period to 30 days are typical in endorsements that modify the basic agreement.

The insuring agreement also provides that it may be amended by later endorsements. Without such permission, a question might be raised as to which provision holds, the basic agreement or later stipulations. It is clear that later amendments govern the coverage, even if they directly contradict earlier provisions, unless the basic agreement specifically prohibits such amendments.

Assignment. Because the insurer wishes to reserve the right to choose the one with whom it will deal, the contract provides that assignment of the policy rights will not be valid without the written consent of the insurer. The personal element in insurance is an important underwriting characteristic and without this provision, the original insured might assign the policy to someone who is a poor moral risk.

The usual reason for an assignment is to transfer an insurance policy to another individual who has purchased the covered property. The assignment avoids the necessity of canceling the existing contract and taking a short-rate return of premium for the unexpired term of protection, only to replace the coverage with a new policy. Usually the insurer will give its permission to make such an assignment.

Conditions and stipulations—165 lines

The New York Standard Fire Policy (1943) contains 165 lines of provisions and stipulations that form the basis of the insurance coverage. Some of the provisions are amended by later endorsement, but by and large the 165 lines "set the pattern" for all later insurance protection and deserve careful attention. Reference should be made to Figure 10–2 for an identification of the lines discussed in the following comments pertaining to the more important conditions of the policy.

Excluded property. Lines 7–10 refer to excluded property, which is divided into two classes—that property which may not be covered at all under the Standard Fire Policy, and that property which may be insured by specific endorsement. Separate coverage is provided for property such as money and securities, because the special underwriting problems that arise make it desirable to give that class of property special attention. Bullion and manuscripts need to be described carefully before insurance can be granted.

Excluded perils. Lines 11–24 name the perils that are excluded from coverage. For example, if there is an invasion or a war that results in a fire and this fire destroys the insured property, it is the position of the insurer that the proximate cause of loss is war, not fire. War is a peril that is almost universally excluded in all private insurance contracts. Likewise, if the insured deliberately fails to call the fire department until after the fire has a good start, coverage will probably be denied because the proximate cause of loss was the willful neglect of the insured to use all reasonable means to save his property.

Excluded losses. Lines 28–37 exclude three types of *losses:* (1) those occurring while the hazard is increased by any means within the control or knowledge of the insured, or (2) those occurring while the building is vacant for a period beyond 60 consecutive days (this period is often extended in some territories), or (3) those occurring as a result of explosion or riot, unless fire ensue and then for the fire loss only. The first type of loss involves situations in which the insured may change the basic character of the risk by some action, such as switching his use of the building from a garage to a manufacturing establishment. The insurer is entitled to be told of this situation, and if it is not, the coverage is suspended. Often this exclusion is waived for residential property.

An unoccupied or vacant building is subject to greater danger of fire than a building in full use. Unless special permission is received from the insurer, the coverage is suspended after 60 days of vacancy or unoccupancy. In the case of explosion or riot, direct loss from these sources is excluded; but in the event that a fire is caused by a riot or an

1 Concealment,
2 fraud. This entire policy shall be void if, whether before or after a loss, the insured has wilfully concealed or misrepresented any material fact or circumstance concerning this insurance or the subject thereof, or the interest of the insured therein, or in case of any fraud or false swearing by the insured relating thereto.

7 Uninsurable
8 and
9 excepted property. This policy shall not cover accounts, bills, currency, deeds, evidences of debt, money or securities; nor, unless specifically named hereon in writing, bullion or manuscripts.

11 Perils not
12 included. This Company shall not be liable for loss by fire or other perils insured against in this policy caused, directly or indirectly, by: (a) enemy attack by armed forces, including action taken by military, naval or air forces in resisting an actual or an immediately impending enemy attack; (b) invasion; (c) insurrection; (d) rebellion; (e) revolution; (f) civil war; (g) usurped power; (h) order of any civil authority except acts of destruction at the time of and for the purpose of preventing the spread of fire, provided that such fire did not originate from any of the perils excluded by this policy; (i) neglect of the insured to use all reasonable means to save and preserve the property at and after a loss, or when the property is endangered by fire in neighboring premises; (j) nor shall this Company be liable for loss by theft.

25 Other Insurance. Other insurance may be prohibited or the amount of insurance may be limited by endorsement attached hereto.

28 Conditions suspending or restricting insurance. Unless otherwise provided in writing added hereto this Company shall not be liable for loss occurring (a) while the hazard is increased by any means within the control or knowledge of the insured; or (b) while a described building, whether intended for occupancy by owner or tenant, is vacant or unoccupied beyond a period of sixty consecutive days; or (c) as a result of explosion or riot, unless fire ensue, and in that event for loss by fire only.

38 Other perils
39 or subjects. Any other peril to be insured against or subject of insurance to be covered in this policy shall be by endorsement in writing hereon or added hereto.

42 Added provisions. The extent of the application of insurance under this policy and of the contribution to

84 relating to the interests and obligations of such mortgagee may be added hereto by agreement in writing.

86 Pro rata liability. This Company shall not be liable for a greater proportion of any loss than the amount hereby insured shall bear to the whole insurance covering the property against the peril involved, whether collectible or not.

90 Requirements in
91 case loss occurs. The insured shall give immediate written notice to this Company of any loss, protect the property from further damage, forthwith separate the damaged and undamaged personal property, put it in the best possible order, furnish a complete inventory of the destroyed, damaged and undamaged property, showing in detail quantities, costs, actual cash value and amount of loss claimed; **and within sixty days after the loss, unless such time is extended in writing by this Company, the insured shall render to this Company a proof of loss,** signed and sworn to by the insured, stating the knowledge and belief of the insured as to the following: the time and origin of the loss, the interest of the insured and of all others in the property, the actual cash value of each item thereof and the amount of loss thereto, all encumbrances thereon, all other contracts of insurance, whether valid or not, covering any of said property, any changes in the title, use, occupation, location, possession or exposures of said property since the issuing of this policy, by whom and for what purpose any building herein described and the several parts thereof were occupied at the time of loss and whether or not it then stood on leased ground, and shall furnish a copy of all the descriptions and schedules in all policies and, if required, verified plans and specifications of any building, fixtures or machinery destroyed or damaged. The insured, as often as may be reasonably required, shall exhibit to any person designated by this Company all that remains of any property herein described, and submit to examinations under oath by any person named by this Company, and subscribe the same; and, as often as may be reasonably required, shall produce for examination all books of account, bills, invoices and other vouchers, or certified copies thereof if originals be lost, at such reasonable time and place as may be designated by this Company or its representative, and shall permit extracts and copies thereof to be made.

123 Appraisal. In case the insured and this Company shall fail to agree as to the actual cash value or the amount of loss, then, on the written demand of either, each shall select a competent and disinterested appraiser and notify

46 policy, may be provided for in writing added hereto, but no pro-
47 vision may be waived except such as by the terms of this policy
48 is subject to change.

49 **Waiver**   No permission affecting this insurance shall
50 **provisions.** exist, or waiver of any provision be valid,
51 unless granted herein or expressed in writing
52 added hereto. No provision, stipulation or forfeiture shall be
53 held to be waived by any requirement or proceeding on the part
54 of this Company relating to appraisal or to any examination
55 provided for herein.

56 **Cancellation** This policy shall be canceled at any time
57 **of policy.** at the request of the insured, in which case
58 this Company shall, upon sur-
59 render of this policy, refund the excess of paid premium above
60 the customary short rates for the expired time. This pol-
61 icy may be canceled at any time by this Company by giving
62 to the insured a five days' written notice of cancellation with
63 or without tender of the excess of paid premium above the pro
64 rata premium for the expired time, which excess, if not ten-
65 dered, shall be refunded. Notice of cancellation shall
66 state that said excess premium (if not tendered) will be re-
67 funded on demand.

68 **Mortgage** If loss hereunder is made payable, in whole
69 **interests and** or in part, to a designated mortgagee not
70 **obligations.** named herein as the insured, such interest in
71 this policy may be canceled by giving to such
72 mortgagee a ten days' written notice of can-
73 cellation.
74 If the insured fails to render proof of loss such mortgagee, upon
75 notice, shall render proof of loss in the form herein specified
76 within sixty (60) days thereafter and shall be subject to the pro-
77 visions hereof relating to appraisal and time of payment and of
78 bringing suit. If this Company shall claim that no liability ex-
79 isted as to the mortgagor or owner, it shall, to the extent of pay-
80 ment of loss to the mortgagee, be subrogated to all the mort-
81 gagee's rights of recovery, but without impairing mortgagee's
82 right to sue; or it may pay off the mortgage debt and require
83 an assignment thereof and of the mortgage. Other provisions

129 interested umpire; and failing for fifteen days to agree upon
130 such umpire, then, on request of the insured or this Company,
131 such umpire shall be selected by a judge of a court of record in
132 the state in which the property covered is located. The ap-
133 praisers shall then appraise the loss, stating separately actual
134 cash value and loss to each item; and, failing to agree, shall
135 submit their differences, only, to the umpire. An award in writ-
136 ing, so itemized, of any two when filed with this Company shall
137 determine the amount of actual cash value and loss. Each
138 appraiser shall be paid by the party selecting him and the ex-
139 penses of appraisal and umpire shall be paid by the parties
140 equally.

141 **Company's** It shall be optional with this Company to
142 **options.** take all, or any part, of the property at the
143 agreed or appraised value, and also to re-
144 pair, rebuild or replace the property destroyed or damaged with
145 other of like kind and quality within a reasonable time, on giv-
146 ing notice of its intention so to do within thirty days after the
147 receipt of the proof of loss herein required.

148 **Abandonment.** There can be no abandonment to this Com-
149 pany of any property.

150 **When loss** The amount of loss for which this Company
151 **payable.** may be liable shall be payable sixty days
152 after proof of loss, as herein provided, is
153 received by this Company and ascertainment of the loss is made
154 either by agreement between the insured and this Company ex-
155 pressed in writing or by the filing with this Company of an
156 award as herein provided.

157 **Suit.** No suit or action on this policy for the recov-
158 ery of any claim shall be sustainable in any
159 court of law or equity unless all the requirements of this policy
160 shall have been complied with, and unless commenced within
161 twelve months next after inception of the loss.

162 **Subrogation.** This Company may require from the insured
163 an assignment of all right of recovery against
164 any party for loss to the extent that payment therefor is made
165 by this Company.

In Witness Whereof, this Company has executed and attested these presents; but this policy shall not be valid unless countersigned by the duly authorized Agent of this Company at the agency hereinbefore mentioned.

Figure 10-2

CONDITIONS AND STIPULATIONS OF THE STANDARD FIRE POLICY

explosion, the resulting loss from fire is covered. This contrasts with other excluded perils, excluded in lines 11–24, in which no loss is covered if it can be traced directly to one of these perils. For example, if an explosion wrecks a building and the wreckage catches on fire and burns, the Standard Fire Policy indemnifies the insured for the value, if any, of the wreckage.

Cancellation. The provisions within lines 56–67 specifically set forth the terms under which the policy may be canceled by the insurer. Termination is effective five days after the written notice of cancellation is communicated to the policyholder. The policy remains in force during the five days, which are counted from midnight on the day in which the notice is received to midnight five days later. The notice must either be accompanied by a return of the unearned premium or contain a statement that the pro rata unearned premium will be returned to the insured. Neither party to the contract is required to give a reason for cancellation. The purpose of the five-day notice is to give the insured an opportunity to place his coverage elsewhere.

Mortgage clause. Lines 68–85 contain the provisions that govern relationships with any mortgagee named in the declaration of the policy. The form that extends the basic fire policy contains further elaboration of the provisions relating to the mortgagee in the so-called Standard Mortgage Clause. This clause has the effect of creating a separate agreement between the mortgagee and the insurer, almost as if the mortgagee had taken out a separate policy covering his interest in the property.

The mortgagee requires some kind of protection because if the property were destroyed, it is much less likely that his debt would ever be paid. A mortgagee has the possibility of protecting his interest in insured property in at least four different ways:

1) Separate insurance for the mortgagee's interest.
2) Assignment by insured.
3) Loss payable clause.
4) Standard Mortgagee Clause.

1) Separate insurance for the mortgagee's interest. The mortgagee can purchase separate insurance covering his interest. This plan has the disadvantage, however, that both the mortgagee and the mortgagor will be placing coverage on the same values, since the mortgagor has an interest equal to the entire value of the property, and not just his "equity." For example, if there is a house valued at $20,000 with a $15,000 mortgage on it, the interest of the mortgagee is $15,000 and the interest of the owner is $20,000. If each purchased separate coverage, there would be a total of $35,000 of insurance on the house, far more than is necessary to protect the value exposed; and it would be difficult to prevent double payment by the insurer.

2) Assignment by insured. The mortgagee could be protected by means of an assignment. The insured could simply take out a policy and then assign its benefits to the mortgagee, after obtaining permission of the insurer. The difficulty with this method is that in case the owner defaults on his premium, or otherwise violates a policy provision, the coverage ceases and with it the protection of the mortgagee. In other words, the mortgagee receives no better protection under an assignment than is enjoyed by the person making the assignment. If the assignor has no rights, he has nothing to assign the assignee.

3) Loss payable clause. The mortgagee could be protected by a loss payable clause. Such a clause simply states that the loss, if any, shall be payable to the person named. However, if the insured were to violate his policy, such as defaulting on his premium, no loss would be payable and the loss payee would receive no payment in most jurisdictions.

4) Standard Mortgagee Clause. The mortgagee may be protected by the Standard Mortgagee Clause, which was designed to overcome the limitations of the other methods and is now in almost universal use. Under the Standard Mortgagee Clause, the mortgagee has certain rights and obligations. Among its rights are:

1. To receive any loss or damage payments as its interest may appear, regardless of any default of the property owner under the insurance contract, and regardless of any change of ownership or increase of the hazard.
2. To receive 10 days' notice of cancellation, instead of five days.
3. To sue under the policy in its own name.

Among the obligations of the mortgagee under the Standard Mortgagee Clause are:

1. To notify the insurer of any change of ownership or occupancy or increase of the hazard that shall come to the knowledge of the mortgagee.
2. To pay the premium if the owner or mortgagor fails to pay it. (In most jurisdictions this has been interpreted to mean that the mortgagee must pay the premium only if it wishes to enjoy the protection under the policy. In some states, and in the forms used widely on the Pacific Coast, the mortgagee covenants to pay the premium on demand, even if it does not wish to maintain the insurance.)

3. To render proof of loss to the insurer in case the owner or mortgagor fails to do so.
4. To surrender to the insurer any claims it has against the mortgagor to the extent that it receives payment from the insurer. The insurer may under some conditions deny liability to the owner or mortgagor and therefore retain, through subrogation, all rights that the mortgagee may have had against the mortgagor. To illustrate, assume that the mortgagee, protected under the Standard Mortgagee Clause, has a $10,000 mortgage on a $15,000 building, and there is a $5,000 fire loss caused deliberately by the insured himself. The insurer denies liability to the insured, but must pay the mortgagee $5,000. The mortgagee must now surrender to the insurer $5,000 of its claim against the mortgagor. Or the insurer has the right to pay the mortgagee the entire $10.000 debt, obtain an assignment of the mortgage, and collect in full against the mortgagor. In this way, the mortgagor does not obtain any of the benefits of payment to the mortgagee through a reduction of his debt. Instead of owing the mortgagee, he owes the insurance company.

Pro rata liability.   Lines 86–89 state that the insurer shall not be liable for a greater proportion of any loss than the amount insured bears to the whole insurance covering the property, whether or not this insurance happens to be collectible. The pro rata liability clause is simply an apportionment clause, which was discussed in Chapter 9. The clause is designed to enforce the principle of indemnity and to prevent the insured from collecting more than one policy covering the property. Thus, if there are three policies in the amount of $5,000, $3,000, and $2,000 covering a loss of $1,000, the insurers are obligated for one half, three tenths, and one fifth of the loss, respectively. If the $2,000 policy is not collectible because the insurer is insolvent, its share of the loss, $200, is not made up by the other policies.

It is worth noting that the pro rata liability clause applies only to all policies that cover the same legal interest. If there is more than one interest involved, such as in the case of a lessee and an owner, and there are two policies on the property, each insurer must pay to the fullest extent of its liability and the payment will not be reduced by action of the pro rata liability clause. For example, suppose a lessee spends $10,000 improving a property on which he has a lease and insures this value. Since the value of all permanent improvements to real estate revert to the landlord upon expiration of the lease, the landlord also has an interest in the improvements, and may insure them. Since there are two interests, there may be two policies of $10,000 each. In the event that a fire destroys the entire property, both insurers would have to pay to the fullest extent of the insurable interest of each insured; the insurers would not contribute to the loss in the proportion that the limit of liability on each policy bears to the total insurance.

Requirements when loss occurs and appraisal. Lines 90–161 of the Standard Fire Policy represent an attempt to spell out in considerable detail the procedures that are to be followed when a loss occurs, in order that disagreements and perhaps expensive court litigation may be avoided. These procedures must be followed before any suit can be filed under the policy.

In case loss occurs, there are several obligations that must be met by the insured. Violation of any of these obligations may jeopardize the protection. They include: (1) giving immediate written notice to the company or its agent, (2) protecting the property from further damage, (3) separating damaged from undamaged property and furnishing an inventory of all property, (4) filing detailed proof of loss within 60 days of the loss, and (5) submitting all evidence available to the insurer's adjuster to aid in determination of the amount of the loss as may be reasonably required.

If the adjusters and the insured cannot agree on the amount of the loss, the policy details the procedures that must be followed before any legal action can be taken. It provides that each party must select an impartial appraiser, who will then select an umpire to arbitrate any disagreements that still exist after the appraisers have rendered their separate judgments as to the amount of the loss. The insurer reserves the right to take over the damaged property and to pay the insured its sound value, or to repair or rebuild it, or to make a cash settlement for the amount of the loss. Normally the last method is used, but sometimes one of the first two is employed. In any case, it should be noted that these are company options, not those of the insured. The insured may not elect to "abandon" to the company, property that has been partially or totally destroyed and demand payment therefor. Once the proof of loss is agreed upon by all parties, payment is due within 60 days. This gives the insurer time to investigate further, if it wishes, or to raise the money for payment in the event the loss is so large as to require liquidation of securities or collection from reinsurers. Finally, the policy provides that any legal suit must be commenced within 12 months of the loss. This provision places a sort of statute of limitations on all disputes and prevents indefinite prolongation of uncertainty about them.

Subrogation. Lines 162–165 provide for subrogation rights of the insurer in case the insured has legal rights against liable third parties for any loss. Subrogation has been explained in detail in Chapter 8.

THE FORM

The fire insurance policy is not complete in itself but is designed for use with appropriate amendments and additional provisions so that it can be made to fit the needs of individual buildings and business situations. In insuring a private residence, for example, many problems are presented that are different from those connected with the insuring of a business building. Likewise, a national chain store organization has many insurance problems which a single store does not face. Therefore, a form, appropriate to each type of risk, is used to amend the basic policy.

There are hundreds of different forms in use, some of which are specially designed to fit a given situation. Most of the forms, however, are printed by a *standard forms bureau,* an association supported by organizations of fire insurance companies.

Forms may be classified according to four different purposes that they serve:

1) To describe accurately the property which is to be covered and to place various kinds of limitations on the coverage of this property.
2) To extend the basic policy to cover additional perils.
3) To allow automatic coverage on property which fluctuates in amount, such as stock in trade or which is situated at different locations and is moved from location to location throughout the term of the policy.
4) To cover losses, such as indirect losses, which are excluded in the basic policy.

The first three types of forms are discussed below, and the fourth is reserved for more detailed treatment in Chapter 11.

1) Describing the property and its coverage

Residences. The typical residence may be insured under several different forms, each of which differs primarily in the degree to which it extends the protection given by the basic fire policy. A typical form will define what is meant by "dwelling coverage" as opposed to "contents coverage"; will define the extent to which coverage is given to trees, shrubs, and plants; will set forth the amount of coverage given to property located away from the main premises; and the amount that can be ascribed to indirect losses, such as rental value or additional living expenses.

Dwelling buildings special form. An example of a typical residence form now in use is the *dwelling buildings special form* introduced in 1954, which is the broadest form available for residential property. In it a dwelling is defined to include not only the home, but also the building equipment, fixtures, and outdoor equipment, and even materials and supplies, located on the premises and intended for construction or alteration of the building. This form allows the insured to apply up to 10 per cent of the amount of insurance as additional insurance on *private structures,* which are defined as other buildings, on the premises, used for nonbusiness purposes. The form permits the insured to apply up to five per cent of the amount of insurance as additional coverage on trees, plants, shrubs, and lawns, if these items of property are damaged by certain specified perils, and not to exceed $250 on any one tree, shrub, or plant. The form is also extended to apply up to 10 per cent of the amount of insurance as additional coverage on rental value and 10 per cent on additional living expenses. These two coverages will be explained in Chapter 11.

Finally, the form adds, with certain limitations, protection known as *replacement cost insurance.* Under this insurance, the company makes no deduction for depreciation if the loss is less than $1,000 and less than five per cent of the amount of the policy. If the loss is greater than either of these two amounts, no deduction for depreciation is made if the insured has been carrying coverage equal to 80 per cent of the full replacement cost of the building. Even if the insured has not been carrying coverage equal to 80 per cent of the full replacement cost, he might not suffer a full deduction for depreciation. Under the terms of the replacement cost protection in the special form, the insured may still make a claim for that portion of the full replacement cost of a loss which the amount of insurance he carries bears to 80 per cent of the full replacement cost of the building. For example, assume that a residence, replaceable at $10,000 and insured for $6,000 on the special form, suffers a fire loss of $1,200. It is agreed that the depreciation applicable to the destroyed portion is $600. Eighty per cent of the full replacement cost is $8,000. The insured may recover six eights (75 per cent) of his $1,200, or $900, providing he actually replaces the property. The actual cash value of his loss is $600. He will never recover less than this amount under his policy, and he may recover more through the operation of replacement cost coverage.

The special form excludes coverage on any seasonal dwelling, unless it is specifically named, and it excludes the first $50 of loss except that resulting from certain specified perils. The special form is not available for residential buildings containing more than four families or more than four apartments, nor for rooming houses with more than 20 rooms, nor for nurses' homes with more than 10 rooms, nor for farm property.

Dwelling buildings and contents—broad form. The broadest form covering the *contents* of a dwelling is called *dwelling buildings and contents—broad form,* also introduced in 1954. This form contains a $50 deductible clause applicable to certain specified perils, and defines contents as all personal property incidental or usual to the occupancy of the premises (except boats and aircraft). Up to 10 per cent of the face amount of insurance on contents may be applied as additional insurance while the contents are located in an area away from the main premises, but within the United States or Canada.

Business property. Forms defining what is to be included as a business building, what must be classified as contents of the building, and what limitations of coverage are imposed, are much more numerous than in the case of residential forms. The reason for this lies in the many varied types of businesses in operation with special hazards applicable to each. Special forms have been designed, for example, for schools, restaurants, service stations, lumber mills, and many other classes of occupancies. In many territories, a so-called *general form* is used and space is left in it to insert the definition and description of the property to be insured, as the case may be.

General form. Since the fire insurance rate applying to buildings is lower than that applying to contents, it is to the insured's advantage to broaden the description of the building as much as possible. A typical description of a building will include permanent attachments such as engines, boilers, pumps, tanks, signs, flagpoles, fences, awnings, and storm windows. Also, fire extinguishers, floor coverings, cooking and cooling equipment, window shades, and even janitors' supplies and employees' uniforms may be counted as a part of the building if they are related to the landlord's servicing of the structure.

The general form describes stock as all merchandise, raw materials, goods in process, packaging materials, labels, etc. It will describe separately all items to be known as furniture, fixtures, and machinery, to include such things as machine parts, manuscripts, electrical appliances, tools, and accounting records. The general form also provides for coverage on what are known as improvements and betterments. These items are usually investments made in the building by the lessee. Even though they will belong to the landlord at the termination of the lease, the tenant may insure their value to him until the lease has expired.

Under the general form, coverage may be on one of three different bases: (1) specific, (2) schedule, or (3) blanket. Under *specific* coverage, separate items of stock, machinery, buildings, etc., are listed on the face of the policy with a definite amount of insurance after each item, which is insured separately. Under *schedule* coverage, which is a variation of specific coverage, property at two or more locations is listed and specifically insured. Under *blanket* coverage, property at several locations may be insured under a single item. For example, the policy could provide $87,500 of insurance on all contents at plants in five different cities. Or under blanket coverage, classes of property usually insured specifically might be lumped together and be insured as a single item, such as $10,000 on stock, furniture, fixtures, and machinery.

Typical clauses in business property forms. Business fire insurance forms often contain important clauses that affect the property to be covered. It is very usual, for example, to find clauses excluding from coverage the cost of excavations, brick or concrete foundations, and underground flues or pipes. The reason for these exclusions is to enable the insured to carry less coverage for purposes of meeting the requirements of the coinsurance clause, since these items are normally not destroyed in a fire. Very often the form will exclude damage to electrical machinery which is caused by electrical short circuits. The form may provide coverage for goods within 100 feet of a building, such as goods that are on platforms or in streets and alleys near the building. It will usually provide a limited amount of protection to cover the cost of removal of debris following a fire.

2) Extending the coverage to additional perils

Residences. It will be recalled that the basic fire policy covers only fire, lightning, and loss while goods are removed from the premises for safety from threatened loss due to the perils insured against. Practically all residential property is protected against many additional perils through the use of one or more of several different forms that offer varying combinations of protection.

Extended coverage endorsement. One of the first, and still the most widely used, endorsements that broaden the list of perils insured against is the *extended coverage endorsement*. This endorsement adds windstorm, hail, explosion, riot, riot attending strike, civil commotion, aircraft, vehicles, and smoke, as defined. The endorsement states that the above-named perils will be substituted for the word "fire" in the basic policy as the case requires. Special definitions of windstorm, hail, smoke, etc., are provided. For example, the term "smoke" means only smoke due to a sudden faulty operation of a heating or cooking unit, and specifically does not mean smoke from fireplaces or industrial apparatus. "Explosion" as a peril does not include bursting of steam boilers, rupture or bursting of water pipes, or concussion, such as a "sonic boom." Loss from vehicles belonging to the insured or loss caused by any vehicle to fences, driveways, walks, or lawns, is excluded. When extended coverage is added to the basic fire policy, it must be written for the entire amount of indemnity as provided against fire. If some policies are written on the property without the endorsement, an apportionment clause, discussed previously, reduces the recovery from any extended coverage loss to that proportion of the loss that the policies having extended coverage bear to the total insurance on the property.

Additional extended coverage endorsement. An *additional extended coverage endorsement,* introduced in 1951, was employed for a few years and then gave way to a still broader form. The additional extended coverage endorsement added such perils as water damage from plumbing and heating systems, vandalism and malicious mischief, damage by vehicles owned by the insured, glass breakage, ice, snow and freezing, fall of trees, and collapse of the building. These additional perils are all subject to a $50 deductible.

Dwelling buildings and contents—broad form. The *dwelling buildings and contents—broad form,* mentioned on page 242, extends even further the coverage against added perils. It lists 20 perils and provides that a $50 deductible will be applicable to certain of these perils. In addition to the perils named above, this form covers loss due to landslide, damage to property done by burglars, glass breakage, and electrical short circuits. It includes broader definitions of explosion and smoke damage than appear in forms which are less comprehensive.

Dwelling buildings special form. An even more comprehensive attempt to broaden the coverage for residential property is found in the *dwelling buildings special form* mentioned on page 241. This form utilizes the "all-risk" approach and attempts to cover all risks of physical loss except those perils and losses specifically enumerated. In other words, if a property is covered by this form and is damaged in any way, the loss may be presumed to be covered unless there is a specific exclusion listed. This form cannot be used to cover contents, however; only buildings may be covered. Typical exclusions include damage due to wear and tear, termites, rust, dry rot, mechanical breakdown, earthquake, flood, radioactive contamination, and war or military action of any kind. In addition, certain types of loss to property are excluded, such as loss to retaining walls by landslide or water pressure, and loss to undrained plumbing or heating systems by freezing while the building is vacant. A $50 deductible applies to all losses except those caused by certain common perils.

Homeowners program.   The ultimate in comprehensive protection for residences, however, is found in what is known as the *homeowners program*. The homeowners program is an outgrowth of several attempts by the insurance industry to provide a "package" of protection for the average homeowner that would provide a more balanced and a more generally adequate program of insurance at a lower cost than would be true if the coverages were purchased separately. Such a policy was made possible by multiple-line legislation, and it is known as a *multiple-line* policy. The homeowners policy was developed in 1958 by the Multi-Peril Insurance Conference, an advisory and rating organization for insurance companies. There is a single standard skeleton policy with which is used one or more of five standard forms together with an assortment of endorsements to provide flexibility in coverage.[4]

A basic objective of the homeowners program is to provide an opportunity for the homeowner to purchase in one policy almost any of the variations of fire insurance and extended peril coverages, previously discussed plus such coverages as personal liability insurance, medical payments insurance, and theft. The distinguishing feature of this type of policy is that *definite amounts of coverage* in each of the above categories may be required and *one indivisible premium* is charged. Thus, the insured must buy a certain minimum "package of benefits" and cannot select specific coverages as he sees fit. Yet, there is sufficient flexibility in amounts required so that the form can fit the needs of most residents.

---

[4] As of 1961, not all states had approved the homeowners program.

The most comprehensive of the five homeowners forms is Form 5, which is similar to a predecessor, *Homeowners Policy C*. Form 5 has the following minimum limits:

Coverage A—Dwelling building, $15,000 (may be increased).
Coverage B—Private structures, 10% of coverage A.
Coverage C—Personal property, 50% of coverage A.
Coverage D—Additional living expense, 20% of coverage A.
Coverage E—Comprehensive personal liability, $25,000 per occurrence.
Coverage F—Medical payments, $500 per person.
Coverage G—Physical damage to property, $250 per occurrence (This coverage provides payment of losses to property of another caused by the insured regardless of legal liability).

Under the homeowners program, the coverage is on an "all-risk" basis, with various exclusions similar to those in the dwelling buildings special form. However, the homeowners form also covers personal property, and thus the homeowner has all-risk protection on all property normally exposed in connection with his home. There is no exclusion for theft, except theft during the course of construction of a building. Flood, earthquake, landslide, war, and vermin are among the excluded perils, although these exclusions do not apply uniformly to all types of property and interests covered under the policy. There is a $50 deductible clause applying for some types of losses, such as windstorm, hail, water damage, glass breakage, and fall of trees.

The chief advantages claimed for insuring under the homeowners program are:

1. The homeowner is able to secure a broad protection at much less cost than if all the various coverages were purchased separately. The "package" contains most of the insurance that the average homeowner needs and should have. However, if he does not want all the protection listed, he must insure on one of the traditional forms.

2. The three-year premium paid under the program might amount to as much as $500 or more, and this is said to provide sufficient commission income to the agent to give him more incentive to service the needs of the average homeowner in a more comprehensive fashion than has been true in the past.

3. Finally, the underwriters secure a broader base of insurance and there is less adverse selection in these policies.[5] It follows that the total loss ratio should be lower for the policy as a whole and

[5] See Chapter 1, page 7.

hence more profitable. To the insured, this means that more liberal underwriting with fewer exclusions is possible.

Business property. Extensions of the basic fire policy to various business exposures have not progressed as rapidly as has been true in the case of personal risks. In general, the subject of extending coverage to additional business property perils breaks down into: 1) extending coverage on buildings, and 2) extending coverage on contents and other items of personal property used by business.

1) Extending coverage on buildings. Coverage on buildings is not generally available on an "all-risk" basis, as it is in the case of personal residences. The businessman may extend his coverage in the standard fire policy through use of the extended coverage endorsement or by means of an "optional perils" policy. Under the *optional perils policy,* protection may be obtained against explosion, riot and civil commotion, vandalism and malicious mischief, and aircraft and vehicle damage. He may also purchase separate protection against such perils as earthquakes; or he may, in some territories such as the Pacific Coast, extend the basic fire policy to cover this peril. Insurance against many other perils, commonly called "allied lines," may be purchased. Thus, damage due to faulty sprinkler systems, or the liability resulting therefrom, may be insured. Special coverages for certain types of property, such as boilers and machinery, have been devised. The more important of these coverages will be discussed in Chapter 18.

2) Extending coverage on personal property. Coverage on personal property belonging to a business enterprise may be purchased on the forms previously described in connection with buildings. In addition, such coverage is available on an "all-risk" basis. There are two basic groups of forms that cover the personal property of business on an "all-risk" basis: (1) one group for establishments carrying stocks of goods held for sale (wholesalers and retailers), and (2) one group for manufacturing establishments.

PERSONAL PROPERTY OF WHOLESALERS AND RETAILERS. Under this group, there are three main types of coverage; namely, inland marine forms, "block" forms designed specially for given types of risks, and forms known as the commercial property coverage program. The first two, inland marine forms and block forms will be discussed in Chapter 13, which deals with inland marine insurance.

The commercial property coverage form, which is attached to the standard fire policy, is designed for a wide range of retail and wholesale merchants, and provides an all-risk coverage on stock in trade, furniture

and fixtures, with improvements and betterments protection available
optionally. The form is available for almost every type of merchant except those specifically named, such as jewelers and furriers, for whom
special inland marine forms are provided; [6] and establishments such as
restaurants, florists, pawnbrokers, and pet shops, which present special
underwriting problems.

The commercial property form has a $50 deductible that applies
to all but certain listed perils. [7] It covers property wherever located in the
United States, and while in transit in Canada. Among the excluded
perils are freezing, flood, rising water, seepage, earthquake, landslide,
war, inherent vice of the goods, radioactive sources, mysterious disappearance, and honesty of the insured or his employee. Most of these
excluded perils do not apply to goods in transit. Certain types of
property are specifically excluded as well, such as unattended property
in a vehicle, damage to steam boilers, automobiles, neon signs, and furs,
jewels, gold, and silver in excess of a limited amount. The commercial
property coverage is written with 80 per cent coinsurance, and various
discounts are available for the use of such loss-prevention devices as
watchman service, burglar alarm systems, and iron protective screens.
For additional premiums, the insured may extend his coverage to such
items as money up to $250 in any one occurrence, personal effects,
debris removal, and damage to the building done by burglars.

PROPERTY OF MANUFACTURING ESTABLISHMENTS. The indus-
trial property policy program of coverage, still in a state of development, is designed for manufacturers and involves more than 20 forms,
endorsements, and blanks for use with the standard fire policy. The program offers coverage for buildings as well as for personal property, improvements, and betterments. Under the basic coverage of the program,
which covers all property at definite insured locations, named peril protection is given. The perils consist of fire and lightning, all those perils
of the extended coverage endorsement, vandalism and malicious mischief, sprinkler leakage, falling objects, burglary, and collapse of building under the weight of ice, snow, or sleet. Certain causes of loss such
as earthquake, flood, and fire resulting therefrom, are excluded. Certain additional perils, such as theft and water damage, may be added to
the basic coverage.

Some special features of the industrial property policy program
should be observed. The policy is a multiple-line contract, since it covers

[6] These forms are the Jewelers Block Policy and the Furriers Block Policy.
[7] For example, fire, extended coverage perils, additional extended coverage perils,
and theft.

perils not traditionally classified as "fire and allied lines," such as burglary. However, liability insurance is not included, but must be written
separately. The industrial property policy is also multiple-location in
nature. Eligible manufacturers must have at least two locations, with values at the second location amounting to at least 10 per cent of overall
values, or $50,000, whichever is lesser. Insurance on personal property is required under this form, but coverage of buildings and improvements and betterments is optional. Certain exclusions in the program
make it clear that the manufacturer still needs marine insurance for
property aboard vessels. Some types of property, such as dies, molds,
patterns, and models, are valued on a replacement cost basis, while
other types of property, such as buildings, are valued on an actual cash
value (indemnity) basis. Minimum premiums are substantial, ranging
from $2,500 for a manufacturer covering personal property only on a
named-peril basis, to $10,000 for coverage on personal property, buildings, and the "special personal property" endorsement, discussed below.

The industrial property policy program permits use of an endorsement known as the *special personal property endorsement*. This endorsement gives broad and "all-risk" protection against the loss of
manufactured finished stock in trade while located anywhere and of
other items of personal property while located anywhere except at the
manufacturer's plant (within territorial limits). Finished stock that is
lost either at the manufacturer's own plant, or at the plant of a processor,
or while in transit, is thus covered. If machinery, conveying equipment,
or other movable items are lost while away from the manufacturer's
plant, all-risk protection is available. This insurance, one of the broadest
types of commercial protection available, is not yet written in every
state.

The "all-risk" protection on manufacturers' personal property is
written with a $100 deductible applying to all losses except those resulting from listed basic perils such as fire and extended coverage. As might
be expected, certain perils, such as flood and earthquake, gradual deterioration, breakage of fragile articles, smoke from industrial operations, war, and mysterious disappearance, are excluded.

3) Covering changing values in varying locations

An important purpose of this type of form is to adjust insurance
protection to business firms that have many plants located in different
geographical areas or that wish protection to be adjusted automatically
to constantly changing values at these plants. It would be cumbersome,

indeed, if a business enterprise carrying on a nationwide operation involving 10 manufacturing or processing plants and 20 warehouses and other distributing centers had to purchase a separate policy for each location. For example, there would undoubtedly be much duplication of coverage when goods were shipped from one location to another (being insured both by the sender and the receiver) and many instances of omission of insurance protection altogether (each party believing the other to have taken care of the insurance).

Reporting forms are designed to adjust insurance coverage to changing property values in different locations. Reporting forms have several advantages: (1) the amount of insurance protection is automatically adjusted to changes in values of property at different locations; (2) new locations are automatically covered; (3) the insured does not have to pay premiums on limits of liability in the policy, but rather pays premiums according to the actual values at risk; and (4) the possibility of having gaps in coverage or duplication of insurance is virtually eliminated.

The industrial property policy program may be written on a reporting basis, as may be the commercial property policy program. In addition, there are in common use many other multiple-location forms, each designed to fit specific types of risks or to allow variations in the way in which values are reported and the premium determined.

A typical multiple-location reporting form is known as Multiple Location Reporting Form 1. When the insured has two or more locations, he estimates the highest value of personal property he will have at each location and pays a deposit premium (there is a minimum premium of $500) based on the average values for all locations. The rate applied is an average rate determined by applying at each territory the rate in that territory multiplied by the average value of the goods to be located there. Each month the insured is required to report to the company what the actual values were at each location on a specific date. If he understates his actual value and later suffers a loss, he is penalized in his recovery and receives only that portion of the loss that the amount reported bears to the actual values at risk. Thus, if the insured reported $50,000 of inventory at location C, and it was determined that the true value was $60,000, he would recover only five sixths of any subsequent partial loss. Also, if the insured fails to make a report on the required date, his recovery is limited to the values reported on the last date he made a report; he is thus denied the feature that gives automatic protection when values rise between reporting dates. For example, if on

January 1 the insured reports correctly $10,000 of values at location D and on January 15 there is a loss of $15,000 (made possible because incoming shipments of goods raised the values exposed), the entire loss is paid if it falls within the limitation of liability at location D. However, if the loss occurred on February 15 and no report had been made on February 1 when it was due, the limit of liability would be $10,000.

To avoid the necessity of making monthly reports and yet to secure the advantage of automatic coverage at newly acquired locations, the insured may elect another type of multiple-location form known as Form 5, in which a coinsurance clause of at least 90 per cent is required. This form is suitable for risks with varying locations and which have little fluctuation in total values and where it is impossible or inconvenient to render monthly reports. If values fluctuate considerably, the insured would be subject to coinsurance penalties unless he constantly adjusts the amount of insurance. However, the insured has automatic coverage at any one location, and thus is fully protected as long as he carries sufficient insurance to avoid coinsurance penalties.

SUMMARY

1. The perils of fire, windstorm, explosion, etc., annually cause great loss of life and property in the United States. Fire loss alone amounts to well over $1 billion annually. Insurance against these losses is among the best developed and widely accepted types of insurance in existence, with the Standard Fire Policy being the basic contract on which most property insurance coverages are based.

2. The Standard Fire Policy is divided into three parts—the insuring agreement, the conditions and stipulations, and the various types of forms. The insuring agreement and conditions form the basic part of the contract and have been standardized throughout the United States. They cover such matters as what basic perils and property are covered or excluded, how losses shall be adjusted, termination of the contract, interests of others including the mortgagee, and rights against negligent parties.

3. The form in fire insurance is necessary to complete any insuring agreement against property losses. It serves four major purposes, the first three of which are discussed in this chapter and the fourth in the next chapter: (a) to describe accurately the insured property and the various kinds of limitations and extensions applying to it; (b) to extend the basic contract to cover additional perils; (c) to give automatic coverage on property which either fluctuates in value, such as stock in trade, or which is moved about from one location to another, *i.e.*, reporting and multiple-location forms; (d) to cover losses which are indirectly a result of fire or other perils.

4. Forms may be analyzed under two main headings, those applying to residences and those applying to business property. The main dwelling forms are the special form, extended coverage endorsement, replacement cost endorsement, dwelling buildings and contents (broad form), and the homeowners program. The chief business forms include the general form, the commercial property coverage program, the industrial property policy program, the multiple location reporting forms, and reporting forms.

QUESTIONS FOR REVIEW AND DISCUSSION

1. It was announced that in a certain state a group of insurers experienced in 1958 a 63.7 per cent loss ratio on "homeowners multiperil" coverage, while the experience on "fire" insurance was 44.5 per cent and the experience on "extended coverage" insurance was 62.6 per cent. Explain why the loss ratios in these types of insurance probably differed so markedly in some instances and were so similar in others.

2. Insurance companies support various organizations such as the National Board of Fire Underwriters and the National Fire Protection Association which aim at reducing the losses from fires that occur annually in the United States.
   (a) A certain agent suggests that this activity, if completely successful, would put insurance companies out of business. Comment.
   (b) Is it in the best interests of insurance companies to attempt to eliminate loss from fire or other perils? Discuss.

3. "Z" owns a 20-year old house. When new, it had a life expectancy of 50 years and was valued at $10,000. What could be collected from a $10,000 fire insurance policy in the event of a total loss, under the assumption that it would take $15,000 to replace the house? Explain your answer.

4. Assume that coverage on "Z's" house in Question 3 is written on the dwelling buildings special form, which provides for replacement cost insurance. The loss is partial, and it is estimated that $2,000 would replace the lost portion with new materials.
   (a) What will the recovery be? Show your calculations.
   (b) How would your answer be changed if it were shown that instead of $15,000 it would take $30,000 to replace the house today? Explain.

5. Mr. Jones' factory is destroyed by fire, and he estimates that it will take three months to rebuild it and to resume operations. He calculates that this delay will cost him $20,000 because of loss of profits and fixed charges that continue regardless of the volume of operations. Is this amount recoverable under the standard fire policy? Explain.

6. "A" owns a residence and insures it for $15,000 on the standard fire policy with extended coverage. He insures his contents, valued at $10,000, for $5,000 on the same policy. Show the extent to which the following losses would be covered and give your reasons in each case:
   (a) Smoke damage from a fireplace necessitates a $70 repainting job in the living room.

(b) A valuable antique wooden table worth $500 is accidentally damaged by heat when it is placed too near a hot air register.

(c) A grass fire threatens "A's" house. For safety, he removes all contents and places them in three warehouses, as follows: Warehouse X, $4,000; Warehouse Y, $3,000; Warehouse Z, $3,000. Water damages the goods at Warehouse Z and causes a $2,000 loss two days after they have been stored there. Also $500 worth of goods is stolen from Warehouse Y on the same day.

(d) A neighbor's house burns. Firemen's trucks gouge deep holes in "A's" yard.

(e) Three teen-age boys "have it in" for "A" and cause $25 of damage to his lawn hoses by slashing them with knives.

7. In a recent case a windstorm damaged the roof of a building, allowing rain to enter. The water caused a short circuit in the electricity. Food in a freezer thawed when the electricity went off and was ordered destroyed by health authorities. The insured carried the standard fire policy with extended coverage. The insurer denied liability under the contract for the loss of the spoiled food.

(a) Upon what probable grounds would the insurer reject the above claim?

(b) Do you agree with the insurer? Why or why not?

8. In a fire the following items were included on a proof of loss form. Discuss the extent to which these losses, if any, are insured under the standard fire policy:

(a) $50 of cash in a locked box.

(b) One share of A. T. and T. in the same box.

(c) A deed to a summer residence.

(d) Loss of a water heater valued at $150 when heat from the fire caused it to explode.

(e) $500 loss of an old oak tree damaged by fire.

9. "D" claims that the exclusion in the standard fire policy for losses due to increase of the hazard by the insured might serve to exclude almost any loss where the insured was negligent, such as fire loss from a carelessly discarded cigarette. Comment.

10. "T" has a house insured for $20,000 with a $15,000 mortgage. The mortgage is protected by a loss payable clause. A fire occurs, and it develops that the $2,000 loss is uninsured because "T" has forgotten to pay the premium and the policy lapsed.

(a) May the mortgagee collect? Why?

(b) What is the most satisfactory way for the mortgagee to protect his interest? Why?

11. What rights and obligations does the mortgagee have under the standard mortgagee clause?

12. Mr. Smith insures his retail building under three policies, as follows: Insurer A, $5,000; Insurer B, $10,000; Insurer C, $15,000. At the time of a $6,000 fire loss, it is discovered that Insurer A is insolvent and is not paying any claims. How much can Mr. Smith collect from each insurer? Why?

13. What is meant by "the form" in fire insurance and what four purposes are served by it? Explain.

14. Mr. Mayer insures his palatial mansion for $50,000 under the dwelling buildings special form. A few months after he spent $20,000 in oriental landscaping, the building was completely gutted by fire and $10,000 worth of landscaping was lost. What limits of liability for this loss exist under the policy? Explain.

15. Mr. Kammack insures his $30,000 private business college building for $12,000 under a policy containing an 80 per cent coinsurance clause. The policy is written on a form that contains a clause excluding the value of foundations from the coverage. If it is determined that the building's foundations are valued at $10,000, what effect does this clause have on the recovery for the loss? Explain.

16. Name the perils covered under the extended coverage endorsement.

17. In California there have been a series of losses due to the slow movement of earth which becomes loosened when water used for lawns seeps down and causes the shale to slip. Mr. Underman's house is one of those affected. When a large crack in the foundation occurred, he submitted a claim. The insurer paid the loss and immediately canceled the policy. A month later Mr. Underman's house fell into the bay when the entire cliff gave way. Mr. Underman made a claim for loss, but the insurer rejected the claim, arguing that the loss occurred after the policy was canceled. Discuss the rights of the parties.

18. What advantages and disadvantages are there for the average homeowner under the homeowners' program that covers multiple-peril risks?

19. What essential difference is there in the operations of manufacturers as opposed to those of retailers and wholesalers that has caused different types of property insurance forms to be devised for them? Name the chief forms used in this connection.

20. Why have reporting forms been developed? Discuss.

21. A certain hardware wholesaler is insured under the Multiple Location Reporting Form 1. He has ten warehouses located throughout the United States. He has been unable to provide satisfactory monthly reports because his accounting system is not arranged to provide the necessary information conveniently. Suggest a different form that will give adequate protection automatically, but that will not require the monthly reports. What dangers may exist in the use of this form? Explain.

Indirect Loss
Coverage

It has been seen that the common contracts of fire insurance cover only *direct* loss from given perils. Direct losses are those where the damage has been caused by the fire either coming into contact with the subject matter or causing an unbroken chain of events leading to the destruction of the subject matter. Direct loss policies invariably exclude losses that result from the peril insured against but not caused *directly* by it. Such losses, which are described as *consequential,* may be added by endorsement to the standard fire policy. To cover consequential losses represents the fourth purpose of the form. The first three purposes of the form—to describe the property and its coverage, to extend the coverage to additional perils, and to cover changing values in varying locations—were explained in Chapter 10.

BASIC CHARACTERISTICS OF CONSEQUENTIAL LOSSES

The nature of consequential losses can best be understood by use of an example. Suppose a small manufacturer suffers a serious fire that shuts down his plant for two months while repairs are being made. He is fully insured against *direct* loss by fire but carries no consequential loss coverage. The fire policy pays for the replacement cost of lost raw materials, goods in process, and finished goods, as well as repairs to machinery and buildings. However, the manufacturer finds that he must continue to keep certain key employees such as plant foremen and salesmen on the payroll to help with the reorganization and to render service to customers. In addition, there are other expenses, such as taxes, insurance premiums, interest, heat, light, power, and depreciation, that are incurred regardless of the volume of operation. Finally, the manufacturer has not been able to earn any profit on the unsold finished goods nor upon the volume of goods that he would normally have produced during this period. The sum of such losses may be so severe that he is unable to continue in business. It is to indemnify him for this type of loss that consequential damage contracts have been devised.

The importance of consequential losses has long been recognized in personal insurance lines. Life insurance, for example, is intended to replace lost income due to the premature death of the breadwinner. Disability income insurance is designed to restore income lost as a result of total disability. In property insurance, however, consequential losses have not generally been recognized for the serious exposure that they really are. In a study of 21 losses of steel manufacturers,[1] for example, it was found that in 15 cases the consequential loss exceeded the direct physical loss. The physical loss was placed at about $381,000, while the consequential losses were estimated to be $2,654,000, or about seven times as great as the direct losses. The largest single direct loss was $86,800, while five of the consequential losses exceeded $400,000, the largest amounting to $675,973. There were many examples where a minor property damage loss resulted in a very substantial consequential loss. In one case $750 direct damage was suffered, but $5,000 indirect loss resulted; in another case $32,511 direct damage was suffered, but $481,634 indirect loss resulted. While comprehensive data on the premium volume from consequential business is not available, there is little question that it accounts for a small portion of the total fire insurance written. The central reason for the failure to insure such an important exposure appears to lie in the somewhat complicated techniques employed to put the coverage into effect. Furthermore, agents have found consequential loss coverage difficult to understand completely and have thus not been able to educate their clients to the need. In addition, loss settlements have been somewhat involved because it has been difficult to determine precisely the true amount of dollar losses. In fact, it is not uncommon to find it difficult to persuade the insurance consumer that such a loss actually exists and is insurable.

In general, consequential loss coverages may be grouped into two categories: (1) time element and (2) nontime element. *Time element* coverages are those contracts which measure the indirect loss in terms of so many dollars per unit of time that passes until the subject matter can be restored. A good example of time element coverage is known as *business interruption* insurance, where the loss is measured by the dollars of profits and continuing expenses lost during the time it takes to repair or to replace the property destroyed. *Nontime element* coverages are those in which the measurement of loss is not a function of elapsed time, but is measured by other means. An example of this would

---

[1] R. E. Lauterbach, "Business Interruption," A.M.A. Insurance Series, No. 115, pp. 43–44.

be *temperature damage* insurance, where the measure of loss is the value of goods destroyed when a fire cuts off the source of power in a cold-storage warehouse and the property stored therein is lost as a result of rising temperatures.

CLASSIFICATION OF CONSEQUENTIAL LOSS CONTRACTS

Consequential loss contracts are usually written as an endorsement to the standard fire policy. The perils insured against generally include fire and extended coverage. The perils of riot, civil commotion, vandalism, and malicious mischief may also be insured against. Thus, if the interruption of business or other consequential loss results from damage to property by any of the major perils in the contracts, the insured is indemnified. The following contracts are discussed herein:

Time element contracts
1) Business interruption
2) Contingent business interruption
3) Extra expense
4) Additional living expense
5) Rental value
6) Leasehold interest
7) Excess rental value

Nontime element contracts
1) Profits
2) Accounts receivable
3) Temperature damage
4) Rain

TIME ELEMENT CONTRACTS

1) Business interruption insurance

Business interruption insurance undertakes to reimburse the insured for profits and fixed charges lost as a result of damage to his property from a named peril. It is generally a contract of indemnity [2] and, thus, one of the important problems in this line of insurance is to acquire a firm understanding of methods to determine losses which, by their very nature, depend on future events. Because the future is an unknown quantity, this problem is sometimes complicated.

Basic characteristics of business interruption insurance. The business interruption contract has certain fundamental provisions that

---

[2] Occasionally valued policies are written in the London Market.

are frequently a source of much misunderstanding. The policy will indemnify the insured subject to the following conditions:

1. There must be physical damage to property by a fire or other insured peril.
2. There must be a shutdown of business and this shutdown must result from the physical damage caused by the named peril (and not from some other cause such as a strike or a shortage of supplies).
3. During the period of shutdown, it must be established that the business would have continued to operate had it not been for the occurrence of the insured peril.
4. The peril must occur during the policy term at the described location.
5. During the period of shutdown, the business would have continued to earn profits and to earn continuing expenses.

If the business had only been breaking even at the time of occurrence of the insured peril, there would be a question raised as to whether any profits would have been earned. If it were found that no profits would have been made even if the business had not been shut down, no real loss from this source would have been incurred, and hence no indemnity for lost profits would be paid. Of course, if the business is earning its fixed charges, these would be reimbursed. Thus, even though a business is losing money, there is an insurable value to the extent that it is earning its fixed charges. As might be surmised, it might be a considerable source of conflict to resolve the question as to what profits might be in the future.

Business interruption value. The value of the possible loss may be measured by different methods, but the central idea is to examine the income statement of the firm and derive from this statement the various items of income and expense that are to be insured. An example of such a technique is presented below:

Total gross earnings from all sources derived from the use and occupancy of
the described building... xxxx
Less:
Cost of materials consumed in the manufacturing process, or the cost of
goods sold in a mercantile business............................xx
Cost of supplies...xx
Sales taxes...xx
Bad debts..xx
Ordinary payroll *..xx
Total... xxx
Remainder—Profits and all other expenses...................... xx

* May be insured for limited periods, if desired, under most forms.

In other words, the process of isolating the insurable value is to deduct from total gross earnings all expenses and costs that are variable —that is, those that may be discontinued if a fire or other peril were to cause a shutdown of the business. The amount so obtained is the *insurable value* and forms the basis of the loss settlement. In some jurisdictions, a form known as the *agreed amount endorsement* is permitted under which the insurer agrees that in the event of interruption, it will accept this statement as the best estimate of future earnings and expenses and settle the loss on that basis. Thus, this endorsement eliminates arguments over what future profits and expenses might be.

Coinsurance. The importance of determining business interruption value (sometimes referred to as use and occupancy value, because all value is supposed to result from the use and occupancy of the damaged building) becomes even more evident when it is realized that most business interruption forms contain a coinsurance clause. Coinsurance requirements vary from 50 per cent upward, depending on the amount of coverage desired. If the business concern elects to take the 50 per cent form, it is required to carry at least 50 per cent of its annual insurable value. Failing to carry this amount, it becomes a coinsurer.

To illustrate, assume that the sum of the annual fixed charges and profits during the prior year is $96,000. When the policy was originally issued, the insurable value was $80,000; the firm now carries $40,000 of business interruption insurance. In the event of a shutdown for three months and assuming an even rate of operations and earnings, the firm will have lost $3/_{12}$ of its year's profits and fixed charges, or $24,000. Does the firm collect this amount? No, because it has not been carrying the amount of insurance required by the coinsurance clause. Since it carries $40,000 and is required to carry $48,000 (one half of its annual insurable value of $96,000), it collects only 40/48 of the loss, or $20,000. To avoid coinsurance penalties of this nature, the insured should either see that the agreed amount endorsement is part of his policy, or that he carries more coverage (say 10 or 15 per cent) than is required by the coinsurance clause in order to provide a margin in case business improves during the year.

How much insurance should be carried? The question frequently arises, "How much business interruption insurance should be carried?" The answer depends upon what the firm believes the maximum loss might be. Coinsurance forms are available that allow the insured to carry as little as one half of its annual insurable value. However, if the firm has reason to believe it might take as much as a year to restore the business to regular operations, it should, of course, carry insurance equal to its full insurable value. Generally, insurance on no more than one year's insurable value is available. It should be remembered that some firms may operate on a seasonal basis, and a few months' operations might account for an entire year's profits. If the peril occurs just before the operating season which lasts only three months, a whole year's profits might be lost and probably a good part of the year's expenditures for fixed charges would not be earned. Such a situation would, of course, justify carrying insurance on the profits and fixed charges of a whole year. The policy does not require that the lost profits or charges be incurred in any particular time period, so long as they do not exceed the time that it reasonably takes to restore the building and to resume operations.

On the other hand, the loss may be only partial; that is, if the business is only partially shut down, indemnity can be collected for the partial loss. If it takes an entire year to make repairs and to restore normal operations and the firm is forced to reduce operations by one fourth of its normal level, the indemnity would be one fourth of the annual insurable value, assuming the operations to be perfectly level throughout the year.

Incurring expenses to reduce loss.   Sometimes it is possible to expedite repairs by incurring costs that would not normally be necessary. For example, special parts might be flown in by air express or overtime allowances may be paid to workmen. If such costs succeed in reducing the time of interruption, they will be reimbursed by the insurer so long as the total amount does not exceed the amount that would have been payable had the expediting funds not been spent. Thus, if it would normally have taken three months to restore operations, but by spending $3,000 extra, the insured is able to reduce the period of interruption to two months, the insurer will pay the insured the $3,000 providing the monthly loss from earned profits and fixed charges would not have exceeded $3,000.

Special provisions.   The business interruption policy limits payments to the length of time it reasonably takes to restore the property to normal operating conditions so that the same quality of service exists as existed before the loss. The insured is given up to 30 days' additional time to process damaged raw stock to the same stage of manufacture as existed at the time of the loss, but no such indemnity is available for finished stock. If a civil authority, such as a local government, prohibits access to the insured's premises because of other damage in the area arising out of the insured peril, the policy provides up to two weeks' indemnity for loss from this source. However, no indemnity is payable in case a building ordinance, strike, or lease agreement results in a delay in rebuilding. Electrical power failure is excluded as a source of loss unless fire ensue and then coverage pertains only to the resulting fire. If a larger building replaces the destroyed structure, indemnity is adjusted for the length of time it would have taken to rebuild a comparable building of the same size as the one destroyed.

Forms available.   The most common forms in business interruption insurance are the *gross earnings form* and the *two item form*.[3] The basic difference between these two major forms lies in the approach taken to the determination of insurable value and of coinsurance requirements.

Gross earnings form.   Gross earnings forms are of two varieties— one for mercantile or nonmanufacturing risks, and one for manufacturing risks. In the mercantile form, gross earnings are defined as the total sales and other earnings less the cost of goods sold, and materials and supplies or outside services, the cost of which may be discontinued in the event of interruption. This definition corresponds generally to a typical accounting concept of gross earnings for a retailer or wholesaler. It is a simple and easily understood concept, and for that reason the gross earnings form has been the most popular type of form used. All that is needed to determine insurable value is to find gross earnings, as defined. The form requires a minimum coverage of 50 per cent of gross earnings in order to avoid coinsurance penalties.

It will be recognized that gross earnings is normally intended to cover all fixed expenses and profits and, in addition, expenses that are *not* usually fixed in nature, such as ordinary payroll. Naturally, ordinary payroll and other similar variable expenses would be eliminated if the business shuts down. Thus, such expenses do not constitute amounts that can be repaid under the policy because they do not constitute a loss. In effect, this means that insurance is being carried on values that will never actually be indemnifiable under the terms of the policy. To correct such a condition, the two item form was developed.

Two item form.   Under the two item form, it is necessary to segregate from the income statement all items of fixed expense and profit,

---

[3] The two item form as such has been dropped in many states, but almost the same coverage is available by means of an endorsement to the gross earnings form.

which are insurable as Item I. The insured may carry coverage on ordinary payroll (up to 90 days) as Item II. Ordinary payroll is often continued for a short time in order to enable the employer to resume operations without delay once the damage is repaired. Under the two item form, the minimum coinsurance requirement is 80 per cent instead of 50 per cent required in the gross earnings form.

The difference in total premium between the two item form and the gross earnings form may be little or nothing for some insureds and a considerable sum for others, depending on whether it is desired to insure ordinary payroll. Because it is more difficult to develop the proper insurable value under the two item form and because it has been confusing to agents and to insurance consumers, the two item form has been abandoned in many territories. New rules have been made to permit the exclusion of ordinary payroll from the gross earnings form. This exclusion accomplishes the same result as was accomplished by the two item form and is somewhat easier to understand. If ordinary payroll is excluded from the new gross earnings form, the coinsurance requirement is increased from 50 to 80 per cent.

To illustrate how a given loss might be handled under the two forms, consider the following financial statement of a retail merchant.

Sales		$200,000
Cost of goods sold		100,000
Gross Earnings		100,000
Expenses:		
Ordinary payroll	$48,000	
Fixed expenses	42,000	90,000
Net profit		$ 10,000

Under the gross earnings form, the insurable value is $100,000. The minimum amount that must be carried would be one half of the gross earnings, or $50,000. Premiums would be developed on this amount. The merchant may submit a claim for such items as clerical salaries if he chooses, in the event that his business is interrupted. He would not, however, normally do so. Hence, he must insure one half of a year's fixed expenses and profits even though he might determine that the period of interruption would never exceed, say, three months.

Under the two item form, the insurable value for Item I would be the sum of the fixed expenses and the net profit, or $52,000. Since 80 per cent of this amount is required, the insured must pay premiums on $41,600 of insurable value. It would appear that the insured can reduce his premium cost by using the two item form, unless it is desired to continue clerical and other salaries in the event of a temporary interruption. If the merchant wishes to do this, he may insure ordinary payroll up to

90 days under Item II. Three months' payroll would amount to $12,-000 (one fourth of an annual payroll of $48,000). Eighty per cent of this would be $9,600. Total insurable value is thus raised from $41,600 to $51,200 under the two item form.

To summarize, if the merchant wishes to insure ordinary payroll, it would probably be better for him to use the gross earnings form, under which he has the option of submitting claims for the cost of ordinary payroll if circumstances warrant. If he wishes to exclude ordinary payroll, he can often reduce his insurance premiums by using the two item form. As indicated above, it is now permitted to accomplish this latter objective and still use the gross earnings form, because new rules permit the exclusion of ordinary payroll from the gross earnings form. At the same time, if this is done, the minimum coinsurance requirements are raised to 80 per cent. In any given case a careful comparison of total premiums under each method is justified. Rates vary according to the degrees of coinsurance and according to the amount of ordinary payroll covered.

2) Contingent business interruption insurance

It sometimes happens that a firm is forced to shut down, not because a peril occurred and damaged its plant, but because a peril forced the shutdown of the plant belonging to a supplier or an important customer on whom the firm depends. Thus, a manufacturer of air conditioners may find that his plant is shut down because his supplier of compressors has suffered a fire. His consequential loss is just as severe, perhaps, as if the fire had occurred at his own plant, because it may require several months to obtain another supplier to meet his requirements. Similarly, a firm may find that its chief customer has canceled orders because of a fire or other disaster at its plant, thus forcing a shutdown on the part of the supplier.

To meet such situations, *contingent business interruption insurance* has been devised. The regular business interruption policy will not cover the losses described above because the insured peril did not cause any damage at the firm's own plant. Insurable value for contingent business interruption insurance is calculated in the same manner as it is for business interruption insurance. Since oftentimes the interruption of a supplier's plant will only reduce the operations of the firm's plant, insurable value may be correspondingly reduced. Of course, the form is designed to cover losses only when the reduction of business stems from the occurrence of an insured peril, and not from any other source. Thus, if a customer decides to buy from another source, such an event is not compensated under this policy. It is only where there is a direct connection between damaged property from an insured peril at another plant and the consequent reduction of business that indemnity is payable. This policy is written separately from the standard fire policy.

3) Extra expense insurance

Certain types of business firms do not find it possible or expedient to close down following the destruction of their physical plants. Such firms as laundries, newspapers, dairies, public utilities, banks, oil dealers, and ice companies will often continue their businesses using alternative facilities. The closing of such firms would deprive the public of a vital service or would involve a complete loss of goodwill or loss of business to competitors. If the firm is not shut down, even if using other facilities, the business interruption policy is not liable. However, the firm may have incurred great costs for such things as rental of new quarters for its staff, purchase of extra transportation facilities, rental of substitute equipment at high cost, and overtime allowances to employees. To cover such expenses when the firm's operations have not been interrupted, the *extra expense policy* has been devised. Some forms of extra expense insurance limit the allowances in such a way that no more than 40 per cent of the policy amount can be paid in any one month and that the total amount must be distributed over at least three months.

Extra expense insurance should not be confused with the expense-to-reduce-loss coverage that is given in connection with a business interruption policy. Extra expense coverage is designed primarily for indemnification of the extra costs of operations that are necessitated by a destruction of physical facilities. Expense-to-reduce-loss coverage repays the insured for extra costs and expenses involved in expediting, at higher than normal costs, the rebuilding of the destroyed facilities in order to reduce the period during which the business is interrupted. Expense-to-reduce-loss coverage is also written in connection with extra expense insurance, and payments are made to the extent that the expenses are incurred to reduce indemnity otherwise payable under the extra expense policy. This gives the insured some incentive to return to normal operations as soon as possible.

4) Additional living expense insurance

Corresponding to extra expense insurance in a business is a coverage known as *additional living expense* that is designed for a homeowner who incurs higher than normal living costs when he is displaced from his home because of fire or other insured peril. Written as an extension of coverage in the usual dwelling contents form, additional living expense insurance pays the difference between an insured's normal living costs and the higher costs that he is likely to incur in temporary quarters, such as in a hotel. The indemnity continues for the time required, with due diligence and dispatch, to repair or replace the insured's destroyed home, or for him to become settled in permanent quarters. Thus, if the insured normally spends $400 each month, including rent, to maintain his home, but is forced to spend $700 each month in a hotel for similar accomodations, the policy will reimburse the insured $300 each month until his home is rebuilt or until he can reasonably move to permanent quarters. Some additional living expense provisions limit the recovery to a certain amount each month, say $\frac{1}{12}$ of the face amount of his policy, while other provisions do not contain this limitation. Generally, there is an aggregate limitation of not over 10 per cent of the face amount of the policy applicable to additional living expense. This is not additional insurance, but is an application of the existing coverage for a certain purpose.

5) Rental value insurance

Rental value insurance, or *rent insurance,* as it is also called, represents a type of coverage that is closely akin to business interruption insurance, but which is usually written for those individuals who would not normally carry business interruption insurance. The insurable interest in rents may be illustrated by two examples. Bob Bickley leases a building under the condition that if the premises are partially or wholly destroyed by fire, the rent payments must continue until the end of the lease. Clearly, if a fire or other insured peril occurs, Bob is deprived of the use of the building but must still pay rent. His loss is insurable under a rent form.

Charles Johnson, on the other hand, being a shrewd businessman, occupies his building under a lease which provides that if a fire occurs and renders the building untenantable, his rent payments stop. Charles loses no rent payments in the event of fire, but the owner loses his rental income and may insure it under a rent form. No matter what the lease provides, someone loses the use of the property if it is destroyed by fire or other insured peril. Among the users of rent insurance are those who depend on rental income of apartments or other business buildings, beneficiaries of estates whose sole source of income is from the rent of real estate, firms that rent portions of their buildings to others, and homeowners whose loss of rental value might exceed by a large margin the fire damage that would force them to vacate their homes.

The question arises, "Doesn't rent insurance duplicate what is already provided for under a business interruption policy?" The answer, as in so many cases, is, "It depends." It depends on whether or not the business interruption form considers rental income as a part of the insured income. If rental income is already counted in the total income of a business, it is not necessary to purchase separate coverage. Sometimes, however, it is to the insured's advantage to purchase separate coverage, because of a cost saving made possible by differences in calculation of the rate in the two forms. In any event, the matter of rental income, which is so important to many individuals, should not be overlooked in the insurance program.

Forms of rent insurance. Rent insurance is generally written on one of three available types of forms:

1. The first type of form provides for reimbursement of rent loss for a specific period of time, usually 12 months.
2. The second type promises to reimburse rent loss for the length of time that it will *reasonably* take to rebuild the property, with no other time limit indicated.
3. The third type of rent form makes no reference to any time limit, but indicates that no more than one twelfth of the amount of insurance may be paid in any one month. Thus, if the amount of insurance is $12,000, no more than $1,000 may be paid in any one month. If the monthly loss is only $500, the policy would reimburse the insured $500 each month until the face of the policy is exhausted, which would take, in this case, 24 months.

Common elements in rent insurance forms. The three rent insurance forms have certain elements in common. The forms are all contracts of indemnity and will not allow payment to the insured of any more than his actual loss. Thus, they generally provide that any expenses which do not necessarily continue during the period of untenantability must be deducted from the rent. For instance, Mary Anderson receives $12,000 a year from renting an apartment building, and pays $2,000 a year for janitorial services. If a fire causes a loss of one year's rental income, she must deduct the cost of the janitorial services since these services are not continued during the period of untenantability. If Mary is forced out of her own home, which has a fair rental value of $150 per month, and it is agreed that $10 a month is the cost of maintenance and repairs (which will not continue during the period of untenantability), she can collect only $140 per month.

All rent forms limit the recovery to that period of time dating from the occurrence of the fire to the time that the property can be restored with due diligence and dispatch. The insured peril must occur during the policy term, but the period of rental loss can extend beyond the expiration of the policy. If the period of loss is extended because of a local ordinance regulating construction or repair, the amount of loss during this period is not recoverable under the policy.

Rent forms may provide (1) that indemnity is payable whether or not the property was actually occupied at the time of its destruction, or (2) that indemnity is not payable unless the property was actually occupied at the time of the loss. While the "rented only" forms are somewhat cheaper, they are not usually satisfactory because the property might be only temporarily vacant when the fire occurred and the owner would be deprived of rentals that he might otherwise have earned. Rental value insurance provided on the dwelling form usually covers the owner whether the property is rented or not.

Rent forms usually contain clauses that are designed to prevent underinsurance. The form that provides a monthly limitation of a given percentage of the total insurance is an example. Thus, if the policy states that not over one twelfth of the face amount is payable each month, the insured is encouraged to purchase adequate total limits in order to receive full indemnity in event the building is rendered unusable for a short period. For example, Jones has a building that is rented for $200 a month, or $2,400 a year. He figures that the maximum rental loss would be $800 because it would not take over four months to rebuild even if the property were completely destroyed. If he carries only $800 of insurance, however, the policy would reimburse not over $\frac{1}{12}$ of $800 each month. If Jones wishes full recovery, he must purchase $2,400 of insurance.

If the policy does not contain the type of limitation mentioned above, it will usually have a coinsurance clause, ranging from 60 to 100 per cent. The insured receives substantial credits in the rate for the use of coinsurance clauses, but he is required to carry an amount of insurance equal to the stated percentage of annual rental value in order to avoid becoming a coinsurer. If annual rents are $2,000 and the policy is written with an 80 per cent coinsurance clause, the insured must buy $1,600 of coverage or be willing to suffer a portion of any partial loss.

The common use of coinsurance clauses in rent insurance makes the "time to rebuild" form undesirable because of the difficulty of estimating precisely the time it takes to restore a building and the consequent danger of underinsuring and suffering coinsurance penalties. For example, delays in construction may throw off estimates of untenantability, and thus reduce recoveries.

Special arrangements can be made in rent insurance when the property is rented on a seasonal basis. A beach house, for example, can be insured under the condition that indemnity is payable only if the untenantable period falls in certain specified summer months. Special provisions in rent forms are possible when rentals are based on a percentage of the tenant's sales instead of a flat amount. In such cases it is desirable to pay particular attention to the problem of avoiding coinsurance penalties by taking out adequate provisional amounts. Usually a deposit premium is required and an end-of-year audit determines the final premium charge.

6) Leasehold interest insurance

A *leasehold* may be defined as an interest in real property that is created by a contractual agreement (a lease) which gives the lessee (the tenant) the right of enjoyment and use of the property for a period of time. A leasehold may become very valuable to the lessee because changing business conditions, improvements in the property, and good management may increase the rental value of real estate considerably above the rental due under the lease. For example, the "Y" Department Store may negotiate a 20-year lease on its store building calling for a rental payment of $12,000 a year. Due to a growing business community, comparable property might rent for $15,000 within five years after the lease has been signed. This increase in value creates what is known as *leasehold interest* or *leasehold value*.

Given the situation described above, what insurance problems are raised? If the lease is lost because of the occurrence of a fire or other physical damage to the building, the "Y" Department Store might be forced to sign a new lease calling for an increased rental of $3,000. It is very common in leases to provide that the agreement is void or voidable if the premises are destroyed by fire, or if a certain percentage of the sound value of the premises is destroyed by fire, or if the premises are so damaged that they cannot be restored within a given number of days. It is this source of loss that is insurable under a form of coverage known simply as *leasehold interest insurance*. In the preceding illustration, such a policy would provide indemnity for the loss of $3,000 a year for the unexpired term of the lease, which is 15 years. The policy, giving consideration to the interest factor, defines the loss as the present value of a sum of payments of $3,000 compounded annually at four per cent. The form provides a table that enables the insured to see what his indemnity will be for each dollar of leasehold interest value. When the policy is written, the value of the lease at that time is estimated and this amount is named as the face amount of the policy. As time goes on, the amount for which the insurer may become liable is diminished, because the remaining period of the lease grows shorter each year. The premium, therefore, is computed on the average leasehold value over the life of the lease.

Leasehold value probably changes constantly just as the market opinions vary daily as to the value of common stocks listed on the stock exchange. While there is no daily market in real estate or in leases that will tell precisely what these fluctuations are, they no doubt occur and should be estimated periodically so that the leasehold interest insurance form can be kept current. Such an estimate should be made by a qualified appraiser at least annually, as the policy is renewed.

Forms are provided for other types of interest in property that result from the loss of a leasehold. For example, an insured lessee might spend $10,000 remodeling the outside of his building. A fire occurs inside and as a result, the lease is canceled. The lessee stands to lose $10,000 because the permanent improvements made by him revert to the landlord at the expiration of the lease. His loss, it will be noted, does not stem from direct damage by fire, but from indirect loss by fire which caused cancellation of the lease. Hence, the indirect loss is not covered under the standard fire policy. Such a loss is insurable, however, under a leasehold interest insurance policy covering tenants, improvements, and betterments. Another similar type of loss, also insurable under such a form, is the loss of prepaid rent that is not returnable in the event the lease is canceled.

Most leases provide that the option to cancel in the event of destruction of the premises lies with the lessor (owner). If the lessor does not cancel the lease, of course there is no loss and, hence, no indemnity is payable under the policy to the lessee. The policy provides that if the lessee cancels, there is no payment due. Normally, if the rental value of the property has increased, it is very likely that the lessor will exercise his option to cancel the lease in the event of fire. If he does cancel, he may still rent the property to the same tenant on a month-to-month basis at a higher rent, in which case the policy pays the lessor the difference between the old rent and the new rent. If the lessor does not cancel, the lessee stands to lose the use of the premises until it is made tenantable again, in which case the leasehold interest policy indemnifies him for the loss of use of the property until it is repaired.

7) Excess rental value insurance

The question arises, "Suppose the rental value of the property has *fallen* since the lease was signed and it is the landlord, not the lessee, who loses by cancellation of the lease in the event of fire, or other insured peril?" In this case, a policy known as *excess rental value* may be written to cover the landlord's loss. Coverage under this policy parallels that given the lessee under the leasehold interest form.

NONTIME ELEMENT CONTRACTS

As explained earlier, there are several types of consequential losses that are not measured as a function of elapsed time. *Nontime element contracts* or coverages are used to insure those losses that result from fire, but where the loss cannot be measured by either direct damage by fire or in terms of elapsed time. The following examples of such coverages are discussed: 1) profits insurance, 2) accounts receivable insurance, 3) temperature damage insurance, and 4) rain insurance.

1) Profits insurance

Profits insurance differs from business interruption insurance in that the latter covers profits that would have been earned in the future had the fire or other insured peril not damaged the firm's plant. *Profits insurance* covers the loss of the profit element in goods already manufactured but destroyed before they could be sold. Suppose that a plant is manufacturing refrigerators and is disabled by fire. Among the lost property, stored in a warehouse, are finished refrigerators with a sales value of $10,000. This figure includes an expected profit of $2,000. The standard fire policy indemnifies the insured only for his replacement cost, which would be $8,000. The business interruption policy would not cover the $2,000 loss of expected profit because the policy applies only to refrigerators which would have been produced during the period of interruption by fire, and not those already produced. To receive full indemnity for his $2,000 loss, the manufacturer would have to be covered by profits insurance.

Profits insurance serves a vital need. If a businessman could re-place the lost finished goods immediately at the same cost, he could realize his expected profit on the new goods. Oftentimes, however, the goods cannot be replaced in time for their expected market. Thus, goods ready for shipment to buyers who need them for a seasonal sale probably cannot be purchased elsewhere in time to realize the expected profit. The purchasers will buy elsewhere and the profit will be lost.

Profits insurance is not generally written for merchants, but only for manufacturers. A merchant would receive the same protection through a business interruption insurance policy since his business *is* the selling of finished inventory and the policy is designed to cover the lost profits and expenses from lost future sales.

In some jursidictions a manufacturer may insure his goods for their selling price rather than for their replacement cost, or cost of production. In such a case, profits insurance is obviously not needed. Profits insur-ance covers only finished goods, not goods in process, which come un-der the loss settlement procedures of the business interruption policy.

2) Accounts receivable insurance

Accounts receivable insurance attempts to indemnify an insured for the loss brought about because of the inability to collect from open account (unsecured) debtors because a fire destroyed accounts receiv-able records. If a catastrophe such as fire makes it impossible to prove the existence of a debt because there are no records of the transaction, some debtors may refuse to honor their obligations. Most debtors are honest and will pay, but a loss from unscrupulous debtors may result as a consequential loss from fire or other peril.

Accounts receivable insurance is written as an *all-risk* cover, with the only exclusions being war and infidelity of the insured's main part-ners or officers. The insured is required to make a deposit premium and to report the value of his outstanding receivables each month. An audit at the end of the year determines the actual premium. Non-audited forms are also available. The coverage applies only while the accounts receivable records are on the premises, but for an additional premium the records may be covered while at another temporary location. It may be required that records be stored in a vault or a safe when the business is closed.

Indemnity under accounts receivable insurance is made for: (1) uncollectible accounts, the sole reason for which is the damage or loss of records, less an allowance for normal bad debts, less any debts that can be re-established or proven by other methods or other records; (2) interest on loans made necessary by the loss; and (3) excess collection expense or the reasonable cost of re-establishing proof of an account. To establish the amount of the loss in the absence of accounts receivable records, projections from accounting data for prior years are made, with adjustments for seasonal or cyclical fluctuations. The rate for this coverage, as is true of most consequential loss contracts, is based on the fire rate in the territory served.

3) Temperature damage insurance

In many types of business firms, such as bakeries, cold-storage plants, dairies, and greenhouses, the maintenance of a certain temperature is vital to the prevention of loss. A fire may disrupt the power supply, and before it can be restored, a rise or fall in temperature may have caused a great loss even though there was no *direct* loss by fire. Such losses would not generally be covered under the standard fire policy. Yet it is vital that their insurance not be overlooked.

In most jurisdictions insurance against such consequential loss from fire is accomplished by means of an endorsement known as the *consequential loss assumption* clause. This clause broadens the definition of loss on the standard fire policy to include many types of damage due to changing temperature. A typical clause, used in the middle western territory reads:

> In consideration of the premium at which this policy is written and subject to its provisions and stipulations, this policy is hereby extended to cover also consequential loss, except as excluded below, to stock . . . or merchandise covered hereunder, caused by change in temperature or humidity resulting from damage by the perils insured against to equipment used for refrigerating, cooling, humidifying, dehumidifying, air conditioning, heating, generating or converting power (including their connections and supply or transmission lines and pipes) only when situated on the described premises or on the premises of the plant of which the building described herein form a part.
>
> If this clause is attached to a policy containing the Extended Coverage endorsement, this company shall not be liable hereunder for any loss specifically excluded under the riot provisions of the extended coverage endorsement or the provisions of the vandalism and malicious mischief endorsement, if also attached.

It will be observed that there must be actual destruction by an insured peril of the cooling equipment or power plant, etc., before indemnity is payable. If someone accidentally shuts off the power, there is no coverage. Also, there is no insurance on apparatus located *off* the main premises. In some jurisdictions, however, this limitation may be removed. In general, insurers make no additional charge for the consequential loss assumption endorsement, but where the endorsement extends to apparatus off the premises, an extra premium is required.

In the second paragraph of the insuring clause, reference is made to the extended coverage endorsement. Such an endorsement denies any coverage of a consequential nature. This limitation may be removed in most states by payment of an additional premium. Thus, in case rioters damage the power plant, the resulting damage to stored goods from temperature change can be recovered. However, as stated before, there must be physical damage to the apparatus; malicious turning off of the power will not be covered.

4) Rain insurance

Rain as such seldom causes any direct damage to property. The accumulation of water due to extended rainfall, of course, does cause much loss to property in the form of flood or rising water, but such coverage is generally not available from private insurers. Rain, itself, however, may be a source of considerable *indirect* loss because its occurrence may greatly reduce the expected profits of promoters of an outdoor or public event. *Rain insurance* is designed to cover the loss of profits and fixed charges or extra expenses due to rain, hail, snow, or sleet of anyone having a financial interest in an event that is dependent on good weather for its success.

Rain insurance forms are designed to cover a variety of different needs. One form covers the loss of fixed charges and expenses in case a scheduled event must be abandoned or postponed because of rainfall. There is also a form to cover the fixed charges and expected profits lost in whole or in part because rainfall reduced the expected attendance at an event. Another form pays a set dollar indemnity in case a specified amount of rain falls. Still another form is intended to compensate advertising publications in case they have to refund advertising revenue for an outdoor event canceled because of rain. Similarly, a form has been designed to compensate promoters who must make ticket refunds when the event is canceled because of rain.

Rain insurance forms are contracts of indemnity and contain several types of limitations. Usually, the indemnity cannot exceed a specified portion of the expected profits from an event and no more than 100 per cent of the fixed expenses. Income in prior years is often used as a guide to the amount of insurance coverage permitted, and the contract reimburses the insured for the difference between expected and actual revenues. Payments may be contingent upon a specified amount of rainfall, say $1/20$ of an inch, as measured either by impartial observers or by official weather stations. The rain must fall during the period of time indicated in the policy, which is usually three or more hours prior to the event and continuing throughout the day.

Rain insurance must be applied for at least seven days prior to the time the event is scheduled, and once issued, the insurance cannot be canceled. This provision protects the insured from having his coverage canceled in case rain threatens, and protects the insurer from demands for premium refunds in case the insured sees that there is not going to be any rain after all and tries to cancel the coverage just before the event takes place.

Rates for rain insurance depend on a number of factors. The longer the period of time during which rain may be registered as satisfying the minimum rainfall specified in the policy, the higher the rate. Naturally, rates are somewhat higher in areas where rainfall is heavy, or where sudden showers are common. Finally, the greater the specified rainfall that must be registered, the less is the rate.

The advisability of purchasing rain insurance depends on the promoter's estimate of the actual effect of rainfall on his anticipated attendance and the resulting profit. In some areas rain is so common that it does not discourage attendance substantially, while in other locations, even a light rainfall will ruin attendance. If an event is very popular and is sold out by advance ticket sales that are nonrefundable, the profit is assured in advance and there is no reason for rain insurance. Among the possible users of rain insurance are sponsors of auction sales, sporting events, boat excursions, carnivals, fairs, conventions, dances, outdoor movies, and resorts.

SUMMARY

1. The major contracts of insurance covering indirect or consequential losses are classified under two headings: time element and nontime element coverages. Time element policies measure the loss in terms of given time periods, while nontime element coverages use some other basis in measuring loss.

2. Consequential losses are often greater than the loss of property destroyed directly by fire or other peril. Yet, they are often overlooked in an otherwise complete insurance program.

3. The most important single type of time element contract is called business interruption, which is designed to indemnify the insured for loss of profits and fixed charges occasioned by stoppage of business due to some named peril.

4. Other time element contracts of insurance are: (a) contingent business interruption, which indemnifies for losses due to interruption of the business of a major supplier or customer; (b) extra expense, which indemnifies for the extra costs when a named peril occurs and while not causing a business shutdown, necessitates a higher cost of operation than normal; (c) additional living expense, which indemnifies for higher living costs necessitated by occurrence of a named peril that renders a home unusable; (d) rental value, which indemnifies for loss of rents when fire renders a building untenantable; (e) leasehold interest, which indemnifies the tenant for loss of a valuable lease canceled before its usual termination, due to occurrence of fire or other named peril; and (f) excess rental value, which indemnifies a landlord who loses a favorable lease due to occurrence of fire or other named peril.

5. Examples of nontime element contracts of insurance are: (a) profits insurance, which indemnifies the insured for loss of profits expected from the sale of finished goods; (b) accounts receivable insurance, which indemnifies for failure to collect accounts rendered uncollectible because a fire or other named peril destroys the records that give evidence of the debts; (c) temperature damage insurance, which indemnifies for loss due to temperature changes brought about by the occurrence of some named peril; and (d) rain insurance, which indemnifies for the loss of profits and expenses incurred when rain or other types of precipitation decrease expected attendance at some public event.

QUESTIONS FOR REVIEW AND DISCUSSION

1. In Palatine Insurance Company v O'Brien (68 Atl. 484), the insurer refused to pay rent indemnity to an insured during the time that the insured property was rendered untenantable, because the city refused to issue a permit while it was considering a change in the zoning law.
   (a) Is such a restriction common in rent forms?
   (b) Why would such a restriction be imposed?

2. A circus owner purchased a rain insurance policy covering the period beginning two hours before his opening and continuing throughout the circus. Early in the morning of the day of the circus it rained heavily and turned cold, but the rain stopped entirely at noon. The grounds of the circus were soaked and the weather continued cold and threatening, but no rain fell during the two-hour period prior to opening nor during the circus. Nevertheless, attendance at the circus was poor. Discuss the liability of the insurer for indemnity to the circus owner.

3. "In a sense, life insurance may be properly termed a consequential loss contract." Explain.

4. Gerdes takes out a business interruption insurance policy against the perils of fire, lightning, riot, and civil commotion. As a result of a riot connected with a labor disturbance, his employees fail to show up for work during the following three days and the plant is closed. Under what conditions may Gerdes apply for loss of profits and fixed charges under his policy? Discuss.

5. Distinguish between time element and nontime element coverages.

6. If business improves considerably during the year, the individual purchaser of business interruption insurance may fail to collect in full for a partial loss under his policy. Why is this possible? Explain.

7. How should a firm go about determining how much business interruption insurance to carry? Discuss.

8. "Z" operates a concession at a beach resort for only four months during the year. His agent recommends a business interruption policy covering an entire year's profits and fixed charges. "Z" objects, saying that if he is interrupted for only four months, the policy indemnifies him for that period only. Discuss.

9. A lumber mill is shut down when a fire destroys its main saw carriage. The daily loss of continuing expenses and profits amounts to $1,000. It is determined that repair parts can be flown in at an extra cost of $500 over rail transportation and if this is done, the mill can resume operations three days earlier than it could if the parts were shipped by rail.
   (a) Under the typical business interruption policy, will the insurer reimburse the mill for the $500 difference? Why?
   (b) In this case, what is the limit of indemnity payable? Explain.

10. A small manufacturing plant is destroyed by fire and it is determined that it will take four months to rebuild it. However, the owner wishes to build a larger plant and it is estimated that the rebuilding time will be five months because of the larger size. For how many months will the business interruption policy apply? Explain.

11. The following financial statement reflects the operating figures for the Atlast Retail Company for the year:

Sales		$150,000
Cost of goods sold		90,000
Gross margin		$ 60,000
Administrative expenses:		
Sales salaries	$10,000	
Buyer's salary	20,000	
Store overhead	10,000	40,000
Net profit		$ 20,000

It is estimated that if the building burns, it would take four months at the most to restore it. The manager feels that he would not retain any of the sales personnel in such an event, but good buyers are hard to find and he would want to keep his buyer on the payroll. Store overhead consists of $5,000 depreciation and $5,000 miscellaneous expenses, such as insurance premiums, interest, taxes, and rent.

(a) Under which of the two most common forms of business interruption insurance would you recommend that the Atlast Retail Company insure? Show your calculations in detail and explain fully.

(b) In the event of a fire loss with a total interruption period of two months, what would be the maximum recovery under the form you recommended in (a)? Under what circumstances might this maximum figure not represent the actual indemnity payable? Explain.

(c) Answer (b) on the assumption that sales had been running at the rate of $200,000 for the whole year at the time of the loss. Assume that the cost of sales is the same proportion of sales as before, but that other items of expense are unchanged.

(d) Would this firm have any need for the following types of insurance? Explain fully in each case, why or why not. If your answer is negative, explain what situations each type fits best and why.

(1) Extra expense insurance.

(2) Profits and commissions insurance.

(3) Leasehold interest insurance.

(4) Contingent use and occupancy.

12. On January 1, 1952, "A" leased his building to "B" under a 20-year nonrenewable lease calling for an annual rent of $1,800. The lease contains a clause under which the lease is terminated in the event that fire destroys 25% or more of the value of the building. On January 1, 1962, "B", realizing that if he had to obtain other comparable quarters in case of a major fire it would cost him $250 a month, seeks an agent's advice concerning his (B's) insurance needs. "B" informs the agent of the above facts and also reports that he has just spent $4,000 to lower the ceiling of the building and to refinish the exterior. Based on these facts, what insurance policies, and in what amounts, should "B" consider? Explain.

13. The Myrtles Dairy asks its agent to look into a business interruption insurance policy, but the agent, upon inquiry, recommends that this type of insurance would not be suitable for the dairy. He recommends another policy. Why might business interruption insurance not be appropriate for the dairy and what other policy would the agent probably recommend?

14. Under what circumstances would a rent insurance policy duplicate the coverage granted under a business interruption insurance policy? Explain.

15. Herman Hendershot purchases rent insurance under a dwelling form that limits the recovery to $\frac{1}{12}$ of the applicable insurance. The applicable insurance is 10 per cent of the face amount of the policy. The fair rental value of his home is $180 a month. His policy is written in the amount of $12,000. It is estimated that $20 per month represents the average cost of maintenance and repairs. How much can Herman collect under his rent insurance if the home is:

(a) completely untenantable because of fire for two months?

(b) tenantable, but approximately one half of the area is unusable until it is repaired, and the repair period will last three months?

16. Answer Question 15 on the basis that Hendershot's policy had been for the face amount of $20,000.

17. The insurance manager of the "T" Manufacturing Company is concerned about the possibility that sales to the chief customer of the firm may be canceled because of fire damage to the customer's plant. He is particularly concerned with the expected profit on a shipment of finished parts ready for sale, parts that would not have a market for any other buyer because of their specialized nature.
    (a) Is such a risk insurable?
    (b) Would profits insurance cover the risk?
    (c) What methods of handling this risk, other than insurance, might be used?

18. Why is profits insurance, as a general rule, not sold to retailers or wholesalers? Explain.

19. The ABC Company sells raw materials on open account to a certain manufacturer. Due to fire in the manufacturer's plant, accounts in the amount of $20,000 prove to be uncollectible by the ABC Company. Is this loss payable under accounts receivable insurance? Why, or why not?

20. The loss of the General Motors hydramatic transmission plant at Livonia, Michigan, in 1953 has often been cited as an illustration of the need for business interruption insurance. Why?

21. A writer stated, "With regard to the settlement of business interruption losses, we have found that the technique is not as proven as that used in the settlement of a property damage loss. Neither is it as readily acceptable to the adjuster. The settlement of our first loss entailed considerable negotiation, but since certain principles were established at that time, future adjustment of losses has been on a more understandable basis." The following example illustrates the method used:

Description of loss: Explosion in No. 4 open hearth furnace
Determination of business interruption value:

Net sales January 1 to March 31	$30,000,000
Net cost of sales	24,500,000
Gross profit	$ 5,500,000
Add back depreciation	500,000
	$ 6,000,000
Less profits from products not having origin in open hearth department.	$ 1,000,000
Total business interruption value	$ 5,000,000
Tons of finished products shipped	200,000
Average business interruption value per ton	$ 25

Basis of settlement:

Period of shutdown	200 hours
Average product of No. 4 furnace per hour	16 tons
Total loss of tons produced	3,200 tons
Average yield from open hearth to finished product	75%
Finished product shipments lost (3,200 × .75)	2,400 tons
Amount of loss (2,400 tons × $25)	$ 60,000

(a) What "principles" did the writer probably refer to as illustrated in the example?
(b) Do you feel that the method of loss determination is sound? Why?

Transportation

12

Insurance

In the preceding chapter, insurance on property in a fixed location was analyzed. The question arises, "What happens if goods are lost while they are being moved from one place to another?" This question has been raised by shippers of goods ever since the beginning of civilization, but in the last analysis, insurance has proved to be the most satisfactory answer.

Insurance on the risks of transportation of goods is one of the oldest and most vital forms of insurance. All types of trade depend heavily upon the availability of insurance for successful and expeditious handling. If it were not possible to trade with others, it would not be feasible to manufacture goods on a mass-production basis. Without mass production, life as we know it would be entirely different and probably not as comfortable and easy.

In history, there is much interesting proof that insurance played a vital part in stimulating early commerce. In Roman times, and earlier, contracts known as *bottomry* and *respondentia* governed the terms under which money was borrowed to finance ocean commerce. Under these contracts, the lender of money took as security for his loan either the ship itself, in the case of bottomry bonds, or the cargo in the case of respondentia bonds. However, if the ship or cargo were lost as a result of ocean perils, the loan was canceled. If the voyage were successful, the loan was repaid and substantial interest charged, mainly because the interest included an allowance for the possibility of loss of the security; this extra charge was essentially an insurance premium.

Today, even as in ancient times, shippers of goods are seldom in a position to assume the risks of transportation perils. They have constantly sought means to transfer these risks to others. The perils of transportation are so many and so varied that the shipper is in no position to make subjective judgments of their importance and to make allowances in his selling prices. In addition, much trade is accomplished with the use of borrowed money. Normally, the lender is unwilling to commit his funds unless satisfactory arrangements have been made to meet the risks of transportation.

THE PERILS OF TRANSPORTATION

The perils that may cause a loss to goods being transported may be appreciated by realizing the failure of man to control adequately or completely the forces of nature, or to prevent human failure as it affects the safe movement of goods. For example, in spite of radar, sonar, the gyroscope, compass, and all the other modern safety devices, frequent ocean tragedies occur. Ocean storms can capsize even the largest ocean vessels. Huge waves driven by hurricane winds often dump tons of sea water on a vessel and cause damage to cargo stowed inside. Engine failure may subject a ship to the mercy of a storm, driving the ship aground, where it quickly breaks up by the pressure of waves grinding it against rocks and sand. Poor visibility still causes collisions, and fires occur frequently. Goods are sometimes lost as a result of basic dishonesty, negligence, or incompetence of the crew handling them or through faults in the management of the vessel. Likewise, loss of goods shipped on land comes from sources such as overturn of the vehicle, collision, fire, theft, flood, rough or careless handling, and unusual delays that result in spoilage.

THE LIABILITY OF THE CARRIER

The question arises, "Is not the carrier of the goods responsible for their safe movement?" The answer is, "Yes, to some extent." The common law liability of the carrier differs depending upon the country in which the transportation conveyances are chartered, the applicable statutes, custom, the type of shipping, and other factors.

The carrier's liability in ocean transportation

In the field of ocean shipping, the carrier, or shipowner, is responsible only for failure to exercise "due diligence." His liability, which is spelled out by the Carriage of Goods by Sea Act, passed in the United States in 1936, is to make the ship seaworthy; to properly man, equip, and supply the ship; and to make all holds and other carrying compartments safe and fit for the goods stored there. In addition, he must exercise due care in loading, handling, stowing cargoes, etc.

The Act lists specific causes for which the carrier is definitely *not* liable. For example, he is not liable for loss resulting from:

1. Errors in navigation or management of the vessel.
2. Strikes or lockouts.
3. Acts of God.

4. Acts of war or public enemies.
5. Seizure of the goods under legal process.
6. Quarantine.
7. Inherent vice of the goods.
8. Failure of the shipper to exercise due care in the handling or packing of his goods.
9. Fire.
10. Perils of the seas.
11. Latent defects in the hull or machinery.
12. Other losses where the carrier is not at fault.

Even though the carrier must prove that he was not to blame, it can be seen that the shipper of the goods has little claim against the carrier for loss of goods by some force outside the control of the carrier, such as windstorm or other perils of the sea.

The carrier's liability in land transportation

The common law liability of the land carrier is considerably greater than that of the ocean carrier, but it is still not absolute. In addition to being responsible for failure to exercise due diligence, the land carrier is responsible for *all loss* to the goods except for the following causes:

1) Acts of God.
2) Acts of public enemy or public authority.
3) Acts or negligence of the shipper.
4) Inherent vice or quality of the goods.

1) Acts of God. *Acts of God* have been interpreted to mean perils such as earthquakes, storms, and floods, which could not have been reasonably guarded against. Fire or lightning is not an act of God and hence the carrier is liable for damage caused by these perils to goods in his custody. However, loss caused by the breaking of a rail due to sudden and intense cold,[1] and loss caused when a train was held up because of a heavy snowstorm,[2] were held to be perils falling within the scope of the definition "act of God" and the carrier was held not liable.

2) Acts of public enemy or public authority. The term *public enemy* has been interpreted to mean the action by forces of men at war with a domestic government, not acts of gangsters, mobs, or rioters. Thus, the carrier is liable for losses of goods by organized criminals as well as by a single thief. However, the carrier is not liable for loss when

---

[1] *McPaddin* v. *New York Central Railway Co.,* 44 N. Y. 478 (1871).
[2] *Ward* v. *Chicago, St. Paul, M & O Railway Co.,* 137 N.W. 995 (Neb. 1912).

the goods are taken from him by legal process against the owner, such as the confiscation of contraband.

3) Acts or negligence of the shipper. Under the heading *acts or negligence of the shipper,* come such causes of loss as improper loading or packing, or where the nature of the goods is concealed. Thus, if packages contain glassware but are not clearly marked "fragile," the carrier may be excused from loss due to breakage. Loss from poor packing that was visible to the carrier when the goods were accepted for shipment falls upon the carrier. But if it can be proved that the loss was caused by improper packing which was not readily apparent to the agent of the carrier when the goods were accepted for shipment, the carrier is excused from liability.

4) Inherent vice or quality of the goods. A loss from the *inherent nature of the goods* may be illustrated by losses due to decay, heating, rusting, drying, or fermentation. In one case the shipper sent a car of Christmas trees from Vermont to Florida. When the trees arrived, it was found that they had sustained damage by mold and rot. Investigation revealed that the trees had been shipped with excessive moisture and were locked in a steel car. As the train proceeded south, temperatures rose and the heat ruined the shipment. The carrier was held not liable because the loss stemmed from the inherent nature of the goods.[3]

Need for transportation insurance

The preceding discussion reveals that many types of transportation losses fall outside the responsibility of the common carrier. Furthermore, common carriers have been slow to settle losses for which they are legally liable. In land transportation it is common, moreover, for the shipper to send goods under what is known as a *released bill of lading.* The effect of shipping goods under a released bill of lading is to limit the dollar liability of the carrier for any loss to the goods. In return, the shipper obtains a lower freight rate. In effect, the difference in freight rates is intended to compensate the shipper for the added risk of loss which he must assume. For these reasons the shipper finds it expedient to use outside insurance to effect the degree of security and safety in commerce that prudent business methods demand.

It is possible, of course, to shift the risk of transportation losses to the consignee of the goods. In this way the shipper may feel that he does not have to worry about insurance. For example, he may ship

---

[3] *Austin* v. *Seaboard Air Line Railway Co.,* 188 Feb. 2d 239 (1951).

under terms such as f.o.b. mill or f.o.b. factory. These terms mean that the selling price does not include the cost of freight or insurance and that the title to the goods is transferred to the buyer when the goods are laid down for shipment at the railway siding or at the pier. However, suppose the buyer does not pay and the goods are returned. The seller is now subjected to the risk of loss while the goods are being sent back. Again, the shipper himself may buy materials on the same terms as he ships. Thus, he becomes liable for loss to incoming shipments. It should be clear that it is not feasible to avoid the risk of loss entirely by trying to shift it to the buyer. There is no satisfactory substitute for insurance as the major way of handling the transportation risk.

OCEAN TRANSPORTATION INSURANCE

Because other methods to obtain protection against the perils of transportation have not proved satisfactory, the insurance method has been developed and has attained a high degree of refinement in modern-day commerce. The oldest type of insurance known was in the field of ocean marine, in the form of the bottomry and respondentia contracts, which were mentioned earlier. This development was natural because most early commerce was carried on by sea; land transportation vehicles had not yet been developed. As world trade grew and values at risk became larger, the need for coverage became more apparent. Larger ships and more refined instruments of navigation made long voyages possible and with this development, insurance protection was looked upon almost as a necessity. The major source of underwriting capacity was in England, probably because England was among the first to develop a refined system of admiralty law, a very necessary adjunct to successful insurance underwriting.

Major types of coverage

The four chief sources of loss to be insured in an ocean voyage are:
1) The vessel, or the hull.
2) The cargo.
3) The shipping revenue or "freight" received by the shipowners.
4) Legal liability for proved negligence.

If a peril of the sea causes the sinking of a ship in deep water, it is possible that one or more of these losses can result. However, as explained on pages 284 and 285, each of these potential losses can be covered under a corresponding insurance policy.

1) Hull policies. Policies covering the vessel itself, or *hull insurance,* are written in several different ways. The policy may cover the ship only during a specified voyage, or it may cover all voyages taken during a given period of time, usually not to exceed one year. The insurance is commonly subject to geographical limits. If the ship is laid up in port for an extended period of time, the contract may be written at a reduced premium under the condition that the ship remain in port. The contract may cover a builder's risk, while the vessel is under construction.

2) Cargo policies. Contracts insuring cargo against various types of loss may be written to cover only during a specified voyage, as in the case of a hull contract, or on an "open" basis. The latter is probably the most common type of contract. Under the *open contract,* there is no termination date, but either party may cancel upon given notice, usually 30 days. All shipments, both incoming and outgoing, are automatically covered. The shipper reports to the insurer at regular intervals as to the values shipped or received during the previous period. The shipper declares the classes of goods in which he deals and the ports between which these goods move. There is usually a limit of values that may be insured on a single vessel and a limit on the goods stowed on deck.

Ocean cargo is often shipped under what is known as a *cargo certificate,* an instrument which entitles the holder to collect any losses that would have been paid under the basic cargo policy covering the goods. The certificate is used because it can be negotiated from one person to another, entitling each subsequent owner of the goods to collect on the insurance in case of loss. In this way the goods may be sold and resold during the course of the shipment. Each seller transfers the certificate of insurance to the buyer, who has assurance that he is protected if the goods are damaged during the time that he owns them. In this way ocean commerce and foreign trade are greatly facilitated because it is unnecessary for each transferee of goods to arrange for insurance; all who have a financial interest in the voyage are automatically protected.

3) Freight coverage. The money paid for the transportation of the goods, known as *freight,* is an insurable interest because in the event that freight charges are not paid, someone has lost income with which to reimburse expenses incurred in preparation for a voyage. Under the laws of the United States, the earning of freight by the hull owner is dependent on the delivery of cargo unless this is altered by contractual arrangements between the parties. If a ship sinks, the freight is lost and the vessel owner loses the expenses that he has incurred plus the expected profit on the venture. The carrier's right to earn freight may be defeated by the occurrence of perils ordinarily insured against in an ocean marine insurance policy. The hull may be damaged so that it is uneconomical to complete the voyage, or the cargo may be destroyed, in which case, of course, it cannot be delivered.

The owner of cargo has an interest in freight arising from his obligation to pay transportation charges. There are two typical arrangements for handling the shipping charges. First, freight may be guaranteed to the carrier, payable in all events. This type of freight is a part of the invoice cost and is insured by the cargo owner as a part of the value of the goods. Since payment of the freight is guaranteed to the carrier, the carrier does not insure its payment. Second, freight may be contingent, payable only if the goods are delivered. The carrier insures this type of freight. However, the cargo owner is normally required to pay freight charges on goods arriving in damaged condition. Thus, he may also insure contingent freight and there then exists a double insurable interest. Freight insurance is normally made a part of the regular hull or cargo coverage instead of being written as a separate contract.

4) Legal liability for proved negligence. In the *running down clause (R.D.C.)* in ocean marine insurance policies covering the hull, the hull owner is protected against third-party liability claims that arise from collisions. Collision loss to the hull itself is included in the perils clause as one of the perils of the sea. The R.D.C. clause is intended to give protection in case the shipowner is held liable for the negligent operation of his vessel, which is the proximate cause of damage to certain property of others. If the vessel owner or his agent fails to exercise the proper degree of care in the operation of the ship, he may be legally liable for damage to the other ship, and for loss of freight revenues. The R.D.C. clause normally excludes liability for damage to cargo, harbors, wharves, piers, or for loss of lives or personal injuries.

To provide liability coverage for personal injuries, loss of life, or damage to property other than vessels, the *protection and indemnity (P. & I.)* clause is usually added to the hull policy. This clause is intended to provide liability insurance for all events not covered by the more limited R.D.C. clause, except liability assumed under contract. (See Chapter 15 for a discussion of contractual liability.) Similarly, the policy may be extended to insure the shipowner's liability under the Federal Longshoremen's and Harbor Workers' Compensation Act.

Perils clause

In 1779, Lloyd's of London developed a more or less standard ocean marine policy containing an insuring clause, the wording of which has been retained almost in its original form in policies issued today. The wording, which has been the subject of repeated court decisions interpreting almost every phrase, is as follows:

> Touching the adventures and perils which we the assurers are contented to bear and to take upon us in this voyage; they are of the seas, men of war, fire, enemies, pirates, rovers, thieves, jettisons, letters of mart and countermart, surprises, takings at sea, arrests, restraints, and detainments of all kings, princes, and people, of what nation, condition, or quality soever, barratry of the master and the mariners, and of all other perils, losses, and misfortunes, that have or shall come to the hurt, detriment, or damage of the said goods and merchandise, and ship, etc., or any part thereof.

It will be noticed that this clause might be interpreted as an all-risk contract since it makes reference to certain named perils "and *all other* perils, losses, and misfortunes." However, the courts have interpreted the quoted phrase as "all other *like* perils." Hence, it cannot be said that the policy is an all-risk contract although it is very broad in its coverage. Essentially, the insuring clause covers perils *of* the sea and not all perils. Perils *on* the sea, those not finding their inherent cause arising out of the sea, are not insured unless they are specifically mentioned. Fire, for example, is a peril *on* the sea and is insured by specific mention. Examples of perils *of* the sea are action of wind and waves, stranding, and sinking. Gradual wear and tear caused by the ocean is not considered a covered peril.

The insuring clause is not interpreted as providing coverage against the perils of war, even though a broad implication is present that such is the intention. Action by pirates, assailing thieves, or overt dishonest actions by the ship's master or crew (barratry) are intended to provide coverage similar to burglary and robbery protection on land and are not losses from war. Pilferage is not covered, but may be added by endorsement. The *free of capture and seizure* (*F.C.&S.*) clause, which is present in most modern policies, specifically excludes all loss arising out of war. War coverage is not available from private insurers today, although the United States government provided this protection during World War II by creation of a special body known as the War Shipping Administration.

Deductibles

Ocean marine insurance policies have several different types of deductible clauses. The three most important of these are the:

1) Memorandum clause.
2) Free of particular average (F.P.A.).
3) General average clause.

1) Memorandum clause. One of the most common of the deductible clauses is known as the *memorandum* clause. Attached to cargo policies, this clause lists various types of goods with varying percentages of deductibles that apply on a franchise basis. Thus, the memorandum clause may specify that there will be no loss payment for loss to tobacco under 20 per cent, nor to sugar under 7 per cent, nor to *any* partial loss to cheese or certain other perishables. This means that if there is a partial loss to a shipment of tobacco and the damage is less than 20 per cent, each package considered separately, no loss will be payable; but if the loss exceeds 20 per cent, the entire amount of the loss will be reimbursed to the owner.

2) Free of particular average clause (F.P.A.). Some policies covering the cargo and the hull may contain a type of deductible known as the *free of particular average* clause. In ocean marine insurance terminology, the word average, stemming from the French word *avarie,* means loss or damage to a ship or a cargo. *Particular average* means a partial loss to an interest which must be borne entirely by that interest. Particular average is contrasted to *general average,* which will be explained shortly. The free of particular average clause (F.P.A.) usually provides that no partial loss will be paid to a single cargo interest unless the loss is caused by certain perils such as stranding, sinking, burning, or collision. Often the F.P.A. clause is limited to those losses under a certain percentage, such as three per cent.

In interpreting what is a partial loss, each package is insured separately. A total loss of one package in a shipment is not considered as particular average but as a total loss of a part. Let us say that the clause reads, "warranted free from particular average under 10 per cent unless general." The shipment consists of 100 bags of coffee. If one bag of coffee is completely destroyed, the policy will cover the loss even though it constitutes only one per cent of the value of the shipment. No indemnity would be paid, however, if there is a partial loss to each unit of an amount less than the stipulated percentage that constitutes the franchise deductible. The words *unless general* mean that if there is a partial loss falling in the category of a general average claim, the loss will be paid regardless of the percentage. The ocean marine insurance policy always provides full coverage for general average claims.

3) *General average clause.* The *general average* clause refers to losses which must be partly borne by someone other than the owner of the goods that were damaged or lost. General average losses may be total or partial, while particular average losses, by definition, are always partial. To illustrate, suppose that a certain cargo of lumber, wrapped in a large bundle, is stored on deck. To lighten the ship during a heavy storm that is threatening the safety of the whole voyage, the captain orders the lumber, worth $5,000, to be jettisoned. His action is successful in saving the ship and all the other interests. Such a sacrifice would be termed a general average and those interests that were saved would be required to share a pro rata part of the loss. Thus, if the ship and freight interests were valued at $100,000, and the other cargo interests at $95,000, the shipowner would have to pay one half (100/200) of the value of the lumber. The other cargo interests would share 95/200 of the loss and the owner of the lumber would bear 5/200 of the loss.

General average claims must meet certain requirements before they can be properly described as "general average." The sacrifice must have been *voluntary;* it must have been reasonably *necessary;* it must have been *successful.* If in the above case the lumber had washed overboard just before the captain ordered it jettisoned, the loss would not be termed a general average because it was not a voluntary sacrifice. This is true even though the result of the loss saves the other interests. Likewise, if the ship sinks, even though the sacrifice was voluntary, there will be no general average contributions because the sacrifice was not successful in saving the other interests.

General average claims extend to many types of loss other than mere jettison. Suppose a fire breaks out and water used to put it out causes loss to otherwise untouched cargo. Since fire fighting is considered to be a voluntary effort and is necessary to save the other interests, such losses would be paid as general average claims, assuming the effort is successful. Again, assume that a ship is stranded and engine damage is sustained in an effort to get the ship free, or that certain expenses are incurred when a ship is voluntarily sent into a harbor for refuge during a storm. These examples may both qualify as general average claims, assuming always that there is absence of negligence on the part of any interest seeking indemnity in bringing about the peril which threatens the voyage. It should be also noted that no general average claims will be paid as a result of sacrifices that are made because of perils which are not covered by the ocean marine contract.

Sue and labor clause

A clause of basic importance to the ocean marine insurance policy is known as the *sue and labor* clause. A typical clause reads:

> And in case of any loss or misfortune, it shall be lawful and *necessary* (to and for the Assured) . . . to sue, labor and travel for, in and about the defense, safeguard and recovery of said goods and merchandises, or any part thereof, without prejudice to this insurance; . . . and to the charges whereof, the said Assurers will contribute according to the rate and quantity of the sum hereby insured.

Under this clause, the insured is required to do everything he can to save and preserve the goods in case of loss. If he fails to do this, he has violated a policy condition and loses his rights of recovery. This means that the insured must incur reasonable expenses such as salvage fees, attorney's fees, or storage, for which he may be expected to be reimbursed by the insurer, even if such expenses fail to recover the goods. It is possible for the insured to recover for a total loss plus sue and labor charges even if the face amount of the policy proceeds is exhausted.

Abandonment

In ocean marine insurance two types of total losses are recognized, actual and constructive. *Actual total loss* occurs when the property is completely destroyed. *Constructive total loss* occurs when, even though the ship or other subject matter of insurance is not totally destroyed, it would cost more to restore it than it is worth. Under American law, before constructive total loss is said to have occurred, the damage must equal 50 per cent or more of the ship's value in an undamaged condition, while under English law, damages must exceed 100 per cent of the ship's sound value. In most hull policies the English rule is stated as a policy provision. Such a provision says that if it costs more to repair the ship than its agreed-on value as stated in the policy, the ship may be abandoned to the insurer and the insured collects the full amount of his policy. The salvage then belongs to the insurer who is usually in a better position to dispose of it than the insured, since the insurer deals with salvors all over the world and is experienced in such matters. Abandonment is not permitted in any line of insurance except marine.

Subrogation

The ocean marine insurance contract provides for subrogation rights against liable third parties for damage to insured property. The principle of subrogation was discussed on pages 182 and 183.

Warehouse-to-warehouse clause

Under the terms of the *warehouse-to-warehouse* clause, such protection as is afforded under the insuring agreement extends from the time the goods leave the warehouse of the shipper, even if it is located far inland, until they reach the warehouse of the consignee.

Other insurance clause

Unlike other forms of insurance, the ocean marine contract specifies that if there shall be more than one insurer covering a given interest, each policy shall contribute to the loss in the order of the date of its attachment. In case two or more policies attached on the same date, each would contribute in the proportion that the face amount of each policy bears to the total insurance. For example, suppose a hull valued at $100,000 is insured for $75,000 by Company A on January 1; for $15,000 by Company B on January 2; and for $10,000 by Company C on January 2. The hull suffers a $60,000 loss. How would the insurers settle the claim? Under the other insurance clause, Company A would have to pay the entire amount, since it had coverage attached before that of Companies B and C. If the loss had been $85,000, Company A would have paid $75,000 and Companies B and C would have divided the remaining $10,000 of loss in the proportion $\frac{3}{5}$ and $\frac{2}{5}$ respectively.

Coinsurance

While there is no "coinsurance" clause as such in the ocean marine policy, losses are settled as though each contract contained a 100 per cent coinsurance clause.[4] Ocean marine contracts are usually "valued." Total losses result in an enforceable claim for the entire limit of liability as stated in the policy, and partial losses are determined, insofar as possible, by sale of the damaged article or by independent appraisal.

---

[4] See page 211 for an explanation of coinsurance.

In general, since it is usual for the insured and the insurer to agree on a full valuation in advance, there are no coinsurance penalties involved. Occasionally, however, the value of a cargo may rise or fall during the course of shipment. Assume that a certain shipment is valued at $1,000 at the time of shipment and at the time of arrival, it is found to be damaged. To determine the loss, the article is sold in damaged condition and brings $600. It is determined that if the article had been undamaged, it would have brought $1,500. Thus, the loss is $900. The ratio of $900 to $1,500, or 60 per cent, is the percentage of sound value which is lost. This percentage is then applied to the amount of original valuation $1,000 and the insured recovers $600 or two thirds of his loss. The insured has received a total of $1,200 on cargo worth $1,500. If he had taken out $1,500 of insurance, he would have received 60 per cent of $1,500, or $900, from the insurer and $600 from the sale of the damaged goods, or a total of $1,500. Since he failed to carry the full value of the goods, even though this failure was inadvertent, he becomes a coinsurer.

Usually cargo policies contain wording which values cargo at "invoice plus 10 per cent." The additional 10 per cent coverage provides a hedge against the possible rise in value of a shipment and the resulting coinsurance penalties. If the value of cargo falls, it is possible, of course, for the insured to collect more than his actual cash loss. Since the insured seldom has control over fluctuations in value or over conditions causing losses, little or no moral hazard exists. The fact that an insured may occasionally collect more than his actual loss is of little significance.

Warranties in ocean marine insurance

There are, in general, two types of warranties in marine insurance —express and implied. *Express* warranties are written into the contract and become a condition of the coverage relating to potential causes of an insured event. *Implied* warranties are an important condition of coverage too; however, they are not written into the policy but become a part of it by custom. Breach of warranty in marine insurance voids the coverage, even if the breach is immaterial to the risk.

Express warranties. Express warranties are often used to effect certain exclusions. Examples of express warranties are:

1) The F. C. & S. (Free of Capture and Seizure) warranty.
2) The S. R. & C. C. (Strike Riot and Civil Commotion) warranty.
3) The delay warranty.
4) The trading warranty.

1) F. C. & S. warranty. Under the *F. C. & S.* warranty, both parties agree that there shall be no coverage in case of loss from such perils as capture, seizure, confiscations, weapons of war, revolution, insurrection, civil war, or piracy.

2) S. R. & C. C. warranty. Under the *S. R. & C. C.* warranty, it is agreed that the insurer will pay no loss due to strikes, lockouts, riots, or other labor disturbances.

3) Delay warranty. Under the *delay* warranty, the insurer excludes loss traceable to delay of the voyage for any reason, unless such liability is assumed in writing.

4) Trading warranty. A class of express warranties known as *trading warranties* is important in ocean marine insurance. Examples of trading warranties are warranties restricting the operation of the ship to a given area, such as a certain coastal route; warranties specifying that the insurance issued represents the true value of the ship or other interests; and warranties restricting the time during which the ship may operate, such as only during the open season on the Great Lakes.

Implied warranties. There are three implied warranties in marine insurance. These relate to: 1) seaworthiness, 2) deviation, and 3) legality.

1) Seaworthiness. If a ship leaves port without being in safe condition, the implied warranty as to seaworthiness has been breached and the entire coverage is immediately void. If the ship were seaworthy when it left port but became unseaworthy later on, the warranty is not breached. Seaworthiness involves such factors as having a sound hull, engines in good running order, qualified captain and crew, proper supplies for the voyage to be undertaken, and sufficient fuel.

2) Deviation. The warranty as to deviation is breached when a vessel, without good and sufficient reason, departs from the prescribed course of the voyage, but without the intention of abandoning the voyage originally contemplated. The liability of the insurer ceases the moment that the ship departs from its course; but mere intention to deviate, not accompanied by an actual change of course, does not relieve the insurer of liability. Undue delay may constitute a deviation. The deviation or delay does not have to increase the hazard of the voyage in order to release the insurer, because, as noted before, any breach of warranty, regardless of whether or not the warranty was material to the risk, voids the contract. Even if the ship later resumes course and then suffers a loss, there is no coverage unless later negotiations with the insurer have restored the insurance.

The ocean marine policy is often written to waive or to alter the implied warranties of deviation and seaworthiness. After all, a shipper of grain from the midwestern part of the United States seldom has any control over the type of ocean conveyance in which his goods are ultimately carried to their final destination. Yet he would be deprived of protection under his cargo policy if it turned out that the shipping company violated one or more of the implied warranties. Therefore, the insurer typically inserts a clause excusing him from the effect of implied warranties. For the hull owner, the policy may provide that permission is granted to "touch and stay" at a certain port en route to the final destination. This does not mean, however, that the ship can stop at any port desired, or even that the ship may stop at the named port for purposes not connected with the voyage. To do so would constitute a deviation.

There are certain causes which will excuse a deviation that has not been authorized by contract. These fall into two main groups: (1) unavoidable necessity and (2) aiding in saving human life. *Unavoidable necessity* may be proved when a ship is blown off her course or puts into a port of distress, deviates to escape capture, is taken over by mutineers, or is carried off her course by a warship. *Aiding in saving human life* is illustrated when a ship deviates to help a vessel in distress. It is to be noted, however, that deviation to save *property* is not permitted.

If a voyage is changed or abandoned, the insurance ceases from the moment the decision is made to alter the voyage. Thus, if a ship leaves from New York and clears for London, but five miles out of port decides to go to Lisbon instead, the coverage stops at that point even though she may proceed on the same track for several days because the route for the two ports is identical for most of the voyage.

The reason for these rather strict rules is that without them, the insurer would never know what his real risk is and would be saddled with risks he never contemplated. Ocean marine insurance rate-making is a highly subjective matter, and each voyage commands a different rate because of different circumstances. It is necessary that the underwriter be able to rely on the knowledge that the voyage for which he has quoted a premium will be the actual voyage undertaken.

3) Legality. The implied warranty of legality is one that is never waived. If the voyage is illegal under the laws of the country under whose dominion the ship operates, the insurance is void. Under the laws of the United States, insurance on a ship engaged in running rum would be void, but such a purpose might not be illegal under the laws of another country, and in that country the insurance contract would be enforceable. To provide insurance against an illegal enterprise is obviously against public policy and this accounts for the fact that the illegality warranty cannot be waived.

LAND TRANSPORTATION INSURANCE

In the early period of industrial development, buyers of goods generally took delivery at an ocean port and conducted most of their business from that port. With the growth of inland centers of commerce, inland shipments of ocean cargo by way of railroad or canal became common and pressure grew for an extension of the ocean marine contract to cover the perils of land transportation. The warehouse-to-warehouse clause was developed to meet this need. But the ocean marine contract was not suited to the needs of land transportation insurance and so there developed a branch of insurance known as inland marine.

The marine definition

Inland marine insurance is defined in what is known as the *nationwide marine definition* of the National Association of Insurance Commissioners. This definition, first formulated in 1933 and completely revised in 1953, serves as a guide for regulatory authorities in governing rating procedures, underwriting methods, contract provisions, and other matters. The five subjects of insurance that are recognized include contracts covering: 1) imports, 2) exports, 3) domestic shipments, 4) instrumentalities of transportation and communication, and 5) "floaters," which are policies on movable property.

One of the important reasons for adopting a uniform definition of what constitutes marine insurance arises from the fact that rate regulation applicable to fire insurers is generally much more rigid than that applicable to marine underwriters. Before the definition was adopted, there was a tendency for marine underwriters to insure subjects, such as property in fixed locations, which normally would have been insured by fire underwriters. The greater flexibility in rating and in coverage enjoyed by the marine underwriters had a tendency to undermine the rating formulas imposed upon fire underwriters who were rapidly losing business. In general, the common requirement of all subjects of insurance in the marine definition is that there must be some element of transportation or communication involved in their handling. This means, for example, that real estate which has nothing to do with transportation or communication cannot be insured under a marine insurance policy. As for personal property, it is possible to insure such goods under either a marine policy or a multiple-line policy, regardless of whether the goods are situated at a fixed location or are in transit. This has been made possible by the adoption of multiple-line laws that give an insurance company the right to design contracts which are all-inclusive in nature.

The nationwide marine definition does not distinguish between inland or ocean marine insurance. It permits insurance on certain classes of goods and contains a section of prohibited risks. In general, the basis for differentiating permitted from prohibited risks is the mobility of the goods.

1) Imports and 2) Exports. Imports and exports may be covered under marine contracts so long as the perils of transportation are included. When goods lose their identity as shipments, they are no longer eligible for coverage under a marine policy. Thus, an import loses its characteristics as an import when it is sold and delivered by the importer, or when it is removed from storage and placed on sale as part of the importer's stock in trade, or when it is delivered for manufacture or processing.

3) Domestic shipments. Domestic shipments may be insured under a marine contract so long as the policy covers the perils of transportation. Goods qualify for coverage while they are in a fixed location of a customer who has them on consignment, or in a warehouse of a carrier where storage is incident to their transportation. However, such goods may not be covered under a marine contract while they are at the factory or warehouse location of the owner.

4) Instrumentalities of transportation and communication. Bridges, tunnels, piers, wharves, docks, pipelines, power transmission and telephone lines, radio and television towers, outdoor cranes, and loading bridges are among the so-called instrumentalities of transportation and communication which may be insured under a marine insurance contract. However, there are some restrictions on the coverage of these objects. For example, bridges and tunnels are not eligible under the marine policy if the only perils to be insured are fire, lightning, windstorm, sprinkler leakage, hail, explosion, earthquake, riot, or civil commotion. In other words, the policy would have to insure such transportation perils as collapse or cave-in, in addition to those listed above, before the property would be eligible for marine insurance.

5) *Floaters.* The marine definition lists 25 different types of floater policies which may be issued. Seven of these policies cover private individuals and the remainder are designed for either business use or personal use. A *floater* policy may be used to insure goods of a movable nature wherever they may be located, whether in transit or in the permanent location. However, floaters are often much more restrictive than this, and cover goods only under certain conditions while away from their normal location. Floaters may be all-risk or specified peril, most being of the latter type. Examples of personal floaters are personal property floater, tourists' floater, personal effects floater, and fur and jewelry floaters. Examples of business floaters are those that cover patterns and dies, contractors' equipment, animals, property on exhibition, jewelers' stocks, merchandise held on a floor-plan financing basis, and signs. Floater policies are analyzed in detail in Chapter 13.

Inland transit policy

A basic contract covering domestic shipments primarily by land transportation systems is known as the *inland transit policy.* Sometimes called the *annual transit floater,* this form of insurance is designed for manufacturers, retailers, wholesalers, and others who ship or receive a substantial volume of goods. The contract usually covers shipments by rail and railway express and may cover coastal shipments by ship between ports on the eastern coast of the United States and the Gulf of Mexico. It covers goods in the hands of other transportation agencies when in connection with rail, railway express, or steamer shipments. Shipments by mail or by aircraft are not usually covered unless specifically named in the policy.

Perils. There is no standard form for the inland transit policy, but all such contracts follow a similar pattern. The contracts are typically written on a named perils basis, covering the perils of transportation, which include collision, derailment, overturning of vehicle, rising water, tornado, fire, lightning, and windstorm. Sometimes the policy covers theft of an entire shipping package, but it seldom covers pilferage except when the goods are shipped by express. In general, the policies exclude loss due to strike, riot, civil commotion, war, delay of shipment, loss of market, illegal trade, inherent vice of the goods, leakage, or breakage unless caused by one of the basic perils insured against. Among the types of property excluded are accounts, bills, deeds. evidences of debt, money, notes, securities, and exports after arrival at seaboard. Variations in these provisions are frequently negotiated between the parties. For example, an all-risk form for the inland transit policy is available for certain types of shippers, with the insuring clause reading "This policy insures against all risks of loss or damage to the insured property from any external cause (including general average and/or salvage charges and expresses) except as herein excluded."

Loss limits. The inland transit policy normally has several types of liability limits. For example, there will be a limit of loss of a given amount, often 5 per cent of the annual estimated shipments, while the goods are in the custody of any one shipping agency. There will be a limit of 10 per cent of the annual estimated shipments in any one casualty. For purposes of loss settlement, goods are valued at invoice cost plus any prepaid or advanced freight or other costs that are due on the goods.

Rates. As noted earlier, if the common carrier assumes the liability for loss of goods at their full valuation, the rates are considerably higher than if the goods are shipped under a released bill of lading, whereby someone else assumes liability for losses above a certain amount. The express agency, for example, charges 10¢ per $100 for any declared valuation in excess of $50, whereas the insurance rate will probably be about half of this amount,[5] depending upon the individual circumstances of the shipper's business. Furthermore, the insurance coverage is broader than the protection given by the express company, which insures only for the amounts for which it is legally liable. This liability is less than complete or absolute, as we have seen.[6] A deposit premium is required by the insurer and, the final premium is determined by audit at the end of the policy year.

Important conditions. The inland transit policy, as is true of most inland marine insurance contracts, is characterized by somewhat different conditions and provisions than prevail in the ocean marine policy. For example, if other insurance is applied on the risk, the policy provides that it is excess only. It is important that two policies with identical provisions not be placed in force or each would be "excess" over the other. The inland transit policy contains a 100 per

---

[5] Rates differ but are usually within the following ranges for each $100 of value: railway express, $.04–$.07; rail freight, $.02–$.04; truck, $.07–$.10; coastal steamer, $.12½–$.18.

[6] See page 281.

cent coinsurance clause, which formalizes the unwritten similar condition in ocean marine contracts. It also has a cancellation clause which provides that either party may end the agreement, with five days' notice thereof being a typical requirement if the insurer cancels. In contrast to the situation in ocean marine insurance, the inland transit policy may not be assigned or transferred without the written consent of the insurer. Unless otherwise provided, coverage under the inland transit policy is limited to the continental United States and Canada.

The inland transit policy, similar to the ocean marine form, contains both a subrogation and a sue and labor clause. In transportation risks, the loss is often caused by neglect of some other party, and so the right of subrogation by the insurer and the activities required by the sue and labor clauses are very important. Sometimes the common carrier insists that the shipper waive his rights of collection against the carrier for loss if an insurance company pays. In such a case, the insurer could not collect for negligence of the carrier, and if this is the situation, the insurer will charge a higher rate than he otherwise would. Often the inland transit policy contains a *no benefit to bailee* clause, under which the insurer retains its rights of subrogation against the common carrier for all loss for which the carrier is legally liable. In such a case, it is important that the insured does not also have an agreement with the common carrier that it shall not be obligated for any losses which the insurer pays. If two conflicting agreements exist, somewhat tedious devices are necessary to effect prompt collection of the loss from the insurer. The insurer, instead of paying the claim, loans the amount of the loss to the shipper-insured, attempts to collect from the carrier in the name of the shipper, and cancels the loan to the extent that collection is not made in full.

The blanket motor cargo policy

Insurance against loss of goods while being transported in a motor truck is written under two major forms, those protecting the interests of the shipper and those protecting the interest of the truckman for his legal liability to shippers in carrying their goods. The common carrier's legal liability to the shipper has been described previously.[7] In most states, a policy covering a truckman cannot be written to name the shipper as an additional insured or contain a clause making any loss payable to a shipper as his interest may appear. Therefore, it is not possible to have one policy do the work of two.

---

[7] See page 281.

The blanket motor cargo policy generally limits its coverage to certain perils, such as fire; collapse of bridges; overturn of the vehicle; collision; perils of the seas, lakes, and rivers, while the trucks are on ferries; flood; explosion; and windstorm. The exclusions vary in different contracts, but usually the following property and perils are not covered: accounts; money; notes; loss by leakage or breakage or to paintings or livestock except as a direct result of an insured peril; loss from egg breakage unless over 50 per cent of the shipping package is broken, and not over a specified sum in any event; strike; civil commotion; war; and illegal trade.

The blanket motor cargo policy is usually a named perils contract, but for trucks operating in interstate commerce, and in many states for those operating entirely within the state, the law requires that cargo insurance covering the trucker's legal liability be endorsed to provide all-risk coverage up to a stated limit, usually $1,000 per vehicle and $2,000 for any one disaster. When such a clause is required, the insurer has an agreement with the insured that if, because of this endorsement, the insurer is required to pay any sums that it otherwise would not have had to pay, the insured will reimburse the insurer for this amount. Thus, the effect of the endorsement [8] is not to give all-risk coverage to the truckman but to provide a guaranty of the truckman's solvency and credit. As such, the endorsement is really a bond. In case of loss not usually covered under the policy, the insurer will pay the claimant and then seek recovery from the insured truckman. The insurer, obviously, must make a careful investigation of the truckman's financial solvency and character before writing the coverage.

The question arises, should a shipper of goods purchase blanket motor cargo insurance in his own name or should he rely on coverage owned by the truckman, particularly if the truckman is required by law to carry all-risk coverage? There are certain dangers in relying upon the truckman's insurance for complete protection. In the first place, the truckman's policy only provides for his *legal liability* to the shipper, and this liability is not absolute. Thus, there would be no protection for loss due to "acts of God." Second, the limits of liability under the Interstate Commerce Commission endorsement are usually very small, much smaller than the value of the goods exposed in a typical shipment. Third, the shipper has no control over the insurance purchased by the truckman. The truckman's coverage could be voided

---

[8] Called the "Endorsement for Motor Common Carrier Policies of Insurance for Cargo Liability Under Section 215, Interstate Commerce Act."

or reduced in amount by nonpayment of premium, breach of warranty, coinsurance penalties, exclusions of various types, or by poor selection of an insurance carrier. A shipper relying on such coverage may discover that his confidence was entirely misplaced. Fourth, if the truckman's insurance is not collectible, it has often been found that the financial position of the truckman makes him more or less "judgment proof." This, of course, is not a generalization to be applied to all truckmen. Nevertheless, in general, truckmen have not enjoyed the same reputation for financial stability as have the railroads.

If the shipper of goods is satisfied in his own mind that none of the disadvantages noted above apply in his particular case, he may rely on the coverage provided by the truckman for at least some degree of protection. Otherwise, he would be advised to carry blanket motor cargo insurance covering his own interest. The rates for such coverage are based on the total value of shipments to be made during the year. A typical arrangement is for the shipper to take out such coverage, the premium being based on the haulage charges or on weights shipped, and to charge the truckman for the cost thereof.

Trip transit insurance

For the individual or business firm that makes only an occasional shipment, the trip transit policy is especially applicable. Covering on a named perils basis, this policy is written for a specific shipment of goods between named locations. The type of conveyance may be either a common carrier or a private carrier of some type, such as a horse-drawn vehicle, a public truckman, or a trailer. It is common to insure household furniture, merchandise, machinery, or livestock under trip transit insurance contracts. The perils insured, conditions, and exclusions are similar to the inland transit and blanket motor cargo contracts previously discussed. For example, leaking, marring, scratching, or breaking is excluded unless caused by certain named perils. This limitation is of special interest to shippers of household goods that are susceptible to damage by freight car movement.

As in other forms of transportation insurance, the trip transit policy is an inexpensive method of obtaining protection as compared to shipping under bills of lading that are not released. In a given situation, the freight charges under a released bill of lading were $1.00 per 100 pounds and charges for full value declared, $1.50. Thus, the carrier in effect charged $.50 per 100 pounds for "insurance" on the full value of the goods. Yet, a trip transit policy was available for only 10 cents per

100 pounds. Therefore, the insured could effect a saving of 40 cents per 100 pounds by using the trip transit policy. In many cases, however, the effect of minimum premiums is such that it may be cheaper not to use a trip transit policy but to rely on full common carrier liability for protection.

SUMMARY

1. Insurance on the risks of transportation, particularly ocean transportation, was one of the earliest forms of insurance to be employed. It has proved vital to an expanding industrial economy dependent on mass production and consequent need for wide distribution of goods.

2. Two of the factors increasing the demand for transportation insurance are the seriousness and frequency of losses from transportation perils and the fact that the legal liability of the common carrier for safe shipment of the goods is neither absolute nor complete.

3. The major types of policies in ocean marine insurance are contracts covering (a) the hull, (b) the cargo, (c) the freight, and (d) legal liability of the carrier for proved negligence. The coverage is broad, but is still on a named perils basis.

4. Ocean marine policies contain many types of deductible clauses. The two most common are the memorandum clause and the free of particular average (F.P.A.) clause. The former clause excludes losses to certain commodities on a franchise basis. Free of particular average conditions means that the policy will not pay for any partial loss to a single interest.

5. General average refers to a situation where all interests must contribute to a voluntary sacrifice, made for the good of all, which is successful in saving the ship from threatening total loss.

6. Warranties in ocean marine insurance are of extreme importance and any breach, no matter how slight, voids the contract. Express warranties are typified by trading warranties of various kinds. The implied warranties are those of seaworthiness, deviation, and legality.

7. Insurance on the perils of land transportation grew out of contracts of ocean marine. The marine definition delineates five types of insurance to be allowed as "marine insurance," with no distinction now being made between ocean and inland marine. The five groups are contracts covering (a) imports, (b) exports, (c) domestic shipments, (d) instrumentalities of communication and transportation, and (e) floater risks. The one element common to all these contracts is that the subject of insurance is essentially mobile, either actually or constructively.

8. The inland transit policy, the blanket motor cargo policy, and the trip transit policy are three basic contracts covering the perils of land transportation. In general, it is cheaper and better to use these policies than to rely on insurance covering the interest of the common carrier or upon the common law liability of the common carrier for safe carriage of the goods.

QUESTIONS FOR REVIEW DISCUSSION

1. A television play recently featured a drama about the experiences of a captain who insisted upon keeping with him at all times an aide whose qualifications as a sailor were in doubt. It developed that the captain was partially blind and relied on the good vision of this aide to help him perform his duties. What insurance implications does this story have to the shipowner? Explain.

2. In a recent case (Bolta Rubber Company v. Lowell Trucking Corporation, 37 N. E. (2nd) 873) a trucking company insured under a motor cargo policy to protect its legal liability as a common carrier. The policy contained a warranty that each insured truck would be equipped with a burglar alarm in good working order. A truck was held up. It was determined that the burglar alarm system had been turned off at the time of the hold up. The trucker was held liable for $1,000. The policy contained the Interstate Commerce Commission endorsement required for truckmen in interstate commerce. Discuss the liability and rights of the insurer and the truckman.

3. List at least six causes of loss for which an ocean-going common carrier is not liable at common law.

4. A ship is lost by collision with an iceberg. The owners of cargo claim that the tragedy would not have occurred if the captain had steered a more southerly course. In your opinion, is the captain guilty of negligence, or is the loss caused by one of the acts of God over which no control is exercised and for which liability does not exist on the part of the common carrier? Discuss.

5. In Vernon v. American Railway Express Company S.W. 913 (Mo. 1920), the court held that extraordinarily hot weather at a particular time was a cause for which the common carrier was not liable. Under what conditions might the court have held otherwise, *i.e.,* that the carrier would be liable for such a loss? Discuss.

6. If the common carrier is responsible for the safe carriage of the goods, why is insurance necessary? Explain.

7. Explain the role of the released bill of lading in transportation insurance.

8. Why is an ocean cargo certificate considered such a valuable device in facilitating foreign commerce?

9. What basic interests are insured in ocean transportation insurance?

10. The antiquated wording in the 1779 Lloyd's ocean perils clause is retained in its essential outline in modern-day policies. Suggest reasons for this.

11. What coverage is added to the ocean marine contract by the R.D.C. clause? by the P.&I. clause? Contrast these two clauses.

12. A shipment of 1,000 bags of flour valued at $5 per bag is shipped by ocean transport from San Francisco to Rio de Janeiro. The shipment is insured under an ocean marine open cargo insurance policy containing the following clause: *"Free of particular average* under 3% unless caused by the vessel being stranded, sunk, burned, or in collision, each package

separately insured." One hundred (100) bags of flour are damaged to the extent of $500, by a peril insured against.

(a) Explain briefly the italicized term, free of particular average, as it is used in ocean marine insurance.

(b) What is the amount of the liability, if any, of the recovery by the shipowner for this damage by fire?

13. A shipowner insures his $100,000 hull under a typical ocean marine hull insurance policy for $75,000. A fire causes damage resulting in a repair cost of $10,000. What is the extent, if any, of the recovery by the shipowner for this damage by fire?

14. The *S. S. Victory* lost all her power after going under the Golden Gate Bridge of San Francisco. The captain immediately tossed out the anchor, but due to the heavy current produced by the tide, found that his vessel was drifting dangerously near the rock-ledged coast. Rather than risk drifting onto the rocks before he could develop any power, he called for two tugs to come out and pull him clear. The cost of this service amounted to $1,120. The *S. S. Victory* is valued at $2 million, the collect freight expected from pursuance of the voyage is stated at $75,000, and the total cargo carried is valued at $725,000. The cargo of the Smith Company is valued at $5,000.

(a) Would Smith Company incur any liability as a result of this action? If so, what would such liability be?

(b) Would the insurer pay such a loss?

15. The *S. S. Victory* runs aground as it enters the harbor at Honolulu. Due to various contingencies, it is impossible to refloat her before a storm strikes. Considerable damage is done to the vessel and the cargo, especially to the Number 3 hold in which the Smith Company's merchandise (pens and pencils) is packed. The pens and pencils are so badly battered that in order to save the shipment from being a total loss, it is necessary that $2,000 be spent on reconditioning them. The Smith Company seeks recovery from the insurer for the entire $5,000 for which the shipment is insured on the grounds that there is actually a total loss. Do you agree? Why or why not?

16. (a) Explain in your own words the meaning of general average.

(b) Why should the various interests be required to pay such claims?

17. "A particular average is not a total loss of a part of a shipment." If this is so, just how would you describe particular average?

18. A ship ran aground and the captain hired salvage vessels to pull her off before an approaching storm broke her upon the rocks. The salvors worked all night, managing to save most of the crew, but the ship was a total loss. Is the recovery under the ocean marine policy limited to the full value of the ship? Explain why or why not.

19. Why is abandonment permitted in ocean marine insurance and not in most other lines of insurance?

20. A shipowner insures his ship with Company T on July 1 for $100,000. Later, on July 5, fearing he does not have sufficient coverage, he takes out

another $50,000 policy with Company U.

(a) In the event of a $30,000 loss to the hull, how would the two companies divide the claim? Explain.

(b) What would the settlement be if the loss were $60,000? Explain.

21. Contrast the situation outlined in Question 20 to a similar case in which a cargo owner insures his cargo under the inland transit policy.

22. A shipper of grain to a foreign port by ocean transportation insured his goods for their full value, $25,000, under an ocean marine cargo policy. When the goods arrived, it was found that they had suffered a 50% damage. However, the price of grain had fallen so that the remaining grain brought only $10,000 on the open market.

(a) For what amount is the insurer liable? Explain.

(b) What would your answer have been if the price had risen instead and the remainder of the shipment had brought $15,000? Explain.

23. Does the fact that most ocean marine policies are "valued" introduce a moral hazard in their underwriting? Explain why or why not.

24. "Warranties in marine insurance are both express and implied." Give examples of each type.

25. A captain received a radio message that a storm had blown overboard valuable boxes of cargo belonging to a ship some 50 miles from his course. The message requested assistance in recovering these goods.

(a) Should the captain respond favorably to this request? Why or why not?

(b) Under what circumstances would you advise him differently than you did? Explain.

26. If a voyage policy contains the statement, "warranted that there shall be a crew of 25 on this vessel" and the vessel sails with 30 in the crew, is the insurance void? Why or why not?

27. (a) What main subjects of insurance are outlined in the nationwide marine definition?

(b) Is there any distinction between ocean marine and inland marine subjects?

28. A shipper purchased an inland transit policy with a "no benefit to bailee" clause. At the same time he had an agreement with the common carrier that in case of loss to the goods, the common carrier would be excused from paying any amounts recoverable from an outside insurer. Is there anything inconsistent in this arrangement? If so, how would the agreement be resolved in case of loss?

29. Is it generally true that it is cheaper to ship under a released bill of lading, and purchase outside insurance than to ship for full value declared? Suggest reasons why the insurance function might be performed cheaper by a party other than the common carrier. Discuss.

30. (a) What advantages, other than cost, are there in using an outside insurer rather than declaring full value with the common carrier?

(b) Why do these advantages apply particularly to truckmen?

Bailee Liability

(13)

and Inland Marine Floater Insurance

The practice of insuring property at a fixed location or while being transported by a common carrier from one location to another is well established. The need for coverage is universally recognized and owners of such goods rely on fairly standard contracts to protect them. Presenting a more difficult insurance problem is the risk of loss associated with property which is either not at a fixed location or is not being transported by a common carrier. How may the owner of such property make sure that he is not exposed to substantial losses?

For example, Contractor Brown owns $50,000 worth of equipment that is used in building bridges and roads. This equipment includes such items as cranes, tractors, diggers, winches, hoists, small tools, cement mixers, and cable. The equipment is being moved constantly from job to job and is exposed to losses from many types of perils, such as landslide, theft, flood, fire, windstorm, collision, explosion, and vandalism. Since the equipment is seldom located at any one place very long, coverage under traditional fire insurance forms is not suitable. Because the equipment is not being moved by, nor is in the custody of, common carriers, the usual transportation insurance forms are not applicable. Clearly, there is a need for giving specialized attention to Brown's problem. The answer is found in a "floater" policy, more particularly in the contractors' equipment floater, which is discussed in this chapter.

Similarly, how may one make certain that he will be reimbursed for loss to his goods while they are temporarily in the care and custody of others? For restitution in case of loss, must one rely solely on the good faith and, perhaps, the generosity of the holders of goods on consignment, goods at the warehouse, or property being repaired? Discussion of these and other questions form the content of this chapter.

The term *floater policy* has never been satisfactorily defined, but it is generally understood to be a contract of property insurance which satisfies three requirements:

1. Under its terms the property may be moved at any time.
2. The property is, in fact, subject to being moved; that is, the property is not at some location where it is expected to remain permanently.
3. The contract insures the goods while they are being moved from one location to another, that is, while they are in transit, as well as insuring them at a fixed location.

Contracts which qualify as floaters have been classified by the National Association of Insurance Commissioners in the nation-wide marine definition under two headings: (1) those covering businesses and/or individuals, and (2) those covering individuals only.

In this chapter we shall consider only a few examples in each of these categories. Under the first heading, bailee liability and business floater policies are analyzed. Under the second, the personal articles floater, the jewelry and fur floater, and the personal property floater are analyzed.

INSURANCE FOR BAILED PROPERTY

Bailee liability

A *bailee* is a person who has possession of property belonging to someone else. The owner of the goods is known as the *bailor*. Bailees include many different types of individuals in business or in personal life. The neighbor who borrows your lawnmower is a bailee, as is the neighbor who gratuitously stores your piano for you while you are away. The launderer, watch repairman, garageman, parking lot owner, dry cleaner, and warehouseman of furniture are all bailees.

The common carrier who transports goods is also a bailee. It is important to distinguish common carriers from other types of bailees primarily because of the difference in legal liability for goods entrusted to each type. As has been observed in Chapter 12, the common carrier is responsible for safety of the goods in his care except for certain definite reasons, such as acts of God, acts of a public enemy or a public authority, inherent vice of the goods, and acts of default on the part of the shipper. The common carrier is thus liable for negligence and also for other perils resulting in losses to goods (for example, fire or theft), unless the loss falls among the exceptions noted. Other bailees, however, such as warehousemen, are liable only when the proximate cause of loss can be traced to their negligence.

Negligence may be defined as the failure by a reasonably prudent individual to exercise the degree of care required by law under the circumstances. The degree of care required of the bailee varies with the conditions that gave rise to the bailment. Three different types of bailments are distinguished:

1) Bailment for the sole benefit of the bailor.
2) Bailment for the sole benefit of the bailee.
3) Bailment for the benefit of both parties.

1) Bailment for the sole benefit of the bailor.   When the bailee agrees to hold the goods of the bailor free of charge and primarily as an accommodation to the bailor, it is said that a *gratuitous bailment* exists. One who agrees to store in his garage his neighbor's trunk without charge is a gratuitous bailee. A minimum standard of care is required of such a bailee. He may not wantonly destroy the trunk, but, on the other hand, if the trunk is stolen from the unlocked garage, it would be difficult to believe that a court would hold him responsible because he failed to lock the building. Liability might exist, however, if the bailee removes the trunk to an unprotected driveway where it is damaged by a passing truck.

2) Bailment for the sole benefit of the bailee.   If a person borrows the property of another for his own use and benefit, he owes the bailor a much higher standard of care than is owed by the gratuitous bailee. The borrower is definitely liable for his own carelessness and owes it to the bailor to return the goods in satisfactory condition within a reasonable time. Thus, if John borrows Jim's lawnmower and while John has it in his possession it is stolen from an unlocked garage, the courts would probably hold John liable for the loss.

3) Bailment for the benefit of both parties.   Examples of bailment for the benefit of both the bailee and the bailor are the most common and of greatest interest. They include situations where the bailment is of a commercial nature, and both parties benefit. Thus, the laundry cleans clothing voluntarily submitted to it for this purpose for a stipulated price. The laundry bailee owes the bailor a reasonable degree of care, but the standard is not so high as when the benefit of the bailment is primarily for the bailee. Failure of the bailee to return the goods, or returning them in a damaged condition, will be interpreted as *prima facie* evidence of negligence unless the bailee can provide facts which reveal that he was not to blame. If the laundry building burns and it can be shown that there was no particular negligence on the part of the laundry, there is no legal liability to make restitution to the bailor. However, the laundry might wish to make restitution voluntarily in order to preserve the goodwill of its customers. It is for this reason that bailee insurance is in demand.

Insurable interest of the bailee

The question arises, is it permissible for a bailee to insure the goods belonging to another, where legal liability might exist for their destruction due to the negligence of the bailee? It has been long established that the answer is affirmative.[1] Ownership of the bailee in the goods is not necessary to establish an insurable interest. If the bailee's negligence causes a loss to the goods of a bailor and the bailee must reimburse the bailor, an insurable event exists because the bailee has suffered a financial loss due to accidental destruction of property.

The situation is not quite so obvious when a loss occurs to the goods of a bailor and it is determined that there is no legal liability on the part of the bailee. If there is no requirement that the bailee actually reimburse the bailor for his loss, has the bailee suffered any loss? If not, would the insurance contract be supported by an insurable interest? Upon reflection, it can be realized that the bailee, resting upon his legal right not to pay in such situations, would subject himself to the loss of the goodwill of his customers. The courts have decided that a contract to insure property of a bailor but issued in favor of a bailee is enforceable even if the bailee himself has no lien interest and is not legally liable for the loss which has occurred.[2]

The above legal doctrine is well established in the courts. The bailee's interest is called a *representative interest,* a name derived from the fact that the bailee, in applying for coverage really *represents* the interest of the bailor. The bailor has an equitable right to the proceeds of insurance collected by the bailee on the loss of goods belonging to the bailor. In other words, the bailee cannot collect on, or for, loss on the bailor's goods and then refuse to indemnify the bailor for his loss on the grounds that he was not legally liable for the loss. To hold otherwise would mean that the bailee would profit from someone else's loss. If the insurance coverage is insufficient to cover the interest of

---

[1] E. W. Patterson, *Essentials of Insurance Law* (New York: McGraw-Hill Book Company, Inc., 1957), p. 117.

[2] *Ibid.,* p. 127, citing *Waring* v. *Indemnity Fire Ins. Co.,* 45 N.Y. 606 (1871); *Fire Ins. Ass'n of England* v. *Merchants & Miners Trans. Co.* 66 Md. 339 (1887); *Home Ins. Co. of N.Y.* v. *Baltimore Warehouse Co.* 93 U.S. 527 (1876); and *Johnson* v. *Campbell,* 120 Mass. 449, 453 (1876).

both bailee and bailor in destroyed goods, the prevailing view is that the proceeds should be divided in proportion to their respective interests.[3]

Bailor coverage

Two interests in bailed property exist, the interest of the bailee and the interest of the bailor. The bailor may insure his property when it is in the hands of a bailee. For example, the typical fire insurance form covering the contents of a dwelling, allows up to 10 per cent of the insurance to be applied to property while it is located elsewhere than on the main premises. Thus, the bailor's interest in property in the hands of a bailee is covered for the specified perils and to a limited degree. The policy states that the coverage so provided shall not be for the benefit of any bailee. If it turns out that the bailee is legally liable for the loss, the fire insurer may, through its right of subrogation, proceed against the bailee for indemnification.

In a similar way, and with fewer limitations, the personal property floater, discussed below, protects the interest of the bailor. To illustrate, assume that Jones has a $10,000 fire insurance contract covering his personal belongings. He sends an expensive rug to the dry cleaners where it is accidentally damaged by fire when one of the cleaner's employees carelessly drops a cigarette on it. Under the terms of his contract, Jones may apply 10 per cent, or $1,000 of the face amount to cover this loss. His insurer will indemnify him and will attempt to determine if the dry cleaner, the bailee, is liable. Under the circumstances it appears that the dry cleaner, through negligence of his employee, is directly responsible for the loss and the insurer may collect the amount it has previously paid Jones. The dry cleaner is not permitted to benefit from insurance carried by Jones.

Bailees' customers contracts

Practically all insurers writing inland marine contracts issue a form of coverage known as the *bailees' customers policy*. While these policies are not standard, their provisions are similar. Written to cover bailees such as laundries, dry cleaners, tailors, upholsterers, cold storage companies, and silversmiths, the policy insures the bailee against losses to customers' property, whether or not the bailee is legally liable for the damage.

---

[3] *Ibid.*, p. 130.

Slightly modified forms are used to fit the special needs of each type of bailee. Although bailees' customers policies are not "all-risk," they cover a long list of perils, including fire, lightning, windstorm, hail, explosion, aircraft, vehicles, smoke, riot, strike, civil commotion, vandalism and malicious mischief, earthquake, sprinkler leakage, flood, theft, transportation perils, and "confusion" of property resulting from any of the above perils. *Confusion* refers to a loss due to the inability to identify the ownership of goods, even though they may not be destroyed.

Among the excluded losses are loss to goods from misdelivery, mysterious disappearance, failure to use all reasonable means to save and preserve the property from further loss at the time of the damage, theft from unattended vehicles, embezzlement or dishonesty of an employee, and while the goods are in permanent storage or in the hands of other processors. For at an additional premium, this latter exclusion may ordinarily be waived by endorsement. The usual policy will contain an exclusion for losses that would have been paid by other contracts had the bailees' customers policy not been in effect.

Bailees' customers policies commonly provide that small losses amounting to $100 or less may be settled with the customers directly by the insured. On larger claims, the insurer reserves the right to settle with the bailee or with the customer directly. Often there is no limit of liability except the actual cash value of the customers' goods destroyed. Rates are based on the fire rate and vary according to the gross receipts of the bailee and upon the particular territory in which the bailee is located. Under some forms, the insured must report gross receipts monthly and pay his premium monthly. Other forms, designed for small businesses, permit the insured to pay a deposit premium; the final premium is determined by an audit of gross receipts at the end of the year. The policy contains no expiration date but is continuous until cancellation by either party on notice ranging from five to thirty days.

Typical of the contracts designed for special classes of bailees' customers is the *furriers' customers policy*. Storage of furs gives rise to large concentrations of values in a single location, and thus is not only a favorite target for thieves but also presents the insurer with exposure to catastrophic loss due to fire and other physical perils. As a result, special provisions are incorporated into the contract. For example, the insurance covers only property for which a storage receipt is given. This receipt must specify to the customer how much insurance is being provided by the bailee on a particular garment and the limit of the furrier's liability for loss. There is a limit of liability for loss at each location used for storage of customers' property, a limit on furs in transit, an aggregate limit for any one loss, and a limit of liability at each location not used for permanent storage. The perils clause is "all-risk" but contains the usual exclusions such as loss due to moth, vermin, damage due to processing or work done on the goods, war, and failure to maintain protective safeguards.

Furriers' customers will often declare a lower value on a fur than its true worth in order to save on storage charges. Since the furriers' customers policy contains a limit of liability for the amount stated on the storage receipt, there is a possibility that if the fur is destroyed because of the negligence of the furrier, the customer can obtain a judgment against the furrier for an amount larger than may be recovered under his policy. To forestall such an event, the furrier is well advised to purchase, by endorsement, what is known as *excess legal liability coverage*. This endorsement, in effect, extends the insurance beyond the limits stated on the storage receipt, but only for losses caused by the negligence of the furrier.

INSURANCE ON FLOATING PROPERTY—BUSINESS

Block policies

The term *block* in insurance language, while having no precise meaning, connotes the general idea of a contract which is somewhat broader than the traditional forms of inland marine or fire insurance. A *block policy* covers *en bloc,* on an "all-risk" basis, the stock in trade or the equipment belonging to a business firm, no matter where the property happens to be located. In Chapter 10 the coverages known as the commercial property program (a development in multiple-line underwriting) were described. This program comes very close to providing for wholesalers and retailers generally what block forms provide for specific types of business firms. Since block policies on jewelers, furriers, camera and musical instrument dealers, and equipment dealers have been issued for many years by inland marine insurers, these and a few other types of firms are not eligible for the commercial property coverage program. Block policies will be discussed in some detail because of this fact and because these forms tend to set the pattern for the more general commercial property coverage program as it is being extended to more and more types of commercial institutions.

Jewelers' block policy. One of the oldest and broadest of all block contracts, the *jewelers' block policy,* is written to insure all the stock in the trade of a typical jeweler on an "all-risk" basis. Thus, such property as jewels, watches, precious metals, glassware, and gift items are covered whether they belong to the jeweler or to a customer, or whether they belong to another firm and are in the store on consignment and the jeweler is legally liable for their safety or has a financial interest in them.

The jewelers' block policy covers not only property belonging to the jeweler as an owner, but also property of the customer bailor. Thus, the jewelers' block policy is another example of bailee liability insurance. Its coverage may be extended to insure property anywhere in the world, and while in transit to or from the jeweler's place of business, such as while the property is in the hands of messengers, salesmen, customers (on approval), common carriers, other jewelers, repairmen, the post office, or the railway express agency.

The jewelers' block excludes the perils of war; dishonesty of the insured; dishonesty of employees (a peril best insured under a bond); inherent vice of the goods; earthquake or flood at the insured's premises; breakage of fragile articles unless occasioned by fire, lightning, and other typical perils; theft from a smashed show window; and mysterious disappearance or inventory shortage. The insured may remove some of these excluded perils, such as theft from a smashed show window or flood at the insured's premises, by paying an extra premium.

Excluded from coverage is certain property such as goods shipped by regular mail shipment instead of registered first-class mail; property left in any unattended vehicle by the insured; or property shipped by express, other than railway express. The policy is subject to certain limits of liability applying to given types of losses. For example, there will be a maximum liability expressed in the policy for property shipped by registered mail or railway express, for shipments handled by customer parcel delivery service, or for property in the custody of the insured's employees who are away from the main premises. In addition, deductibles ranging from $500 to $5,000 for any one loss are available (but not required), a feature which enables the insured to assume part of his own risk in exchange for a reduction of premium. A typical annual premium for the jewelers' block policy may range from $100 to $150, depending on the individual situation.

Because of the all-inclusive nature of the risk, the applicant for a jewelers' block policy is required to give in a proposal form complete information concerning his type of operation, system of accounting, description of safes and vaults, type of burglar alarm system, loss experience, personnel, nature of shipments, and inventory. Any misrepresentation by the insured on such an application voids the policy because the proposal is made a part of the contract.

It may appear that such elaborate contractual precautions are unnecessary and represent a suspicious attitude on the part of the underwriters of jewelers' block insurance. However, values in the jewelry business are very large and small packages may contain hundreds of thousands of dollars' worth of gems. In issuing coverage, the underwriter must rely on strong enforcement of safety precautions. For example, a central alarm system is perhaps the most effective means of detecting criminal action in a store. Special circuits, activated by such devices as electric eyes or wires attached to closed windows and doors, signal a central station which transmits any message to the police department for immediate action. Proper maintenance of such a system can easily mean the difference between success or failure of the burglar or robber, who as a class seems especially attracted to jewelry stores and the promise of easy riches. Therefore, the underwriter protects himself by inserting contractual provisions that require, as a condition of coverage, certain minimum standards of operation and safeguards on the part of the insured.

Camera and musical instrument dealers' policy. Another significant example of the "block" idea in inland marine insurance is the *camera and musical instrument dealers' form.* An all-risk policy, it covers all goods typically stocked by camera and musical instrument dealers while the goods are in transit or at any location in the United States or Canada. Like the jewelers' block policy, it covers both owned property and goods of others in the insured's custody for repair, delivery, or storage. To be eligible for this policy, the dealer must have at least 75 per cent of his business in cameras or musical instruments, as the case may be. Radios, television, and phonograph sets are not considered musical instruments, but for insurance purposes they may be stocked by musical instrument dealers and insured under the policy so long as their sale does not exceed 25 per cent of the dealer's total sales. Certain types of property, such as goods delivered to customers on conditional sales contracts, goods in the course of manufacture, accounts, bills, money, furniture and fixtures, and tools and machinery, are excluded.

Among the perils that are excluded from the policy are war; theft in unattended, unlocked vehicles; earthquake and flood at the dealer's premises; breakage of fragile articles (unless occasioned by physical perils such as fire, lightning, theft, windstorm, or collision of conveyances); mysterious disappearance; wear and tear; and dishonesty of the insured or his employees. These exclusions are similar to those in the jewelers' block form and are typical of most block policies.

Among the conditions of the camera and musical instrument dealers' form are:

1. A $25 deductible is applied to all losses except those from major physical perils such as fire, lightning, the perils of extended coverage, and burglary and holdup.
2. Detailed, up-to-date records of insured property both on and off the premises, as well as records of all sales, must be maintained.
3. The policy is considered excess over any other applicable insurance.
4. The insured must maintain any watchman service, burglar alarm system, or other protective devices as were in effect at the time the policy was taken out.
5. For forms written on an annual basis with a specified premium, an 80 per cent coinsurance clause is required and adequate insurance limits on all property, both in transit and at the premises, must be maintained. (The insured may use a reporting form under which he reports values monthly, and in this event, the coinsurance clause is not required.)

The camera and musical instrument dealers' form is subject to a minimum premium of $100. The rate is based on the fire rate in the territory served, and total premiums depend on the limits chosen by the insured. There are several types of limits, both specific and aggregate, within the form. For example, the policy provides a limit of liability on property while situated at the insured's premises, while in transit, while in the custody of employees away from the premises (for example, salesmen's samples), and while off the premises and not in the custody of an employee (for example, goods sold on approval).

Equipment dealers' policy. A third example of an "all-risk" block form is the *equipment dealers' policy,* designed for retailers and wholesalers of heavy agricultural and construction equipment, such as road scrapers, bulldozers, pneumatic tools, compressors, harvesters, tractors, binders, reapers, plows, and harrows. The policy covers property belonging to others in the insured's control, but excludes automobiles, trucks, motorcycles, aircraft, or watercraft, which are insured under automobile forms. Covered territories include the United States and Canada, except for shipments via the Panama Canal. Other provisions are similar to the two block forms already discussed.

Scheduled property floater risks

Many types of movable business property are insurable under a form known as the *scheduled property floater,* a general or skeleton form to which is attached an endorsement describing specific types of property and the conditions under which they are insured. The basic form contains fairly standard provisions such as subrogation, appraisal, loss adjustment, cancellation, and misrepresentation and fraud clauses. Losses are settled on an actual cash value basis. The policy provides that it is to be excess over any other collectible insurance on covered property. Some of the scheduled floaters are all-risk, but a majority are on a named-peril basis.

Included among the various types of property insured under the scheduled property floater are: contractors' equipment, mobile agricultural equipment, office machinery, salesmen's samples, theatrical equipment, railroad rolling stock, oil-well drilling equipment, patterns and dies, goods on exhibition, neon and mechanical electric signs, radium, livestock, and instrumentalities of transportation and communication. Because inland marine floater forms covering these types of property are similar in nature, only two commonly used floaters—contractors' equipment floater and the livestock floater—will be discussed here.

Contractors' equipment floater. One of the most important classes of property insured under the scheduled property floater form is *contractors' equipment.* The contractors' equipment floater is typical of most of the floaters on scheduled property that are listed above. Contractors have a special need for protection against the many perils that can cause loss to movable equipment. Very large sums are often invested in a single piece of equipment which is used under conditions that are basically dangerous. For example, road-building caterpillars are commonly valued from $40,000 upward. Fire, landslide, collision with other equipment, falling rock, and flood are not uncommon causes of total loss.

Contractors normally work under time deadlines, with severe penalties applying if they are not met. If important items of equipment are damaged or destroyed at a time when the owner has most of his ready capital already invested in the job, the need for immediate indemnity for the loss becomes apparent. Without insurance, the contractor may lose not only the funds invested in equipment, but also the profits on the job in which the funds were employed because of construction delays incurred while credit arrangements are made for equipment replacements.

Not all contractors' equipment floaters are the same, but, in general, the following perils are covered: fire, lightning, collision or overturning of a vehicle on which the equipment is being transported, explosion, collapse of bridges, windstorm, earthquake, landslide, flood, and theft. Sometimes deductibles are applied to certain types of perils, such as theft and collision. The form usually contains the following perils exclusions: wear and tear, war, riot, strike, civil commotion, infidelity of employees, overloading of lifting equipment, and damage to electrical apparatus unless caused by fire.

The contractors' equipment floater insures such items as tractors, steam shovels, cement mixers, scaffolding, pumps, engines, generators, hoists, drilling machinery, hand tools, cable, winches, and wagons. In fact, all items of equipment used by a contractor, except motor vehicles designed for highway use, such as trucks, trailers, and road tractors, are covered. The contractor may schedule all items, with a given amount for each, or he may name a blanket amount of coverage, in which case an 80 per cent (or higher) coinsurance clause is required. The floater covers property whether it is owned, leased, or borrowed. Insurance attaches no matter where the property is located. However, property permanently situated at a given location is not eligible for coverage under this floater. Property such as designs, plans, surveying equipment, and underground cable, is usually excluded.

While there is no standard rating system for the contractors' equipment floater, the fire rate in each territory usually serves as a basis. The rate is then modified on a judgment basis according to the particular perils and exclusions stated on the given contractors' equipment floater and according to the type of equipment mainly involved. The annual premium will typically range between one and three per cent of the value of the equipment insured.

Livestock floater. Illustrating the flexibility of coverage that is possible in inland marine floaters on scheduled property is the *livestock floater,* available to owners of cattle, horses, hogs, sheep, and mules, whether these animals are kept for farming purposes or otherwise. This floater, which is on a named-peril basis, gives world-wide insurance to the owner against loss of death or destruction of the animal due to such perils as fire, lightning, windstorm, hail, explosion, riot and civil commotion, smoke, aircraft, collision with vehicles, theft, overturn of conveyances, earthquake, flood, and sinking or stranding of vessels while the animals are being transported.

Among the excluded perils are war, mysterious disappearance, escape, and infidelity of an employee or a person to whom the property is entrusted, except a carrier for hire. Certain types of losses are excluded, such as loss of use, extra expense occasioned by loss of the animal, and accidental shooting by the insured. Neither death due to sickness or disease nor veterinarian expenses are covered under this form, unless the proximate cause of the loss is one or more of the perils insured against.

An optional perils rider, available at extra cost, may be endorsed on the livestock floater to cover death or destruction due to accidental shooting by someone other than the insured or his employees, attack by dogs or wild animals, collapse of building, drowning, and by artificially generated electricity.

The livestock floater can be written to cover newly acquired animals up to 30 days after their acquisition. However, not all types of livestock may be insured. Race horses, for example are not eligible, nor is livestock belonging to others under policies issued to auction houses, veterinarians, or humane societies. Circus, carnival, or theatrical animals; livestock being transported to or from stockyards; and livestock turned out on winter ranges are not eligible. Special forms are available for these classes.

The *winter range livestock floater* covers herds of cattle or sheep turned out during the winter from October to May at given range locations against death or destruction from the same perils insured under the livestock floater (except riot, earthquake, and theft), and in addition, against freezing, smothering, or blizzards. The winter range livestock floater, however, has no provision for adding coverage against accidental shooting or drowning, or attack by dogs or wild animals as is true in the livestock floater. Furthermore, the policy will not restore more than 75 per cent of the actual cash value of any animal lost. Young animals under 60 days of age and sheep without at least 60-day fleece are not covered, nor is loss due to the failure of the insured to use all reasonable means to save and to preserve his property from the perils insured against.

The rates which apply to the livestock floater range from three fourths of one per cent of exposed values, without the optional perils endorsement, to two per cent, with the endorsement. The rate applicable to the winter range livestock floater is two and one half per cent of exposed values for the season, with a minimum premium of $100. In consideration of these rates, the livestock floater is written with an 80 per cent coinsurance clause. If the policy covers animals of others in the custody of the insured, care should be taken to provide coverage of at least 80 per cent of the maximum values exposed in order to avoid coinsurance penalties.[4]

Miscellaneous business floaters

There is a wide variety of miscellaneous business floaters, each designed to meet a specific need for insuring property in a given situation. While no attempt will be made to list them all, or even to classify them, two will be discussed as examples of the wide range of risk management problems which can be at least partially solved by the use of inland marine floaters.

The conditional sales floater—its economic rational. Of all retail sales of consumer goods, it is estimated that approximately one third represent credit sales, and that of all credit sales, one third are installment sales. Thus, the value of unpaid-for property in the hands of credit buyers is tremendous. In July, 1961, there was $10.6 billion of installment credit outstanding on goods other than automobiles.[5] The question arises, who loses if the goods are destroyed by some insurable peril before they are paid for. Clearly, the seller has an interest in the goods to the extent of the unpaid balance, and the buyer has an interest to the extent of his equity. Legally, the buyer is required to pay for the

---

[4] This problem, which is common to other types of insurance arrangements in which the coinsurance clause is operative, may be illustrated briefly as follows: Assume that an insured covers $10,000 worth of livestock under a floater with an 80 per cent coinsurance clause. The policy is written to cover animals sold to others but awaiting delivery. The policy has a face amount of $8,000 and thus meets the coinsurance requirements. However, the insured purchases $5,000 worth of new animals which he immediately resells to a buyer for delivery in four weeks. The total value of the insured's herd is now $15,000 and under the terms of the coinsurance clause, 80 per cent or $12,000 of insurance is required. In the event of loss, the insured may collect only $\frac{8}{12}$ of his loss. The policy should be written to adjust automatically to this situation by means of a reporting form, or should have a sufficiently large face amount to cover the maximum value of the herd at any one time. Of course, an alternative method of coverage would be to exclude animals not belonging to the insured, placing this responsibility on the buyer.

[5] *Federal Reserve Bulletin*, (September, 1961), p. 1084.

goods even if they are destroyed, because he usually signs a note for the unpaid balance and is obligated to repay the note regardless of what happens to the goods. In practice, however, it may turn out that he has no funds and is more or less "judgment proof." The loss then falls on the seller. It must be admitted that it is often difficult for the seller to collect for a "dead horse."

Aside from the fact that collection of debts for goods that have been destroyed may be difficult and expensive, many sellers hesitate to force collection because of the danger of losing the goodwill of a customer who may not consider that it is fair to make payment for goods that "still belonged to the finance company." These customers need replacements for the lost property and represent a source of continued business which normally will be profitable. An antagonistic debt collector may cause the loss of this business.

Finally, many sellers consider it illogical to insure stock "to the hilt" while it is in their possession, only to expose the goods to possible loss when they are in the home of a customer with little or no equity in them and with the attitude of indifference toward loss which often characterizes an individual in these circumstances. Furthermore, scheduled property forms and block policies usually exclude from coverage property sold to others. For example, the jewelers' block policy excludes property sold on the installment plan. A conditional sales floater is necessary for complete coverage for the jeweler who sells a substantial volume of goods on credit.

Because of these considerations, the conditional sales floater has assumed somewhat greater significance as a tool of risk management among manufacturers selling on installment contracts and sales financing institutions and retail credit stores.

Basic provisions of the conditional sales floater. The conditional sales floater may be written to insure: 1) only the seller's interest in the goods, in which case the floater is known as a *single interest* form; 2) both the seller's and the buyer's interest, under what is called *double interest* form; or 3) on a *contingent* basis, where indemnity is paid to the creditor only if the debtor cannot be made to pay.

1) SINGLE INTEREST FORM. If a loss occurs under a *single interest* form, the customer's debt is canceled and the seller recovers the amount of the unpaid balance. There is no insurance on the customer's equity in the goods as is true in the double interest form.

2) DOUBLE INTEREST FORM. In the *double interest* form, if goods are destroyed by an insured peril, both the equity of the buyer in the goods and the unpaid debt are covered. For example, suppose Keeling has purchased a stereo set for $500 and still owes $300 on it at the time the set is destroyed by fire due to overheating in a tube. Fortunately, his creditor carries insurance on the double interest form of the installment sales floater. Keeling may recover the $200 he has already paid and the store recovers the $300 unpaid balance. The remaining debt of $300 is canceled. The policy is considered excess over any other insurance which covers the goods, so if Keeling is able to collect $500 from his fire policy covering building contents, there is no collection from the installment sales floater. Once the full purchase price has been paid, the installment sales floater coverage is terminated.

3) CONTINGENT FORM. Under the *contingent* form, the customer's debt is not canceled, nor is his equity in the goods covered. The seller is obligated to make full effort to collect the unpaid balance due. If the unpaid balance proves uncollectible, the insurer reimburses the seller for his loss. Contingent forms are written at a rate equal to approximately two thirds the rate of the other forms because the insurer expects to pay only for losses where the seller's customer is financially insolvent or has disappeared.

Although conditional sales floaters are not standardized, they usually cover the perils of the extended coverage endorsement to dwelling policies, perils of fire and lightning, transportation perils, water damage, earthquake, collapse of building, breakage in transit, and theft. Some insurers write "all-risk" coverage on certain goods, such as household appliances. Typical perils excluded are stealing by the buyer, inherent vice of the goods (for example, scratching, bending, and breakage of fragile articles), faulty internal wiring of electrical appliances, war, and illegal trade. Sometimes a flat dollar deductible is used for goods such as musical instruments, which are especially subject to breakage or other typical loss.

Shipments by mail. The United States Post Office is not a common carrier and has no liability for the loss of goods entrusted to it unless they are insured by the Post Office, therefore, anyone using the mails, and especially those sending a considerable volume of shipments annually by the mails, is in need of obtaining protection for his shipments. The insurance industry has designed forms to meet the needs of almost everyone, from the person sending only a relatively small volume of mail, to the shippers of very large values of securities and currency. The following list summarizes the major policies of this nature:

1) Parcel-post policy—covers merchandise shipments only.
2) First-class mail floater—three forms are available for different classes of customers sending securities, coupons, stamps, and other papers of value by first-class or certified mail.
3) Registered-mail floater—covers bonds, stocks, currency, bullion, precious metals, warehouse receipts, and other valuable shipments by registered mail or express.

Policies issued by private insurers generally offer the advantages of greater convenience, broader coverage, lower cost, and faster claims service than Post Office coverage. These advantages are more apparent to the large shipper than to the occasional shipper. For example, shipments under a registered-mail policy are covered from the moment they leave the premises of the sender until they arrive at the premises of the addressee, and not only during the time they are in the hands of the Post Office or the express company. Under the first-class mail floater, it is not necessary to wait in line at the Post Office to purchase insurance each time a shipment is mailed nor to trust a messenger to make proper arrangements each time. Each of these policies discussed below is "all-risk," with the chief exclusion being for the peril of war.

1) Parcel-post policy.   Covering shipments on an all-risk basis from the time they are in the custody of the post office until final delivery, the *parcel-post policy* is available for merchandise but not for money or securities. Perishable merchandise, packages not labeled "return postage guaranteed," packages bearing descriptive labels on the outside, and shipments not made in accordance with the General Parcel Post Act of 1912 are among the excluded items of property. There is a limit of liability of $100 on unregistered mail, and of $500 on registered mail.

Rates are less if shipments are registered or if government insurance is purchased. If government insurance is purchased, the amount must be for at least 50 per cent of the stated value of the shipment if the value is under $100; for values exceeding $100, at least $50 coverage must be purchased. Small shippers generally purchase the parcel-post policy on a coupon basis, whereby the shipper buys coupons costing 5 cents each and places these coupons on the package.

For ordinary mail (uninsured and unregistered), if the shipment is valued at $25 or less, one coupon is required; for values between $25 and $50, two coupons are required; and for values between $50 and $100, five coupons. For registered or government-insured parcel post, the cost is: for each package valued at $50 or less, one coupon; for each package valued between $50 and $100, two coupons; for each package valued over $150 but under $250, five coupons; and for each package over $250 and up to $500, eight coupons. Larger shippers generally buy the parcel-post policy on an annual or open form whereby monthly reports are made to the insurer for all insured shipments and premiums are paid on this basis.

2) First-class mail floater. Uses of the *first-class mail floater* enjoy all-risk coverage on incoming or outgoing shipments by first-class or certified mail. While the rates are somewhat higher than those charged for the registered-mail policy, considerable savings and added conveniences are effected for certain types of shipments by the use of first-class mail instead of registered mail. There are three forms of the first-class mail floater: Form A, Form B, and Form C.

FORM A. *Form A* allows coverage up to $50,000 per package and $500,000 per addressee, applying from the moment the package is placed in the hands of a messenger for mailing until it reaches the addressee. Government bonds and their coupons are not covered under this form. The insured is not required to insure every item of first-class mail he sends, but only those items on which he records and renders payment of premium to the insurer. No insurance is given to shipments not thus recorded. Rates are a flat charge per $1,000 of declared value. In one category, for example, rates range from 2 cents for nonnegotiable securities sent by certified mail to 48 cents for coupons sent by first-class airmail on shipments to specified financial institutions.

FORM B. *Form B* of the first-class mail floater enables the insured to avoid the requirement of recording each shipment and of paying a premium based on the values thus recorded. Under this floater, there is a flat charge of 10 cents per package for first-class mail or airmail, and 8 cents per package for certified mail, subject to a $50 minimum annual premium. However, there is a limit of liability of $500 per package under this form, and an exclusion for all currency and checks. Furthermore, Form B covers only shipments made by the insured, whereas Form A covers both incoming and outgoing shipments.

FORM C. *Form C* of the first-class mail floater is designed for bond indenture trustees, transfer agents, and registrars who send by first-class mail issues of their own securities. The top limit of recovery for a single package is $100,000. The policy gives the insured the right to have lost securities duplicated or reissued on behalf of the issuing company, and the insurer agrees in the contract to pay for this cost and to guarantee against any loss resulting from negotiation of the lost securities in case they fall into unauthorized hands. The rate for Form C is 7 cents per package, subject to a minimum annual premium of $50.

3) Registered-mail floater. The *registered-mail floater,* one of the oldest of inland marine floater policies, gives all-risk protection to a wide variety of shipments by either registered mail or express. Depending on the rate charged, coverage may be world-wide or restricted territorially. Except for currency, there are no stated limits of insurance; the coverage is equal to the values reported by the insured. For currency, the policy usually specifies a limit on any one shipment, often $250,000. If it is determined that the insured reported the full market value of securities at the time of mailing and the value of these securities had risen by the time of the loss, the amount payable to the insured may be higher than the original declared amount, subject to a maximum of 105 per cent of full market value at the time of shipment. Rates are based on each $1,000 of valuation and approximate 6 cents per $1,000 for registered mail or express, for shipments within the United States. Premiums may be quoted on a flat amount per package if desired.

INSURANCE ON FLOATING PROPERTY—PERSONAL

Personal articles not only represent a more sizable investment than many homeowners realize, but they are also subject to many more hazards, both physical and moral, than is true of real property. Theft of real property, for example, is next to impossible; but theft of movable property is not uncommon, as F. B. I. reports document all too well.[6] Water damage, freezing, and breakage are among the other perils especially destructive to personal property. A person who purchases a home on a long-term mortgage with a relatively low down payment will have only a small investment in his home, but he will probably have

---

[6] See page 436.

several times that amount invested in furniture, clothing, garden equipment, jewelry, and other articles. Underwriters estimate that in a typical room in the home of a middle-class family of four, the contents could not be replaced for less than $3,000 to $9,000 at 1961 price levels. Accurate data as to the average amount of physical peril insurance on personal property do not exist, but the experience of local agents generally will place the average amount at far less than the true replacement cost of the property.

Gradually, however, more people have become aware of the facts of underinsurance and the growing cost of replacing personal property. There exists a substantial demand for comprehensive insurance contracts that will cover personal articles of all types. Several approaches have been used by underwriters in meeting this demand. One approach has been the use of endorsements that extend the scope of the basic fire policies on dwelling contents, as described in Chapter 10. Another approach has been to offer inland marine floater policies on specific types of property, such as jewelry, furs, golfer's equipment, cameras, stamp collections, musical instruments, and outboard motor boats. A third approach has been the sale of comprehensive, all-risk floaters that cover personal property of almost any description, wherever located.

Personal articles floater

The *personal articles floater* is a skeleton form with basic provisions applying to endorsements that give coverage to specific items of personal property formerly insurable only under separate floaters, each with a minimum premium. The personal articles floater corresponds to the scheduled property floater for business discussed on page 315. The personal articles floater has a single minimum premium and gives an individual a chance to insure only the specific items of property he desires on an all-risk, world-wide coverage basis. This floater is used for one or more of the following types of property: furs, silverware, cameras, musical instruments, jewelry, fine arts, stamp and coin collections, and sporting goods. Newly acquired property of the same type as that insured under the floater is automatically covered for a period of 30 days. Typical excluded perils are war, wear and tear, gradual deterioration, moths, vermin, and inherent vice.

Personal jewelry and fur floater

The *personal jewelry and fur floater* may be written separately or attached to the personal articles floater. It gives all-risk coverage on scheduled items of jewelry and furs belonging to the insured and members of his family, no matter in what location or situation the items may be. Each article must be completely identified in the schedule, together with the value attributed to it. Usually, an independent appraisal of all insured items must be submitted with the application for the policy, along with a signed personal application giving full details as to the applicant's occupation, financial capacity, family background, etc. These precautions are necessary because of the great physical and moral hazard to which property of this nature is subject. Insurers generally refuse to write this type of insurance without the best of references and recommendations by agents who know the applicant's background. Annual rates for the personal jewelry and fur floater are established on a sliding scale, and range from 1.2 per cent for the first $5,000 of exposed values to .5 per cent for values in excess of $50,-000. There is a minimum premium of $10. A premium reduction of 10 per cent is given if the applicant accepts a $50 deductible.

The personal property floater

For those desiring an all-risk policy covering personal property on a "blanket" basis, the *personal property floater* (*PPF*) has been devised. One of the oldest of the inland marine floaters, this contract has gained widespread acceptance, and because of its basic importance, it will be analyzed in detail.

The basic distinction between the personal property floater and the personal articles floater is that the former may be written to cover not only specific items of property for stated amounts, but it may also cover *all* other nonbusiness personal property without scheduling each item separately. While there are different versions of the personal property floater, depending on which company issues the floater and which rating organization happens to sponsor it, the contract has become quite standardized. Figure 13–1 shows the first page of a typical form. The main features of this floater are discussed under the headings:

1) Property covered and excluded.
2) Limits of liability.
3) Perils excluded.
4) Coinsurance and deductibles.
5) Rating.

1) Property covered and excluded. The personal property floater covers personal property of a nonbusiness nature belonging to or borrowed by the insured or members of his household. Also included,

Figure 13–1

PERSONAL PROPERTY FLOATER

INLAND MARINE

PPF 1335
PERSONAL PROPERTY FLOATER

Attached to and forming part of Policy Number

issued to Frank Johnson
by National Insurance Company   at its Agency
located (city and state) New York, New York   Date March 12, 19--

PROPERTY COVERED

1. Personal property owned, used or worn by the person in whose name this policy is issued and members of the Assured's family of the same household, while in all situations, except as hereinafter provided.

PERILS INSURED

2. All risks of loss of or damage to property covered except as hereinafter provided.

AMOUNTS OF INSURANCE

3. Insurance attaches only with respect to those items in this paragraph for which an amount is shown and only for such amount.

ITEM	AMOUNT	
(a)	$ 6,000	On unscheduled personal property, except as hereinafter provided.
(b)	$ none	On personal jewelry, watches, furs, fine arts and other property as per schedules attached hereto. Each item considered separately insured.
(c)	$ none	On unscheduled personal jewelry, watches and furs, in addition to the amount of $250.00 provided in Paragraph 5 (b), against fire and lightning only.
TOTAL	$ 6,000	

(See other side for Paragraphs 4, 5 and 6)

DECLARATIONS OF THE ASSURED

7. The following are the approximate values of the unscheduled personal property, other than jewelry, watches and furs, as estimated by the Assured, at the time of issuance of this policy:

	Wherever Located	(Of which the following amounts involve personal property ordinarily situated throughout the year at residences other than principal residence.)
(a) Silverware and pewter	$ 365.00	($)
(b) Linens (including dining room and bedroom)	$ 385.00	($)
(c) Clothing (men's, women's, children's)	$ 610.00	($)
(d) Rugs (including floor coverings) and draperies	$ 750.00	($ N)
(e) Books	$ 150.00	($)
(f) Musical instruments (including pianos)	$ 200.00	($)
(g) Television sets, radios, record players and records	$ 250.00	($ O)
(h) Paintings, etchings, pictures and other objects of art	$ 375.00	($)
(i) China and glassware (including bric-a-brac)	$ 300.00	($)
(j) Cameras and photographic equipment	$ 150.00	($ N)
(k) Golf, hunting, fishing and other sports and hobby equipment	$ 215.00	($)
(l) Refrigerators, washing machines, stoves, electrical appliances and other kitchen equipment	$ 525.00	($)
(m) Bedding (including blankets, comforters, covers, pillows, mattresses, and springs)	$ 225.00	($ E)
(n) Furniture (including tables, chairs, sofas, desks, beds, chests, lamps, mirrors, clocks)	$2,625.00	($)
(o) All other personal property (including wines, liquors, foodstuff, garden and lawn tools and equipment, trunks, traveling bags, children's playthings, miscellaneous articles in basement and attic) and professional equipment, if any, covered under Paragraph 6(b)	$ 375.00	($)
TOTAL	$7,500.00	($)

NOTE: If the total value ordinarily situated throughout the year at residences other than the principal residence exceeds ten per cent of the amount of the insurance granted under Item (a) Paragraph 3, such excess value is not insured hereunder unless specifically endorsed hereon.

THE PROVISIONS PRINTED ON THE BACK OF THIS FORM ARE HEREBY REFERRED TO AND MADE A PART HEREOF.

....*Richard Roe*................Agent.

at the insured's option, is the property of visitors while on the described main premises, and even property of servants while located off the premises, if the servant is actually engaged in the insured's service and has the property in his physical custody at the time of the loss. In Figure 13–1, typical items of unscheduled property covered under the form are shown. This list is not intended to be all inclusive, however, since jewelry, furs, watches, and fine arts do not appear on the list but are covered just the same, subject to a limitation of amount. The policy also covers loss to the real property of the insured if it is damaged in the course of a theft or attempted theft.

Various items of personal property are excluded from coverage because other types of insurance are designed for them, or because their use involves hazards too great for an all-risk type of policy. For example, automobiles, aircraft, and motorcycles are excluded because special forms of coverage are designed for them. Animals, business or professional equipment (except books and instruments in the insured's residence at the time of loss), and property at an exhibition are subject to unusual hazards and are covered under more limited policies.

Certain types of property are excluded from coverage unless the loss is caused by certain named perils. Thus, eyeglasses, glassware, statuary, marble, bric-a-brac, porcelains, and other similar fragile articles (watches, jewelry, and cameras excepted) are not covered unless the loss was occasioned by theft, vandalism or malicious mischief, fire, lightning, windstorm, earthquake, or other listed perils.

2) Limits of liability. The personal property floater has many different types of clauses that limit the liability of the insurer for losses. The most important ones are listed below.

1. There is an aggregate limitation of the face amount of the policy, applying to all losses of scheduled property (see Section 3, Item (a), of Figure 13–1).
2. There is a limitation of $250 applying to any one loss of *unscheduled* items of jewelry, watches, or furs, unless this amount has been increased under Section 3, Item (c), in Figure 13–1. Under another endorsement the coverage on jewelry, furs, and watches may be increased on an all-risk basis to $1,000, subject to a $250 limit per item. Section 3, Item (b), of the floater (see Figure 13–1) provides for an aggregate limit on all *scheduled* property. The insurance liability for loss cannot exceed the stated value of each scheduled item.

3. Liability for loss cannot exceed 10 per cent of the aggregate amount as regards property ordinarily kept at residences other than the principal residence. This limitation does not apply to property kept at another residence on a temporary basis. However, it is expected that if two permanent residences are maintained, separate policies will be purchased in order to avoid granting free insurance.

4. There is a limit of liability of $100 on any one loss of money or $500 on any one loss of notes, securities, stamps, transportation tickets, or other valuable documents. Note that throughout the policy year, the insured could collect on several losses of $100 in money, but not more than $100 each time.

5. The limitation on recovery for loss cannot exceed the actual cost to repair or to replace with materials of like kind and quality at the time of the loss. In the past there has been a tendency for some insurers not to make any deduction for depreciation, especially for items insured on a scheduled basis, but the policy definitely provides that it is to be considered a contract of indemnity.

6. On permanent improvements to dwellings not owned by the insured, there is a limitation of liability of 10 per cent of the aggregate amount of insurance applying to damage caused by certain named perils.

7. Outboard motor boats may be endorsed to the property item, but not to exceed $500. Coverage on boats is on a named-peril basis.

3) Perils excluded. Like every all-risk policy, the personal property floater has a number of excluded perils. Among these are war, mechanical breakdown, extremes of temperature, deterioration, moths, vermin, inherent vice, damage caused by refinishing, renovating or repairing, and nuclear fission. In addition, certain types of water damage to unscheduled property are excluded. Prior to 1959, there was no exclusion for flood, surface water, waves, backing up of sewers or drains, or seepage. Losses from this source were so serious that it was decided to eliminate this coverage, but only in so far as the loss is caused at the premises owned or controlled by the insured. Thus, property away from the residence is still covered for water damage. A final exclusion is that of loss caused by animals kept by an insured or a residence employee.

4) Coinsurance and deductibles. The personal property floater does not contain a coinsurance clause, but the rules provide that the policy may not be issued unless the insured purchases limits equal to or exceeding 80 per cent of his exposed values. The purpose of this rule is to help overcome the problem of underinsurance. It is to be noted that the values stated by the insured in Figure 13–1 for each type of property are only estimates and are not a binding limit upon his recovery; nor will a coinsurance penalty for breach of warranty be involved if these estimates are incorrect, or if the insured later acquires values beyond those stated. However, there are exceptions to this general statement in certain territories, such as in four metropolitan counties of New York where the amounts stated are converted into actual limits, and newly acquired property is covered only to the lesser of two amounts, 10 per cent of the amount of the policy or $2,500.

The personal property floater permits the use of a $50 deductible against each loss, for which a rate credit of 40 per cent is given. This deductible applies only to *unscheduled* property and the rate credit is applied to the premium charges for that property (Section 3, Item (a), in Figure 13–1). Furthermore, it is not a flat deductible that applies to all losses to unscheduled property, because losses from certain named perils are not subjected to the deductible. These perils include theft, fire, lightning, windstorm, hail, smoke, explosion, riot, civil commotion, aircraft, vehicles, and rupture of a steam or hot water heating system. The deductible applies to theft from an unattended and unlocked automobile and to mysterious disappearance, and all losses except from the above-listed perils. Although the deductible is generally optional, it is mandatory in some jurisdictions, such as in the four metropolitan counties of New York referred to previously.

5) Rating. The personal property floater rate is computed by adding a "loading" to the basic contents fire rate. The *loading* is a charge based upon the amount of insurance and upon the territory in which the principal residence is located. In metropolitan areas, for the first $5,000 of coverage, the loading ranges from nearly 2 per cent of the stated values in New York to 1.3 per cent in Oregon. Rates for the next $5,000 of coverage are approximately one half of the rates for the first $5,000. After credits are applied for the $50 deductible, the annual rate for the personal property floater may vary from 1.5 to 3 per cent of the values exposed. Considering that the personal property floater provides the equivalent of fire, extended coverage, theft, and transportation insurance, plus the all-risk feature which takes care of unknown perils, the premium seems reasonable.

SUMMARY

1. Bailments of property give rise to a demand for property insurance on bailed goods even though oftentimes no legal liability exists on the part of the bailee for damage to the goods of others which are in his custody. The bailee has a representative insurable interest in such goods if he is not legally liable for their destruction.

2. Coverage on bailed property may be provided by either or both the bailee and the bailor. Bailees' customers policies are designed to pay for the loss of bailed goods from specified perils regardless of the legal liability of the bailee. Typical among the many types of bailees' customers forms is the furriers' customers policy, an all-risk contract designed to cover the concentrations of values in furs left for storage or for repair at furriers.

3. Block policies, issued on an all-risk basis to specific types of retail and wholesale concerns by inland marine insurers, are significant because they have tended to set the pattern for all-risk insurance on floating business property, issued under the commercial property policy program. Common block policies are the jewelers' block, the camera and musical instrument dealers' block, and the equipment dealers' block.

4. In contrast to block forms, scheduled property floaters, generally issued on a named-peril basis, cover an extremely wide variety of floating business property. Examples of the different needs met by these forms are the contractors' equipment floater and the livestock floater.

5. Because of the increasing importance of credit sales in the United States, the conditional sales floater, covering unpaid-for property in the hands of buyers, has assumed great significance as a tool of risk management in retail stores, in sales finance institutions, and for others who take installment sales risks. The conditional sales floater insures the goods against loss from named perils and may cover the interest of the buyer, the seller, or both.

6. The parcel-post policy, the first-class mail floater, and the registered-mail floater, used by those who ship valuables by mail, may be arranged in an economical and convenient manner to meet the widely varying needs of these individuals.

7. Of the various floater policies covering personal nonbusiness property belonging to an individual, the best known and most widely used is the personal property floater (PPF). This form, written on a "blanket" basis, insures on an all-risk, world-wide basis with relatively few exclusions applying to either property or perils.

QUESTIONS FOR REVIEW AND DISCUSSION

1. (a) Explain carefully the difference between the legal liability of an ordinary bailee and the legal liability of a common carrier.

   (b) Upon what does the degree of care required of a bailee depend?

2. If a bailee does not own goods entrusted to his care, how is it possible for him to have an insurable interest in them? Explain under the headings: (a) Where the bailee is legally liable for negligence, and (b) Where he is not legally liable for negligence.

3. Is there a duplication of coverage carried by a bailee under a bailee's customers policy and the insurance provided for a bailor under a personal property floater? Explain.

4. A furrier did repair work on a fur coat of which the declared value was $100. The actual value, however, was $2,000. The coat disappeared before it could be placed in the vault for storage. The court, holding that the $100 value limitation applied only to the contract for storage and not to the contract for repairs, awarded the customer a judgment of $2,000.
   (a) How much, if anything, would the furriers' customers policy pay?
   (b) What additional coverage, if any, would be necessary for full indemnification? Discuss.

5. (a) Draw up a list of (1) excluded perils, (2) excluded property, (3) excluded territories and, (4) type of loss limitations found in common "block" type floaters that cover business property.
   (b) What similarities and dissimilarities among block policies can you observe? (Do not confine your inquiry necessarily to forms discussed in the text.)

6. (a) What is the chief difference in approach used by draftsmen of block policies and those of scheduled property floaters?
   (b) Suggest reasons for not using the block idea for users of scheduled property forms.

7. (a) Select three examples of scheduled property floaters *not* discussed in the text and compare them under the headings: (1) covered property, (2) covered perils, and (3) loss limitations and exclusions.
   (b) What other factors do these forms have in common? (You may use forms supplied you by a local agent or a home office in your area.)

8. The West Furniture Store has a conditional sales floater issued on a contingent basis. John Homan has just taken advantage of the generous credit terms offered by this store and furnished his home with $2,000 worth of furniture, with a down payment of $200. Returning from a short vacation, John finds his house burned to the ground. Since he has not taken out fire insurance on the goods that he assumed to be owned by the West Furniture Store, he shrugs his shoulders over the $200 loss and goes on another shopping trip, only to be met by West's credit manager at the door demanding the next installment before any further credit is extended.
   (a) If the credit arrangements by West are typical, is John required to pay his unpaid debt? Why?
   (b) What type of conditional sales floater available to West would have made John's shopping trip more enjoyable? Why?

9. The firm of Overman, Meyer, and Mann, security dealers, does not wish to ship ordinary stock certificates to customers by registered mail because of the inconvenience and expense involved in this type of shipment. Yet, they do not wish to send these securities uninsured in the ordinary mail.

(a) Suggest a policy that will fit their needs.

(b) What form of this policy do you recommend? Why?

10. The Alamo Jewelry Company sells valuable diamonds and watches by mail.

(a) Why would the parcel-post policy not be an appropriate solution to Alamo's insurance needs?

(b) What policy would you recommend? Why?

11. Indicate, with your reasons, which, if any, of the following losses are covered under a personal property floater written with a $50 deductible:

(a) A dog belonging to the neighbors has chewed up the insured's patio lounge pad.

(b) Same situation as in (a), only it is determined that the insured's own dog is responsible.

(c) A squirrel has gnawed a hole in an expensive coat left on an outdoor table.

(d) Thieves take $75 from an insured locker in an athletic club. Six months later another $80 is taken in the same manner.

(e) Valuable carpeting, sent to the cleaners, was damaged by a moth-proofing process.

(f) Thieves stole some blank checks belonging to a church, filled in various amounts, and negotiated the checks.

(g) A rug was damaged by discoloring when a servant used household ammonia and water to clean it. The insurer denies payment on the grounds that the loss was not accidental and that the insured could have prevented the loss by a quick application of acetic acid but failed to do so.

(h) Wind caused a hole in a roof during a storm; water seeped in and caused an electrical short circuit; a freezer, filled with frozen food, warmed up and the meat spoiled. The insurer denies recovery because of the exclusion for "mechanical breakdown."

(i) A toilet runs over and water seeps through ceiling joists and damages a valuable chair below.

(j) The insured borrows some silverware from his neighbor for use at a party. Thieves ransack the house that night and the silverware is among that taken. They also take a fur coat belonging to one of the guests who is staying overnight.

(k) A $500 watch disappears mysteriously. It was not scheduled on the insured's PPF.

(l) In estimating his unscheduled property, the insured forgot to list a $1,000 living room rug; this rug is damaged when indelible ink is spilled on it.

(m) The insured moved an unscheduled $1,500 piano to a summer beach house with the intention of moving it back in the fall. It is warped in the damp air.

(n) The insured acquires new property so that his total values are $10,-000, but his total insurance under the PPF is $7,000. What effect will this acquisition have on any loss adjustment? Explain.

The Liability

(14) Risk

One can scarcely pick up a newspaper without reading stories of one person bringing an action at law against another for damages arising out of some alleged negligence. A review of jury action on personal injury cases will bring to light situations similar to the following in which substantial sums have been awarded the plaintiff.[1]

Bernard v. Railway Express—$22,662. Plaintiff, an employee, put his hook into a box of frozen fish and pulled. The box broke, causing the plaintiff to fall backwards off the loading dock and onto the street four feet below. He fractured his wrist and ribs. There was $750 in medical bills. Suit was based on the alleged failure of the employer to provide sufficient help to move the shipment.

Dowell v. Mossberg—$6,000. Plaintiff alleged the defendant had treated him but failed to diagnose diabetes, resulting in nontreatment of the disease until it had reached a more serious stage, causing permanent artery damage, possible retina detachment, and kidney injury. Suit was based on breach of contract, but defense contended that the evidence proved only negligence, which was barred by the statute of limitations.

Elliot v. Butler—$18,000. Plaintiff, a professional baseball player, sustained a severe broken arm when defendant ran a stop sign and struck his vehicle. The medical testimony was that the plaintiff would have permanent disability as a pitcher and further surgery on the arm was recommended. The verdict included $6,743 special damages.

When one becomes a defendant in actions such as these, immediate financial problems arise. Defense attorneys must be retained; court costs and judgments must be paid if the verdict goes against the defendant. Time is lost from one's work, and loss of efficiency may stem from the resulting worry. The rise of automobile accident frequencies and the increasing cost of settling damages from this source force the conclusion that getting into a situation such as the one described is by no means a rare occurrence.

---

[1] Reported by G. G. Talboy, "Review of Jury Action on Personal Injury Cases," *Insurance News* (February, 1959), pp. 59–61.

This chapter traces the underlying legal basis for negligence actions and the losses which may result from them. Analysis of the insurance contracts that are designed to provide protection against the financial catastrophe of court judgments for negligence and other related losses is given in Chapter 15.

BASIC LAW OF NEGLIGENCE

The basic law of negligence has many threads which are sometimes difficult for the layman to disentangle. To see what this central law is all about, one needs first to understand what conditions must be met before an act is considered such that it gives rise to actionable negligence on the part of a plaintiff. Next, one must appreciate what defenses are recognized by the courts for the protection of defendants. No matter how wrong a defendant may have been, if he can raise a suitable defense which satisfies the law, he may be absolved. Finally, it is necessary to appreciate how this interaction of negligence and defenses operates in the many different sets of relationships that make up our culture—that is, relationships such as the employee-employer relationship, the landlord-tenant relationship, the buyer-seller relationship, the principal-agent relationship, and the driver-pedestrian relationship. Different standards of conduct are applied in each different relationship. The law is extremely complex and is changing constantly; therefore, only a summary of the highlights can be given in this text.

TORTS

A *tort* is an injury to another that arises out of actions other than breach of contract. A legal *injury* results when a person's rights are wrongfully invaded. Examples of such rights are the right of personal privacy, the right to enjoy one's property unmolested, and the right to be free from physical injury. Examples of torts are libel, slander, assault, and *negligence*. Torts may give rise to criminal action, civil action, or both, against the offender. We are concerned here with protection against the financial consequences of civil action arising out of only one of these torts, negligence. Insurance against other torts is generally not available because the requirement that an insurable event must be fortuitous is not met. In other words, libel, slander, and assault are not accidental occurrences and hence are not insurable events.

THE NEGLIGENT ACT

By *negligence* is meant failure to exercise the degree of care required by law. What is required by law is understood to be the conduct expected of a reasonably prudent individual in the same circumstances. What constitutes negligence, of course, is not spelled out in any set of statutory laws but is judged in accordance with the standards that society has come to observe in different situations.

A negative act

A negligent act is essentially a *negative* one. It is characterized by the *failure* to do something as much as it is by the positive doing of something. One may drive an automobile into the rear of another car. As such, this is a positive act. In this case, negligence may appear as the *failure* to drive carefully.

A voluntary act

A negligent act is one which is done *voluntarily*. If an act is done involuntarily, the interpretation may be that the act was excusable. If such were the case, the plaintiff could not collect damages. For example, it is easy to see that if one person puts a gun into the hand of another, directs his aim at a target, and helps him pull the trigger, the second person is hardly a free agent; and if the shot injures a person, there is doubt that the second person is necessarily negligent. Or, as another example, if a person who is standing on a mountain side loses his balance and in attempting to regain it clutches at another person and causes him to fall too, there is a question that the act is voluntary. Even a reasonably prudent man would have behaved similarly. An involuntary reaction is not one which gives rise to legal negligence.

A negligent act, it should be noted, is not excused because it is *unintentional*. Intentional injury to another may give rise to both criminal and civil action at law. Negligent acts are essentially those in which the defendant may try to excuse himself by saying "I didn't mean to."

The law does not expect perfection to be the standard by which a negligent act is judged. The degree of care expected of a trained physician who is a specialist may be higher than that expected from an intern or even a general practitioner. The degree of care expected from a child is different from that expected of an adult. The degree of care expected of an automobile driver is not interpreted in the light of what might have been, had the driver taken full advantage of hindsight in avoiding an accident, but in the light of the decision that any reasonable person would have made in an emergency when there was no time to consider all the possible alternatives.

An imputed act

A negligent act may be *imputed* from another person. Thus, one is liable not only for his own acts, but also for the negligent acts of servants or agents legally representing him. If a bus driver physically strikes a passenger to keep him quiet, the bus company is considered to be negligent for hiring someone who exercises such bad judgment in carrying out his duties of keeping order on the bus. Negligence may be imputed because of a contract with another to assume the liability that would normally be ascribed to the other person. Thus, a baseball club may be held liable for accidents arising out of the use of a ball park owned by the city and leased from it, simply because the club had assumed such liability under the lease. A father may be held legally liable for the acts of his child who drives the family automobile because the state law requires that the father assume such liability when the child is licensed to drive.

Proximate cause of the loss

A negligent act, to give rise to action for damages, must of course be the *proximate cause* of the loss. There must be an unbroken chain of events leading from the negligent act to the damage sustained. Suppose "A" negligently damages "B's" car and as a result, "B" is late for an important business engagement. "B" charges that, as a result, he loses a sale which would have netted him $10,000. Can "B" add $10,000 to his claim for damages? The courts would probably require proof that the accident was the sole, or at least the chief, cause of losing the sale. It would be difficult to demonstrate this because many factors, other than "B's" tardiness, could have lost the sale. Carrying the example further, suppose "B" claims that not only did he lose the sale, but as a result of losing it, he also lost his job. Further, because of the lost job his wife had to go to work, necessitating the expense of purchasing a second automobile and the hiring of a nurse for the children. May "B" also add these expenses to his claim? It is clear that the court must draw a sharp line in determining proximate cause, or a host of sources for damage claims would open up. However, the preceding comments should not be construed to mean that the courts never go beyond the immediate demonstrable loss from the negligent act.

COMMON LAW DEFENSES

Even if a person is guilty of a negligent act, there are certain defenses that he can erect against the successful prosecution of a suit for damages by the injured party. At common law, these defenses are three: 1) contributory negligence, 2) assumed risk, and 3) fellow servant rule.

1) Contributory negligence

At common law, if both parties are to blame in a given accident, neither party may collect from the other for damages arising out of negligence. One must come into court with "clean hands." If one is partially to blame, it is said that he was contributorially negligent and may not collect against another, even if the other person was 90 per cent to blame and the plaintiff was only 10 per cent to blame.

2) Assumed risk

Under certain circumstances a defendant may erect the defense that the plaintiff has no cause for action because he assumed certain risks when he entered upon the defendant's premises; and if he sustained damage, it was the result of his own actions and not those of the defendant. The assumed risk defense may be illustrated in the case of a theater fire. People in a crowded theater often panic in case of fire, jam the exits, and perish. May relatives of the deceased sue the theater management for having an inadequate number of exits? Assuming that there is no negligence for the start of the fire, that the conduct of the defendant was otherwise without fault, and that the number of exits prescribed by law had been provided, it is likely that the relatives will have no case, since the defense of assumed risk will probably hold. Managements of baseball parks are sometimes sued when baseballs hit members of the viewing crowds. Assuming that reasonable care has been exercised in providing appropriate wire screens, courts usually hold that when a person views a ball game he is assuming the risks normally attributed to viewers and must accept the consequences of any normal result of a baseball game. Employers have in the past been able to use the doctrine of assumed risk to defeat negligence actions by employees, but through statutory enactments and common law decisions, the defense has been considerably weakened in the case of employers.

3) Fellow servant rule

Before the passage of workmen's compensation and emloyer's liability statutes, employers were often able to prevent successful negligence actions by employees for occupational injuries by showing that the cause of the accident was traceable to another worker. So long as the employer was found to use reasonable discretion in hiring workers who were competent for their jobs, he was safe from judgments that might otherwise have been handed down. This defense has been largely removed.

THE TREND TOWARD ABSOLUTE LIABILITY

There is evidence that the traditional concepts of what constitutes actionable negligence are being altered so that not only are more acts being interpreted as negligent acts, but the defenses formerly available to defendants are also being weakened. Furthermore, the damages awarded to plaintiffs have tended to be greater and are allowed for a wider variety of losses than was formerly the case.[2] Some of the evidences of these trends are discussed below.

Weakening of defenses

Reference has already been made to the fact that the assumed risk and the fellow servant defenses, as they apply to employers, have been altered by workmen's compensation and employer's liability statutes. The area of workmen's compensation, discussed in a later chapter, was the first major example of social insurance in the United States. All states have now passed this type of legislation, which represents an abandonment of the principles of negligence law in settling occupational injury cases. Before these laws were passed (most such laws were enacted in the decade 1910–1920), the principles of negligence governed and an employee had to seek damages at law from his employer for occupational injuries. Because this system proved inefficient, time consuming, and generally unsatisfactory, especially for the employee, it was at least partially abandoned. The employee now receives a payment for on-the-job injuries according to a schedule set up for this purpose, regardless of who is to blame, if anyone, for the injury.[3]

The defense of contributory negligence likewise has been weakened in various ways. In a few states, statutes have been enacted that replace this principle with one termed *comparative negligence*. Under the doctrine of comparative negligence, which has been the basis of many out-

---

[2] Harold Chase, "Changing Concepts of Legal Liability and Their Effect on Liability Insurance," *Proceedings,* 82d Annual Meeting, Fire Underwriters Association of the Pacific (March 5–6, 1958), pp. 14–25.

[3] This statement should not be interpreted to mean that an employee can no longer bring action against his employer for negligence. In many circumstances he can, as will be seen later.

of-court settlements, damages are awarded according to the degree of negligence assessed after the facts are known. For example, the plaintiff may be found to be 10 per cent to blame, in which case he would be required to pay 10 per cent of the defendant's damages, while the defendant who was 90 per cent to blame would have to pay 90 per cent of the plaintiff's damages. Under contributory negligence, neither party would be able to collect anything from each other.

Another way in which the defense of contributory negligence has been weakened is in the *last clear-chance* rule. Under this rule, a plantiff who was contributorially negligent may still have a cause of action against the defendant if it can be shown that the defendant had a last clear chance before the accident to avoid injuring the plaintiff, but failed to do so. Thus, it is possible that a jaywalker may collect if the motorist who hit him had a chance to swerve, but failed to do so.

Additionally, a wife may, in some jurisdictions, bring an action against a negligent third party for damages even though her husband was contributorially negligent in the case. For example, a husband and wife are involved in an automobile accident with another car, whose driver is found to be negligent in the operation of his car. It is found that the husband was also contributorially negligent. The wife, nevertheless, may sue the driver of the other car. Formerly the negligence of one spouse was imputed to the other in such cases, for to allow the wife to collect would be tantamount to allowing the husband to benefit from his own negligence. This rule has now been abolished by statute in some areas under the theory that each spouse has separate property and that to enable one spouse to obtain judgments in such cases is not benefiting the other spouse.[4]

Res ipsa loquitur

Another illustration of the trend toward absolute liability lies in the more frequent use of a rule known as *res ipsa loquitur*—"the thing speaks for itself." Under this rule, a plaintiff may sometimes collect without actually proving negligence on the part of the defendant. It should be noted that under common law, before an action can be sustained against a negligent party, it must be shown that there was some failure on the part of the defendant to use the degree of care required of a reasonably prudent man in the same circumstance. Testimony of witnesses and of the injured parties must usually be brought to bear upon the case. Suppose, however, that the injured person is found bleeding by the

---

[4] Chase, *op. cit.*, p. 20.

roadside, having been struck from behind by an automobile, and there are no witnesses other than the defendant to testify about what happened. The plaintiff did not see what happened. Under such circumstances, liability of the defendant is presumed to exist because under ordinary circumstances of a similar nature, no accidental injuries occur.

Res ipsa loquitur may be applied to establish a case against the defendant when (1) the defendant is in a position to know the cause of the accident and the plaintiff is not, (2) the defendant had exclusive control of the instrumentality which caused the accident, and (3) the use of the instrumentality would not normally cause accidental injuries without the existence of negligence in its operation. As may be guessed, this doctrine has been used frequently in automobile accident cases. It is also being employed frequently in aviation, occupational, malpractice, faulty product, and railway cases. In one case, a railroad was held liable for injuries under this doctrine when the plaintiff was injured in a boxcar that had been struck by another boxcar, thus causing the fall of the plaintiff.

Vicarious liability

Still another evidence of the stricter view of negligence taken by society today is the passage of what are known as *vicarious liability* laws, discussed in more detail below. The effect of vicarious liability laws is to place liability on the *owner* of the car for the negligence of the *driver*. About 35 states have such laws. Thus, in these states, under certain circumstances, an owner of a car may be embroiled in a damage suit simply because in good faith he loaned his car to another.

Changing concepts of "damage"

Another factor worth noting in assessing the trend toward absolute liability is the more liberal interpretation of what type of damages may be allowed in negligence actions. Courts generally allow as damages claims for medical bills, loss of income, loss of life, property damage, and other losses for which the proximate cause was negligence. Thus, damages have usually been allowed for such things as pain and suffering, and loss of the conjugal relation by a husband. However, more recently, damages have been awarded for such intangible losses as *mental anguish,* presumably under the theory that pain and suffering need not be physical to establish damages.[5] Furthermore, courts have awarded damages to a *wife* for loss of conjugal relations with her husband.[6]

---

[5] *Ibid.*, p. 24.
[6] *Ibid.*, p. 21.

Increased damage awards

Not only have the courts tended to widen the type of cases for which damages are awarded, but they have also tended to increase greatly the amount of these damages. While there are no comprehensive data available to establish this point conclusively, some examples will illustrate it. In 1902 a court awarded $3,000 for the loss of a worker's leg and broken ribs.[7] In 1949 the same court awarded $100,000 for a similar injury.[8] One may observe that such large judgments are by no means uncommon.[9] For example, in one case a court awarded the plaintiffs $400,000 for the accidental death of a husband, $79,600 for injuries to the wife, and $70,000 for injuries to a chauffeur.[10]

Various reasons have been advanced for the tendency of courts to be more generous than they formerly were in assessing the awards given in negligence actions. The effect of inflation in reducing the purchasing power of the dollar has undoubtedly had a considerable effect. The existence of liability insurance, it is claimed in some quarters, has caused juries to be more generous than they would be if it were known that the plaintiff himself would have to pay damages. An organization of attorneys known as the National Association of Claimant's Compensation Attorneys (N.A.C.C.A.) has had some influence in obtaining larger judgments for claimants. This organization has been instrumental in advancing the use of ideas and methods known to be successful in obtaining larger awards than would otherwise be the case. The use of visual aids in a courtroom to illustrate vividly the scope of the damage done, and the seriousness and reality of pain and suffering, is an example of such methods.[11] The N.A.C.C.A., greatly criticized by some for its activities in attempting to increase court judgments, vigorously defends its methods as only a realistic approach to what it feels is the task of raising awards that were in the past, and still are, too low for adequate compensation of injured plaintiffs.[12]

---

[7] *The Iroquois,* 113 Fed. 964.

[8] *Guthrie* v. *Southern Pacific Co.,* No. 28106 G.

[9] A review of the "Actual Large Judgments" section of the *Fire, Casualty, and Surety Bulletins* (National Underwriter Co., Cincinnati, Ohio), is convincing evidence of this statement.

[10] *O'Toole* v. *United States,* 7 (CCH Auto, 2d., 734); 140 F. Supp. 642 (1956).

[11] An amusing treatment of the courtroom antics and graphic, if not too dignified, methods sometimes used by attorneys in injury cases is given by Alexander Rose, *Pay the Two Dollars* (New York: Simon and Schuster, Inc., 1957).

[12] For an able presentation of the view on this subject taken by a member of the N.A.C.C.A., see Leo S. Karlin, "Bodily Injury Awards—Where Are We Going?" *Insurance Law Journal* (September, 1957), pp. 568–569.

Guest-host statutes

About the only significant exception to the general trend toward absolute liability in our society has been the passage of what are known as *guest-host statutes*. These laws relate to the standard of care owed by an automobile driver to a passenger riding with him in the car. The general effect of the laws is to reduce the standard of care owed to a "guest" in a car in such a manner that the guest, in order to prove liability for the negligence of a driver, must prove that the driver was guilty of gross negligence, or willful injury, such as might be the case if the driver were intoxicated.[13] Under the guest-host laws, ordinary negligence will not be sufficient to sustain a case against the driver.

EMPLOYER LIABILITY

As noted above, the law of negligence applies to various classes of individuals in different ways. Employers are still subject to the law of negligence in spite of the universal adoption of workmen's compensation laws. These laws, which are analyzed in detail in Chapter 24, do not, however, cover many classes of employees. For example, oftentimes farm workers and workers of an employer who hires less than a specified number of people, are excluded from coverage. Railroad employees and seamen are also exempt from workmen's compensation statutes. Furthermore, in many states an employer may elect not to participate in the workmen's compensation system. Finally, workmen's compensation laws usually provide for common law suits by employees against employers in given instances, such as when the employer has willfully injured the worker or has failed to comply with certain provisions of the law. In these and other cases, it is of interest to inquire as to the nature of the application of the law of negligence to employers.

The standards of care owed by an employer to his employees, breach of which may give rise to damage suits against him, are governed by the following:[14]

1. The employer must provide a safe place to work.
2. The employer must employ individuals reasonably competent to carry out their tasks.

---

[13] An interesting exception to this general rule was illustrated in a case in which the plaintiff had given several drinks to the defendant and afterward rode with him as a guest in his car. There was an accident and the plaintiff was injured. In denying the recovery under the states guest-host statute, the court held that the plaintiff knew the defendant was intoxicated and thereby assumed the risk of riding with him. *Sanderson* v. *Frawley*, 7 (CCH Auto, 2d) 513.

[14] Thomas Gaskell Shearman and A. A. Redfield, *A Treatise on the Law of Negligence*, Vol. I, p. 438; Vol. II, pp. 441–42.

3. The employer must warn of danger.
4. The employer must furnish appropriate and safe tools.
5. The employer must set up and enforce proper rules of conduct of employees, as they relate to safe working procedures.

To illustrate the operation of these standards, if a garage provides a jack to raise automobiles and the employee using this jack is injured because the jack breaks due to no fault of the worker, the employer has probably breached his common law duty to his employee. If an employer fails to warn a new employee of the existence of explosives in a storehouse, or hires an untrained worker to handle explosives, with resulting injury to an innocent worker, grounds exist for damage suits. If the employee disregards danger signals, or if he fails to use the tools provided, and injures himself, he is guilty of at least contributory negligence, and under common law cannot recover. Normally, the worker would receive something under workmen's compensation, which does not use the law of negligence as the basis for payment. As has been observed, however, not all workers are covered under these statutes.

The employer may utilize the three common law defenses in suits against him by employees, providing he has not lost these defenses for one reason or another. For example, a worker brings an action against an employer for some breach of care and the employer argues that the worker was partly to blame (contributory negligence defense); or the worker was accidentally injured by another worker who was reasonably competent, but just had an accident (fellow servant defense); or the worker should have known there were certain risks on the job when he took it and cannot complain because one of these risks materialized (assumption of risk). These defenses, while they have been limited by statute and by the courts in various ways,[15] are still powerful weapons of defense in the hands of a skilled attorney.

LIABILITY OF LANDLORDS AND TENANTS

In situations that involve the operation of real property, the owner or tenant owes a certain degree of care in his relationships with those who enter on the premises. The degree of care is governed by the status of the person who is involved. The law recognizes three classes of individuals, members of the public who enter on fixed premises—invitees,

---

[15] See C. A. Kulp, *Casualty Insurance* (3d ed.; New York: Ronald Press Company, 1957), pp. 62–64, for a good discussion of these modifications.

One of the most important areas of limitation is the employer's liability act, passed in a number of states. These acts spell out the standards of care required of the employer and either eliminate or place limitations on common law defenses.

licensees, and trespassers. The degree of care owed to an invitee is highest, and to a trespasser, lowest.

An *invitee* is an individual who is on the premises for his own benefit as well as for that of the landlord or tenant. Typical invitees are customers in a retail store, guests in a private home, and guests at a hotel or at a public meeting. *Licensees* are those who are on the premises for a legitimate purpose. Typical licensees are milk deliverymen, messengers, and meter readers. *Trespassers* include all those other than invitees and licensees who are on the premises.

No positive standard of care is owed a trespasser, but the owner cannot set a trap or deliberately injure a trespasser. If the trespasser injures himself by or through some hidden hazard, the landlord or tenant is not liable. In only slightly higher status is the licensee, to whom the landlord owes the duty to warn of danger, but otherwise to whom no positive standard of care is owed. Ordinary care is owed an invitee. It is not sufficient only to warn the invitee of danger; in addition, positive steps must be taken to protect him from injury from the known danger.

Illustrating the above concepts, consider the owner of a retail store who has just polished the floors to such a high degree of slickness that they constitute a definite hazard to safe walking. A burglar enters the store at night, slips, and breaks his leg. Clearly the owner is not required to pay any medical bills or otherwise compensate this trespasser. If a deliveryman had a similar accident, the courts would probably hold the owner innocent of negligence providing he had taken reasonable steps to warn people that the floors were slick. However, if a customer slips and breaks his leg on a slick floor, the courts would probably award damages unless it could be shown that something more than just danger signs had been posted. If the owner has provided rails to hold on to, or has taken similar measures, he has lessened the danger of a successful suit against him by an invitee.

An additional illustration of negligence actions involving landlord and tenant liability is the case of a house guest who fell down a flight of stairs, mistaking a basement stairway door for a door to a closet in which her coat was hung.[16] A successful damage suit resulted. In another case a painter had climbed upon a canopy to finish a painting job.[17] He was injured when the canopy collapsed under his weight. Although the painter was a licensee, he sustained a successful action against the homeowner because of the latter's negligence in erecting faulty supports for

---

[16] *Maher* v. *Voss*, 2 (CCH Neg. 2d) 320 (1953).
[17] *Hall* v. *Holland*, 18 (CCH Neg.) 794 (1950).

the canopy and in his failure to warn the painter. In another case, when leaving a church service, a woman was pushed down the stairs by the crowd and was injured. She based her suit on the allegation that she was an invitee and that the church was negligent in not providing safeguards against such accidents. The court ruled that legally she was a licensee and no special degree of care was owed her.[18]

Assumption of liability by tenant

If a landlord leases his building, the question arises, to what extent is the landlord responsible for injuries to tenants though he is no longer in control of the premises? In general, when the landlord releases custody of the building, the tenant takes on whatever duty the landlord owes to members of the public. The tenant is the owner's licensee in the building and the owner owes no particular standard of care except to warn of danger. Very often, however, the courts hold that the landlord does not succeed so easily in transferring his liability to the tenant because it is held that the landlord has not abandoned all the premises to the tenant. For example, in the hallways of an apartment house occupied by several tenants, and in the general building maintenance, the owner has been held liable for negligence to tenants and to members of the public. In one case involving a tenant who tripped and fell over a crack in a cement slab leading to her apartment, a substantial judgment was rendered when the tenant's leg had to be amputated.[19] In another case the landlord was held liable when a tenant was injured by a loose front porch floor board which had been poorly repaired by the owner.[20]

In most states it is common and it is legal to require, by terms of the lease, that the tenant assume whatever liability the landlord may have had (or to reimburse the owner for liability he is required to accept) for injuries to members of the public or to employees of the tenant. However, there are some types of liability of an owner that cannot be so shifted. Examples are the violation of a safety ordinance, the failure of a subcontractor to comply with such ordinances, or his failure to exercise reasonable care in excavations, blasting, or the use of fire.

Attractive nuisance doctrine

Under a doctrine which has become known as the *attractive nuisance doctrine*, the liability of a landlord to children may be changed so

---

[18] *McNulty* v. *Most Reverend Bishop of the Diocese of St. Augustine*, 7 (CCH Neg. 2d) 473.
[19] *Petrillo* v. *Maiuri*, 20 (CCH Neg.) 572.
[20] *Koleshinske* v. *David*, 20 (CCH Neg.) 264.

that a trespasser who happens to be a child is considered, in many jurisdictions, to be an invitee. Various legal fictions have been invented to accomplish this result, among which are those that a child is not capable of contributory negligence; that there is an implied invitation to children; and that there is an intention to harm because the landlord has placed an allurement of some kind known to attract children, who are incapable of recognizing or appreciating the danger involved. The courts, in utilizing the attractive nuisance doctrine, usually consider the age of the child in rendering judgments. The decisions in the field of attractive nuisance are contradictory among the various states, and in some jurisdictions the doctrine is not recognized at all. Judgments have been rendered in favor of children for injuries received when the child has ventured on a railroad track that was supposed to be fenced,[21] and when a child was lighting matches over the gas tank of an abandoned vehicle in a vacant lot. In these cases it is clear that an ordinary trespasser would have no claim, but because the trespasser happened to be a child, damages were awarded.

PRODUCT LIABILITY

A manufacturer, wholesaler, or retailer is required to exercise reasonable care and to maintain certain standards in the handling and selection of goods in which he deals. If injury to person or property results from the use of a faulty product, there may be grounds for legal action in the courts. Such actions are generally based on one of two grounds: 1) breach of warranty or 2) negligence.

1) Breach of warranty

A warranty, as noted in Chapter 8, may be express or implied. Oftentimes a seller gives a written or an express warranty on goods or services he sells, and it is the breach of this written contract that may give rise to a court action. However, under the Uniform Sales Act, which has become law in most states, the seller is held to have made certain unwritten or implied warranties concerning his product. These warranties are two: (1) the seller warrants that the goods are reasonably fit for the purpose for which they are intended, and (2) the seller warrants, that

---

[21] However, a court refused to charge a railroad with negligence when an 11-year-old boy was injured on an overhead wire as he climbed atop one of the railroad's freight cars. The court said it would be asking too much to require the railroad to make its property "child proof" along its 275 miles of track. *Dugan* v. *Pennsylvania Railroad,* 6 (CCH Neg. 32d) 443.

when the goods are bought by description instead of by actual inspection, the goods are salable in the hands of the buyer. Breach of the first implied warranty is most often used as the basis of suits for faulty products.

Actions for breach of the implied warranty that the goods are fit for their intended purpose are usually brought against the person who sold the goods and presumably knows their intended purpose. The buyer, relying on the superior knowledge of the seller, who takes the goods and is thereby injured, may establish a case against the seller.

In a famous early case it was held that a manufacturer or a vendor has no liability for negligence unless he had a contractual relationship with the injured party.[22] Thus, an injured person could bring action only against a retailer with whom he had had a contractual relationship, and not against the manufacturer. Later cases brought about a relaxation of this defense, known as lack of privity between the injured party and the manufacturer. A landmark case, *MacPherson* v. *Buick Motor Company*,[23] in which a defective wheel broke, established the precedent that in the court's language, "If the nature of a thing is such that it is reasonably certain to place life and limb in peril when negligently made, it is then a thing of danger." It should be emphasized, however, that a manufacturer or a seller does not guarantee the safe *use* of his product. For example, a court refused to indemnify damage incurred when a sparkler set fire to a child's dress. The court reasoned that there would have been little danger if the article had been used properly.[24]

The following cases illustrate the liability of a manufacturer for faulty products. These cases may be brought by the injured consumer directly or by a retailer who has paid a judgment as a result of selling a faulty product, particularly in the case of foods, medicine, explosives, or weapons. For example, a manufacturer paid a judgment of $111,000 when a fire resulted from the heating of some roofing primer in order to thin it.[25] The manufacturer had provided no warning that the mixture would release explosive gases when heated. Under similar actions, manufacturers have paid the following losses: $11,330, when contaminated feed caused the death of five horses; $35,609, when 2,138 lambs died from a disease against which they had just been vaccinated by a faulty serum; $312,000, when an abrasive wheel on a cheap bench saw flew into the eye of its operator, causing blindness.

---

[22] *Winterbottom* v. *Wright,* 10 M.&W. 109, 152 Eng. Rep. 402 (Ex. 1842).
[23] 217 N. Y. 382.
[24] Suel O. Arnold, "Products Liability Insurance," *Insurance Law Journal* (Oct., 1957), p. 618, citing *Beznor* v. *Howell,* 203 Wis. 1, 233 N.W. 758.
[25] *Panther Oil & Grease Mfg. Co.* v. *Segerstrom,* 224 Fed. (2d) 216.

Retailers have paid losses in the following cases resulting from their handling of products. A tree worker fell to the ground when a metal hook attached to his safety belt snapped. The retailer was held to have assumed what might otherwise have been the liability of the manufacturer because the retailer represented that the hook was capable of sustaining a man's weight. In another case, a dealer sold floor stain under his own private brand. Due to faulty manufacture, the mixture exploded, causing a loss to the user; but the court held that the dealer was liable because he must answer for a product he has accepted as his own. Breach of the implied warranty of fitness has formed the basis of most suits against restaurants that serve poisoned food, and against drugstores that sell faulty medicines or cosmetics.

2) Negligence

Many product liability suits are based on the common law of negligence as well as on breach of implied warranty. Since it is usually difficult to prove negligence in cases where the plaintiff claims he found a nail or a piece of glass in the bread, or a mouse in a bottle of carbonated beverage, and suffered injury from it, the doctrine of *res ipsa loquitur* is commonly used. As noted previously, this doctrine enables the plaintiff to *infer* negligence from the facts observed and it may be difficult for the defendant to prove that he was *not* to blame for the alleged defect.[26]

Examples of successful actions of this nature are illustrated by a case in which both a manufacturer and a dealer in plastic combs were held guilty of negligence in failing to warn a user who was burned when the combs caught fire while her hair was being dressed. The court said:

> It is settled that a person who sells an article which he knows is dangerous to human life, limb, or health to another person, who has no knowledge of its true character, and fails to give notice thereof to the purchaser, is liable in damages to a third person who while in the exercise of due care is injured by use of it which should have been contemplated by the seller.[27]

PROFESSIONAL LIABILITY

Closely related to product liability is the area of negligence law known as professional liability. Just as a manufacturer is required to make a product reasonably fit for its intended purpose, so is the seller of

---

[26] Arnold, *op. cit.*, p. 648, citing *Ryan* v. *Zureck-Wollenberg Co.* 3 (CCH Neg. 2d) 724; 266 Wis. 630 (1954).

[27] *Farley* v. *Tower Co.* (Mass.) No. 18431 (1930).

services required to use reasonable care not to injure others in the performance of his services. There are two variations of this type of liability: 1) the liability of individuals such as physicians, accountants, insurance agents, lawyers, pharmacists, and others who render a professional service, and 2) the liability of contractors who perform work which, when completed, results in injury to someone. Insurance against the former has been identified as *malpractice insurance,* while contracts covering the latter type of liability are known as *completed operations insurance.*

1) Malpractice liability

The standard of care required of a physician, accountant, attorney, or other professional person is broadly interpreted to mean that the individual must possess the degree of skill, judgment, and knowledge appropriate to his calling and conduct himself accordingly. This standard naturally varies from profession to profession and is changing constantly as each particular field develops. Failure to take X-rays of a patient's hip cost one physician a judgment of $38,000. The injury was diagnosed as a bruise instead of a fracture, and resulted in severe complications.[28] It is doubtful that the same failure, prior to the time that it was considered standard procedure to take X-rays following accidents, would have been interpreted as negligence.

In the field of medical malpractice, damage claims appear to be especially persistent and serious in recent years. In one jurisdiction it was estimated that about one in every thirty-five medical doctors is sued annually for malpractice. Although only in about one out of seven or eight cases examined by a special study group was there any substantial evidence of negligence by the practitioner, yet in about one fourth of the suits the doctor-defendant lost.[29] Malpractice verdicts have often been catastrophically large,[30] and the standards imposed have tended to become stricter. For example, in a California case, the physician, a specialist in vascular surgery, employed a standard diagnostic procedure to determine the specific nature of the patient's difficulty. This procedure involved the injection of certain drugs, which for unknown reasons caused the permanent paralysis of the patient from the waist down. The physician had previously performed 50 such injections with no adverse effects. The doctrine of *res ipsa loquitur* was employed, thus permitting the jury

---

[28] *Agnew* v. *Larson,* 5 (CCH Neg. 2d) 23.

[29] R. Crawford Morris, "Medical Malpractice—A Changing Picture," *Insurance Law Journal* (May, 1956), p. 319.

[30] *Ibid.,* Morris cites cases occurring over a two-year period involving verdicts of courts as follows: San Francisco, $250,000; San Diego, $210,000; Tennessee, $200,000; Texas, $100,000; Wisconsin, $97,000; federal jury, $123,000.

to find for the plaintiff unless the doctor could prove no negligence. A verdict of $250,000 was handed down, but it was later reduced to $215,-000. Use of the doctrine of *res ipsa loquitur* in medical malpractice cases appears to have had the effect of turning the doctor into an insurer, and may result in his unwillingness to try new procedures and treatment for fear of financial bankruptcy if the treatment backfires.[31]

2) Completed operations liability

If a contractor carelessly installs a water boiler or an electrical appliance that later explodes or causes a fire and resulting damage to the property or person of another, he may be held liable for negligence arising out of his faulty installation. This is known as completed operations liability, under which the damage must occur after the contractor has completed his work and it has been accepted by the owner or abandoned by the contractor. The liability law is governed by the same rules that apply to product liability. Examples of completed operations liability include the following cases: A contractor was held liable for extensive property damage when a rubber hose connection broke in an air-conditioning system several months after the installation and admitted many gallons of water to the attic.[32] In another case, a contractor was involved in litigation 17 years after he repaired an iron railing; it was alleged that his faulty repair work caused injury to a person leaning on the railing.[33] An electrical contractor paid $12,000 for the death of a three-year-old child electrocuted by an improperly installed outlet on which the work had been completed 15 months prior to the accident.[34]

It should be noted that if the negligence of a contractor causes injury while the contractor is still in control of the operation, the liability is similar to that of an owner or a tenant of real property. Insurance contracts differentiate, however, between these two types of liability.

LIABILITY FOR ACTS OF AGENTS

Under the doctrine of *respondiat superior,* a master is liable for the acts of his servants under two conditions: (1) if the servant or agent is acting within the scope of his authority, (2) if the servant or agent is acting within the scope of his employment.[35] An employee thus binds

---

[31] *Ibid.,* Morris gives an excellent bibliography of legal cases on medical malpractice including 61 cases in which it was held that the doctrine of *res ipsa loquitur* is applicable to doctors.
[32] *Saunders* v. *Walker,* 86 Sou. (2d) 89.
[33] *Hanna* v. *Fletcher,* 8 (CCH Neg. 2d) 1017.
[34] *Kurdziel* v. *Van Es,* 6 (CCH Neg. 2d) 1080.
[35] *Singer Mfg. Co.* v. *Rahn,* 132 U. S. 158.

his employer for third party negligence liability even if the employee is acting contrary to instructions, so long as he is doing his job. If an employee is told to solicit orders for a product, and in so doing he injures a customer by striking him when he refuses to buy, the employer will probably be required to answer for his agent's act. If the employee is instructed not to call on "X," but he calls on "X" and injures him, the employer cannot plead in defense that the agent acted contrary to instructions. However, if the employee also represents another firm (in violation of his employment contract with his first employer) and is trying to sell the other firm's product to "X," the court may find that the employee is acting outside both the scope of his authority and outside the scope of his employment with the first employer and hold the first employer innocent. It is to be understood that when a servant or an agent quits his employer's business and is carrying out his own business, he no longer binds his former employer for any negligence.

There is a distinction between acting as an agent or a servant and acting as an independent contractor. In the former, the employer not only controls what is to be done, but also directs the manner in which it shall be done. In the latter, the employer pays the contractor for completing a certain job, but does not exercise any control over how it is done. It is logical that the employer is not held liable for the carelessness of an independent contractor to the degree that he is held liable for the carelessness of an agent or a servant.

LIABILITY OF AUTOMOBILE OWNERS AND OPERATORS

Under common law an automobile owner or operator is required to exercise reasonable care in the handling of automobiles. Three situations may be distinguished in this important area of negligence:

1) Liability of the operator.
2) Liability of the owner for negligence of others who are operating his car.
3) Liability of nonowners for negligence of servants or agents using automobiles in the furtherance of their employer's business.

1) Liability of the operator

The typical damage suit in the field of automobile liability is one which charges the operator with carelessness, which is the proximate cause of either bodily injury or property damage to an injured third party. As in the other areas of liability, it is impossible to lay down a comprehensive statement of what constitutes negligence in the operation of an automobile. What is negligence varies with the laws of the jurisdiction in which the accident occurs, the interpretation of the events by witnesses, the attitude of juries, and many other factors. For example, in some areas a traffic violation is almost sufficient to establish negligence, but in other localities it is only one piece of evidence to consider. While the operator may still attempt to rely on the defense of contributory negligence in most areas, some jurisdictions limit this defense by adoption of the rule of comparative negligence and the last clear-chance doctrine.[36] There is a tendency to allow automobile cases to go to the jury to determine who is at fault, instead of permitting a "directed verdict" whereby the judge determines the blame when there is no substantial conflict in testimony concerning the facts of the case.[37] In certain cases, guest-host statutes have operated to lessen the degree of care required of operators for passengers.

2) Liability of the owner who is not the operator

The question arises, under what conditions can an automobile owner be held liable for damages when he was not personally to blame for the alleged negligence? If one gives a loaded gun to a boy and tells the boy to entertain himself and the boy accidentally injures or kills someone, the owner of the gun might well be held guilty of negligence. Does the same situation hold if one lends his car to a person without investigating this person's qualifications to handle the car and there is a subsequent injury to another through the operator's negligence? At common law the courts have generally agreed that the automobile is not a "dangerous instrumentality" in itself and that one is justified in assuming that a borrower of an automobile is competent to handle it unless there is obvious evidence of incapacity or known recklessness. Illustrating this is the case of an employer who successfully defended an action charging him with negligence in failing to examine a bus driver who, having recently returned to work from an illness, suffered a fatal heart attack and crashed his bus, causing injuries to the plaintiffs.[38]

There are, however, several exceptions to the general rule that an owner is not liable for acts of operators of automobiles. In 25 states [39] so-

---

[36] See pages 338 and 339 for a discussion of these concepts.
[37] Kulp, *op. cit.*, p. 65.
[38] *General Electric Company* v. *Rees,* 5 (CCH, Auto Cases, 2d) 330.
[39] Arizona, Arkansas, California, Colorado, Connecticut, Delaware, Florida, Hawaii, Idaho, Indiana, Kentucky, Louisiana, Maryland, Mississippi, Montana, Nevada, New Mexico, North Dakota, Ohio, Oklahoma, Rhode Island, Tennessee, Texas, Utah, and Wisconsin.

called vicarious liability laws have the effect of making the parent of a minor child liable for damage done by negligent operation of the car by a minor. Usually the owner-parent has signed the minor's application for a driver's license, and in so doing, binds himself to be responsible for the minor's negligence. In six states,[40] any person furnishing a car to a minor is liable for the minor's negligence. In 13 jurisdictions,[41] the owner is liable for personal injuries or property damage done by the negligence of *any* driver.

In addition, there is a tendency for courts to rely more and more on the doctrine of *respondiat superior* in deciding the liability of the owner for negligence of an operator driving with the owner's permission. There is no question about the right of an injured third party to sue the employer of a negligent employee in the course of his employment, but some have questioned the propriety of making an owner liable for the acts of a gratuitous borrower of his car. Yet, there is a tendency for the courts to decide that the permissive user is really the agent of the owner and hence the owner must answer for his agent's carelessness.[42] The inconsistency in this viewpoint was stated as follows:

> If I agree to take friends in my automobile to visit their relatives or am otherwise on a mission for their convenience and benefit, it is hard to see that an agency relation exists, much less that of master and servant. Any benefit accruing to me or any "business" that I may have is the purely social end of accommodating not myself but my friends. Under these facts, then how can I suddenly become the master by relinquishing the operation of the automobile to the friend? Yet decisions so finding are almost universal, including the appellation of "gratuitous servant or agent." [43]

Another application of the agency relationship in establishing liability of an owner for negligence of an operator is the so-called *family purpose doctrine*. Under this doctrine, an automobile is looked upon as an instrument to carry out the common purposes of a family. Therefore, the owner ought to be responsible for its use when any member of the family uses it, because this member is actually the agent of the family head and is carrying out a family function. Yet the courts have not seen

---

[40] Delaware, Idaho, Kansas, Maine, Pennsylvania, and Utah. Arizona and Virginia provide that liability exists only if the minor is not licensed.

[41] California, Connecticut, District of Columbia, Florida, Idaho, Iowa, Massachusetts, Michigan, Minnesota, New York, North Carolina, Rhode Island, and Tennessee.

[42] R. Parke and M. Orona, "Automobile Owner's Liability: Anomaly or Enigma?," *Insurance Law Journal* (March, 1957), p. 155.

[43] *Ibid.*, p. 155, citing *Mazur* v. *Klewans,* 34 (CCH Auto Cases) 180; *Droppelman* v. *Willingham,* 17 (CCH Auto Cases) 421; and *Flynn* v. *Kurn,* 1 (CCH Auto Cases) 387.

fit to extend this doctrine to any instrument or possession, such as a bicycle or a boat, in common use by a family. It would appear that the family purpose doctrine is a legal fiction to establish the liability of the person most likely to be able to respond financially for damages incurred in the use of the automobile. In support of this conclusion, other examples can be cited. In an Illinois case, a car owner was even held liable to a third party for the negligent driving of a thief who took a car in which the owner had left ignition keys, in violation of an ordinance to the contrary.[44] Likewise, some statutes place special requirements on owners such as used-car dealers to exercise care in inspecting the cars they sell lest an innocent third party be injured because of some mechanical deficiency in the car.

3) Liability of nonowners

Even those who do not own automobiles may be liable for damages through their negligent operation if by some legal construction the nonowner can be shown to be responsible. The legal construction normally employed is *respondiat superior*. The employer is liable for the negligent actions of his employees whether their acts were in or out of an automobile. The ownership of the automobile is immaterial in such cases. In a famous early case, a life insurance company was held liable for a $10,000 judgment arising from the negligence of one of its salesmen driving in his own car on the way to a convention.[45] The defendant's argument that the salesman was really an independent contractor whose actions are not binding on the insurer was dismissed. In general, the courts are not sympathetic to the independent contractor argument. Thus, when the employee of a holder of a parking concession at a hotel was involved in negligence action after parking a car belonging to one of the guests, the hotel was found to be liable.[46] A California court held a central church organization responsible when due to the negligence of a volunteer worker of a small church, a child was injured while being driven from the church to a playground.[47] This case casts doubt on the universal exemption from liability of nonprofit organizations.

MISCELLANEOUS LIABILITY

The preceding examples illustrate the major areas of negligence liability. In a similar way, legal decisions form the framework of the

---

[44] *Ney* v. *Yellow Cab Company*, 3 (CCH Auto Cases 2d) 888.
[45] *Dillon* v. *Prudential Insurance Co.*, 242 Pac. 736 (1926).
[46] *Stuyvesant Corporation* v. *Stahl*, 62 Sou (2d) 18 (1953).
[47] *Malloy* v. *Fong*, 232 Pac. (2d) 241 (1951).

common law of negligence of many other types of relationships in modern society. For example, there is a body of decisions (and some statutory enactments) surrounding the area of liability of a parent for the negligent acts of children, of the liability of a trustee to beneficiaries for mishandling of trusts, and of the liability of owners of animals for destruction or injuries caused by these animals. Detailed inquiry into the liability law for these and other areas is beyond the scope of this text. However, the same principles that govern the development of liability law in the areas illustrated above apply generally to all cultural relationships in society. Certainly, the unpredictable nature of jury trials and their outcome suggest that comprehensive insurance protection against liability judgments is vital to business and personal solvency.

SUMMARY

1. Negligence is the failure to exercise the degree of care normally expected of a reasonably prudent individual in the same circumstances. Negligence, which is the proximate cause of injury to the property or possessions of another, may, in the absence of effective defenses, give rise to substantial court judgments against the responsible party.

2. The common law of liability is not so strong that one is expected to go through life running no risks at all. In general, three defenses, known as common law defenses, are available to turn an otherwise negligent act into an excusable act. These defenses—contributory negligence, assumed risk, and fellow servant rule—are employed by various classes of individuals in different ways.

3. There is an unmistakable tendency for courts to be more severe in their interpretation of what constitutes negligence than they have in the past. That is, there is a trend toward "absolute" liability. Evidence of this trend includes a weakening of the common law defenses, greatly increased damage awards, and broadened definitions of situations that permit negligence suits to be brought.

4. An employer owes his employees certain standards of care, breach of which may give rise to damage suits against him, in spite of the universal adoption of workmen's compensation statutes.

5. The degree of care owed by a landlord or a tenant to members of the public and others who are on private property depends on whether the person is said to be an invitee, a licensee, or a trespasser. The highest degree of care is owed to an invitee; the lowest degree of care is owed to a trespasser.

6. Liability of a vendor for damage caused by faulty products is well established. Negligence actions are based on either some failure on the part of the vendor to exercise reasonable care in the manufacture of his product, or on the breach of express or implied warranty concerning its appropriateness for its intended use.

7. Professional liability exists for individuals holding themselves out as qualified to render a professional service but who fail to meet the standards of care or practice looked upon as normal by other members of their profession.

8. It is well established that under *respondiat superior,* a master is liable for the negligent acts of servants or agents performed while the employee is acting within the scope of his employment. This holds true even if the employee is acting contrary to instructions. The master is released only when the employee quits his employer's business and begins his own. It is under this doctrine that an employer not owning any automobiles is usually held liable for the negligence of an employee who is driving an automobile while performing his employer's business.

9. An automobile operator is liable for negligence in the operation of his car; and in many cases the owner of the car, if someone other than the operator, may be held liable as well. The family purpose, last-clear chance, and *respondiat superior* doctrines, along with vicarious liability laws, have all operated to extend and to tighten the liability law applicable to owners, nonowners, and operators of automobiles.

QUESTIONS FOR REVIEW AND DISCUSSION

1. In the year 1466 a legal case known as "the case of the thorns" arose in which the court said: "The defendant pleads that he hath an acre lying next the said five acres, and upon it a hedge of thorns, and he cut the thorns, and they *ipso invito* fell upon the plaintiff's land, and the defendant took them off as soon as he could . . . adjudged for the plaintiff; for though a man doth a lawful thing, yet if any damage do thereby befall another, he shall answer for it. . . . If a man shoot and hurt another unawares, an action lies. . . . If a man assault me, and I lift up my staff to defend myself and in lifting it up hit another, an action lies by that person, and yet I did a lawful thing. And the reason of all these cases is, because he that is damaged ought to be recompensed. . . ."
   (a) What "standard of care" was apparently required of human beings during the period in which this case was decided? How does this standard compare with the standard normally insisted upon in today's courts?
   (b) Discuss the social and economic background which might have justified the court's attitude in the case of the thorns.
   (c) Do you observe any evidence that present-day courts are returning to the philosophy expressed in the case of the thorns? Explain. Indicate any possible reasons for this trend.

2. A writer stated, "At first the courts were extremely suspicious of the liability insurance contract. Some courts held that it would be against public policy to permit a person to insure himself against the results of his negligence, on the theory that such insurance would have the effect of encouraging recklessness."

(a) What attitude seems best to characterize the courts in modern society on this subject?

(b) How does this attitude compare with that expressed in the quotation? Discuss.

3. Many states have passed guest-host statutes, which have the effect of converting a rider in an automobile from the status of an invitee (guest) to the status of a licensee. Does the existence of such laws represent an additional evidence of the "trend toward absolute liability?" Why, or why not?

4. In connection with guest-host statutes, referred to in Question 3, a court held that an owner is not a guest in his own car even though the trip is purely social.

(a) If he is not a guest, what status does he presumably occupy?

(b) What is the significance of the fact with regard to the possibility of an owner suing for damages if a friend of his is driving the car and is involved in an accident in which negligence is proved?

(c) How would the situation differ if the owner were driving and the friend were suing for damages?

(d) Discuss the implications of this case to the "trend toward absolute liability."

5. Some courts have held that if the state workmen's compensation board issues a safety order to regulate the conduct of employees on the job, and if a member of the public is injured as a result of the violation of this order by an employee, the employer is liable unless he can prove his negligence was excusable. Is this an example of the "trend toward absolute liability," or is it a normal consequence of the common law duty of an employer to protect members of the public from harm? Discuss.

6. Look up the employer's liability statute, if any, in your state or in a nearby state. To what extent does the statute eliminate or change the common law defenses of the employer?

7. In a famous English case in 1837 (Priestly v. Fowler, 3 M and W 1; 150 Eng. Rep. 1030), a worker was injured when the employer's wagon in which he was riding broke and collapsed. He sued his employer for damages and won in a lower court, only to have the decision reversed in the higher court, in which the judge ruled: (1) that to allow damages would result in a host of cases in which an employer could be held liable for almost any negligence or omission on the part of any of his employees, (2) that it would mean that the employer had to take better care of his servant than he did himself, and furthermore, (3) that the employee was not bound to accept service with the employer and if he wished to avoid danger to himself he could refuse to take such service.

(a) Which of the three common law defenses does this case illustrate?

(b) Did this decision put the employee in a better or a worse position than a member of the public?

(c) It had been suggested that this decision grew out of the laissez faire economic philosophy which was at its height at the time this decision was rendered. Explain why this might be true.

8. In a recent study by Dr. Hans Zeisel, 500 trial judges were asked to keep a record of personal injury cases, noting how the jury decided the case and how the judge would have decided it without a jury. The findings were: (1) In 79 per cent of the cases, both judge and jury agreed—for the plaintiff in 50 per cent of the cases, and for the defendant in 29 per cent of the cases. (2) In 21 per cent of the cases they disagreed, the judge finding for the plaintiff in 10 per cent of the cases while the jury found for the defendant, and vice versa in the remaining 11 per cent. In case of disagreement it was found that if the defendant was a corporation, the jury tended to favor the plaintiff by a substantial margin; and if the defendant was a governmental body, the jury favored the plaintiff by an even greater margin.

   (a) If you were a plaintiff in a personal injury trial, do you think it would generally be to your advantage to seek a jury trial, according to the above findings? Why, or why not?

   (b) Do you believe that the above study supports the often-heard statement that juries have a "soak-the-rich" attitude? Why or why not?

   (c) What relevance, if any, does this study have to liability insurance and its influence on the outcome of jury trials? Discuss.

9. In the case of Union Carbide v. Stapleton (6 CCH Neg. 2d, 337), the employer gave an employee a physical examination upon his leaving the employment of the employer due to illness. The worker was found to have been suffering from tuberculosis, but he was not informed of this fact. In your opinion, was this a breach of one of the common law standards of care required of employers? Discuss.

10. A worker was hired to mow a lawn with a power mower and was injured when his foot slipped under the skirt at the rear of the mower. He sued his employer and the vendor of the machine, claiming that the mower lacked certain specific safety features, such as guards, which would have prevented the accident.

    (a) In your opinion should the worker win his case?

    (b) If so, what implications would this have for the manufacturers of goods intended for buyers of relatively inexpensive merchandise?

11. The owners of a swimming beach were sued by the parents of a boy who drowned when he swam into deep water and the lifeguard failed to reach him in time to save him. The plaintiffs argued that the defendant beach owners should have had more lifeguards. The defendants argued that they had enough guards for normal needs and that the boy was guilty of contributory negligence in swimming out into deep water which, rather than the absence of a sufficient number of lifeguards, was the cause of his death [Spiegel v. Silver Lake Beach Enterprises (CCH 6 Neg. 2d, 874)].

    (a) Decide who should win this case. Why?

    (b) How does this case illustrate the basic requirements of a negligent act?

12. In the case of Jamieson v. Woodward & Lothrop (CCH, 6 Neg. 2d, 1172) a manufacturer of rubber ropes with loops at each end, designed

as an exerciser, was sued by a user of its product. The plaintiff's eye was injured when the end of the rubber rope slipped from her foot as she was performing an exercise illustrated in the instruction booklet. The plaintiff alleged that the manufacturer did not warn of the possibility of such danger in his instructions. Who should win this case? Give your reasons based on your knowledge of product liability.

13. In Stewart v. Rudner [Mich. Sup. Ct. (CCH 7 Neg. 2d, 325)], the argument concerned the case of a woman who charged that failure on the part of her physician to provide for a Caesarean operation caused her mental anguish. The woman had had two stillbirths previously and arranged with her physician to have her third child delivered by Caesarean. The physician failed to carry out these arrangements. The physician defended on the ground that the baby's death was not connected with failure to have a Caesarean, and that the plaintiff should not be allowed to recover for mental anguish because the baby was not born alive.

   (a) Decide who should win this case, stating your reasons.
   (b) What implications does this case have (1) to the trend toward absolute liability and (2) the growth of professional liability claims?

14. In Carter v. United Novelty & Premium Co. (CCH 7 Neg. 2d 325), it was held that both the tenant and the building owner were liable for the death of one of the tenant's employees when an elevator broke loose. It was found that both defendants knew that certain safety devices were inoperative. What does this case illustrate about the negligence liability of an owner for accidents on leased property? Discuss.

15. What is the main distinction between the following: (a) product liability, and (b) completed operations liability? Explain with illustrations.

16. In 1958 an accounting firm in Illinois was ordered by the supreme court to pay $24,265 to a firm for which it had undertaken annual audits for several years. During this time a bookkeeper had managed to embezzle a large sum of money, undetected by the auditors. In your opinion, was this decision instrumental in turning a C.P.A. firm into an insurance company? Discuss.

17. In Ward v. Arnold (8 CCH Neg. 2d 790), a woman hired an attorney to draw up a will for her husband, making her the beneficiary of his estate. The attorney drew up the will and mailed it to the husband with instructions to sign it in the presence of three witnesses. The husband signed it, but no witnesses were present. When the husband died, his will was ruled invalid and the property was distributed as though the husband had died intestate. As a result, the husband's brother inherited $15,262, half the estate, which would have otherwise gone to the wife. The wife sued the attorney for malpractice. Do you think her suit should succeed? Why?

18. The doctrine of comparative negligence has replaced the contributory negligence rule in some jurisdictions and has long been used as an informal method of settlement. Consider the equity of this doctrine in the following case: A wealthy defendant causes $100 of damage to the automobile of a poor plaintiff, who has been adjudged 10 per cent to blame

for the accident. There is $4,000 of damage to the car of the defendant who was 90 per cent to blame.

   (a) How much will each party pay under the doctrine of comparative negligence?

   (b) Is this fair? Discuss.

19. A plaintiff alleged that while walking across a street, he was struck by a car which had first been hit by the defendant's car. The plaintiff received a concussion, a sprained foot, and bruises. Doctor bills were $118. The defendant's car had been stolen and the plaintiff charged negligence and violation of a city ordinance because the defendant had left his keys in the ignition, making it easy for a thief to steal the car. Decide this case, giving full reasons.

20. Locate a few cases in each of the areas listed below and write a summary of these cases together with your evaluation of what constitutes a reasonable standard of care.

   (a) Trustee liability.

   (b) Parents' liability.

   (c) Liability for damage done by animals, either domestic or wild.

21. A woman purchased a refrigerator and three years later received a severe electric shock when she grasped the door handle. The manufacturer argued that after purchase, the door handle had been serviced because it didn't close properly and that, therefore, the manufacturer did not have exclusive control over the machine and, hence, could not have been directly liable for the damage [Ryan v. Zweck Wollenberg Co. (3 CCH Neg. 2d 724)]. Decide the case, stating the principles of negligence governing your answer.

22. "A's" automobile was struck by an approaching vehicle belonging to "B," who had swung out of his lane to avoid striking another vehicle whose driver "C" was negligently backing out of his driveway without looking. "A" sued "B" for damages, but "B" defended on grounds of no negligence. "A" contended that it was "B's" car that actually did the damage. Who should win this case? Why?

23. Can it be established that violation of a traffic ordinance, *per se,* should constitute proof of negligence? Discuss the pros and cons of this argument.

24. Is there any "justice" in holding one parent liable for a son's careless driving, and absolving another parent, whose son's carelessness in the use of a horse he is riding causes the injury of another person? Discuss.

25. A writer stated: "Automobile insurance is based on the common law principles of liability. However, the mere fact that a person owns an auto does not establish liability where persons or property are injured due to the negligence of another." (a) If mere ownership of the automobile is not direct evidence of liability for injuries to persons or property, what *would* constitute such evidence? Explain. (b) What classes of persons would most likely be purchasers of nonownership liability insurance in connection with automobile liability? Why?

Liability Insurance

Contracts

Liability insurance is an outgrowth of, and is in fact an inevitable result of, those legal relationships in society which permit the bringing of successful lawsuits against individuals for negligence. This is a key factor in understanding the scope of and the reasons for the liability contracts to be discussed in this chapter. As it became recognized that inexcusable negligence formed the basis for a damage suit based on tort, a demand arose for some protection against the financial consequences of such suits.

At first the courts frowned upon liability insurance in the belief that contracts of this nature would tend to encourage reckless conduct and thus result in more injuries to persons and property. Later it was recognized that there was a true need for financial protection and that existence of insurance did not cause an unwarranted degree of irresponsible conduct. Today the law takes the attitude that *failure* to obtain liability insurance against the consequences of negligence does in itself constitute irresponsible financial behavior. For example, all states have enacted legislation imposing penalties for failure to provide some sort of financial protection against negligence in the operation of automobiles.

The seriousness of the need for liability insurance did not become widely apparent in the United States until a highly industrialized economy began to emerge around 1900. At this time juries began to realize that if a person were permanently injured, it meant a definite, calculable loss in money to the individual concerned. Since then, as we have seen, demands for higher amounts of compensation have steadily increased, which along with the mounting costs of legal defense, may result in a financial loss amounting to thousands of dollars. The amount of these claims are determined mainly by the *actual damage done* and not by the ability to pay of the *tort-feasor,* as the defendant in such actions is called. In other words, the impecunious circumstance of the tort-feasor, while it may discourage a suit in the first place, does not put a limit on the amount of damages which may be assessed. Once a judgment is handed down, the plaintiff may use any available legal means to collect it, such as obtaining a lien on the property or upon the salary of the unfortunate defendant. The judgment may usually be renewed over the years until it is finally paid. Thus, one accidental slip or monetary failure may mean a lifetime of payments in liquidating a judgment. Even bankruptcy is not always a way out. Not only does bankruptcy cast a cloud on the otherwise good credit standing of a person, but it is also not available in cases of debts owed for willfully inflicted personal injuries. While it may not appear that an accidental but negligent injury is "willful," nevertheless, courts have been known to interpret as "willful" negligent acts which the layman would classify as just another accident with no malice aforethought. Thus, among the evils facing the tort-feasor, leaving the country may seem the least undesirable.

MAJOR CLASSES OF LIABILITY INSURANCE CONTRACTS

Liability insurance contracts have developed to parallel the major classes of legal liability, as described in Chapter 14. As may be expected, the insurance industry has formulated hundreds of different policies, but it would be superfluous to consider them all. The classification below gives typical examples of each major class of contract. Only a few of these policies have been selected for analysis here, with the emphasis being placed on elements that are common to all.

The major types of liability insurance contracts are:

1. Business liability:
   (a) Employers' liability and workmen's compensation.
   (b) Owners', landlords', and tenants' liability.
   (c) Manufacturers' and contractors' liability.
   (d) Products and completed operations liability.
   (e) Contractual liability.
   (f) Contingent liability.
   (g) Comprehensive general liability.
2. Professional liability (malpractice):
   (a) Physicians', surgeons', and dentists' malpractice.
   (b) Lawyers' professional liability.
   (c) Insurance agents' and brokers' errors and omissions liability.
3. Personal liability:
   (a) Comprehensive personal liability.
   (b) Special liability contracts.
4. Automobile insurance.

In the classification above, automobile insurance has been singled out for special attention in Chapter 16 because of its economic importance and the particular hazards and problems surrounding this line of insurance. Actually, of course, the automobile risk is a type which is common to each of the three other classes—business, professional, and personal liability. In addition, types of coverage other than liability, for example, physical damage and medical payments, are discussed as they apply to automobile insurance.

SOME ELEMENTS COMMON TO ALL LIABILITY INSURANCE CONTRACTS

Insuring agreements

Practically all liability insurance contracts include three similarly worded insuring agreements that set forth: 1) the insuring clause, 2) the defense, settlement, and supplementary payments, and 3) the definition of the insured.

1) *The insuring clause.*

To pay, on behalf of the insured, all sums which the insured shall become legally obligated to pay as damages because of bodily injury, sickness or disease, including death at any time resulting therefrom, or because of injury to or destruction of property, including loss of use thereof, sustained by any person and caused by accident.

Sometimes there are two separate agreements for bodily injury and property damage, and sometimes the two are combined into one insuring clause as shown above. The following points may be observed in interpreting this typical agreement:

1. The policy of liability insurance almost invariably states that the insurer is bound only to pay sums which the insured is *legally obligated* to pay. Unless specifically insured, voluntary payments are not covered, even if made in good faith because of what is felt to be a moral obligation to the injured party. This, of course, does not mean that every case must be brought into court to determine legal obligation—it is estimated that over 95 per cent of all cases are settled out of court—but it means that there must be some breach of care giving rise to actionable negligence.
2. There is no limitation or restriction of coverage as to *whom* it is that the legal obligation may be owed. In other words, if the insured injures a man, rich or poor, important or unimportant, native or foreigner, sane or insane, and it is determined there is a breach of care giving rise to actionable negligence, the policy covers.

3. The act causing the injury must be accidental. Otherwise, the insured would be covered for torts other than negligence, such as libel, slander, assault and battery, which are not accidental. It will be recalled that a basic requirement of an insurable peril is that it be fortuitous in nature. In spite of this, some liability policies now appear without the "caused by accident" clause. Instead, wording is substituted under which the insurer is liable for any "occurrence" giving rise to legal liability. Even though these policies declare that injuries caused intentionally by the insured are excluded, there is the probability that use of the "occurrence" wording does give more coverage than the "caused by accident" wording. The word "accident" suggests a sudden, unexpected, and abnormal event, while the word "occurrence," when modified to exclude intentional acts, connotes unexpected and abnormal events, but not necessarily "sudden" events. For example, suppose a contractor is blasting for an excavation for a new building and, while there is no immediate damage observable to a neighboring property, over a period of days the earth is so shakened that the foundations of the nearby building are damaged. Under "caused by accident" wording, there may be some doubt that this injury is covered since the contractor should know the probable consequences of his actions and there is no *sudden* damage due to the blasting. Under the "occurrence" wording, unless it is demonstrated that the contractor deliberately continued actions known to be destructive, the liability for the damage would be covered.

2) *Defense, settlement, and supplementary payments.* With respect to such insurance as is afforded by this policy for bodily injury liability and for property damage liability, the company shall:

1. Defend any suit against the insured alleging such injury, sickness, disease, or destruction and seeking damages on account thereof, even if such suit is groundless, false, or fraudulent; but the company may make such investigation, negotiation, and settlement of any claim or suit as it deems expedient.
2. Pay all premiums on bonds to release attachments for an amount not in excess of the applicable limit of liability of this policy, all premiums on appeal bonds required in any such defended suit, but without obligation to apply for or furnish such bonds.
3. Pay all expenses incurred by the company, all costs taxed against the insured in any such suit and all interest accruing after entry of judgment until the company has paid or tendered or deposited in court such part of such judgment as does not exceed the limit of the company's liability thereon.
4. Pay expenses incurred by the insured for such immediate medical and surgical relief to others as shall be imperative at the time of the accident.

5. Reimburse the insured for all reasonable expenses, other than loss of earnings, incurred at the company's request; and the amounts so incurred, except settlements of claims and suits, are payable by the company in addition to the applicable limit of liability of this policy.

In words substantially similar to those above, all contracts of liability insurance provide in the insuring agreements to pay for the legal defense of the insured and other related costs. The importance of this agreement is indicated by the fact that liability insurance has sometimes been termed "defense" insurance because in a majority of cases liability suits are settled out of court by negotiation between attorneys, and the insured knows that the worry and care of negotiations is assumed by the insurer. The following points concerning the defense clause are worth noting:

1. The fact that the insurer agrees to defend any suit, even if it is groundless, false, or fraudulent, relieves the insured of the worry and expense of nuisance cases, where the plaintiff is relying on the fact that in many cases a reputable business house will settle a small but groundless claim rather than go to the expense of defending itself in court. The insurer already has a legal staff, the cost of which is distributed over many similar claims in a given year and can thus handle each case economically. Without insurance, a defendant might wish to retain counsel even if the amount involved were small. It should be noted that the word *any* does not mean that the insurer will defend a court action falling outside the scope of a negligence action. If the insured is sued for bigamy, he cannot look to his liability policy for protection even though he may be liable to someone for damages.

2. Sometimes courts require that the tort-feasor post a bond to guarantee that, pending the outcome of a negligence action, he will not dispose of property subject to confiscation if the case goes against him. In cases where a decision has been lost in the lower court and is appealed to a higher court, a bond must be posted to guarantee that if the defendant loses in the higher court, he will pay the judgment. The insurer agrees to pay the premium on these bonds, plus any accrued interest after the date of the judgment.

3. Under the other terms of the liability policy, the insurer has the right to require the insured to appear in court personally in in legal actions arising under the policy.

4. The insurer agrees to pay for such immediate medical relief to others as shall be necessary at the time of the accident.

5. The insurer does not deduct the cost of defense from the applicable limit of liability for damages, but instead pays for these costs over and above all limits of liability for damages. It may turn out that the defense costs exceed the judgment finally handed down.

3) Definition of the insured. All contracts of liability insurance specifically set forth who is to be considered the insured. The concept of the insured individual in liability policies is generally very broad, and the wording differs for each type of policy. In the case of a business firm, the intent is to include all partners, officers, directors, or proprietors in their capacity as representatives of the particular business. In personal liability insurance, the policies include as insureds all members of the family who are permanent residents of a single household. It is not uncommon to write liability contracts naming other parties as additional insureds, for payment of an extra premium.

Exclusions

Among the various liability insurance contracts, certain exclusions appear almost universally. Among these are:

1. In the case of business policies, all nonbusiness activities giving rise to damage suits are excluded. In personal contracts, all business pursuits giving rise to damage suits are excluded.
2. There is an attempt in each policy to exclude all sources of liability intended to be covered in other contracts, or intended to be covered by a special provision for an extra premium. Thus, the comprehensive general liability policy covers products or contractual liability only if specific payment is made for this coverage and it excludes professional liability since this is insured under separate contracts (see page 377).
3. Nearly all liability contracts exclude damage to property belonging to or rented to the insured, or property in his care, custody, or control, under the general theory that a person cannot be liable to himself for his own negligence. The insured is expected to obtain physical damage insurance, such as fire or lightning insurance, to cover the accidental loss of property which he owns or for which he is legally liable for loss.

The question sometimes arises as to the conditions under which property is in the care, custody, or control of the insured. For example, if a mechanic is working on the fan belt of an engine in a customer's car, and the fan blade accidentally breaks off and puts a hole in the radiator, is the damage covered under the garage liability policy or is it excluded under the construction that the car is in the care and custody of the insured and hence damage to any part of the car is excluded? A liberal policy interpretation would hold that the damage is covered and that only damage to property actually being worked on is excluded. Thus, in one case a contractor installed a heat exchange unit. While it was being tested, but before the job was abandoned, damage resulted. The court held that the damage was covered.[1] In another case, however, the court held that damage to a concrete retaining wall by a bulldozer was excluded because the wall was "in the care, custody, and control" of the contractor at the time of the damage.[2] There seems to be no general rule applicable to such cases, except the general rule that always applies— ambiguities in contractual language will be construed against the insurer. In other words, when the court is in doubt, the insurer will usually be required to pay the claim.

Some insurers offer broadened policies under which the "care, custody, and control" exclusion is considerably liberalized. Of special interest to contractors, the *broad form property damage liability* program, as it is called, spells out in considerable detail just what property is covered and under what terms. Under this program, for example, a contractor has coverage on borrowed tools or equipment while they are not being used by him.

Limits of liability

Under all policies of liability insurance there are limits of liability of various sorts. For example, in the comprehensive general liability contract, the limits might be $100,000 for bodily injury liability for any one person, and $300,000 for each accident. For property damage liability there might be a limitation of $50,000 for each accident. This means that if three or more of the insured's customers are injured in a single accident, there is an aggregate limitation of $300,000, with no coverage for each individual claim to be in excess of $100,000. If there is more than one insured named in the policy, the question arises, Are these limits of liability applicable to each insured, thus doubling or tripling the stated limits? The answer is "No."

The question also arises as to whether a given accident can be interpreted as a *series* of accidents so as to apply the limit of liability per person or per accident to each separate "accident," thus greatly increasing the insurer's liability. In a famous case a truck negligently ran into a

---

[1] *Boswell* v. *Travelers Indemnity Company,* 8(CCH Fire and Casualty Cases) 936.

[2] *Jarrell Construction Company* v. *Columbia Casualty Company,* 8 (CCH Fire and Casualty Cases) 642.

train derailing 16 freight cars.[3] In its action against the insured truck owner, the railroad argued that since the cars were owned by 14 separate owners, in reality there were at least 14 separate accidents and the insured's limit of liability applied to each one of them. This contention was rejected and the court held that there was only one accident within the normal meaning of the word. This principle is also applied to the field of products liability insurance, where the liability limits apply to all claims arising out of any one batch or lot of goods or products. Let us say that a manufacturer with a $50,000 limit of coverage for products liability, sells a bad lot of a certain medicine and 1,000 injured customers make claims of $1,000 each over its use during the ensuing six months. The maximum amount the insurer will pay for damages arising out of these 1,000 claims is $50,000 not $1 million. One accident is defined in such a way that it applies to one lot of goods. Since there might be many claims arising out of the use of one lot of goods and since the limits of liability apply to the sum of these claims, the need for much higher limits than are commonly purchased in products liability is apparent. The manufacturer might be severely underinsured in the mistaken belief that his liability limits apply to each and every claim.

Subrogation

Practically all contracts of liability insurance are subject to the right of subrogation by the insurer against any liable third party. This right is very important. It may turn out, for example, that while the insured is held legally liable for some act of negligence, someone else had agreed to assume this liability by contract or is held liable because the insured is his agent or servant. If the insurer pays the claim, it has a right to any such claims that the insured may have had against others.

Notice

Like all insurance policies, liability contracts require immediate notice of accident and notice of claim or suit. It is especially important that this condition be complied with since otherwise available witnesses may be dispersed and evidence dissipated so as to make it difficult or impossible to determine later what actually happened. Such information is vital to the successful defense of the insured and without prompt notice, the insurer is greatly handicapped.

---

[3] *St. Paul-Mercury Indemnity Company* v. *Rutland Railroad,* 5(CCH Auto 2d) 894.

BUSINESS LIABILITY INSURANCE

Among the business liability contracts listed on page 362, we shall give somewhat detailed consideration only to the comprehensive general liability policy because this contract includes all the perils covered by the others except the employers' liability and workmen's compensation policy, which will be discussed in a later chapter.

Comprehensive general liability

The *comprehensive general liability* policy [4] (abbreviated CGL) is a scheduled form that permits the insured to combine many types of liability coverage in one contract. It is issued on an all-risk basis so that if legal liability arises out of some event not listed, but also not specifically excluded, coverage is provided. The policy is issued to a wide variety of business enterprises.

The following classes of liability are insured under the CGL:

1. Liability arising out of use of a premises.
2. Liability arising out of manufacturing, contracting, or other business activities of the insured.
*3. Medical payments.
4. Elevator liability.
5. Contingent liability.
6. Teams liability.
*7. Products liability.
*8. Contractual liability.
* Optional coverages.

In addition, it is usually possible to insure all automobile liability under a form which is a combination of the CGL and the comprehensive automobile liability policy. Insurance on the exposures listed above may also be purchased separately under separate contracts. For example, the first type of liability listed is essentially the coverage provided in the owners', landlords', and tenants' liability policy which insures liability arising out of the ownership, maintenance, and use of a premises. The second listed coverage is that provided by the manufacturers' and contractors' liability policy which insures liability arising out of manufacturing or contracting operations. Examples of suits arising from these sources have been given in Chapter 14. The phrasing of the coverage in the CGL is such that claims arising out of any operation in any way connected with or required by the insured's business are covered. Thus, a claim arising

---

[4] For a more detailed consideration of this contract, see Mark R. Greene, *Comprehensive Liability Insurance, Lectures and a Case Study* (University of Oregon, 1957).

out of a roadside sign is covered, because the sign would be interpreted as "incidental or necessary" to the business operation.

It is significant that for each of the perils named, the CGL provides automatic coverage on newly acquired premises, elevators, or other hazards arising during the policy term. Thus, if a new building is purchased or leased, a new elevator installed, or even if a new type of business is purchased or begun, the insurance adjusts automatically to provide coverage. Naturally, when the policy is audited at the close of the year, an additional premium is charged for any such new exposures. The automatic coverage applies only to exposures falling within the class of those already insured. For example, if the insured had elected not to take products liability insurance, there would be no automatic coverage for claims arising from this source.

Medical payments

A typical agreement covering medical payments under the CGL reads as follows:

> To pay all reasonable expenses incurred within one year from the date of accident for necessary medical, surgical, and dental services, including prosthetic devices, and necessary ambulance, hospital, professional nursing and funeral services, to or for each person who sustains bodily injury, sickness, or disease, caused by accident and arising out of the ownership, maintenance, or use of the premises, or operations necessary or incidental thereto.

Medical payments coverage applies only to expenses incurred within one year of the accident, and payments are made only to individuals *other than the insured,* regardless of the legal liability of the insured for the accident. The purpose of medical payments coverage is to compensate the insured for costs he would normally incur when members of the public are injured on his property, regardless of his legal liability. Of course, the injured person may feel that he has a legal claim for further damages, in which case there is nothing to prevent him from bringing an action, even after he has received medical care under the medical payments section of the policy. Medical payments claims do not affect the liability sections of the CGL.

The medical payments coverage as commonly attached to the CGL has some important limits and exclusions. There is a dollar limit per person, usually $250 or $500, and a dollar limit per accident, commonly $25,000 or $50,000. Medical payments claims arising from use of faulty products or in connection with elevator accidents are usually excluded.

There is no coverage applicable to tenants who do not reside on the premises, and no coverage to tenants living off the premises for accidents incurred on those parts of the premises rented to them. All medical claims arising from the use of automobiles are excluded, inasmuch as separate coverage for automobiles (discussed in the following chapter) is available. Automobile medical payments coverage, incidentally, is generally much more comprehensive than other medical payments insurance.

Elevator liability

The liability in connection with the use of elevators on a premises is singled out for special coverage because of the obvious danger surrounding the use and maintenance of elevators, especially those not properly maintained or where safety precautions are not always observed. A special additional premium is charged where elevators are present, and credits to this premium are granted for provision of safety features. The insurer often provides regular inspection service for the elevator, the cost of which is included in the premium. In elevator liability, by special provision, coverage is granted on damage to property belonging to the insured or in his care, custody, or control in event of an elevator collision.

Contingent liability

Contingent liability is the liability imposed on the insured by law for actions of his independent contractors. As noted previously, not all liability can be passed on by an owner to the contractor, even if the contractor is willing to assume it by agreement. The building owner, for example, may still be held liable to members of the public if an independent contractor engages in hazardous activities such as blasting. Contingent liability insurance covers this risk.

Teams liability

Strange as it may seem to some, there are still several hundred thousand horses in the United States, and claims sometimes arise out of their use as draft animals. For the sake of completeness, the CGL lists this type of liability as one of those covered and separate charges may be computed in the premium. A *team* is defined as a wagon with one or more animals, the number of which need not be specified; nor is it necessary to identify each animal since the team is looked upon as a unit.

Products liability

As written in the CGL, *products liability* includes the liability of the manufacturer or the vendor arising out of the handling of faulty products, as well as completed operations. This coverage is vital to most insureds and a careful study of it is warranted.

Products liability is distinguished from general liability in that the accident must arise *away* from the premises of the insured and after the insured has relinquished possession and control of the product which caused the loss.[5] In one case, for example, a plaintiff tapped a glass jar lightly and the jar exploded, cutting her seriously. The court found the manufacturer liable because the explosion was caused by a faulty annealing process in the manufacture of the glass.[6] If an accident similar to this had occurred *on the premises* of the vendor, the general premises liability portion of the CGL would have covered the loss. Since it is common to purchase different limits of coverage on different types of liability exposures, it makes a difference as to which liabiltiy coverage is applicable to a given loss. A firm may have $100,000 limits for general premises coverage but only $25,000 on products liability.

Similar reasoning holds for services performed by the insured on the premises of others. If a loss occurs while the worker is engaged in his job, the general liability section of the CGL would cover. Once he has quit the job, the products liability (completed or abandoned operations) section covers the loss. However, losses arising from pick-up or delivery operations, existence of tools left on the job, and uninstalled equipment or left-over materials, are covered under the general liability portion, by contractual provision.

The fact that the insured intends to perform additional work in the future does not necessarily mean that the job is unfinished and that, therefore, the general liability portion of the policy covers. If, for example, a flooring contractor installs a new floor in the living room, intending to do the dining room at a later time, but leaves the job for a temporary period, it will be considered that the living room has been completed, and any losses arising from defective workmanship are covered under the completed operations liability.

In one case a salesman applied some wax on a customer's floor but did not remove it. Later on someone slipped on the floor and a claim

---

[5] There is an exception to this general rule for restaurants, where coverage attaches for accidents occurring while food is being consumed on the premises.

[6] *Trani* v. *Anchor Hocking Glass Corp.,* Conn. Sup. Ct. of Errors (July 12, 1955) 5(CCH Neg. cases 2d) 34.

for injuries resulted. The salesman's employer carried general liability coverage but did not carry completed operations liability. The court found that the installation was one of completed operations and that no liability under the general liability policy existed.[7] Because of the fine distinction that exists between the general liability coverage and the products liability coverage, it is advisable that a company carry both types of insurance so as to prevent possible disagreements over the question as to who, if anyone, is to pay the loss.

Unless the CGL is written on an "occurrence" basis (for which an extra premium is generally charged), the products liability coverage is good only if the loss is "caused by accident." Sometimes confusion has existed regarding whether negligence, the natural result of which is damage to someone's person or property, is truly accidental. One court said, for example, that if a carpenter erects a roof with rafters too thin to hold it and later on the roof collapses, there is no accident because the collapsing of the roof is the natural and usual consequence of the use of weak rafters. A better opinion, however, seems to be that an ordinary person would consider such an event an accident, and the insurer would be liable unless it could be proved that the carpenter deliberately intended the fall of the roof when he erected it. In one case a distributor sold a new type of plaster totally unsuitable because after it was applied, it shrank and cracked, necessitating its removal. A contractor using the plaster sued the distributor for damages, but the distributor's liability insurer denied liability on the ground that the loss was not accidental. The court held that the insurer was liable because the damage caused by the defective plaster was a completely unexpected and unintentional result.[8]

Since the CGL excludes damage to property in the care of the insured, there would be no possibility in the case just cited for the distributor to have recovered for the loss of the plaster itself. Only liability for damage to the person or the property of third parties due to defective products is covered.

Products liability insurance applies equally to damages caused by the container of the goods as well as by the goods themselves. Thus, if a bottle of liquid explodes and the glass causes injuries to the holder, the policy covers the resulting damages.

---

[7] *United States Sanitary Specialities Corporation* v. *Globe Indemnity Company,* 7(CCH Fire and Casualty Cases) 1193.

[8] J. W. Wheeler, " 'Caused by Accident' As Used in Comprehensive Liability Policies," *Insurance Law Journal* (February, 1956), p. 98, citing *Hauenstein* v. *St. Paul Mercury Indemnity Company,* 8(CCH Fire and Casualty Cases) 370 (Minn. 1954).

Products liability insurance applies to all accidents that give rise to losses suffered during the policy term regardless of when the article or service causing the accident was sold or rendered. It is not unusual for products liability claims to arise several years after the goods are sold. The insurance applies not only to the goods that were sold but also to any free samples or premium merchandise given away with the goods.

Major exclusions. Liability in connection with vending machines is not covered unless this type of protection is specifically included at an extra premium. All liability assumed under contract, except for warranties of goods or products, is excluded from the products liability section of the CGL; such liability is covered under contractual liability, which is discussed below. Finally, liability arising from the responsibility imposed by a liquor law is excluded. Known as the *dram shop* exclusion, this provision appears in most liability contracts because in some states the so-called dram-shop laws make the seller or the distributor of alcoholic beverages liable for losses which can be traced to the use of alcohol sold or distributed by him. Thus, a person, "under the influence," may leave an establishment dispensing liquor, and in his intoxicated state may injure someone or destroy property. Under the state's dram shop law, the liability might be traced back to the insured establishment. This liability is excluded under the policy but may be covered by payment of an additional premium.

Vendors' endorsement. Because of the importance of the products liability hazard, many retailers refuse to handle the goods of a manufacturer or a wholesaler unless they are provided with evidence that the distributor has protected them with products liability insurance. This is usually accomplished by naming the retailer as an additional insured on the wholesaler's or the manufacturer's products liability policy. This endorsement covers not only claims based on breach of the manufacturer's warranty, but also those claims based on the retailer's negligence, or upon the retailer's own warranty of the goods. An extra premium is, of course, charged for this endorsement. Since the retailer often carries his own products liability insurance as well, the effect of this endorsement is to provide higher limits of liability for products hazard claims.

Contractual liability

A source of liability that is often overlooked by business firms stems from agreements they have signed with others assuming liability that might otherwise be attributed to someone else. Typical examples are railroad spur track agreements, lease agreements, contracts with suppliers of goods or services, contracts with municipalities for the performance of certain services (say, snow removal) or for construction, elevator maintenance agreements, and purchase order agreements. Under these agreements the liability assumed is not necessarily restricted to negligence liability, but may be for any accidental occurrence, such as fire.

Railroad spur track agreements. One of the oldest and best known sources of contractual liability arises out of agreements with railroads to "hold harmless" the railroad for certain losses growing out of the installation, maintenance, or use of a spur track run into the insured's property for his convenience in loading and unloading materials and supplies. These contracts are not standardized but usually provide that if one of the railroad's locomotives causes fire damage to the property of some third party, or if accidental injury results from the use of the spur track, the property owner will be responsible for the resulting expenses and losses.

Even if *both* the railroad and the property owner have general liability insurance, the property owner has no coverage against these claims unless he has contractual liability coverage insuring such contracts. Let us assume that due to the negligence of the employees of both the railroad and the property owner, someone is killed by one of the railroad's engines. A judgment is obtained against both the railroad and the property owner and is paid by each party's liability insurer. The railroad's insurer now sues the property owner for recovery of the amounts paid on behalf of the railroad, arguing that the railroad's liability was assumed by the property owner under the hold harmless agreement. The property owner must pay this amount and may not look to his insurer for legal defense unless he has purchased contractual liability insurance, either separately or under the CGL. Note that both parties were protected by general liability insurance, but that because of the hold harmless agreement, the property owner suffers an additional loss.[9]

Lease agreements. Under the typical lease, the lessee agrees to assume any liability that would otherwise be attributable to the lessor for any damage caused by the lessee or by any other person due to poor building maintenance or due to the neglect of any person, including tenants or occupants of the building. It is significant to note that the agreement provides that if *anyone* causes a loss for which the lessor is

---

[9] A case very similar to this actually occurred and is described in *St. Louis Police Relief Association* v. *Aetna Life Insurance Co.,* 154 S.W. (2d), 782.

held liable, the lessee must pay. Thus, even if a landlord is held directly liable at law for negligence, the lessee or his insurer must reimburse the landlord. The same principle applies to most contractual liability agreements. In a leading case, for example, an electrical contractor had assumed liability in a construction contract with the city of New York. Through negligence of one of the city's employees, the city was held liable for a judgment of $85,000, which it was able to collect from the contractor under the hold harmless clause of its construction contract.[10]

Underwriting requirements and limitations. It is ironic that it is possible for both parties to a business arrangement to be amply protected by public liability insurance and physical damage insurance and yet be required to carry contractual liability insurance. The question arises as to why business practice dictates that a hold harmless clause be required at all under such circumstances. If both parties have ample liability insurance, it would appear somewhat redundant to require that one party assume the liability which would otherwise be paid by the other party's liability insurer. Eliminating the hold harmless agreement would result in a saving of insurance premiums. After all, if contractual liability insurance is purchased, eventually one of the insurers pays the loss. However, as long as hold harmless agreements are in use, it is vital that contractual liability insurance be carried.

When the CGL is written with contractual liability, the policy requires that all hold harmless agreements, or other contracts under which liability is assumed by the insured, be listed. Since there are many variations of agreements, even those that are supposed to be standardized in nature, the insurer sometimes insists that copies of the actual agreements be supplied to it upon request before it will underwrite the agreement. For similar reasons, ordinarily no automatic coverage is given on agreements of a type not named and insured and undertaken during the policy term.

The CGL normally lists and insures without extra charge five types of contractual liability agreements: lease of premises, sidetrack agreements, elevator and escalator maintenance agreements, easement agreements in connection with a railroad grade crossing, and agreements required by municipal ordinance in connection with work for the municipality. The policy automatically covers all *written* agreements of these types during its policy term. Any other agreements, such as those arising

---

[10] *Thiebault* v. *City of New York,* reported in 135 New York Law Journal 108.

out of the use of leased equipment, must be covered by separate endorsement and a premium paid therefore. Insurers are generally not willing to issue a blanket endorsement covering any and all types of agreements which might be signed during the policy term.

Because contractual liability insurance is not designed to guarantee the proper performance of a contract by the insured or to replace defective products, the contractual liability portion of the CGL contains exclusions for damage *to* property in the insured's control and for accidents arising out of products handled or work completed by the insured. Even though the insured may have a written contract guaranteeing his work, the contractual liability insurance will not pay for this type of liability.

Contractual liability insurance does not exclude the insured's liability for fire damage or automobile damage assumed under contract. Sometimes a separate contract known as fire legal liability on contractual obligation is purchased because either the general liability insurer will not grant sufficiently high contractual liability limits to cover the fire exposure or because the insured is renting or holding property of others which is in his care, custody, and control, and which is therefore excluded under the contractual liability portion of the CGL. Suppose the insured is leasing some industrial equipment and has agreed in writing to be responsible for all accidental loss, including fire. Coverage of this exposure might be obtained by purchasing fire insurance directly on the equipment with a trust and commission clause attached. The *trust and commission* clause of the fire insurance form grants fire insurance on leased property provided the insured has a legal obligation for the safety of the goods. A special rider to the CGL might be obtained granting contractual liability on this exposure, or fire legal liability insurance could be purchased.

PROFESSIONAL LIABILITY (MALPRACTICE) INSURANCE

Because general liability policies usually contain exclusions for all claims arising out of error, or mistake, of a professional person in the performance of the duties of his profession, separate policies covering this important form of legal liability have been developed. These contracts are sometimes referred to as *malpractice* and sometimes as *errors and omissions* policies, depending upon the type of professional person utilizing them. Essentially the two contracts are quite similar, however, and have many provisions in common. Examples of three of these policies follow, with the peculiar characteristics of each analyzed.

Professional v. other liability contracts

Important differences between professional liability and other liability insurance contracts exist:

1. In professional liability insurance, the insurer often does not have the right to settle claims out of court by tendering sums in return for releases of liability by the plaintiff, unless the prior consent of the professional person involved is obtained. The practice of out-of-court settlement is very common in other liability claims, but it is easy to see that to allow this in the case of professional liability would tend to damage the reputation of, say, a doctor who might become known as a person who admits his constant malpractice by settling claims in this manner. Therefore, even though it might be less expensive for the insurer just to pay a claim regardless of whether it is valid or otherwise, the professional person has the right to insist that the insurer defend him in the courts.

2. The professional liability policy is usually written with only one major insuring clause, with no distinction made between bodily injury or property damage liability, and with no limit *per accident*. Usually there is a limit of liability *per claim* stated. Thus, if the policy has a $25,000 limit of liability per claim and a $100,000 aggregate limit, and two damage suits arise out of a single error, say one by the patient and another by his wife, the limits of liability would be $50,000 ($25,000 per claim). Other liability policies, on the other hand, invariably state the limits of liability in terms of so much per accident or per occurrence.

3. The professional liability policy does not restrict its coverage to those events that are "caused by accident" because usually the act which gives rise to a claim is deliberate. The event has an unintended *result* but may not always be described as accidental. For example, a druggist may sell a patent medicine for the relief of itching. If this medicine causes a severe allergic reaction in the customer, certainly the result is unintended, but the act of selling the drug was deliberate. Medical malpractice insurance would cover such a loss. However, the policy always excludes illegal or criminal acts from its coverage.

4. The professional liability policy usually does not exclude damage to property in the care, custody, or control of the insured, as do general liability contracts. Normally this type of loss will be at a minimum since, for the most part, the contracts cover personal injuries.

5. Unlike other liability policies and products liability in particular, professional liability contracts insure all claims which had their basis in the service or the acts performed during the policy term.

It is not necessary for the claim itself to be made during the policy term, but the professional error must have been committed during the policy period.

6. The products liability policy insures claims arising out of a breach of warranty of the vendor regarding the goods. If a retailer says a product is good for a certain purpose and it turns out to be definitely wrong for this purpose, "an action lies" for which the policy must respond. In the professional liability policy, however, there is generally an exclusion for any agreement guaranteeing the result of any treatment. A suit by a patient, irritated because the treatment failed when the doctor promised it would succeed, is thus not covered under the policy. The policy responds to suits based on a physician's error, mistake, or malpractice in rendering the service, but not to any warranty on his part for successful results, which after all cannot be guaranteed. Similar clauses are found in other types of professional liability contracts.

Medical malpractice insurance

One of the major professional liability contracts is the physicians', surgeons', and dentists' liability policy. In it the insurer agrees to pay:

> All sums which the insured shall become legally obligated to pay as damages because of injury arising out of malpractice, error, or mistake in rendering or failing to render professional services in the practice of the insured's profession described in the declarations, committed during the policy period by the insured or by any person for whose acts or omissions the insured is legally responsible.

The insuring clause refers to "injury" and not to bodily injury. Thus, the clause covers a broad range of claims, such as mental anguish, false imprisonment, slander, and libel, based on professional acts. The insuring agreement refers to acts arising in the "practice of the insured's profession." If a patient slips on a wet doormat while entering the premises, however, this is not part of a professional service and the malpractice policy would not cover any damages. The professional person thus needs premises liability insurance as well as professional liability coverage. Very often professional liability insurance is provided by a rider on the general liability policy, and thus in practice there is normally little difficulty arising from problems of this sort.

The insuring agreement covers the insured's liability for the act of a nurse, assistant, technician, etc., but does not cover the personal liability which might attach to such a person. The nurse, assistant, or technician is expected to provide his own professional coverage separately. Often the insurer permits this coverage to be endorsed on the employer's policy.

Lawyers' professional liability

Another example of malpractice insurance is found in a more or less standardized contract that covers the professional liability of lawyers and attorneys. This contract is now offered by most liability insurers on a form developed by the National Bureau of Casualty Underwriters. The contract is similar in wording to other professional liability contracts, with adaptations to fit the particular needs of lawyers. The insuring agreement is very broad, covering liability "because of any act or omission of the insured, or of any other person for whose acts or omissions the insured is legally responsible, and arising out of the performance of professional services for others in the insured's capacity as a lawyer." Like other contracts, it makes no reference to "accidents," and the insurer may not settle a claim without the permission of the insured.

The contract covers claims arising out of any act if the act occurred during the policy term, with no time limit as to when the claim must be presented. Thus, if lawyer Brown fails to carry out properly a divorce proceeding for client Smith and ten years later it develops that Smith, having been illegally remarried, is charged with being a bigamist, the insurer will defend the suit and pay any judgment that arises even if the insurer is no longer carrying the policy on Brown. On the other hand, if Brown had never carried professional liability insurance before, and during the policy term he is sued by Smith for damages, the present liability insurer will still pay the claim providing it can be shown that when the policy went into force, Brown did not know nor could he reasonably have foreseen that his earlier omission would have caused the suit by Smith. However, if Brown drops his policy after one year and Smith's suit is brought after the policy has expired, there is no coverage, as there would have been had the original error occurred during the policy period. If at the time Smith's suit is brought, Brown has his policy with another insurer, the first insurer must respond (providing the professional mistake occurred duing the period the first policy was in force) and the second insurer's coverage is considered excess in case the limits of liability of the first insurer are insufficient.

The lawyers' professional liability contract may be written to cover additional interests. Thus, all the attorneys in a given partnership may be insured under the same policy, with automatic coverage applying to new partners or employees. The limits of liability, like other professional liability contracts, are on a per claim basis, not on a per occurrence basis. Thus, if an attorney makes an error in drawing up a trust agreement adversely affecting the rights of several beneficiaries, this single mistake could result in successful damage claims by each of the injured parties. Each such claim would be subject to the per claim limit stated in the policy.

The lawyers' professional liability contract contains certain important exclusions. Of considerable interest is the exclusion for damage to physical tangible property and for *bodily* injury to others. This exclusion emphasizes (1) the fact that most errors and omissions contracts are intended to cover loss to intangible property caused by professional mistakes, and (2) the consequent continued need for general liability insurance against claims arising from the operation of any business establishment. If attorney Carr strikes someone as a result of careless driving, his act may be a "professional mistake" in a general sense; but as it does not arise out of his professional practice *in his capacity as a lawyer,* it would be excluded from coverage. The policy also excludes liability resulting from fraudulent, criminal, dishonest, or malicious acts or omissions, since presumably such acts are within the control of the insured, and hence are basically uninsurable.

Insurance agents' and brokers' errors and omissions liability

It has been established in the courts that, like other persons offering professional services, insurance agents and brokers are liable to members of the public for losses caused by professional error or mistake. If an insurance agent agrees to place insurance on a client's house and through some oversight either by himself or his employee, the coverage is not placed or the client is not notified of his inability to obtain coverage, the agent may be required to respond to his client for damages.[11] If the agent places the insurance, but does it incorrectly, so that the insurer is not bound by the contract, the agent is liable for damages.[12] This might occur when an agent fails to describe the insured property accurately; fails to add an endorsement covering some peril, such as windstorm, even though the coverage was requested; or arranges policies on a single property in such a way that through nonconcurrency the insured is penalized in a loss settlement. Because of the increasing complexity of insurance, professional errors of this type are not uncommon.

An insurance agent is also subject to damage suits by the insurers he represents for failing in a common law duty, such as loyalty or obedi-

---

[11] See *Burroughs* v. *Bunch,* 210 S.W. (2d), 211, and *Coffey* v. *Polimeni,* 7(CCH Fire and Casualty Cases) 519.

[12] *Shapiro* v. *Amalgamated Trust & Savings Bank,* 283 Ill. App. 243.

ence, which an agent owes to his principal. For example, the insurer may prohibit the agent to bind coverage on a certain class of property. The agent, in disobedience to these instructions, writes the insurance and a loss develops before the insurer has an opportunity to cancel the policy. Because the agent was the authorized representative of the insurer and had the power to bind it and bcause members of the public are not bound by private instructions of a principal to his agent, the insured has a legal right to collect. The insurer may then come against the disobedient agent for indemnification.

The agents' and brokers' errors and omissions policy insures the agent against all loss which the agent must pay because of negligent acts, errors, or omissions of his employees to members of his clientele. Whilc these contracts are not standardized, most insurers give the agent the option of protection against similar claims from the insurance companies he represents. Usually the contract is written with a substantial deductible amount, say $500 or $1,000. The policy pays only if legal liability on the part of the agent can be proved, and does not respond to payments made to customers voluntarily in order to preserve goodwill. Like other professional liability contracts, errors and omissions insurance covers only *professional* mistakes, and general liability insurance is still necessary.

In order for the agent to collect, he need only show that the claim against him occurred during the policy term, regardless of when the professional mistake occurred. However, for the protection of the agent, the contract requires that if the insurer refuses to renew, the coverage is extended for one year against claims arising from mistakes occurring during the policy term. It might happen, for example, that an agent realizes on December 28 that he has committed an error for which he is liable, there having occurred a loss which, because of his mistake, was left uninsured. The professional liability insurer, learning of this, might refuse to renew the errors and omissions policy in the knowledge that a claim would not be submitted before the expiration of the policy on December 31. The provision granting coverage on such claims thus protects the agent from being unjustly denied recovery on his errors and omissions contract.

PERSONAL LIABILITY INSURANCE

Most insurance coverage on one's *personal* (nonbusiness) liability for negligence, other than automobile, is written on the comprehensive personal liability policy (abbreviated CPL), first introduced in 1944.

Individual contracts on particular types of personal liability, such as golfer's liability, sportsman's liability, and dog liability, are occasionally written but will not be discussed here. The comprehensive personal liability policy is an all-risk contract and has few exclusions. It is intended primarily for legal liability risks arising from the maintenance of a home, but also covers the insured's nonbusiness liability away from his residence.

Insuring agreements

The insuring agreements of the comprehensive personal liability policy parallel those of the CGL in most respects, but with the following differences:

1. The insuring agreement makes no reference to acts "caused by accident." Therefore, the coverage is on an occurrence basis (see page 364).
2. Property damage and bodily injury liability are covered in one insuring clause and a single limit applies to both types. This procedure is becoming more common in liability policies, although at one time only the CPL was written in this manner.
3. Medical payments coverage is not optional as it is on the CGL, and it amounts to $250 per accident, unless the policy is endorsed for higher limits. The following medical payments claims, which must be based on an accident, are covered: (a) losses to persons on the premises with permission of the insured, (b) losses away from the premises if they were caused by activities of the insured, his children, his servants, or by any of his animals, (c) losses on premises where the insured is temporarily living (providing he does not own the premises) or on vacant land belonging to the insured. Medical payments on the CPL do not cover the cost of accidents to the insured himself or to anyone else residing with the insured. As will be seen in the following chapter, this restriction does not apply to medical payments as it is written on automobile liability contracts.
4. In defining the insured, the CPL includes not only the named insured but also his wife and the relatives of either who are residents; together with any person under 21 living at the residence; and, with respect to the use of certain farm and garden implements, employees.
5. Liability *to* employees for injuries incurred are covered unless a workmen's compensation policy is in force or is required under the laws of the state.

Exclusions

The major exclusions of the CPL are:

1. Business activities and professional activities are specifically excluded, as on the CGL personal liability is excluded. However,

the CPL covers business activities ordinarily incident to non-business pursuits. Thus, if the insured walks downtown on personal business but goes to his office on an errand and bumps into another person when rounding a corner, his CPL covers any resulting claim.

2. Liability arising out of the use of aircraft or automobiles away from the premises.

3. Liability arising out of the use of large boats. The policy generally covers the average small pleasure boat, so long as it does not exceed certain dimensions. Liability arising out of the use of larger craft must be handled by a separate contract or by a special endorsement to the CPL.

4. Destruction of property in the care, custody, or control of the insured.

5. Contractual liability except those contracts of liability relating to the premises, as might be the case under a typical lease.

6. Liability arising out of intentional acts of the insured. The question has arisen as to whether intentional acts of children giving rise to parental liability are covered. It has been held that since the parent did not perform the intentional act, the CPL applies to such cases as far as the *parent's* liability is concerned.[13] Presumably suits against the *child* would not be defended where the child intentionally causes some loss, even if the child cannot know the full consequences of his act because of his age.

7. Liability arising from secondary residences, such as beach houses or mountain cabins *if owned* by the insured. The insured is expected to purchase a separate policy for such property. Since in most areas the rates for the CPL are less than $15 a year for basic limits, this requirement does not impose an undue cost.

SUMMARY

1. The major classes of liability insurance contracts are (a) business, (b) professional, (c) personal, and (d) automobile. The latter class has applications in each of the first three classes but, because of its special importance, is singled out for separate discussion in Chapter 16.

2. All liability contracts have certain elements in common. For example, the insuring agreements are fairly well standardized. The major differences lie in whether the event giving rise to a legal claim is interpreted to be an "occurrence" or an "accident." The occurrence basis, being broader than the accident basis, is a preferred wording from the viewpoint of the insured. Liability contracts vary in the definition of who is insured. All liability contracts guarantee that the insurer will bear the cost of defense in addition to paying any judgments up to the limits of liability.

---

[13] *Arenson* v. *National Automobile & Casualty Insurance Co.* 286 Pac. (2d) 816.

3. Common exclusions peculiar to liability contracts include (a) nonbusiness activities in the case of business liability policies, and business activities in the case of nonbusness liability contracts, and (b) damage to property in the care, custody, and control of the insured. Because of its inherent ambiguity, the latter exclusion has resulted in much litigation.

4. The comprehensive general liability contract (CGL) is one of the major policies of business liability insurance. A scheduled form written on an all-risk basis, the CGL insures premises liability; liability arising out of manufacturing, contracting, or other business activities of the insured; elevator liability; contingent liability; teams liability; medical payments; products liability; and contractual liability. The latter three coverages are optional. Any of the coverages are available on separate contracts.

5. Products liability insurance, which may be written with the CGL, is distinguished from general liability insurance in several ways, chief among which is that the accident giving rise to the claim must occur away from the main premises of the business and must arise out of a faulty product sold or a service rendered by the insured after the insured has completed his work. Products liability insurance covers the loss no matter when the deficient product was sold or the faulty service was performed. It never covers loss to the product itself but only damage caused by its faulty manufacture.

6. Contractual liability insurance is necessitated by the existence of agreements whereby one party assumes the liability of another party by contractual agreement, often termed a "hold harmless agreement." Such an obligation is not covered under the concept of "legal liability" that applies to the general provisions of liability contracts and, therefore, special coverage is required.

7. Professional liability (malpractice) insurance covering liability for claims arising from professional errors or mistakes is distinguished from other liability contracts in a number of ways. Generally, professional liability contracts do not permit out-of-court settlements without the permission of the insured, are issued on a per-claim basis instead of a per-accident basis, and do not restrict their coverage to accidental occurrences. Professional liability policies will not cover dishonest or criminal acts nor will they insure any claim arising out of any guarantee that professional services rendered will accomplish a specified result.

8. Most personal liability insurance is written on the comprehensive personal liability policy (CPL). This contract, similar in wording to the CGL, is designed to meet the needs of the typical householder for premises liability as well as for other liability arising from ordinary nonbusiness pursuits, such as sports, hobbies, and ownership of animals.

QUESTIONS FOR REVIEW AND DISCUSSION

1. In Employers Insurance Company of Alabama Inc. v. Rives 8(CCH Fire and Casualty Cases) 676 (1955), a contractor installed some gaso-

line pumps and, due to his failure to tighten connections, gasoline leaked out underground and contaminated the well of a nearby property owner.

(a) Would the contractor's products liability policy cover this loss?

(b) If you were the attorney for the insurer, on what grounds might you attempt to deny liability under the policy? Explain.

2. In Great American Indemnity Company of New York v. Saltzman 8(CCH Fire and Casualty Cases) 388, an insured had a general liability policy. He entered an airplane belonging to another person to inspect it (without permission) and started the engine. Because of his unfamiliarity with the controls, the insured could not stop the plane, which crashed into a hangar and caused substantial damage. The insurer refused to defend the insured in the resulting suit for damages.

(a) On what grounds is it likely that the insurer relied? Explain, with reference to appropriate policy provisions of the typical business liability policy.

(b) Do you think that the defense in (a) should be found to be good? Discuss.

3. The druggists' liability policy is a combination of professional liability and products liability, with the professional liability portion covering errors in compounding, delivery, or other handling of prescriptions or drugs. This policy gives the insurance company the sole right to settle claims. Is this provision typical of most professional liability contracts? If so, what dangers lie in it? If not, suggest a reason why the insurer might so provide.

4. "A," a local agent, places "Y's" general liability insurance in the Shifting Sands Insurance Company. "Y" has an accident in which he is held to be legally liable for $5,000 damages. When he submits his claim, it is discovered that the Shifting Sands Insurance Company is bankrupt. So "Y" sues "A" for $5,000 claiming that "A" negligently placed his insurance with an unsound insurer and is therefore guilty of breach of professional duty.

(a) In your opinion is "A" negligent? Why or why not?

(b) Assuming "A" is negligent, would his errors and omissions policy respond to this claim?

(c) Assuming "A" is not legally negligent but tenders "Y" $5,000 anyway because of what he feels is a moral obligation, will the errors and omissions policy cover the payment?

5. On his way to a meeting with a client, an attorney injures a third party in an automobile accident.

(a) Does such an occurrence arise out of the attorney's professional practice? If so, would the professional liability policy respond in damages? Why?

(b) Would your answer be different if the accident occurred because the attorney and his client were discussing a legal question while driving along and as a result of not paying attention to driving, the attorney caused the accident? Discuss.

6. In one case, a patient, "P," alleged that his physician agreed to remove a growth by a method known as fulguration for a fee not to exceed $150. The physician promised that the plaintiff would be cured in a few days and could resume his work, because the procedure would not involve any cutting into the abdominal wall. The procedure failed and as a result, "P" was required to have an operation and spend a large sum of money. In addition, he was hospitalized for one month and could not return to work for a considerable period of time. "P" based his complaint on breach of contract—Robins v. Finestone, 5(CCH Negligence Cases 2d) 16.

    (a) Would the physicians' professional liability policy cover this loss?

    (b) Would your answer have been the same if the suit were based on the fact that the physician had performed the operation in an unskillful and unworkmanlike manner? Explain.

7. What are the central differences between professional liability contracts and other liability contracts? Discuss each.

8. Do professional liability insurance policies usually exclude damage to property in the care, custody, or control of the insured? Discuss.

9. In Providence Washington Indemnity Co. v. Varella, 8(CCH Fire and Casualty Cases) 117, the insured had a CPL policy covering her residence and a hairdressing shop at another location. Later she moved her business to her home and after this relocation of the business, a patron was injured in a stairway accident. The insurer denied liability under the CPL. The insured claimed that the CPL applies to all activities connected with her home, including business activities incidental to nonbusiness pursuits. Hence, her hairdressing activities were really incidental to running a home and should be covered. Is the insurer on sound grounds in denying liability? Why?

10. "C," on a business trip, rents an outboard boat for some pleasure fishing. Due to careless handling, the boat runs into a swimmer, causing severe injuries. Will the CPL pay the claim? Why or why not?

11. A department store has a CGL policy with products liability covered. A woman came into the store to look at an automatic washer. After she purchased the washer, she asked to see once again how the bleach dispenser operated. During the demonstration of the machine, a metal strap snapped out and bruised her hand. Medical attention was necessary and a claim for damages resulted.

    (a) Under which portion, if any, of the CGL policy would this claim be paid, if it is found that negligence exists?

    (b) How, if at all, would your answer have changed if the accident had occurred after the washer had been delivered at the home of the buyer?

(c) What difference does it make as to which portion of the policy pays the loss? Explain.

12. The city of "Y" hires a contractor, "C," to perform some work, and specifies that "C" name "Y" as an additional insured under his CGL. "Y" also requires "C" to sign a hold harmless agreement to the effect that "C" will assume any liability that "Y" might have arising out of the work which "C" is performing. "C" points out that such an agreement is unnecessary and, in fact, dangerous because the city would in effect be holding itself harmless for any liability arising out of the work.
(a) Do you agree? Why?
(b) In your opinion should the city not only require a hold harmless agreement but also be named as an additional insured? Discuss.

13. A commercial dock operator contracting to handle blocks of army cargo is asked to sign a somewhat lengthy contract, part of which states:
    During any period or periods of time under this contract . . . the contractor shall, at his own expense, procure and maintain insurance as follows:
    (1) Bodily injury liability insurance in an amount not less than $50,000 for any one person and $250,000 for any one accident.
    (2) Property damage liability insurance, which shall include any and all property, whether or not in the care, custody, or control of the contractor, in an amount of not less than $250,000 on account of any one accident.
    . . . it is expressly agreed that the provisions contained in . . . this article shall not in any manner limit liability or extent of liability of the contractor. . . .

(a) Should the dock operator sign this contract? Why or why not?
(b) If he does sign it, what difficulties might be encountered when he attempts to fulfill the contract? Explain.

14. A writer stated "If both buyers and sellers, contractors and owners, and landlords and tenants will simply agree each to assume full responsibility for his own obligations according to law and each to rely on his own insurance for protection, the necessity for any sort of hold harmless clause in purchase orders, contracts, and leases will instantly cease." Do you agree? If so, why? If not, why not?

15. Which of the following claims, if any, would be defended under the CPL: (Give your reasons in each case.)
    (a) A boy riding a bicycle struck and injured a pedestrian. The boy's parents were sued, but the supreme court found the boy and not the parents liable.
    (b) A boy struck another boy and threw him down an embankment, breaking his leg. The court found the parents liable because of their knowledge of the vicious propensities of the child.

(c) Two hunters, firing at the same time at a quail, injured a third hunter, who obtained a $10,000 judgment from each.

(d) The insured was sued when a guest tripped on steep stairs leading to the beach from an oceanside cabin which the insured maintained as a second residence.

(e) The insured's dog bit a "tresspasser" who turned out to be the meter reader.

(f) The insured's dog, a police dog, killed another smaller dog in a somewhat uneven fight.

16. A customer of a department store purchased an electric heater which overheated and set fire to his home due to a failure in the electrical circuit. The customer brought action against the store for damages to his home plus the cost of a new heater. To what extent will the products liability policy of the store respond to this claim? Why?

17. A customer of the store in Question 16 hires one of the store's workmen to apply some ceramic tile to the bathroom wall. Three weeks after the job is completed, one section of the tile comes loose and falls into the bathtub. Will the store's products liability policy respond to this claim? Why, or why not?

18. The XYZ Manufacturing Company has purchased a CGL but has not bought contractual liability coverage with it. One day, the landlord informs XYZ that a nearby concern has brought an action against him arising out of XYZ's maintenance of the premises. It appears that XYZ's failure to control smoke emission has ruined certain raw materials through smoke deposits. The landlord observes that XYZ has agreed in the lease to hold him harmless for any claim arising out of the maintenance of the premises. Does XYZ have any protection against this claim under its CGL? Why, or why not?

19. What is the significance of the fact that subrogation is almost a universal privilege retained by the insurer in liability contracts? Discuss.

20. Which, if any, of the following medical payments claims, would be paid under the CPL? Give your reasons in each case.

(a) A high school boy hired by the day is injured in a fall from a ladder while cleaning out a gutter.

(b) A union painter, one of four hired to paint the insured's home, is injured in a fall from a ladder.

(c) The insured's son injures a classmate in a hockey game.

(d) The insured's son is injured in a fall on the steps of a skiing cabin rented for a weekend.

(e) The insured's electric fence electrocutes a thief trying to enter the premises at night.

(f) The suitor of the insured's daughter, repeatedly warned to stay off the premises, is injured when he trips over the electric fence.

21. (a) For each of the cases given in Question 20, suggest reasons why the insurer has included the particular policy provisions which governed your answer.

    (b) If you were drafting a new "competitive" contract, would you include the same provisions? Why?

22. (a) Why are the supplementary payments portion of the insuring agreement in liability contracts especially important?

    (b) If you were drafting a new "competitive" contract, would you charge extra for the supplementary payments portion? Why?

Automobile

16

Insurance

Automobiles, not an unmixed blessing in Twentieth Century America, were introduced in the United States at a time when mass-production methods were just becoming technically feasible. As a result, large numbers of automobiles were produced and sold before roads could be built or before other facilities were available to cope with the traffic problem. The industry has been able to accelerate the pace of manufacture of vehicles with a degree of speed and power that has tended to outpace the skill of their drivers and the capacity of the highways. These two conditions, coupled with the fact that automobiles were cheap enough for nearly everyone to own, created an ideal climate for the growth of losses from liability claims, from collision, and from bodily injuries and deaths due to accidents. Insurance premiums have grown from an insignificant amount to a level where they are among the largest costs of owning and operating a car. Measured by premium volume, automobile insurance is, furthermore, by far the largest single segment of all property and liability insurance business, being almost as large as all other lines combined.[1]

THE HIGH COST OF AUTOMOBILE ACCIDENTS

Some specific notion of the extent of growth of the automobile industry and the high cost of automobile accidents may be seen from certain facts collected by the National Safety Council. It was estimated that in 1959, for example, there were 84 million licensed drivers in the United States, operating 70.4 million registered vehicles, and over 20 per cent of these drivers were involved in some kind of accident causing either bodily injury or property damage. A classification of the type of loss is given in Table 16–1, while Table 16–2 presents the 1913–1959 record of death rates.

---

[1] In the period 1953–1957, stock companies reported by *Best's Insurance Reports, Fire and Casualty,* collected a total of $16.7 billion in the field of fire, extended coverage, inland marine, workmen's compensation, ocean marine, and miscellaneous bodily injury liability. During the same period, automobile premiums amounted to $15.4 billion, of which $9.1 billion was for liability insurance and $6.3 billion was for physical damage insurance.

Table 16–1

DEATHS AND INJURIES FROM AUTOMOBILE ACCIDENTS, 1959

Number of deaths:		Number of accidents causing	
Pedestrians................. 7,750		Deaths................. 32,300	
Nonpedestrians.............30,050		Nonfatal injuries.......... 900,000	
37,800		Property damage.......... 9,300,000	
		Total accidents.............10,232,300	
Number of deaths:			
Urban.....................10,000		Number of injuries causing	
Rural.....................27,800		disability for one or more	
37,800		days.................... 1,400,000	

	Number of Deaths	Per Cent of Total
Type of accident causing deaths:		
Collision between motor vehicles.......................15,100		39.9
Noncollision (overturn, running off roadway, etc.)..........11,600		30.7
Pedestrian... 7,750		20.5
Collision with fixed objects............................ 1,650		4.4
Collision with railroad trains.......................... 1,135		3.0
Collision with bicycles................................ 480		1.3
Other collisions...................................... 85		.2
Total...37,800		100.0

Source: National Safety Council, *Accident Facts, 1960.*

Table 16–1 shows that an overwhelming majority of accidents resulted in property damage alone, but about nine per cent of all accidents resulted in bodily injuries, and of these injuries, about 3.6 per cent resulted in deaths. A death occurred in 1959 once in every 314 accidents and about one out of every 180 persons was an automobile accident victim. Table 16–2 gives a long-run picture of death rates from automobile accidents expressed in three different ways. It is encouraging to note that the death rate per one hundred million vehicle miles traveled has declined steadily over the period 1913–1959 to a point that it is now only one third the rate that existed in the 1920's. However, the death rate expressed as a percentage of population has remained fairly constant. Automobile deaths constituted about 40 per cent of the total accidental deaths in 1959.

The cost of these deaths and injuries has been mounting in both absolute and relative terms. Automobiles accounted for nearly half of the total cost of accidental deaths and injuries in 1959. The physical damage caused by automobiles in 1959 is estimated by the National Safety Council at $2.1 billion, which, when added to the $4.1 billion cost of deaths and injuries, amounts to $6.2 billion, or approximately $120 per family. Rising repair costs, use of more expensive cars, and a

Table 16–2

DEATH RATES IN FATAL AUTOMOBILE ACCIDENTS, AND THEIR ESTIMATED COSTS, 1913–1959

Year	Death Rates			
	Per 10,000 Motor Vehicles	Per 100,000,000 Vehicle Miles	Per 100,000 Population	Cost (in Billions)
1913–1917 Av............	23.8	...	6.8	...
1918–1922 Av............	13.9	...	11.9	...
1923–1927 Av............	11.1	18.2	18.8	...
1928–1932 Av............	12.1	15.6	25.3	$1.30
1937....................	13.2	14.7	30.8	1.80
1942....................	8.6	10.6	21.2	1.60
1947....................	8.7	8.8	22.8	2.65
1952....................	7.1	7.4	24.3	3.75
1957....................	5.8	6.0	22.7	5.30
1958....................	5.4	5.6	21.3	5.60
1959....................	5.4	5.4	21.4	6.20

COST OF ACCIDENTAL INJURIES BY MAJOR TYPE, 1959

Motor vehicle accidents
Lost wages.....................................$1,600,000,000
Medical expenses...............................   150,000,000
Overhead of insurance companies................. 2,350,000,000
    Total motor vehicle accidents..................$4,100,000,000

Other accidents
Public nonmotor vehicle accidents.................$ 850,000,000
Home accidents................................   900,000,000
Work accidents................................. 2,100,000,000
    Total other accidents........................ $3,850,000,000
    Total all accidents *........................$7,800,000,000

* Duplications between motor vehicle, work, and home are eliminated in the total.
Source: National Safety Council, *Accident Facts, 1960*. Data collected from the National Office of Vital Statistics, except 1959, which was estimated; motor vehicle registrations and vehicle miles from United States Bureau of Public Roads.

higher proportion of newer cars being driven are among the explanations of the rising physical damage costs of accidents.

CAUSES OF AUTOMOBILE ACCIDENTS

There is no generally accepted or proved basic reason for accidents of any type, including, of course, automobile accidents. Explanations that automobile accidents are a result of psychological insecurity which is manifested by irrational behavior behind the wheel are interesting but unproved.

Certain statistical data are available that reveal the various conditions under which accidents occur, the types of drivers involved in the most accidents, etc. These data cast a shadow of doubt on oft-expressed statements that accidents are caused by defective mechanical condition of cars, night driving, women drivers, wet highways, too many trucks and inexperienced drivers. Statistics collected by the National Safety Council reveal, for example, that most accidents occur when the roads are dry, the weather is clear, and the condition of the car is apparently good. Furthermore, drivers with less than one year of experience, constituting about seven per cent of all motorists, are involved in only about three per cent of the accidents. Men have roughly twice the accident rate per 1,000 drivers as women, but data are lacking on vehicle miles driven by men and women; so no final conclusion can be drawn on the perennial claim about "women drivers."

Data on the ages of drivers involved in accidents, summarized in Table 16–3, reveal that age appears to be a factor in automobile accidents. For example, drivers under age 20 constituted 7.2 per cent of all drivers but were involved in 11.6 per cent of fatal accidents and 13 per cent of all accidents, resulting in an "accident index" figure of 1.81. On the other hand, drivers aged 70–74 were involved in accidents not nearly in proportion to their numbers, having an accident index of only .52. Drivers between the ages 25–49 accounted for 56.2 per cent of all drivers and were involved in 52.6 per cent of all accidents, resulting in an accident index of .94.

One study, the results of which appear in the last column of Table 16–3, reveals that in those cases where it could be determined that a driver was to blame for an accident, there was a significant difference in the percentage of faulty drivers in various age groups. In general, the groups most culpable were those drivers under 20 and over 70. It is interesting to observe, however, that in only about half of the cases was it determined that either driver was to blame. This fact is of significance to those who favor elimination of the negligence system as a basis for allocating the costs of automobile accidents in favor of a compensation system similar to workmen's compensation. The significance lies in the fact that a basic strength of the compensation system is that it is not necessary to determine fault. Indemnity is paid regardless of fault.

One conclusion which should be drawn from the above discussion is that while the data observed have been used for rate-making purposes in automobile insurance, they are still not explanations of the *cause* of automobile accidents. Just because a driver is youthful is no reason to

Table 16–3

AGE AS A FACTOR IN AUTOMOBILE ACCIDENTS, 1959

Age	% Distribution 84 Million Drivers	% in Fatal Accidents	% in All Accidents	Accident Index *	% at Fault †
Under 20.........	7.2	11.6	13.0	1.81	61.9
20–24............	19.2	16.8	15.0	1.34	56.5
25–29............	12.7	13.4	14.1	1.11	50.4
30–34............	12.5	11.5	11.2	.90	47.2
35–39............	11.6	9.1	10.2	.88	46.8
40–44............	10.3	8.9	9.0	.87	46.2
45–49............	9.1	7.8	8.1	.89	47.2
50–54............	7.8	5.9	6.2	.79	47.1
55–59............	6.2	4.6	4.8	.77	49.6
60–64............	4.7	3.9	3.4	.72	53.2
65–69............	3.1	2.9	3.0	.97	56.3
70–74............	2.1	2.1	1.1	.52	62.2
75 and over......	1.5	1.5	.9	.60	70.6

* Ratio of per cent in all accidents to per cent of all drivers in each age group. 1.00 is average; the larger the ratio, the poorer the experience.
† Based on a study of California drivers and reported in *1956 Annual Statistical Report*, Department of California, Highway Patrol. The average of this column is 51.6%.
Source: National Safety Council, *Accident Facts, 1960*, p. 53.

suppose he is therefore almost sure to cause accidents. The National Safety Council estimated that 16 per cent of all fatal auto accidents and 10 per cent of total auto accidents involve nonresidents of the state, but this is not convincing proof of a cause-and-effect relationship, or that out-of-state drivers should be barred at the borders. One theory of the business cycle was developed when an observer noted a correspondence between sun spots and the high and lows of business activity. It would be wrong to conclude, however, that sun spots *cause* business cycles. Nevertheless, observation of data similar to those we have been considering have led to increased insurance rates for youthful drivers and for drivers with past records of repeated involvement in accidents, because until more is known as to the cause of accidents the rate-maker must, in the interest of equity, assign the cost to those groups where more than proportionate amounts of accidents have occurred.

THE NEED FOR INSURANCE

In the face of mounting costs of automobile accidents and the substantial probability of being involved in one, what should the average driver do to protect himself against the financial consequences of risk? For nearly everyone the answer has been insurance, in spite of its in-

creasing cost. As we shall see, not only is insurance almost a legal requirement in most states, but it is also far superior to the method of
running the economic risks without any protection (assumption of risk).
Since most individuals own at most two automobiles, there is an insufficient exposure to allow for the method of self-insurance.[2] Because of
the personal catastrophic loss hazard involved in the liability risk, insurance is the only feasible solution.

As for physical damage coverage, the wisdom of the insurance
method depends on the size of the exposure. For example, most persons
could not easily afford to lose a $3,000 automobile in a wreck; but if one
can afford a $300 second car, its possible destruction might not be suf-
ficiently serious to warrant collision or comprehensive insurance. The
annual cost of collision insurance on a $300 vehicle might be $50 or
more, even for $50 deductible coverage. The rate is thus much higher
than if the auto were worth $3,000, for which the premium might be
$75.

ANALYSIS OF THE FAMILY AUTOMOBILE POLICY (FAP)

Most automobile insurance contracts are written on two major
forms—the *family automobile policy* (FAP) and the *1955 version of the
standard automobile policy*. The FAP was introduced in 1956, and revised in 1958, as the basic coverage for noncommercial vehicles. The
1955 standard automobile policy, which formerly served both the needs
of private and commercial automobile owners, is now employed primarily
for commercial vehicles only. The provisions of the two contracts are
similar in most basic respects. An analysis of the FAP is given here because of its wide general use. Individual insurers often use slightly different forms to meet particular needs, to make their forms more salable,
or to simplify them. Broadly speaking, however, an understanding of the
FAP will enable the reader to analyze nearly any automobile contract.
The five basic parts of the policy form, reproduced in Figure 16–1, are:
  1) Part 1—Liability
  2) Part 2—Medical payments
  3) Part 3—Physical damage
  4) Uninsured motorist endorsement
  5) Part 4—Conditions

---

[2] See Chapter 1 for a discussion of the methods of handling risk.

1) Part 1—Liability

Considerable similarity between the insuring agreements in Part 1 of the FAP and the insuring agreements in the liability contracts discussed in Chapter 15 are observable. Coverage is on an occurrence basis and the agreement to defend each suit arising out of the ownership, maintenance, or use of the owned, or of any nonowned automobile, is made part and parcel of the general insuring agreement to pay all bodily injury or property damage claims against the insured. The purpose here is to forestall the possibility that the insurer will be called upon to defend a suit against the insured even though the limits of liability under the contract have been exhausted or even though the suit did not even involve an automobile. Some courts have held that in liability policies the agreement to defend the insured is separate from the agreement to pay damages which the insured is legally obligated to pay. As a result of a decision of this type,[3] the FAP has combined its insuring agreement to reflect what has been the actual intention of the insurer all along.

Illustrating these points, suppose that John carries liability limits of $10,000/$20,000 bodily injury ($10,000 each person, and $20,000 each occurrence) and $5,000 property damage. He is found to be negligent in an automobile accident and is required to pay a judgment of $4,000 to Jim, $3,000 to Sam, $11,000 to Harry for bodily injuries, plus $5,000 for the loss of Sam's building which was burned when John crashed into it. The FAP will respond in the amount of $17,000 for bodily injury liability, covering all of Jim's and Sam's claims, but only $10,000 of Harry's claim. Sam's property damage claim of $5,000 will be paid, plus all court costs and attorneys fees involved, if any. Later on, suppose Sam sues for an additional $3,000 under property damage liability when it is found that the fire also burned his new automobile. The FAP's limits have been exhausted as to that accident and the insurer is not required to defend the second suit.

Persons insured.[4] The FAP defines an insured in a very broad manner. Not only are all members of the named insured's household covered automatically, but so is anyone who is driving the owned auto with permission of the named insured or his spouse.[5] Furthermore, the policy covers a person who is legally responsible for the use of the car, or

(Continued on page 406)

---

[3] *American Employers Insurance Company* v. *Goble Aircraft Specialties, Inc.* 8(CCH Fire and Casualty Cases) 437.

[4] Coverage of individuals other than the named insured is sometimes referred to as the *omnibus clause.*

[5] Note that the definition of "named insured" includes his spouse or a resident of the same household. Note also that no one else is empowered to give such permission.

Allied Insurance Company

(A stock company, herein called the company)

Agrees with the insured, named in the declarations made a part hereof, in consideration of the payment of the premium and in reliance upon the statements in the declarations and subject to all of the terms of this policy:

Part 1 — Liability

Coverage A—Bodily Injury Liability; Coverage B—Property Damage Liability

To pay on behalf of the insured all sums which the insured shall become legally obligated to pay as damages because of:

A. bodily injury, sickness or disease, including death resulting therefrom, hereinafter called "bodily injury," sustained by any person;

B. injury to or destruction of property, including loss of use thereof, hereinafter called "property damage";

arising out of the ownership, maintenance or use of the owned automobile or any non-owned automobile, and the company shall defend any suit alleging such bodily injury or property damage and seeking damages which are payable under the terms of this policy, even if any of the allegations of the suit are groundless, false or fraudulent; but the company may make such investigation and settlement of any claim or suit as it deems expedient.

Supplementary Payments

To pay, in addition to the applicable limits of liability:

(a) all expenses incurred by the company, all costs taxed against the insured in any such suit and all interest on the entire amount of any judgment therein which accrues after entry of the judgment and before the company has paid or tendered or deposited in court that part of the judgment which does not exceed the limit of the company's liability thereon;

(b) premiums on appeal bonds required in any such suit, premiums on bonds to release attachments for an amount not in excess of the applicable limit of liability of this policy, and the cost of bail bonds required of the insured because of accident or traffic law violation arising out of the use of an automobile insured hereunder, not to exceed $100 per bail bond, but without any obligation to apply for or furnish any such bonds;

(c) expenses incurred by the insured for such immediate medical and surgical relief to others as shall be imperative at the time of an accident involving an automobile insured hereunder and not due to war;

(d) all reasonable expenses, other than loss of earnings, incurred by the insured at the company's request.

Persons Insured

The following are insured under Part I:

"**trailer**" means a trailer designed for use with a private passenger automobile, if not being used for business, or commercial purposes with other than a private passenger, farm or utility automobile, or a farm wagon or farm implement while used with a farm automobile;

"**automobile business**" means the business or occupation of selling, repairing, servicing, storing or parking automobiles;

"**use**" of an automobile includes the loading and unloading thereof;

"**war**" means war, whether or not declared, civil war, insurrection, rebellion or revolution, or any act or condition incident to any of the foregoing.

Exclusions

This policy does not apply under Part I:

(a) to any automobile while used as a public or livery conveyance, but this exclusion does not apply to the named insured with respect to bodily injury or property damage which results from the named insured's occupancy of a non-owned automobile other than as the operator thereof;

(b) to bodily injury or property damage caused intentionally by or at the direction of the insured;

(c) to bodily injury or property damage with respect to which an insured under this policy is also an insured under a contract of nuclear energy liability insurance issued by the Nuclear Energy Liability Insurance Association or the Mutual Atomic Energy Liability Underwriters and in effect at the time of the occurrence resulting in such bodily injury or property damage; provided, such contract of nuclear energy liability insurance shall be deemed to be in effect at the time of such occurrence notwithstanding such contract has terminated upon exhaustion of its limit of liability;

(d) to bodily injury or property damage arising out of the operation of farm machinery;

(e) to bodily injury to any employee of the insured arising out of and in the course of (1) domestic employment by the insured, if benefits therefor are in whole or in part either payable or required to be provided under any workmen's compensation law, or (2) other employment by the insured;

(f) to bodily injury to any fellow employee of the insured injured in the

thereof is with the permission of the named insured;

(b) With respect to a non-owned automobile,
(1) the named insured,
(2) any relative, but only with respect to a private passenger automobile or trailer, provided the actual use thereof is with the permission of the owner;

(c) Any other person or organization legally responsible for the use of
(1) an owned automobile, or trailer,
(2) a non-owned automobile, if such automobile is not owned or hired by such person or organization,
provided the actual use thereof is by a person who is an insured under (a) or (b) above with respect to such owned automobile or non-owned automobile.

The insurance afforded under Part I applies separately to each insured against whom claim is made or suit is brought, but the inclusion herein of more than one insured shall not operate to increase the limits of the company's liability.

Definitions

Under Part I:

"named insured" means the individual named in Item 1 of the declarations and also includes his spouse, if a resident of the same household;

"insured" means a person or organization described under "Persons Insured";

"relative" means a relative of the named insured who is a resident of the same household;

"owned automobile" means a private passenger, farm or utility automobile or trailer owned by the named insured, and includes a temporary substitute automobile;

"temporary substitute automobile" means any automobile or trailer, not owned by the named insured, while temporarily used as a substitute for the owned automobile or trailer when withdrawn from normal use because of its breakdown, repair, servicing, loss or destruction;

"non-owned automobile" means an automobile or trailer not owned by or furnished for the regular use of either the named insured or any relative, other than a temporary substitute automobile;

"private passenger automobile" means a four wheel private passenger, station wagon or jeep type automobile;

"farm automobile" means an automobile of the truck type with a load capacity of fifteen hundred pounds or less not used for business or commercial purposes other than farming;

"utility automobile" means an automobile, other than a farm automobile, with a load capacity of fifteen hundred pounds or less of the pick-up body, sedan delivery or panel truck type not used for business or commercial purposes;

employee;

(g) to an owned automobile while used in the automobile business, but this exclusion does not apply to the named insured, a resident of the same household as the named insured, a partnership in which such resident or the named insured is a partner, or any partner, agent or employee of such resident or partnership;

(h) to a non-owned automobile while used (1) in the automobile business by the insured or (2) in any other business or occupation of the insured except a private passenger automobile operated or occupied by the named insured or by his private chauffeur or domestic servant, or a trailer used therewith;

(i) to injury to or destruction of property owned or transported by the insured, or property rented to or in charge of the insured other than a residence or private garage.

Financial Responsibility Laws

When this policy is certified as proof of financial responsibility for the future under the provisions of any motor vehicle financial responsibility law, such insurance as is afforded by this policy for bodily injury liability or for property damage liability shall comply with the provisions of such law to the extent of the coverage and limits of liability required by such law, but in no event in excess of the limits of liability stated in this policy. The insured agrees to reimburse the company for any payment made by the company which it would not have been obligated to make under the terms of this policy except for the agreement contained in this paragraph.

Limits of Liability

The limit of bodily injury liability stated in the declarations as applicable to "each person" is the limit of the company's liability for all damages, including damages for care and loss of services, arising out of bodily injury sustained by one person as the result of any one occurrence; the limit of such liability stated in the declarations as applicable to "each occurrence" is, subject to the above provision respecting each person, the total limit of the company's liability for all such damages arising out of bodily injury sustained by two or more persons as the result of any one occurrence.

The limit of property damage liability stated in the declarations as applicable to "each occurrence" is the total limit of the company's liability for all damages arising out of injury to or destruction of all property of one or more persons or organizations; including the loss of use thereof, as the result of any one occurrence.

Other Insurance

If the insured has other insurance against a loss covered by Part I of this policy the company shall not be liable under this policy for a greater proportion of such loss than the applicable limit of liability stated in the declarations bears to the total applicable limit of liability of all valid and collectible insurance against such loss; provided, however, the insurance with respect to a temporary substitute automobile or non-owned automobile shall be excess insurance over any other valid and collectible insurance.

Figure 16-1

THE FAMILY AUTOMOBILE POLICY (FAP), page 2

Part 2 — Expenses for Medical Services

Coverage C—Medical Payments

To pay all reasonable expenses incurred within one year from the date of accident for necessary medical, surgical, X-ray and dental services, including prosthetic devices, and necessary ambulance, hospital, professional nursing and funeral services:

Division 1. To or for the named insured and each relative who sustains bodily injury, sickness or disease, including death resulting therefrom, hereinafter called "bodily injury," caused by accident, while occupying or through being struck by an automobile;

Division 2. To or for any other person who sustains bodily injury, caused by accident, while occupying

(a) the owned automobile, while being used by the named insured, by any resident of the same household or by any other person with the permission of the named insured; or

(b) a non-owned automobile, if the bodily injury results from (1) its operation or occupancy by the named insured or its operation on his behalf by his private chauffeur or domestic servant or (2) its operation or occupancy by a relative and it is a private passenger automobile or trailer not regularly furnished for the use of such relative.

Definitions

The definitions under Part I apply to Part II, and under Part II:

"**occupying**" means in or upon or entering into or alighting from;

"**an automobile**" includes a trailer of any type.

Exclusions

This policy does not apply under Part II to bodily injury:

(a) sustained while occupying (1) an owned automobile while used as a public or livery conveyance, or (2) any vehicle while located for use as a residence or premises;

(b) sustained by the named insured or a relative (1) while occupying an automobile owned by or furnished for the regular use of either the named insured or any relative, other than an automobile defined herein as an

"owned automobile," or (2) while occupying or through being struck by (i) a farm type tractor or other equipment designed for use principally off public roads, while not upon public roads, or (ii) a vehicle operated on rails or crawler-treads;

(c) sustained by any person other than the named insured or a relative, resulting from use of (1) a non-owned automobile in the automobile business or as a public or livery conveyance, or (2) a non-owned automobile in any other business or occupation, except operation or occupancy of a private passenger automobile by the named insured or by his private chauffeur or domestic servant, or of a trailer used therewith, or with an owned automobile;

(d) sustained by any person who is employed in the automobile business, if the accident arises out of the operation thereof and if benefits therefor are in whole or in part either payable or required to be provided under any workmen's compensation law;

(e) due to war.

Limit of Liability

The limit of liability for medical payments stated in the declarations as applicable to "each person" is the limit of the company's liability for all expenses incurred by or on behalf of each person who sustains bodily injury as the result of any one accident.

Other Insurance

If there is other automobile medical payments insurance against a loss covered by Part II of this policy the company shall not be liable under this policy for a greater proportion of such loss than the applicable limit of liability stated in the declarations bears to the total applicable limit of liability of all valid and collectible automobile medical payments insurance; provided, however, the insurance with respect to a temporary substitute automobile or non-owned automobile shall be excess insurance over any other valid and collectible automobile medical payments insurance.

Part 3 — Physical Damage

"utility automobile," "automobile business," and "war" in Part I apply to Part III, and under Part III:

"**insured**" means (a) with respect to the owned automobile (1) the named insured and (2) any person or organization, other than a person or organiza-

Coverage D (1)—Comprehensive—Excluding Collision •
(2)—Personal Effects

(1) To pay for loss caused other than by collision to the owned automobile or to a non-owned automobile. For the purpose of this coverage, breakage

(2) To pay for loss caused by fire or lightning to robes, wearing apparel and other personal effects which are the property of the named insured or a relative, while such effects are in or upon the owned automobile.

Coverage E—Collision

To pay for loss caused by collision to the owned automobile or to a non-owned automobile but only for the amount of each such loss in excess of the deductible amount stated in the declarations as applicable hereto.

Coverage F—Fire, Lightning and Transportation

To pay for loss to the owned automobile or a non-owned automobile, caused (a) by fire or lightning, (b) by smoke or smudge due to a sudden, unusual and faulty operation of any fixed heating equipment serving the premises in which the automobile is located, or (c) by the stranding, sinking, burning, collision or derailment of any conveyance in or upon which the automobile is being transported.

Coverage G—Theft

To pay for loss to the owned automobile or to a non-owned automobile caused by theft or larceny.

Coverage H—Combined Additional Coverage

To pay for loss to the owned automobile or a non-owned automobile caused by windstorm, hail, earthquake, explosion, riot or civil commotion, or the forced landing or falling of any aircraft or its parts or equipment, flood or rising waters, malicious mischief or vandalism, external discharge or leakage of water except loss resulting from rain, snow or sleet whether or not wind-driven; provided, with respect to each automobile $25 shall be deducted from each loss caused by malicious mischief or vandalism.

Coverage I—Towing and Labor Costs

To pay for towing and labor costs necessitated by the disablement of the owned automobile or of any non-owned automobile, provided the labor is performed at the place of disablement.

Supplementary Payments

In addition to the applicable limit of liability:

(a) to reimburse the insured for transportation expenses incurred during the period commencing 48 hours after a theft covered by this policy of the entire automobile has been reported to the company and the police, and terminating when the automobile is returned to use or the company pays for the loss; provided that the company shall not be obligated to pay aggregate expenses in excess of $10 per day or totaling more than $300.

(b) to pay general average and salvage charges for which the insured becomes legally liable, as to the automobile being transported.

Definitions

The definitions of "named insured," "relative," "owned automobile," "temporary substitute automobile," "private passenger automobile," "farm automobile,"

the permission of the owner;

"**non-owned automobile**" means a private passenger automobile or trailer not owned by or furnished for the regular use of either the named insured or any relative, other than a temporary substitute automobile, while said automobile or trailer is in the possession or custody of the insured or is being operated by him;

"**loss**" means direct and accidental loss of or damage to (a) the automobile, including its equipment, or (b) other insured property;

"**collision**" means collision of an automobile covered by this policy with another object or with a vehicle to which it is attached or by upset of such automobile;

"**trailer**" means a trailer designed for use with a private passenger automobile, if not being used for business or commercial purposes with other than a private passenger, farm or utility automobile, and if not a home, office, store, display or passenger trailer.

Exclusions

This policy does not apply under Part III:

(a) to any automobile while used as a public or livery conveyance;

(b) to loss due to war;

(c) to loss to a non-owned automobile arising out of its use by the insured in the automobile business;

(d) to damage which is due and confined to wear and tear, freezing, mechanical or electrical breakdown or failure, unless such damage results from a theft covered by this policy;

(e) to tires, unless damaged by fire, malicious mischief or vandalism, or stolen or unless the loss be coincident with and from the same cause as other loss covered by this policy;

(f) under coverage E, to breakage of glass if insurance with respect to such breakage is otherwise afforded.

Limit of Liability

The limit of the company's liability for loss shall not exceed the actual cash value of the property, or if the loss is of a part thereof the actual cash value of such part, at time of loss, nor what it would then cost to repair or replace the property or such part thereof with other of like kind and quality, nor the applicable limit of liability stated in the declarations; provided, however, the limit of the company's liability (a) for loss to personal effects arising out of any one occurrence is $100, and (b) for loss to any trailer is $500.

Other Insurance

If the insured has other insurance against a loss covered by Part III of this policy, the company shall not be liable under this policy for a greater proportion of such loss than the applicable limit of liability of this policy bears to the total applicable limit of liability of all valid and collectible insurance against such loss; provided, however, the insurance with respect to a temporary substitute automobile or non-owned automobile shall be excess insurance over any other valid and collectible insurance.

Figure 16-1

THE FAMILY AUTOMOBILE POLICY (FAP), page 3

Part 4 — Protection Against Uninsured Motorists

Coverage J—Damages for Bodily Injury

To pay all sums which the insured or his legal representative shall be legally entitled to recover as damages from the owner or operator of an uninsured automobile because of bodily injury, sickness or disease, including death resulting therefrom, hereinafter called "bodily injury," sustained by the insured, caused by accident and arising out of the ownership, maintenance or use of such uninsured automobile; provided, for the purposes of this coverage, determination as to whether the insured or such representative is legally entitled to recover such damages, and if so the amount thereof, shall be made by agreement between the insured or such representative and the company or, if they fail to agree, by arbitration.

Definitions

The definitions under Part I, except the definition of "insured," apply to Part IV, and under Part IV:

"insured" means:

(a) the named insured and any relative;

(b) any other person while occupying an insured automobile; and

(c) any person, with respect to damages he is entitled to recover for care or loss of services because of bodily injury to which this coverage applies.

The insurance afforded under Part IV applies separately to each insured, but the inclusion herein of more than one insured shall not operate to increase the limits of the company's liability.

"insured automobile" includes a trailer as defined under Part I and means:

(a) an owned automobile provided the use thereof is by or with the permission of the named insured, or

(b) any automobile not owned by the named insured while being operated by the named insured;

but the term "insured automobile" shall not include:

(1) any automobile or trailer owned by a resident of the same household as the named insured, or

(2) any automobile while used as a public or livery conveyance.

"uninsured automobile" includes a trailer of any type and means:

(a) an automobile with respect to the ownership, maintenance or use of which there is no bodily injury liability bond or insurance policy applicable at the time of the accident with respect to any person or organization legally responsible for the use of such automobile, or

(b) a hit-and-run automobile;

(c) so as to inure directly or indirectly to the benefit of any workmen's compensation or disability benefits carrier or any person or organization qualifying as a self-insurer under any workmen's compensation or disability benefits law or any similar law.

Limits of Liability

(a) The limit of liability for uninsured motorists coverage stated in the declarations as applicable to "each person" is the limit of the company's liability for all damages, including damages for care or loss of services, because of bodily injury sustained by one person as the result of any one accident and, subject to the above provision respecting each person, the limit of liability stated in the declarations as applicable to "each accident" is the total limit of the company's liability for all damages, including damages for care or loss of services, because of bodily injury sustained by two or more persons as the result of any one accident.

(b) If claim is made under this Part and claim is also made against any person insured under Part I because of bodily injury sustained in an accident by a person who is an insured under this Part:

(1) any payment made under this Part to or for any such person shall be applied in reduction of any amount which he may be entitled to recover from any person insured under coverage A; and

(2) any payment made under coverage A to or for any such person shall be applied in reduction of any amount which he may be entitled to recover under this Part.

(c) Any loss payable under the terms of this Part to or for any person shall be reduced by the amount paid and the present value of all amounts payable to him under any workmen's compensation law, exclusive of non-occupational disability benefits.

Other Insurance

With respect to bodily injury to an insured while occupying an automobile not owned by the named insured the insurance hereunder shall apply only as excess insurance over any other similar insurance available to such occupant, and this insurance shall then apply only in the amount by which the applicable limit of liability of this Part exceeds the sum of the applicable limits of liability of all such other insurance.

With respect to bodily injury to an insured while occupying or through being struck by an uninsured automobile, if such insured is a named insured under other similar insurance available to him then the damages shall be deemed not to exceed

but the term "uninsured automobile" shall not include:

(1) an automobile defined under Part IV as an "insured automobile";

(2) an automobile or trailer owned by the named insured or by any resident of the same household;

(3) an automobile or trailer owned or operated by a self-insurer within the meaning of any motor vehicle financial responsibility law, motor carrier law or any similar law;

(4) an automobile or trailer owned by the United States of America, Canada, a state, a political subdivision of any such government or an agency of any of the foregoing;

(5) a land motor vehicle or trailer, if operated on rails or crawler-treads or while located for use as a residence or premises and not as a vehicle; or

(6) a farm type tractor or equipment designed for use principally off public roads, except while actually upon public roads.

"hit-and-run automobile" means an automobile which causes bodily injury to an insured arising out of physical contact of such automobile with the insured or with an automobile which the insured is occupying at the time of the accident, provided: (a) there cannot be ascertained the identity of either the operator or the owner of such "hit-and-run automobile"; (b) the insured or someone on his behalf shall have reported the accident within 24 hours to a police, peace or judicial officer or to the Commissioner of Motor Vehicles, and shall have filed with the company within 30 days thereafter a statement under oath that the insured or his legal representative has a cause or causes of action arising out of such accident for damages against a person or persons whose identity is unascertainable, and setting forth the facts in support thereof; and (c) at the company's request, the insured or his legal representative makes available for inspection the automobile which the insured was occupying at the time of the accident.

"occupying" means in or upon or entering into or alighting from.

"state" includes the District of Columbia, a territory or possession of the United States, and a province of Canada.

Exclusions

This policy does not apply under Part IV:

(a) to bodily injury to an insured while occupying an automobile owned by the named insured and principally garaged in a state which has not authorized the issuance of this coverage;

(b) to bodily injury to an insured, or care or loss of services recoverable by an insured, with respect to which such insured, his legal representative or any person entitled to payment under this coverage shall, without written consent of the company, make any settlement with or prosecute to judgment any action against any person or organization who may be legally liable therefor;

the higher of the applicable limits of liability of this insurance and such other insurance, and the company shall not be liable under this Part for a greater proportion of the applicable limit of liability of this Part than such limit bears to the sum of the applicable limits of liability of this insurance and such other insurance.

Subject to the foregoing paragraphs, if the insured has other similar insurance available to him against a loss covered by this Part, the company shall not be liable under this Part for a greater proportion of such loss than the applicable limit of liability hereunder bears to the total applicable limits of liability of all valid and collectible insurance against such loss.

Arbitration

If any person making claim hereunder and the company do not agree that such person is legally entitled to recover damages from the owner or operator of an uninsured automobile because of bodily injury to the insured, or do not agree as to the amount of payment which may be owing under this Part, then, upon written demand of either, the matter or matters upon which such person and the company do not agree shall be settled by arbitration in accordance with the rules of the American Arbitration Association, and judgment upon the award rendered by the arbitrators may be entered in any court having jurisdiction thereof. Such person and the company each agree to consider itself bound and to be bound by any award made by the arbitrators pursuant to this Part.

Trust Agreement

In the event of payment to any person under this Part:

(a) the company shall be entitled to the extent of such payment to the proceeds of any settlement or judgment that may result from the exercise of any rights of recovery of such person against any person or organization legally responsible for the bodily injury because of which such payment is made;

(b) such person shall hold in trust for the benefit of the company all rights of recovery which he shall have against such other person or organization because of the damages which are the subject of claim made under this Part;

(c) such person shall do whatever is proper to secure and shall do nothing after loss to prejudice such rights;

(d) if requested in writing by the company, such person shall take, through any representative designated by the company, such action as may be necessary or appropriate to recover such payment as damages from such other person or organization, such action to be taken in the name of such person; in the event of a recovery, the company shall be reimbursed out of such recovery for expenses, costs and attorneys' fees incurred by it in connection therewith;

(e) such person shall execute and deliver to the company such instruments and papers as may be appropriate to secure the rights and obligations of such person and the company established by this provision.

Figure 16-1

THE FAMILY AUTOMOBILE POLICY (FAP), page 4

Conditions

(unless otherwise noted, the conditions apply to all Parts)

1. Policy Period, Territory. This policy applies only to accidents, occurrences and loss during the policy period while the automobile is within the United States of America, its territories or possessions, or Canada, or is being transported between ports thereof.

2. Premium. If the named insured disposes of, acquires ownership of, or replaces a private passenger, farm, or utility automobile or, with respect to Part III, a trailer, he shall inform the company during the policy period of such change. Premium shall be adjusted as of the date of such change, in accordance with the manuals in use by the company. The named insured shall, upon request, furnish reasonable proof of the number of such automobiles or trailers and a description thereof.

3. Notice. In the event of an accident, occurrence or loss, written notice containing particulars sufficient to identify the insured and also reasonably obtainable information with respect to the time, place and circumstances thereof, and the names and addresses of the injured and of available witnesses, shall be given by or for the insured to the company or any of its authorized agents as soon as practicable. In the event of theft the insured shall also promptly notify the police. If claim is made or suit is brought against the insured, he shall immediately forward to the company every demand, notice, summons or other process received by him or his representative.

If, before the company makes payment of loss under Part IV, the insured or his legal representative shall institute any legal action for bodily injury against any person or organization legally responsible for the use of an automobile involved in the accident, a copy of the summons and complaint or other process served in connection with such legal action shall be forwarded immediately to the company by the insured or his legal representative.

4. Two or More Automobiles. When two or more automobiles are insured hereunder, the terms of this policy shall apply separately to each, but an automobile and a trailer attached thereto shall be held to be one automobile as respects limits of liability under Part I of this policy, and separate automobiles under Part III of this policy, including any deductible provisions applicable thereto.

5. Assistance and Cooperation of the Insured—Parts I and III. The insured shall cooperate with the company and, upon the company's request, attend hearings and trials and assist in making settlements, securing and giving evidence, obtaining the attendance of witnesses and in the conduct of any legal proceedings in connection with the subject matter of this insurance. The insured shall not, except at his own cost, voluntarily make any payment, assume any obligation or incur any expense other

The insured and every other person making claim shall submit to examinations under oath by any person named by the company and subscribe the same, as often as may reasonable be required. Proof of claim shall be made upon forms furnished by the company unless the company shall have failed to furnish such forms within 15 days after receiving notice of claim.

The injured person shall submit to physical examinations by physicians selected by the company when and as often as the company may reasonably require and he, or in the event of his incapacity his legal representative, or in the event of his death his legal representative or the person or persons entitled to sue therefor, shall upon each request from the company execute authorization to enable the company to obtain medical reports and copies of records.

10. Appraisal—Part III. If the insured and the company fail to agree as to the amount of loss, either may, within 60 days after proof of loss is filed, demand an appraisal of the loss. In such event the insured and the company shall each select a competent appraiser, and the appraisers shall select a competent and disinterested umpire. The appraisers shall state separately the actual cash value and the amount of loss and failing to agree shall submit their differences to the umpire. An award in writing of any two shall determine the amount of loss. The insured and the company shall each pay his chosen appraiser and shall bear equally the other expenses of the appraisal and umpire.

The company shall not be held to have waived any of its rights by any act relating to appraisal.

11. Payment of Loss—Part III. The company may pay for the loss in money; or may repair or replace the damaged or stolen property; or may, at any time before the loss is paid or the property is so replaced, at its expense return any stolen property to the named insured, or at its option to the address shown in the declarations, with payment for any resultant damage thereto; or may take all or such part of the property at the agreed or appraised value but there shall be no abandonment to the company. The company may settle any claim for loss either with the insured or the owner of the property.

Part IV. Any amount due is payable (a) to the insured, or (b) if the insured be a minor to his parent or guardian, or (c) if the insured be deceased to his surviving spouse, otherwise (d) to a person authorized by law to receive such payment or to a person legally entitled to recover the damages which the payment represents; provided, the

than for such immediate medical and surgical relief to others as shall be imperative at the time of accident.

6. Action Against Company—Part I. No action shall lie against the company unless, as a condition precedent thereto, the insured shall have fully complied with all the terms of this policy, nor until the amount of the insured's obligation to pay shall have been finally determined either by judgment against the insured after actual trial or by written agreement of the insured, the claimant and the company.

Any person or organization or the legal representative thereof who has secured such judgment or written agreement shall thereafter be entitled to recover under this policy to the extent of the insurance afforded by this policy. No person or organization shall have any right under this policy to join the company as a party to any action against the insured to determine the insured's liability, nor shall the company be impleaded by the insured or his legal representative. Bankruptcy or insolvency of the insured or of the insured's estate shall not relieve the company of any of its obligations hereunder.

Parts II and III. No action shall lie against the company unless, as a condition precedent thereto, there shall have been full compliance with all the terms of this policy nor, under Part III, until thirty days after proof of loss is filed and the amount of loss is determined as provided in this policy.

7. Medical Reports; Proof and Payment of Claim—Part II. As soon as practicable the injured person or someone on his behalf shall give to the company written proof of claim, under oath if required, and shall, after each request from the company, execute authorization to enable the company to obtain medical reports and copies of records. The injured person shall submit to physical examination by physicians selected by the company when and as often as the company may reasonably require.

The company may pay the injured person or any person or organization rendering the services and such payment shall reduce the amount payable hereunder for such injury. Payment hereunder shall not constitute an admission of liability of any person or, except hereunder, of the company.

8. Insured's Duties in Event of Loss—Part III. In the event of loss the insured shall:
(a) protect the automobile, whether or not the loss is covered by this policy, and any further loss due to the insured's failure to protect shall not be recoverable under this policy; reasonable expenses incurred in affording such protection shall be deemed incurred at the company's request;
(b) file with the company, within 91 days after loss, his sworn proof of loss in such form and including such information as the company may reasonably require and shall, upon the company's request, exhibit the damaged property and submit to examination under oath.

9. Proof of Claim; Medical Reports—Part IV. As soon as practicable, the insured or other person making claim shall give to the company written proof of claim, under oath if required, including full particulars of the nature and extent of the injuries, treatment, and other details entering into the determination of the amount payable.

company may at its option pay any amount due in accordance with division (d) hereof.

12. No Benefit to Bailee—Part III. The insurance afforded by this policy shall not enure directly or indirectly to the benefit of any carrier or bailee liable for loss to the automobile.

13. Subrogation—Parts I and III. In the event of any payment under this policy, the company shall be subrogated to all the insured's rights of recovery therefor against any person or organization and the insured shall execute and deliver instruments and papers and do whatever else is necessary to secure such rights. The insured shall do nothing after loss to prejudice such rights.

14. Changes. Notice to any agent or knowledge possessed by any agent or by any other person shall not effect a waiver or a change in any part of this policy or estop the company from asserting any right under the terms of this policy; nor shall the terms of this policy be waived or changed, except by endorsement issued to form a part of this policy signed by a duly authorized representative of the company.

15. Assignment. Assignment of interest under this policy shall not bind the company until its consent is endorsed hereon; if, however, the insured named in Item 1 of the declarations, or his spouse if a resident of the same household, shall die, this policy shall cover (1) the survivor as named insured, (2) his legal representative as named insured but only while acting within the scope of his duties as such, (3) any person having proper temporary custody of an owned automobile, as an insured, until the appointment and qualification of such legal representative, and (4) under division 1 of Part II any person who was a relative at the time of such death.

16. Cancellation. This policy may be canceled by the insured named in Item 1 of the declarations by surrender thereof to the company or any of its authorized agents or by mailing to the company written notice stating when thereafter the cancellation shall be effective. This policy may be canceled by the company by mailing to the insured named in Item 1 of the declarations at the address shown in this policy written notice stating when not less than ten days thereafter such cancellation shall be effective. The mailing of notice as aforesaid shall be sufficient proof of notice. The time of the surrender or the effective date and hour of cancellation stated in the notice shall become the end of the policy period. Delivery of such written notice either by such insured or by the company shall be equivalent to mailing.

If such insured cancels, earned premium shall be computed in accordance with the customary short rate table and procedure. If the company cancels, earned premium shall be computed pro rata. Premium adjustment may be made either at the time cancellation is effected or as soon as practicable after cancellation becomes effective, but payment or tender of unearned premium is not a condition of cancellation.

17. Declarations. By acceptance of this policy, the insured named in Item 1 of the declarations agrees that the statements in the declarations are his agreements and representations, that this policy is issued in reliance upon the truth of such representations and that this policy embodies all agreements existing between himself and the company or any of its agents relating to this insurance.

Figure 16-1

THE FAMILY AUTOMOBILE POLICY (FAP), page 5

a temporary substitute automobile. Thus, if an insured drives his car on an errand for his employer, the contract will cover the employer because the employer would be legally responsible for the claim.

With respect to nonowned automobiles (cars not belonging to the insured *or* any relative), the coverage is not quite so broad as it is with owned automobiles. The insured is covered under his policy while driving any nonowned car. In addition, relatives who are residents of the named insured's household are also covered while driving a nonowned car providing this car is not regularly furnished for their use. To illustrate, assume that the named insured's son borrows a neighbor's car to run an errand and has an accident. The neighbor's car would be a nonowned car and hence the son is insured. However, if the neighbor's car were a truck, the situation is different. The truck is not a private passenger automobile and coverage is not provided. The son would be insured under the neighbor's policy as a person driving with permission.

Suppose the father is borrowing a car regularly for going to work. The 1958 edition of the FAP defines a nonowned automobile as "an automobile or trailer not owned by the named insured or any relative, other than a temporary substitute auto." [6] Clearly the father is covered under his FAP if he borrows a car regularly to go to work. However, the father is not covered under his FAP if he borrows his son's car, because this car is neither owned nor nonowned under the definitions. If the son had the FAP in his own name, the father would be insured as a person driving with permission under the son's insurance.

Notice that a relative is defined as a person related to the insured and who is a resident of the same household. It follows, therefore, in the above case, that if the son were no longer living in the same household and the father borrows his son's car, the father's FAP grants coverage because the car now is nonowned. It will be observed that the definition of a nonowned automobile refers to "an" automobile, whereas the definition of an owned automobile refers to a "private passenger, farm or utility automobile or trailer." The distinction means that the insured is covered for *any* type of nonowned automobile.

Because of the very broad definition of insured, in some cases an insurer may be required to pay liability claims which one insured may have against another insured. For example, the named insured lends his car to a neighbor who in negligently backing out of the garage strikes and injures the named insured. The named insured may now bring an

---

[6] The policy requires that any use of nonowned cars must be with the owner's permission. If an insured takes another car without the owner's permission, he is denied coverage under both his own FAP and the coverage applying to the nonowned car.

action against the neighbor who is also an insured under the policy. The insurance company is required to defend the neighbor and pay any judgments which may be handed down in favor of the named insured. In other cases, the named insured and his wife may own two cars and have a collision. One spouse may bring an action against the other in such cases; the insurer must of course defend the suit.

What is an automobile? The FAP contains definitions of different types of automobiles, but does not define an automobile itself. Under existing rules, however, the FAP insures the following: private passenger cars, station wagons, jeeps, pick-up trucks or farm trucks with a load capacity of 1,500 pounds or less, trailers designed for use with private passenger automobiles, and farm wagons or implements (for liability and medical payment only). Motorcycles, motor scooters, and other vehicles of less than four wheels must be insured under the 1955 standard automobile policy.

Exclusions of the FAP. In general, the exclusions in the FAP serve the purpose of delineating the coverage of the automobile policy so that wasteful duplication of insurance does not result. For example, using a private car as a taxi or a public livery is excluded because this represents a business risk for which special coverage is designed. (But note that if the insured is held legally liable for an accident while riding as a passenger in a taxi, his FAP covers him.)

Liability for damage to property in the insured's care, custody, or control is excluded because physical loss of movable property is usually covered under fire insurance forms (for example, loss from vehicles in the extended coverage endorsement). Workmen's compensation claims likewise are excluded as are accidents for which an automobile business liability policy (for example, garage liability) would normally respond. Thus, if a service station employee is driving an insured's car while testing it and has an accident, there is no coverage under the FAP, since it is assumed that the station's garage liability policy will cover this type of claim. However, use by the insured of his private passenger car in his occupation or profession is not excluded, nor is his similar use of a non-owned private passenger car.

Financial responsibility laws. The FAP provides that in states with financial responsibility laws (see page 418 for a discussion of these laws) it will "comply with the provisions of such law to the extent of the coverage and limits of liability required by such law." It is possible, for example, that the insured might have violated certain conditions in the policy, thus negating his coverage, but under the laws of the state the insurer is required to make payment to an injured party regardless of its right to deny liability on the insured's behalf because of the violated conditions.[7] In such a case the insurer will make the required payment to an injured third party but may bring an action against the insured for reimbursement. The purpose of this provision in the policy is to make the FAP conform to those laws of the state that regulate financial responsibility of motorists within that state.

Other insurance. The other insurance clause, which is very important, provides that if more than one policy applies to a given loss involving an owned car, the FAP will contribute on a pro rata basis with such other contracts. However, with respect to nonowned cars or temporary substitute automobiles, the FAP is to be considered excess. Thus, if Henry borrows Joe's car and negligently injures someone, both owners being covered by the FAP, Joe's policy is responsible to the extent of the limits of liability carried, and if damages exceed these limits, Henry's policy then contributes.

2) Part 2—Medical payments

Medical payments insurance is automobile insurance designed to pay for medical claims *of occupants* arising from automobile accidents without regard to fault. Payment is made for *"reasonable* expenses incurred within one year from the date of accident for *necessary* medical, surgical, X-ray, and dental services, including the cost of burial in case death results." Medical payments insurance covers all persons, including the named insured and residents of his household, who are injured while "occupying" the automobile (meaning entering, leaving, or while in or upon the vehicle) regardless of the question of negligence.

There are at least three important reasons for medical payments coverage. First, there is the fact that guests in an automobile might feel hesitant in bringing legal action against their host for negligent driving, in order to recover for their medical bills. Yet, such action is technically required under the legal liability portion of the contract. Also, guest-host statutes in many states prevent successful negligence actions against drivers of automobiles unless *gross* negligence can be proved. Thus, without medical payments coverage, many medical bills simply would not be covered. Second, a negligent host would normally feel a moral

---

[7] *United States Casualty Co.* v. *Timmerman* (180 Atl. 629, 1935) was one of the first cases upholding this provision.

obligation to provide for at least the medical bills of his guests, even if it is determined that he is not to blame for the accident. But in the absence of negligence, the insurer has no obligation to pay for such costs under the liability portion of the automobile contract. Third, experience indicates that if prompt settlement of all medical costs is made, there is much less likelihood that injured guests will bring negligence action, with its resulting defense costs and possibility of large judgments for such factors as loss of income and mental anguish. Medical payments coverage thus tends to minimize liability losses under the policy, with a resulting lower premium for the insured.

Limits of liability. Medical payments insurance is written with limits of liability between $500 and $5,000 *per person*. If there are six passengers in a vehicle and the owner has elected to purchase limits of say $2,000, there would be a total limit of $12,000 for all necessary medical costs arising from a single accident. It is possible that a passenger could collect under medical payments and also bring a negligence action against the driver and recover again for the same costs.[8] Medical payments insurance is actually a health insurance contract, which is not a contract of indemnity. The insurer reserves no right of subrogation in claims arising under the medical payments section, and if a passenger brings a successful action against the host, say for gross negligence, the insurer has no right to any collections made by the injured passenger. The probability of this result is statistically small, however, and no substantial moral hazard is introduced thereby.

Persons insured. The contract of medical payments is in two sections, Division 1 for the named insured and members of his household, and Division 2 for other persons.

Division 1 provides broad coverage, and compensable accidents are not confined to situations where the insured is a passenger in a car, but occur when the insured is occupying or is struck by *an automobile*. Thus, the insured's family is covered for almost any automobile accident, while a passenger or a pedestrian.

Division 2, covering medical costs of other passengers, gives complete coverage for injuries arising in the insured's owned automobile so long as the car is being operated by an authorized person (that is, the insured or persons driving with permission of the insured). As for nonowned cars, passengers are covered only if the insured, his servants, or his relatives are driving the nonowned car.

---

[8] This principle was upheld in *Severson* v. *Milwaukee Automobile Insurance Co.* 3(CCH Auto 2d) 1011.

Exclusions. There are certain limitations on the application of medical payments insurance as outlined in the exclusions. For example, since use of the vehicle as a taxi or a public livery is excluded, medical payments insurance does not apply in such cases. The exclusion denying coverage to a named insured or relative "while occupying an automobile owned by the named insured or any relative, other than an automobile defined herein as an 'owned automobile,' " is confusing until one recalls that the contract defines an owned automobile as a private passenger or utility automobile or trailer. The intent of this exclusion is to deny medical payments coverage to the named insured while he is operating a commercial vehicle (such as a truck) which he also owns. Also, if the insured is operating a nonowned car in his business, medical payments coverage is denied for injuries to passengers if the nonowned car is a commercial vehicle, but not if it is a passenger type vehicle. It is well to recall that a vehicle belonging to a relative in the same household is neither owned nor nonowned under the definitions. Hence, no medical payments coverage is applicable to such vehicles, since it is expected that each owner will insure his automobile separately.

Other insurance. The medical payments section provides that if medical payments insurance applies to a loss suffered when the insured is driving a nonowned automobile or a temporary substitute automobile, the other owner's coverage, if any, applies first and the insured's medical payments coverage is excess. Thus, if John, who has his FAP written with $500 medical payments, borrows Jim's car which is covered for $1,000 medical payments and has an accident which necessitates the expenditure of $1,250 in medical bills, Jim's policy will pay $1,000 and John's FAP will pay the remaining $250.

3) Part 3—Physical damage

The FAP combines in one contract not only liability and medical payments coverage but in addition provides for indemnification of the insured in case his automobile is damaged by almost any type of peril, regardless of the insured's fault. It is obvious that the insured will not always be able to recover from a third party for damage to his vehicle. For example, the insured could be contributorially negligent, or the loss could be caused by perils other than collision (say theft). Thus, it may be seen that the FAP is really a schedule policy on which the insured may purchase insurance against loss due to legal liability, fire and related perils, medical costs, and theft. In other words, the FAP insures the automobile owner against almost every type of loss to his automobile or to himself that arises out of the use of an automobile.

Physical damage coverage includes several types of indemnity, as follows:

Comprehensive loss.

Collision loss.

Fire, lightning, and transportation loss.

Theft.

Combined additional coverage.

Towing and labor costs.

Supplementary payments.

Comprehensive loss. *Comprehensive coverage,* as it applies in the FAP, covers all loss to the insured vehicle other than collision (subject to certain exclusions). To clarify what is meant by comprehensive, the contract specifies certain sources of loss which are to be construed as comprehensive and not as collision. Thus, breakage of glass caused by missiles, falling objects, fire, theft, explosion, earthquake, windstorm, hail, water, flood, malicious mischief, riot, and civil commotion are to be construed as comprehensive and not as collision losses.

Since the various coverages on the FAP are optional, some insureds may carry collision with a deductible amount and comprehensive with no deductible. Hence, cases have been tried over the distinctions between these two terms. In one case a large piece of ice came loose from a moving bus, struck the insured's car, which then went off the road and collided with the embankment. The court held that the entire loss, both the damage done by the ice and the collision with the embankment, was to be classified as a comprehensive claim, under the general theory that the ice, a falling object, was the proximate cause of loss.[9] In another case a child entered a car, released the brakes, and the car rolled down a hill and collided with another vehicle. The court held that the proximate cause of the loss was vandalism, not collision, and hence the comprehensive coverage applied.[10] In a case where the vehicle went off the road into the river and was damaged by water, the court held the damage to be done by collision and comprehensive insurance did not cover it.[11] Because of a lack of consistency in such cases and the resulting difficulty in predicting what a jury will decide, it would appear advisable that if an insured desires complete physical damage protection against loss, he should take both collision and comprehensive insurance. Insurers are continually paying "unusual" claims under comprehensive coverage, thus illustrating the need for protection against the many hazards that

---

[9] *Gruenther* v. *American Indemnity Co.* 17 N.W. (2d) 570.

[10] *Unkelsbee* v. *Homestead Fire Insurance Co.* 41 Atl. (2d) 168.

[11] *Ringo* v. *Automobile Insurance Co.* 22 Pac. (2d) 887.

cause loss to automobiles. Examples include damage to paint by dust storms, vandalism, or hail; damage to upholstery by burns, oil, or acids; windshields broken by flying rock or falling trees; cars being blown into rivers or lakes by hurricanes; and theft damage.

Collision loss. Collision with another object or upset of the automobile is normally subject to a flat dollar deductible amount of $50 or $100. Larger deductibles are permitted and corresponding reductions in the premium are granted. Collision coverage applies to a utility trailer, subject to an upper limit of $500. For large and valuable trailers, such as mobile homes, separate collision coverage must be purchased. Coverage against collision loss extends to nonowned cars that the insured or any relative is driving, but such coverage is excess over any other valid and collectible collision insurance.

If it is determined that another driver is legally liable for collision damage, the insured may elect to make a claim under his collision coverage, or he may make a claim directly against the insurer of the other vehicle. Normally he does the latter because in this manner he is not subject to a deductible amount. If the insured makes a claim under collision coverage, normally his insurer will cover the loss, less any deductible amount, and proceed under its subrogation rights against the liable third party. If collection is made in full, the question arises as to whether the insurer refunds the deductible amount to the insured. Practices differ among insurers, some retaining the entire amount as partial compensation for the costs of collection against the liable third party, and some dividing the deductible amount in the proportion that each party has suffered loss.

Collision is not defined in the policy, but interpretations have made it clear that the insured car need not be in motion itself nor does the collision have to be with another vehicle. For example, if a car strikes a cement barrier in the middle of the road and 20 miles later it is discovered that the engine is ruined because of a hole in the oil pan, the loss may be collected under collision insurance. Parked cars that are struck by another vehicle suffer collision damage.

Fire, lightning, and transportation loss. If one does not wish to purchase a full, comprehensive coverage, as described above, he may secure a more limited coverage against the perils of fire, lightning, smoke or smudge due to faulty operation of heating equipment in the premises in which the automobile is located, and by the stranding, sinking, burning, collision, or derailment of a conveyance in which the car is being transported.

The FAP provides a very limited coverage on personal effects damaged while they are in or upon the automobile. Loss is covered only if caused by fire or lightning, while the effects are in or upon an *owned* car, and is subject to a limit of $100. Thus, property burned while temporarily out of the automobile, or belonging to guests, or belonging to the insured while driving a nonowned car would not be covered. No extra charge is made for this insurance, since it is a part of the comprehensive coverage.

Theft. If a car is stolen, all direct loss is covered under the comprehensive section of the FAP. In the FAP, *theft insurance* can be purchased separately from comprehensive insurance. Approximately 300,000 cars valued at $250 million are stolen annually in the United States, or roughly one in every 800 cars. The theft peril is real but small, especially since about 94 per cent of the stolen value is recovered.[12]

Combined additional coverage. Instead of buying comprehensive coverage, the insured may secure coverage described in the section entitled Coverage H—Combined Additional Coverage. This clause lists certain perils such as windstorm, hail, earthquake, explosion, riot or civil commotion, falling of aircraft, flood, vandalism, and certain water damage. There is a $25 deductible applied against any loss caused by malicious mischief or vandalism. It is very likely that the insured could secure comprehensive coverage as cheap as or cheaper than the combination of the three coverages fire, lightning, and transportation; theft; and combined additional coverage.

Towing and labor costs. Under the FAP the car owner may elect to insure against towing and labor costs that result from a breakdown of the car. Even if this coverage could be purchased for $1, it is doubtful if it is justified under basic insurance buying principles because the loss, even if it occurs, is too small to cause financial embarrassment to the insured.

Supplementary payments. The FAP provides for compensation to the insured for loss of use of a stolen car at the rate of not over $10 per day, subject to an aggregate limitation of $300. The payment begins after a 48-hour waiting period and ceases when the car is returned to use or when the insurer settles with the insured for the lost vehicle.

The FAP agrees to reimburse the insured for his liability for general average or salvage claims arising out of the transportation of the automobile. Such claims may arise, for example, when the vehicle is being transported on a ferry and there is a voluntary but necessary sacrifice of

---

[12] Federal Bureau of Investigation *Uniform Crime Reports,* based on 1957 data.

goods to save the ship during a storm. Each owner of cargo is required to contribute pro rata to the owner of the jettisoned property. The insurer of the car owner with such a liability must meet this demand.[13]

Physical damage exclusions. Among the excluded perils of Part 3 of the FAP are war, use as a public livery, wear and tear, freezing, and mechanical or electrical breakdown. Damage to tires is excluded under the comprehensive coverage unless this damage is caused by certain described perils, namely, fire, vandalism, theft, or unless it is coincident with some other loss covered by the policy. For example, if the car is stolen and as a result the motor freezes up, or the tires are ruined through speeding over a rough road, the damage would be covered. The same damage caused by the insured's carelessness would be excluded.

Part 4—Uninsured motorist endorsement

The uninsured motorist endorsement is a fairly recent innovation in automobile insurance. The basic reasons for its existence are analyzed later in this chapter. Essentially the endorsement says, "If you should be struck and injured by a negligent motorist who happens to carry no liability insurance, you may bring legal action against your own insurer just as though your insurer covered the other party as well as yourself." Coverage under the endorsement, abbreviated UME, is limited to bodily injury claims. If an uninsured motorist is responsible for damage to your automobile or to other property, the UME gives no protection. It is expected that the insured will carry physical damage coverage on his own property.

Coverage under the UME is extended to the named insured and any relative, passengers in the insured automobile, and other persons who would have a legal right to collect for bodily injuries suffered through the negligence of the uninsured motorist. Thus, the father of a minor child who was injured as a passenger would be protected under the UME. The uninsured automobile is defined to include hit-and-run automobiles, and other cars which are being operated without any applicable insurance protection. What constitutes an uninsured auto is carefully spelled out. For example, cars owned by the named insured, cars owned by political subdivisions or governmental agencies, trailer houses being used as a residence, or farm-type tractors or equipment except while operating on public roads, are not "uninsured autos" within the meaning of the UME.

The UME contains certain limitations. For example, if the insured was entitled to recover under a workman's compensation law for the

---

[13] See Chapter 12 for a discussion of general average.

bodily injuries he suffered at the hands of the uninsured motorist, any liability under the UME is reduced by the amount of such compensation. Coverage under the UME is excess over any other coverage available to the insured as an operator of a non-owned car. If the negligent uninsured motorist has other assets which are later attached by the insured, the insurer can recover the amounts paid under the UME to the extent of any recoveries so made by the insured against the guilty party.

Part 5—Conditions

The major conditions of the FAP are similar to those of other insurance policies and the following comments concern those conditions which require special comment as they apply to automobile insurance.

Premium. Because the FAP applies automatically to all owned and nonowned cars and does not require as a condition of coverage that the insurer be notified within a specified number of days when a new car is purchased or an old one is disposed of,[14] there is a requirement that the insured notify the insurer of the acquisition or replacement of all cars during the policy period. The premium is adjusted as of the date the new vehicle was acquired or the old one disposed of. Without such a provision, the insured would be granted free coverage on newly acquired cars during the policy term.

Two or more automobiles. The FAP requires that if there is more than one automobile covered, the limits of liability apply separately to each vehicle unless a car and a trailer are involved in the same accident. In that event the liability limits apply as though there were just one vehicle involved, but the physical damage limits apply as if there were two vehicles involved. The effect of this is that any deductibles for physical damage insurance would apply separately to the car and to the trailer, but existence of a car and a trailer would not serve to double the liability limits.

Assistance and cooperation. The assistance and cooperation condition is quite typical in all insurance contracts. In automobile insurance, it is particularly important because of a sentence stating:

> The insured shall not, except at his own cost, voluntarily make any payment, *assume any obligation,* or incur any expense other than for such immediate medical and surgical relief to others as shall be imperative at the time of accident.

---

[14] Under the 1955 standard policy, newly acquired cars must be reported within 30 days. Some states require that this be done under the FAP.

It is common for individuals involved in accidents to say something like this to the other driver, "I'm very sorry. It was all my fault. My insurer will see that everything is taken care of." Oftentimes it is discovered that it was not the insured's fault at all but that because of his statement admitting guilt (which unhappily may be witnessed), the court finds him guilty. In such cases the insurer appears to be justified in denying liability.

Subrogation. The FAP reserves the right of subrogation against liable third parties for both physical damage and liability insurance, but not in the case of medical payments. If the insured does anything to prejudice such rights, a warranty has been violated and the insurer may deny liability under the policy.

Business v. nonbusiness forms

The FAP, as the name suggests, is available only for nonbusiness consumers. Business consumers either take coverage under the 1955 standard automobile policy, or under an increasingly popular form known as the comprehensive automobile liability policy. In general, the provisions of the FAP and these two policies are similar, the chief differences arising from the fact that business vehicles tend to be more varied than is common for nonbusiness vehicles. The comprehensive automobile liability policy, for example, grants automobile insurance on power cranes, welding trucks or machinery, and air compressor trucks or spray rigs either while such vehicles are being towed or are under their own power being driven to and from a job. However, such equipment as crawler type tractors, concrete mixers, and graders, designed for use off public roads, are not considered to be automobiles unless they are being towed or carried to and from a job. Liability for such equipment is intended to be covered under the comprehensive general liability policy.

Nonownership liability insurance

As we have seen in Chapter 15, individuals may be liable for the use of automobiles even if they do not personally own vehicles of any sort. A person may be responsible because he is directing the driving of a car, or because someone else is driving a car on his behalf.

There is automatic protection for nonownership liability under the FAP for the insured and his spouse with the exception of cars furnished for their regular use, cars being driven without permission of the owner, or commercial-type vehicles used in business. By payment of additional premiums, an endorsement called *extended nonowned automobile cover-*

age may be added to the FAP granting coverage for cars regularly furnished to the insured and for business use of commercial vehicles. The same endorsement may be written to cover relatives in the same household. A similar endorsement may be added to the 1955 standard automobile policy. Also, nonownership liability coverage may be obtained for officers of corporations, partners of the insured, and co-owners of automobiles by endorsement to the basic contract covering operation of the vehicle.

If an individual does not own a vehicle, he may secure coverage for nonownership liability by use of the named nonowner endorsement on a standard contract which assumes that no automobile is owned. This coverage, like all nonownership liability insurance, is excess over other applicable insurance.

Hired cars

An individual or business firm may feel that proper liability protection has been secured for all owned vehicles and all nonowned vehicles, but there may still be doubt about the status of vehicles hired from others. Nonownership liability insurance generally excludes such vehicles from coverage. A business firm may conclude that its liability for hired cars does not arise except in connection with the operations of independent contractors, and in that event it is felt that the contractor is liable for the use of such vehicles.

There are several instances when liability for the use of hired cars may arise and will be uninsured unless the individual has purchased the *hired-cars endorsement* or has such exposure covered automatically under a form such as the Comprehensive Automobile Liability policy. First, it may turn out that a certain job is given to a hired truckman who the employer thought was an independent contractor but who is not legally liable because the employer has exercised certain controls over the use of the trucks. Even if it turns out that the truckman is an independent contractor, a court litigation and its attendant cost may be necessary in order to resolve the question of independence. Second, a salesman might hire a "U-drive" car in the name of the employer, thus creating an exposure that is excluded under nonownership liability. Third, the employer may borrow a truck or vehicle from someone. Such exposures are also excluded under nonownership liability, which covers only if an *employee* borrows a car or a truck and not if the employer himself borrows one.

Hired-car coverage is becoming more important with the growing business practice of leasing fleets of automobiles under terms whereby the user is responsible for the insurance.

AUTOMOBILE INSURANCE AND THE LAW

In every state and in all the provinces of Canada, legislatures have passed some form of automobile insurance law designed to solve in some manner the problem of the uncompensated victim of financially irresponsible automobile drivers. Many studies [15] have been made confirming what anyone might expect from his knowledge of human nature; namely, that without some organized plan such as liability insurance, it is difficult at best for an automobile accident victim to collect for his damages from the guilty party. If there is no insurance, the innocent victim probably will not press for payment at all even if he has an airtight legal case, in the knowledge that if he does go to the expense of reducing his claim to a judgment, the judgment is likely to remain unsatisfied. In other words, the law has stepped in because without some system of financial guarantees, the motorist is forced to use the method of assumption of risk whether he is financially able to or not. Most often he is not. Accordingly, legislatures have attempted various methods to cope with the problem. Laws have taken the following forms:

1) Financial responsibility laws.
2) Compulsory liability insurance laws.
3) Unsatisfied judgment fund.
4) Uninsured motorist endorsement.
5) Compensation laws.

1) Financial responsibility laws

Financial responsibility laws represent by far the most common approach to the general problem of the uncompensated victim of the financially irresponsible motorist. There are two basic requirements of most such laws:

1. Motorists without liability insurance who are involved in an automobile accident must obtain and maintain liability insurance or other proof of financial responsibility (say, a surety bond) of a specified character for a given period, usually three years, as a condition of continued licensing of the operator and registration of the vehicle.

---

[15] See, for example, Report of the *Joint Legislative Committee to Investigate Automobile Insurance,* State of New York, Legislative Document No. 91 (1938), p. 197.

2. Motorists without liability insurance who are involved in an automobile accident must pay for the damages they have caused, or give evidence that they were not to blame, as a condition for the continued operation of their vehicle.

In their early development, financial responsibility laws often contained only the first requirement; but gradually the second requirement, called *security provisions,* was added. Financial responsibility laws have no penalty other than the suspension of driving privileges, and hence are not guarantees that the uncompensated victim will actually be paid. The effectiveness of the laws in this regard rests upon the hope that most drivers will be led to purchase insurance rather than face possible loss of their driving privileges.

Financial responsibility laws have the following points in common:

1. A majority specify that insurance policies must have limits of $5,000/$10,000 bodily injury and $5,000 property damage liability, although many states have increased the limits to $10,000/$20,000 bodily injury liability.
2. A majority of laws do not apply to accidents where less than $100 (or $50) of property damage is caused and there is no bodily injury caused by the accident.
3. Most laws apply to both the owner and the driver.
4. A majority of laws specify that both the driver's license and the vehicle registration be suspended for violation of the law.
5. Over 90 per cent of all laws provide that the insurer may not deny liability to the accident victim even if it is not liable to the insured because of some breach of policy condition. The insurer must pay the claim but may, of course, attempt to recover from the insured for payments made under these conditions.
6. About two thirds of the laws require that insurers participate in an assigned risk plan whereby drivers who have been refused coverage from one insurer may obtain coverage, sometimes at a higher rate, from another insurer. Each insurer agrees to take a certain number of so called "bad risks."
7. About 80 per cent of the laws require that proof of future responsibility be maintained regardless of the negligence of the operator. Thus, if an owner does not carry liability insurance and he is involved in an accident causing bodily injury to others through no fault of his own, he is still required to maintain proof of responsibility for the specified future period.
8. Driving privileges are restored to a driver once he has paid the amount of liability specified by the maximum legal limits, even though the actual judgment is much larger and is still unsatisfied. For example, if a $50,000 property damage judg-

ment is obtained against Doe, Doe can get back his driver's license once he has paid the $5,000 which is usually specified as the maximum property damage liability limit.

9. Three fourths of the laws have reciprocity provisions whereby suspension of privileges in another state applies in the home state as well. Thus, if Doe is involved in an accident while on his vacation in another state, and a judgment is rendered against him in this state for damages he caused, his home state treats this as though the violation had occurred there and will also remove his driving privileges until the judgment is satisfied.

10. It is common to allow certain exceptions under the law, such as when the vehicle is legally parked at the time of an accident, or if the vehicle is legally owned by some governmental agency, or if it is being driven by a person using it without permission. Under such conditions the owner is not subject to the provisions of the financial responsibility law.

Effectiveness of financial responsibility laws. Financial responsibility statutes have been criticized on a number of grounds. Opponents who urge the strengthening of these laws point out that the laws give no guarantee that the accident victim will be compensated because there is no guarantee that insurance will actually be carried or that, if it is, that legal liability will exist, a necessary condition of the applicability of liability insurance. For example, hit-and-run drivers, drivers of stolen vehicles, and out-of-state drivers may cause accidents; and no certain means exist to assure payment of the cost of accidents they cause because either the guilty party cannot be located or he is judgment proof. Opponents raise questions about the certainty of punishment of offending drivers, pointing to daily lists of individuals caught driving in violation of suspension orders. Opponents also criticize the basic premise of financial responsibility laws, that they rest upon the common law of negligence and that proving negligence is as difficult, expensive, and time consuming as it is uncertain to compensate the innocent victim. They argue that since automobiles are necessities and their operation is basic, some socialized method should be worked out to handle this problem.

Those in favor of financial responsibility statutes are usually opposed to any further strengthening which probably would lead either to compulsory insurance or a compensation system similar to workmen's compensation laws. The proponents point out that these laws, where they have been enforced effectively and are doing a good job of meeting the problem, have generally resulted in a very high percentage of insured drivers.

A study has been made in Oregon which brings some objective analysis to bear on the effectiveness of the law in that state. The study,[16] covering a five-year period, 1952–1957, revealed that the percentage of motorists involved in accidents who could not prove financial responsibility declined from 6.2 per cent in 1952 to 3.0 per cent in 1957. Analysis of the damage caused by the uninsured motorists in 1957–1959 showed that 20 per cent of the damage claims were paid when the enforcement agency issued suspension orders. The remaining 80 per cent amounted to $287,992, of which 75 per cent was damage to motor vehicles, 3 per cent was other property damage, and 22 per cent was damage resulting from personal injuries. A classification of the individuals causing the damage revealed that out-of-state drivers accounted for 21.2 per cent; minors, 12.7 per cent; persons driving under suspended licenses, 11.2 per cent. In about half the cases, the files did not reveal sufficient information to classify the type of financially irresponsible motorist with any degree of precision. It seems clear that a small minority of drivers—less than 3 per cent—constituted a hard core of motorists in Oregon whose financial responsibility is doubtful and who probably would not purchase insurance even under a compulsory insurance law.

The Oregon study reveals some interesting new evidence about the effectiveness of financial responsibility laws. The percentage of financially irresponsible motorists in a state with many years of experience with a typical law is likely to be fairly low. When it is realized that a significant part of the 3 per cent of all financially irresponsible motorists may not have been legally to blame for the damage caused, it is apparent that compulsory liability insurance would not have increased the recoveries to any significant degree. If the compulsory liability insurance law were of the type in Massachusetts, where compulsory insurance does not include property damage liability, the effect would have been almost nil, since three fourths of the damages done by the uninsured motorists in Oregon was damage of this type. When compared to such criteria as personal income, the damage done by financially irresponsible motorists is infinitesimal, amounting to .009 per cent of Oregon's personal income during the year 1957–1958. Furthermore, the size of the average claim was small. It was found that 56 per cent of the unsettled cases were under $250, 33 per cent were between $251 and $500, 7 per cent between $501 and $1,000, and 4 per cent over $1,001.

---

[16] Raymond C. Rauch, *The Problem of the Uninsured Motorist in Oregon* (Bureau of Business Research, University of Oregon, Eugene, Oregon, 1959).

While it should not be concluded that these results are necessarily general and apply to all financial responsibility laws, nevertheless they point to the possibility that perhaps the financial responsibility laws can be reasonably effective and that no social problem of great dimension exists which would warrant the adoption of some of the stricter measures discussed below.

2) Compulsory liability insurance laws

Three states—Massachusetts, New York, and North Carolina—have gone one step further than the passage of financial responsibility laws and have adopted compulsory liability insurance statutes. In these states every resident must have purchased a specified type of liability insurance *before* he is given a registration certificate or driving privileges. Connecticut, Maryland, and Rhode Island have laws that make the purchase of insurance compulsory for minors, with certain exceptions, while Illinois requires all trucks registered in the state to be covered by liability insurance, with certain exceptions.

Compulsory liability insurance has been in force in Massachusetts since 1927 and represents the only law with a considerable record for evaluation. New York's law, effective in 1957, and North Carolina's law, effective in 1958, attempted to remedy some of the defects inherent under the Massachusetts system; but it is too early to tell just how successful these laws will be. Since apparently little in the way of objective analysis of the effectiveness of their financial responsibility statutes preceded the passage of the compulsory laws, an evaluation of the success of the laws will be more difficult than it might otherwise have been.

In Massachusetts every application for registration of a vehicle must be accompanied by evidence of bodily injury liability insurance with limits of $5,000/$10,000. The limits in New York and North Carolina are double those of Massachusetts. Property damage liability insurance is not required in Massachusetts [17] as it is in New York and North Carolina. The insurance must be written to cover others driving the car with permission, but is not required to cover accidents occurring off public highways nor to guests riding in the car. Insurance rates are set by the insurance commissioner in Massachusetts, but the rates are set by insurance companies in New York and North Carolina.

---

[17] A separate law requires the suspension of driving privileges of any person failing to pay judgments for property damage. In effect, this accomplishes in Massachusetts what financial responsibility statutes accomplish in other states in stimulating automobile drivers to respond to damages they cause.

Criticisms of compulsory liability insurance. Opponents of compulsory liability insurance have been predominantly the insurance companies themselves. This may seem strange since it would appear that insurers would have a "built-in" sales system if everyone were required to purchase their product. However, the opposition points out that once compulsory insurance is "in," political influences are immediately felt in such vital matters as rate-making, underwriting, selection of insureds, and policy provisions.[18] If the private insurers resist such influences too strongly, there is always the threat that the state will organize its own insurance organization and eventually lead to socialization of insurance in other lines as well. Such a result might spell the end of free private enterprise in the insurance industry altogether.

Opponents of compulsory automobile liability insurance also cite the experience in Massachusetts to support their fear of the system. In this state the insurance commissioner sets the rates for the forthcoming year about September 15 following public hearings. Since this is near election time, it is only natural that the commissioner is under pressure by the party in power not to announce substantial increases in insurance rates. Because rising accident rates and inflation have necessitated steady increases in rates and because the commissioner has consistently set rates lower than those requested by insurance companies, substantial and consistent underwriting losses have resulted.[19] (In spite of this, bodily injury insurance premiums in Massachusetts still tend to be higher than those of nearby states.) Apparently because of underwriting losses, many insurers have withdrawn entirely from Massachusetts. For example, less than half as many insurers do business in Massachusetts as are operating in nearby states. Some insurers operate at a profit, however, through careful underwriting and strict selection standards. Others continue to operate because to quit automobile insurance underwriting would mean the loss of other more profitable lines to companies willing to underwrite all lines. It is pointed out that if all insurers ceased to write Massachusetts compulsory automobile liability insurance, a state fund

---

[18] For a detailed discussion of this point, see C. A. Kulp, *op. cit.,* pp. 203–210.

[19] In the six-year period 1951–56, for example. losses exceeded premiums collected each year but one, resulting in a total deficiency of $24.3 million, not counting expenses. In 1957, when the commissioner again set rates far below the request of insurers, the insurers brought legal action and the state supreme court ordered the commissioner to set "new and adequate" rates because it found that the commissioner had ignored heavy losses in 1955–56.

See *The First Thirty Years,* a commentary on the operation of the Massachusetts Compulsory Automobile Liability Insurance Act (Casualty Insurance Companies Serving Massachusetts, 8 Beacon Street, Boston, Massachusetts, 1957), p. 21.

would almost certainly be established, a result that most insurers wish to avoid at all costs.

Another factor in the vicious circle of rising accident rates that goes unreflected in premiums is the assertion that under compulsory insurance the public is more claims-conscious than in such states with no compulsory coverage. For example, claim frequency per 100 cars in 1953, 1954, and 1955 in New York State was 4.2, 4.6, and 5.4 respectively, as compared to 6.1, 6.0, and 6.5 respectively for Massachusetts.[20] It is doubtful, however, that the higher claim frequency observed in Massachusetts can be proved to be a direct consequence of compulsory insurance. The quoted data stand only as a basis for an inference for which there is no other ready explanation. Much additional research is needed on this point.

Critics of compulsory insurance also make the claim that compulsory insurance does not solve the basic problem, namely, the growing trend of the increased cost of automobile accidents and compensation of their victims. Furthermore, even if every resident is required to take out insurance as a condition of driving, there will still be accidents caused by out-of-state drivers, hit-and-run drivers, drivers of stolen cars, and drivers who operate in violation of suspension orders or with false license plates.

In answer to some of these criticisms, it may be pointed out that the political influence can be minimized by appropriate statutory provisions that set up hindrances to inside manipulation of the rating structure and that guarantee independence of insurer operation as is the case in New York where insurers set their own rates independently. Also, as was done in New York in 1959, a separate fund can be set up to respond to damages that are uncollectible from insurance companies, those stemming from hit-and-run drivers, out-of-state drivers, and stolen car accidents. Compulsory insurance also has the effect of providing fines and jail sentences for violation of the act, whereas financial responsibility laws merely suspend driving privileges.

The argument that compulsory automobile insurance does not attack the basic problem of preventing accidents and of compensating those who suffer financial losses thereby is really not an argument against compulsory insurance as such but an argument against the system of legal liability upon which both compulsory liability insurance laws and financial responsibility laws are based. Insurers who argue in

---

[20] *Ibid.,* p. 33.

this manner might be interpreted to be in favor of a compensation system, a position they would usually oppose strenuously.

3) Unsatisfied judgment fund

The *unsatisfied judgment fund* (*UJF*) is a fund set up by a state to pay certain judgments arising out of automobile accidents, claims which cannot be collected by any other means.[21] Thus, if the negligent motorist is insolvent, does not carry liability insurance, has voided his insurance through some violation of a policy provision, or if his insurer is insolvent, the injured victim may collect his claim from the unsatisfied judgment fund providing he has exhausted every other means of collection. In a sense the UJF is broader than compulsory insurance, since it covers cases where insurance was carried but the damage was still uncollectible. However, the UJF is based on the principle of negligence and if there is no legal liability, there can be no collectible judgment from the fund. Furthermore, the UJF reserves through the right of subrogation to collect from the negligent motorist if and when he acquires property on which liens may be obtained. In any case the insolvent motorist loses his driving privileges until the fund has been repaid.

The UJF may be maintained by assessments from insured motorists, from insurance companies, and from motorists who are uninsured at the time they make application for license plates. Although the assessments received from uninsured motorists are greater than those levied against insured motorists, they are not, of course, equivalent to insurance premiums. There is a common tendency, however, for the uninsured motorist to believe that he has actually paid for liability insurance when he pays his assessment.

Criticisms which have been levied against the UJF include:

1. It is inequitable for the insured motorists to pay, directly or indirectly through their insurers, costs that are properly assessable to the uninsured motorists. Such a procedure will eventually encourage recklessness and irresponsible conduct among uninsured motorists who have "nothing to lose." Under such a procedure, it is possible for one uninsured motorist to collect for an accident involving another uninsured motorist, all at the expense of those who are prudent enough or perhaps ignorant enough to pay insurance premiums.

---

[21] Unsatisfied judgment funds exist in New Jersey, Maryland, North Dakota, Manitoba, Alberta, British Columbia, Newfoundland, Nova Scotia, Ontario, and Prince Edward Island.

2. The UJF is at a substantial disadvantage in defending claims. By the time a claim is made, witnesses have dispersed and the record of the accident is "cold." Thus, it is difficult or impossible to determine whether or not legal liability actually exists.

3. Like compulsory liability insurance, the UJF resembles socialization of insurance and is subject to possible unwarranted political influence and public misunderstanding. For example, the uninsured driver may not understand why his driving privileges are suspended when the state fund has paid his judgment, why the state fund does not automatically pay medical or repair bills sent to it, nor why the state fund seeks reimbursement from him after paying a judgment. Consequently, it is likely that public pressure will be brought to bear upon the UJF to pay unwarranted claims, or to enforce collection procedures against negligent drivers.

In favor of the UJF, it may be observed that in the long run, society must pay for the cost of irresponsible conduct behind the wheel in one way or another. It is no more unfair for motorists as a whole to pay for these claims than it is for the claims to be paid out of general taxes, or by the families of those who are injured. The criticisms about the difficulty of determining legal liability can probably be rectified by statutory amendments. The UJF has certain characteristics of a socialized scheme of insurance, but it does not go so far as it might in this direction, for the UJF still rests on the legal liability system and not on the compensation principle. Even if the UJF were to be considered a step in the direction of socialized insurance, this is not necessarily an argument against it, providing such a step is generally good for the people as a whole.[22]

4) Uninsured motorist endorsement

The solution to the problem of the uncompensated victim of the uninsured motorist has been proposed and supported by private insurance companies in the form of an endorsement to the automobile policy known as the *uninsured motorist endorsement (UME)*, which was discussed earlier in the chapter. Under the terms of this endorsement, which applies only to bodily injury claims, if it is determined that an insured driver is injured by another driver who is uninsured, the insured driver's

---

[22] An analysis of the New Jersey UJF law was made by David Green, "An Insurer Looks at the New Jersey Unsatisfied Judgment Fund Law," *Insurance Law Journal,* November, 1957, pp. 728–732. The author concludes that the law is a step in the right direction although he recommends several changes.

company will act as the insurer of the negligent motorist and pay any legal liability that he would be obligated to pay. The insurer naturally has the right to collect from the negligent uninsured motorist for any damages paid to the insured motorist.

It may be immediately observed that a conflict of interest might arise over the UME, with the insured claiming that the other driver was liable and with the insurer disagreeing. The UME provides that the insured may not make a settlement with the uninsured motorist without the consent of the insurer. Without such a provision there would be nothing to prevent the insured from convincing the negligent party to agree to an unrealistically high settlement in the mistaken assumption that "he has nothing to lose." Therefore, the UME provides that if there is a disagreement between the insured and the insurer as to who is liable or as to the amount of damages, the question will be resolved by arbitration according to the rules of the American Arbitration Association. However, experience indicates that the conflict of interest problem is more theoretical than real, for very few cases go to arbitration but are settled without difficulty.[23]

Several states have already amended their financial responsibility laws to require attachment of the UME to each automobile liability policy issued within the state. In New York an amendment effective January, 1959, in effect gives uninsured motorist's protection to every resident of the state regardless of whether he owns an automobile.[24] Nonowners in other states may purchase a special form of the UME which is similar to nonownership liability insurance discussed earlier. The UME is issued for liability limits not to exceed those of the state's financial responsibility law.

The UME does not go so far as the UJF or compulsory liability insurance in solving the problem of compensating innocent victims of uninsured motorists, but it does overcome an important weakness in the typical financial responsibility law. For an annual flat charge of approximately $4, an individual may protect himself against bodily injury damage caused by uninsured motorists at least for minimum limits. While he does not receive similar protection for property damage, he can always purchase physical damage insurance if he desires protection against the accidental loss of his property.

---

[23] Henry S. Moser, "The Uninsured Motorist Endorsement," *Insurance Law Journal,* November, 1956, pp. 719–722, indicated that out of 1,000 cases involving the UME by one large insurer, only "a handful" went to arbitration.

[24] This coverage, provided under the Motor Vehicle Accident Indemnification Corporation, applies only to accidents occurring within the state.

5) Compensation laws

The *compensation principle* relates to the argument that the economic importance of automobile accidents is such that we can no longer trust the legal liability system with the task of solving the problem of compensating the victims. It is argued that it is impossible to determine the precise degree of negligence in a given accident, even if any existed, and that too often the automobile accident victim is without any means to meet the costs involved. It is the person with the best lawyer and the most cooperative witnesses who is compensated, and the "scientific method" is conspicuous by its absence. The concept of fault in a society on wheels is not a workable principle.

On the side of the compensation principle, one can point to the successes of the workmen's compensation laws. Ideally, the administration of similar laws for automobile accidents would be much simpler than the negligence system since everyone who is disabled by an automobile accident would receive a schedule of benefits set forth by the law of the state. Payments would be made regardless of fault and would depend on the seriousness of the injury instead of the income of the victim, and his skill at obtaining good legal talent or favorable witnesses. The upward trend of automobile insurance coverage would be stopped in its tracks, or even reversed. The existence of insurance would not be a factor in influencing the size of the judgment because there would be no insurance or trial. Best of all, the car driver and his family would never be called upon to bear the entire cost of an automobile accident over which he has little or no control, as is now the case when he is injured by a financially irresponsible motorist.

At present only the province of Saskatchewan has adopted this principle as the basis for compensating automobile accident victims; but it is not the only remedy, since it is supplemented by private insurance coverage for certain types of damage and for bodily injury damages in excess of certain limits of legal liability. In other words, the compensation principle has not replaced the legal liability principle, but has only supplemented it. The same thing has happened in the field of workmen's compensation, where in many cases workers can bring legal action against their employers despite the universal existence of workmen's compensation statutes. A few states have established funds for payment of limited types of automobile claims. An example is the Oregon Motor Vehicle Accident Fund, which compensates hospitals, doctors, and nurses for costs incurred in automobile accidents that involve indigents who are unable to pay for these expenses. The law deviates from the compensation principle in that (1) the injured person may not make a claim himself, and (2) in case the hospital, doctor, or nurse recovers from the patient, the fund must be repaid; and if the patient is later able to pay, he must reimburse the fund.

Opponents of the compensation principle, chiefly commercial insurers, point out that there are vast differences between the problem of industrial injuries and highway accidents and there is no reason to suppose that the administration of a compensation system in the automobile accident field will be as simple a matter as its proponents believe. The system would undoubtedly be in addition to and not in place of the present legal liability method and the cost of two duplicating methods of handling accident claims might be more confusing and costly than the present method, with all its wastes and inefficiencies. Furthermore, and perhaps most important, such a step would be an additional move toward the socialization of insurance, a result which private companies almost universally oppose.

SUMMARY

1. The cost of automobile accidents, in both absolute and relative terms, has been rising steadily in the United States for many years, posing a serious problem as to the most efficient and equitable manner in which the economic burden can be borne. Although the analysis in this chapter is concerned with this problem and not with the more basic problem of what can be done to reduce the severity, frequency, and cost of automobile accidents, this latter problem is the one about which more must be known before any ultimate solution to the problem of distribution of costs can be developed.

   If we knew the real causes of accidents, steps might be taken to handle the risk by placing greater emphasis on the method of reduction of hazard and less emphasis would have to be laid on the reduction of risk to the individual through private insurance, a state fund of some sort, or assumption of risk by a person unable to bear it. One example of the significance of this point is the relationship of age to the probability of having an automobile accident. At present all that insurers seem to do is assign higher rates to certain classes of youthful drivers without any real knowledge as to what causal factors there are in youthful drivers that result in higher accident rates.

2. Because the cost of a single automobile accident may be catastrophically expensive to the victims and because of the relatively high probability of

loss, insurance is the only feasible method commonly available to protect against the risk involved.

3. The provisions of the Family Automobile Policy (FAP) are representative of those found in most contracts covering the use of automobiles. The FAP is one of the most comprehensive contracts ever devised, insuring against losses due to legal liability for negligence, medical payments, and physical damage to the vehicle. Under the terms of the FAP, the words "insured" and "automobile" are defined broadly enough to give the average car owner almost complete protection no matter what car he is operating, and to give nearly the same protection to anyone else driving his automobile with his permission.

4. Liability coverage under the FAP covers against loss due to legal liability for damage to the person or property of others arising out of the ownership, maintenance, and use of the automobile. Medical payments coverage insures the loss due to accidental bodily injuries of occupants of a vehicle regard'ess of any negligence of the insured driver. Physical damage insurance reimburses the owner for physical loss of his vehicle from almost any peril, regardless of the insured's fault in causing the accident.

5. Because the definitions, exclusions, and conditions are as important as they are basic to an understanding of the FAP, they must be studied carefully to ascertain the scope of coverage under the contract. In general, coverage granted when the insured is driving nonowned cars is less comprehensive than when he is driving his own car.

6. Because of the economic importance of automobile accidents, it has been found socially desirable that each motorist be financially responsible for his negligent operation of vehicles. In general, the approach used in the United States has been to remove the motorist's driving privileges if it is determined that he either cannot respond financially for damages caused or does not carry liability insurance. There is some evidence that financial responsibility laws have been reasonably successful in their objective of seeing that drivers are able to pay for the increasing costs of automobile accidents.

7. A few states have gone a step further than the passage of financial responsibility laws and have made the purchase of liability insurance a prerequisite to licensing of the vehicle. Experience with this plan in Massachusetts since its adoption in 1927 does not support the conclusion that governmental control of automobile insurance is a more effective or desirable method of handling claims than well-enforced financial responsibility statutes. It is too early to tell whether more recent laws, designed to correct some of the weaknesses in the Massachusetts system, will provide better answers to the problem than financial responsibility laws alone.

8. A few states and several provinces in Canada have adopted unsatisfied judgment funds, which go even a step further than compulsory liability

insurance in that the funds represent an ultimate source from which payments can be made for the losses caused by financially irresponsible motorists.

9. So far no state has adopted the compensation principle in automobile insurance, although the province of Saskatchewan has a law based upon this idea. It seems certain that adoption of such laws would not replace our present system based on negligence law, but would only supplement it. It is not clear why the compensation principle should be adopted as long as there is no serious failure evident in the operation of financial responsibility statutes. If these laws are amended from time to time to meet such inadequacies as might appear, such as has been done in a number of states by requiring the uninsured motorist endorsement, the burden of proof that stricter legislation is needed should fall upon those who can demonstrate its need.

QUESTIONS FOR REVIEW AND DISCUSSION

1. Among the exclusions of the liability portion of the FAP are injuries to or destruction of property in charge of the insured "other than a residence or private garage." Reasoning from general insurance principles, would you argue that this quotation implies that the policy intends to cover an insured's damage to his own garage in, say, backing out and ruining the garage door? Explain your reasoning.

2. Since "Y's" car is broken down, "Y" borrows his son's car to run an errand. The son, who lives with "Y" in the same household, does not have his car insured. If "Y" had an accident, would his FAP cover him? Explain why or why not.

3. "X" borrows a neighbor's small garden tractor and while returning it, runs over a sled belonging to a third party. Will "X's" FAP cover the loss? Why or why not?

4. "G's" son gives permission for a neighbor to borrow his father's car, thinking it will be all right because the neighbor is a good friend of his family. Under the terms of the FAP, will the neighbor be covered while driving "G's" car? Why?

5. Discuss the basic reason for the exclusion in the FAP of injury to employees of the insured.

6. Speaking before the fourth annual Insurance Buyers' Conference of the American Society of Insurance Management, an executive of a large insurance company stated that the public is now prepared to consider a *basic change in the law of torts* and that in the near future it is possible that the *compensation* concept will replace the present system, even though some might oppose it on the ground that it would *relieve a man of the consequences of his own guilt.*

    (a) Explain what the speaker had in mind for each of the italicized phrases. Do you agree with his statements?

    (b) What are the arguments for and against a compensation system?

7. "Y" pulls a large house trailer behind his vehicle each year on a winter vacation which lasts four months.

    (a) Assuming limits of $5,000 property damage, what coverage is granted to "Y" under the FAP if the trailer sideswipes another car, causing a $1,000 loss to the trailer and a $2,000 loss to the other car?

    (b) Would your answer be different if the trailer had been a small two-wheel camping trailer with sleeping accommodations for two? Why?

8. An insured's mentally deranged son, after becoming intoxicated, broke into the insured's locked vehicle, and while driving it at high speed, wrecked the vehicle. If the insured had comprehensive insurance but not collision insurance, what line of reasoning might lead to the conclusion that the damage was covered under the FAP? Discuss.

9. A thief steals the insured's car and wrecks it. Is this a collision loss or a theft loss? Discuss.

10. In Harris v. Allstate Insurance Company (309 N. Y. 72), the insured had driven rapidly over a portion of highway inundated by water. He lost control and the car went over an embankment. There was no collision insurance, but the insured had comprehensive insurance. Should the insurer pay the claim?

11. Many cases have been concerned with claims originating when an animal jumps on top an automobile. In your opinion, is this a falling object or a collision? What difference does it make? Discuss.

12. An insured heard a large bang under his car, but continued to drive. After he had gone a mile or so, the motor stopped. The insured did not examine the car, but had it pushed to the nearest garage, where it was determined that all the oil had leaked out of a hole in the oil pan and the engine was burned out. Is the insurer liable? If not, why not? If so, under what type of auto coverage? Why?

13. In view of the data in Table 16–3, page 395, can it be concluded that drivers in certain age classes cause more than their share of automobile accidents? Discuss, giving examples. If so, may it also be concluded that age is a factor in the cause of accidents? Discuss the pros and cons of this question.

14. (a) Is it true that women cause more accidents than men? Is it true that women have a higher accident rate than men? What information should you have before drawing any conclusions about the accident rate of men v. women? As a project, consult a source such as the latest edition of *Accident Facts* of the National Safety Council for such data as will support an unbiased position on this question.

    (b) Perform a similar investigation to secure answers to the question "Should farmers be charged more than city dwellers for automobile insurance?"

15. John has $50 deductible collision insurance on his car, while Jack carries $100 deductible. If John borrows Jack's car and has a collision in which $200 damage is done, which policy must respond and in what amounts? Why?

16. In the case of Farm Bureau Mutual Automobile Insurance Company v. Boecher 48 N.E. (2d) 895, the insured worked for an automobile dealer and was involved in an accident when driving a car made available for employees by the dealer. The insured, who had never driven this particular vehicle before, applied for coverage under his private automobile policy and was denied protection on the grounds that the policy excluded coverage on nonowned cars. With reference to the provisions of the FAP, discuss the correctness or incorrectness of the position taken by the insurer.

17. A trade publication reported the following story:

> A new approach to automobile insurance is being tried by one group of insurers. In their contracts the individual operator is covered, regardless of what vehicle he is driving, in contrast to the usual practice of "insuring the automobile" regardless of who is driving it. The proponents of this plan argue that the present wave of granting rate credits "to an automobile" (under various "safe driver" plans) regardless of who is driving it, is unsound. The new contract covers only the named insured and does not extend to anyone else unless the other person is driving and the insured is a passenger.

   (a) Is it true that it is the usual practice to issue insurance "on the automobile?" What is the fallacy involved here?
   (b) What is meant by the argument that rate credits granted under merit rating plans now being tried are unsound?
   (c) Would you feel that the new contract approach described here meets the needs of the average family? Why, or why not? Would it meet the needs of the average business? Discuss the pros and cons.

18. It has been urged that a way of reducing insurance premiums under a compulsory automobile liability insurance law would be to "insure the driver instead of the car." In Massachusetts, for example, since in one year there were 2,150,000 licensed drivers and about 1,500,000 registered vehicles, it was argued that the insurance premium for each driver would be only 70 per cent of the current rate. Is the conclusion of the above argument sound? Discuss some of the possible fallacies in it.

19. A method proposed to reduce the cost of automobile liability insurance is to issue all policies with a deductible clause of, say, $50 or $100. It is urged that this would not only make drivers more careful if they knew they had to pay the first $50 or $100 themselves in any liability claim for property damage, but would also reduce the cost to insurance companies of paying small claims.
   (a) Do you agree that these are sound arguments? Why, or why not?

(b) What would be the probable attitude of accident victims under this arrangement?

20. It has been pointed out that the four most densely populated states in the United States—Rhode Island, New Jersey, Massachusetts, and Connecticut—are also the states with the lowest traffic death rate. What aspect of automobile accident statistics does this information illustrate? (See Table 16–1, page 392.)

21. (a) Criticize automobile fatality rates as the best single measure of the accident problem.
    (b) What other measure might be substituted? Would it have any weaknesses? Discuss.

22. Some states have installed "no fix" traffic ticket systems, whereby once a citation is issued, a court has complete jurisdiction; and any attempt to "fix" a ticket may result in a contempt of court charge. There is evidence that the frequency rates of automobile insurance claims in these states are much lower than in states without such a system.
    (a) Suggest possible reasons why there might be a connection between these two phenomena.
    (b) What evidence would you require to say without equivocation that "putting in a 'no fix' system will reduce automobile accidents"?

23. The text states "there are vast differences between the problem of industrial injuries and highway accidents and there is no reason to suppose that the administration of a compensation system in the automobile accident field will be as simple a matter as its proponents believe." Point out one or more of the differences that might be relevant to the administration problems referred to. Do you agree that these differences make a compensation system in automobile accidents difficult or impossible to administer? Why?

24. A writer stated, ". . . our present system of jurisprudence must either be made to work more effectively in the evaluation and settlement of bodily injury claims or it will inevitably give way to some system of compensation regardless of fault, or a set schedule of payments, or some other means yet to be devised. . . . We surely cannot believe the public is going to permit costs to continue to rise as they have been indefinitely, for the public bears the cost, and their annual liability premium notices are forceful reminders to them of the costs they bear."
    (a) Do you agree that the main factor in causing bodily injury premiums to rise is our "present system of jurisprudence?" Why?
    (b) Do you believe that the writer above is taking the position that the costs of automobile accidents can be kept down by imposing a set schedule of benefits for car accidents that are lower than those which are allowed under our legal liability system? If so, what is your estimate of the possibility of success of a compensation system? Discuss.

25. "Z" backs out of his driveway across the street and slams into a parked car belonging to a neighbor. Occupants of the car are injured to the

extent that the medical payments limits in the FAP are insufficient to cover the damage. In your opinion may "Z" make a claim under the medical payments section of his comprehensive personal liability policy to supplement these payments? Why, or why not?

26. In the case of Arnold v. Goldstein (Michigan Supreme Court, 1955, 5 CCH Auto Cases, 2d, 1302), a plaintiff testified that he was attempting to cross a street when he noticed a truck approaching from the north. Turning around to return to the curb, he saw another car coming from the other direction and decided to stand on the white center line, hoping that neither car would hit him. However, the cars hugged the white line, collided with each other, and struck the plaintiff. The insurers of the two vehicles claimed no liability on the grounds of contributory negligence on the part of the plaintiff for standing motionless on a public thoroughfare.
    (a) Decide with reasons, the question of who, if anyone, is liable in this case.
    (b) If the FAP terms governed the insurance in this case, would there be any costs incurred by the insurer? If so, under what parts? Discuss.

27. "A" owns an automobile protected by the family automobile policy, with liability limits of $10,000/$20,000 bodily injury and $5,000 property damage. He is aware that the policy covers individuals other than himself and the insurer agrees to indemnify for more than liability claims alone, but "A" is not sure just how far his coverage extends. Indicate, *with reasons* based on the insurance given under his policy, the extent to which, if any, the following claims would be paid:
    (a) "A's" wife takes the car to the service station and an attendant, while driving it, collides with another vehicle, damaging "A's" car to the extent of $300. The service station seeks to hold "A's" insurer liable.
    (b) "A" has an accident with another car and injures a driver. "A" calls an ambulance to take the other driver to the hospital, where he is discharged after minor treatment. The hospital bills "A" for $75. It is never determined whether "A" is liable for the accident or not. "A" makes a claim under his policy.
    (c) "A" lends his car to "B." "B" drives the car to another city and lends it to his friend "C," who has an accident involving damage to "D's" property in the amount of $500. "C" does not own a car himself and asks "A's" insurer to pay.
    (d) "A," in driving his car at his place of work, runs into another employee who was moving some boxes on a hand truck and failed to see the automobile. Hospital bills are $150, and "A's" employer asks "A's" insurer to pay the bills.
    (e) "A's" minor son takes the car without permission and is involved in an accident that results in a suit against "A" for $12,000 for damage to the driver of the other car. In addition, the cost of defense is $3,000. "A" asks his insurer to pay these claims.

Insurance Against

Dishonesty and Human Failure

Crime in the United States is not only one of the most serious perils causing loss to property, but it is also one of the most underinsured perils. It is estimated that only one fifth of all losses from this source are covered by insurance or bonds. Reporting stock insurers incurred losses in the following categories in 1959; $46 million in burglary and theft insurance, $32 million in fidelity bonds, and $50 million in surety bonds, for a total of $128 million.[1] If only one fifth of the actual losses are insured, this would mean that, at a minimum, actual losses are in the range of approximately $500 to $600 million annually. Because crime losses are not so well publicized as other insured losses, and because of the tendency for people to ignore a source of loss of which they are not constantly reminded, the crime peril is often left uninsured.

THE STATISTICS OF CRIME LOSS

Burglary, robbery, and theft

The Federal Bureau of Investigation crime reports document all too well the feeling that crime is increasing, despite generally good business conditions in the United States. Each year there are more major crimes committed than the year before. In 1960, for example, the number of robberies, burglaries, and thefts of $50 or more increased 23 per cent, 24 per cent, and 22 per cent, respectively, over the average number in the period 1957–59. These data are based on the number of crimes actually reported to the Federal Bureau of Investigation, but it is estimated that a substantial number are unreported, which would increase the total number of crimes by approximately 30 per cent. Measured by these data, it is estimated that crime increased much more rapidly than total population in the period 1950–1958. The rate of burglaries, robberies, and larcenies per 100,000 population increased from 1,301 in 1950 to 1,766

---

[1] *Best's Fire and Casualty Aggregates and Averages* (1960), p. 28.

in 1958, an increase of 35.7 per cent. During this same period, population increased an estimated 15 per cent.

As shown in Table 17–1, there are wide differences in the crime rate geographically, which ranges from 235.9 per 100,000 population in Mississippi to 1,336.4 in California, for a national average of approximately 701.9 per 100,000 population. States with higher than average rates of burglary, robbery, and larceny are not necessarily the most populous, but they are those states in which the greatest population gains have been registered since 1950. This is not surprising since growing areas are generally likely to suffer maladjustments in community services, such as police enforcement.

Table 17–1

BURGLARY, ROBBERY, AND LARCENY RATES PER 100,000 PEOPLE, BY STATES, 1958 NATIONAL AVERAGE, 701.9

700 or more	500 to 700	Less than 500
California...........1,336.4	New York...........689.0	Minnesota...........492.9
Nevada.............1,260.6	Wyoming...........687.6	Alabama.............491.0
Arizona............1,159.5	Michigan...........681.9	Arkansas.............486.4
Florida............1,066.2	Utah...............633.2	Kentucky.............485.2
Colorado............ 912.1	Oregon.............646.7	Pennsylvania.........484.7
Rhode Island........ 819.1	Delaware...........635.2	Missouri.............472.6
Washington......... 784.2	Indiana............628.3	South Dakota........398.5
New Mexico......... 761.6	Montana...........609.7	North Carolina.......383.5
Nebraska............ 745.0	Illinois............608.2	Iowa................367.0
Texas.............. 739.0	New Jersey.........604.4	Vermont.............365.0
Oklahoma.......... 734.3	Maryland...........587.7	Maine...............355.9
	Tennessee..........584.8	Wisconsin............355.9
	Georgia............576.7	New Hampshire.......332.6
	Virginia...........561.9	West Virginia........313.0
	South Carolina......551.3	North Dakota........309.3
	Idaho..............542.4	Mississippi..........235.9
	Ohio...............533.7	
	Massachusetts.......527.1	
	Connecticut.........518.2	
	Louisiana...........516.3	
	Kansas.............503.9	

Source: Federal Bureau of Investigation 1958 Uniform Crime Reports.

Federal Bureau of Investigation estimates place the total known annual property losses due to burglary and robbery at $120 million, excluding automobile theft. Six times as much property is stolen through burglary as through robbery, but the average amount per burglary ($170) is 85 per cent of that taken through robbery ($200). The following table gives the value of property stolen and the percentage recovered based on reports from 407 cities.

Table 17–2

VALUE OF PROPERTY STOLEN AND PERCENTAGE RECOVERED—1960

(407 Cities over 25,000; Total Population 56,000,000)

	Value of Property Stolen (Millions of Dollars)	Per Cent of Total Property Stolen	Per Cent of Property Recovered
Cash.............	$ 34.2	24.0	9.1
Jewelry...........	24.4	17.2	8.2
Furs.............	7.7	5.4	5.2
Clothing..........	13.1	9.2	10.7
Miscellaneous......	63.0	44.2	19.0
Total..........	$142.4	100.0	52.2

Source: Federal Bureau of Investigation as reported in *Fire, Casualty, and Surety Bulletin* (National Underwriter Company).

Relatively little stolen property is ever recovered, with the exception of automobiles, which are not included in the figures above. As might be expected, cash, jewelry, and furs account for nearly half of all lost property. Federal Bureau of Investigation data show that only about one fourth more burglaries of residences take place at night than in daytime, indicating that burglary is not just a peril that strikes at night. However, in the commercial area, the burglary rate is about ten times as great by night as by day. Commercial robberies are over twice as numerous on highways as they are in buildings.

Embezzlement

Even more serious than burglary, robbery, and larceny losses are those from embezzlement and forgery. Unfortunately there are no uniform data available which permit reliable estimates to be made of the total loss from embezzlement and forgery over the years. What information is available suggests that stealing by employees and forgery losses conservatively amount to several times the annual losses from burglary, robbery, and larceny. Comparing estimated fidelity losses with the losses reported by fidelity insurers leads one to believe that only a small portion of the total losses is insured, less than 10 per cent. Part of the reason for this lies in the reluctance of owners of many business firms to admit even to themselves that employees chosen by them might not be honest. Even when an embezzlement is discovered, there is a tendency to hush up the matter for fear that publicity among customers, creditors, or other employees might be damaging to the firm's best interests. Unfortunately it is in the smaller firm, where losses can be least afforded, that the attitude of "it can't happen here" tends to be most strong.

A study of individual cases concerning the dishonesty hazard is perhaps more revealing than is a quotation of aggregate statistics. One such study described the typical embezzler as follows: [2]

> The typical defaulter is in his thirties, is married, has one or two children. He lives in a respectable neighborhood, drives a medium-price car, and once in a great while travels on the weekend. Whatever his secret life, he usually looks like a good mixer and is active in the community; often as not, he's a church officer. Temperately, he takes an occasional drink. Usually he's had a couple of job promotions, partly because he's been around the firm for awhile, and partly because he has slightly better than average ability, works hard, and seems to accept responsibility. In one study of 1,001 cases, 270 of the embezzlers held supervisory or executive positions.

Thus, the average embezzler is not an unusual type of person, but is a "regular" person, a hard worker, a social mixer, a trusted and intelligent worker. If he were not trusted, he would have little chance to steal. His reasons for embezzling are as numerous as they are varied. Expensive hobbies, the desire for a higher standard of living, or just to save money for an undetermined purpose are common motives stated by those who are apprehended. Usually the embezzler convinces himself that he has a need for money which is obtainable in no legitimate manner, sees and takes an opportunity for stealing, and then rationalizes his behavior by telling himself that he is not stealing—only borrowing. One of the most common types of embezzlement is that depicted by an individual, not uncommonly a bank employee, who believes that his employer is exploiting him and decides to get even by stealing. One unusual example of this was the case of a man earning $2,500 a year who felt he deserved $4,500 in order to live properly. He therefore stole the difference between these two amounts, reducing his thefts as his salary was increased. Finally his salary exceeded the $4,500 per year and he began to repay the $25,000 he had stolen until, at the time his embezzlements were discovered, he had reduced the "debt" to $3,000.[3]

An interesting fact about embezzlements is the enormous sums that can be stolen before the thefts are discovered. One of the most publi-

---

[2] "Embezzlers, the Trusted Thieves," *Fortune* (November, 1957), p. 143.
[3] *Ibid.*, p. 144.

cized cases in recent years was the theft of $2,919,000 by a woman executive in a savings and loan association. The thefts went undiscovered over a period of 23 years. Another example was that of a large national wholesale drug chain in which, while being reorganized, the auditors uncovered a gigantic theft by the president of the company running into millions of dollars. The embezzlement had been hidden by falsifying inventory records. In another case, a bank officer managed to steal $678,000 within a five-year period. He went unsuspected in spite of his purchase of seven homes and expensive race horses while earning only a modest salary. When he was discovered, the bank had to close its doors.

These examples could be multiplied many times if space permitted. They suggest the wisdom of securing large limits of financial protection through fidelity bonds, and of bonding even those who are trusted completely, in the realization that, in the last analysis, only the trusted employees are in a position to succeed in such large thefts. In addition, it is undoubtedly true that the existence of fidelity bonds, as well as other protective devices, tends to discourage embezzlement in the first place. This follows because the average embezzler, valuing his position of respectability, is more easily discouraged by means of preventive measures than the so-called hardened criminal. Existence of a bond requirement within the firm undoubtedly puts a would-be embezzler on notice that all employees are subject to careful controls.

Forgery

Forgery losses involving the passing of illegal checks are among the most common types of dishonesty engaged in and yet are among the easiest to prevent. Most such losses are caused by so-called amateurs, since it is estimated that only one third of the total check losses are caused by "professionals." Forgery most commonly involves the issuance of entirely fictitious checks, although the alteration of and false signatures upon legitimate checks are frequent. Most false checks are cashed in supermarkets, department stores, service stations, and taverns where large volumes of small transactions take place and where it is fairly uncommon to require a very careful identification of the passer. Installation of devices to take photographs of every person cashing a check, together with his fingerprints, and of the check to be cashed has reduced false check passing tremendously in stores where this method has been adopted. However, most business firms, especially small ones, seem unwilling to take the necessary steps to prevent these losses. In addition to the objection that it is expensive to install control measures, it is likely that in the desire to make sales, the store owner feels that to require identification of the customer might incur public ill will.

INSURANCE AGAINST CRIME

There are two basic types of financial protection that are available as bulwarks against the catastrophic losses which can be caused by crime: (1) surety and fidelity bonds, and (2) burglary, robbery, and theft insurance. *Surety and fidelity bonds* provide guarantees against loss through the dishonesty or the incapacity of individuals who are trusted with money or other property and who violate this trust. *Theft insurance,* on the other hand, provides coverage against loss through stealing by individuals who are not in a position of trust when performing thefts.

BONDS

Characteristics of bonds

In Chapter 3 certain differences between contracts of insurance and contracts of suretyship, that is, bonds, were discussed.[4] These distinctions will now become clearer as we consider in detail the nature of bonds. Strictly speaking, all bonds are surety bonds, but in practice it is convenient to classify them as fidelity bonds and surety bonds.

Fidelity bonds indemnify an employer for any loss he has suffered at the hands of dishonest employees. As such, the bonds are hardly distinguishable from insurance as far as the employer is concerned. While technically there are three parties to a fidelity bond—the employer (obligee), the employee (obligor), and the insurer (surety)—in practice the main parties are only two, the employer and the surety. The employees are often not even referred to by name, since they are covered on a blanket basis. The bond may be cancelled by either the surety or the employer, the surety has the right of subrogation against defaulting employees, and in other details fidelity bonding follows insurance practice.

Surety bonds, sometimes known as *financial guaranty bonds,* are contracts between three parties—the principal (obligor), the person protected (obligee), and the insurer (surety). Under the contract the surety agrees to make good any default on the part of the principal in his duties

---

[4] See page 55.

toward the obligee. For example the principal might be a contractor who has agreed with the obligee for a given consideration to construct a building meeting certain specifications. The owner-obligee requires the contractor to "post a bond" to the effect that he will faithfully perform this contract. If the contractor fails in some way, the surety must "make good" to the owner and then has the right to recover any losses from the contractor.

Fidelity v. surety bonds

Fidelity and surety bonds have certain differences which may be contrasted. First, fidelity bonds are purchased by an employer for his own benefit, but surety bonds are purchased by the obligor for the benefit of some other party, the obligee. Second, fidelity bonds are concerned only with the honesty of the employee and not with his ability to perform certain work. In surety bonds, the obligee is concerned not only with the obligor's honesty but also with his *capacity* to perform. Hence, the risk to the underwriter is greater on the surety bond than it is on the fidelity bond. Third, the surety "expects no losses" in the case of the surety bond, since it is assumed that if the surety must make good the default of the principal, the principal will reimburse the surety. If it were otherwise, the surety would be a sort of "business partner" to the principal, a partner with great financial resources, to absorb any and all losses for the principal but without the chance of sharing in the principal's profits. In fidelity bonding, the surety's only hope of reimbursement is to recover from the defaulting employee; hence, losses are expected and planned for in the premium charged.

Requirement of collateral

As an outgrowth of the fundamental nature of a surety bond, the surety often requires collateral before it will issue the bond. The surety bond is an instrument for lending the superior credit of the surety to the obligor in return for a premium payment. The surety may decide that the credit position of the obligor is strong enough so that definite collateral in the form of cash, securities, or property is unneeded; but in many cases such collateral is required as a matter of routine to protect the surety against losses, particularly in risky ventures. It may be inquired as to why an obligee requires a bond at all. If the obligee wants security, why does it not accept the collateral of the obligor directly? The answer lies basically in the fact that the obligee is usually in no position to assess the value of the many varieties of collateral that might be offered nor to attend to the details involved in obtaining legal security. The bonding company can perform the function much more economically and more efficiently than the typical obligee. Furthermore, many surety bonds are required by statute, and collateral may not be acceptable under the statute. Examples of these kinds of bonds are court bonds and fiduciary bonds, to be discussed later.

Major types of fidelity bonds

Fidelity bonds may be classified in two groups: 1) those bonds in which an individual is specifically bonded, either by name or by position held in the firm, and 2) those bonds which cover all employees of a given class, called *blanket bonds.*

1) Bonds in which an individual is specifically bonded. Bonds in which an individual is specifically bonded may be further classified according to whether they are individual bonds or schedule bonds.

Individual bonds. *Individual bonds* name a certain person for coverage. If the employer suffers any loss through any dishonest or criminal act of the employee, either alone or in collusion with others, while the employee holds a position with the employer, the surety will be good for the loss up to the limit of liability, called the *penalty* of the bond.

Schedule bonds. *Schedule bonds* may list many employees by name and bond them for specified amounts, in which case the bonds are known as *name schedule bonds.* Additional names may be added or old names deleted upon written notice to the surety.

Position schedule bonds are those which list positions to be bonded and any employee in these positions is automatically covered. The employee is not identified by name in the bond, only by his position. This form is especially suitable for the employer who has a rapid turnover of employees. The employer may add coverage for positions that are created from time to time.

Some schedule bonds grant automatic coverage for a limited period on new names or new positions which may be introduced in order to grant a more complete protection to the employer using these bonds. The term of years for which coverage is provided varies from company to company.

2) Blanket bonds. *Blanket bonds* have the following advantages over individual or schedule bonds which cause their use to be heavily favored among most business firms:

1. Automatic coverage of a uniform amount on all employees is given, thus eliminating the possibility that the employer may select the "wrong" employee for bonding. An employer might believe, for example, that a common laborer is in no position to steal and thus fail to list him under the bond or perhaps bond him for a very low amount. Yet it may turn out that this person is the one who admits thieves to the premises or cooperates with other employees in a plan to steal inventory.
2. New employees are automatically covered without need of notifying the surety. Thus, there is no need for setting up special records to handle premium adjustments when employees come and go or when seasonal help is hired. The only requirement is that each new employee fill out an application form in order that the bonding company may investigate him.
3. If a loss occurs, it is not necessary to identify the employees who are involved in the conspiracy in order to collect, as is required on the individual or schedule bonds. It need only be shown that the loss was due to employee infidelity.
4. Because blanket bonds are subject to rate credits for large accounts, the cost may be no more than that of schedule bonds.

Types of blanket bonds. There are two major types of blanket bonds: the blanket position bond and the primary commercial blanket bond. These two bonds, whose terms are standardized by the Surety Association of America, differ primarily in the manner in which the penalty of the bond is stated. The *blanket position bond* has a penalty, ranging in amounts from $2,500 to $100,000, that applies to each *employee*. The *primary commercial blanket bond* has a penalty, ranging upward from $10,000 that applies to *any one loss*.

To illustrate this difference, consider the case of an employer who discovers a $20,000 loss involving three employees, each equally liable. Under a blanket position bond written for a $5,000 penalty, the maximum recovery would be $15,000. If only one employee had been involved, the recovery would be $5,000. The total limit and recovery for any one loss depends on the number of employees responsible for it, assuming all employees are equally to blame. Under the primary commercial blanket bond, the penalty of the bond is the limit of liability. The $20,000 loss would be covered fully if the penalty of the bond were $20,000 or more, regardless of the number of employees involved.

In deciding which type of bond is more appropriate, it should be noted that in case an employee or employees cannot be identified, the blanket position bond limit per employee is all that can be collected, even though it is known that more than one employee is involved. This factor necessitates a higher penalty per employee than might otherwise be carried, and may result in a somewhat larger total premium on the blanket position bond than on the primary commercial blanket bond. The total premium on the blanket position bond is also slightly greater because of the higher maximum potential penalty that could be paid under this bond. This follows from the fact that there is no limit on the number of employees covered, and hence no limit on the aggregate loss that could be paid in any given time period.

Important provisions of fidelity bonds

Continuity of coverage. Most fidelity bonds are continuous until cancelled by either party. They have no expiration date, only an anniversary date. The premium may be paid annually, or a three-year premium may be purchased at the cost of two and one-half times the annual premium. In the latter case, the premium is due either in a lump sum at the beginning or it may be spread out over the period of the bond, 50 per cent of the premium payable the first year, 30 per cent the second year, and 20 per cent the third year. The bond itself does not expire automatically on the anniversary date as do most insurance contracts. However, coverage on any one employee is automatically cancelled once an employer learns of any dishonest or fraudulent act committed by an employee either before or after the employee was hired. Thus, if an employer learns of a theft committed by an employee five years before he was hired but decides to forgive the employee and give him a second chance, he does so at his own risk for any later stealing.

Noncumulative penalty. The penalty of the bond is the maximum amount payable for any one loss or for any one employee. The employee may steal $5,000 each year over a long period of time under a bond where the penalty is say $5,000, but the total amount payable for losses traceable to him remains at $5,000.

Losses covered. Fidelity bonds generally cover losses occurring while the bond is in force and discovered during this time or within a certain period, known as the *discovery period,* usually of two years' length, after the bond has been discontinued. If the loss occurs *before* the bond is effective, the loss is not covered under the typical fidelity bond. Some bonding companies write what are known as *discovery bonds,* whereby the loss is covered if it is discovered either during the period of the bond or within any discovery period following its cancellation, regardless of when the loss occurred. Discovery bonds are recommended for employers who have not previously bonded their employees, since there is no way of knowing in advance how long an employee has been stealing.

Sometimes a bond may be cancelled in one company and replaced by another bond in another company. In such instances, the *superseded suretyship clause* provides that if a loss is discovered during the term of the second bond (but after the discovery period has elapsed under the first bond) and if the loss would have been paid under a prior bond had this bond been continued in force, the second surety will pay the loss. In this way an employer who wishes to change sureties may do so without fear of losing continuity of coverage. In effect, the superseded suretyship clause converts the second bond into a type of discovery bond.

Perils covered. Most fidelity bonds cover any dishonest act or any criminal act of covered employees, but some bonds are restricted to certain crimes such as larceny and embezzlement. The difficulty with specifying such crimes is that there are different legal definitions for these crimes in varying jurisdictions. Thus, an employer can never be certain that he is insured for all dishonest acts. Therefore, such restrictive wording should be avoided wherever possible. All blanket bonds use the broad wording in the insuring agreement.

Salvage. Recoveries of stolen property from employees, after the surety has fully indemnified the employer, are, of course, returned to the surety. If the surety has not fully indemnified the employer, say because the loss exceeded the penalty of the bond, some bonds require, under a *full salvage clause,* that any recoveries go to the employer until he has been fully restored for his loss. This clause is similar to the rule in subrogation recoveries in insurance. Other bonds contain a *pro rata salvage clause,* which provides that such salvage will be divided between the surety and the employer in the proportion that each has suffered loss.

Suppose Jack takes $10,000 from the cash drawer one morning, goes on a wild spree in Florida, and when the surety's detectives arrive a month later, he has only $6,000 left. In the meantime Jack's employer has been paid $5,000, the penalty under the bond. If the bond had been written with a pro rata salvage clause, the $6,000 would be split evenly between the surety and the employer because up to that time each has suffered a $5,000 loss. Under the pro rata salvage clause, the surety and the employer each would have lost $2,000. Under a full salvage clause, $5,000 would be returned to the employer and $1,000 would go to the surety. In this way, the employer would be fully restored and the surety would have lost the $4,000 that Jack squandered. It obviously makes a substantial difference to the employer which type of salvage clause is used.

Property covered.   Bonds covering employee dishonesty do not restrict the type of property for which indemnification is payable. Stealing of cash, inventory, equipment, securities, or any other property is covered. The property does not have to be owned by the insured, but may be merely held by him in trust for others to whom he may or may not be legally responsible. Sometimes there are territorial limits as to where the stealing may be insured. Usually, full coverage applies in the United States or its possessions or while the employee is temporarily in another country. Coverage for employees permanently located outside the United States should be arranged for by separate negotiations with the surety.

Restoration.   When a loss is incurred, the question arises as to what happens to the amount of bond penalty available for other losses. In blanket bonds there is an automatic reinstatement of bond limits (or restoration clause) immediately after the payment of any loss. For example, under the primary commercial blanket bond written with a $50,000 limit, payment of $30,000 for one loss from one employee does not reduce the $50,000 penalty applicable to thefts by other employees. As to the employee who stole $30,000, however, only $20,000 remains as coverage for other peculations of his, no matter when they are discovered. Of course, all coverage in the future for this employee is cancelled. Since the blanket position bond limits apply separately to each employee, there is no need for a restoration clause.

Excess insurance.   Under bonds written with limits that apply to individual employees, it may sometimes be desirable to place larger limits on certain employees on an *excess* basis. Such coverage can be arranged without disturbing the primary bond and without, therefore, increasing the limits of the primary bond for all employees. Use of excess insurance on certain employees, while it may be more economical than increasing the limits of the primary bond, means that the employer must single out certain employees for higher coverage, an uncertain process at best since it cannot be predicted in advance which employee will steal.

Inventory shortages. One of the most common types of loss from employee dishonesty is that of stealing various items of inventory. Yet, the existence of an inventory shortage does not necessarily mean that an employee is to blame; shoplifting, sneak thievery, or natural evaporation or spoilage may account for the loss. In individual and schedule bonds there is no recovery under the bond for any loss unless the defaulting employee can be identified positively, including, of course, cases where the accounting system reveals an inventory shortage. In blanket bonds, where identification of the individual employee causing the loss is not a requirement, a question arises as to whether the bond will pay for a loss where an abnormal inventory shortage exists and where no explanation other than employee dishonesty could account for it. The bond provisions state that there must be "conclusive" proof that employees have been responsible for the shortage.

Major types of surety bonds

Surety bonds may be classified under three major headings:

Construction bonds
1) Contract
2) Bid
3) Completion
4) Owners' protective

Court bonds
1) Fiduciary
2) Litigation

Miscellaneous surety bonds
1) License and permit
2) Lost instrument
3) Public official

Construction bonds.

1) Contract construction bonds. From the standpoint of premium volume, probably the most important type of surety bond is the *contract construction bond* (sometimes called a *final* or *performance bond*). The contract construction bond guarantees that those principals (contractors) involved in construction activities will complete their work in accordance with the terms of construction contracts and will deliver the work to the owner free of any liens or other debts or encumbrances. To the owner, particularly in the case of corporate or municipal owners who let contracts for large projects to the lowest bidder, the construction bond is an indispensable financial security mechanism. Only through use of a third-party guarantee, namely the guarantee of the surety company, can the owner realistically give a contract to the lowest bidder. Without the bond, the owner could not be sure that the lowest bidder would be able to perform the contract at the price stated. There is the possibility that he has bid low just to get the work, and will be unable to finish the job at his bid price. With a bond the owner knows that if the contractor fails to perform, the surety will make good any loss involved. The cost of the bond is returned many times by the fact that owners are in a position to take advantage of the savings involved in competitive bidding. From the viewpoint of the contractor, the bond is highly desirable because the bond places each contractor on an equal footing in his bid, which can be calculated in the knowledge that a bid will not necessarily be looked upon with suspicion because it is low.

Even if the contract is not let for competitive bidding, requirement of the contract construction bond is looked upon as a highly desirable business practice because it transfers the risk involved in construction to an institution that specializes in this area. The owner is not often in a position to judge adequately the risks taken by a contractor in the performance of his work. Each job is different from the one before; it may be carried on in a remote part of the world under unfamiliar conditions; it may involve a new type of architectural problem; it may involve the use of unusual building materials. What appears to be an adequate financial position of the contractor before the job may turn out to be sadly inadequate as these new problems are faced. The owner probably has only limited experience with contractors and looks upon the surety as a specialist who passes his judgment on the ability of the contractor and backs it up with a promise of monetary indemnity if he is wrong. The contract construction bond is thus required in practically all public work and in most commercial work.

2) Bid bond.   A *bid bond,* in contrast to a contract construction bond, guarantees that if the bidder is awarded the contract at the bid price and under the terms outlined, he will sign the contract and post a construction bond. The bid bond thus involves the same risk as the contract construction bond.

3) Completion bond.   Both bid and contract construction bonds are required for the protection of the owner. The *completion bond,* on the other hand, is required by the lender or the mortgagee, who also may have an interest in the property because of financing arrangements. The completion bond guarantees that the person who borrows the money for the project (this may be either the contractor or the owner) will use the money only for the project and will ultimately turn over to the lender the completed building or project, free of any liens, as security for the loan. The completion bond, which is required only in case of private work, is a guarantee of the honesty and ability of both the borrower and the contractor, if they are different parties. A single job may involve all three types of construction bonds—the contract, the bid, and the completion bond.

4) Owners' protective bond. A form of the contract construction bond known as the *owners' protective bond* is issued for private construction only. The owners' protective bond provides that if the principal defaults, the surety has a direct obligation to take over and to complete the contract or to pay the owner his loss in cash. This bond differs from the usual form of contract bond in which the owner has to take over himself and complete the work in order to determine the loss. If the surety elects a cash settlement, the amount payable is the reasonable cost of completion, less the unpaid balance of the contract price, as determined by taking bids from at least three responsible contractors. The owners' protective bond differs also from other contract bonds in that unpaid laborers or material men may take direct action against the surety instead of filing a lien and foreclosing as is often the case under other contract bonds. The owners' protective bond further requires that the work must be performed under the supervision of an architect.

Court bonds.

1) Fiduciary bond. A *fiduciary* is a person appointed by a court to manage the property of another person, and in that capacity the fiduciary owes a very high degree of care to the beneficiary of his trust. Unless the provision is excused by an authorized person, courts universally require that a fiduciary be bonded. Thus, if there is a failure in the degree of care owed by the fiduciary, the surety will make good any resulting liability for loss. Examples of fiduciaries are executors of estates, guardians over the estates of minors or incompetents, and receivers in bankruptcy proceedings. Each of these classes of individuals is responsible for honest and capable conduct while managing the property under his care. In fact, the degree of care owed by a fiduciary, the highest owed by any class of individual, is one of undivided loyalty to the beneficiary.[5] This increases the risk to the surety because conduct which might not involve any legal liability under a less stringent standard may result in a loss to the surety on a fiduciary bond.[6]

Because of the risk involved, it is common for sureties to require that estate funds be deposited in a joint bank account with the surety and that disbursements be made only on the signature of both the fiduciary and the agent of the surety. Known as *joint control,* this practice assures that all legal formalities will be complied with in disbursement of funds and that liability will not result from unintentional actions on the part of the executor, who is not infrequently inexperienced in legal formalities. Normally the court itself determines the form of bond to be required and the penalty for which it is to be written. The bond is continuous until the court releases the fiduciary of all his obligations.

It is common for executors of estates and other fiduciaries of probate courts to ask a good friend to be the surety in an estate which they are administering. The friend, believing he is guaranteeing only the honesty of the executor, signs as surety, and is usually ignorant of the substantial risk he is taking. The surety, as has been seen, guarantees both the honesty *and the ability* of the fiduciary in the performance of his duties. Thus, he is subjecting all his own property to possible attachment in case there is a loss caused by some failure on the part of the executor, however innocent or unintentional this failure might be. Personal suretyship is generally unsatisfactory to the beneficiaries of the estate because oftentimes the personal surety is financially unable to respond for damages that might result from the incompetence of the fiduciary. In spite of these difficulties, and in spite of age-old warnings against suretyship which appear in the Bible,[7] personal suretyship is still common in the United States.

2) Litigation bond.   *Litigation bonds* include all those bonds required by the court in certain legal proceedings involving civil and criminal suits. The bonds are required whenever one party to a suit requests the court to do something which he claims is his legal right, but which would result in an unjust loss to the other party in case the court decides, after due consideration, that he does not have such a right. Litigation bonds may be divided into two groups; defendants' bonds and plaintiffs' bonds.

---

[5] For an excellent discussion of this point, see G. T. Stephenson, *Estates and Trusts* (New York: Appleton Century Crofts, 1955), Chapter 22.

[6] One example of how large this risk can be occurred in 1957 when Charles H. Barnard, former president of the state senate in New Hampshire, embezzled $245,624 from an estate for which he was the executor.

[7] For example, "He that hateth suretyship is sure," *Proverbs* 11; and "A man void of understanding striketh hands, and becometh surety in the presence of his friend," *Proverbs* 17; to "strike hands" means to become security for another's obligations.

DEFENDANTS' BONDS. The best known example of defendants' bonds is a *bail bond,* in which the court requires the deposit of a bond to guarantee that the defendant will appear in court at the time scheduled or forfeit the penalty of the bond.

Other examples of defendants' bonds are appeal bonds, removal bonds, and release attachment bonds.

Appeal bonds are required when a defendant who has lost a case in a lower court wishes to appeal the case to a higher court. In case the appeal loses, the court requires security that the amount of the judgment, interest thereon, and court costs will be paid.

Removal bonds are required when the defendant wants to have the case moved from one court to another, say from a state court to a federal court. The bond guarantees that if the defendant loses, the costs of moving the case will be paid.

Release attachment bonds are required when the defendant's property has been attached under some prior legal proceeding and the defendant seeks the court's approval to have the continued use and control of the property pending the outcome of the case. The court will grant such approval if the defendant will post a bond to the effect that if the case goes against him, the amount of the judgment plus court costs will be paid.

Many defendants' bonds, such as the appeal bond, are quite hazardous since there is great likelihood that if the defendant has lost in one court, he will also lose in another. Usually the surety requires 100 per cent collateral in such cases.

PLAINTIFFS' BONDS. Examples of plaintiffs' bonds are attachment bonds, replevin bonds, and injunction bonds.

Attachment bonds are required when the plaintiff is bringing suit to attach certain property belonging to the defendant so that the defendant cannot sell or otherwise dispose of the property. It may be, for example, that a creditor seeks to attach the bank account of the debtor to prevent the debtor from transferring his account to someone else so as to avoid payment of the debt. In such cases the attachment bond is required to guarantee that if the plaintiff loses his action, he will pay the defendant any damages suffered because his property was attached. Without the bond, the court will not permit the attachment proceedings to go through.

Replevin bonds are required when the plaintiff is seeking to recover specific property which he claims is wrongfully in the possession of the defendant. If the plaintiff posts a replevin bond, the court will permit him to repossess his property pending the outcome of the case. If the case goes against him, the bond guarantees that he will pay any damages the defendant has sustained. Suppose, for example, a finance company has repossessed an automobile which the plaintiff argues has already been paid for. The court, after the posting of a replevin bond, will permit the plaintiff to retake his car pending the outcome of the case. If he loses, he must pay any damages that the finance company has suffered by being deprived of the car during the time of the appeal.

Injunction bonds guarantee that if the plaintiff obtains a temporary injunction by a court prohibiting the defendant from performing a certain act, and it turns out that after hearing all the facts, the court refuses to issue a permanent injunction, the damages suffered by the defendant during the temporary injunction will be restored. Thus, an injunction bond may be issued when an employer obtains a court order to stop the picketing of his establishment by union members pending a full consideration of the case. If the picketing is fully within the rights of the union, the union may obtain damages from the employer, payment of which is guaranteed by an injunction bond.

It should be stressed again that a bond is not an insurance policy that pays the damages referred to in the above cases. A bond is only a guarantee that if the principal does not pay, the surety will. The surety will usually require a deposit of full collateral in case there is any doubt of the ability of the principal to respond to any damages that may be levied against him. The bond is required because the court will not accept collateral directly.

Miscellaneous surety bonds. We shall illustrate the many miscellaneous types of surety bonds with three examples: 1) license and permit, 2) lost instrument, and 3) public official bonds.

1) License and permit bonds. Many governmental bodies use the *license* or *permit bond* to obtain assurance that owners of certain business enterprises will obey the law and will be responsible for any damages caused through violation of a license or a permit under which they do business. Sometimes the bond must also guarantee the payment of taxes and fees. It is common to license such business people as auctioneers, building wreckers, plumbers, sign hangers, small loan companies, employment agencies, boxing gyms, detective agencies, and insurance adjusters. The license or permit bond is noncancellable. A secondary purpose is served by the bond during the investigation of the background of applicants for coverage. In this way persons of doubtful reputation are refused permission to operate.

2) Lost instrument bonds. If a person has lost a valuable paper, such as a stock certificate, a corporate bond, a warehouse receipt, a railroad ticket, a pawnshop ticket, or a money order, there is always the possibility that it will fall into unauthorized hands and be passed on to an innocent third party for value. If the institution which issued the lost paper in the first place is requested to reissue it or to pay an obligation under it, there is a possibility that the original document will turn up in the hands of a *bona fide* holder for value and will impose an obligation on the institution to restore this bona fide holder as well. Therefore, before they will reissue or pay for the document, many institutions require that a *lost instrument bond* be posted to guarantee against any loss imposed if and when the document is found. Rates for these bonds depend on the character of the lost document. Thus, the rates for negotiable instruments are much higher than for nonnegotiable instruments. Naturally, if the surety suffers a loss, it may seek reimbursement from the original owner who lost the document.

3) Public official bonds. Elected or appointed officials at every level in government—city, county, state, and federal—are generally required to furnish a *public official bond* guaranteeing that they will honestly and faithfully perform the duties of their office according to law. An official may be completely honest but may fail in some legal responsibility and thus cause a liability to the surety. For example, the official is usually responsible for the acts of certain deputies or subordinates, and losses caused by their dishonesty would be paid under the public official bond if the official has failed in his legal duty to see that each deputy is bonded as well. Another example would be where the public official has failed to deposit public monies in approved depositories, failure of which is his personal responsibility.

The form of public official bond is usually prescribed by statute and the surety must provide protection accordingly. The bonds are non-cancellable until the end of the official's term of office.

Forms are also provided for bonding on a blanket basis all public employees other than certain positions, such as treasurer and tax collector, who are required by statute to furnish an individual bond. The bonds are sometimes written only to cover employee dishonesty, and at other times to cover both dishonesty and lack of faithful performance. They may be written with a penalty applying on each loss in the aggregate, or with the penalty applying to each employee, in the same way that the penalty applies under the primary commercial blanket bond or under the blanket position bond, respectively.

BURGLARY, ROBBERY, AND THEFT INSURANCE

Definitions

As used in insurance contracts, the meaning of the terms burglary, robbery, and theft are important in the understanding of the extent of coverage. These terms always refer to crimes by persons other than the insured, his officers or directors, or employees, coverage on which is provided by fidelity bonds.

Burglary.   *Burglary* is usually defined somewhat narrowly to mean the unlawful taking of property from within a premises, closed for business, entry to which has been obtained by force. There must be visible marks evidencing the forcible entry. Thus, if a customer hides in a store until after closing hours, or enters by an unlocked door, steals some goods, and leaves without having to force a door or a window, the definition of burglary is not met under a burglary policy covering the store.

Robbery.   *Robbery,* on the other hand, is defined to mean the unlawful taking of property *from another person* either by force or by threat of force or by violence. Personal contact is the key to understanding the basic characteristic of the robbery peril. However, if a burglar enters a premises and steals the wallet of a sleeping night watchman, this crime is not one of robbery because there was no violence or threat thereof. The person robbed must be cognizant of this fact. On the other hand, if the thief knocks out or kills the watchman and then robs him, or the owner, the crime would be classed as a robbery. Robbery thus means the forcible taking of property from a messenger or a custodian. Many contracts further define robbery according to whether it occurs outside the premises or inside, a higher rate being charged for outside robbery.

Theft.   *Theft* is a broad term which is generally undefined in the insurance contract. Theft includes all crimes of stealing, not leaving out robbery or burglary. Theft is a "catch-all" term and is usually not distinguished from larceny. Thus, any crime not meeting the definition of burglary or robbery will be a theft. Therefore, confidence games or other form of swindles are thefts, not robberies or burglaries.

Special characteristics of the crime peril

Certain provisions that will be observed in crime policies result from the following special characteristics of the crime peril.

1. A high moral hazard surrounds the business. Since crime is difficult to detect, it sometimes is difficult to distinguish crime by outsiders and crime by insiders. It may be tempting for an unsuccessful merchant to "arrange" a theft in an attempt to profit both from the insurance and from the subsequent sale of the "stolen" articles.

2. There is a high element of adverse selection among applicants for coverage. Those most likely to suffer loss are first to apply for coverage. Stores in poorly lighted neighborhoods may tend to be robbed more often than other stores. Stores with high-value, easily transportable merchandise like jewelry or clothing are especially susceptible to loss. It is only natural that these institutions are among the first to seek insurance protection. To encourage loss prevention. insurers grant substantial rate discounts for the maintenance of safety devices, such as burglar alarms, watchman services, guards, and burglar-resistive safes.

3. The burglary and robbery insurance business tends to suffer more from underinsurance than other types of insurance businesses. An owner of goods feels certain that thieves cannot or will not steal the entire contents of the store at one time. because of physical limitations. He therefore seeks to purchase insurance equal in value to only a fraction of the value of the entire stock of goods. Because of these factors, premium rates for crime coverages tend to be high and underwriting restrictions tend to be rigid. Stores with repeated loss records or owners with doubtful backgrounds may be excluded from coverage altogether. Yet, these same factors indicate the extreme seriousness of the crime peril and the desirability of insuring against it by most property owners.

Business coverages

There are many varieties of contracts covering the peril of crime for businesses. We shall examine only a few as typical examples. Ranging from least comprehensive coverage to most comprehensive, these contracts are:

1) Safe burglary policy.
2) Mercantile open stock burglary policy (MOS).
3) Storekeepers' burglary and robbery policy.
4) Money and securities broad form policy.
5) Dishonesty, disappearance, and destruction policy (3D).

1) Safe burglary policy. The *safe burglary policy,* one of the oldest business crime policies, restricts its coverage to loss of property taken by forcible entry from a safe or a vault described in the declarations as the insured safe. Visible marks, such as those made by tools, explosives, electricity, or chemicals, must evidence the entry. If the safe combination is used or if the lock is manipulated, there is no coverage. If the property owner is forced to give the combination, there is no coverage; such a loss is covered under a robbery policy. However, the safe burglary contract covers the loss when the entire safe is taken from the premises, even if the evidence is never found. The loss must be capable of being determined through books and accounts kept by the insured. Loss of these books in the safe are excluded property; separate contracts (for example, valuable papers and accounts receivable) are available for this type of loss.

Damage to the safe or vault, to the building or to furniture, fixtures, equipment, or other property in the premises but outside the safe or vault is covered under the safe burglary policy, providing of course there has been evidence of an actual safe burglary. Any type of property (except books and records) stolen in a safe burglary is covered, not just money or securities; but if the burglar takes other property outside the safe, there is no coverage. Rates for this coverage depend on the fire and burglar-resistive properties of the safe, and upon the degree of hazard attached to the particular type of business involved. Discounts are granted for policies covering more than one safe, or where certain types of property, such as securities, constitute a given percentage of the total values exposed, or when certain protective devices are used.

2) *Mercantile open stock burglary policy.* Demand for crime insurance against the loss of stock on merchants' shelves as well as property contained in a safe gave rise to the *mercantile open stock burglary policy* (abbreviated *MOS*). The MOS covers loss by *burglary* (as usually defined) or by *robbery of a night watchman,* while the premises are not open for business, of merchandise, furniture, fixtures, and equipment within the premises or within a showcase or show window. (The showcase may be outside the main premises, but must be within the building line of the premises.) Money and securities are not insured, nor are books, records, manuscripts, or furs taken from a showcase that was broken into from the outside. There is a limitation of $50 on any article of jewelry and $100 on any loss from a showcase that does not open directly into the building from the interior. The policy covers all loss incurred through damage to the premises and to other property during the covered burglary or robbery. However, vandalism and malicious mischief, war, loss occurring during a fire or when the hazard is in-

creased, and loss to plate glass or its lettering are among the sources of loss excluded by the policy.

The MOS is written with a coinsurance arrangement under which the insured is required to purchase coverage equal to the lesser of the following: (1) A certain percentage, ranging from 40 to 80 per cent, of the value of the exposed property, or (2) A dollar amount, called the *coinsurance limit,* which varies with the type of merchandise and its location. Failing to carry this amount, the insured may collect only that proportion of his loss as the amount of insurance he carries bears to the amount required.[8] This provision, which is designed to prevent under-insurance, may be illustrated as follows: A hardware store owner with $20,000 of stock may decide that thieves could never carry away more than $5,000 worth of merchandise at one time, and so this is the limit of coverage he purchases. However, the MOS contract has a coinsurance percentage of 40 per cent and a $10,000 coinsurance limit. Since 40 per cent of the value of his stock is $8,000, and this is less than $10,000, the merchant would collect from the insurer only $5,000/$8,000, or $\frac{5}{8}$ of any loss. To avoid coinsurance penalties, the merchant must carry at least $8,000 insurance in this case. The merchant may obtain reductions in his rate by accepting higher coinsurance percentages or higher coinsurance limits.

For an additional premium of approximately 75 per cent, the retail merchant may by endorsement broaden the coverage under the MOS to include any kind of theft, not just burglary or robbery of a night watchman. This additional charge amounts to 40 per cent of the burglary premium for wholesale merchants or manufacturers. The size of these premiums gives a rough idea of the estimate that actuaries place on the additional perils introduced by broadening the coverage from burglary to theft.

3) Storekeepers' burglary and robbery policy. The *storekeepers' burglary and robbery policy* is a "package" policy designed especially to fit the typical requirements of the small retail establishment. It covers in one policy seven different types of perils: (1) safe burglary, (2) mercantile open stock burglary, (3) damage to money, securities, merchandise, furniture, fixtures, and equipment caused by burglary or robbery, (4) theft of money or securities from a residence or night depository of a bank, (5) kidnapping, meaning compelling a messenger or custodian to give the thief access to the premises for purpose of taking

---

[8] See page 211 for a full explanation of coinsurance, its theory, and its application.

money, securities, merchandise, or equipment, (6) robbery, outside the premises, of the insured or his messenger, and (7) robbery inside the premises.

For each of the perils above, the policy contains a limit ranging from $250 or multiples thereof up to $1,000. There is a loss limit of $50 applicable to burglary of money or securities outside a safe, such as from a cash drawer or cash register. There is also a provision which limits the number of insured messengers at any one time to two for each location covered. Thus, if a retailer has this contract written for limits of $1,000, and two messengers each take $1,000 to a bank for deposit, the retailer is fully insured against robbery if both should be robbed. Premiums for the storekeepers' burglary and robbery contract vary with the class of risk, the territory, and the limits purchased. The premiums may range from a minimum annual premium of $12.50 to $82.50 for the first $250 of coverage. The charge for $1,000 of coverage is approximately two and one-half times the premium for $250 of coverage.

4) Money and securities broad form policy.   The storekeepers' burglary and robbery policy gives limited protection against one of the chief crime perils facing a business enterprise—theft of money or securities. The *money and securities broad form policy* is designed to meet the needs of any business enterprise for money and security protection in any limits desired. Furthermore, the peril under this form is broader than just theft, and includes loss of money or securities due to destruction of any kind, including fire, and almost any type of disappearance or wrongful abstraction. Thus, if paper money blows out a window while it is being counted, if fire or flood ruins securities and paper money, or if money mysteriously disappears, the policy will respond. If money is taken from a cash drawer or a safe by manipulating the lock, the safe burglary policy would not apply since this is not a burglary under the definitions; but the money and securities broad form policy would cover the loss. In addition, coverage is given for damage to the premises or to furniture or equipment caused by burglary or robbery, and for loss of merchandise due to interior robbery. Notice that loss of merchandise due to *burglary* is not insured, and therefore there is still the need for the MOS burglary policy which insures this loss.

The main perils excluded under the money and securities broad form policy are war, forgery (may be insured separately), fire (this exclusion does not apply to money and securities), and employee dishonesty. Property such as manuscripts and records, plate glass and its lettering, money in a vending machine (unless the machine has a continuous recording and counting device) is excluded. Losses due to purchase or exchange of property, or due to arithmetical errors or omissions are also excluded. Thus, if a clerk accidentally gives the wrong change, or if money is given as the purchase price for property whose value has been fraudulently misrepresented, these are not losses under the policy. However, if a thief poses as a bank messenger and thereby steals a sum of money intended for deposit, the loss is covered even though the owner voluntarily surrendered the cash to the thief.

The money and securities broad form policy is divided into two parts—loss inside the premises and loss outside the premises. Coverage outside the premises is limited to actual destruction, disappearance, or wrongful abstraction of money or securities from a messenger, armored car company, or from the home of a messenger. Loss of other property by robbery is only covered if it occurs in conjunction with the robbery of money or securities, or as the result of a theft in the home of a messenger. Coverage on the premises for property other than money and securities is limited to damage resulting from actual or attempted safe burglary or holdup, or by interior holdup.

If a loss occurs under the money and securities broad form policy, there is no reduction in the amount of insurance for subsequent loss. Furthermore, there is a one-year discovery period after expiration of the policy within which losses that occurred during the policy term may be discovered and paid.

5) *Dishonesty, destruction, and disappearance policy (3D)*. The dishonesty, destruction, and disappearance policy, commonly abbreviated 3D, is a package contract with five parts: (1) employee dishonesty, (2) money and securities broad form, inside the premises, (3) money and securities broad form, outside the premises, (4) money orders and counterfeit paper currency coverage, and (5) depositors' forgery.

The first three parts of this comprehensive contract will be recognized as forms already analyzed in this chapter. The fourth coverage indemnifies the insured for loss in case he accepts, in good faith, in exchange for merchandise, money, or services, counterfeit money or illegal or counterfeit money orders.

The fifth coverage, *depositors' forgery*, also known as *outgoing forgery*, covers the insured for losses suffered when: (a) checks are endorsed, (b) when a check is issued to a person posing as a legitimate payee and the legitimate payee's signature is forged on the instrument, or (c) when a check legally issued by the insured to a legitimate payee is endorsed and cashed by someone else without the authority of the legitimate payee. Court and legal costs involved in any suit over an allegedly forged instrument are also covered under the policy.

For an additional premium, an endorsement may be added to the 3D policy giving the insured protection in case of *incoming* check forgery. For example, losses incurred when the insured accepts a forged check in payment of merchandise or services may be insured. Incoming forgery coverage is somewhat hazardous in that it might encourage careless procedures in cashing any and all checks presented to the insured. For this reason checks cashed purely as an accommodation are excluded. Recovery on checks given for merchandise is limited to 75 per cent of the insured's pecuniary interest in the check. Thus, if a customer gives a $100 check in payment for $75 of merchandise and receives $25 in change, the insured's pecuniary interest is $100 and his recovery is limited to $75. This limitation on recovery helps to encourage careful check-cashing procedures.

In addition to incoming check forgery, mercantile open stock burglary, mercantile open stock theft, and certain other crime coverages may be endorsed on the 3D policy. Thus, the insured is provided a means of covering practically all his crime exposures in one contract.

Personal coverages

Broad form personal theft policy. The *broad form personal theft policy* is the major form of theft insurance written for the typical homeowner. The broad form personal theft policy, defining theft as "any act of stealing," covers against loss by either theft or mysterious disappearance of any property from a private home, or from another depository such as another private dwelling, a public warehouse, a bank, or a trust company. The policy provides for limits of liability under the categories: loss *on* the premises or loss *off* the premises.

Loss on the premises. Although jewelry and furs must be named for separate limits of coverage, for all other property, personal theft insurance on the premises applies on a blanket basis. "Other property" includes money up to $100 and securities up to $500 for any one loss. Damage to the premises and to insured property by theft is also covered, whether it is due to the theft peril or simply to vandalism. Thus, if a burglar enters a premises and, finding nothing of value, decides in his disappointment to smash anything in sight, the resulting damage is insured. If property mysteriously disappears, the insurance applies, since it is assumed that theft is the reason for the disappearance. Property simply lost, or where there is a known explanation for its disappearance, is, of course, not covered.

Loss off the premises. The broad form personal theft policy gives fairly complete protection for property away from the premises. It covers, for example, property taken from unattended automobiles, property taken while being moved from one premises to another, property taken from a son's fraternity house while the son is at college, and property taken while the premises are rented to another. Furthermore, the coverage is worldwide, a feature which attracts individuals who travel to the far corners of the earth.

There are, however, some limitations on coverage while the property is located elsewhere than on the main premises. For example, the contract excludes coverage on: (1) property pertaining to a business, (2) property in a secondary residence, except when the insured is temporarily residing there (The insured is supposed to buy another policy for this residence.), (3) property of a residence employee unless he is in the employment of the insured while away from the premises, (4) property in the custody of a laundry, cleaner, dyer or tailor, except by robbery or burglary, and (5) property lost in the mails.

The policy also contains some general exclusions. For example, loss of aircraft, automobiles, trailers, motorcycles, animals, birds, or salesmen's samples are not covered. Note, however, that boats are not excluded. The mysterious disappearance of a precious stone from its setting is excluded, as is loss sustained by a boarder or roomer (not a relative), loss due to war, or loss committed by an insured. The contract defines an insured as the named insured and any permanent member of the named insured's household other than a residence employee or a roomer and boarder. If a wayward son living at home takes his father's watch and sells it, there is no claim under the policy.

An insured can always specifically insure certain property for limits greater than the blanket limit of the policy. In this event the specific amount named is the maximum recovery if the item comes up missing. Thus, if James has a $2,000 boat that he wishes to insure, he may name it specifically. If he has general limits of $1,000 under his contract, he must still pay for coverage of $2,000 on the boat. He may not use any of the $1,000 general limits as coverage for the boat.

Personal theft policy. A more limited coverage available to the general householder is offered by a contract known as the *personal theft* *policy.* Coverage under this policy is about the same as the broad form personal theft contract except in the following major particulars:

1. It does not cover mysterious disappearance. Thus, it is necessary to prove theft in order to collect for a loss.
2. There is only one insuring clause covering both on and off the premises.
3. Loss of boats or their equipment, loss from unlocked and unattended automobiles, and loss from dormitories, fraternity or sorority houses are excluded.

SUMMARY

1. Crime statistics show that the peril of dishonesty and human failure cause more total losses than other major perils. Yet the crime peril is greatly underinsured. Prominent among the reasons for this underinsurance are the tendency for business firms to refuse to recognize that trusted employees can and do steal, and the lack of publicity that attends these crimes.

2. The two major types of crime protection are bonds, and burglary, robbery, and theft insurance. Bonds give protection against losses due to defalcations of persons in a position of trust, while theft insurance gives protection against crimes of so-called "outsiders."

3. There are some important differences between bonds and insurance, and an understanding of these differences is vital to an understanding of how crime protection contracts operate. Basic is the fact that bonds provide the surety's financial guarantee of the principal's honesty and ability, with the understanding that if there is a loss, the surety can attempt to recover from the principal.

4. Fidelity bonds, which are similar to an insurance contract in their operation, appear in many forms which may be adapted to the needs of the particular business firm. They cover against loss due to dishonesty of employees, while surety bonds provide financial guarantees of both the honesty and the ability of the principal to perform according to a given agreement.

5. Fidelity bonds are continuous in term until cancelled, but their penalties are not cumulative from year to year. They generally cover only those losses that occur during the currency of the bond and which are discovered within a two-year period after its cancellation. The method of distributing any salvage under fidelity bonds may make a substantial difference to the employer in his compensation for loss. The employer should give careful consideration to the method by which he intends to prove that losses have occurred. Proving losses under a fidelity bond is usually much more difficult than in other types of insurance.

6. The major classes of surety bonds are contract construction, court, and miscellaneous. Contract construction bonds have an important economic

influence in all contract construction and in its financing in two ways: they facilitate competitive bidding and enable free competition to flourish in this important industry; they enable the transfer of construction risk to parties better able to handle it, thus facilitating the growth of this industry and reducing the cost of construction. Surety bonds thus exert a much deeper economic influence than merely protection against crime.

7. Three major types of crime loss from "outsiders" result from burglary, robbery, and theft. These perils are usually defined carefully in insurance contracts and their meanings differ from the meanings commonly ascribed to them by the layman, who may make no differentiation among them. Crime policies have certain major underwriting characteristics that help to explain the insurance practices involving their use. Chief among these characteristics are the existence of underinsurance, a high degree of moral hazard, and a tendency toward adverse selection.

8. Contracts of insurance against each of the three major crime perils are available, both for personal and business use. In addition, all-risk coverage against loss of money and securities is available. The best known comprehensive crime policy for business is the 3D—dishonesty, destruction, and disappearance contract, which covers in one scheduled form fidelity insurance, broad form money and securities destruction insurance, and forgery and counterfeit money insurance. The broad form personal theft policy is probably the best known and most widely used form of theft insurance for individuals.

QUESTIONS FOR REVIEW AND DISCUSSION

1. An employer discovered that one of his employees "borrowed" a small amount of cash from the company without prior permission. The employee repaid the sum and the employer kept him on the payroll. Two months later the employer applied for and received a bond covering all employees, but did not state anything about the incident. Later on, the same employee was caught in another theft, but the bonding company denied recovery. On what grounds did the surety do this? Explain.

2. An employer has a blanket position bond with a $10,000 penalty. Three employees are caught in a scheme whereby fictitious employees are kept on the payroll and their names are forged on paychecks by the group. The total amount of theft is $36,000, of which $12,000 is finally recovered by the surety.
   (a) What is the amount payable to the employer under the bond? Explain your answer.
   (b) How would the salvage be divided under a bond with (1) a full salvage clause? (2) a pro rata salvage clause? Explain all calculations.

3. (a) Assuming no salvage in the case in Question 2, would the employer have been financially better to have secured a primary commercial blanket bond written for a penalty of $25,000? Why, or why not?
   (b) Discuss the merits of the two types of bonds—blanket position bond and primary commercial blanket bond. Which would you prefer?

4. The restoration clause has no applicability to the blanket position bond, as it has with the primary commercial blanket bond. Why?

5. Federal Bureau of Investigation reports indicate that in 1937 there were 137,700 burglaries, as compared with 247,845 in 1957. During the same period robberies increased from 26,700 to 34,600. These data were based on 343 large cities. Suggest possible reasons for the much greater growth of the crime of burglary than of robbery.

6. Federal Bureau of Investigation reports indicate that in 1932 there were 554 bank robberies in the United States. By 1943 this figure had fallen to only 24. This crime then began to rise after 1943 and the number of robberies reached 81 by 1950, and 346 by 1959, for a total "take" of about $1.4 million in 1959.
   (a) Suggest possible reasons for the tremendous growth of bank robberies.
   (b) Do you think these crimes are largely the work of professional criminals? Why or why not?

7. A news item from Roscoe, Pennsylvania, February 5, 1960, gave an account of a bank robbery as follows "Two men age 21 and 18, violated every rule in the bandit's handbook. They entered the bank during the afternoon rush hour. One kept yelling 'more' after two women clerks threw $5,000 into his paper bag. Then, instead of ignoring the bank manager who pleaded with him not to take the money, the robber wasted time arguing with him. The robber forgot to load his gun. He turned his back to the entrance and was overpowered by two passers-by who saw the holdup. The other robber in a lavender-colored getaway car was soon captured after he was hampered by the heavy traffic." What aspect of the current bank robbery problem does this story illustrate?

8. Summarize the essential differences between: (a) surety bonds and fidelity bonds and (b) the bond and the insurance contract.

9. A certain dairy bonded all its financial personnel as well as its driver-collectors on a position schedule bond. A laborer in the yard made arrangements to purchase empty wooden butter cartons at five cents each for his "hobby." It turned out some months later that he had systematically stolen several thousand dollars' worth of butter in the "empty" boxes as he passed through the check gate. How could the dairy automatically have protected itself against such a loss?

10. An insured, a retail store, carried a blanket position bond. At the end of a year it discovered a substantial stock shortage when inventory as revealed by the accounting records was compared with a physical inventory. Checks indicated that accounting errors were small, and there was no evidence of unusual shoplifting by customers. The discrepancy was large, even after considering normal spoilage. There was no evidence incriminating any employee, but the insured claimed that there was no other explanation, and made a claim for indemnification under the bond. In your opinion do the above facts establish a case of conclusive evidence that employees were responsible? Discuss.

11. An employee is bonded for $10,000. In one year he steals $6,000; in the next, $3,000; in the next $4,000; and in the next, $2,000, before he is finally detected. The insured claims full indemnity, but the surety refuses to pay. How much must the surety pay? Give reasons why the insured is right or wrong in his contention.

12. Writing on the subject of the tendency of management to ignore danger signals from dishonesty losses, an author stated: "Besides overlooking obvious danger signals, management often places undue confidence in its alarm systems. The principal alarms for embezzlement are the accounting system and the auditor. Both, for this purpose, are overrated. Most large embezzlements are hidden in accounting systems, remaining hidden through one audit after another. The internal accounting systems are not primarily established to detect fraud, and auditors can't audit what they can't find. More embezzlements are discovered by good luck than by good accounting." Comment. Does this imply that audits are completely useless? If not, what value might they have?

13. Judge Louis D. Brandeis was reported to have called fidelity insurance "an abomination," stating that it is ridiculous "to think of insuring management against the consequences of its own failure to know and supervise its trusted employees!"
    (a) Discuss arguments for and against this position.
    (b) Do the facts support Brandeis' opinion?
    (c) What relationship does this argument have to the increasing dominance of professional managers in business as opposed to the former eminence of individual entrepreneur-owners? Discuss.

14. One case of employee embezzlement was revealed when a secretary in Jersey City stole nearly $5,000 from stamp money over a period of five years. What might this case illustrate in deciding upon the type of bond to procure? Why?

15. Among the common devices to conceal stealing are the following: manipulation of inventory records to conceal stolen merchandise; forging of checks and destroying them when returned by the bank; padding bills for goods purchased and obtaining a kickback from the supplier; taking money from the cash register and correcting the tape; and returning goods to suppliers but failing to record this act, thus enabling the theft of an equivalent amount of cash without unbalancing the records.
    (a) How might an accountant or an auditor prevent such acts from succeeding? Discuss.
    (b) If you could find methods for preventing each of the above methods from succeeding, does this mean that you would not recommend to the firm's management the purchase of a dishonesty bond? Why?

16. In contrast to the relatively low percentage of middle-aged persons arrested in such crimes as robbery, burglary, and theft, Federal Bureau of Investigation reports show that over 80 per cent of all those arrested for embezzlement and fraud were 25 years of age and over, with the maximum number of arrests being made in the age group 30–34. Suggest reasons for the age distribution reported.

17. On January 1, 1962, an employer changes his fidelity bond, a primary commercial blanket bond, from one surety to another. Two months after this change, on March 1, 1962, it is discovered that Jones, the cashier, has stolen $7,000 over a period of ten years as follows, 1951, $2,000; 1956, $3,000; 1961, $1,000; February 1, 1962, $1,000. The first bond had been in force continuously since January 1, 1954.
    (a) Assuming the limits of both bonds are $10,000, which surety must pay for which losses?
    (b) How would your answer have been changed, if at all, if the losses had not been discovered until 1965? Explain, with reference to the pertinent bond provisions which govern your answer.

18. The text states: "The cost of the (contract construction) bond is returned many times by the fact that owners are in a position to take advantage of the savings involved in competitive bidding."
    (a) Explain what is meant by this statement.
    (b) In constructing a building, what risks are taken by an owner who accepts a low bid only after investigating the successful contractor very carefully?

19. It is fairly common for the maker of a will to excuse the executor from the requirement that he be bonded. This is done to save costs and is commonly justified by the belief that the executor is an honest person and does not have to be bonded. Criticize this position.

20. In a famous decision Judge Cardozo stated, "Many forms of conduct permissible in a workaday world for those acting at arm's length are forbidden to those bound by fiduciary ties. A trustee is held to something stricter than the morals of the market place. Not honesty alone, but the punctilio of an honor the most sensitive, is then the standard of behavior. . . ." (Meinhard v. Salmon, 62 A.L.R. 1, 1928). Of what significance is the above quotation to the underwriter of surety bonds? Explain.

21. "Y," a trustee for an estate, is directed by the court to dispose of certain real property. "Y" decides that he would like to have this property himself and so purchases it at a public auction at a fair price. Six months later "Y" sells the property at a profit.
    (a) Applying the principles stated in Judge Cardozo's opinion as quoted in Question 20, would you say this represents defensible conduct on the part of "Y"?
    (b) As judge of the court having jurisdiction over the estate, would you attempt to force "Y" to distribute the profits of his transaction to the beneficiaries, or failing in that, would you attempt to collect an equivalent amount from the surety? Why?
    (c) Is the surety liable? Why? If so, under what type of bond?

22. John Jones, a general contractor, submits a bid plus a bid bond, for a certain job in the amount of $100,000. He is awarded the contract, but goes into bankruptcy after $75,000 of the work has been put into place. It is estimated that $35,000 will be required to complete the work.
    (a) What is the liability, if any, of the surety under the bid bond?
    (b) What is required under a bid bond?

23. (a) Assuming in Question 22 that the proper bonds have been issued, what action is required of the surety?

   (b) What liability, if any, would exist if the estimate for completion of the work after Jones' bankruptcy were $15,000 instead of $35,000?

24. In an address to local agents, a bond underwriter stressed the following: "In looking over an application for a bond, the underwriter's first question is, 'Who is going to pay if the principal does not?' " Does this statement imply that the surety is not going to meet its obligations under the bond if a loss develops? If not, explain what steps the surety takes to insure that a loss to it will not occur.

25. (a) What particular advantages over other types of contract bonds are there in the owners' protective bond to (1) the owner and (2) the labor or material supplier?

   (b) Suggest possible reasons for the requirement under this form that construction be handled under the supervision of an architect.

26. Identify briefly the main differences in the following:

   (a) Contract construction bond v. completion bond.

   (b) Fiduciary bond v. litigation bond.

   (c) Public official bond v. individual fidelity bond.

   (d) Attachment bond v. release attachment bond.

   (e) Appeal bond v. injunction bond.

   (f) Removal bond v. replevin bond.

27. Why does the surety under an appeal bond consider this type of bond especially hazardous from an underwriting standpoint?

28. In the automobile insurance policy, the insurer has a clause stating that if it is required to make any payment under a financial responsibility act, which it would not have had to make except for this provision, the insured will reimburse the insurer for the amount so paid.

   (a) Under what conditions might the payment referred to arise? (See Chapter 16.)

   (b) What similarities, if any, are there in this provision to a surety bond?

29. Jack Smith cannot find a policy covering his house against the peril of fire.

   (a) As his insurance adviser, inform him as to the desirability of securing a replacement policy.

   (b) Would a lost instrument bond be required before the insurer will replace the policy? Why, or why not?

   (c) Would your answer be the same if Jack had lost a stock certificate showing him to be the owner of 100 shares of General Motors? Why?

30. The XYZ Finance Company, discovering that John B. is two days late in making his final monthly car payment, sends its investigator to pick up the car. Later John discovers that his car is missing when he unsuccessfully attempts to get into another car looking just like his. John brings action to recover his car, complaining that the final monthly payment was remitted on time. But the finance company insists on keeping the car, arguing that $498.03 in back carrying charges is due. John asks the court to allow him the use of the car until the case can be decided.

   (a) What type of bond might John have to put up in order to get back his car?

   (b) Why is this bond required?

31. A burglar enters a jewelry store at night by forcing a window. Just as he begins his work of forcing open the safe, he is surprised by a night watchman. There is a struggle, the watchman is knocked unconscious, and the burglar escapes with his haul of gems taken from the safe. Is this crime compensable under the usual burglary policy? Why or why not?

32. The Ace Department Store, which has an annual sales volume of $1.5 million, applies for a storekeepers' burglary and robbery policy. The agent discourages this purchase and recommends the money and securities broad form in combination with the MOS contract. Would you agree that Ace's idea is better, or that the agent's recommendation is better? Or would you recommend some other form of protection against crime? Why?

33. The manager of Ace's Department Store (Question 32), rightly or wrongly, finally buys the money and securities broad form contract. Shortly thereafter, a slick promoter, fraudulently representing that certain land in Florida would make a fine site for a branch store (the land is under water 90 per cent of the time), causes the manager to part with $10,000. Is the loss covered? Would it be covered under any other crime policy that Ace might have purchased? Discuss.

34. Robbery, burglary, and theft policies almost uniformly require that the insured be able to prove his loss by means of records and accounts. In one case a retailer maintained a dollar inventory record under which he could determine the dollar value of his stock at any given time, but could not determine the number of pieces of each item of goods in his store. The insurer claimed that this record was not sufficient to determine the exact amount of loss under the policy and refused to pay. How should this case be decided? As a juror, what criteria might you apply to determine a fair answer? Discuss.

35. Apply the criteria determined in Question 34 to the following case: A retail store owner discovered one morning that the previous day's receipts had been stolen from his safe. His only record of the amount was a cash register tape, which had also been stolen. The manager claimed that the amount of the cash was substantially higher than any amount he had ever taken in and, furthermore, it included cash received for sales made outside the store and not recorded on the cash register.

   (a) How should the manager's claim be determined? Explain.

   (b) What lessons in accounting might be learned from this example? Discuss.

36. An employer gave a messenger an envelope containing $1,000 for delivery at a certain location. When the messenger arrived, the envelope was missing. Under what policy, if any, would this loss be covered?

37. Indicate some of the possible weaknesses or limitations in the storekeepers' burglary and robbery policy from the viewpoint of the insured.

38. The manager of a men's clothing store maintains an average inventory of $15,000. He purchases an MOS policy of $6,000 with a coinsurance percentage of 60 per cent and a coinsurance limit of $10,000.
    (a) How much may he collect in the event of a $1,000 loss caused by robbery? Why? For a $2,100 loss caused by burglary? Why?
    (b) How could the manager have made sure that he would collect in full for these losses? Explain.

39. (a) Distinguish, with an example, between incoming forgery and outgoing forgery.
    (b) Which is the more hazardous from an underwriting standpoint? Why?

40. Max has experienced the following losses in the previous year and requests your advice as to which form of personal coverage he should consider purchasing:
    (a) In January a prowler stole a battery-operated pump from his sailboat. In the process a hole was gouged in the bottom of the boat.
    (b) In February Max's son reported $105 missing from his wallet. His son lives in a dormitory in college.
    (c) In April Max's wife discovered a package missing from the car when she returned from a shopping trip. The car was unlocked, but all the windows were rolled up.
    (d) When Max started out on his vacation in July, a $75 tent was found to be missing from its storage place in the garage.
    (e) When Max returned from his vacation, he found that someone had attempted to open a window, and apparently disgruntled at failure, threw tar on the outside of the house.
    (f) In November, returning from a hunting trip, Max noted that one of his rifles was missing, apparently left in the woods.
       Advise Max as to which of the above losses, if any, would have been covered under the personal theft policy; which would have been covered under the broad form personal theft policy, but not under the personal theft policy; and which would not have been covered at all. Which contract, if any, do you recommend? Why?

41. Brown has a beach cottage at which he vacations two months each year. One year prowlers stole a $450 outboard motor from the cottage the night before Brown arrived. They also took $300 worth of power tools which Brown uses in his business. The next night they returned and stole the boat. Brown carries a personal theft policy on his principal residence.
    (a) To what extent, if any, will the personal theft policy respond to the losses indicated? Why?
    (b) What additional collection, if any, could Brown have made under the broad form personal theft policy? Why?

Insurance and

Service Guarantees

Insurance companies are not infrequently in a position to render certain services to an insured other than strict indemnification for loss due to insurable perils. In some cases certain contracts of insurance are purchased as much as or more for these corollary services than for the indemnity payable in the event of loss. The nature of these services is not always apparent from reading the insurance contracts. The contracts discussed below illustrate a few examples of this phenomenon and point up the fact, stressed frequently in this text, that a full understanding of insurance involves more than a knowledge of the contract. The contract must be interpreted in the light of the economic and social environment within which it is operative.

We have selected for analysis four types of insurance which are "miscellaneous" in that they do not readily fit into the ordinary types of insurance usually offered in the various departments of insurance companies. These miscellaneous insurance contracts are:

1. Credit insurance.
2. Title insurance.
3. Boiler and machinery insurance.
4. Plate glass insurance.

These contracts have in common, however, the fact that the insurer offers more than indemnification for loss. In each type there are somewhat different underwriting problems involved, and the element of services of the insurer assumes special importance to the insured.

CREDIT INSURANCE

Types of credit risks

Use of credit in modern economic societies is universally recognized as a key factor in facilitating growth.[1] Without credit it is very doubtful that the modern industrial economy could have developed at all. How-

---

[1] One of the earliest works on credit insurance was published in 1848 by Robert Watt, and was entitled *Principles of Insurance Applied to Mercantile Debts.*

ever, the use of credit has created many complex problems, not the least of which is the risk that debts will not be paid because of the occurrence of some peril that is oftentimes outside the control of the debtor. Among these perils are:

1. Death or physical disability of the debtor.
2. Destruction of accounting records which prevent the creditor from proving his right to collect from a debtor.
3. Failure of a financial institution in which funds have been deposited.
4. Failure of a business firm to repay a bank loan because of insolvency.
5. Failure of a homeowner to repay a housing loan because of his insolvency.
6. Political action which prevents the debtor from repaying his debts to creditors in a foreign country.
7. Insolvency of a business firm to which merchandise credit has been extended.

We shall be concerned primarily with the last type of credit risk, namely, the risk that commercial debtors will be unable to meet their obligations due to business failure of one type or another.

Credit life insurance and credit accident and sickness insurance. Insurance exists in one form or another for all the credit risks listed above. Insurance against failure to pay a debt because of death of the borrower is known as *credit life* insurance. Because this contract is not basically different from any contract of life insurance except for the manner in which it is arranged and marketed, we will not analyze it further. Suffice to say that credit life insurance should not be confused with other forms of credit insurance. A similar comment applies to *credit accident and sickness* insurance, which is arranged to liquidate payments on an installment debt during the time the debtor is disabled because of accident or sickness.

Accounts receivable insurance. Insurance protecting the creditor against failure or inability to collect a debt because accounting records have been destroyed by certain listed perils is known as *accounts receivable* insurance and has been analyzed in Chapter 11.

Deposit insurance. Insurance against the loss of deposits due to the failure of a bank or a savings and loan association is known as *deposit* insurance and is written only by agencies of the United States government. The Federal Deposit Insurance Corporation insures bank deposits in all federally chartered banks and in most of the state chartered banks up to a maximum limit of $10,000. A depositor may obtain up to $10,000 coverage in each of any number of different accounts he wishes to maintain. Similar coverage is given to deposits in savings and loan associations by the Federal Savings and Loan Insurance Corporation. Deposit insurance proved its worth following the depression of the 1930's. After large numbers of people lost their life savings in banks which failed during this depression, the government created these insurance corporations in order to restore confidence in the banking system.

From the time its operations began in 1934 through 1956, the F.D.I.C. had handled 431 bank failures, in which losses to depositors amounted to only .5 per cent of insured deposits. These losses were suffered by .9 per cent of all depositors. Thus, the $10,000 limit of liability has been adequate for a vast majority of depositors. In 1956 the agency insured nearly $220 billion of deposits in covered banks, which represented 55 per cent of the total deposits in those banks.[2] Only 975 banks and banking offices out of a total of 22,314 at the end of 1956 were not insured.

Cash loan credit insurance. The United States government, through such agencies as the Federal Reserve System, the Veterans Administration, and the Small Business Administration, has sponsored various programs to insure cash loans made by banks to certain business enterprises that are unable to secure credit in any other way. While these guarantees are not strictly insurance (being more in the nature of a bond), they nevertheless serve the same purpose, namely, to facilitate the creation of credit.

The economic significance of credit insurance in effecting the willingness of banks to lend to business may be illustrated by the record of the "V" loan program, administered by the Federal Reserve Board during World War II. Loans to business for purposes of carrying out war contracts were insured under the program. It was estimated that in 1944 the volume of insured loans reached $2.1 billion, representing two thirds of all bank loans for war purposes.[3] Under this program the maximum amount that could be guaranteed was 90 per cent of a loan and over half of the total loans were insured for this maximum in spite

---

[2] *Annual Report of the Federal Deposit Insurance Corporation,* 1956, p. 16.
[3] Susan Burr and Elizabeth Sette, *A Statistical Study of Regulation* v. *Loans* (Washington, D. C.: Board of Governors, Federal Reserve Board, 1950), p. 19.

of the higher guarantee fees which this involved, thus indicating the importance that lending institutions attached to credit insurance. Losses due to business failures in the entire program over the five-year period, 1941–1945, during which it was in force, amounted to .6 per cent of the total loan authorizations.[4]

   Home loan credit insurance.   Another credit insurance program of considerable significance is that of the United States Federal Housing Administration and the United States Veterans Administration in insuring long-term loans to homeowners. The F.H.A. insured $3.7 billion of mortgage loans in 1957 and since its formation in 1934 had, by the end of 1957, insured $47 billion of these loans of various types. In the period 1939–1941, the F.H.A. insured about one fifth of all home mortgages, but this proportion later declined, reaching nine per cent in 1957. In 1957 the Veterans Administration insured 27 per cent of all nonfarm homes.[5] The influence of credit insurance in home lending is greater than these figures would suggest, however, because a substantial proportion, about one half, of the new homes built under the F.H.A. program are ultimately financed by private lending agencies. It is doubtful that long-term amortized mortgages would have been nearly so prevalent in the United States had it not been for the availability of insurance which guaranteed the lender that someone would ultimately repay these loans. As it has turned out, the homeowner has proved himself to be a good risk. Foreclosures accounted for only 1.8 per cent of F.H.A. home mortgage terminations for the period 1934–1957. In the year 1957, only .45 per cent of the 2,310,367 mortgages in force defaulted. Foreclosures were made on about 10 per cent of these defaulted mortgages.[6]

   Export credit insurance.   Protection is available for the exporter who wishes to insure against two basic perils, insolvency of a debtor and political action taken by the government of the debtor's country which prevents payment of debt. Known as *export credit* insurance, this coverage is of varying importance in world commerce. Governmental bodies generally are the only agencies willing to cover the political risk, which is essentially uninsurable for the private company. Private insurers generally are willing to assume the risk of business insolvency. Both private and governmental agencies operate in the field of export credit insurance.

---

[4] *Ibid.,* p. 57.
[5] *Annual Report, Federal Housing Administration,* 1957 (United States Government Printing Office, 1958).
[6] *Ibid.,* p. 48.

In Great Britain the Export Credits Guarantee Department, an agency of the British Government, issues policies of credit insurance for the British exporter covering losses caused by the following:

1. Insolvency of the buyer.
2. Failure of the buyer to pay for delivered goods within 12 months of due date.
3. Exchange restrictions, or a shortage of exchange in the buyer's country, that prevent the transfer of sterling to the United Kingdom.
4. War between the buyer's country and the United Kingdom.
5. War, rebellion, revolution, etc., in the buyer's country.
6. Cancellation of an export license or imposition of restriction on the export of goods not previously subject to license.
7. Irrecoverable extra delivery charges occasioned by diversion of the voyage.
8. Any other cause outside the United Kingdom which is beyond the control of the exporter or the buyer.

Indemnity is payable for 85 per cent of the loss due to peril (2) and 90 per cent for all other causes.[7]

In the United States, export credit insurance is offered through the Export-Import Bank, an agency of the federal government, and by one private insurer, the Intercredit Agency, Incorporated, in New York City, a subsidiary of Continental Casualty Company. Although plans are under way to extend the export credit insurance facilities available to exporters from the United States, as yet it cannot be said that this type of insurance is widely used or available in this country.

Credit insurance through the United States Export-Import Bank covers the "political risk," by which is meant loss through inconvertibility or nontransferability of foreign currencies, loss through imposition of law or regulation beyond the control of the exporter or buyer which prevents delivery of goods, loss due to cancellation of an import license, loss due to war, and expropriation of exported items by foreign authorities.[8] The limit of recovery in the above cases is 90 per cent.

---

[7] The Trade Indemnity Company, Ltd., of London, a private insurer, offers export credit insurance as well, but does not cover against the political risk. In France, there are two credit insurers, one, *Société Francaise d'Assurances pour Favoriser le Credit*, insures only buyers at home, while *the Compagnie Francaise d'Assurance pour le Commerce Exterieur*, with the help of reinsurance from the government, covers export transactions. Export credit insurance is sold in Belgium, Sweden, Austria, Switzerland, Germany, Holland, Ireland, Italy, Spain, Norway, and Denmark, generally by agencies owned or backed by the governments. For a summary of the international credit insurance market and its operations, see Hans Karrer, *Elements of Credit Insurance, an International Survey* (London, Sir Isaac Pitman & Sons, Ltd., 1957), especially Chapter 3.

[8] Loss due to expropriation of funds or goods by the "Exim bank" should not be confused with insurance offered through the Investment Guaranties Division of the International Cooperation Administration, which protects an investor in fixed plant and equipment in a foreign nation against loss due to expropriation, war, and inconvertibility of currency.

Thus, if a foreign buyer deposits his payment with the exporter in his local currency, but is later unable to convert that deposit into United States dollars, the Export-Import Bank will indemnify the exporter for 90 per cent of the amount deposited. The premium for export credit insurance of the "political risk" varies with the length of credit terms granted. For example, the fee for accounts sold on terms not over 30 days is 25 cents per $100 of gross invoice value. If terms are between 61 and 90 days, the premium is 35 cents. For terms between 151 and 180 days, the premium is 50 cents. Premiums for medium-term credit, ranging from 180 days to five years, is approximately ¾ of one per cent per year on the outstanding balance.

The Intercredit Agency of New York offers the exporter a contract protecting him against the "commercial risk," that is, the risk that a foreign buyer will go insolvent (as defined) or who simply fails to pay his account, under certain conditions. The contract offers protection up to 85 per cent of the amount of credit outstanding at rates ranging from 20 to 40 cents per $100 on the monthly outstanding balances. Coverage extends to all countries where effective bankruptcy laws exist. It is possible for the seller to exclude certain accounts from coverage and to include sales made in foreign currencies or by foreign subsidiaries of American companies. The policy is a yearly contract and is not cancelable. It is possible to obtain protection against both the commercial risk and the political risk in one package through the Intercredit Agency, which has been appointed as an agent of the Export-Import Bank for purposes of handling the political risk.

Domestic merchandise credit insurance. In the United States, Canada, and Mexico, as well as in most European countries, sellers may obtain insurance against the insolvency of domestic debtors on credits arising out of the sale of merchandise on an unsecured basis. Such coverage has been sold in the United States since 1890. Insurance against failure to repay a cash loan is generally not available in the United States, except as it is applied for through a governmental agency in special programs such as those mentioned above carried on by the Federal Reserve System, the Federal Housing Administration, the Veterans Administration, and the Small Business Administration. The volume of merchandise credit insurance is generally quite small, when compared with other major lines of insurance. Because it is so specialized in nature, relatively few insurers in each country compete for the business and those who write it make it their chief line. In most countries credit insurers give only limited coverage, in that only certain business consumers, such as manufacturers and wholesalers, are eligible. Not all types of transactions are insured, not all perils are covered, and losses are not indemnified 100 per cent. In the United States, for example, there are only two private insurers, the American Credit Indemnity Company and the London Guarantee Company. In 1957 their total premium volume, including amounts reinsured, was about $9 million, which was a small fraction of other types of insurance premium volumes. (For example, stock insurers wrote $40 million of premium in glass insurance alone in 1957.) The major insurer, the American Credit Indemnity Company, writes three fourths of all the merchandise credit insurance in the United States; and its contracts, which are very similar to those of the London Guarantee Company, are analyzed below.

Types of credit insurance contracts

Credit insurance contracts as written in the United States may be classified in four ways:

1) Back coverage contracts.
2) Forward coverage contracts.
3) General coverage forms.
4) Individual account forms.

1) Back coverage contract. Credit insurance contracts termed *back coverage* apply only to *losses* incurred either during the policy term (one year) or during a short period prior to its inception, not exceeding three months. Under these policies it does not matter particularly that the sale giving rise to the account did not take place during the policy year. Back coverage contracts account for a majority of all credit insurance in force.[9]

2) Forward coverage contract. Under the terms of *forward coverage* contracts, the policy indemnifies the insured for losses stemming only from accounts which were created by *sales* made during the policy term. Accounts already on the books when the policy is purchased, are, accordingly, not insured. However, if on the last day of the policy term a credit sale is made which ultimately becomes a bad debt, the contract is applicable even if it is not renewed. There is usually a time limit within which the account must be filed with the insurer as a claim in order to establish some termination of the insurer's liability.

---

[9] In the American Credit Indemnity Company, back coverage policies account for over three fourths of the company's total business.

3) General coverage form. Under *general coverage* policies, insurance is not granted on specific debtors by name, but covers all debtors falling into given (and insured) classes of credit ratings on a blanket basis. Thus, the policy may specify that $100,000 of coverage applies to the bad debts of any debtor that has an AaA1 Dun and Bradstreet credit rating. The blanket coverage is scaled down for firms with lower credit rating. For example, the insurer may be willing to grant only $500 of insurance on all debtors that are not rated by a general credit agency or that have a K3 Dun and Bradstreet rating. All back coverage policies are of the general coverage type.

4) Individual account form. *Individual account* policies are designed to cover a specifically named debtor of the insured. Use of these forms is generally discouraged by the underwriter because of the moral hazard involved. In cases where an insured seeks specific coverage on one account only, to the exclusion of other accounts, there is some justification for the belief among underwriters that this insured probably fears for the solvency of the account and is trying to shift the potential loss onto the insurer. Certainly there exists an element of adverse selection against the insurer on such forms and the risk tends to be uninsurable. Where these policies are issued, there is usually the requirement that a large initial loss first be borne by the insured and the insurer then takes on the excess. The insurer will require that the debtor named have a high credit rating, and oftentimes will also require that the insured cover his other accounts as well, usually under a general coverage form.

It is unfortunate that individual account forms are considered somewhat hazardous by underwriters because it is under these forms that credit insurance can serve its clientele in a very advantageous manner. Individual account forms, designed primarily for the catastrophic type of loss, are very useful for creditors whose entire sales are made to one or two accounts, the failure of which would bankrupt the creditor. It is in just such a situation that the seller will normally seek a method of risk transfer. Such a situation need not necessarily be one fraught with moral hazard. The debtor account could have the highest of credit ratings and yet some unusual event could lead it into bankruptcy and resulting loss to the creditor. Files of credit insurers are full of such examples.[10] Through riders of various kinds, credit insurance under-

---

[10] One of the most celebrated credit insurance loss payments was in the case of the failure of the company whose product, *Hadacol,* was such a success that the concern was given the highest Dun and Bradstreet credit rating. The advertising agency extending credit received a loss payment of $298,000.

writers can provide extra coverage on certain debtors named on a general coverage policy. In this case, though, the insured is required to pay premiums covering accounts, no one of which is large enough to cause him serious loss and which he would probably be qualified to self-insure in many cases.

Establishing a loss

To establish a loss the insured must first show what credit rating the debtor had at the time the goods were shipped. It is this rating which determines the limit of coverage under the credit insurance policy, unless the particular debtor has been specifically named for additional coverage beforehand. The policyholder must show that a legal obligation exists and that the debt arose because of bona fide sales of merchandise or services normally dealt in by the seller. Under the terms of the contract, a loss is said to have occurred under two general situations: (1) a debtor simply does not pay his account by the due date but is not insolvent, and (2) a debtor becomes legally insolvent as determined by specific events listed in the contract.

If the debtor is not insolvent but refuses to pay a legal obligation as defined in the contract within a period of not over 90 days after the debt is due under the original terms of sale, the insured may file the account with the insurer as a claim. In other words, if a seller grants 60-day credit terms, the account is past due after 60 days. If the account is not paid within 150 days from the date of shipment (60 days' normal credit plus 90 days over the overdue time), the insured may file this account with the insurer who will then make an attempt to collect it. Failing to do so, the insurer will indemnify the insured for his loss, subject to the other terms of the policy. Because some insureds fear they will offend their debtor by such an action, they hesitate to file the account for collection with the insurer. If the account is not filed within the specified period (forward coverage policies require that this be done, however),[11]

---

[11] This is done to establish some final date after which the insurer will have no further liability under the policy. Under one form of forward coverage written by the American Credit Indemnity Company, known as the "H" form, the insured *must* file claims only at the expiration of the policy. However, during the policy term, if the insured delays filing of past-due amounts beyond three months after the original due date, an additional coinsurance deduction of one fifth of one per cent is added for each day, thus creating an additional incentive for prompt filing. This form yields approximately 15 per cent of the insurer's gross income, and accounts for about 13 per cent of all policies issued. Forward coverage policies as a rule are written for firms having terms of sale no longer than four months from the date of shipment, and they allow an additional period of up to three months for the final filing of claims with the insurer for collection. Thus, a claim for a sale that took place on December 31 in a firm with four months' credit terms could be filed with the insurer no later than July 31 of the following year. After this date there is no further liability under the policy.

the insured must then wait until the occurrence of one of 12 conditions defining the insolvency of the debtor. These 12 conditions, as they appear in the credit insurance policy, are as follows:

1. The debtor shall have absconded.
2. A sole debtor shall have died.
3. A sole debtor shall have been adjudged insane.
4. A receiver shall have been appointed for a debtor.
5. The stock in trade of a debtor shall have been sold under the bulk sales act.
6. The business of a debtor shall have been sold under a writ of attachment or execution, or the writ of execution returned unsatisfied.
7. A debtor shall have made a general offer of compromise to his creditors for less than his indebtedness.
8. Possession shall have been taken under a chattel mortgage given by a debtor on his stock in trade.
9. A debtor's business shall have been assigned to or taken over by a creditors' committee for the sole purpose of liquidation.
10. Possession shall have been taken of a debtor's assets under an assignment or a deed of trust executed by the debtor for the benefit of his creditors.
11. A voluntary or an involuntary proceeding shall have been instituted to adjudge a debtor bankrupt.
12. A proceeding for an arrangement of the debts of a debtor shall have been instituted in a court of bankruptcy.

In other words, if the insured does not file the account for collection with the insurer within the time specified, he must wait until one of the above formal events has taken place in order to establish the fact that insolvency has actually occurred. Payment for losses occurs within a set time period after the end of the policy unless, for additional premium, a rider is attached entitling the insured to an interim settlement.

After the account has become over 90 days past due, the insured has lost his right to file the account as a loss simply because the debtor did not pay within the time granted under the creditor's terms of payment. However, he has the option of filing the account for collection with the insurer after the 90 days is up and the insurer will charge a stated fee for any amounts collected. In this way the insured does not have to wait until formal bankruptcy has occurred before receiving at least part of his money. If the insurer cannot make the collection, the insured must wait until one of the 12 events above has occurred before he has the right to collect the amount as a bad account under the terms of the contract.

Deductibles

Most loss settlements under the credit insurance contract are subject to one or both of two different kinds of deductibles; a stated dollar amount, and a percentage, usually 10 per cent of the individual loss. The *dollar deductible,* called the *primary loss,* is intended to represent the normal credit losses of the firm. Since these losses are expected and are in the nature of a certainty, they are excluded from coverage. The amount of normal loss varies with the industry and is adjusted according to the experience of the individual insured. It is applied to the total of the insured's losses in a given policy term.

The *percentage deductible,* called *coinsurance,* is a flat deductible that applies to each individual loss. It is intended to control the moral hazard, the tendency that would otherwise exist for the insured to be careless in granting credit in the knowledge that if the debtor did not pay, the insurer would. The reasoning is that if the insured knows he can at best collect only 90 per cent of a given account from the credit insurer, he will be less tempted to sell to marginal credit risks, since collection of only 90 per cent of an account from the insurer will usually not leave any profit. The coinsurance for poorly rated or nonrated accounts is increased to 20 per cent.

As an example of these deductibles, assume that a firm has five bad debts in a given year totaling $15,000, and that the contract is written with a $4,000 primary loss deductible. Assume further that all these accounts are filed with the insurer before they are 90 days past due under the original terms of sale. The settlement would be as follows:

Bad debts	.$15,000
Less: Normal loss	. 4,000
	$11,000
Less: Coinsurance (10%) . . .	. 1,110
Loss payment	.$ 9,900

Collection service

Various studies in the field of credit insurance have documented the conclusion that many insureds look upon the collection services of the credit insurer as a very important part of the benefits secured under the contract.[12] Part of the efficacy of the efforts of insurers in this regard

---

[12] See James G. Sheehan, *Credit Insurance from the Policyholder's Point of View,* Unpublished doctoral dissertation, The Ohio State University, 1955, and John A. Churella, *An Evaluation of Credit Insurance and Its Effects on Business Management* (Baltimore, American Credit Indemnity Co., 1958), and Mark R. Greene, *An Analysis of Credit Insurance,* Unpublished doctoral dissertation, The Ohio State University. 1955.

is due to the fact that failure to collect accounts placed with them by policyholders will normally result in a loss under the policy. Hence, the credit insurer has a greater stake in a given account than a typical collection agency, and will make strong efforts not only to collect the account but also to preserve the customer's goodwill in the knowledge that if the goodwill is sacrificed in the process of collection, the insured *and* the insurer may lose a good customer. One writer stated,[13]

> It would appear that the use of credit insurance tends to make the policyholder more conscious of past-due accounts and causes him to take constructive collection action sooner than he might otherwise do. It further appears that the insuring companies, by using only the best available collection attorneys to handle both insolvencies and delinquencies, collect a greater portion of accounts filed than the policyholder might be able to collect through other means. . . . It would appear that this phase of credit insurance use is one of the most practical uses of coverage, other than for the basic insurance purposes involved, and involves values and considerations of considerable importance to the policyholder as they affect both costs and credit department operations.

The services rendered by the credit insurer may be thus employed to bring about collections from distant buyers in an economical manner, a service of special importance to the small localized firm. It should be mentioned that the use of credit insurance does not permit a firm to disband its collection department or to dismiss its credit manager, since the insurer relies on careful credit screening as a basis for issuing the contract.

Advantages and limitations of credit insurance

In view of the apparent usefulness of credit insurance, both to the firm which wants to protect itself against catastrophic credit losses brought on by the insolvency of some large accounts and to the firm which seeks to make use of the extensive collection facilities of the credit insurer, one may wonder why credit insurance has not been used more widely. The following arguments in favor of the use of merchandise credit insurance have been put forth:

1. It is illogical for a firm to insure its inventory against loss arising from various perils only to ignore the substantial possibility of loss when the inventory is sold and is represented on the books by accounts receivable. Records of bad debt losses show that the peril is very substantial.

---

[13] John Churella, *op. cit.,* p. 31.

2. The use of credit insurance has important psychological benefits in reducing the fear of bad debt losses, thus removing a hindrance to expanded sales. A "run" of credit losses will thus not cause the credit manager to "tighten up" on all applications for credit, regardless of merit.

3. Use of credit insurance may in some cases enable the firm to accept applications for credit which would otherwise have been refused, because investigation of the account by the credit insurer reveals conditions which justify credit. Thus, the existence of the insurance may lead to expanded sales, or, on the other hand, may result in limiting the amount of credit extended to firms that the insurer's investigation reveals would have resulted in loss had it been granted.

4. The use of credit insurance enables a firm to stabilize its operations by placing definite limits on the size of bad debt losses. The efficacy of the insurer's collection service is important to many users.

On the other hand, it appears that the following factors have been instrumental in limiting the growth of merchandise credit insurance in spite of the advantages claimed for it:

1. The sale of credit insurance is limited to certain types of business firms—wholesalers, manufacturers, and certain firms providing services such as advertising agencies. Retailers are excluded because they sell to the final consumer whose credit is not normally believed to be insurable.

2. Many business firms feel they are better able to self-insure the credit risk because of the basic diversification of their accounts. The credit insurance contract best fits the firm that sells large quantities of goods on credit to relatively few customers, the failure of any one of which would jeopardize the firm's own solvency. If this condition is not met, as it very frequently is not, the firm sees no particular advantage in credit insurance, and relies on its own credit management staff to control unusual bad debt losses.

3. The operation of the deductibles in the credit insurance contract tends to limit recoveries in a typical year so that the insured usually pays most of the loss himself. This, of course, is the result of the way in which the insuring arrangement is planned because it is intended to cover only abnormal, excess, and unusually large losses, not the average normal credit loss. Nevertheless, many insureds have not understood this basic point and reject the insurance because the "price is too high."

4. Credit insurance has not been promoted vigorously and the advantages claimed for it are relatively unknown by the overwhelming majority of business firms. Because it is a specialized and complex line of insurance, few general or local agents

handling other lines of insurance are in a position to sell it to their customers. This situation is reinforced by the fact that the line is considered too hazardous to give the field agent authority to bind coverage without home office approval. The credit insurance contract is noncancelable, once issued, and must be tailored carefully to meet the individual needs of its user.

5. Conservative underwriting, brought on partly by lack of sufficient loss data to establish rates in which great confidence may be taken, and partly by the element of adverse selection against the underwriter, has limited the growth of credit insurance. Competition of other insurers in the field is virtually nonexistent because of the specialized nature of credit insurance. On the other hand, factors, particularly in the textile trades, have combined the financing and the insurance functions in the outright purchase of a seller's accounts, thus eliminating the credit risk for many types of potential credit insurance users.

TITLE INSURANCE

Title insurance is a device by which the purchaser of real estate may protect himself against losses in case it develops that the title he obtains is not "good" or can be made "good" only after certain payments are made. Defects in titles may stem from a number of sources, such as forgery of public records, forgery of titles, invalid or undiscovered wills, defective probate procedures, and other court proceedings under which transfer of real estate may have been erroneously made. Thus, a person may occupy his real property for years only to find that the one who conveyed him title was not the rightful owner, that true ownership lies in the possession of another, say a former wife who had been wrongfully deprived of her rights in the property.

Usually all rights in real property, such as encumbrances, liens, and easements, must be duly recorded in the court house of the county or the parish in which the real estate lies. Before title insurance became common, the real property buyer usually retained an attorney to search these records and render an opinion, called an *abstract*, that the title was or was not marketable, or that it was transferable subject to certain recorded rights of others. If an abstract turned out to be in error, the attorney was liable only if it could be shown that he was negligent in his title search. Unusual, unrecorded defects in the title, not discoverable by a reasonable and diligent search, were not the responsibility of the abstract attorney. Thus, the need for a formal guarantee of the accuracy of the title search arose. Title insurance is essentially this guarantee.

The title insurance policy does not insure the soundness of a title, but only those losses arising from the fact that the title is not sound. If a rightful owner turns up, he may repossess the property; and the title insurance will indemnify the insured for his loss, which is usually the purchase price of the real estate. The insured may not insist on continued possession of the property.[14]

Special characteristics of title insurance

Some of the differences between title insurance and other contracts of property and liability insurance may be summarized as follows:

1. The premium for title insurance is almost entirely intended to cover the necessary services in investigating possible sources of loss of title marketability, and not an expected loss. The title insurance company, in fact, expects no losses, feeling that if an adequate job of investigation is performed before the policy is issued, there will be no loss to pay on the policy. Some title insurance firms maintain extensive "plants" of real estate records in their area, and retain a staff of expert title attorneys, so as to render more rapid service to the purchaser.

2. Title insurance covers only title defects which have occurred *before* the effective date of the policy but which are discovered *after* the effective date of the policy. Most other types of insurance cover only losses which occur after the effective date of the policy, and not before, under the general theory that to do otherwise would be to cause insurance to be taken out to cover a known loss. In the case of title insurance, the defect which causes a loss is not known at the time of the issuance of the policy. If the defect is known, it is excluded as one of the sources of loss not covered.

3. Title insurance contracts are not cancelable by either party, and the premium is full earned once it is paid, that is, there is no refund of premium under any conditions.

4. Title insurance has no expiration date; the coverage is effective indefinitely. In other words, if a person finds that his title is clouded 20 years after the effective date of his policy, and the

---

[14] Under the Torrens system, an applicant has a title registered after proving to a court that he is the rightful owner. An insurance fund is accumulated from the registration fees and anyone who later can prove he has an interest in the property is compensated out of this fund. The advantages of the Torrens system include the simplification of title transfers, reduction of legal controversy, and the increase in certainty (reduction of risk) concerning the owner's right to the property. The disadvantages include the fact that Torrens titles are not available everywhere. And even in the areas where they are available, they cannot be made compulsory for everyone due to legal obstacles, existence of which tend to remove the finality of title, which is the chief merit of Torrens titles. In addition, it cannot be denied that title insurance companies are not anxious to promote a system which might materially reduce their business.

defect causing this cloud occurred before this date, the policy covers any loss incurred. The policy contains no limitation as to when a claim can be made following a loss.

The title insurance contract

There is no standard title insurance contract, but the general form of the insuring clause is fairly uniform. The insurer agrees to indemnify the owner against any loss he may suffer "by reason of unmarketability of the title of the insured to or in said premises, or . . . from all loss and damage by reason of liens or encumbrances, defects, objections, estates, and interests, except those listed in Schedule B."

Schedule B is a separate endorsement on which is listed all title defects or rights in the property found during the title search. The most usual of these defects are easements, mortgages, assessments, and tax liens. Often Schedule B will exclude from coverage those losses arising from "easements, liens or encumbrances, including material or labor liens, which are *not* shown by the public records, rights or claims of persons in possession or claiming to be in possession not shown of record, water rights, mining claims, taxes not yet payable, zoning laws, and any state of facts which an accurate survey and inspection of said land would show." The intent of these exclusions is to remove from coverage certain sources of defect in the title which exist at the time of title transfer, even if the title search did not reveal them.

The title insurance contract is certainly not an all-risk agreement, even with respect to the *unknown* defects. To illustrate, assume that Smith buys some land with the intent of constructing an apartment house. Unknown either to Smith or to the insurer, just before title is transferred, a zoning ordinance is passed prohibiting this type of construction on the land. Even though a loss accrues to Smith and it was unknown at the time of transfer, there is no liability under the title insurance contract.

Defense. Under the typical policy the insurer agrees to defend the insured in any legal proceedings brought against him concerning the title, assuming that the action involves a source of loss not excluded under the contract. The insured is required to notify the insurer of any such proceedings and to cooperate fully in any legal action taken by the insurer.

Premium. The premium in title insurance is paid only once, and it keeps the policy in force as to the named insured for an indefinite period.

If the property is transferred, a new premium must be paid for the protection of the new purchaser. The old policy is not assignable to the new buyer. Usually there is no reduction in premium, even if the property is transferred a short time after the prior purchase. Thus, if a residence is built in one year and is resold five times in the next five years, a title insurance premium might be charged five times. Since the premium presumably is charged chiefly for making the search, and since there is obviously less work to do on each succeeding title search (because less time has elapsed during which defects could have arisen), it would appear inequitable to charge the same premium for each policy. Premiums charged for a $20,000 policy might cost approximately $130. Premiums are based on the face amount of the policy, the territory, and on whether the insured is an owner or a mortgagee.

BOILER AND MACHINERY INSURANCE

The hazard of loss

Explosions caused by steam boilers, compressors, engines, electrical equipment, fly wheels, air tanks, and furnaces constitute a serious source of loss which the layman often does not recognize. Examples of these losses include the following:

1. A hot water tank in a variety store suddenly exploded, killing five people, injuring 50 others, and causing $130,000 of property damage.
2. A hose connection on an air-conditioning system gave way and water poured through the dwelling, causing over $10,000 of damage.
3. Workmen removed a plug from the top of a gas conversion burner, allowing gas to accumulate in the combustion chamber. Later this gas was ignited, and in the resulting explosion one man was killed and two were injured.
4. In attempting to light a gas heater, two workmen were seriously injured when the heater exploded. A total judgment for $301,-000 was handed down for these injuries.

Since the causes of boiler and machinery explosions are technical in nature, the danger is usually minimized by the would-be insured. Contrary to common belief, for example, danger of explosions in a low-pressure tank may be just as great as in a high-pressure tank. Water under pressure is "hotter" than water not under pressure. When the pressure is reduced, water boils at a lower temperature than it would if the pressure were higher. When pressure is reduced suddenly, as it might be with a broken connection, water turns into steam rapidly, expands hundreds of times its original volume, and creates an explosion.

Special characteristics of boiler and machinery insurance

Boiler and machinery insurance has been developed along somewhat different lines than the usual insurance contract. First, recognizing that prevention of losses is even more important than indemnification of loss, insurers have combined with the pure insurance function the service of inspection and servicing of boiler operations and technical machinery. Approximately one fourth of the total premium collected is used for the service function.[15] The insurer typically sends an inspector to the plant of the insured two or more times each year, depending on the size of the firm. In many states these inspections substitute for an inspection required by law. Technical specialists examine boilers and pressure vessels both internally and externally, using special equipment to detect minute cracks, crystallization, deterioration of insulation, vibration, and general wear. Failure of a vessel to pass an inspection may mean imminent danger of continued operation. As a result, the insurer reserves the right to suspend coverage immediately if recommended repairs or replacements are not made.

Second, because of the technical nature and diversity of the many types of boilers, tanks, furnaces, and electrical equipment in use, the boiler and machinery policy specifies by endorsement the exact definition of "accident" applicable to each insurable "object." The insurer requires a series of separate endorsements describing in detail the nature of the insured "object" and what will constitute an "accident." An insured may have ten different types of objects with a different definition of accident for each one. There is no blanketing of coverage for all machines and pressure vessels on one form. For example, one endorsement might list on a schedule of reciprocating pumps and compressors a "two cylinder York ammonia belted compressor" with the definition:

> "object" shall mean the complete unit which is designated and described in this schedule, including the shaft of said unit; but shall not include any electrical machine, nor any piping leading

---

[15] For example, in 1957, aggregate premium collections by 124 stock insurers amounted to $51,527,000, of which 30.3 per cent went for "general expenses." Typical charges under this category are about seven per cent for other lines of insurance. Thus, the difference may be said to approximate the amounts expended for inspection services. Losses incurred to premiums earned were only 30 6 per cent, considerably lower than for other property insurance lines, a fact which reflects in a sense the efficacy of loss-prevention efforts. Data from *Best's Fire and Casualty Aggregates and Averages, 1958,* p. 134.

to or from the unit, nor any structure or foundation supporting the unit, nor any mechanism, appliance, or shaft connected to the unit.

"Accident" shall mean:

1. A sudden and accidental breaking of the Object, or any part thereof, into two or more separate parts, but not the breaking of any gasket, gland packing, shaft seal or diaphragm, nor the loosening of any assembled parts; or
2. A sudden and accidental burning out of the Object, or any part thereof, but not the burning out of any gasket, gland packing, or shaft seal; or
3. A sudden and accidental deforming of any shaft or rod of the Object, not caused by the cracking of such shaft or rod.

An Accident arising out of a strike, riot, civil commotion or acts of sabotage, vandalism, or malicious mischief, shall be considered "accidental" within the terms of this definition.

It may be appreciated that without such a careful definition, it might be possible for an insured to require the insurer to compensate him for expensive machinery that actually did not break down but merely wore out.

Third, because the damage caused by an exploding boiler may result in legal liability for damage to the property or persons of others as well as direct loss to the property of the insured, and in addition may cause substantial indirect loss due to a shutdown of the plant, the single boiler and machinery contract provides coverage at once against many different types of losses. Thus, the following types of insurance may be found in a single boiler and machinery policy:

1) Loss of the boiler or machinery itself due to accident, as defined.
2) Expediting expenses.
3) Property damage liability.
4) Bodily injury liability.
5) Defense, settlement, and supplementary payments.
6) Automatic coverage of newly installed machinery for a period of 90 days.
7) Business interruption insurance.
8) Outage insurance.
9) Power interruption insurance.
10) Consequential loss due to spoilage of goods, from the accident, such as when a refrigeration system fails and meats spoil as a consequence.
11) Furnace explosion.

Because of the comprehensive nature of boiler and machinery insurance, there may be some overlapping of coverage with other property and liability insurance contracts. To avoid this as much as possible, the boiler and machinery contract contains provisions to the effect that for certain losses, such as property damage and bodily injury liability, the boiler policy is to be considered excess over any other applicable insurance. The policy also contains a unique feature in that an aggregate limit of loss is stated for the first four coverages listed above and loss payments are to be satisfied out of this aggregate limit in numerical order. Thus, if a policy has a $50,000 limit and $40,000 is paid out under the first coverage, $10,000 remains for the second. If no liability exists for this, the $10,000 is available to satisfy any liability for the third coverage, and so on, until the $50,000 is used up, after which the limits are exhausted for that particular accident. Separate limits of liability are commonly stated for all coverages from the sixth on. The insurer pays all defense, settlement, and supplementary payments over and above the aggregate limit. The net effect of these provisions is to maximize the benefits of the contract for the use of the insured in allowing him to apply the policy limits where they are needed, and to avoid paying for duplicating coverage. All loss from the peril of war is excluded.

Insuring agreements

The following comments will elaborate briefly upon each of the coverages commonly found in boiler and machinery policies, with emphasis on any unusual features.

1) Loss of property of insured. Perhaps the chief reason for the purchase of boiler and machinery insurance is to replace, in the event of sudden or accidental loss, damaged machinery belonging to the insured, or to prevent the occurrence of such a loss. The insuring clause excludes loss when the proximate cause is fire, since fire losses are paid under the standard fire policy. Indirect losses are excluded but may be insured separately by endorsement. The insurer reserves the right to replace or to repair the property or to indemnify for its actual cash value.

2) Expediting expenses. Under this clause the insurer agrees to pay for the reasonable extra cost of temporary repair or the extra costs of expediting the repair of the machinery, including overtime costs and the extra costs of express or other rapid means of transportation. Payments under this section may not exceed $1,000, or the amount payable under the first section, whichever is less.

3) Property damage and 4) bodily injury liability. This coverage is identical to the typical agreement contained in the comprehensive general liability policy discussed in an earlier chapter. The property damage liability contributes pro rata with any other applicable coverage, but the bodily injury liability is considered as excess. Bodily injury liability coverage may be eliminated by endorsement, and a premium reduction granted in return.

5) Defense, settlement, and supplementary payments. This coverage, too, is identical to the typical agreement in general liability insurance coverages. The insurer assumes all legal defense of liability suits caused by the occurrence of an accident, as defined in the policy. This cost is paid over and above any amounts payable under other agreements.

6) Automatic coverage. Under this endorsement the insurer agrees to cover accidents from all machinery of the same type as those specifically listed in the endorsement. (The coverage does not extend to just *any* additional equipment purchased.) The insured is required to apply for coverage on any additional equipment thus acquired within 90 days and to pay an additional premium thereon.

7) Business interruption insurance. One of the important types of loss stemming from the failure of a steam boiler or from other vital machinery is the shutdown of an entire plant. Thus, business interruption insurance, usually called *use and occupancy* in this line of insurance, is commonly added by endorsement to the boiler and machinery contract. The contract is similar to business interruption insurance as written in connection with fire insurance (see Chapter 10). It is available on the valued form or on an actual loss sustained basis. On the valued form a daily indemnity is stated, say $1,000 a day, with an aggregate limit, say $50,000. This amount is paid without proof of loss in case the plant is totally shut down. Proportionate parts of this amount are paid for partial shutdowns, which are measured by the reduction of sales or production due to the accident. Only shutdowns caused by described accidents are covered. The cost of this endorsement may be reduced by acceptance of waiting periods until indemnity begins.

The actual loss sustained form for power plant business interruption is gaining in popularity among many business firms, in spite of its greater complexity. The valued form is simple to apply in the event of total shutdown, but for partial shutdowns it is not satisfactory for many types of firms. Partial shutdowns are much more common than total shutdowns. The measure of the shutdown is in terms of lost production, measured in physical units. It may turn out that some types of production in a diversified plant are much more valuable than others and a 50 per cent reduction in over-all physical volume means a much greater financial loss than 50 per cent of the daily indemnity because certain types of valuable output might be the most affected. The actual loss sustained form can be made to fit such a situation. It also adapts automatically to seasonal fluctuations in output, so that if the firm is shut down during a busy season, the loss can be fully compensated.

8) Outage insurance. *Outage* refers to insurance against loss incurred during the time that a piece of machinery has been put out of commission by the described accident. It is similar to extra expense insurance described in Chapter 11 in that it is intended to cover the extra expenses of operation after an accident when the business is not wholly or partially shut down. For example, a heating plant boiler may fail, thus forcing the business to install temporary alternative methods of heating at considerable expense. A power plant failure may force the firm to purchase stand-by power from another source at extra cost. Outage insurance may be endorsed on to the boiler and machinery policy to pay a set amount for each hour the "object" is "out" to pay for these extra expenses. Outage insurance is especially appropriate for office or apartment buildings, schools, and stores where failure of an insured object would not usually stop operations, but would cause considerable extra cost in keeping everything running.

9) Power interruption insurance. The *power interruption endorsement* is available on a boiler and machinery contract to provide coverage for two types of losses stemming from interruption of electricity, gas, heat, or other energy from public utilities: (a) loss from interruption of operations and (b) loss from damage through spoilage to property of the insured. The first type of loss is paid on a valued basis, and it is not necessary to prove any losses. All that must be shown is that the outside power source failed for a period longer than five minutes. Indemnity is paid according to the length of time of the interruption. This type of loss is actually a combination of power plant business interruption and outage losses, but the contract makes no distinction between the two; and there is no necessity of proving that an actual loss was sustained.

The second type of power interruption loss is on an actual loss sustained basis and if the power or energy source is cut off for longer than a five-minute period, the insured may claim any amount of indemnity up to the policy limits, assuming he can prove that spoilage of goods actually occurred. In other words, the actual loss sustained, rather than time, is the element that decides the amount of a valid claim. Thus, if a high wind destroys the power company's distribution facilities and electricity is cut off for ten hours, the insured may lose an entire cold-storage warehouse of perishable foodstuffs, and might collect the entire amount of the policy.

10) Consequential damage.   Coverage similar to the second type of power interruption loss described above, but due to failure of an insured "object" *within* the insured's own premises, is provided on the *consequential damage endorsement*. In the case where an insured has a cold-storage warehouse filled with perishable foodstuffs and the refrigeration system is inoperative due to failure of the compressor system within the insured's plant, indemnity would be payable under a consequential damage endorsement but not under a power interruption endorsement. Firms such as cold-storage warehouses, brewers, creameries, florists, ice plants, and hothouses are among the more potential candidates for consequential damage and power interruption coverage.

11) Furnace explosion.   Coverage for losses resulting from the explosion of furnaces, as opposed to explosion of the boilers which they may service, is generally provided in one of the fire insurance forms or liability contracts covering the property. Alternatively, this coverage is available as an endorsement to the boiler and machinery contract. No general rule can be laid down as to which method is preferable, other than care should be taken to see that this peril is recognized and that insurance against it, but not duplicating coverage, is provided.

PLATE GLASS INSURANCE

The hazard to loss

Plate glass in modern architecture has assumed much greater significance than it formerly enjoyed. Use of plate glass assumes much greater signficance than mere physical protection against the elements, because of its great advertising value. Use of plate glass in show windows of large department stores, for example, is of tremendous significance in successful merchandising.

There are many uses of glass and types of glass objects, other than for plate glass windows, in which large investments are made and for which insurance is sought. Examples include glass signs, motion picture screens, halftone screens and lenses, stained glass windows, glass bricks, glass doors, neon signs, showcases, counter tops, and insulated glass panels.

Glass is susceptible to loss from many sources other than the usual perils of fire, windstorm, riot and civil commotion, and vehicles. Breakage from such sources as improper setting, excessive heat or cold, flying rock, and sonic boom illustrate the somewhat unusual nature of the many perils which destroy glass. Of basic importance to the insured is the prompt repair of broken plate glass.

Since loss settlement procedures, common under insurance contracts of fire and related lines, are often somewhat delayed, a special contract known as the *comprehensive glass policy* has been developed under the rules of the National Bureau of Casualty Underwriters and the Mutual Insurance Rating Bureau. Under this policy the insured may purchase all-risk insurance against breakage [16] of glass from any source except fire or nuclear reaction. As is true in fire insurance, the insurer reserves the right to settle losses either in cash or by repairing or replacing the glass. Unlike fire insurance loss settlement procedures, however, it is the practice of insurers to replace the glass insured under the policy, and to so immediately after the loss. The insurer commonly has agreements with glass repair firms to handle all work. In this way it is usual to get the work done at discounts below what regular customers can obtain and, in addition, to provide immediate service, which is the paramount consideration. Insurance on the replacement glass continues as before without extra premium.

The insuring agreement

The comprehensive glass policy provides a place in the declarations for a detailed description of each plate of glass, the value of lettering and ornamentation, its position in the building, and its size. The insuring clause indicates that the insurer agrees:

1. To pay for damage to the glass and its lettering or ornamentation by breakage of the glass or by chemicals accidentally or maliciously applied.
2. To pay for the repair or replacement of frames when necessary.

---

[16] Scratching or defacing is not the same as breakage, and is not insured.

3. To pay for installation of temporary plates or boarding up of windows, when necessary.
4. To pay for the removal or replacement of any obstructions made necessary in replacing the glass.

Each of the last three agreements is subject to a loss limitation of $75 per occurrence. There is no dollar amount of liability stated.

Duplication of coverage

When an insured purchases fire insurance on his building, he commonly adds extensions of coverage, very comprehensive in nature, from such perils as windstorm, explosion, smoke and hail. Since it is not practicable to exclude glass from this coverage, there is the strong likelihood that the comprehensive glass policy duplicates to some extent the insurance granted by the extensions of coverage usually purchased with the basic fire policy. The insured may still purchase glass coverage, even though he has glass insurance under a broad fire form because of the replacement service of the glass insurer and because the other contracts do not usually grant all-risk coverage on glass, but rather only specified peril insurance.

In settling losses, an agreement between insurers writing plate glass insurance and those writing the insurance on fire and related lines has been worked out as follows: The insurer of plate glass agrees to pay all glass losses (other than fire) up to $1,000. If the loss is over $1,000 and if there is contributing insurance, the entire loss is settled according to the *limit of liability rule.* The operation of this rule may be best explained by an example. Assume a glass loss of $2,000 from explosion. There is coverage under an extended coverage endorsement attached to the standard fire policy and also coverage under the comprehensive glass policy. If the $2,000 loss is fully insured under the extended coverage, each policy would be liable for $2,000, the full loss. Equal apportionment would mean that each insurer then pays $1,000, half the loss. Under the limit of liability rule, each insurer's maximum liability for the loss is determined as if there were no other insurance and the loss is apportioned accordingly. If it should turn out that the extended coverage endorsement contained a $100 deductible clause for glass losses, the limit of liability under this contract would be $1,900. The limit of liability under the glass policy is $2,000. The total limits of liability under the two contracts is $3,900. The two insurers would then apportion the loss as follows: The extended coverage insurer pays 19/39 of the loss and the glass insurer pays 20/39 of the loss. A similar method would be used to apportion the loss if the fire insurer's limit of liability were reduced because of coinsurance penalties. If the loss had been under $1,000, the glass policy would have paid the entire amount.

SUMMARY

1. Credit, title, boiler and machinery, and plate glass insurance all have the common element that the insurer renders certain collateral services in addition to the indemnification and risk-reduction function.

2. There are at least seven different kinds of credit insurance in existence. Merchandise credit insurance, issued to cover bad debts arising from unsecured open accounts with debtors who have become insolvent, is perhaps the oldest and best known type. While this coverage has existed for over 70 years in the United States, it has not become widely adopted.

3. Credit insurance seems useful when a firm has a few large accounts, the failure of any one of which would cause a severe and crippling loss, or when it is desired to use the credit and collection services of the insurer. It is necessary that a careful analysis be made of the firm's exposure to loss and that the policy be tailored to fit these specific needs.

4. Some of the reasons that account for the relatively small volume of credit insurance business stem from the complicated nature of the contract, the use of deductibles that tend to place the average policyholder in the position of bearing most of the loss himself, conservative underwriting, absence of strong promotive efforts, and the tendency for most business firms to self-insure the credit risk or to handle it by loss-prevention methods.

5. Title insurance is purchased largely for the title investigation that accompanies it, although, of course, the protection it gives against losses caused by discovery of defects that impair the marketability of the title is also important.

6. Title insurance is distinguished from other insurance contracts in that it applies only to certain losses that existed before, but which are undiscovered at the time the policy is issued. Title insurance has no expiration date and the premium is paid only once. Far from all-risk in nature, title insurance excludes all known sources of loss as well as many unknown sources.

7. Boiler and machinery insurance exists because of the severe and crippling losses that can stem from an exploding boiler or broken machinery. Not only direct losses but also many types of indirect losses are so caused. Inspection of boilers and other insured machinery is an important feature of the boiler contract and accounts for a substantial element of cost in the premium.

8. The comprehensive glass insurance contract is a type of coverage that seems to find its justification more in the convenience it provides in the

replacement of broken glass and in the comprehensive nature of its coverage than in the risk-reduction function, since it generally duplicates at least to some extent glass coverage granted on other contracts.

QUESTIONS FOR REVIEW AND DISCUSSION

1. The text points out that the percentage of total loans insured by the Federal Housing Administration has declined over the years.
   (a) Does this imply that credit insurance on home loans is "on its way out"? Why?
   (b) What factors may account for the trend noted?

2. The text states: "Protection is available for the exporter who wishes to insure against two basic perils, insolvency of a debtor and political action taken by the government. . . . Governmental bodies generally are the only agencies willing to cover the political risk, which is essentially uninsurable for the private company."
   (a) Indicate the requirements of insurable perils and explain why political risks are "essentially uninsurable" by private concerns.
   (b) Why are they apparently insurable by governmental concerns?

3. Mr. E. M. Shenkman, in describing the policies of the first credit insurance company in Great Britain (formed in 1820), the British Commercial Insurance Company, stated that "The company undertook to make good losses incurred by any debtor who became bankrupt, or sought relief under any Act of Parliament. But the insured must prove that the credit was given to the debtor when the latter's financial position was unimpeachable." How does this practice contrast with present-day methods of proving loss?

4. It has been suggested that the chief value of export credit insurance would be to enable the exporter to obtain immediate payment for his exports from the bank, which presumably would be willing to extend a loan because of the existence of the insurance. In this way an exporter could increase the size of his business because of greater credit resources. Is this a sound argument? Discuss.

5. A writer stated, "The main cause of uncertainty in economic life is time. The function of insurance in an organized society consists in overcoming the disadvantage of time in the same way in which the means of transportation overcome the disadvantage of space."
   (a) In what way is credit insurance an instrument to overcome the disadvantages of time? Explain.
   (b) Can you say that this statement is true for other kinds of insurance? Why?

6. To what extent, if any, are bad debt loss reserves a substitute for credit insurance? Explain.

7. A writer stated, "Credit risk cannot . . . be transferred entirely to an external agency. . . . Some residual risk must always rest upon the shoulders of the independent businessman as a necessary consequence of his engaging in business." Explain why this is true or untrue.

8. In a letter to Senator Charles Tobey published in the Senate hearings on the Export Insurance Act of 1946, a representative of the Motor and Equipment Manufacturers Association stated, concerning the bill:

> It would saddle the bad debt losses of American suppliers for export upon the backs of the American taxpayers. It would be an inducement to careless credit granting by those who might wish to take advantage of this coverage. Manufacturers in this industry carefully check the standing of their overseas customers and are perfectly willing to stand these losses, if any, themselves as a common business risk.

Is this statement in agreement with sound principles of insurance? Why or why not?

9. In another letter concerning the Export Insurance Act of 1946, the writer, president of the Export Managers Club, stated:

> Government insurance would protect American exporters against unilateral action taken by other governments. . . . To rule *a priori* that a scheme cannot be satisfactory because it is government managed is not a sound way of reasoning. . . . That government losses would have to come out of the taxpayers' money is undeniable, but why should we export men object to it? Doesn't the government use taxpayers' money to subsidize other interests, such as agriculture, mining, transportation, etc.? Why shouldn't the taxpayers' money be used to assist us in promoting foreign trade which, in turn will help the taxpayers by making high employment possible?

Do you agree with the above position? Discuss.

10. Identify at least seven different varieties of credit insurance and indicate briefly their major differences.

11. (a) To what extent, in your opinion, should a bank be more willing to lend money to a firm whose open account credit is insured?
    (b) Is there any evidence that banks pay any attention to this matter?

12. In view of the outstanding record of repayment of long-term home loans by homeowners, why, in your opinion, is credit insurance necessary?

13. Why are retail business firms not eligible for merchandise credit insurance?

14. The Jones Furniture Manufacturing Company, operated by Mr. A. M. Jones, has a credit insurance policy of the back coverage general form. The company's terms of sale call for a payment within 90 days after shipment. A sale is made to the Smith Retail Company, whose credit rating at the time of sale is A1 in Dun and Bradstreet, a rating to which

$10,000 of credit insurance liability applies under the terms of Jones' policy. The sale was for $20,000. Payment is not made within the 90 days and Jones decides to wait a while. Thirty days later, payment still has not been received.

(a) Advise Jones as to what rights he has under his credit insurance contract.

(b) If the Smith Company does not pay within 90 days after the due date, what rights does Jones have under his credit insurance policy if he has not filed a claim by then?

(c) For what reason might Jones have hesitated to file the account as a claim with the insurer? Are these reasons valid? Why?

(d) What payment will be made by the insurer if this is the only claim of Jones during the year and if the contract is subject to a $3,000 primary loss and ten per cent coinsurance? (Assume no recoveries of any sort.) Does use of these deductibles follow sound insurance practice? Why?

(e) Could Jones have obtained full coverage on this account?

15. How does the factor enter in as a competitor to credit insurance companies? (Consult an elementary credits and collection or finance text for reference to the operations of factors.)

16. Summarize the advantages and limitations of credit insurance as it is now written. As a project, consult a business firm or a local agency in your area that uses this type of insurance and obtain their evaluation and reaction to the arguments used in the text.

17. "A" objects to certain wording that he sees in his title insurance contract which states that he may recover for no losses that are discovered after issuance of the policy. "A" claims that there has been a mistake and what the insurer really intended was to eliminate all losses occurring before the contract is issued. Is "A" correct? If not, why not?

18. Of what benefit is title insurance if the insurer excludes all losses occurring after the policy is issued and in addition all losses known to exist before the policy is issued? Explain.

19. (a) It is claimed that the premium for title insurance is unfairly high when the property is transferred frequently. Do you agree?

(b) What justification could the title insurer have for not making any reduction in premium when the property is transferred frequently?

20. A dishonest bookkeeper concealed the presence of tax arrears on a certain property in order to prevent discovery of an embezzlement. Under what is known as *in rem* legislation, the property is sold for taxes and cannot be recovered by its former owner. In the transfer an agreement between the former owner and adjacent property owners regarding access rights to their rear driveway and garage is canceled. The adjacent property owners find themselves without the legal right to cross the property and to enter their garages. This loss may be traced directly to tax liens existing on *neighboring* property. Assuming that one of these adjacent property owners purchased his property at the time these liens were in

existence, and assuming the title insurance contract does not contain exclusions for tax liens of this nature, would the loss be normally recoverable under title insurance? Why, or why not?

21. Under the Torrens Title system, a property owner deciding to register his property so notifies the court and submits all evidence of his title. A hearing is held for all interested parties, a tentative title is issued, and this title becomes final after a given period of time. All subsequent changes in title are registered with the court, and ownership is a public record. What advantages might this system have over the use of title insurance?

22. What three special characteristics of boiler and machinery insurance exist that distinguish this type of insurance from other lines? Explain each characteristic.

23. Distinguish between outage insurance, power interruption, and power plant business interruption.

24. (a) Why is power plant consequential damage insurance vital in many types of business firms?
   (b) Which types of firms would you specify as candidates for this type of coverage?

25. A writer reported on the following incident: A department store in a small city had, within a fairly short period, three explosions of fuel oil vapor in the furnace of its boiler. In one of these accidents $25,000 of damage was caused, including the loss of plate glass windows. Many people, frightened by these explosions, stopped trading at the store and even crossed to the opposite side of the street to avoid passing near the store. What moral do you see in this incident for the insurance manager of the department store?

26. Explain why plate glass insurance is purchased separately even though its purchase often duplicates coverage granted under the standard fire policy and its extensions.

27. A large department store has purchased the comprehensive glass policy. A vehicle smashed into a show window at night. The local agent is called and before opening hours the next day, arrangements have been made to wall off the window and to replace the glass by noon. The bill is $350. The store has the standard fire policy with extended coverage and thus has two policies covering this loss.
   (a) How is the loss settled?
   (b) If the loss had been $1,200, how would it have been settled? Explain fully.

Nature and Extent of

⑲ Loss of Human Values

So far in this book we have mainly considered those problems caused by the destruction of property values, and the contributions of insurance to the solution of these problems. We shall now discuss some of the problems caused by the destruction of human values. Human values, aside from being more important to us from a personal standpoint, are far greater and more significant than all the different property values combined. The true wealth of a nation lies not in its natural resources or its accumulated property, but in the inherent capabilities of its population and the way in which this population is employed. The preservation of human life is the basic occupation of all of us. A careful study of the specific types of economic loss caused by the destruction of life or health is vital to an understanding of the insurance methods available to offset these losses.

LIFE VALUES

A human life has value for many reasons. Many of these reasons are philosophical in nature, and would lead us into the realm of religion, esthetics, sociology, psychology, and other behavioral sciences. Of greatest interest here are economic values, although, of course, it is difficult to separate the discussion in such a way that an economic analysis would have no implications or overtones for other viewpoints.

A human life has economic value to two central economic groups —the family and the employer. To the family, the economic value of a human life is probably most easily measured by the value of the earning capacity of each of its members. To the employer, the economic value of a human life is measured by the contributions of an employee to the success of the business firm. If one argues that in a free competitive society a worker is paid what he is worth and is not exploited, his contribution again is best measured by his earning capacity. It develops that earning capacity is probably the only feasible method of giving measurable economic value to human life. This concept is not so strange, since the same idea is used in determining the value of property. Thus, the price that an investor is willing to pay for a business, a share of stock, or an apartment house, depends mainly on what the earning capacity of the property is. If the "market rate" of return for a given type of business is 10 per cent, for example, and we are told that the business should earn, on the average, $10,000 a year, we would be willing to pay $100,000 for it. By the same reasoning, if a human life or health is destroyed, both the family and the employer are deprived of the earning capacity of this "human engine," the value of which may be determined by an appropriate capitalization process, as shown below.

There are four main perils that can destroy, wholly or partially, the economic value of a human life. These are:

1. Premature death.
2. Loss of health.
3. Old age.
4. Unemployment.

We shall discuss in this chapter only those problems arising from the first three of these perils. The peril of unemployment is reserved for analysis in Chapter 24.

PREMATURE DEATH

Loss of values to the family

The main economic problem arising when someone in the family dies, particularly if it is the chief breadwinner, is the loss of earnings of this person.[1] The present value of these earnings is then the measure of loss. A method of determining this value is to find a sum of money, which when paid out in installments representing both principal and interest over the remaining working life of the worker, will produce, after taxes and allowances for the support of the worker, the same net income as he earned before. This amount, once calculated, represents the amount of life insurance that would be necessary to insure the full economic value of the person and to replace the net income which he formerly produced.

To illustrate, suppose a breadwinner age 35 is expected to earn an annual fixed amount, say $10,000, over his remaining working years. Assuming that his retirement age is 65, his remaining working years

---

[1] Loss to a family caused by the death of dependents is, generally speaking, not susceptible to measurement by loss of earnings. There are definite measurable losses, nevertheless, such as the loss of investment in education, loss of unpaid for services, and the cost of a funeral.

number 30, and the worker would normally be expected to earn a gross amount of $300,000. From this sum the following deductions would be made: (1) An allowance for taxes, business expenses, etc., and (2) An allowance for the worker's own maintenance.

Assume that these items total $4,000 annually. The question is, what sum of money now on hand would produce a payment of $6,000 a year and would last exactly 30 years? If one assumes 3.5 per cent interest, reference to an annuity table indicates that it would take exactly $112,435 to produce this income. This sum, when compared to the average life insurance per family in 1960 of $10,200,[2] indicates to some degree the extent of underinsurance of the human life value for the peril of premature death.

Several underlying factors in the above calculation should be observed. First, the peril of premature death always produces a *total* loss of human life value. There are no cases of *partial* loss, as in property insurance. Second, the human life value declines with age, since each year that goes by means that the worker has one less year of income to earn. Third, the calculation of the human life value must assume a given value for the interest, the size of the worker's contribution to his family, future income tax rates, and a given level of total earnings. Changes in these and other factors could produce substantially different results in the final figure for human life value. For this reason, the calculation produces only a rough estimate of human life value, which is a very personal matter. Life insurance designed to offset the loss of human life value must take into consideration these and many other factors and should always be tailored to fit individual needs.

Needs approach

Another method of measuring the loss to the family in the case of death of a person lies in what has been termed the *needs approach*. From this viewpoint, value lost is estimated in terms of the various uses to which the earnings would have been put had the individual lived to produce them. Thus, the value lost is measured by adding together sums necessary to meet certain family needs for income during various periods of life. For example, to pay last expenses such as funeral, debts, and taxes, $3,000 may be required. The sum necessary to provide a monthly income of $200 to the family during a 15-year child-raising period at 3.5 per cent interest, is about $30,000. The sum necessary to

---

[2] See *Life Insurance Fact Book,* published annually by the Institute of Life Insurance, for current information about this amount and for other life insurance statistics.

continue a monthly income of $150 to the widow for the remainder of her life, beginning after the 15-year family-raising period, would come to about $37,000 if the widow were 50 years of age at the time the income payments began. To provide a college education for two children, an additional sum of say $10,000 (depending upon the school selected and the spending habits of the children) might be needed. These needs total $80,000, a minimum figure as an estimate of the value lost when a breadwinner dies.

The following are examples of needs for income and cash which the life insurance estate may fill:

Income Needs	*Cash Sum Needs*
Readjustment income to ease the family adjustment to a lower income level.	Death expenses (funeral, doctor bills, debts, cemetery lot, taxes, etc.)
Family income during child-raising period.	Mortgage redemption.
Income to widow for life.	College education fund.
	Gift fund.
Retirement income for insured.	Fund for emergencies.

An advantage of the needs approach to an estimation of human life value is that it may focus attention on specific objectives in the purchase of life insurance. Life insurance purchased for a certain need can be arranged in the most appropriate way to provide funds for that need. Insurance bought to provide an income for children's education can be set up so that the insurer holds the funds until a given date and then pays out the income during the college period. Insurance is often purchased to offset high estate and inheritance taxes levied on the person's property after his death. Without ready cash to pay these taxes, the asset might have to be sold at forced sale, thus causing unnecessary losses to dependents. Life insurance bought for this purpose can be paid in a lump sum to the estate of the deceased, and thus be made available for taxes and other costs. Life insurance purchased to pay off a mortgage can be set up so that no matter when the property owner may die, there is a sufficient amount of life insurance to liquidate the outstanding balance of the mortgage. The needs approach thus motivates the purchase of insurance for a given objective. Since these needs arise at different times throughout life, the needs approach also provides a guide as to which type of need should have priority and the type of insurance which should be purchased.

Naturally this technique produces a different figure than the capitalization of income approach because of the different assumptions underlying it. The needs approach seems to be a more realistic approach to the problem. Both methods reveal clearly that a human life is much more valuable economically than many realize, and that this value exceeds the amount for which life is commonly insured. It has been rightfully declared that private life insurance represents one of the greatest areas of underinsurance in existence.

Loss to business

A business firm has a somewhat more difficult task in determining the life value of a key employee, or of a partner, or of an important stockholder in a closely held corporation. If a key person dies, the firm may lose valuable customers whose loyalty depends on this individual. Plans on which the individual was working and in which the firm had invested much money may have to be abandoned. The extra cost of training or hiring a replacement may be very substantial. Key employees may quit because of the death of a partner or an officer with whom they were closely associated. Each firm must make the best estimates it can of the loss exposure and insure accordingly.[3]

Another source of loss to a business when a partner or a stockholder dies stems from the fact that his ownership in the business may pass to persons unfriendly to the firm, or may even result in liquidation of the assets in order to pay estate obligations. For example, in order to raise money, a deceased partner's widow may wish to sell her part of the assets of the partnership for cash, resulting in liquidation of the business. Competitors may obtain controlling ownership of the firm by purchasing shares from families of deceased stockholders. Those who have inherited the deceased stockholder's shares may enter the business but, because of inexperience, may cause losses or even bankruptcy. Life insurance arranged to offset or to prevent these losses is appropriately called *business continuation insurance*.

In a business continuation plan funded by life insurance, usually the owners of a business agree in advance as to what is to be done with the ownership shares in the event of death. For example, two partners own equally a business valued at $100,000. The chief asset of the business is a factory building. Neither partner has any family member capable of stepping into management in case of his death. Yet it is realized that the premature death of a partner will force the sale of the

---

[3] In one survey of the field of business life insurance, it was found that of 214 enterprises studied, only three eighths carried some form of business insurance. Three times as many firms carried key man life insurance as other forms. Robert I. Mehr and Hugh G. Wales, *Business Life Insurance and Its Economic Applications* (Urbana: University of Illinois, Bureau of Economic and Business Research, 1950), p. 31.

building to obtain money to retire his share of the business and to make money available for the use of his family. If the building were sold at forced sale, it is doubtful if $50,000 would be realized. To prevent this loss the partners enter into a *buy and sell agreement,* in which each agrees to buy the interest of the other if either dies. To fund the agreement and to insure that money for this purpose will be available, each buys life insurance of $50,000 on the life of the other. The buy and sell agreement binds each partner's estate to accept a certain valuation for his share and to sell it according to the terms of the contract.

The probability of loss

What is the probability that a person will die prematurely? Recall, that for determining the economic loss of human life value we are not interested in *whether* a person will die, but *when* he will die. The probability is 100 per cent that he will die sometime, but no one can predict when a given individual will die. Even life insurance company examiners, who examine a person's application for insurance with utmost care, continually accept insureds who die within a year after taking out a policy in spite of their appearance of good health. For large numbers of people, however, actuaries have developed *mortality tables* on which scientific life insurance rates may be based. These tables, which are revised periodically,[4] state the probability of death both in terms of deaths per 1,000 and in terms of expectation of life. Reference to Table 19–1 will be instructive at this point.

Table 19–1 shows that a young person age 20 has an expectation of living for 50 years. At this age only 179 persons in every 100,000 are expected to die before they become 21. The probability of death at age 20 is thus .179 per cent. At age 96 the death rate is slightly over 40 per cent, since 400.56 per 1,000 are expected to die during that year. At age 100 it is assumed that death is a certainty. The probability of death expressed in a mortality table is based on *insured* lives and not the whole population; thus the death rate is generally overstated. Death rates are purposely "loaded" to take care of certain contingencies (such as unusual fluctuations in death rates in a given year) and to make sure that all insurers, large and small, may use the table with safety. Death rates for the whole population consider young and old, sick and well,

---

[4] The table in current use is the Commissioners Standard Ordinary Table (CSO), 1958, which is based on death rates recorded by insurance companies during the years 1950–1954. The CSO 1958 table replaced the CSO 1941 table, which was based on experience of the period 1930–1940. The 1941 CSO table replaced the American Experience Mortality Table, which was based on data collected between 1843 and 1858. Different tables are used for different purposes, such as for annuities.

Table 19–1

COMMISSIONERS STANDARD ORDINARY MORTALITY TABLE (1958)

Age	Deaths Per 1,000	Expectation of Life-Years	Deaths Per 1,000	Expectation of Life-Years	Age
0	7.08	68.30	9.11	22.82	51
1	1.76	67.78	9.96	22.03	52
2	1.52	66.90	10.89	21.25	53
3	1.46	66.00	11.90	20.47	54
4	1.40	65.10	13.00	19.71	55
5	1.35	64.19	14.21	18.97	56
6	1.30	63.27	15.54	18.23	57
7	1.26	62.35	17.00	17.51	58
8	1.23	61.43	18.59	16.81	59
9	1.21	60.51	20.34	16.12	60
10	1.21	59.58	22.24	15.44	61
11	1.23	58.65	24.31	14.78	62
12	1.26	57.72	26.57	14.14	63
13	1.32	56.80	29.04	13.51	64
14	1.39	55.87	31.75	12.90	65
15	1.46	54.95	34.74	12.31	66
16	1.54	54.03	38.04	11.73	67
17	1.62	53.11	41.68	11.17	68
18	1.69	52.19	45.61	10.64	69
19	1.74	51.28	49.79	10.12	70
20	1.79	50.37	54.15	9.63	71
21	1.83	49.46	58.65	9.15	72
22	1.86	48.55	63.26	8.69	73
23	1.89	47.64	68.12	8.24	74
24	1.91	46.73	73.37	7.81	75
25	1.93	45.82	79.18	7.39	76
26	1.96	44.90	85.70	6.98	77
27	1.99	43.99	93.06	6.59	78
28	2.03	43.08	101.19	6.21	79
29	2.08	42.16	109.98	5.85	80
30	2.13	41.25	119.35	5.51	81
31	2.19	40.34	129.17	5.19	82
32	2.25	39.43	139.38	4.89	83
33	2.32	38.51	150.01	4.60	84
34	2.40	37.60	161.14	4.32	85
35	2.51	36.69	172.82	4.06	86
36	2.64	35.78	185.13	3.80	87
37	2.80	34.88	198.25	3.55	88
38	3.01	33.97	212.46	3.31	89
39	3.25	33.07	228.14	3.06	90
40	3.53	32.18	247.77	2.82	91
41	3.84	31.29	265.93	2.58	92
42	4.17	30.41	289.30	2.33	93
43	4.53	29.54	316.66	2.07	94
44	4.92	28.67	351.24	1.80	95
45	5.35	27.81	400.56	1.51	96
46	5.83	26.95	488.42	1.18	97
47	6.36	26.11	668.15	.83	98
48	6.95	25.27	1,000.00	.50	99
49	7.60	24.45			
50	8.32	23.63			

insurable and uninsurable, and therefore are generally higher than for the insurable population. Nevertheless, for most purposes, the mortality table is a fairly accurate representation of the death rate.

The probability that a person will live is one minus the probability that he will die. There is a much greater *likelihood* of a breadwinner living to retirement age than dying before that time.[5] Current mortality tables show that out of every 100 persons age 20, 62 will live to age 65. Table 19–2 gives estimates of the expectation of life at birth for

Table 19–2

EXPECTATION OF LIFE AT BIRTH IN THE UNITED STATES

Year	White		Nonwhite	
	Male	Female	Male	Female
1900	46.6	48.7	32.5	33.5
1920	54.4	55.6	45.5	45.2
1930	59.7	63.5	47.3	49.2
1940	62.1	66.6	51.5	54.9
1950	66.5	72.2	59.1	62.9
1957	67.1	73.5	60.3	65.2

Source: National Office of Vital Statistics, United States Department of Health, Education, and Welfare.

selected years since 1900. This table reveals the great improvements that have been made in lowering the expected mortality rates over the years. It will be observed that since 1900 the expectation of life for white males has increased about 44 per cent, compared to a 49 per cent increase for white females. Life expectancy for nonwhite persons has increased at a much higher rate, approaching 85 per cent for males and 95 per cent for females. At the present time a white female can be expected to outlive a white male by about six years. These data have important effects in life insurance and annuity rate-making. For example, life insurance rates for women should be lower than for men. Furthermore, a woman can expect to outlive her husband by at least six years if they are the same age. However, since it is common for a man's age to exceed that of his wife by a few years, it appears that a considerable period of widowhood is in store for the average wife. Thus, husbands should observe that, unless some provision is made, the probabilities are that the average wife will be a dependent widow for several years. The need for life insurance becomes immediately apparent and, because

---

[5] The *risk* is infinite, however, for no one person can say whether he will be among the unfortunate ones who pass on. All that is known for sure is that among a large group of persons randomly distributed, the mortality table will tell us, within a narrow range of error, how many will die.

women live longer than men, the amount of insurance necessary to provide a given income is greater than it would be if the beneficiary were a man.

Improvement in longevity has taken place at a much more rapid rate at lower ages than at higher ages. For example, the American Experience Mortality table, based on data collected in the period 1843–1858, reveals that a child of two had an average life expectancy of 50 years, while the Commissioners Standard Ordinary (CSO) 1958 table shows a two-year-old child with a life expectancy of nearly 67 years, a 34 per cent increase. At age 50, however, under the American Experience Mortality Table, a person had an expectancy of living about 21 more years, while under current conditions the person may expect to live 23.6 years, an increase of only 12.4 per cent over 100 years ago. Much of the explanation for this phenomenon lies in the fact that medical science has made its greatest strides in controlling diseases which do not primarily affect older age groups. As shown in Table 19–3,

Table 19–3

**DEATH RATES AMONG INSURED INDIVIDUALS FROM SELECTED CAUSES
1950 AND 1960**

Cause of Death	Death Rates Per 100,000 Lives Exposed	
	1950	1960
Cardiovascular-renal diseases:		
Cerebral hemorrhage	53.2	52.0
Diseases of the heart	252.4	253.1
Nephritis and nephrosis	10.9	5.3
Other	27.5	25.4
Total	344.0	335.8
Cancer	104.2	112.7
Pneumonia and influenza	11.7	19.2
Tuberculosis	7.8	1.8
Diabetes	7.7	6.0
Pregnancy and childbirth	.8	.3
Total	132.2	140.0
External causes:		
Motor vehicle accidents	18.8	17.5
Other accidents	21.5	18.7
Suicide	13.2	11.0
Homicide	1.6	1.4
Total	55.1	48.6
All other causes	74.5	78.1
Total, all causes	605.8	602.5

Source: Institute of Life Insurance.

death rates today arise out of diseases such as heart trouble and cancer, which account for a majority of all deaths. These diseases primarily afflict older people. It will be observed that over the eleven-year period, 1950–1960, total death rates did not change significantly, but there were some significant changes in causes. Considerably fewer deaths were caused in 1960 by nephritis, tuberculosis, diabetes, and pregnancy and childbirth than in 1950. Data such as these influence underwriting practices in life insurance, so that it has become possible to issue policies on many more individuals with histories of certain diseases than was true before medical advances were able to control these diseases effectively.

The probability of death rises rapidly with age. Chart 19–1 is a sketch of CSO 1958 death rates, on a semilogarithmic scale, with age levels represented on the horizontal axis and death rates on the vertical axis. Death rates during the first few years of life are higher than they are following ages 9 or 10. The death rate at age 1 is approximately the same as at age 19, with lower death rates falling in between these ages. After age 25, death rates increase at an increasing rate until age 40, but are still relatively low. At age 60, the death rate is over twice the rate at age 50, and by age 70 the death rate is nearly 2.5 times the rate at age 60. Thus, it is seen that after age 60 the death rates climb geometrically, until at age 99, the rate is assumed to be 100 per cent.

Premium rates for life insurance tend to follow the same pattern as the curve represented in Chart 19–1. They rise steeply after age 40 until they tend to become prohibitive for new policyholders entering the insured group at advanced ages. For this reason very few people can afford to take out life insurance at an advanced age and most underwriters refuse to accept applications for term insurance from persons past age 65 because of the tendency for adverse selection beyond that age. Thus, if a person seeks life insurance at a time "when he needs it," it is not available to him. He must purchase it at a time when the probability of death is quite low. This same truth was observed in other lines (for example, fire insurance is not available after the house catches fire), namely, that insurance is a commodity the purchase of which must be arranged before the loss occurs or before it becomes highly probable.

Chart 19–1

THE MORTALITY RATE, CSO 1958 MORTALITY TABLE

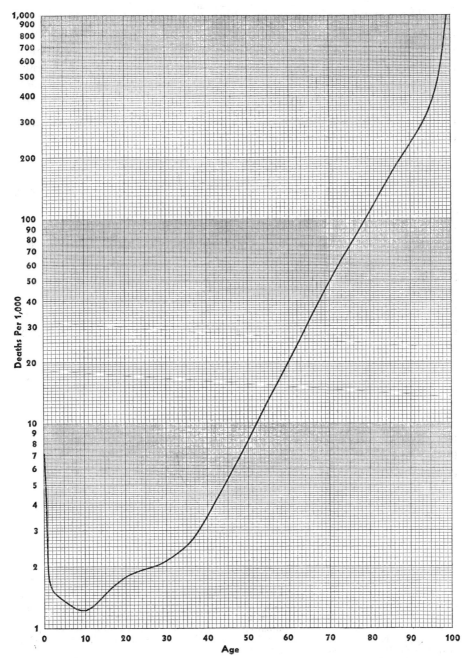

LOSS OF HEALTH

The second major way in which human life value may be destroyed is through loss of health. Loss of health is in many ways a more serious peril than the premature loss of life, because if a person is incapacitated from accident or sickness, not only is his earning power either cut off completely or reduced greatly, but in addition it becomes necessary to pay for medical and hospital bills and to care for the individual during his illness. This imposes a considerable financial drain on his family and upon society.

Income loss

Losses from destruction of health may be measured in two different ways: (1) loss of earnings due to disability and (2) expenditures for medical care. The Social Security Administration, which makes annual estimates of total income loss from short-term nonoccupational disabilities (illness lasting six months or less), estimated this loss to be $7.5 billion in 1957. Of this amount about 25 per cent was insured, and only about 16 per cent of the total insurance was represented by individual policies; the remainder was provided under group coverages of various types.[6] Occupational injuries and nonoccupational long-term disabilities account for many more billion dollars of income loss, but no precise measurements of it exist. One estimate is that temporary illness is responsible for about 20 per cent of all nonoccupational income losses; partial disability cases, 50 per cent; and long-term total disability cases, 30 per cent.[7] On this basis, total nonoccupational illness would have caused an estimated $37.5 billion of income loss in 1957. This does not include occupational disability income loss, which was estimated to be about one per cent of the national income in 1952.[8] If this same relationship held in 1957, another $3.6 billion would be added to the total, making total income losses from disability approximately $41 billion, or 10 per cent of the national income in that year. Such estimates, of course, do not take into consideration the vast amount of indirect losses from disability, such as lowered production efficiency and

---

[6] *Health, Education, and Welfare Trends, 1959 Edition* (Department of Health Education and Welfare, 1959), p. 57. Private group plans accounted for 52 per cent of the total insurance, and government employees' sick-leave plans accounted for 32 per cent.

[7] J. G. Turnbull, C. A. Williams, and E. F. Cheit, *Economic and Social Security* (New York: The Ronald Press Company, 1957), p. 298, citing Commission on Health Needs of the Nation, *Building America's Health, IV* (Washington, D. C.: United States Government Printing Office, 1957), p. 303.

[8] *Ibid.*, p. 247.

other additional expenses borne by employers and by families of disabled workers, nor do they count the loss of services of unpaid individuals such as housewives or other dependents.

Total income losses have been rising in the United States, primarily because income has been rising steadily. An additional factor arises out of the fact that medical science has kept disabled people alive for longer periods than before. Thus, the decrease in death rates brings about an increase in disability rates.

Medical costs

Estimates place the expenditures for medical care in the United States at $11.9 billion in 1958. On a per capita basis, this represents an outlay of $95.65 for every person in the country, an increase of 81.6 per cent over the $52.68 per capita spent in 1948, ten years earlier. Table 19–4 summarizes some of the more important statistics relating to medical cost expenditures. Data from this table support the following conclusions:

1. Expenditures for hospital services are now the largest single item of medical care, accounting for 31.1 per cent of total such expenditures in 1958 as compared to 24.6 per cent ten years earlier.
2. Expenditures for physicians' services now account for slightly over one fourth of the total medical care costs, slipping from nearly a third of the total medical care costs ten years earlier.
3. There was little change in the relative cost of medicines, dental services, and other professional medical services in the ten-year period. These items together accounted for 42.7 per cent of the total medical bill in 1958, with medicines costing as much as all physicians' services.
4. The total expenditures for medical care are only about one fourth as large as the total loss of income through loss of health, $11.9 billion *versus* $41 billion.
5. Most medical expenditures are met directly, but payments through insurers are increasing rapidly. Insurance benefits in 1958 were three times as important as they were in 1948 and accounted for nearly one fourth of all payments in 1958. This increase has been most marked in the area of coverage for physicians' services. In 1948 doctors received only two per cent of their fees through insurers, as compared with 7.8 per cent in 1958.
6. Paying medical bills through insurance is not without its costs, but these costs are not so high as commonly assumed. Expenses of insurers, as measured by the difference between earned pre-

Table 19-4

PRIVATE EXPENDITURES FOR MEDICAL CARE AND VOLUNTARY
INSURANCE, 1948–1958

Type of Expenditure (Millions of dollars)	1948			1958		
	Columns					
	1	2	3	4	5	6
Direct payments..........................	$6,785	88.7	3.6	$11,900	72.6	3.8
Insurance benefits.........................	606	7.9	.3	3,877	23.6	1.2
Expenses for prepayment*.................	256	3.3	.1	620	3.8	.2
Total................................	$7,647	100.0	4.0	16,397	100.0	5.2
Hospital services..........................	$1,881	24.6	1.0	$ 5,102	31.1	1.6
Direct payments.........................	1,234	16.1	.7	2,170	13.2	.7
Insurance benefits........................	455	6.0	.2	2,591	15.8	.8
Expenses for prepayment..................	192	2.5	.1	341	2.1	.1
Physicians' services.......................	$2,424	31.7	1.3	$ 4,290	26.2	1.4
Direct payments.........................	2,209	28.9	1.2	2,725	16.6	.9
Insurance benefits........................	151	2.0	.1	1,286	7.8	.4
Expenses for prepayment..................	64	.8	...	279	1.7	.1
Medicines................................	$1,897	24.8	1.0	$ 4,362	26.6	1.4
Dentists.................................	900	11.8	.5	1,674	10.2	.5
Other professional services†..............	445			769		
Nursing homes...........................	100	7.1	.3	200	5.9	.3
Total................................	$7,647	100.0	4.1	$16,397	100.0	5.2

* Represents expenses of the insurer as measured by the difference between earned premiums and benefits paid.
† Services of osteopaths, chiropractors, podiatrists, etc.
Key: Columns 2 & 5—Per cent of total.
        3 & 6—Per cent of total Disposable Personal Income.
Due to rounding, subtotals do not add to totals.
Source: Agnes W. Brewster, "Voluntary Health Insurance and Medical Care Expenditure" 1948–1958,
    Social Security Bulletin (December, 1959), pp. 4–9.

miums and benefits paid, represented 3.8 per cent of the total
medical bill in 1958, compared with 3.3 per cent in 1948.

7. The total cost of medical care is not only rising in an absolute
sense, but also is rising relative to disposable personal income.
In 1958 the nation devoted 5.2 per cent of disposable personal
income to medical care, compared with 4 per cent in 1948,
a rise of 30 per cent in ten years.

Life v. health loss

The total economic loss through destruction of human life values
from health loss is estimated to be $52.9 billion. What is the economic
loss from the destruction of human life values through premature

death? Unfortunately, no definitive studies on this point have been undertaken, but a very rough estimate can be made by assuming that the average loss upon the death of a breadwinner is 20 years' disposable income. It follows that life insurance in force should equal 20 years' disposable income. However, the life insurance in force in private insurers and through social security [9] was only about one sixth of this amount in 1958. If the amount of death benefits paid by life insurers was normal in 1958, the benefits represent, under these assumptions, roughly one sixth of the economic loss from premature death. In 1958 private insurers paid death benefits of $2.9 billion, and an additional $1.7 billion were paid to survivors under the Social Security Act. If these benefits are divided by one sixth, one arrives at a total of $27.6 billion. Actually, this estimate is considerably overstated because no adjustment is made for the fact that many death benefits were made to aged people, whose earning years had passed, and no adjustments were made to reflect the refinements necessary to arrive at a true estimate of capitalized earning value, as explained previously. It may be concluded that the total economic loss due to destruction of human life value is undoubtedly much less than the loss due to destruction of human life value through loss of health.

The probability of loss

The data above show the tremendous aggregate cost of the loss of income through illness and accident and medical care expenditures. What is the probability that a person will be among the unfortunate individuals who are struck down annually? Again, there is no complete answer to this question, since data on illnesses and accidents are not nearly so well classified as mortality data. Preliminary data from the United States National Health Survey on the amount of worktime missed by employed persons (including the self-employed) because of illness or injury [10] suggest that the annual expectation of loss was nine workdays per year in 1957 and eight days in 1958.

Even though the average expected length of disability is not long, unfortunately a few individuals may be expected to be disabled much longer. In the 1935–1936 National Health Survey, for example, it was reported that 1.2 per cent of those interviewed had been disabled for an entire year or longer. Of those disabling illnesses lasting a week or

---

[9] See Chapter 22 for estimates of life insurance in force through the Social Security Act.
[10] Public Health Service, *Health Statistics from the United States National Health Survey,* Preliminary Report on Disability, United States July–September, 1957, Series B-4 (June, 1958).

longer, the average period of disability was nearly two months. In the 1949–1950 survey it was brought out that while only about 4 per cent of the population between ages 14 and 64 is disabled at any one time, three eighths of those disabled have been so for over one year. The Social Security Administration reported that in 1954, 2.9 million persons between the ages of 14 and 64 had been disabled six months or more. Of those 65 years of age and over, 15.7 per cent had been disabled for more than six months.[11]

Similar findings have been made for medical bills. In a survey of 2,809 families in 1953, it was verified that health losses are not suffered uniformly by the population. While 8 per cent of the families experienced no medical costs in that year, 11 per cent incurred charges exceeding $495, or 43 per cent of the total charges for all families. It was found that while 53 per cent of the families paid out less than 5 per cent of their incomes in medical costs, 2 per cent incurred charges exceeding 50 per cent of their incomes.[12] Thus, the *average* medical bill may not be excessive, but the variation is very great, and an unfortunate minority will suffer an inordinate loss each year. Such a skewed distribution of medical costs lends itself to a solution *via* the insurance device in an admirable way.

Some of the findings of various health surveys that have been made [13] suggest the following facts about the illness peril:

Illness is more severe among nonwhites than whites; among low-income groups than high-income groups; among unemployed persons than employed persons; among the very young and the very old than middle-aged persons. Females have more illnesses than males but are disabled for shorter periods of time. Single people have more illnesses than married persons.

Causes of illness

An indication of the causes of serious illness may be seen in Table 19–3 (page 509) which shows the chief causes of death. The same factors also cause illness, of course, but the whole story is not told. For ex-

---

[11] A. M. Skolnick, "Estimated Prevalence of Long-Term Disability, 1954" *Social Security Bulletin* (June, 1955), pp. 20–21.

[12] Odin W. Anderson and J. G. Feldman, *Family Medical Costs and Voluntary Health Insurance: A Nationwide Survey* (New York: McGraw-Hill Book Company, Inc., 1956), pp. 134–135.

[13] Three extensive studies of national health have been made: by the Committee on the Costs of Medical Care, covering 8,758 families over the period 1928–1931; the National Health Survey, covering 703,092 households in 18 states in 1935–1936; and by the United States Public Health Service, the Social Security Administration, and the Office of Vocational Rehabilitation, covering 25,000 households in 1950.

ample, in 1957, records show that 623,938 individuals, or 475 per 100,-
000 of civilian population, were confined in various mental hospitals in
the United States. About one third of these persons represented new ad-
missions during the year. There were 86,861 cases of tuberculosis reported in 1957.[14] The importance of economic losses caused by these
illnesses are not entirely revealed by mortality data. The National Health
Survey findings attributed to the following illnesses the longest average
periods of disability: [15]

Orthopedic impairments	344 days
Tuberculosis	246 days
Nervous and mental diseases	189 days
Cardiovascular-renal diseases	122 days
Rheumatism and allied diseases	120 days
Cancer and other tumors	100 days

Thus, it may be observed that the impairments causing the most
lengthy periods of disability are only partially reflected in mortality
statistics. Cancer and heart trouble, major causes of death, are not so
serious as other disabilities in causing time loss due to impaired health.

A study by the United States Department of Health on the annual
days of disability caused by different illnesses according to age, revealed
that certain ailments, such as heart disease, cancer, arthritis, hyper-
tension, accidents, diabetes, bronchitis, and nephritis, are much more
severe at ages 45 and above than they are below this level. On the other
hand, mental disorders, rheumatic fever, colds, pneumonia, and other
contagious diseases affect more young people than old persons.[16]

OLD AGE

Old age is a peril that destroys earning capacity just as does premature death or loss of health. Old age, in contrast to the two perils
previously described, is a certainty for everyone and as such may be
planned for in advance. Because there is no uncertainty about old age, it
may be inquired as to why it is even considered in a text in insurance.
The concept was developed in Chapter 1 that one cannot successfully
insure certainties. Nevertheless, old-age dependency is a condition
against which much life insurance is directed. Life insurance is commonly arranged so as to build up cash values with which to meet income

---

[14] *Health, Education, and Welfare Trends, 1959 Edition, op. cit.*, pp. 36 and 38.
[15] G. W. Bachman and Lewis Meriam, *The Issue of Compulsory Health Insurance*
(Washington, D. C.: The Brookings Institution, 1948), Chapter VI.
[16] *Health and Demography* (Washington: United States Department of Health,
Education and Welfare, National Office of Vital Statistics, October, 1946).

needs in old age. The uncertainty lies in whether or not this income will serve its purpose. What is needed is the scientific liquidation of these values so as to guarantee a life income to the beneficiary. Thus, the uncertainty lies in how long a person will live and not in how soon he will die. As we shall see, this uncertainty can be successfully met through the combination method of handling risk.

Extent of old-age dependency

Although everyone knows that some day he will get old and will be dependent unless he makes provision for himself in some manner, statistics show that all too often the arrival of the date of retirement finds the individual with little guaranteed income and very little money. This situation has become of major economic interest because of the growth in the proportion of aged persons to the total population, the declining number of employment opportunities for these persons, and the increasing length of life which extends the average period during which they will be dependent on others. In 1900 only 4.1 per cent of the population was age 65 or over. By 1958 this percentage had grown to 8.6, and actuarial projections place it at 10.6 by 1980.[17] In 1958 there were over 15 million people age 65 and over in the United States. The average life expectancy at age 65 is 12.7 years for white males and 15.4 years for white females. Due to the increasing adoption of compulsory retirement rules, it is becoming more and more difficult for aged persons to continue working, even if they are physically able to do so.

Income status

Tables 19–5 and 19–6 provide an indication of the income status of people age 65 and over.

Without considering that some of these aged individuals have two or more sources of income, it may be observed that roughly 20 per cent of the aged population are still working, and 60 per cent receive a pension from social insurance. Those receiving public assistance, 13.5 per cent, must pass a "needs" test, and presumably are penniless or nearly so. Only 8.7 per cent have incomes solely from other sources, such as their own savings, or from children, relatives, or others. Some are apparently receiving no income. There are many more women than men in these latter two categories, indicating a somewhat more desperate plight for aged women.

---

[17] Census Bureau, *Current Population Reports, Population Estimates,* Series P-25 No. 98, 114, 170, and 187.

Table 19–5

NUMBER OF PERSONS AGED 65 AND OVER RECEIVING INCOME, 1958

Source of Income	Men	Women	Men and Women	Per Cent of Total
Employment.................	2,110	1,570	3,680	19.7
Social insurance..............	5,420	5,410	10,830	58.1
Public assistance..............	940	1,570	2,510	13.5
No money income, or income solely from other sources.....	240	1,370	1,610	8.7
Total	8,710	9,920	18,630	100.0
Less: Those receiving income from more than one source...	1,720	1,530	3,250	17.5
Total aged...............	6,990	8,390	15,380	

Source: L. A. Epstein, "Money Income of Aged Persons: A 10-Year Review, 1948 to 1958," *Social Security Bulletin,* June, 1959, percentages calculated.

Table 19–6

MONEY INCOME OF PERSONS AGED 65 AND OVER, 1949 AND 1959
(IN TERMS OF 1959 DOLLARS)

Income	1949*	1959*
Zero..	30.7	15.1
$1–499...	24.2	13.1
$500–999...	19.4	26.9
$1,000–1,499......................................	7.1	15.0
$1,500–1,999......................................	5.4	8.3
$2,000–2,999......................................	6.2	8.9
$3,000–4,999......................................	4.8	6.7
$5,000–and above.................................	2.1	6.1

*Based on 11,270,000 aged in 1949 and 15,260,000 in 1959.
Source: L. A. Epstein, "Money Income of Aged Persons, Mid-1960," *Social Security Bulletin,* January, 1961.

That these individuals are not receiving substantial incomes is well documented in Table 19–6, which shows that while the situation has improved over the period 1949–1959, 28 per cent of all aged persons are still receiving less than $500 annually in money income, and 70 per cent receive less than $1,500 annually. Fewer than one in 17 persons aged 65 and over live on a standard of living which could be purchased by an income of $5,000 a year or more in 1959.

Aged women are in a much worse position than men from an income standpoint. In 1957, 37.7 per cent of the men received less than $1,000 annually compared with 79.3 per cent of the women in this group. It might be supposed that many of the women are still married and are dependent on their husband's income. However, data reveal that of the 7,720,000 aged women in 1957, only 37 per cent were married. Surveys show that aged husband-wife families appear to be in a better financial condition than single persons. For example, a 1956 study [18] showed the following distribution of income for aged couples living without relatives in the household:

Less than $2,000	48.3%
$2,000–3,999	29.7
$4,000–5,999	12.6
$6,000–or more	9.4
Median Income	$2,080

It is reliably estimated that between 33 and 39 per cent of the total income of aged individuals is received under social insurance programs.

Net worth position

How many individuals are able to save a substantial amount for their old age? The dependence of most aged people on continued employment or on social insurance schemes as a means of livelihood suggests that very few are able to "retire," in the normal sense of the word, on the fruits of their labors. The Social Security Administration made a survey of old-age and survivors insurance beneficiaries in 1957 and discovered that the major asset acquired by most of their pensioners was a home.[19] Yet only half of all aged beneficiary groups owned their homes. The median equity in their homes was about $8,000, and it was estimated that four fifths of these homes had no mortgage on them.

Some of the other findings from this survey were revealing. The retired worker with a wife, called a beneficiary couple, had a median net worth of $9,620. Only 12 per cent of these couples had no net worth at all or had debts. Yet a fourth of this group had no liquid assets, indicating that what little they had was probably tied up in a home. Seven in 10 couples carried some life insurance (median face value, $1,810) yet only 10 per cent of the aged couples had life insurance with a face value of $5,000 or more, and 44 per cent had no life insurance or had policies with a face value of less than $1,000.

In the survey a single retired worker with no dependents was in considerably worse circumstances than a retired worker with a wife.

---

[18] L. A. Epstein, "Money Income of Aged Persons: A 10-Year Review 1948 to 1958," *Social Security Bulletin* (June, 1959).

[19] "Assets and Net Worth of Old-Age and Survivors Insurance Beneficiaries: Highlights from Preliminary Data, 1957 Survey," *Social Security Bulletin* (January, 1959).

The median net worth for single retired men was $800, and for single retired women, $2,080. However, 37 per cent of the single retired men and 29 per cent of the single retired women had no net worth or had debts. It was found that 44 per cent of the single retired workers had no liquid assets. Half of the retired single workers carried life insurance (median face value, $930). However, only two per cent of these workers had life insurance with a face value of $5,000 or more and 77 per cent had no life insurance or had policies with a face value of less than $1,000.

The survey showed that only one in 10 of all aged beneficiary groups had $10,000 or more in liquid assets or $25,000 or more in total net worth. Only a fourth of them had total net worth positions of $13,700 or more. On the other hand, a fourth of the group had net worth positions of less than $177. While this group may not be representative of all aged persons, this survey, concerned with O.A.S.I. beneficiaries, is very indicative of the general conclusion that the net worth position of most persons 65 years of age or over is not one that will be eagerly anticipated by most people.

Causes of old-age dependency

The data cited above show beyond any reasonable doubt that on the whole, people have not succeeded in preventing old-age dependency. There have been a number of "explanations" for this, some of which are given below.

1. The American economy is based on a high consumption pattern and people are urged through constant advertising to spend freely. In the effort to "keep up with the Joneses," saving for old age is ignored.
2. A long-term decline in interest rates has prevented people from saving enough for their old age.
3. A long-term inflation has reduced the ability to save because prices rise faster than wages.
4. Children no longer feel obligated to care for their parents nor are they able to do so.
5. The depression of the 1930's and personal misfortunes caused a loss of the life savings of many.
6. People do not earn enough to save sufficient amounts for old age.
7. Unions are responsible for declining employment opportunities of aged people.
8. Adoption of pension plans by business firms has caused the forced retirement of people able to work.

It will be recognized that these explanations are, at least in some respects, more in the way of excuses than they are valid explanations of a cause which is outside the control of the individual concerned. Perhaps they might best be summarized under the heading, "refusal of most people to plan ahead," or the "tendency to live for today only," or the attitude "we'll get by somehow." Regardless of the merit, or even the truth of the above explanations, the fact remains that while most people fail to save for a rainy day, a few succeed. The few who succeed generally have plans for succeeding, and often as not, the insurance mechanism is an integral part of these plans. In the next three chapters the use of insurance in solving some of the problems outlined in this chapter will be explored.

SUMMARY

1. Human life values, often overlooked in the task of obtaining adequate insurance protection against financial losses, are undoubtedly more important and far greater than all property values. Four perils cause destruction of human life values—premature death, loss of health, old age, and unemployment.

2. Premature death causes great loss to families and to employers, a loss which may be objectively measured and insured. The probability of premature death is substantial in spite of striking improvements in longevity since 1900. According to current mortality tables, approximately 38 of every 100 people aged 20 will die before they retire at age 65. Data on the causes of illness suggest that major reductions in the mortality rate in the future will come when medical science conquers such afflictions as heart disease and cancer.

3. Increase in longevity has brought with it a rise in the rate of observable loss of health, since many who formerly would have died from illness are now kept alive, but in a state of semihealth. The loss of health causes more economic loss than the loss of life.

4. Ill health brings two major types of losses—loss of income during the period of disability, and medical costs. Both types of loss have increased rapidly in the United States. While precise estimates of these costs are not available because of the many types of unmeasurable losses, it seems clear that losses of over 12 per cent of the national income are being registered in the United States annually. The aggregate loss to the economy because of income loss is about four times the cost of medical care, $41 billion versus $12 billion respectively.

5. Long-term disability and partial disability cases account for 80 per cent of the loss of income from sickness and accident, while hospital and physicians' services account for about 60 per cent of all medical care expenditures.

6. Most medical expenditures are still being met directly, but an increasing proportion of them are being met through insurance. About half of all hospital bills and 30 per cent of physicians' bills are now paid through insurance, with insurance on physicians' services increasing more rapidly.

7. Several studies have verified the finding that while medical costs and income losses, *on the average,* do not cause an intolerable financial burden, a disproportionate amount of the burden falls on relatively few individuals. This fact has undoubtedly stimulated the use of insurance as a method of spreading the loss more evenly.

8. The probability of living to old age is nearly twice as great as the probability of premature death. The extent of old-age dependency suggests that not only are people failing to save sufficient amounts for their declining years, but they have also tended to rely primarily on social insurance as a method of handling the risk of outliving their income. Relatively few old persons have annuities or life insurance proceeds on which to retire. Fewer than one in ten aged people have a net worth of $25,000 or more. Nearly three fourths of all aged persons had total money income of less than $1,500 in 1959. Only 20 per cent of aged people are still in the labor force. Unless the retired person is willing to live on the somewhat low standard of living provided by social insurance plans of different kinds, it is apparent that more voluntary savings are necessary than have been amassed in the past.

QUESTIONS FOR REVIEW AND DISCUSSION

1. It has been urged that an average businessman would not think of leaving his factory building uninsured, but he neglects to insure the lives of his important key executives who may be more valuable than the building. Do you agree? In what way might a key executive be more valuable than the building? Discuss.

2. How can the economic loss of a family breadwinner be measured? Explain fully.

3. It is estimated that about one third of all women and about 20 per cent of married women are employed outside the home.
   (a) In your opinion, does the earning capacity of a working wife give rise to economic value for which she should be insured?
   (b) Should the life of a wife and mother not employed outside the home be insured? Why or why not?

4. John is about to purchase a clothing business priced at $50,000, of which $10,000 represents inventory and fixtures. The remainder of the purchase price is attributable to goodwill. The business is expected to net $5,000

each year, after all expenses including the manager's salary have been paid.

(a) If John believes that an appropriate capitalization rate for funds employed in similar enterprises is 15 per cent, is the price of this business reasonable? If not, what is a "fair price"?

(b) Would you expect to find a person whose earning capacity is $5,000 a year insured for a similar amount?

5. (a) In what way does the death of a partner or of a stockholder in a closely held corporation cause a loss to the business firm?

(b) How can life insurance be employed to offset this loss?

6. Referring to Table 19–1, page 507, state the probability that (a) a person age 18 will live until he is 19, and (b) a person age 97 will live to age 99.

7. (a) What explanations can you offer for the fact that the longevity for nonwhite people has increased at a faster rate since 1900 than for white people?

(b) What significance does this have for life insurance?

8. Do observable data support or weaken the statement made in the text that "a considerable period of widowhood is in store for the average wife"? Why is this true or false?

9. The following statements were made by an investment analyst concerning a large industrial concern and the investment merit of its securities: ". . . the company shifted to a decentralized type of organization about six years ago. This move, however, did not yield the desired improvement in efficiency. . . . The deficiencies arising from too few centralized controls are now being corrected. A little more than a year ago a new president took office. Since then the company has come a long way in tightening up its organization. . . . The company is fortunate in having a well-qualified chief executive to direct its improvement program . . . he combines a broad education in business with solid practical experience . . . he developed a central staff of experts to provide the specialized control and knowledge that formerly were lacking. . . ." What are the implications of this analysis with respect to a dependence on human life values?

10. With the tremendous strides in medical science, longevity has increased very significantly, especially at younger age levels. What is the chief reason for this and what implications does it have for life insurance?

11. Why is it difficult for a person past age 60 to purchase life insurance? (Refer to Chart 19–1, page 511.)

12. The text states "Thus, the decrease in death rates brings about an increase in disability rates."

(a) How is this true?

(b) What other factors have brought about an increase in disability rates?

13. Suggest possible reasons for the increase in the proportion of disposable income spent for medical care in the period 1948–1958.

14. (a) How can one obtain a comparison of the economic costs of loss of health versus the economic costs of the loss of life? What are the assumptions underlying this method?

(b) What conclusions, if any, may be drawn concerning this comparison?

15. A survey completed in 1950 indicated that 13.6 per cent of the disabled civilian noninstitutionalized population aged 14–64 in the United States in 1949 had been disabled 10 years or over at the time they were interviewed. Another 22.5 per cent had been disabled over 18 months but under 10 years. What important fact do these data illustrate about the probability of disability?

16. "A skewed distribution of medical costs lends itself to a solution *via* the insurance device in an admirable way." Explain why this is true.

17. A recent study revealed that 80 per cent of the aged who are not in the labor force left because of their health or because their employer asked them to leave. Over 77 per cent of those aged individuals who are not in the labor force do not feel well enough to work. Finally, most aged persons discover that their occupational skills are obsolete.
    (a) What implications does this study have to the problem of old-age dependency?
    (b) Are these implications supported by any other findings? Discuss.

18. Summarize the major factors in our economy that create an economic problem of old-age dependency.

19. Much has been heard of a "population explosion" throughout the world. What implications does this have for the problem of old-age dependency?

20. An employer is requested to adopt the policy of dropping the age 65 compulsory retirement rule in his plant in order to permit many able-bodied older workers to continue working. The employer refuses, stating that the morale problem at younger age levels would be too severe if he did so.
    (a) Why might a morale problem exist if this were done?
    (b) What arguments would you use to counter the employer's position?

21. Evaluate the various "explanations" offered for the existence of old-age dependency. From your personal experience, give an example of an aged person who is dependent and your explanation of the reasons for his dependence.

22. In your opinion what part should the government assume in the task of maintaining aged people? What disadvantages might there be in such a plan?

23. A writer stated, "The 50 per cent of disabled persons who suffer an income loss of four months' earnings or more are those upon whom the impact of disability is heaviest. In addition to the loss of earnings, they also incur costs for medical care, which tend to increase with increasing disability duration, although less than proportionally. The psychological disintegrating effects of disability also increase with duration." Suggest some of the possible factors referred to in the phrase "psychological disintegrating effects of disability." Why might they increase with the duration of disability?

Life

Insurance

Because human life is generally recognized to have great value, a demand has grown for insurance to indemnify those who suffer loss because of the destruction of this value. Few industries have equalled the consistent record of the long-term growth of life insurance. Yet, as we have seen, when measured against the potential market for life insurance, the sales of this product have fallen far short of that market. No small reason for this is the failure of the consuming public to understand what life insurance really is, what it will do, why it is needed, and how it may be arranged. Part of the difficulty lies in the traditional methods of distribution which have been justified on the grounds that "life insurance is not bought; it is sold." In this chapter we will analyze life insurance contracts and their purposes from the viewpoint of the consumer, and assess the role that life insurance now plays in the development of personal financial protection and in the establishment of family financial security.

WHAT IS LIFE INSURANCE?

As a social and economic device, *life insurance* is a method by which a group of people may cooperate to even out the burden of loss resulting from the premature death of members of the group. The insuring organization collects contributions from each member, invests these contributions and guarantees both their safety and a minimum interest return, and distributes benefits to the estates of those members who die.

Viewed from an individual standpoint, life insurance is a method of creating an estate. It is a method of seeing to it that plans for accumulating property for the benefit of others, chiefly the family, are realized, regardless of whether the breadwinner dies prematurely or lives to "a ripe old age." The word "estate," unfortunately, carries a suggestion of death since the word is often employed to describe the aggregate property belonging to a *deceased* person. The meaning of *estate* is much broader, however, and will be used here to mean an aggregate of property, including income-producing property, whether it is to be used before or after the death of a person. In the last analysis, property is accumulated for the benefit of the *living,* not the dead, and the various plans for building an estate should recognize this fundamental precept.

It has been stated that most workers have two central types of estates—the present or actual estate and the future or potential estate. The *present* or *actual estate* is the property that one has actually accumulated for his dependents or himself for the time when his earning capacity will be cut off by premature death or old age. The *future* or *potential estate* refers to the property that one will normally accumulate to provide financial security for his dependents if he lives long enough. Premature death means that the potential estate is never realized. Life insurance is a way of creating an actual estate for the benefit of dependents if the worker does not live to realize his potential estate, and it is a way of saving money for the actual estate to be used as a source of income in old age.

Life insurance is nothing more than a plan to accumulate property, or, if death intervenes, to insure that the property will be available for the purpose intended. Life insurance may, in a sense, be viewed as a postdated check for a certain sum of money, payable to one's dependents or other beneficiaries only at death, or otherwise redeemable for value by oneself at a later time. Unfortunately, this picture is true only if the proper types of life insurance contracts are purchased, and if these types are arranged suitably and skillfully in a *program* designed to fulfill the intended purposes. Too often, life insurance is not purchased, arranged, and planned properly, and thus its chief benefits may thereby be lost.

Protection v. savings needs

Because a clear understanding of the two purposes of life insurance mentioned above is of such fundamental importance in appreciating what various contracts of life insurance will accomplish, these purposes are deserving of special emphasis. Life insurance can accomplish two objectives: (1) to guarantee the existence of an estate out of which one's dependents may meet debts and receive an income if the breadwinner dies and (2) to save money as a part of one's own *living* estate, which is created for future needs for income. The first objective may be termed the *protection need* and the latter, the *savings need.*

Life insurance policies, which are analyzed in detail later in this chapter, may be purchased to reflect each of these needs in varying proportions. *Term insurance* in its various forms is wholly dedicated to the protection need. Generally, there are no cash values whatever in term insurance and hence no possibility of the savings need being met.[1] Term insurance, thus, is designed entirely for death protection and to create an estate only in the event of premature death. On the other hand, *whole life insurance* is available in different forms to meet both the savings and the protection needs. These contracts may be arranged so that the savings need can receive as much emphasis as is desired, within certain limits. All whole life contracts have an element of protection which extends for the whole of the insured's life. *Endowment policies* emphasize the savings need, with only a small element of protection. Endowments and *retirement income* contracts are primarily savings contracts for a definite span of years with the added guarantee that if the insured does not live during this period to complete his savings plan, the insurer will complete it for him. These relationships are shown schematically in Figure 20–1, which is intended to convey the basic concept that different life insurance contracts contain varying proportions of savings and protection.

Ideally, a program of estate building should provide both savings and protection, savings if the estate builder lives, and protection if he dies. Some individuals prefer to use term insurance for protection and to emphasize other types of investments, such as stocks, bonds, savings accounts, or real estate, for the savings portion of their plans. Others desire to combine protection and savings in one contract, and will use one or more of the whole life policies. Still others may arrange their programs to include pure term insurance for the protection element and endowments for the savings element. There is no limit, of course, to the many different combinations which can be made.

Permanent v. temporary needs

Another way of thinking about the uses of various contracts of insurance is to consider whether the need is *temporary* or *permanent*. Unfortunately, these terms have different meanings to different people, and what would be a temporary need to one is a permanent need to another. Generally, whole life and retirement income contracts are considered to serve permanent needs, and term and endowment contracts are considered to serve temporary needs; hence these types of contracts have become known as permanent insurance and temporary insurance respectively. This is an unsatisfactory classification, however, because essentially all needs could be classed as temporary since, as Lord Keynes

---

[1] Certain long-period term insurance contracts have a small cash value, as will be explained later.

Figure 20–1

PROTECTION V. SAVINGS IN LIFE INSURANCE

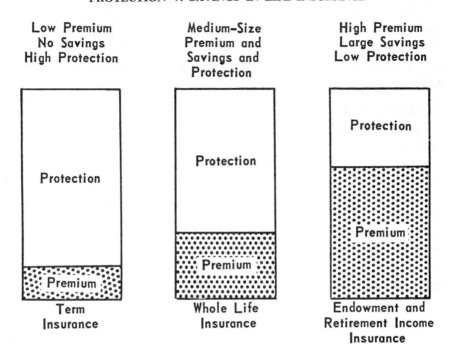

Low Premium No Savings High Protection	Medium-Size Premium and Savings and Protection	High Premium Large Savings Low Protection
Term Insurance	Whole Life Insurance	Endowment and Retirement Income Insurance

pointed out, "in the long run we are all dead." Term insurance is truly temporary, however, in the sense that it is not usually issued past the age of 65. Any life insurance needs which exist past this age will have to be satisfied by other contracts, which may be described as permanent since they may be kept in force for as long as is desired. All permanent contracts have an element of savings in them, for reasons which will be described below.

To illustrate, examples of temporary needs would include the following: (1) John Roman wishes to borrow $5,000 for a period of four years for the purpose of attending medical school. His uncle is willing to lend the money if John will take out a life insurance policy in favor of the uncle should John die before he graduates and is able to repay the loan. The protection is needed for five years only. John will probably find that a five-year term policy will be the most economical form of insurance for his purpose. (2) Erik Stone, age 35, is raising a family and his youngest child is now age five. He wishes to guarantee his family a minimum of $400 a month for 15 years in the event of his death. A term policy may be arranged to fill this need. On the other hand, if Erik wishes to guarantee his wife a minimum income of $200 a month for the rest of her life in the event of his death, a term policy will not work satisfactorily since this need is continuous until Erik's death. As we have seen, Erik has a much greater probability of living to age 65 than of not living until that age. Hence, he would have to purchase a whole life contract, which may be kept in force indefinitely.

The level premium concept

Life insurance is usually issued on a *level premium basis,* which means that the same premium is charged throughout the term of the contract. This was once a startling innovation, since it was reasoned that due to the rising probability of death with age, it would be impossible to charge a flat premium which would compensate for the rising mortality costs. The first life insurance policies were issued for one year only and were renewable at the end of this year at a higher rate, providing the insured was still in good health. These contracts are still issued and are known as *yearly renewable term policies.*[2] The level premium idea is considered one of the most basic advances ever made in the development of life insurance. With this concept it became possible to issue policies for longer and longer periods until finally whole life contracts were made a regular part of the business. Actuaries, using refined mortality statistics, could calculate exactly how much had to be charged in the early years of the contract in order to make up for the rising mortality costs of the later years. This idea is illustrated in Figure 20–2.

Figure 20–2 gives a comparison of the annual rates charged for a level premium contract, term to 65, and the one-year renewable term policy per $1,000 of face amount. The insured, age 20, has his choice of purchasing the former contract at an annual premium of $6.47 for 45 years, or of paying successively higher rates which began at $4.17 and graduate to $35.68 at age 64. This ever-increasing rate follows the upward curve of mortality plotted on Chart 19–1, page 511. At age 40 the *break-even point* of these two contracts is reached. Above this age, the rate for a one-year renewable term policy rises above the rate for the level term. The "overpayments" in the early years of the term to 65 policy, together with interest, represented by the shaded area to left of the break-even point in Figure 20–2, balance the excess "underpayments" area shown by the shaded area to the right of the break-even point.

---

[2] However, modern contracts are practically always guaranteed renewable for specified periods without evidence of continued good health.

Figure 20–2

**COMPARISON OF ANNUAL NONPARTICIPATING PREMIUMS ON THE
ONE-YEAR RENEWABLE TERM CONTRACT AND THE LEVEL PREMIUM,
TERM TO 65, CONTRACT**

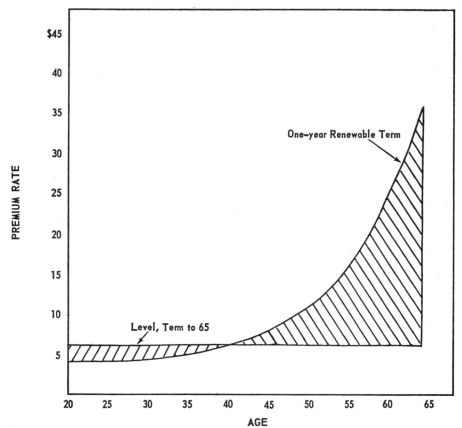

The insured would pay smaller total amounts under the one-year renewable term contract if his intention is to let the contract lapse before the size of the shaded area to the left of the break-even point is counterbalanced by an equal area to the right. It will be seen that the shaded area on the right is larger than that on the left. This difference is roughly accounted for by interest earnings on the overpayment funds held by the insurer and compounded over the years that the policy is in force. Age 64 is the last date on which the one-year renewable term contract may be renewed. Protection under the term to 65 contract expires at age 65.

The overpayment in the early years of a level premium life insurance policy is not really an overpayment in the sense that the insured is paying more than he should for his protection. The insurer acts as a trustee of the premium funds, which belong to the policyholders as a group, and reduces the premium to reflect the interest earnings. The accumulation thus made is known as the *cash surrender value,* or the *reserve.*[3] If the insured desires, he may borrow this value or may recapture it completely upon lapsing the policy. In term policies which span many years, the size of the cash surrender value is relatively small; and for bookkeeping reasons, the insurer does not return any of these amounts to the insured, although the premium is reduced below what it would be without the interest earnings that are made. On permanent contracts the size of the cash surrender value is substantial and constitutes the savings element referred to before.

The reason for having a savings element in life insurance, thus, is to smooth out premium payments over a long period of years. The insurer does not accumulate reserves merely to have funds with which to engage in the investment business or to set itself up as a savings bank. The reserve has its main purpose in meeting the very substantial burden of high mortality costs in the later years of the contract. Without the reserve, it would be impossible to offer continued protection beyond a certain age, roughly age 65. There are many needs for life insurance which extend beyond this age, such as the need for a death expense fund, the need for a fund to provide income for a widow, and for tax purposes.

MAJOR TYPES OF CONTRACTS

As explained previously, the major contracts of life insurance are of three types—term, whole life, and endowment. There are also "package" contracts which represent combinations of these three basic types. Countless names are applied by individual insurers for specific policies issued, but all policies are simply combinations of the three basic types. Some of the more important of these combinations, which are listed below, and their uses will be analyzed in this chapter:

Term Insurance
Level-term contract
Decreasing-term contract

Whole Life Insurance
Ordinary life contract
Limited-payment life contract

---

[3] There is a technical difference between the cash surrender value and the reserve, which will be explained in Chapter 27.

Endowment Insurance
Short-term contract
Retirement income contract

Package Contracts
Family income policy
Family maintenance policy
Specials
Modified life insurance policy
Multiple protection insurance policy
Juvenile insurance
Family group policy

Table 20–1 indicates the relative importance of these contracts as measured by the total face amount of life insurance in force by major category in 1957. Term insurance and whole life insurance shared an approximately equal part, each accounting for about 45 per cent of the total; endowment insurance constituted but 10 per cent of the total. It should be remembered, however, that the average premium for an endowment contract is much higher than that for a whole life contract or for a term contract; thus, from the viewpoint of premium volume, endowments are more significant than this table would indicate. Nevertheless, it seems obvious that a great majority of life insurance is purchased on the term or whole life plan. Combination contracts have been incor-

Table 20–1

MAJOR TYPES OF LIFE INSURANCE IN FORCE, BY PRIVATE INSURERS 1957

Type of Insurance	(Millions of Dollars)	Per cent of Total
Term insurance		
Individual policies..............	$ 56,200	12.3
Group policies.................	151,900	33.0
Total.......................	$208,100	45.3
Whole life insurance		
Ordinary life...................	$126,700	27.1
Limited payment life............	81,200	17.5
Total.......................	$207,900	44.6
Endowment insurance		
Endowment....................	$ 30,600	7.7
Retirement income..............	11,700	2.4
Total.......................	$ 42,300	10.1
Grand total..................	458,300	100.0

Source: *Life Insurance Fact Book, 1959*, p. 14. Percentages calculated.

porated into these totals according to the basic type of insurance of which they are composed. It is likely that term insurance would not loom so important as it does without the large growth in group term and credit insurance [4] which has taken place since 1950. The 1957 level of these types was three times its 1950 level, compared with only a 50 per cent increase in the level of whole life coverage in the same period. Insurance in force under endowments and retirement income policies showed only a 10 per cent rise in the period 1950–1957, indicating that the insuring public apparently preferred other methods of saving during this period. Some of the reasons for these preferences will be explored in Chapter 22.

When confronted with the task of purchasing an appropriate type of insurance, the buyer is usually presented with information such as the premium rates at different ages together with statements of the savings element in each type of contract. He must then decide which type is best for him. However, this selection may be difficult to make without further knowledge. Typical participating premium rates for common policies of insurance, issued at age 30, together with their cash values after 10 and 20 years, are shown below:

Type of Insurance	Annual Premium Per $1,000	Cash Value in 10 Years	Cash Value in 20 Years
5-year term....................	$ 6.46	0	0
Ordinary life...................	21.53	$178.43	$ 370.83
20-payment life................	32.37	295.51	661.69
20-year endowment............	47.43	431.69	1,000.00

Thus, the 5-year term policy is seen to be the least expensive, but it has no cash values. The ordinary life contract costs over three times as much as the 5-year term contract, but the insured may recover a substantial part of this premium (an average of $17.84 per year of the total premium of $21.53 after ten years) by cashing in his policy for its cash value. In addition he will be entitled to dividends. In the long run, therefore, the insured's financial condition may be improved by purchasing ordinary life insurance rather than term, if he can afford the higher initial rate. The rate for 20-payment life insurance is about 50 per cent greater than ordinary life insurance, but its guaranteed cash value is about 65 per cent higher than that of ordinary life, after ten years. The 20-year endowment policy costs about 45 per cent more than the 20-

---

[4] See Chapter 21 for a discussion of group insurance.

payment life contract, and its cash values are correspondingly higher than the 20-payment life policy. Some of the reasons for these relationships will be explored below.

Term insurance

As indicated before, *term insurance* contracts are issued for a specified number of years and do not contain any savings element. In this regard they are similar to other types of insurance in property and liability lines. Term contracts therefore provide a greater amount of pure protection per premium dollar than any other type of insurance. For example, a $100 annual premium would purchase approximately $11,000 of coverage on a person age 30, on a 10-year level-term contract. The same premium spent on whole life insurance would purchase about $5,300 of coverage, slightly less than half as much as that provided under the term contract. For this reason term insurance is used most often when:

1. The maximum coverage is desired and the amount available for premiums is limited.
2. The period during which the protection is needed does not extend past age 65.

Level-term contract. A *level-term contract* is issued for a constant amount during its term. Examples are 5-year renewable term, 10-year renewable term, 20-year renewable term, and term to 65. Level-term contracts are practically always *renewable* without evidence of insurability; thus, an objection is removed that was formerly attributable to this type of contract in that a person's policy could expire and leave him without protection in case he was then uninsurable. *Uninsurability* in life insurance generally means that a person's physical condition is such that he fails to meet the minimum medical and other selection standards on which mortality tables are based. Other factors, such as occupation and credit standing, also enter into the meaning of uninsurability. About three per cent of all applications for life insurance are rejected because of uninsurability. About five per cent of all applications are accepted at an extra premium for unusual risk.[5] The probability of uninsurability, while not great, is nevertheless important and so the right of renewal without medical examination is an important feature. In the case of most insurers, however, this right expires at age 60 or 65.

---

[5] *Life Insurance Fact Book*, 1961, p. 94.

Decreasing term. When the amount of pure death protection gradually declines each year on a term contract, the policy is described as one of *decreasing term.* The premium payable may be constant over the term, but the insurance protection decreases. A good example of the use of decreasing term insurance is in credit life insurance and in mortgage protection insurance. As an insured repays an obligation, such as a mortgage debt, the amount of coverage decreases steadily, corresponding to the declining balance of the debt. In this way the coverage is tailored to meet the need for which the insurance was designed. Since the face amount of decreasing term insurance is, on the average, considerably less than the face amount involved in a level-term contract, the premium is correspondingly lower. Another manner in which decreasing-term insurance is employed is in the family income policy, to be discussed later.

Convertibility. Most term insurance policies are *convertible,* that is, they may be changed into a permanent form of coverage at or before the date of their expiration, without evidence of insurability. In this way a person may take out term insurance with the idea of maximizing his coverage during a period when his protection needs are at a maximum, and then convert his insurance to a permanent form of insurance for use in later years.[6]

Some contracts may be converted retroactively; that is, the insured may pay a sum of money representing the accumulated difference between premiums actually paid and premiums which would have been paid at the age of issue had a permanent form of coverage been purchased. In this way one may obtain a permanent form of insurance at a lower premium (the rate at the original age of issue) than would be possible if he converted his contract as of his attained age. It is doubtful if such a procedure is to be recommended, however, unless the individual wishes to use the insurance as a method of saving money. This question is discussed in Chapter 22.

Whole life insurance

As the name suggests, *whole life insurance* may be kept in force for as long as is desired or until the contract expires, which is never past age 100. There are many different ways of arranging premium payments for whole life insurance, ranging from continuous installments over a person's entire life (ordinary or straight-life plan) to a single installment (single-premium whole life). In other words, an insured, at age 35, may

---

[6] Some term policies require conversion before the protection period expires. Thus, the conversion and protection periods do not necessarily coincide.

pay a single sum, say $5,000 for a $10,000 policy, and never pay another premium. At his death the insurer pays the insured's beneficiary, $10,000. If the insured does not have $5,000 with which to pay the single premium (and few are those who are able to do so), he may pay in installments over whatever length of time is desired.

An *ordinary* or *straight life* contract is one so arranged that the premiums are payable as long as the insured lives. The contract is not "paid up" until one reaches age 100 or dies, whichever event comes sooner. (Sometimes additional cash payments or the use of dividends to "pay up" the contract will effectively convert the true ordinary life policy into a "paid up" policy sooner than this.) A *limited payment life policy,* on the other hand, is one which is so arranged that the insured pays a higher premium than he would on the ordinary life plan so that a definite termination date can be established beyond which no further payments are due. The most common limited installment plans are 20-payment life, 30-payment life, and life paid up at age 65.

Figure 20–3 illustrates the various plans of whole life insurance. On the left vertical axis may be read the face amount of the policy. This amount is made up of two parts, the amount "at risk" and the amount in the reserve fund. For example, line SP shows that if one pays for his whole life policy in one lump sum, he has immediately after purchase a reserve fund of approximately $500. If he should die the next day, the insurer would pay his beneficiary the face amount of the policy, $1,000. It may be seen then that the *amount at risk* to the insurer was really only $500. On the other hand, for the ordinary life policy, represented by line OP, if the insured pays one premium, he has no reserve fund available to him at that time; but if he should die the next day, the insurer would pay his beneficiary $1,000. Thus, the amount at risk is almost the full face of the contract. As time goes on, the reserve fund grows, since the premium paid in the early years exceeds the amount needed for mortality expenses. If the insured is fortunate enough to live to age 100, his reserve fund reaches the full face of the policy and the insurer will consider the contract to have matured and will pay the insured $1,000. Occasionally this actually happens, and when it does, the lucky individual's picture usually appears in the newspaper with an official of the insurer handing him a check.

There is a difference between a policy that is *paid up* and one that is *matured*. When conditions occur to obligate the insurer to pay the *face amount* of the policy, the contract is said to have matured and, hence, terminated. This occurs in the event of death or when the cash

Figure 20–3

HOW PREMIUM PAYMENT ARRANGEMENTS AFFECT RESERVE VALUES IN COMMON LIFE INSURANCE CONTRACTS

The shaded portion represents the reserve fund in the ordinary life policy at different ages. The reserve fund in other policies is represented by total area beneath each line, OE, SP, OAP, and OBP respectively.

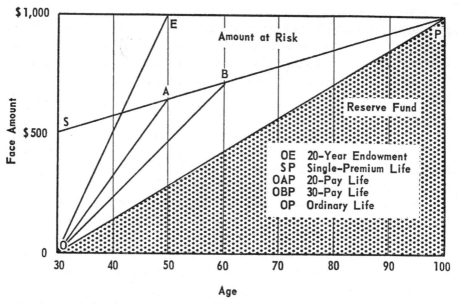

values equal the face amount of the contract. Line OE in Figure 20–3 represents the reserve line of the 20-year endowment contract. This line rises steeply so that 20 years after issuance of the contract, the cash values equal the face amount and the contract is terminated by maturity. Line OAP, on the other hand, representing the 20-pay life contract, rises to a certain point (point A) after which the policy is paid up. This means that the cash values, together with the interest which may be earned on this amount, will be sufficient to enable the insurer to meet its obligations to all policyholders, to contribute each year a share of the mortality expenses, and to build up the principal so that *at age 100* the cash values will equal the face of the policy, $1,000. After age 50 (point A) the insured need pay no more premiums, but his cash value is not equal to the face of the policy, as it is in the 20-year endowment policy. For a typical insurer, the 20-pay life contract with a face of $1,000 has a cash value of about $600 after it is fully paid. A whole life contract is really "endowment at age 100" and is in fact sometimes referred to in this way, because the face amount of the policy is equal to its cash value at age 100.

Figure 20–3 illustrates the fact that the shorter the premium payment period, the higher the premium and the more rapidly the build-up of cash values. Thus, line OAP rises faster than line OBP since if the insured wishes to pay all premiums in a 20-year span, he must naturally pay more than he would (and he saves faster) if he had elected to pay the premiums over a period of 30 years. Of course, the faster the premium is paid up and the faster the reserve is built up, the less is the amount at risk. In any of the plans illustrated, at the time of death the insurer must pay $1,000 to the insured's beneficiary. However, the insurer "loses" less with the high-premium policy than it does with the low-premium policy. That is to say, the $1,000 paid to the beneficiary is made up of two parts—the reserve element and the protection element. The beneficiary collects the insured's own savings and in addition receives a contribution from the other insureds. If the insured lives to age 100, he receives back his own money. Consideration of this point shows why it is that the reserve is not entirely used up to compensate for the high mortality rate experienced by the insurer in the later years of the contract. We saw previously (Table 19–1) that the mortality rate at age 80 is 5½ times as great as the rate at age 60. At age 80 the mortality cost per $1,000 might be approximately $220 or higher. Thus, the reserve would be gone in a year or two if the full $1,000 were at risk. Actually, the amount at risk declines sharply as the reserve rises, and so the mortality costs are kept within bounds. Finally, at age 100 the mortality element is extinguished entirely. This is as it should be, for at age 100 actuaries consider death a certainty. As we have learned, it is not feasible to insure against certainties. The older one becomes, the more and more probable death becomes each year, and the amount at risk in the contract thus declines steadily in permanent whole life contracts.

Endowment insurance

Endowment contracts are primarily savings contracts with an element of pure protection incorporated into the policy so that if the insured dies before his savings plan is completed, the insurer "completes it for him."

To see how an endowment contract works, assume that Adam Jones, age 35, sets for himself the goal of saving $1,000 in 20 years. If Adam could receive four per cent interest in a savings institution, he would have to make annual deposits of $36.13 for 20 years for a total of $722.60 in order to reach his goal. Now assume that he wishes to have a guarantee that in the event of his death before the 20 years have passed, his wife will still receive $1,000. If he purchases renewable term insurance each year for the difference between $1,000 and the amount currently on hand, the total cost of the insurance would be about $163. The total outlay to him would be $885.60. If Adam purchased a 20-year endowment policy,[7] he accomplishes this same goal for an annual premium of $46.50, or $930 for 20 years. While the endowment contract may cost him somewhat more, there are certain features in this contract which partially offset the added cost. A more complete analysis of these features in the insurance policy and the use of life insurance as a savings method will be treated in the next two chapters.

Short-term endowment contracts are those for a given period of years, usually 5, 10, 15, 20, or 30 years. A very common period is 20 years. Endowments are commonly used as savings for some specified purpose, such as for educational purposes, retirement, or travel funds. In this way, if the saver dies before the period has expired, the purpose for which the savings plan was set up can often be accomplished by the insured's dependents.

Retirement income policy. *Retirement income policies* are similar to endowments except that the former are arranged so that their cash values mount to a sum sufficient to provide $10 a month life income at retirement age, usually 65, for each $1,000 of face amount. Endowment policies are purchased for varying periods, such as a 10-year endowment, 20-year endowment, 30-year endowment, and endowment at age 65. They mature for their face value at the end of this term. At maturity, retirement income policies have a cash value equal to about $1,700 for each $1,000 of face amount (some policies have different face amounts). The reason for this is that it requires about $1,700 to purchase a life annuity of $10 a month at age 65. The face amount of the retirement income policy is still $1,000 so that if death occurs before retirement, the insurer will pay $1,000 or the cash value, if it is greater. Since cash values mount rapidly under the retirement income policy, the insurance element in the contract is relatively small. Annuities are analyzed in Chapter 22.

Package contracts

Family income policy. A *family income policy* is a combination of decreasing-term insurance and ordinary life insurance. It is nearly

---

[7] The rates quoted assume 3 per cent interest on reserves, CSO 1941, nonparticipating.

always issued on a level-premium basis. As its name suggests, the family income policy is designed to provide a large amount of pure protection during a time when children are young and at the same time to provide some permanent insurance. The *base* of the contract is usually ordinary life insurance, to which is added a decreasing-term *rider*. The insurance under the rider is commonly expressed as so many units of income at $10 a unit. Thus, a family income policy may be composed of $10,000 ordinary life insurance plus 10 units of decreasing-term insurance, $15,000 of ordinary life insurance with 15 units of decreasing-term insurance, etc. The policy is usually arranged so that the beneficiary receives $100 (or $150) a month for a specified period, and then $10,000 (or $15,000) at the *end* of this period. The $10,000 ($15,000) is held by the insurer, and interest on this sum is used to help make the income payments.

The term rider is "decreasing" because the period during which the income would be payable in the event of death decreases as time goes on. For example, let us say that Jack takes out a $10,000 family income policy with a 20-year decreasing-term rider when he is age 25 and his youngest child is age one. The income is payable to his family from a period dating from his death until the time he would have been 45, or until the youngest child is 21. If Jack dies 10 years after the policy is issued, the payments are made for 10 years. If he dies 15 years after the policy is issued, the payments are made for five years, after which the $10,000 payable under the ordinary life insurance portion is settled. At the end of 20 years, if Jack has survived the period, the term rider expires and this portion of the policy is terminated. The premium is usually reduced accordingly and Jack may continue the ordinary life insurance portion as long as he wishes.

The family income policy is one of the most popular contracts of life insurance sold because it constitutes a small program of insurance in itself. It represents a balanced solution to the twin needs of both temporary and permanent life insurance. The term rider is generally available for varying periods—5, 10, 15, or 20 years—so that income may be provided until the children reach a certain designated age. Some insurers offer the term rider by itself without the necessity of the insured purchasing any permanent insurance along with it. Many insurers will also issue a term rider that may be attached to any permanent policy already issued on the life of the insured.

Family maintenance policy. The *family maintenance policy* is a combination of ordinary life insurance and level-term insurance and should not be confused with the family income policy. Under the family maintenance policy, in the event of the insured's death before the expiration of a certain period, the income payments are made for a stated number of years. In the family income policy, however, the income is paid only until the end of a stipulated period.

In the preceding example, if Jack has a 20-year family maintenance policy and dies 15 years after the policy is issued, the income is paid for 20 years, and not just five. However, if Jack survives the 20 years, the rider expires and he may continue only the basic policy.

The family maintenance policy has an advantage over the family income policy in that the widow may receive the payments for the full 20 years in the example above or for however long the income period may be. Of course, the family maintenance policy will cost more than the family income policy because of this feature. Since the family maintenance policy differs but little from the two contracts of which it is composed, if bought separately, the insured will frequently prefer the added flexibility of buying the protection separately. The family maintenance policy has not been widely used.

Specials. Many insurers issue what have become known as *specials* —life insurance contracts with a specified minimum face amount at reduced prices. The economy rates involved in specials may stem from a number of sources. For example, it costs less to issue one policy for $5,-000, or $10,000, than it does to issue 5 or 10 policies of $1,000 each. Reductions in cost may also be made because the contracts are issued only to *preferred risks,* individuals who pass very rigid underwriting standards. Savings may also stem from a reduction of the agent's commissions on the sale of the contracts. Each of these sources of economy appears to be a legitimate method of reducing the cost of distributing life insurance. Some insurers, however, make "savings" in what appear to be less legitimate ways. For example, specials may contain reduced schedules of cash values, fewer settlement options, less generous settlement options, or reduction of other services. It is not easy for the typical buyer to evaluate the differences, with the result that misleading comparisons may be made with regular contracts. Even though abuses of this kind may occur in the offering of specials, it appears desirable that insurers tailor their offerings to fit as closely as possible the varying needs of the public, particularly when reductions in distribution costs become possible.

Modified life insurance contracts. *Modified life insurance contracts* are those in which the premiums are arranged so that they are smaller than average for the first 5 or 10 years of the policy and slightly larger than average for the remaining years of the contract. This is done by combining term insurance with some form of permanent insurance so that the insured pays more than the term policy would cost at his age, but less than the cost of the permanent insurance at his age. Modified life contracts thus enable the insured to obtain a permanent insurance policy at a cost which is usually one half of what he would normally pay for the first five or ten years. The contract fits the needs of the young married man with a limited income who wants to develop a permanent insurance program but cannot afford to do so until his income rises. The solution could also be found in the purchase of straight convertible term insurance, but human nature being what it is, many persons would fail to convert term insurance into a permanent form because the premium increase is quite substantial. The modified life contract has the advantage that it is not necessary for the insured to take any positive action to convert the contract to a permanent form.

Multiple protection insurance contract. The *multiple protection insurance contract* employs term insurance to grant double, triple, or some multiple of the face amount of a permanent insurance policy for a set period, from 5 to 20 years, after which the protection is reduced to the face amount of the permanent policy. Thus, instead of using the term principle to reduce the cost of a set amount of coverage, as is true of modified life insurance, the multiple protection contract grants added coverage in a way very similar to the family maintenance policy.

Juvenile insurance. Life insurance issued on children is called *juvenile insurance.* For very young children, say between the ages of 1 and 4, it is common to provide graded death benefits, so as to limit the life insurance coverage to modest amounts, such as less than $500. As the child gets older, the coverage increases automatically until it reaches some limit, say $1,000, or a multiple thereof. Normally this coverage is issued only on some permanent insurance form.

Jumping juvenile insurance. A package contract, sometimes called *jumping juvenile,* is issued in units of say $1,000 at some early age. The amount automatically increases to say $5,000 at age 21, without increasing the premium and without evidence of insurability. Oftentimes this insurance is sold as a savings program for college education.

The jumping juvenile insurance plan has certain advantages, but also some serious disadvantages. The advantages include the fact that it provides some permanent life insurance protection even if the child should become uninsurable later on; it instills the savings habit at an early date; and it enables the establishment of an insurance program at a low premium age. The disadvantage is that this plan takes away insurance dollars that probably ought to be spent on the breadwinner. All the advantages are lost, however, if the child should die; but if the father dies and the mother is unable to support the child through primary and secondary schools because the father left little or no income security, nor money to pay the premiums on the child's contract, then it is clear that juvenile insurance will not serve its purpose. In view of the great under-insurance which exists on human life generally, it is doubtful if much money for juvenile coverage can be justified in most homes, particularly when it is issued in substantial amounts on forms that are primarily savings contracts.

Payor clause.   Insurers offer what is known as a payor clause on a juvenile policy which states that if the owner (usually the father) dies before the policy matures, all future premiums are waived until the child reaches age 21. This clause really amounts to additional insurance on the life of the father.

Family group policy. One of the most successful life insurance packages introduced in recent years is the *family group policy,* in which each member of the family is insured for different amounts. The head of the family normally obtains the most coverage and insurance on the spouse and children is limited to smaller amounts. Not uncommonly, if the owner of the policy is covered for $5,000, the spouse and the children will have $1,000 each. The $5,000 contract may be term or permanent insurance, but coverage on the spouse and the children is usually convertible term insurance. One premium is charged for the entire package which solves a common need, that of a limited amount of protection for the breadwinner's dependents, combined with insurance on the family head.

SUMMARY

1. Life insurance is a method of creating an estate of income-producing property. It is the only method of creating an immediate estate in case of premature death; it serves as a hedge against the possibility that the insured may not live to carry out his property accumulation plans.

2. The chief purpose of life insurance in estate planning is to provide for dependents in case of death of the breadwinner. A secondary purpose of life

insurance is to save money for one's retirement or for other purposes. Policies are available which meet these twin purposes with many different degrees of emphasis.

3. Life insurance is commonly issued on a level-premium basis. Because death rates rise substantially over a long period of years, more money must be collected in the early years to offset the higher mortality costs of the later years. For this reason all policies except pure term insurance accumulate a cash value known as the reserve.

4. The reserve in life insurance not only serves to keep the premium level throughout the premium-paying period, but it also serves many other purposes. The insured may view the reserve as a savings fund to draw on in emergencies, as a buffer against the possible lapse of the policy, as collateral for a bank loan, or as a retirement fund. The reserve makes possible the continuance of life insurance beyond age 65, a period in which there are still many needs for protection.

5. The major types of life insurance—term, whole life, and endowment—may be purchased separately or in many different combinations to meet the specific needs of insureds. Measured by the face amount of protection outstanding, term and whole life insurance each share about 45 per cent of the total market, while endowment contracts account for the remaining 10 per cent. Of the three types, term insurance has grown most rapidly since 1950.

QUESTIONS FOR REVIEW AND DISCUSSION

1. (a) What is meant by the future estate? the present estate?
   (b) How does life insurance protect these estates?

2. It has been stated that life insurance is property. What general characteristics of property are possessed by life insurance?

3. It has been stated that the trouble with life insurance is that one has to die in order to collect. Is this an accurate statement? If so, why? If not, restate it more correctly.

4. "What is temporary for one person may be permanent for another." Explain, giving examples, what you consider to be a permanent need as opposed to a temporary need for life insurance.

5. All permanent life insurance contracts have cash values, but not all contracts with cash values are permanent. Do you agree? Why?

6. Why do life insurers issue contracts with an overcharge in the premium, while property and liability insurers do not? Explain.

7. A critic of life insurance stated, "If you die . . . the cash values die with you. Your cash values are ever hopelessly trapped. When you borrow

this money, your own very hard-saved dough, they charge you interest on it. Did you ever hear of such a slick deal—paying somebody interest to borrow your own money?" As a student of life insurance, answer this criticism.

8. The critic referred to in Question 7 also stated, "Whereas that actuarial table of 1941 states that 4.59 out of every 1,000 men starting their 35th year would die in that year, as a matter of fact the experience of several large companies suggests that on the average only 2.9 out of every 1,000 men actually did die. Thus, you come upon the first of a series of life insurance overcharges. The major companies were tucking away $1.69 per annum per $1,000 in a perfectly obvious overcharge." Is this statement true or false? Would you draw the same conclusion from it as has been apparently drawn by the author of the remarks? Why?

9. Obtain the latest *Life Insurance Fact Book* and compare recent trends in the growth of each major type of life insurance—term, whole life, and endowment—for the last 20 years.
   (a) What do you observe?
   (b) How do you account for the trends noted?

10. "The idea of paying up a policy in 20 years rather than 'paying all my life' is appealing, but it has certain drawbacks which often make this course of action of doubtful merit." Mention some of the drawbacks to which reference is made.

11. For what major purposes should term insurance be used? whole life insurance? endowment insurance? Defend your answers.

12. John Smith, age 30, has a family of five, with children aged three, five, and ten. He earns $7,000 per year and figures that he can devote $500 a year to life insurance. He is covered by social security, and has a group life insurance certificate for $7,000 in connection with his employment.
   (a) For what types of life insurance would you recommend that John spend his insurance budget? Defend your choices.
   (b) How much death protection will your selections provide if John should die tomorrow?

13. Would your answer be any different in Question 12 if John Smith earned $15,000 and his three children were aged, 22, 24, and 29?

14. Payments cease 20 years after a 20-pay life or a 20-year endowment contract is issued, but at that time one is matured, while the other is paid up. What is the difference between a policy that is paid up and one that is matured?

15. A critic of life insurance asked, "Why is it that whole life policies endow at age 100 when most men are dead?" How would you answer him?

16. If one were to draw the appropriate line of a term-to-65 policy on Figure 20–3, page 538, where would the line be drawn? Why?

17. "Z" bought a $1,000 ordinary life policy at age 30 for an annual premium of $21.53. In five years its cash value was $86.66; in 10 years, $178.43; in 15 years, $273.82; and in 20 years, $370.83. A $1,000 term policy could have been purchased for a cost of $6.46 per year the first five years; $7.31 per year for the second five years; $9.87 per year for the third five years; and $13.02 per year for the last five years.
    (a) What is the net cost of "Z's" protection under each plan after (1) 5 years, (2) 10 years, (3) 15 years, and (4) 20 years? (Net cost = Premiums − Cash Value)
    (b) How do you account for the differences noted?

18. "A" requests information concerning the family income policy. He wants to know (a) why the company does not pay the proceeds of the base policy immediately upon death of the insured, instead of at the end of the time period, and (b) why the income does not continue for a full 20 years from date of death, instead of stopping after the elapse of a 20-year period dating from the issuance of the contract. Can you suggest reasons why these conditions prevail?

19. A certain insurer offers a family income policy with the following conditions: No base policy is required and the policy can be arranged so that the income may continue for any number of years desired, but not to exceed the period which would require payments after the insured reaches age 65.
    (a) What type of basic life insurance is being used in this plan?
    (b) What advantages, if any, does it have over the usual family income policy?

20. One of the advantages claimed for permanent insurance is that it provides an automatic protection against lapse. How might this be done?

21. A certain insurer offers an ordinary life policy at age 25 at the rate of $18.56 per year per $1,000, and offers an "economy size" policy with a minimum face amount of $3,000, at the rate of $16.20 per year per $1,000.
    (a) Explain the possible sources from which these savings might stem.
    (b) Are all these sources legitimate ways in which the insured may economize?

22. (a) What objections might there be to the purchase of juvenile insurance?
    (b) Are there any advantages to its purchase? Discuss.

Contractual Provisions

of Life Insurance

The contractual provisions of the life insurance policy are of special significance to the insured because it is through a wise use of certain of these contract rights that some of the most valuable benefits of the protection can be obtained. Furthermore, there are few contracts of insurance which contain more provisions directly bearing on the welfare of the insured. Life insurance is usually a long-term contract effective long after the death of the insured, and a clear understanding of at least the more important provisions is vital if the services of the insurer and the agent are to be employed effectively in carrying out the intentions of the insured regarding his estate. Among the more important of these provisions, many of which are standardized and required by law, are:

    I. Nonforfeiture options
        A. Cash and loan value option
        B. Extended term option
        C. Paid-up insurance option
    II. Settlement options
        A. Lump sum
        B. Fixed period option
        C. Fixed amount option
        D. Interest option
        E. Life income option
    III. Clauses designed primarily for protection of insureds and beneficiaries
        A. Incontestable clause
        B. Suicide clause
        C. Reinstatement and grace period clause
        D. Automatic premium loan clause
        E. Misstatement of age clause
        F. Entire contract clause
        G. Spendthrift trust clause
    IV. Miscellaneous contractual provisions
        A. Dividend options
        B. Extensions of coverage
            1. Waiver of premium rider
            2. Disability income rider
            3. Double indemnity rider

C. Assignments
D. Premium payment
E. Excluded perils
F. Change of beneficiary

NONFORFEITURE OPTIONS

The *nonforfeiture options* in life insurance are so named because they guarantee that the reserve element in the policy will not be forfeited to the insurer under any circumstances, but will always accrue to the benefit of the insured. There are three ways in which the insured may receive the reserve: 1) a lump sum paid in cash, 2) extended term insurance, and 3) paid-up insurance of a reduced amount.[1]

1) Cash and loan value option

The *cash and loan value option* enables the insured to remove his savings from the contract either with or without terminating the contract. If emergency cash is needed, but it is not desired to terminate the policy, the cash value may be borrowed from the insurer and interest paid on this loan. Since the insurer has calculated the original premium under the assumption that interest would be earned on reserves, interest is charged to anyone, including the insured himself, who uses these reserves. At the time the insured is using his own reserve in this manner and paying interest on it, the insurer is crediting the insured's account with interest that it is earning on its assets. Thus, the insured may be paying five per cent interest on his insurance loan and receiving three per cent interest in the form of credits to his reserve account. The loan thus costs him only two per cent interest. This cost is necessary because policy loans are offered as an accommodation to the insured and are expensive to administer. The above arguments destroy the oft-expressed fallacy that it is inequitable for the insurer to charge the insured for the loan of his own money. It is not actually the insured's money but that of the policyholders as a group. If the insured dies with an outstanding loan on his policy, the amount of the loan is subtracted from the policy proceeds. Otherwise, there is never any obligation to repay the loan. If the entire cash value has been borrowed, it is necessary, of course, for the insured to pay the annual interest in cash in order to avoid lapse.

---

[1] Before the advent of nonforfeiture options (which are required by law in all states), there were cases where aged persons agreed to sell their policies to speculators when they could no longer continue the premium payments. The speculator's offer depended on the physical condition of the aged person, and a public sale often took place with the aged person present so he could be examined. Needless to say, the insured seldom fared well in these transactions. Elizur Wright, an early insurance commissioner in Massachusetts, was instrumental in outlawing these practices.

2) Extended term option

If the insured has made no selection as to which option he wishes, most insurers automatically use the *extended term option*. The cash value of the contract at the time of lapse is used to purchase a term policy for as many months or years as are allowed by the rates in effect at the insured's age when the lapse occurred. A table in the contract states just how long this period is at various ages. Thus, for one insurer an ordinary life policy issued at age 35 in force for 20 years has a guaranteed cash value of $370.83 per $1,000. If the insured wishes to terminate the contract, he may take the money in cash or he may receive term insurance of $1,000 for 16 years and 325 days.

3) Paid-up insurance option

The insured in the example above might select the *paid-up insurance option* and thus receive a paid-up ordinary life policy of $561. This means that no further permium payments would be necessary and that the insurer would pay $561 upon the insured's death no matter when it may occur. This is almost the same as if the insured had purchased a single-premium ordinary life policy of $561 face amount for a lump-sum premium of $370.83.[2]

The nonforfeiture options are very important to the insured. The insured cannot "lose" his savings because of his inability to continue premium payments, and in addition he has the right to continue his insurance protection in two different ways if he so desires. This exposes a fallacy often heard in reference to ordinary life insurance, namely, that the trouble with it is that one has to pay premiums "all his life." Actually, one may stop paying premiums at any time and elect one of the nonforfeiture options. The extended term option has benefited many a widow who discovered that a policy which she thought had lapsed because of nonpayment of premiums was actually still in force under the extended term option. The paid-up insurance option is especially valuable when old age reduces the ability to continue payment of premiums and yet when continued protection is needed for a dependent wife.

SETTLEMENT OPTIONS

Settlement refers to the way in which the insurer pays the proceeds of the contract. The *settlement options* describe the different ways in which the insured may elect to have the proceeds of his policy paid to

---

[2] However, the insured pays no acquisition expenses for insurance purchased under dividend options or nonforfeiture options, and so it might be said that this is a very economical way to acquire insurance.

his beneficiaries or to himself, whether the proceeds be death proceeds or a liquidation of the cash values of the contract. There are many settlement options and combinations thereof, but the most common are: 1) lump sum option, 2) fixed period option, 3) fixed amount option, 4) interest option, and 5) life income option.

1) Lump sum option

Under the *lump sum option,* proceeds of the life insurance are paid in a lump sum, and the insurer's obligations are ended. The insurer exercises no further control over the money and the various services offered in connection with other options are lost. For this reason lump sum settlements are employed most often when the insured or his beneficiary needs the money for a purpose which may be best served by a cash amount, such as for liquidation of a mortgage, for payment of last expenses, and for paying taxes. A vast majority of all life insurance policies are settled under this option.

2) Fixed period option

Rather than being paid in a lump sum, the insured may select the *fixed period option* under which he directs the insurer to pay the policy proceeds in installments over a set time period. Under this option the insurer issues a supplementary contract (the old policy having been terminated) in which it agrees to pay the proceeds as directed. No extra charge is made for this service, although if a separate trust would have had to be set up to accomplish the same thing, a substantial cost would be involved.

As an example of a situation in which the fixed period option would be used, consider the following case. An insured who, having provided for his family during the period when the children are young, wishes to set up an income for his wife, now age 36, to begin after their 7-year old child is 18 and to continue until the wife is aged 62. Social security income ceases during this period and the insured observes that, without at least a minimum income, the wife may be unable to meet current expenses even if she works, since help from the children is generally not likely to be substantial. The problem then is to provide an income to begin after a set number of years have passed and to continue for a given number of years. Using the fixed period option, the insured instructs the insurance company that if he should die, the proceeds of the policy are to be held at interest until the wife is age 47 and then paid out to her over a 15-year period. At the end of this period the wife will be 62 and social security retirement income payments will commence. The

amount of insurance proceeds necessary to accomplish this purpose may
be calculated from special programming tables designed for this purpose.
Thus, at three per cent interest, it can be calculated that it would require
$7,459 of proceeds to provide $100 per month for 15 years, the first
payment being due at the beginning of the eleventh year, and the fund
being exhausted at the end of the fifteenth year of payments.[3]

3) Fixed amount option

The *fixed amount option* is similar in purpose to the fixed period
option except that under the former option, payment of the proceeds is
arranged to provide a set income, with the *length of time* varying with
the interest assumptions and the total funds available. An insured may
wish to provide a certain minimum income to his family and will instruct
the insurer to pay this income for as long as the proceeds may last. Any
excess interest will lengthen the period, but not vary the amount.

4) Interest option

Under the *interest option,* the insurer holds the proceeds of the
policy and pays an income consisting of interest only. The recipient of
the income may have the right to withdraw the principal. This option is
often used in the following cases:

1. The proceeds of the policy may be intended to pay for last expenses, but it is not known just when these expenses will be payable. The proceeds are thus held at interest until needed and
   then withdrawn whenever the beneficiary wishes.

2. The proceeds of the policy are intended for use as an emergency
   fund for the wife. The policy is settled under the interest option
   with the right of withdrawal of principal as needed.

3. Interest is needed to supplement family income, but the principal is intended to go to a child when he becomes age 21. The
   proceeds are left under the interest option with interest payable
   to the wife, but without the right of withdrawal except by the
   named child when he becomes 21.

4. It is desired to use the principal to meet income needs at a later
   time, but to pay out interest currently to supplement family income. The proceeds are left under the interest option until a
   certain time has elapsed, and are then settled under the fixed
   period option, the fixed amount option, or the life income option.

---

[3] Not all insurers will accumulate interest on death proceeds of insurance.

5) Life income option

Under the *life income option,* the proceeds may be left in an annuity to guarantee the beneficiary a life income with or without any minimum number of guaranteed installments. Annuities will be analyzed in detail in Chapter 22.

Significance of settlement options

In 1959 it was estimated that 17 per cent, or $770 million, of the funds most likely to be used for income purposes (death benefits, matured endowments, and cash surrender values) was set aside for future payment under income settlement options. The remaining 83 per cent was paid in lump sums.[4] By the end of 1959 only $7.4 billion of funds had been accumulated for the purpose of settlement options and $980 million was paid out in 1959. It seems apparent from these data that either life insurance is being used primarily for lump-sum needs, or that policyholders as a group are somewhat unaware of the advantages of using income settlement options, or that alternative uses of insurance proceeds offer advantages, or that some combinations of these conditions are present.

By the use of settlement options, insurance can be arranged to guarantee the income security of which it is capable. It has been stated previously that the central purpose of life insurance is to replace income lost because of the premature death of the insured. If this is true, it is through income settlement options that the lost income can be replaced most economically and efficiently for the average person. Emphasis on settlement options furnishes a rationale for the purchase of life insurance and a guide for determining how much life insurance to purchase. In other words, the answer to the question of "How much life insurance should I buy?" may be answered "It depends mainly on how much income you wish to provide for yourself or your dependents." The principal sum necessary to furnish a given income level for different periods is then readily ascertainable.

Use of insurer services in managing the proceeds of the insurance costs the insured nothing extra. The proceeds are preserved from mismanagement by inexperienced beneficiaries, or from depletion by preying relatives or swindlers. The insured can rest in complete knowledge that fluctuations of the stock or bond market, a business depression, or other investment hazards will not interrupt the flow of income that he wishes to provide for his beneficiaries. Other advantages of the settlement

---

[4] *Life Insurance Fact Book, 1960,* p. 46.

options will become apparent from the material presented below and in Chapter 22. For example, there are tax advantages in the use of settlement options and the law has offered life insurance protection from certain hazards that beset other types of investments.

CLAUSES PROTECTING THE INSURED AND THE BENEFICIARY

In addition to the inherent protective features involved in nonforfeiture and settlement options, there are other important clauses in the life insurance contract. Some of these clauses, which have as their purpose to guarantee that the life insurance contract will accomplish the purposes for which it is intended, are required by law.

1) Incontestable clause

The *incontestable clause* states that if the policy has been in force for a given period, usually two years, and if the insured has not died during that time, the insurer may not afterward refuse to pay the proceeds nor may it cancel the contract, even because of fraud. Thus, if the insured is found to have lied about his physical condition at the time he applied for life insurance, but this misrepresentation is not discovered until after the expiration of the incontestable clause, the insurer may not cancel the policy nor refuse to pay the face amount if the insured has died from a cause not excluded under the basic terms of the policy.[5] Thus, the incontestable clause serves as a time limit within which the insurer must discover any fraud or misrepresentation in the application or be barred thereafter from asserting what would otherwise be its legal right—namely, the right to cancel the agreement. However, this provision is not typical of most insurance contracts. The legal justification for this clause in life insurance lies in the purpose of protecting beneficiaries from doubtful claims by an insurer that the deceased had made misrepresentations, after it becomes impossible for the deceased to defend himself or to deny the allegation.

2) Suicide clause

The *suicide clause* partially protects the beneficiary from the financial consequences of suicide. The clause states that if the insured does not kill himself for at least a stated period, usually two years, after issuance of the contract, the insurer may not deny liability under the policy

---

[5] Sometimes the policy excludes death from war or from certain aviation accidents. Refusal to pay claims resulting from these excluded perils would not be in violation of the incontestable clause no matter when the death occurred.

for subsequent suicide. If suicide occurs within two years of the issuance of the policy, the insurer's only obligation is to return without interest the premiums that have been paid. A one- or two-year period is justified on the grounds that if the applicant's plans to kill himself have motivated the purchase of life insurance, it is likely that these plans will be changed after a period as long as one or two years.

3) Reinstatement and grace period clauses

Under the *reinstatement clause,* contracts may be reinstated within a certain period after lapse, usually three or five years, upon evidence of insurability. The policy lapses for nonpayment of premium, but the *grace period clause* always gives the insured an extra 30 days in which to pay any premium which is due before lapse takes place. Once the policy has actually lapsed, special application must be made under the reinstatement clause to restore coverage. Sometimes a new medical examination must be taken, but usually the insured is only required to state that he is in good health at the time of reinstatement. All premiums in arrears plus interest must be paid. Reinstatement reopens the incontestable clause for another two years, but generally the suicide clause is held not to be reopened since it is the old policy which is restored and not a new policy. It is sometimes desirable to reinstate the old policy rather than to take out a new one because the old policy may have certain provisions, such as more favorable settlement options, immediate eligibility for dividends, or higher interest assumptions, which are not available in the new policy. Furthermore, no new acquisitions costs have to be paid on the reinstated policy as they would on a new form. Since acquisition costs are substantial, amounting to about one year's annual premium, this is an important saving.

4) Automatic premium loan clause

As we have learned, the nonpayment of a premium involves a lapse after expiration of the grace period. If the policy has a surrender value at the time of lapse, it may be surrendered for cash, changed into a different contract under extended term insurance, or become paid-up insurance of a reduced amount. To prevent lapsation, most insurers encourage the use of an *automatic premium loan provision,* which automatically authorizes the insurer to use cash values to pay the premium and thereby to establish a loan against the policy just as though the insured had borrowed this amount for another purpose. In this way the old policy continues as before without interruption, the only change being that there is now a loan against the policy.

5) Misstatement of age clause

Misrepresenting one's age in life insurance is material to accepting the risk and normally would become a defense against payment of the proceeds if it were not for the incontestable clause. Without some control over this hazard, it would become possible for people to lie a little about their age for the purpose of obtaining a lower premium for life insurance and to overstate their age for the purpose of receiving a larger retirement income. Proof of age is therefore required before proceeds are paid. Under the *misstatement of age* clause, if it is determined that the person's true age has been misrepresented, the insurer adjusts the amount of proceeds payable rather than cancel the agreement altogether. The actual amount payable is the amount of insurance which would have been purchased for the premium paid had the true age been stated. For example, if the premium at the true age is $30 and the premium at the stated age is $25, the insurer will pay only $\frac{5}{6}$ of the death proceeds otherwise payable.

6) Entire contract clause

The policy of life insurance generally contains an *entire contract clause,* which provides that the policy together with the application, constitutes the entire contract between the parties. This clause is desirable for the protection of the insured and the beneficiary because, without the clause, it might be possible to affect the rights of the respective parties through changes in the bylaws or in the charter of the insurer. In the case of fraternal insurers, the insured's rights can be changed if the fraternal organization's charter is duly changed.[6]

7) Spendthrift trust clause

One of the legal rights granted to the life insurance owner in most states is the exemption of death proceeds and cash values from the claims of creditors. Creditors of the insured cannot attach the cash value of life insurance for the payment of the insured's debts unless the insured has wrongfully bought or paid up his life insurance with money rightfully subject to creditors' claims. Neither may the insured's creditors attach the death proceeds of life insurance. This is an important right since the beneficiary is thus protected from the claims of the *insured's* creditors, and the indiscretions of the insured are not allowed to wreck the income security of his beneficiaries.

---

[6] See Chapter 5, pages 102 and 103.

The question arises, however, what about the *beneficiary's* creditors? May the beneficiary incur large debts using as security his right to receive income from life insurance proceeds? This is technically possible unless the state law has a provision to the contrary, or unless the law has permitted the attachment of what is called the *spendthrift trust clause*. If the spendthrift trust clause is attached to a life insurance policy, the beneficiary's rights to the promised income cannot be attached by creditors in any court in the state or residence. Such a clause is a valuable security measure, for without it there might be a temptation for an unscrupulous creditor to persuade a beneficiary to purchase goods beyond his ability to pay, secure in the knowledge that he could attach the life insurance trust. Thus, society grants to life insurance special status not given to other types of investments. Endorsement of the spendthrift trust clause is legal in most states. To qualify for this clause, the proceeds must usually be settled under an income option. Once the income has been paid to the beneficiary, the protection is lost when and if the money loses its identity as life insurance proceeds. This may occur when the insurance check is deposited in the beneficiary's checking account or is mingled with other funds.

MISCELLANEOUS CONTRACTUAL PROVISIONS

1) Dividend options

Participating policies [7] are those under which dividends are payable to the owner of the contract. The dividend is actually a partial return of the premium payment and reflects the experience of the insurer with regard to mortality and overhead costs and net investment income. All participating life insurance contracts provide certain options in the use of the dividends. In general, the insured may: (1) take the dividends in cash, (2) leave them with the insurer at interest, (3) use them to buy paid-up additions, (4) use the dividends to reduce premium payments, or (5) use them to help pay up the contract sooner than it would otherwise be paid, if it is a permanent contract.[8]

Dividends may be substantial in size and so the proper choice of a dividend option is important. For example, the average dividends paid

---

[7] See Chapter 6 for an analysis of this subject as it affects the problem of selecting an insurer.

[8] In 1960, dividends in life insurance were used for these purposes in the following proportion: taken in cash, 19%; left at interest, 30%; used to buy additional units of paid-up insurance, 19%; used to pay premiums, 32%; *Life Insurance Fact Book,* 1961, p. 46.

by four large mutual insurers during the period 1948–1958 on a $10,-000 ordinary life policy issued at age 35 amounted to $478. Thus, the insured who held one of these policies would have been able to obtain an additional $1,000 of paid-up ordinary life insurance, or to reduce his total premium payments by about 20 per cent. The use of dividends helps to pay up an ordinary life contract and in some cases may enable the insured to increase the reserve of his policy so that no more payments are necessary after age 65. (Contracts paying no dividends cost less initially and are known as nonparticipating insurance.)

The use of dividends to purchase paid-up additions has four important advantages:

1. Since no acquisition charges are made in such cases, it is an economical way to buy additional life insurance.
2. Since no medical examination or other evidence of insurability is required, use of this option may enable the purchase of insurance when it is impossible to obtain coverage in any other way. Such use of dividend options is of obvious importance to persons in a doubtful state of health. Sometimes the insurer will require evidence of insurability if this option is selected after the policy is first taken out.
3. The paid-up additions themselves have a cash value which may be borrowed. Thus, the insured has available a large portion of his dividends if he wants to borrow the cash value of the paid-up additions. In the event of the insured's death, the beneficiary receives the additional life insurance (less the amount borrowed) even though the insured had the use of most of the dividend payments while living.
4. For individuals in the higher income-tax brackets, paid-up additions have a further advantage in that the interest earned on the dividends so employed has a tax-free status, whereas if they were left to accumulate at interest, the interest would be taxable. Dividends themselves, being considered a return of premium, are not taxable.

2) Extensions of coverage

For an additional premium, most insurers will permit riders, which are actually in the nature of health insurance, to be attached to the life insurance policy.

Waiver of premium rider. The *waiver of premium rider,* which costs about 50 cents per $1,000 per year at age 30 for ordinary life policies, will excuse the insured from paying any further premiums under the policy in the event of his total and permanent physical disability from any cause before a certain age, usually age 60.[9] The policy will have the same cash values, death benefits, and dividends as it would have had if all premiums had been paid. Normally there is a waiting period of six months before the insurer starts to waive the premiums. The use of such a rider is to be recommended as a way of assuring that the life insurance estate will remain intact regardless of what happens to the insured's health.

Disability income rider. Carrying the waiver of premium idea a step further, most insurers will endorse the life insurance policy to provide a monthly income of $5 or $10 for each $1,000 of face amount in the event that the insured is totally and permanently disabled. Known as the *disability income rider,* this endorsement becomes effective after a four or six months' waiting period, and terminates if disability has not occurred before the insured has reached age 55 or 60, or at the maturity date of the policy if this comes sooner. The income continues as long as the insured remains totally and permanently disabled, for life if necessary.

Double indemnity rider. The *double indemnity rider* is an additional extension of coverage under which the insured's beneficiary may receive twice (and sometimes triple) the face amount of the policy if death occurs through accidental means. However, there are numerous restrictions on this benefit. For example, accidental death from suicide, death which occurs after 90 days following an accident, death from all illnesses, death with no visible evidence of wounds or contusions, and accidental deaths which do not satisfy the definition of accidental means [10] are not covered. While the charge for the double indemnity clause is not high, usually amounting to about $1.25 per $1,000 of face amount, coverage under the clause has the unfortunate tendency of leading the unsophisticated insured into believing that he has doubled his death protection for a very small extra charge. Such could not be further from the truth. As we have seen, not only are accidents far from the leading cause of death, but accidents that satisfy the definitions of the double indemnity clause are also an even rarer cause of death.

---

[9] What constitutes total and permanent disability varies according to the interpretation by an individual insurer. A common definition is that the insured shall be considered unable to engage in his regular occupation or any other occupation for profit or remuneration. Total loss of eyesight, or loss of use of both hands or both feet, or one hand and one foot commonly constitutes evidence of total disability.

[10] See Chapter 23, page 608, for an analysis of this clause.

3) Assignments

Rather than cash in a life insurance policy or borrow from the insurer, the insured may wish to *assign* his benefits to another, say a lender of money. This might be done because the bank may refuse to lend money to the borrower without insurance, or the borrower may have insufficient collateral to cover the loan, or the borrower is uninsurable for new coverage to protect a loan. Permission of the insurer is not necessary for the insured to assign his life insurance policy. However, the insurer must be properly notified in writing of an assignment, or the insurer is not bound by it. In the event of the insured's death, the usual procedure is for the insurer to pay to the holder of the assignment that part of the proceeds equal to the debt and the remainder to the named beneficiaries. In other words, the assignee of a life insurance policy normally may recover only that part of the proceeds "as his interest may appear." The assignee need not have an insurable interest in the life of the insured so long as the assignment is made for a legitimate business purpose and is not made to circumvent the law of insurable interest or to convert the policy into a gambling contract.

4) Premium payment

Most life insurers give the policyholder the right to pay premiums annually, semiannually, or quarterly. Many give the right to pay monthly. There is an extra charge, however, for paying other than annually. For example, if the annual premium is $100, the insurer may quote a semiannual premium of say $51. This is equivalent to charging $2 extra per year for the use of $49 for six months.[11] Reduced to simple interest terms, the cost is 4.08 per cent for six months, or 8.16 per cent annually. However, it may be worthwhile to the insured to pay at this rate because of the advantages of making installment payments as part of his budgeting program.

5) Excluded perils

It is not common for life insurers to exclude many perils from coverage. Some insurers exclude deaths caused by airplane accidents except for regularly scheduled flights on established airlines. Some exclude only aviation deaths while on military activities. In wartime many insurers

---

[11] If the insured now has $51 to make his premium payment and is required to pay the rest of the $100 premium in six months, we may accurately state that if the insured were willing to pay an additional $49 now, he would need no credit. Thus, the amount of the credit needed to take advantage of the semiannual premium payment plan is $49.

exclude deaths caused as a result of war. There is little uniformity in the excluded perils clauses and the practices of each insurer should be studied carefully to ascertain the coverage. If a peril is excluded in a life insurance policy, the fact that there is an incontestable clause does not prevent the insurer from denying liability since it is held that the incontestable clause applies only to deaths from perils not excluded by the policy. Technically, the policy is not being "contested," because the insurer has simply elected not to cover certain causes of death. Fortunately, the average life insurance policy contains very few such exclusions. It is virtually a true all-risk agreement.

6) Beneficiary designation

The insured may name anyone he wishes as beneficiary of his policy. The beneficiary does not have to have an insurable interest in the life of the insured. One of the great advantages of using life insurance as a method of estate creation is that the contract simultaneously provides for both the accumulation *and the distribution* of the property. The proceeds are payable directly to the beneficiary and do not pass through a probate court; hence the proceeds are not subject to the costs and delays that probate procedures sometimes involve. However, attention should be given to the way in which the beneficiary designation is made.

For example, a vague beneficiary designation, such as "to the wife and children," should be avoided because it does not identify which or whose wife or children are to be paid. At the time of death there may be an additional newly born child to consider; or the insured may have had more than one wife; or the children may be his wife's children by a former marriage. The ambiguity thus inherent in a vague beneficiary designation could cause a lawsuit over the distribution of the proceeds.

Change of beneficiary. The insured has the right to change beneficiaries without notice to those affected providing he has not named any beneficiary irrevocably. A *revocable beneficiary* has no control over the policy and has only contingent rights. Naming a beneficiary *irrevocably,* however, practically amounts to transferring all ownership rights in the contract to the person so named. It is done only when the insured wishes to give up all incidents of ownership, as, for example, when it is desired to prevent life insurance proceeds from being taxed as part of the estate of the insured.

Secondary beneficiaries. It is common to name *secondary* or *contingent beneficiaries,* so that if the primary beneficiary is not alive at the time of the insured's death, the proceeds will go to them. Since secondary beneficiaries are often children, care should be taken to name a guardian to receive the funds.[12] Otherwise, the court may appoint someone who would not be satisfactory to the insured were he alive to object. Also, if both the insured and his wife, who is the primary beneficiary, were to die in the same accident and it is not determinable who died first, the general rule is that the funds shall go to the secondary beneficiary.[13] However, if the wife survives the insured, even for a little while, and then dies, the insurance proceeds go to the wife's estate and would be inherited by her family. If the insured husband wishes to avoid this, he may use what has been termed the *common disaster clause,* which specifies that the insurance proceeds will be held under the interest option for a specified time, say two months, and if the primary beneficiary is alive then, the proceeds will be distributed to her; otherwise they will go to secondary beneficiaries or to the husband's estate.

INDUSTRIAL AND GROUP LIFE INSURANCE PROVISIONS

Industrial insurance

About seven per cent of all life insurance in force by private insurers in the United States takes a form known as industrial insurance. *Industrial insurance,* sometimes called *weekly premium insurance,* is that form of life insurance in which the policies are typically less than $1,000 in amount and for which the premiums are quoted on a weekly basis, such as five or ten cents a week, instead of so much per $1,000 of face amount as is true in ordinary life insurance. The premiums are typically collected directly by a salesman who goes from house to house on a route known as a *debit.* Industrial insurance was originally designed as a burial policy for a wage worker who would otherwise buy no insurance because of difficulties in budgeting the premium payments involved. Today, however, it cannot be said that only industrial workers have this type of coverage, for almost all classes of workers purchase industrial insurance. The rate of growth in this field of insurance has leveled off and the amount in force declined slightly for the first time in 1958. Part of the reason for this decline is that the large insurers who

---

12 This is usually done in a will.
13 This result is governed by the Uniform Simultaneous Death Act, which has been passed in most states.

specialize in this business [14] have reclassified their business, formerly called "industrial," to "ordinary." It is possible to obtain ordinary life insurance for face amounts of less than $1,000. Furthermore, the economic status of most individuals in the industrial market has improved to the point where the chief selling feature of industrial insurance—its convenient premium—is no longer so important as it once was.

The industrial contract of life insurance, being sold door to door and hence necessitating an expensive form of distribution, costs more than ordinary life insurance. There is no general agreement as to how much of a differential there is in cost between the two, since so many factors enter into a valid comparison of costs.[15] It seems proper to conclude, however, that the cost differentials, whatever they are or have been, have tended to narrow as the methods of doing business in the two areas, industrial insurance and ordinary life insurance, have become more and more similar.

The industrial life insurance policy differs from the ordinary contract in a few particulars, mostly stemming from the small amounts of insurance involved in a typical industrial policy. For example, in industrial insurance the policy must usually be in force three to five years before cash values are available. There are no loan values and no optional modes of settlement. There are, however, the usual nonforfeiture provisions. The policy does not contain a suicide clause and under the incontestable clause, the policy is incontestable after one year instead of two. It may usually be reinstated with no evidence of insurability. A double indemnity clause is included in the regular premium. The industrial policy is commonly issued without a medical examination, although the insured is required to make declarations about his health. Most policies contain a *money-back clause,* under which all premiums are refunded within the first few weeks if the insured is not satisfied for any reason.

An unusual clause in the industrial insurance policy is the *facility of payment* clause, under which the proceeds of the policy may be paid to the beneficiary, or to any person "appearing to the company to be equitably entitled to it by reason of having incurred expense on the behalf of the insured for maintenance, medical attention, or burial." Thus, if there is no named beneficiary, the proceeds may be paid to any person who has borne any expense of the deceased. In this way, the proceeds are not subject to the costs and delays involved in probate procedure.

---

[14] The developers and by far the largest insurers of industrial insurance are Metropolitan Life, Prudential Life, and John Hancock Life, in that order.

[15] See Chapter 6.

Group life insurance

Not to be confused with industrial insurance, *group life insurance* is commonly sold to employers of groups of workers ranging in size from ten to millions.[16] Unlike industrial insurance, group life insurance has shown a tremendous increase in the United States and at the end of 1960 constituted 30 per cent of the total life insurance in force. Ten years prior, group insurance constituted 21 per cent of the total, and in 1940, only 13 per cent of the total.

Group life insurance is almost always issued on the term plan. The employer receives a master contract which outlines the provisions of coverage, and the employee receives a certificate that evidences his participation in the plan. The amount of insurance usually depends on the employee's salary or job classification and may range from $1,000 to $100,000 or more. However, the typical amount per employee will ordinarily range from $3,000 to $10,000.

Group insurance generally costs the employee much less than an individual policy and has other advantages for several reasons:

1. The insurance is written without medical examination. If the employee is able to work, he is deemed well enough to receive coverage. If he leaves his employment, his insurance under the plan ceases; but he may convert his policy to an individual policy without evidence of insurability.

2. Other acquisition costs, such as sales commissions and policy issuance expenses, are greatly reduced.

3. The employer often contributes to the cost, either directly by paying part of the premium, or indirectly by bearing part of the administrative costs.

4. Mortality costs are lower because working groups are usually composed of active, healthy persons who are "preselected." Furthermore, a purpose for their organization exists other than to secure insurance.

Group life insurance can usually be arranged under one of the settlement options offered by the insurer under ordinary policies, although the master contract itself often provides fewer settlement options to choose from than are available on individual contracts. In the event of total and permanent disability on the part of the worker before a certain age, the usual group contract provides what amounts to a waiver of premium benefit.

---

[16] The largest single group is composed of all federal civil service employees.

Some of the reasons for the growth of group life insurance are:

1. Group life insurance solves a business need for providing non-salary inducements to productivity.
2. "Passing the hat" when an employee dies is no longer necessary.
3. The benefits are made available in a form that is nontaxable to the employee and yet the premiums are deductible to the employer.
4. Unions have very successfully promoted so-called fringe benefits, including group life insurance.

Group coverage now forms an important part of the life insurance programs of many individuals.

SUMMARY

1. The nonforfeiture options in the life insurance contract refer to those provisions that grant three methods of benefiting from life insurance with an accumulated reserve when one no longer desires to continue the original contract or is unable financially to do so. Cash value may be: (a) taken in a lump sum, (b) used to purchase extended term insurance, or (c) used to convert the existing policy into a paid-up policy of a reduced amount. Realization of this fact ends the fallacious common belief that one has to "pay all my life" on a whole life policy.

2. Settlement options refer to the contractual provisions under which the insured or the beneficiary may elect to receive the death proceeds or the cash values of life insurance. The insurer will agree to act, at no extra fee, as trustee of the proceeds for the benefit of the insured's family, holding the funds at interest, or distributing them as a guaranteed life income over a fixed period or as a fixed amount for as long as the proceeds last. Thus, the insured may economically plan the distribution of the estate he has created in such a way as to guarantee that it will serve the purpose he intended and will not be lost through mismanagement, theft, or other investment hazards.

3. In the typical life insurance contract, there are many clauses designed primarily for the protection of the insured and his beneficiary and which give the life insurance contract a preferred legal status over other types of property. Among these clauses are the incontestable clause, suicide clause, reinstatement privilege, the grace period, automatic premium loan clause, misstatement of age clause, entire contract clause, and the spendthrift trust clause. These agreements reflect the basic social purpose of the life insurance institution to provide for dependents who often would otherwise become a burden on the state.

4. Proper use of certain options can multiply the benefits to be received from the life insurance contract. The size of the insurance estate may be increased substantially through appropriate use of dividend options. The waiver-of-premium rider guarantees that the estate accumulation plans

of the insured will not be interrupted because of permanent and total disability. The disability income rider replaces income lost because of permanent and total disability and is offered primarily as a means to prevent lapse of the insurance estate. The double indemnity rider is available to multiply death protection in the event of death through accidental means.

5. Since life insurance is usually purchased for the benefit of someone else, careful attention should be paid to the naming of beneficiaries and in planning for various contingencies so that the insurance estate will be distributed according to the wishes of the insured.

6. Industrial life insurance, which describes that type of insurance sold in amounts smaller than $1,000 and at a premium quotation of so much per week, appears to have neared the limit of its natural growth. It was designed for low-income individuals who could not purchase life insurance in any other way, and now constitutes only seven per cent of all private life insurance in force.

7. In contrast to industrial insurance, group life insurance has been expanding rapidly and now constitutes 30 per cent of all life insurance in force. Sold only to groups of individuals, this type of coverage appears to be filling the place formerly occupied by industrial insurance in supplying life insurance to the working class at low costs. However, group life insurance, which is practically always issued on the term plan, is not by any means confined to the working class, but is used quite generally to insure all employees of a business firm.

QUESTIONS FOR REVIEW AND DISCUSSION

1. (a) Differentiate between nonforfeiture options and settlement options.
   (b) What are the chief advantages of using income settlement options?
2. A certain insurer features in its advertising that under its policies extended term insurance can be cashed in at any time, and that it will also participate in dividends.
   (a) What is extended term insurance, and why are these features an advantage to the insured?
   (b) Check the wording on a life insurance policy available to you to see if you can ascertain how the insurer handles these questions.
3. In a survey of insurers it has been determined that about one fourth will consent to adding a spendthrift trust clause to their policies only upon request of the insured, while the remaining insurers include such a clause automatically.
   (a) What is the purpose of a spendthrift trust clause, and why is it a good idea to include this clause?
   (b) When can the clause be used?
4. A valuable use of the interest option is to leave the proceeds of the insurance at interest until the end of a specified period or until any minor beneficiary has reached his majority, at which time the amount accumulated is distributed under another option, such as life income or fixed period. Yet,

a survey of 100 insurers indicates that less than half of them will allow such a use.

(a) For what reasons is this use of the interest option valuable?

(b) Check a life insurance policy available to you to see if the insurer will allow this use of the interest option.

5. In order to join an insurance plan, the insured misstated his age to be 50 when he was actually 51. The oldest age permissible for entering the plan was age 50. After the lapse of the incontestable period, the insured died. When proofs of age were submitted, the insurance association denied liability and offered to return all premiums. The estate of the insured brought suit, complaining that both the misstatement of age clause and the incontestable clause prevented the insurer from denying liability. Apply your knowledge of these two clauses to decide this case. State the reasons for your decision.

6. Dividends in life insurance stem largely from mortality savings and excess interest earnings. If this is true, which types of policies may be expected to produce the greatest dividends in periods of general shortage of investment funds? in periods of oversupply of investment funds? Why?

7. In 1958 a new mortality table, replacing the 1941 CSO table, was developed to reflect the declining mortality experience. What effect on dividends might be expected from the adoption of the new 1958 CSO mortality table? Why?

8. Smith requests your advice as to whether his life insurance dividends, which amounted to $1,000 last year, are taxable under the federal income tax law. Smith was credited with $1,000 in dividends on his policies and under the option he has selected, these dividends are held at interest and have earned $50 interest. Smith is in poor health and does not wish to surrender any of his life insurance. Smith received no money in cash.

(a) Advise Smith about the taxability of these sums.

(b) Is Smith making the best use of his dividends? Why?

9. Jack learns that he may pay his premium quarterly instead of semiannually, as he has been doing. His annual premium is $40.42 per $1,000; $20.61, semiannually, and $10.51, quarterly. Calculate the simple interest cost involved for the privilege of paying quarterly instead of semiannually; semiannually instead of annually.

10. The insured had a policy with a double indemnity rider that provides twice the payment of the face amount if the insured were to come to his death by drowning, directly, independently, and exclusive of all other causes, or of an injury by external, violent, and accidental means. The insured was found dead, immersed in his bathtub. He was in apparently good health, and there was no evidence as to whether death had resulted from an accident exclusive of all other causes.

(a) Would the question of whether or not the incontestable period had elapsed bear on this case? Why?

(b) Should the insured's beneficiary be able to collect this claim? Why or why not?

11. An insured failed to pay a quarterly premium due on February 12. The automatic premium loan provision kept the policy in force until May 12, at which time the cash value was $4.74, insufficient to pay an additional quarterly premium. Accordingly, the policy lapsed and the insurer purchased extended term insurance with the $4.74, thus extending the insured's coverage for 92 days. The insured died September 2. The insured's beneficiary claimed that the 92 days ran from the date of the expiration of the grace period, which would have meant that the insurance was still in force at the date of death. The insurer claimed that the 92 days ran from May 12. How should this case be decided? Why?

12. A writer argued that there are many advantages to borrowing on life insurance policies as compared with borrowing from a bank or another lender, such as ease and speed of the process, cheapness of interest, and lack of any pressure to repay. On the other hand, can you think of any disadvantages?

13. A policy lapsed October 25 and the insured sent a note to the insurer on November 6 saying, "I wish to drop my policy under the above number." The insurer wrote back and said, "As you requested, your policy was permitted to lapse on October 25." On November 14 the insured was accidentally killed. Should this claim be paid? Why or why not?

14. An insured was divorced and upon his remarriage he changed the beneficiary designation of his life insurance from his first to his second wife. The second marriage lasted five months, and in the divorce decree the second wife gave up all rights she might have had to any life insurance belonging to the husband. When the insured later died, it was found that he had not changed the beneficiary designation from the second wife and there was a court contest between the first wife and the second wife for the proceeds. Who should receive the proceeds? Why?

15. A court ordered an insured to use the cash surrender value of his life insurance if necessary to pay arrearages, amounting to $1,058, for his wife's support. The cash surrender value of the insurance was $14,725. The policies were in possession of the insured's son. The insured appealed this decision to a higher court. Do you think the court order should stand? Why?

16. An absolute assignment is one in which all rights in the property assigned are transferred to another person. In one case life insurance with a face amount of $110,000 was assigned as collateral to secure an $85,000 loan. The insured died and the insurance company paid $110,000 to the assignee. The insured's beneficiaries brought suit for the difference between the loan and the face amount of the insurance, claiming it was unjust for the assignee to keep all of it. How should the case be decided? Why?

17. The insured had elected to use his dividends to pay the premiums on a $5,000 life insurance policy. However, he failed to pay a premium of $16.05 due May 24. By June 24 the premium had still not been paid, so under the nonforfeiture option selected, the company applied the cash value to purchase paid-up insurance. On July 5 the insured sought reinstatement of the policy, but died the day before the application for rein-

statement was approved. The insurer tendered to the beneficiary $639.25, which was the amount of the paid-up insurance plus accumulated dividends of $31.25. The check was refused and the beneficiary claimed the full $5,000. State with reasons how you think this case should be decided.

18. An insurer filed suit to rescind and to cancel a life insurance policy on the ground that the insured gave false answers to some questions about his heart and blood condition. The insured died within a year of issuance of the policy, which had been "rated up" because of physical conditions revealed to the insurer by the examining physician.
    (a) What right, if any, does the insurer have to cancel this policy?
    (b) Do you think there might be some valid defenses on the part of the beneficiary which might force payment of this policy? Explain.

19. An insured died of sunstroke two hours after being exposed to temperatures of 109 degrees. The court upheld the refusal of the insurer to pay double indemnity under the typical double indemnity clause in the life insurance policy.
    (a) For what probable reason did the insurer refuse to pay?
    (b) Under what conditions is it possible that a death could have been caused by sunstroke and still obligate the insurer to pay double indemnity? Explain.

20. Do the same conditions exist today which gave rise to the sale of industrial insurance? If not, do you expect the gradual disappearance of this kind of coverage? Why?

21. In what ways are industrial insurance and group insurance different? similar? Explain.

22. What are the sources of economy in group life insurance and the sources of high cost in industrial life insurance? Explain.

23. In group life insurance it is a basic rule that there must be some reason for the existence of the group other than the purchase of life insurance. Explain why this rule is insisted upon.

24. For each of the following policies, indicate which of the premiums listed below should apply at an issue age of 20: ordinary life, 20-pay life, 20-year endowment, life paid up at 65, endowment at age 65 and 5-year renewable term. (a) $16.19, (b) $17.27, (c) $19.35, (d) $26.45, (e) $46.14, and (f) $51.01.

25. For the policies (a), (b), and (c) in Question 24, suggest reasons for the relatively similar premium applicable to each.

26. A salesman presented two plans of life insurance to an insured. In each case the premium was the same—$351.40 for a person aged 40. Plan I provided $10,000 protection under the 20-pay life plan and Plan II provided $15,180 protection under the ordinary life plan. In 20 years the paid-up insurance under Plan I was $10,000 and under Plan II, $8,956. Which plan is the better? What advantages do you claim for your choice? Explain.

Annuities and Life

Insurance Contracts As Investments

As we have seen, life insurance contracts issued on a permanent basis have cash values which may be used for many different purposes, including that of providing retirement income. Separate contracts called annuities may also be purchased for retirement purposes. These contracts have no pure protection element and many authorities do not refer to them as life insurance. The important fact is, however, that one may combine life insurance protection with a savings plan for retirement, or he may save by methods which contain no pure protection. Life insurance companies offer both types of plans as well as combinations of each. The suitability of various methods of saving for retirement is an important consideration in an analysis of how well the problem of old-age dependency may be solved.

The desirability of using life insurance and annuity contracts as a means of saving, especially as a means of saving for retirement, has been attacked by many who claim that other methods are superior. One of the major criticisms has been that the steady inflation experienced in the economy "eats away" the value of these savings more quickly than the low interest rates paid on them accumulate. In other words, it is argued that, over a period of time, the average price level rises faster than the average income level, and that the purchasing power of accumulated savings is thereby lessened.

The inflation controversy has undoubtedly overshadowed many other very important considerations which ought to be taken into account in deciding the place of insurance and annuities in one's investment program. We shall first describe the various annuity uses of life insurance proceeds and other retirement contracts and then analyze these instruments as investment media, with special emphasis on the inflation controversy.

THE ANNUITY CONCEPT

Definitions

An *annuity* may be defined mathematically as a series of equal payments made at equal intervals of time. This is indeed a broad definition since it includes regular payments (called *rent* of the annuity) of almost any type and for any length of time and with no restriction on the length of the time interval. In the field of life insurance, we are primarily concerned with annuities of equal payments by an insurer to an insured (called the *annuitant*) on an annual basis (although the annual payments are usually expressed in terms of monthly installments) with the payment, composed of both interest and principal, due at the *end* of the year (or month).

Often the word annuity also conveys the idea of lifetime payments, although mathematically the term of the annuity may be any length of time. In the following discussion we will use the expression *life annuity* to mean an ordinary annuity payable for life, that is, where the payment period, or *term,* is for the life of the annuitant. Income paid by an insurer for a specified length of time is usually referred to by one of the settlement options, such as fixed period or interest option, which are discussed in Chapter 21. Broadly speaking, however, such payments constitute an annuity for a temporary period and are also called *short-term annuities*.

The *present value* of an annuity, or the cash equivalent of an annuity, is the amount of money that the insurer must have *now* in order to be able to pay the promised amounts over the term of the annuity. Due to the interest factor, the present value is, of course, smaller than the sum of all the promised payments. Thus, the present value of an annuity whose rent is $100 a year for 35 years at 6 per cent interest is $1,449.82, less than half of the sum of all the payments, which total $3,500.[1] If the insurer has the sum of $1,449.82, it will be able to make payments to the annuitant of $100 a year, due at the end of the year, for 35 years, thereby exhausting the principal at the end of this time.

In the long run, the interest assumed in the annuity agreement makes a substantial difference in the present value of the annuity. For example, the present value of an annuity of $100 a year for 35 years at

---

[1] Most mathematical handbooks contain tables for the present value of an annuity of $1 a year for varying periods. The formula for this value is:

$$a_{\overline{n}|i} = \frac{1 - (1 + i)^{-n}}{i},$$

which is read, "*a* sub *n* at rate *i* equals. . . ." In this expression *n* is the number of payment periods in the term of the annuity, and *i* is the rate of interest assumed. If one wishes to find the present value of an annuity of any amount for a given period, he simply multiplies the amount desired by $a_{\overline{n}|i}$ for $1.

2.5 per cent interest is $2,314.51, whereas at 3 per cent, the present value is $2,148.72, some 7.5 per cent lower. Thus, the rate of interest earnings is a vital factor in the choice of an insurer of an insurance or annuity contract.

Annuities compared with life insurance. A life annuity, guaranteeing that the annuitant cannot outlive his income, is the reverse of the life insurance contract where the risk is not how long a person will live to receive an income, but whether he will die before the expiration of a given term of the policy. Thus, it has been facetiously said that life insurance is insurance against "dying too soon," while annuities are insurance against "living too long." A mortality table is the basis of both life insurance and annuity contracts, although in the case of annuities, the tables employed reflect the greater longevity of annuitants. Since the cash values of the life insurance contract are often turned into annuity contracts at retirement age, or the death proceeds of the life insurance contract are settled on a *life income* settlement option (actually nothing more than a life annuity), there is an intimate relationship between life insurance and annuities.

The life insurance contract, as noted earlier, has two central purposes—to hedge against premature death and to accumulate funds for a later purpose. In either case, the goal to provide for is the existence of an estate of income-producing property at the time of death, no matter when this may be. The annuity is essentially a method of *distributing* this estate, either to beneficiaries or to the insured for his retirement. The life annuity accomplishes this task in such a way that all payments are guaranteed, with a minimum guaranteed interest rate, for the lifetime of the annuitant. The insurer liquidates the accumulated sums over the remaining lifetime of the annuitant group, taking amounts left over from the estates of those who die early to pay incomes to those who live beyond their normal life expectancies. Thus, an annuity is a device for creating certainty out of uncertainty. Since one cannot know how long he will live after retirement, he hedges, agreeing that a portion of his estate shall be used for those who live long in return for the promise that if he should be one of the fortunate ones to live long, he will receive contributions from those who die early. Under the annuity an insured receives a *certain* smaller income in return for an *uncertain* but larger income.

For example, according to mortality tables, a man age 65 has an average life expectancy of about 14 years. If he has accumulated $10,-

000 and employs a settlement option under which he receives a fixed amount over a period of 14 years at 3 per cent, he will receive $72.60 each month for the 14 years. If he dies before 14 years have passed, someone, say his beneficiary, will receive the remaining installments. Now, if he uses the $10,000 to purchase a straight life annuity based on a 3 per cent interest guaranty, he will receive about $74 per month; [2] but in case of death, his estate receives no remaining installments. However, he is guaranteed the $74 each month for life, so if he outlives his expectancy, he has the assurance that others in the insured group will "make good" his income. Note that if he elects to invest the $10,000 at 3 per cent, he will receive only $25 each month, but there is no reduction of the principal amount and at his death the entire $10,000 can be left to some beneficiary.

TYPES OF ANNUITIES

Life annuities may be classified in the following ways:

1) According to the period during which a minimum number of payments is guaranteed.
2) According to when the rent begins.
3) According to the method of paying premiums.
4) According to the number of lives insured.

1) Guaranteed payments

The four major types of annuities classified according to the guarantee of payments are:

1) Straight-life annuity.
2) Period-certain life income annuity.
3) Installment refund and cash refund annuities.
4) Temporary life annuity.

1) Straight-life annuity. A *straight-life annuity* is one in which the rent of the annuity is paid only during the lifetime of the annuitant, with no minimum number of guaranteed installments. If the insured dies the day after purchasing the annuity, there is no obligation for the insurer to return any of the purchase price. The sum paid in is held for the benefit of other annuitants. In the straight-life annuity, the annuity principle operates in its purest form. However, many individuals hesitate to use this form, particularly if they have heirs or dependents who would

---

[2] This amount varies, depending on the insurer.

naturally like to participate in the estate upon the death of the insured. Under the straight-life annuity, the rent is higher than in the forms discussed below, where some minimum number of payments must be made.

2) *Period-certain life income annuity.* When it is desired to obtain some minimum number of guaranteed payments, several different arrangements can be made. Under the *period-certain life income annuity,* the insurer agrees to guarantee 10, 15, or 20 years of payments to someone, and if the annuitant outlives this period, for his lifetime. If the annuitant is young (as would be the case of a young widow receiving life insurance proceeds on a life-income basis), there is very little difference in the annual rent of a period-certain annuity and a straight-life annuity. In this example, there is a very high probability that the annuitant will outlive the guarantee period and therefore there is little reason to reduce the rent of the annuity significantly. In this case, the insured should obviously select the period-certain annuity. However, if the annuitant is at retirement age, the annual rent of a 20-year period-certain annuity will be approximately 25 per cent less than the rent of a straight-life annuity. At this age there is a substantial probability that under the guaranteed installment arrangements more will have to be paid out than would have been paid with no such guarantee, because the annuitant is not likely to live until he is 85.

3) *Installment refund and cash annuities.* Other arrangements to guarantee a minimum number of payments under an annuity are the *installment refund* and the *cash refund annuities.* Under the refund annuity, the insurer subtracts from the value of the annuity at its starting date (that is, the present value) the total of all rents paid to the annuitant at the time of death. Any difference is paid to a beneficiary in cash or in installments as the case may be. Slightly larger annuities are given for the installment refund type because the insurer will retain the funds for a longer period of time. If the insured spends $10,000 for a cash refund annuity at age 65 and draws $57 a month for 10 years, he would have received $6,840 in all. His beneficiary would obtain a cash refund of $3,160.

4) *Temporary life annuity.* Assume that it is desired to guarantee an income for the life of the annuitant, but to cease payment in any case after a certain period. This situation might arise if the annuitant knows he has a given income at some future period, say from a trust which matures in 15 years, or from social security benefits. If he survives the 15

years he has no need for rent from the annuity. If he dies before this time, the annuity will cease at that time. Such an arrangement is known as a *temporary life annuity* and is mentioned at this point only to illustrate the many different arrangements for guaranteed payments which can be worked out to fit different needs for income.

2) Period when the rent begins

The rent of an annuity can begin as soon as the annuity is purchased, in which case the transaction is called an *immediate annuity*. Alternatively, the rent can begin at some future time, in which case the annuity is called a *deferred annuity*. Often the rent begins at retirement.

3) Method of paying premiums

An annuity can be wholly paid up in a lump-sum payment, or can be purchased in installments over a period of years. If the annuity is paid up at once, it is called a *single-premium annuity*. If it is paid for in installments, it is known as an *annual-premium annuity*. It is possible to view a permanent life insurance policy as a deferred annual-premium life annuity since the life income option permits the insured or his beneficiary to accept the proceeds as a life annuity as one of the settlement options. A similar observation applies to the retirement income policy, discussed in Chapter 20. Single-premium deferred annuities are common methods of funding group pension plans, discussed below. The pension of the employee is made up of the rents from a series of single-premium deferred annuities bought over the working years of the employee.

4) Number of lives insured

Two major types of annuities under which more than one life is covered are 1) joint and last survivorship, and 2) group annuity.

1) Joint and last survivorship annuity. An annuity may be issued on more than one life. For example, the agreement might be to pay a given rent during the lifetime of two individuals, as long as either shall live. This, a very common arrangement, is known as a *joint and last survivorship annuity,* because the rent is payable until the last survivor dies. The rent may be constant during the entire period or may be arranged to be reduced by, say, one third upon the death of the first annuitant. Thus, a husband and a wife both age 65 may elect to receive the proceeds of a pension plan on a joint and last survivorship basis, with an income guaranteed as long as either shall live.

To illustrate a comparison of rents, one insurer offers the following monthly rents at age 65 per $1,000 of proceeds:

1. Annuity 20 years certain and life $4.98
2. Installment refund and life 5.70
3. Annuity 10 years certain and life 6.30
4. Joint and ⅔ to survivor for life 5.88
5. Straight life, no refund 6.97

If the wife is considerably younger than the husband, the rent on a joint and last survivorship annuity is quite low because of the obligation of the insurer to continue payments until the wife dies. Nevertheless, the joint and last survivorship annuity serves a vital function in removing the risk of having one person dying and leaving the other without a means of support.

2) Group annuity. The *group annuity* is in principle the same as the individual annuity except that the employer usually contributes to its cost and contractual provisions may be varied to fit the different needs of the group. The group annuity is the oldest and best known method of funding a private pension plan. A master contract is issued to the employer, as in group life insurance. Under a common arrangement, known as the *unit-purchase plan,* the annual contributions are used to purchase a single-premium deferred life annuity on the life of each employee at his then-attained age. The employee's rights in the annuity, if he dies before retirement or leaves the group for other reasons, depend on the particular provisions of the group contract. If his rights are fully *vested,* he is full owner of the annuities purchased for his credit. If his rights are vested only after a given period of service or upon reaching a certain age, he may get nothing if he leaves the group before this time, except a return of his own contributions plus interest. If he dies before retirement, the insurer normally permits any vested rights he may have to be settled in an annuity for his surviving spouse. Usually the employee has no withdrawal rights before retirement unless he leaves the group, and sometimes not even then.

The cost of a group annuity is often lower than that of an individual annuity for the following reasons:

1. The group annuity plan may provide that if the employee leaves the group before retirement or until a certain period has elapsed, the employer's contributions will be lost to the employee (that is, the plan is not vested). This means that the remaining employees who do not leave may receive a higher annuity, or the employer may reduce his cost, or both.

2. The plan may provide that if the employee dies before retirement, there is no benefit to survivors; this need will be taken care of by group life insurance bought separately. In this case a given sum of money can purchase a much larger benefit, or the employer's cost can be reduced, or both.

3. If the plan qualifies under tax regulations, the employee does not have to pay income taxes on the value of the employer's contributions on his behalf. In this way the federal government subsidizes a group annuity plan in a way that is presently denied an individual annuity arrangement.

4. The employer usually handles some of the administrative duties in connection with the plan, a factor which reduces the amount of overhead which must be charged by the insurer.

5. Certain operating costs are reduced under a group annuity. Reduced agents' commissions are allowed and reduced handling costs are made possible by the fact that no individual contracts are sent out.

6. Since at least 75 per cent of the employed group are required to participate in the plan (if both employee and employer contribute), there is less adverse selection against the insurer and resultant savings are made, which may be passed on in the form of higher benefits or lower costs, or both. In individual annuities there is a tendency for only "the healthy ones" to apply for coverage. This means that, on the average, individual annuitants tend to live longer than other people. (There is a saying among underwriters that "annuitants never die.") The longer the insured group lives, the longer the average payments must be made. This, of course, raises the cost of the annuity. In a group coverage, however, both healthy and nonhealthy workers are insured, thus averaging out the element of long life which characterizes individual annuitants.

Under the unit-purchase plan, the employer normally uses his contributions to purchase a nonrefund annuity, the least expensive form. The employee, therefore, cannot enjoy the flexibility that is inherent in other settlement methods. A group annuity is sometimes arranged on a *money-purchase* plan, whereby individual paid-up annuities are not purchased annually; but a sum of money is accumulated by a trustee and annuities are purchased for each employee at time of retirement according to whatever settlement basis is desired, refund or period certain, or joint and last survivorship. While the money-purchase plan offers this advantage to the employee, it has the disadvantage that it is difficult to predict with certainty just how much of a pension will be forthcoming, since no one can guarantee longevity nor the amount of interest earnings and expenses. The insurer, of course, guarantees a minimum rate of interest and the safety of the funds, but does not guarantee future mortality rates.

Usually a minimum pension is guaranteed, but how much the pension will be above the minimum, if any, is unknown.

Group annuities are often combined with other private pension plan arrangements under which many variables are introduced. The contributions of the employer may vary from year to year, and the proceeds may be invested in securities other than the fixed-interest bonds which dominate life insurance company portfolios. Many pension plans are invested at least partly in common and preferred stocks, or hinge on profit-sharing arrangements which may not permit a guaranteed pension to be promised. Sometimes the group plan is funded through life insurance issued on some permanent plan instead of term insurance, with the cash values of the life insurance being used for retirement purposes. The details of these plans, known as group permanent, are too numerous for analysis here, and may be studied in more specialized treatments of the subject.[3]

PROBLEMS IN SAVING FOR RETIREMENT

Although permanent life insurance and annuity contracts generally have cash values which may be used at any time, their chief purpose lies in long-term savings. As such, they have certain advantages and disadvantages which will be analyzed below. These factors may be appreciated more fully if some of the problems attending any program of long-term savings are first reviewed. These problems include:

1. Handling one's personal finances in such a way as to provide a certain amount, even though it is small, for regular and consistent savings.
2. Investing these savings in such a manner as to achieve *reasonable safety*. In judging safety, the fact that we are dealing with long periods of time should be considered, and hence investments that appear safe today may not be so in five years. Thus, there is a need for constant review and careful investment management.
3. Investing savings so as to achieve *reasonable liquidity*. Again, since long time periods are involved, it is not necessary that all accumulated savings be made in investments that may be turned into cash at a moment's notice. Such a high degree of liquidity is almost invariably associated with a low interest rate. Of course, a certain portion of savings should be in a highly liquid form so as to provide emergency funds when needed.

---

[3] J. A. Hamilton and D. C. Bronson, *Pensions* (New York: McGraw Hill Book Company, Inc., 1958), Dan M. McGill, *Fundamentals of Private Pensions* (Homewood, Illinois: Richard D. Irwin, Inc., 1955), and Kenneth Black, Jr., *Group Annuities* (S. S. Huebner Foundation, 1955).

4. Making investments so as to achieve as *large a return as is consistent with safety and liquidity.* It is usually agreed that safety and liquidity should not be sacrificed to any great extent for the sake of a high promised return. This is not to shrug off return as the least important of the three elements. As we have seen, even a small difference in the interest return makes a substantial difference in retirement income over a long period of years.

5. Developing sound plans *for use* of the savings so as to achieve the desired objectives, such as making provision for dependents and for one's old age. Problems in this area include the development of plans to minimize taxes, to insulate the estate from common investment perils, to minimize estate settlement costs, and to provide sufficient flexibility in the administration of an estate so that if conditions change after the estate planner is deceased, the plan may be altered according to the needs of the beneficiaries.

6. Securing *protection against inflation.* This is just the reverse of our criterion of safety, which is looked upon as merely securing protection against deflation. Either inflation or deflation may destroy the value of a savings program unless it is properly "hedged." A high-grade bond is a good hedge against deflation because its value will usually rise as the general price level falls. On the other hand, the value of a well-chosen common stock will tend to rise with the general price level while the value of the high-grade bonds declines.

To illustrate this point, consider the experience of United States savings bonds during the period 1940–1950. These bonds were sold at a discount and matured to their face value in 10 years. A $100 bond could be purchased in 1940 for $75 and redeemed in 1950 for $100, yielding 2.9 per cent interest. However, during this time the general price level index (see Table 22–2, page 587) rose from 59.9 to 102.8. Thus, the $100 received in 1950 purchased goods approximately equivalent to what $60 would have purchased in 1940. The saver experienced what amounts to a *negative rate of real interest income.* The interest return was insufficient to offset the decay of savings through inflation, since the loss of real principal was 20 per cent in 10 years ($15 "loss" divided by $75, the original investment). On the other hand, a well-known industrial common stock index doubled during the period 1940–1950, affording the saver in common stocks more than enough protection against the rising price level. (See Table 22–3, page 593.)

While the above list of problems is not meant to be all inclusive, it is suggestive of the complexities that face the saver if he wishes to achieve success in his long-term savings program. With these problems in mind let us now assess the advantages and disadvantages of permanent life insurance and annuity contracts as vehicles for long-term savings.

Life insurance as an investment

Among the advantages and disadvantages of permanent life insurance as a vehicle for long-term savings, the following are cited:

1. The purchase of life insurance lends itself to a regular, consistent savings plan since it may be purchased in any denomination to fit the savings budget of individuals with varying incomes. The plan fits the psychological needs of most savers for a regular savings plan with a semicompulsory flavor. As premiums come due, they are looked upon as any other bill and are paid more or less automatically. Where the saver might well omit making a monthly deposit in a savings bank, he thinks twice before permitting his life insurance policy to lapse. The policy is looked upon as more than just a savings medium, and indeed it is. The consistency record in life insurance savings has been unusually good, even in depression times. The premium income of life insurance companies in the United States, having increased in every year but two since 1911, has shown a consistent growth. In 1932 income declined 4.2 per cent below 1931, and in 1933, it declined 5.3 per cent below 1932. In all other years premium income increased, and the ratio of premiums to disposable personal income has remained fairly constant since 1943. Between 1940 and 1959, this ratio ranged from a low of 3.3 per cent in 1943 and 1944 to a high of 5.1 per cent in 1940. In the period 1951–60 the ratio has climbed gradually from 3.4 per cent to 3.8 per cent.[4]

2. The safety record of the life insurance investment has been above reproach. This factor was evaluated in Chapter 6, page 141, where it was concluded that the probability of loss to policyholders from life insurance company failures, while not zero, is so close to zero as to enable an evaluation of the risk as negligible.

3. The liquidity of the life insurance investment is guaranteed by contract; the only qualification is that the policy contains a *delay clause* which gives the insurer a period of six months or less, if necessary, in which to make a cash loan for a purpose other than payment of the premium. While this clause is seldom invoked by the insurer, it is there as a precautionary measure in case of repetition of a "run" during a financial panic similar to that which occurred during the depression of the 1930's.

   The high liquidity of the life insurance investment, while admirable in most respects, is achieved at the expense of other desirable qualities of an investment. The liquidity is made possible by the fact that the investments of life insurance companies

---

[4] *Life Insurance Fact Book, 1961,* p. 53.

are almost entirely in bonds of one kind or another. Bonds pay fixed interest returns and carry a guarantee of maturity at the end of a bond period for the face amount. Because of this feature, good bonds are considered almost as cash equivalents and may be sold by the insurer, if necessary, to meet demands for liquidity on the part of the policyholders. Because bond prices do fluctuate in response to fluctuations in the interest rate (as interest rates rise, bond prices fall, and *vice versa*), insurers seldom cash bonds but rather hold them until maturity. In the past practically all demands on insurers for liquidity have been more than met by the inflow of premium and investment income. Since insurers can only rely on a return of the face amount of their investment in bonded indebtedness, life insurance contracts are made to promise only so many dollars of cash value. Hence, the life insurance and annuity contract is not a hedge against inflation, but is in the same category as a savings instrument like a United States savings bond, namely, a hedge against deflation.

4. The interest return on a life insurance investment, reflecting the character of the investments made by the insurers of policyholders' funds, is comparable to the interest return on bonds, that is, conservative. It is tempting for the uninformed to attempt to calculate interest return by determining what rate of interest, when applied to the annual premium payments would accumulate to the guaranteed cash values of the contract. This method is, of course, incorrect. A more accurate method would be to subtract from each premium payment that portion which is being paid for the pure protection under the contract, add back any dividends paid in that year, and determine the interest rate which would make this net amount accumulate to the guaranteed cash values for varying periods. A variation of this method is illustrated in Table 22–1. Unfortunately, the average insured cannot know in advance what the dividends will be, nor can he determine without considerable difficulty what the cost of pure protection is. One estimate of actual return under the policy can be determined from the interest earnings on the insurer's investments. For all United States life insurance in 1960, the average earnings on investments, before income taxes, were 4.11 per cent.[5] Investment income has been rising steadily each year since 1947. It is uncommon for an insurer to *guarantee* more than 2.5 per cent on most permanent contracts of life insurance. It is clear that the actual earnings of policyholders are substantially higher than the minimum guarantee, with dividends reflecting the difference between the actual earnings and the guaranteed earnings.

---

[5] Estimates of investment income after federal taxes are not available because of uncertainties as to the final effect of the Life Insurance Company Income Tax Act of 1959.

Buy term and invest difference argument. Because of misunderstandings concerning the true nature of interest return on a life insurance contract, it has been argued by some that it would pay to buy term insurance for the protection element and invest separately the difference in premiums between term insurance and ordinary life insurance. The argument runs as follows: If the premium for ordinary life insurance is $25 and the premium for 20-year insurance is $7, it would pay to buy term insurance for $1,000 and invest the $18 difference in comparable investments elsewhere; and in the end a greater cash value will be obtained than if the entire $25 were used to purchase $1,000 ordinary life policy. Table 22–1 shows a detailed analysis of this argument.

Column (1) in Table 22–1, lists the dividends estimated (but not guaranteed) for a $10,000 ordinary life policy whose gross annual premium is $248.70. Column (2) shows the annual net payments after dividends, it being assumed that the dividends are used to reduce premium payments. Column (3) shows the accumulated net payments for the policy over the 20-year period. The total paid by the end of this period is $3,759.40. Column (4) shows the guaranteed cash values under the policy each year. At the end of the 20 years, the cash value is $3,720. Column (5) shows the cumulative net cost of the policy—the difference between the amounts in Column (3) and Column (4), the cumulative difference between net premium payments and cash values. By the end of the period, the policyholder has paid in only $39.40 more than his guaranteed cash value. Column (6) shows the net insurance protection each year. This amount is the difference between $10,000, the face amount of the policy, and the guaranteed cash value in Column (4). If the insured dies at any time during the 20 years, his estate receives $10,000, which is made up of the net insurance protection and the cash value.

Now assume that the insured decides he will be financially better by purchasing term insurance for the protection element and investing separately the difference in premiums between term insurance and ordinary life insurance. In order to secure a proper comparison, he must buy term insurance each year in the amounts shown in Column (6). If he purchases $10,000 of term insurance, he will have an estate, in case of death, amounting to $10,000 plus whatever he has saved on the side. The total amount so provided will exceed the estate created by the ordinary life policy, and the comparison will not be accurate.

Column (7) shows the term premium per $1,000 for the net insurance protection needed. Column (8) results from multiplying Column

Table 22-1

ORDINARY LIFE PLAN V. DECREASING TERM AND A SEPARATE INVESTMENT OF THE "DIFFERENCE" IN PREMIUMS

Policy Year	(1) Dividend	(2) Annual Net Payment	(3) Total Net Payments	(4) Cash Value	(5) Cumulative Net Cost	(6) Net Insurance Protection	(7) Term Premium Per $1,000	(8) Total Term Premium for Net Protection	(9) Net Payment for Ordinary Life Less Cost of Pure Term Insurance	(10) Accumulation of Column (9) at 4%
1	$ 21.00	$227.70	$ 227.70	$ 80.00	$147.70	$9,920.00	$ 6.36	$ 63.09	$ 164.61	$ 171.19
2	24.80	223.90	451.60	300.00	151.60	9,700.00	6.56	63.63	160.27	344.72
3	28.60	220.10	671.70	530.00	141.70	9,470.00	6.79	64.30	155.80	520.54
4	32.40	216.30	888.00	700.00	188.03	9,300.00	7.05	65.57	150.73	698.12
5	36.50	212.20	1,100.20	880.00	220.20	9,120.00	7.34	66.94	145.26	877.12
6	40.50	208.20	1,308.40	1,070.00	238.40	8,930.00	7.66	68.40	139.80	1,057.59
7	44.60	204.10	1,512.50	1,250.00	262.50	8,750.00	8.02	70.18	133.92	1,239.17
8	48.70	200.00	1,712.50	1,430.00	282.50	8,570.00	8.42	72.16	127.84	1,421.69
9	52.90	195.80	1,908.30	1,620.00	288.30	8,380.00	8.86	74.25	121.55	1,604.97
10	57.20	191.50	2,099.80	1,810.00	289.80	8,190.00	9.34	76.49	115.01	1,788.78
11	61.50	187.20	2,287.00	2,000.00	287.00	8,000.00	9.88	79.04	108.16	1,972.82
12	65.90	182.80	2,469.80	2,190.00	279.80	7,810.00	10.49	81.93	100.87	2,156.64
13	70.70	178.00	2,647.80	2,380.00	267.80	7,620.00	11.17	85.12	92.88	2,339.50
14	75.30	173.40	2,821.20	2,570.00	251.20	7,430.00	11.92	88.57	84.83	2,521.30
15	80.40	168.30	2,989.50	2,760.00	229.50	7,240.00	12.74	92.24	76.06	2,701.26
16	85.40	163.30	3,152.80	2,950.00	202.80	7,050.00	13.66	96.30	67.00	2,878.99
17	90.30	158.40	3,311.20	3,140.00	171.20	6,860.00	14.68	100.70	57.70	3,054.15
18	94.90	153.80	3,465.00	3,340.00	125.00	6,660.00	15.81	105.29	48.51	3,226.77
19	99.40	149.30	3,614.30	3,530.00	84.30	6,470.00	17.04	110.25	39.05	3,396.45
20	103.60	145.10	3,759.40	3,720.00	39.40	6,280.00	18.37	115.36	29.74	3,563.24
Total	$1,214.60							$1,639.81	$2,119.59	

Notes:
Column (2)—$248.70 gross premium of ordinary life plan at age 35, $10,000 face amount, less contemplated dividends in Column (1).
Column (6)—$10,000 less Column (4).
Column (9)—Represents the difference between Column (2) and Column (8). This column then is the amount available for outside investment, the insured enjoying the same net protection as he enjoys with the ordinary life plan.

Source: Adapted from materials furnished by the Standard Insurance Company, Portland, Oregon.

(6) by Column (7), and shows the total premium for the term insurance plan. Note that while the term insurance premium per $1,000 almost triples over the 20-year period due to age increases, the total premium outlay is slightly less than double, because the net amount of insurance purchased declines steadily. By the end of the period, a total of $1,639.81 has been expended on the term insurance plan to provide the same net insurance protection as that which has been provided by the ordinary life plan.

Column (9) gives the difference between the cost of the term plan and the ordinary life premium, and is determined by subtracting each item in Column (8) from each corresponding item in Column (2). It is this sum which is available for separate investment. Column (10) shows how this investment will accumulate at an assumed interest rate of four per cent. Comparing Column (10) with Column (4), one may see that the ordinary life cash values in Column (4) accumulate at about the same rate as the separate investment in Column (10), and in fact exceed it by $157 at the end of 20 years. One may conclude that the insured has earned slightly more than four per cent on the *net investment element* in his ordinary life contract. Of course, he has not earned four per cent on his entire premium expenditures, since a substantial sum had to go to provide the pure insurance protection.

The insured who elected the plan of "investing the difference" and earned four per cent has not only failed to do better than he would have under the ordinary life plan; he has done worse. First, the accumulation under the ordinary life plan is tax free, but under the separate plan, it is not. Thus, the four per cent return on a separate investment, assuming the insured could earn this amount, is reduced by the amount of income taxes payable by the saver. If the saver is in the 25 per cent income tax bracket, he would have had to earn 5.33 per cent on his separate investment to equal the ordinary life performance. The higher his tax bracket, the greater is the net advantage of the ordinary life plan. Second, the saver runs the risk of (1) not maintaining his savings on a regular basis, (2) not finding outlets for savings in convenient denominations so that full interest is earned and compounded regularly on all savings, and (3) losing part of his principal through mistakes in investment judgment. Third, the saver is denied use of the settlement options available in the ordinary life policy for the ultimate disposition of cash values. Fourth, the saver has the option, under the ordinary life plan, of continuing his insurance protection indefinitely, while under the other plan the insurer may not obtain protection past age 65.

We may conclude that the return on the life insurance investment is reasonable considering the safety and liquidity of principal that it provides. It should be noted, however, that dividend schedules are not guaranteed and the return may not be as high as is often assumed. Furthermore, one should never fall into the error of assuming that his entire premium is available for investment and represents his savings, since the element of insurance protection must be paid from it. Likewise, one must not assume that the cost of the insurance protection is measured by the net cost figure such as $39.40 in Table 22–1 [see Column (5)]. The net cost in that example is $1,639.81, the total of Column (8), or 44 per cent of the total net premiums of $3,759.40.

Advantages of estate planning

As pointed out in Chapter 21, life insurance has long enjoyed a favored legal position which gives it advantages over other investments in arrangements which can be made for the eventual *use* of the savings. There is an unfortunate tendency for savers to ignore the problems involved in planning the wisest use of the fruits of their thrift. A lifetime savings program may be greatly diminished or its purpose deflected entirely by careless planning for the eventual settlement of the proceeds. For example, poorly drawn wills may cause the estate to be distributed to parties never contemplated by the saver. Imprudent tax planning may cause the forced liquidation of assets at a fraction of their true value. Creditors' claims, attorneys' fees, court costs, and other claims may deplete the estate more than would be the case if careful attention had been given to estate planning.

A full development of the legal and tax advantages of life insurance in estate planning is outside the scope of this text, but the following comments may be helpful in visualizing the nature of the problems which are encountered and the potential uses of life insurance in meeting these problems.

Life insurance contracts provide a semiautomatic way of planning the disposition of an estate in such a way as to overcome many of the hazards that confront other estates not so planned. The life insurance estate is liquid so that it is not necessary to convert the assets into any other form in order to provide an income to the dependents. The estate is usually immune from creditors' claims. Interest credited on cash values is exempt from federal income taxes during the accumulation period. During the settlement period the annuity receives favorable tax treatment under current tax regulations.[6] Since life insurance proceeds are paid directly to the beneficiary, there are no probate or court costs or attorney's fees connected with this part of the insured's estate. Because the contract provides settlement options, no trustee's fees are assessed for the administration of the estate; the insurer performs these functions at no added cost. Estate and inheritance taxes can also be reduced through proper use of life insurance. Most states exempt from inheritance taxes life insurance proceeds made payable to named beneficiaries. Federal estate tax regulations do not exempt life insurance from this important tax, but it is possible to transfer a life insurance policy to a beneficiary while the insured is still living and thus remove assets from the insured's estate so as to avoid the estate tax.[7] Such a transfer may result in a gift tax, but gift tax rates are much less than estate tax rates and exemptions are more generous.

One disadvantage of life insurance in estate planning is the matter of inflexibility in the administration of the estate proceeds after the death of the insured. Life insurers will seldom permit arrangements other than the stated settlement options, and once determined, these options cannot be changed by the beneficiary. The insured, for example, may leave his widow a lifetime income of $200 each month. Even if inflation reduces the purchasing power of this sum by one half, the insurer will not alter the arrangement to pay additional amounts for a shorter time period, or permit emergency withdrawals not provided for in advance by the insured. As another example, the insured may have purchased a policy to

---

[6] Tax regulations change constantly, but at the time of this writing, a life insurance investment, after being exempt from income taxes on interest accumulations, may often be distributed either to the insured or to beneficiaries with a low taxation burden. The present rules provide that the total cost of the contract shall be determined by adding all the premiums paid in. If the policy is cashed in, the gain, if any, is arrived at by subtracting the total cost from this cash value. Since the cost includes the amounts paid for pure protection, in effect, a tax deduction is given for the pure insurance element. However, there will seldom be an excess of cash values over total cost and, thus, little if any tax will commonly be due.

If the proceeds of a life insurance or an annuity contract are taken in installments, tax regulations are much more complicated. However, the basic principle currently used is relatively simple. Suppose the insured elects a life annuity with no refund. Assume the cash values are $17,000. He will receive a life annuity of about $100 per month at age 65. Tax authorities recognize that the $100 is part interest and partly a return of capital, and they, of course, tax only the interest. To determine the amounts representing capital, the $17,000 is divided by the approximate life expectancy (using tax tables) of the taxpayer. At 65 this period is 15 years. Thus, $1,133 is considered return of capital and the balance is therefore interest, which is fully taxable as ordinary income. Even if the insured outlives his life expectancy, he is still taxed on only $67 a year. Because of these rules, taxes on life insurance are postponed to a time when other income of the annuitant is probably low, and his exemptions would be such that probably no taxes would have to be paid, assuming he has no other taxable income. Note that if the saver had put his $17,000 in the bank and had received three per cent interest, his taxable income would amount to $510 annually. By purchase of an annuity with the proceeds, his taxable interest income is only $67, because of the operation of tax regulations.

[7] This may be done even though the insured continues to pay the premiums.

provide for a son's education and settled it so that the insurer pays the son $1,000 a year for four years, to begin at a stated time. If the college chosen by the son has raised its tuition or other costs have risen, the insurer will not settle the amount, say, at $2,000 a year for two years to accommodate these changes. To avoid these difficulties it is not uncommon to have part of the insurance proceeds made payable to a trustee who may be instructed to use individual judgment in the administration of the money.

Life insurance and inflation

Up to this point we have examined the investment advantages and disadvantages of life insurance and annuity contracts as long-term savings methods from every viewpoint except how well they serve in an economy which in the past has been characterized by long-term inflation. This is obviously an important consideration, and it has caused much concern among life insurance and other "fixed-dollar" savers.

Inflation protection refers to the ability of an investment to withstand the long-term average decline in purchasing power of the currency. Life insurance and annuity contracts give no inflation protection in the usual sense of the word. The savings in these contracts, being invested largely in bonds, is protected against deflation, but not against inflation. The fact that if the insured dies, his estate is often enhanced by a very large multiple of the amount of premiums he has paid in, constitutes a speculative element in the contract which has been equated to inflation protection by some, but this simile does not seem proper.

The inflation peril. How serious is the peril of inflation in robbing the fixed-dollar investment of its purchasing power? A measure of this threat may be observed by noting the rise of price indexes as seen in Table 22–2, which presents the figures of the Bureau of Labor Statistics

Table 22–2

CONSUMER PRICE INDEX, (ALL ITEMS) 1929–1959 (1947–1949 = 100)

1929	73.3	1937	61.4	1945	76.9	1953	114.4
1930	71.4	1938	60.3	1946	83.4	1954	114.8
1931	65.0	1939	59.4	1947	95.5	1955	114.5
1932	58.4	1940	59.9	1948	102.8	1956	116.2
1933	55.3	1941	62.9	1949	101.8	1957	120.2
1934	57.2	1942	69.9	1950	102.8	1958	123.5
1935	58.7	1943	74.0	1951	111.0	1959	124.5
1936	59.3	1944	75.2	1952	113.5		

Source: *1959 Statistical Supplement to the Survey of Current Business*, p. 30.

Consumer Price Index since 1929. A long-term investment begun in 1929, with interest compounded at 3 per cent, would have amounted to $49 in 1959 for every dollar saved annually between 1929 and 1959. However, the price index rose from 73.3 to 124.5. In terms of 1929 dollars, our $49 would be worth only 59 per cent (73.3/124.5), or about $29. This is slightly less than the actual number of dollars saved ($30) and so we might say that inflation has almost consumed any interest earned during the period.

Some of the limitations of this measure of inflation should be considered. First, the index may not measure prices of the type of commodities in which the saver is interested. The index is based on the so-called "market basket" of a city wage-earner or a clerical worker and does not reflect differences in the amounts of goods people buy, or geographical differences in prices. The weights used in deciding how important each type of commodity is in the total market basket may not correspond with the weights of actual purchases of a retired person. In the December, 1958, index, for example, the following weights (in percentages) were used: food, 28.7; housing, 32.7; clothing, 8.9; transportation, 11.7; medical care, 5.4; personal care, 2.2; reading and recreation, 5.3; other goods and services, 5.1. A retired person may find that the prices of the things he is interested in have not risen so drastically, and furthermore he may not be a large purchaser of those items which have increased most in price. For example, a retired person may not spend any where near one third of his budget on housing, as the index assumes, nor 11.7 per cent on transportation, nor 28.7 per cent on food. On the other hand, his expenditures for medical care might well exceed 5.4 per cent, and more might be spent on reading and recreation than 5.3 per cent.

Goods which may be heavily weighted in 1929 might not be important in 1959, nor may the quality of these goods be reflected in the price index. For example, the housing and house furnishings in 1929 did not include many of the conveniences that are taken for granted today. The price of today's housing, while higher, may not therefore reflect inflation so much as it reflects a higher standard of living. As someone has said, "it's not the high cost of living, but the cost of high living," which counts.

In assessing the future seriousness of inflation, it should be recalled that the period under review, 1929–1959, was one of almost continual price increases. With the exception of the period 1929–1933, 1938, 1949, and 1955, prices rose every year. This may not be an entirely typical period, since it encompassed the most devastating depression in

United States history as well as two major wars. If one examines price changes since 1850, one observes large swings in price trends, which include long periods of decline. For example, commodity prices generally fell during the period following the Civil War until 1900, a span of over 30 years. Commodity prices also generally declined following World War I, until 1933. If one had retired at the beginning of a long period of declining prices, after having saved money during a period of rising prices, he would fare very well indeed with a program of fixed-dollar savings. In other words, there is no guarantee that inflation is a continuous phenomenon, uninterrupted by periods of deflation.

On the other hand, many believe that there is a built-in inflationary bias in the United States economy that results from certain factors which were not present during past periods in which prices declined for substantial periods. For example, under the Full Employment Act of 1946, the federal government is committed to a policy of using federal powers to ensure full employment. This implies public works, taxation, and money management policies which aim at preventing price declines and accompanying depression. Strong labor unions reinforce the inflationary pressures by exerting an upward influence on wage rates. Continuance of defense expenditures necessitated by a "cold war," which gives no signs of letting up, tends to encourage federal budget deficits. This causes constant new injections of credit for defense expenditures, which generate demand for scarce consumer goods and service. Thus, more money and credit in circulation compete for existing commodities and drive prices upward. The management of a huge war-induced public debt tends to favor policies which will keep interest rates lower than they might otherwise become, thus encouraging "easy money," a policy which encourages inflation.

It may be concluded that the inflation peril may not be so inevitable or serious as some would predict. It would certainly be a folly to decide that fixed-dollar type savings have no further place in a long-term savings program because of creeping inflation. Yet, the observed long-run rise in prices is too much in evidence to ignore in plans for retirement. Ideally, one should hedge both ways. *The long-term saver needs protection against both inflation and deflation.*

The life insurance industry is only beginning to make overtures in the general direction of recognizing that the permanent life insurance contract and the annuity contract do not meet the inflation peril at all. For example, one proposal is that of a *purchasing power policy*, and another is the *variable annuity*.

The purchasing power policy. It has been proposed, although no United States life insurer has offered such a contract, that a life insurance policy be issued with an automatic annual increase in the face amount and cash values to reflect an assumed annual rate of deterioration in the purchasing power of the dollar. Thus, a 30-year endowment policy issued on such a basis would mature for approximately twice its initial face amount, assuming an annual rate of inflation of 2.5 per cent. The premium on such a policy would, of course, be higher than on an ordinary endowment policy. It could be set up on a level-premium basis, or on some other basis, similar to the way in which present contracts are arranged.[8]

Many difficulties would be experienced in the proposal to offer a purchasing power policy. First, the policy does not actually offer the policyholder anything he cannot arrange (at least approximately) with present contracts. It suggests that the obvious course to follow is simply to buy more life insurance and so save more money to meet inflation. The new policy offers a convenient way in which to accomplish this task neatly, since it provides an automatic method of keeping constant the purchasing power of the proceeds of the insurance. The insured is enabled to add small amounts of savings and death protection each year, but the new policy does not propose that the savings of the insured be invested in inflation-proof investments. All it suggests is that the life insurance industry should offer a contract enabling the insured to save additional amounts which will be invested in the same way as is done for present contracts. Second, the proposal assumes that the rate of inflation which has been observed in the past will be true in the future. If this assumption proves incorrect, the contract will not adjust itself to the actual inflation, if any, which occurs in practice. Third, the proposal offers no protection against inflation during the time that the proceeds are being used by the beneficiaries or by the insured. In other words, the insured might save enough to offset inflation during the accumulation period, but in retirement he receives a set amount, which may or may not be adequate during the 15 or 20 years of his remaining life expectancy.

The variable annuity. A much more ingenious scheme than the purchasing power policy and one which is in actual use among a few United States life insurers in a few jurisdictions, is the variable annuity.[9]

---

[8] Walter G. Bowerman, "Purchasing Power Policies," *The Spectator* (October, 1958). This article illustrates that such a policy is actuarially feasible.

[9] The variable annuity was originated by the College Retirement Equities Fund. The Fund is a subsidiary organization of the Teachers Insurance and Annuity Associa-
(*continued on next page*)

The objectives of the variable annuity are to offer a method by which the long-term saver may accumulate his funds in *equities,* securities whose value tends to follow the fluctuations in the general price level. The basic idea is that if the general price level rises over the accumulation period, the value of savings will also rise, thus maintaining their purchasing power at a fairly constant level. If the general price level falls, the value of the savings will also fall, but their purchasing power will still remain fairly constant. In other words, the variable annuity attempts to provide funds for a retirement income which would have a varying dollar value but a *constant purchasing power*. The regular annuities discussed previously in this text provide an income with a *fixed-dollar value,* but a varying purchasing power. It is presumed that it is more desirable for the retired person to have an income whose value in real terms is constant, than to have an income whose amount is fixed but whose real value fluctuates.

In practice, the details of the variable annuity are somewhat involved, but the general way in which they operate may be described by an illustration. Suppose "A" had purchased a variable annuity contract in 1929 when he was 35 and made annual premium payments of $1,000. Each year the premiums are invested by the insurer in common stocks. Specific stocks are not bought for "A's" account but for the account of the insurer, and "A" owns a small fraction of every security owned by the insurer. Thus, "A" owns a cross section of a broadly diversified common stock portfolio, similar to what he would own if he had purchased shares in a mutual fund. In a mutual fund "A" could cash in his shares at any time without restriction, but in the variable annuity there will be certain limitations on this freedom in order to discourage the use of the variable annuity as a device to "play the stock market," since its basic purpose is to enable the saver to accumulate a retirement fund.

During the 30 years that "A" pays his premiums, he would have deposited a total of $30,000. If the annual premium of $1,000 had been saved at 3 per cent compound interest, the value of the fund when "A" becomes 65 would be approximately $49,000. However, let us assume that due to inflation the value of the stocks is $84,000. This would represent nearly perfect adjustment to the rise in the consumer price index,

---

(continued)
tion, a life insurance company selling life insurance only to faculty members of institutions of higher education. It has offered variable annuities to faculty members since 1947. Among other things, difficulty in securing legal permission to offer variable annuities has prevented most other life insurers from entering this field. The Prudential Life Insurance Company of New Jersey has led a nationwide campaign to secure legislative approval for variable annuities, and in 1959 secured clearance from the New Jersey legislature to offer them.

since the value of "A's" stocks, after depreciation for the declining value of the dollar, would be about $49,000 in terms of 1929 purchasing power.[10]

Assuming that "A" used a traditional annuity or a life insurance contract as the method of saving, he would have taken his $49,000 and accepted a life annuity, 10 years certain, of about $330 per month. This amount is based on the quoted rates of a large insurer for policies issued in 1929. These policies assumed a higher interest rate than is available today. If the $49,000 were used to purchase an annuity at rates existing in this same insurer after 1954, only $295 per month could be received.

Under the variable annuity, the insurer would express the $84,000 in terms of so many *units* whose value can be any arbitrary amount, say $10. Then "A" would have 8,400 units to his credit, and he would be guaranteed a life annuity in terms of these units. If we assume that his life expectancy is 15 years, he would then receive approximately 8,400/15, or 560 units a year for life. The first year he would receive an annuity of 560 units whose value is $10 each, thus receiving $5,600. In the second year, the value of each unit is recalculated to reflect changes in the value of the underlying securities. Let us say that the stock market rose 3 per cent, reflecting a rise in the general price level. Then each unit is worth $10.30, and "A's" annuity for the second year is 560 units times $10.30, or $5,768, an increase of 3 per cent over the previous year. On the other hand if the stock market fell 10 per cent in the third year, "A's" annuity would be reduced accordingly. In any given year, of course, the stock market may not reflect changes in the price level with any degree of precision. For example, the 10 per cent decline in the stock market may actually be accompanied by a *rise* in the general price level. This is one of the weaknesses of the variable annuity. It assumes that the stock market is a nearly perfect reflection of consumer price changes, an assumption which has been true in the long run, but may not be true in the short run.

The above example was hypothetical, of course. What would have actually happened to the value of a constant dollar investment of $1,000 in common stocks begun in 1929, the peak of the stock market boom, and continued until 1959? The results may be seen in Table 22–3. It will be observed that the total investment is comprised of the $1,000 annual savings plus all dividends, less certain expenses including income taxes. Thus, the plan is roughly comparable to a life insurance plan in which the interest earnings are nontaxable. In comparing Column (1)

---
[10] Refer to the example on page 588. $84,000 × .59 equals approximately $49,000.

Table 22–3

RESULTS OF A CONTINUOUS INVESTMENT IN COMMON STOCKS

Year	(1) Total Invested *	(2) Average Stock Price, July 1 †	(3) Total Shares Acquired	(4) December 31 Market Value
1929	$ 1,000	$ 48	20.0	$ 714
1930	2,014	33	50.0	1,321
1931	3,068	24	92.4	1,217
1932	4,154	7	225.5	2,579
1933	5,252	20	282.3	5,476
1934	6,396	18	343.2	6,634
1935	7,600	20	401.3	10,943
1936	8,899	29	445.1	15,413
1937	10,517	33	491.9	11,097
1938	12,341	25	566.7	15,669
1939	13,768	23	624.8	16,400
1940	15,396	19	697.4	15,565
1941	17,243	20	782.6	14,947
1942	19,152	17	885.2	18,783
1943	20,852	26	955.4	24,009
1944	22,607	27	1,020.6	28,546
1945	24,478	30	1,083.6	38,218
1946	26,423	37	1,136.1	35,707
1947	28,606	32	1,204.0	38,202
1948	31,120	35	1,279.1	40,713
1949	34,145	30	1,374.5	48,093
1950	37,808	37	1,475.7	65,048
1951	42,155	45	1,572.1	80,632
1952	46,783	53	1,660.1	93,646
1953	51,544	51	1,744.9	92,985
1954	56,557	62	1,834.8	142,600
1955	62,256	91	1,905.1	192,929
1956	69,199	106	1,972.2	206,312
1957	76,554	108	2,041.2	184,953
1958	83,857	102	2,118.8	251,015
1959	90,842	134	2,168.5	272,466

* Assumes that $1,000 is invested on July 1 each year and that all dividends, less brokerage commissions and federal income taxes, are reinvested. Federal income taxes are based on the taxes which would apply to a married man with an $8,000 salary with two children for the year in which the dividends are received. The 1959 market value is as of July 1.
† Based on the average price of those stocks comprising the Standard and Poor's Industrial Stock Price Index.
Source: *The Outlook*, Standard and Poor's Corporation, Winter, 1959–1960, Annual forecast number, p. 516.

with Column (4), it can be seen that if the plan had been terminated during the first four years or in 1941 or 1942, a substantial loss of principal would have taken place due to the decline of the stock market during those years. However, due to a strong upward basic trend in the stock market following World War II, the value of the investment reached the astounding sum of $272,466 on December 31, 1959, three times the total invested, 5.6 times the $49,000 which would have been saved by traditional methods, and 3.4 times the $84,000 which would have been necessary just to offset the rise in consumer prices which occurred during the period. This astonishing performance is due to a combination of factors, such as the monetary effect of two major wars, an unprecedented rise of general business activity spurred on by an explosive population growth, and many important economic and scientific breakthroughs.

Another factor which makes possible a result such as the one observed in Table 22–3 is a process called *dollar cost averaging,* which refers to the fact that if a constant sum is invested regularly, more shares of a given stock are purchased when the price is low than when the price is high. Thus, the *average* cost of the acquired stock is always lower than the average price which prevailed for this stock. To take a simple example, if $1,000 is used to buy a stock at $100, 10 shares are acquired. Next year the price may be down to $50; and if $1,000 is again invested, 20 shares are acquired. The investor now has 30 shares for which he paid $2,000, for an average cost of $66.67 per share. Yet, the average price of these shares is $75. If the price had gone up to $200, only five shares would have been purchased the second year, and the investor would have acquired 15 shares at an average cost of $133.34. The average price was $150. Thus, no matter whether the price of the stock goes up or down, the average cost is always less than the average price. The variable annuity plan thus enables the investor to utilize the dollar cost averaging principle to compound the value of his investment over the years. It also encourages regularity in the investment program, a principle which must be strictly observed if the benefits of dollar cost averaging are to be achieved.

Arguments for the variable annuity. We may summarize the chief arguments for the variable annuity as follows:

1. It enables the saver to obtain protection against the long-run decline in the purchasing power of the dollar both during the saving years and during retirement years.
2. It permits the saver to share in the economic growth of the nation in a way not possible with fixed-dollar investments. In this way he obtains participation in higher living standards as well as protection against lower living standards due to inflation. The variable annuity may result in the annuitant receiving fewer dollars in some periods than he would with a regular annuity, but the average purchasing power of these dollars should remain fairly constant. Even if it does not, the annuitant will still fare better since if past trends are any indication, he will have much more value on hand at the beginning of his annuity income period than he would have under a fixed-dollar accumulation plan.

Arguments against the variable annuity.   Opponents of the variable annuity stress the following arguments:

1. Issuance of these contracts by life insurance companies which have always been associated with secure, guaranteed investments may result in an adverse public reaction against established life insurance programs, especially among individuals who were sold a variable annuity as a result of the overzealous promises of a salesman anxious to make a sale.

2. Due to an unfamiliarity with the basic assumptions of a variable annuity, many savers might be misled into believing that the value of the investment will always rise. If the stock market declines, they might become discouraged and drop the plan, thus losing any advantages they might have obtained from dollar cost averaging.

3. Since it is recognized by everyone that the stock market is an imperfect instrument in measuring changes in purchasing power, there will be some periods when the value of the annuity may bear no resemblance to actual changes in prices. An annuitant who had relied exclusively on this method as a way of retiring would face a serious dilemma if, for example, prices rose while the stock market fell, as happened in 1946 (see Tables 22–2 and 22–3).

4. There exists a risk that if the annuitant retires at the time of a severe stock market slump, he may not realize enough to retire on and thus suffer loss of substantial principal.

5. There is no guarantee that all insurers who offer variable annuities will be able to achieve satisfactory investment results even in times when the general stock market index moves upward. Judging from the spotty record of the managements of mutual funds, who face the task of continuous investment of shareholders' funds, largely in common stocks, there is little doubt that some managements of variable annuity plans would not achieve so good a result as is achieved by stock market averages.[11]

6. It is argued by some that if life insurers sold variable annuities, it would amount to an admission that the fight against inflation had been given up, an impression that trustees of over $100 billion of policyholders' funds invested conservatively in bonds wish to avoid at all costs. These individuals question the basic assumption that continued creeping inflation is inevitable. They point to the period from 1952–1955, when the consumer price index moved upward only one point, as an example of what can be achieved even at the height of a business boom. In support of this evidence, they cite the efforts of the federal government to employ anti-inflation measures.

---

[11] In 1959, for example, the average market performance for each of four major types of funds fell below the Dow-Jones industrial stock average. See *Business Week* February 20, 1960, p. 166.

Conclusion. A basic conclusion which emerges from this discussion is that in all likelihood there will be continued periods of prosperity and depression, inflation and deflation. The variable annuity, which has much to recommend it, has enough weaknesses so that, if and when it becomes generally available, it ought not to be relied upon as the sole vehicle for retirement. Fixed-dollar investments continue to have an important place in the long-range savings program, and life insurance is one of those investments.

An analysis of the manner in which people in the United States have saved their money reveals some interesting facts. Table 22–4 presents a

Table 22–4

DOLLAR SAVINGS BY INDIVIDUALS IN THE UNITED STATES IN SELECTED MEDIA 1948, 1958

(Billions of Dollars)

Media	Total Assets 1948	Per Cent of Total	Total Assets 1958	Per Cent of Total
Life insurance..................	$ 47.1	23.4	$ 86.6	24.2
Time deposits:				
Commercial banks.............	35.8	17.8	63.2	17.6
Mutual savings banks..........	18.4	9.2	34.0	9.5
Postal savings................	3.3	1.5	1.1	.0
United States savings bonds.......	47.8	23.6	47.7	13.2
Savings and loan associations......	11.0	5.5	47.9	13.2
Government pension and trust funds	36.4	18.0	64.9	18.2
Investment companies...........	2.2	1.0	14.8	4.1
Total	$202.0	100.0	$360.2	100.0

Sources: Compiled from *Economic Almanac, 1960* (New York: National Industrial Conference Board) and *Investment Companies 1959* (New York: Arthur Wiesenberger & Company). Percentages calculated.

comparison of the total assets in the various media available to savers in 1948 and 1958. These data clearly reveal the growth of investor interest in mutual funds, whose primary assets are composed of common stocks. Investments of this type were four times as large, percentage wise, in 1958 as in 1948. Yet, they still constitute only about four per cent of the total dollar savings. It is also clear that savers have not by any means lost interest in traditional conservative fixed-dollar investments. Life insurance constitutes the largest single method of fixed-dollar saving. It appears that savings and loan associations have experienced the largest growth of any of the traditional savings institutions, having grown at the expense of United States savings bonds.

Table 22–4 does not reveal the growth of savings in equity-type investments, such as individually held real estate and common stocks, which together constitute a very important segment of total assets of individuals. For example, in 1959 it was estimated that 58 per cent of all nonfarm family units owned homes with an average value of $12,900 and with a mortgage averaging 47 per cent of the housing value.[12] The value of preferred and common stocks owned by individuals was estimated at $212 billion in 1954 and $335 billion in 1958.[13]

Unfortunately, no reliable data exist as to how widely these stocks are held nor as to what concentration of values exist in higher income classes. Nevertheless, it is significant that both equities and fixed-dollar investments constitute an important part of the holdings of individuals. In view of the considerable uncertainty as to the course of future economic events, this is as it should be, since a hedge against both inflation and deflation is desirable.

SUMMARY

1. The annuity principle, the reverse of the life insurance principle, provides for an orderly *liquidation* of an estate in such a way that the annuitant cannot outlive his retirement income. An annuity generally provides about twice the retirement income that can be provided by interest alone since the annuity contemplates the gradual depletion of principal.

2. The funds for the purchase of an annuity may be accumulated through permanent life insurance contracts, by separate annuity contracts, or through savings plans other than those sponsored by life insurance companies.

3. Saving for retirement through a life insurance or an annuity contract has many advantages over traditional methods of saving; but, in common with investment media such as savings accounts, savings bonds, and other fixed-dollar methods, it contains no protection against loss of values through gradual inflation.

4. While the inflation peril is probably not the absolute certainty that many believe, its threat is sufficiently serious to warrant careful attention to various methods designed to cover it. In an attempt to "beat inflation," the saver should not lose sight of the other important desiderata in an investment program for retirement.

5. There are at least six major objectives to consider in a long-term savings program: (a) safety of the principal, (b) liquidity of the investment, (c) reasonable interest return, (d) choice of a plan most likely to lead to consistent savings, (e) formulation of sound plans for the eventual distribution of the estate, and (f) protection against inflation.

---

[12] "1959 Survey of Consumer Finances, Housing of Nonfarm Families," *Federal Reserve Bulletin* (September, 1959), pp. 1107–1108.
[13] *Economic Almanac, 1960.*

6. Traditional life insurance and annuity contracts lend themselves extremely well in meeting the first five objectives listed on page 597, but make no attempt at meeting inflation. The purchasing power policy and the variable annuity have been proposed to remedy this defect, with most interest being centered in the variable annuity.

7. The variable annuity, perhaps the most radical departure from traditional life insurance economics ever contemplated, is not a cure-all; but it holds sufficient promise to warrant careful investigation and experimentation as a way to permit the small saver to share in the long-term economic growth of the country. Variable annuities should not be viewed as a substitute for, but rather as a complement to, traditional fixed-dollar investments, of which life insurance is the most important single example.

QUESTIONS FOR REVIEW AND DISCUSSION

1. (a) A life insurance agent presented a client with the following figures concerning the purchase of ordinary life insurance versus term insurance:

Annual premium for $20,000 ordinary life, age 35, $373. Annual premium for $20,000 term to age 65, $226. Difference available for outside investment, $147. Amount to which $147 per year will compound in 30 years at 5 per cent interest, $10,213. Cash value of ordinary life policy in 30 years, $10,560. Conclusion, the client would need to earn 5 per cent after taxes and investment expenses to equal the cash value of the ordinary life policy after 30 years.

Criticize the agent's presentation and his conclusion. If the agent's presentation were amended, what conclusions might you make about the wisdom of "buying term and investing the difference"?

(b) The agent continued his presentation by stating that ordinary life insurance is a superior plan for retirement provision. He indicated that the $10,560 cash value of the ordinary life policy would provide $67.73 a month, while the separate savings fund would require a capital amount of $16,255 to equal this monthly income at an interest rate of 5 per cent. Explain why the ordinary life plan is able to accomplish this feat.

(c) The agent made the following comparison of ordinary life insurance and a retirement income policy:

	PLAN I RETIREMENT INCOME POLICY	PLAN II ORDINARY LIFE
Total premium payments....................	$ 3,186.40	$ 3,189.60
Amount of protection.......................	40,000.00	180,000.00
Cash value at age 55.......................	79,840.00	65,520.00
Paid-up insurance at age 55................	122,200.00	108,360.00
Monthly life income at age 55 (10 years certain).	400.00	328.26

(1) The client's main objective is to provide for his own retirement although he has four sons and would like to give each of them a substantial inheritance if he should die. The client is age 33 and wishes to retire at 55. In your opinion, which plan is superior as an all-round estate accumulation plan. Why?

(2) A salesman from a stock brokerage house approaches the client after the life insurance agent has left. He observes the agent's cash value figures and notes that if the client has $80,000, he could invest this money in a "blue chip" security whose dividends have averaged 6 per cent for many years. Thus, the client would receive $4,800 a year in dividend income and preserve all the principal. What risks would the client run if he took the broker's advice?

2. In the United States there has been a downward trend in long-term interest rates for many years, and mortality rates have also declined steadily. In possession of these facts, if you were offered the choice of a 35-year deferred annuity whose rent is guaranteed and one whose price is 10 per cent lower but whose rent depends on conditions in existence at the time of retirement, which one would you take? Why?

3. An economist, writing on the future of the dollar, observed that when the public begins to lose faith in the currency, wasteful consumption and misdirected investments suddenly become rational actions, compared with the foolishness of saving money that is becoming worthless. Do you agree? Why, or why not? What type of investments becomes "rational" in this situation? Why?

4. A writer stated, "To the advocates of creeping inflation, full employment and monetary stability are incompatible." Do you agree? In your answer explain why some might advocate creeping inflation as a desirable alternative to less than full employment.

5. It has been pointed out that since inflation is not self-regulating, the only way to keep inflation within predetermined limits is to impose restrictions on the volume of borrowing, and perhaps to exercise other economic controls. This leads to a fundamental inconsistency in the arguments of those who favor creeping inflation as a preferable alternative to less than full employment. Explain why this might be true.

6. One argument which has been used against the variable annuity is the fear that life insurance companies might gain voting control over companies in whose stocks they have invested. This, it is argued, would place insurance companies in fields in which they have no experience, to the detriment of the policyholder. What points might be raised for and against this argument?

7. One of the arguments for the variable annuity is that it should enable the long-term saver to share in the economic growth of the nation. If you were an opponent of the variable annuity, how might you answer this argument?

8. A salesman of a mutual fund points out that there is little in a variable annuity not already available from a mutual fund, and that his company

will agree to pay the proceeds of a savings program in as many installments and in whatever amounts are desired over a retirement period.
What factor is the salesman overlooking in his argument?

9. (a) In what way is the purchasing power policy a protection against inflation?

(b) What are the shortcomings of this policy as such a protection?

10. A financial writer stated, "Insurance has always been a contract in dollars.
When it is no longer that, it becomes a mixture of investment trust and an
insurance contract—neither fish, fowl, or good red herring. The danger, it
seems to this writer, is that people purchasing the variable annuity may do
so under the impression that it provides the safety of an ordinary insurance
policy. This can only be true if the days of deflationary and heavy declines
in stock prices are entirely of the past." Do you agree? Why?

11. Roger Babson, whose prediction of the 1929 stock market crash helped
bring him fame in the field of finance, wrote in the *Commercial and
Financial Chronicle* on January 7, 1960, "I don't see how buying Dow-
Jones common stocks now can be a hedge against inflation. This is not to
say they may not go higher, but these stocks are already too inflated to be
bought as inflation hedges by intelligent people." What bearing, if any,
does this statement have on the wisdom of purchasing a variable annuity
at the time of that writing? Explain.

12. "A" argues that through dollar cost averaging he can always be assured
that the average cost of the securities he purchases will be less than the
average price of these securities, regardless of whether the market rises
or falls.

(a) Explain how this can be true, using a numerical example.

(b) Does this mean that "A" cannot lose on his investment? Why?

13. A life insurance actuary stated, "If we are willing to face the truth for our-
selves, we must admit privately that life insurance and pension funds as
now issued are something of a gamble insofar as the proceeds have any
definite foreseeable purchasing power." Formulate a reply to this argument from the viewpoint of one strongly committed to fixed-dollar savings
as an exclusive method of saving for retirement.

14. A life insurance company in Chile is said to have introduced a life insurance contract that provides a face amount which varies each year according to a cost of living index in the city of Santiago. The premium is
increased or decreased according to changes in the face amount and age
changes. Nonforfeiture values are not provided. What weaknesses and
strengths do you see in such a plan?

15. An opponent of variable annuities stressed that the risk that a person
would not live to complete a savings program in common stocks is substantial. Furthermore, an analysis of the stock market fluctuations in the
period 1900–1960 reveals eight times when stocks fell by 40 per cent or
more in a relatively short time and that the period it took for market
averages to regain their previous high ranged from 32 to 302 months. In
the event of death before these peaks were regained, the investor might

lose part of his principal. How might these arguments be answered by the proponent of variable annuities?

16. Explain in your own words why it is that the present value of an annuity becomes less as the rate of interest assumed becomes greater.

17. "A life annuity is the reverse of a life insurance contract." Explain.

18. One use of a regular annuity is to enable a father to distribute part of his estate to his heirs while he is still living and yet enjoy the same retirement income from the remainder of his estate as he would have received from the entire estate invested conservatively.
    (a) How can this be true?
    (b) What advantages or disadvantages might there be for the heirs? Discuss.

19. One insurer quotes the following annuity rents on a female, age 30: 10 years certain and life, $3.22 per $1,000 of proceeds; 15 years certain and life, $3.20; 20 years certain and life, $3.18; installment fund, $3.12. No quotation is available for a straight-life annuity at this age. Explain (a) why there is such a small difference in rents between these various annuity plans and (b) why the insurer does not publish quotations for the straight-life annuity at this age.

20. Differentiate between the 15-year temporary life annuity settlement and the fixed-period option for 15 years.

21. Would you logically expect to receive a higher or a lower life annuity from $10,000 of cash value in an ordinary life insurance policy or $10,000 of outside savings invested in an annuity when the annuitant reaches retirement age? Why?

22. Why would one logically expect to receive a higher income from a group annuity than from an individual annuity (assuming the same cash values available)? Explain.

23. Account for the substantial growth of group annuities in recent years as compared with the growth of individual annuities.

24. "A" states that in his opinion the safety factor in a long-term investment has been interpreted much too narrowly. Most investors interpret safety to mean protection against loss of values through the bankruptcy of a debtor firm. What is needed is a broader meaning of the word safety so as to include protection against loss of values through inflation as well. Do you agree? If so, will the same type of investment serve as "safe" in both senses?

Health

Insurance

Of the major types of insurance against perils which destroy income, health insurance has shown the most rapid increase in public acceptance since the end of World War II. For example, during the period 1948 to 1958 when the purchase of life insurance policies rose at the same rate as personal income, expenditures for health insurance were of such magnitude that the percentage of total medical expenditures met by insurance increased from 7.9 per cent to 23.6 per cent, a threefold increase.[1] (See Table 19–4, page 514.) Such rapid public recognition of the increased peril and of the method of insurance to meet it has seen few equals in the history of insurance. In this chapter we shall examine the major types of health insurance contracts, together with the many problems involved in the implementation of these contracts.

CATEGORIES OF HEALTH INSURANCE

Health Insurance may be defined broadly as that type of insurance which provides indemnification for expenditures and loss of income resulting from loss of health. Unfortunately there is no sharp distinction among the various contracts as to the *type* of medical expense for which indemnity is payable. For example, hospitalization policies usually pay not only for hospital services but also for medicines used in the hospital, physicians' services rendered in the hospital, and other items. In general, however, we may recognize five different types of health insurance benefits which may be offered on separate contracts or in different combinations on a single contract:

1) Hospitalization.
2) Surgical.
3) Regular medical.
4) Major medical.
5) Loss of income.

---

[1] Agnes W. Brewster, "Voluntary Health Insurance and Medical Care Expenditures, 1948–1958," *Social Security Bulletin* (December, 1959), p. 9.

1) Hospitalization

The *hospitalization contract* is intended to indemnify the insured for necessary hospitalization expenses, including room and board in the hospital, laboratory fees, nursing care, use of operating room, and certain medicines and supplies. The agreement may set dollar allowances for the different items or may be on a "service" basis. Typical contracts offered by insurance companies, for example, may state that the insured will be indemnified "up to $15 a day" for necessary hospitalization, while Blue Cross arrangements may provide for "full hospital service in a semiprivate room."

2) Surgical

The *surgical contract* provides set allowances for different surgical procedures performed by duly licensed physicians. In general, a schedule of different operations is set forth, together with the maximum allowance for each operation. Thus, the $300 schedule may provide $150 for an appendectomy, $25 for a tonsilectomy, $10 for the lancing of a boil, and $300 for a lobotomy. The $300 limit is the maximum allowance and applies only to a few specified surgical procedures.

3) Regular medical

The *regular medical contract* refers to that contract of health insurance which covers physicians' services other than surgical procedures and is to be sharply distinguished from the major medical contract, which is defined below. Generally, regular medical insurance provides allowances for physicians' visits, such as $3 or $5 per visit, regardless of whether the visits are made in the hospital, at home, or in the doctor's office. Normally, but not always, regular medical insurance is written in conjunction with other types of health insurance and is not written as a separate contract.

4) Major medical

The *major medical contract,* a relatively new type of health insurance, is designed to meet very large medical bills, on a blanket basis with very few sublimitations imposed on specific expense items. The contract is issued subject to substantial deductibles of different sorts and with a high maximum limit. A major medical policy might have a $10,000 maximum limit for any one accident or illness, have a $500 deductible for any one illness, and contain an agreement to indemnify the insured for a specified percentage of his bills, such as 80 per cent over and above the amount of the dollar deductible. A few insurers offer a variation of the major medical contract, known as *comprehensive*, which reduces the deductible to $25 or $50.

5) Loss of income

The *loss of income contract* agrees to indemnify the insured for loss of income due to illness or accident. Usually there is a waiting period before the income payments commence and the disability must be one that prevents the insured from carrying on his usual occupation. Most policies continue payment of the benefits for only a specified maximum number of years, but lifetime benefits are available in some contracts. However, under all loss of income policies, the benefits are terminated as soon as the disability ends.

METHODS OF PAYING FOR HEALTH LOSS

In general, we may say that there are two broad methods of arranging for the payment of medical bills—individually and through some insurance plan. Three fourths of all private medical bills are estimated to be paid individually, and one fourth, through insurance methods.[2] These figures exclude expenditures of public health agencies, public assistance programs, government hospitals, medical research, and services rendered by private agencies without charge.

The insurance plans may be further subdivided into social insurance and private insurance arrangements. Social insurance methods, which include workmen's compensation, compulsory nonoccupational disability plans, and social security, are discussed in Chapter 24. Private arrangements are of two types—individual contracts and group contracts. *Group contracts* include Blue Cross and Blue Shield plans, private group clinics, college health plans, consumer sponsored plans, industrial plans, and community plans, as well as insurance company group contracts.

Data collected by the Health Insurance Council in 1959 indicate that approximately 128 million people were covered for hospital expenses, 117 million for surgical expenses, 82 million for regular medical expenses, 22 million for major medical expenses, and 43 million for loss of income. Included in these totals are Blue Cross and Blue Shield policies covering 57 million people for hospitalization, 49 million people for surgical expenses, and 43 million people for regular medical expenses.

---

[2] *Ibid.* p. 9.

Group insurance contracts cover many more persons than individual contracts. Although the data for the number of individuals covered are only approximate, it may be said that only one in four people covered for hospitalization and surgical expenses has an individual policy, while one in three having coverage for loss of income has an individual contract. In terms of dollar amounts, it was estimated that in 1959 approximately $2.8 billion in benefits was paid to individuals under insurance company plans, and another $2.3 billion under independent group, Blue Cross, and Blue Shield plans.[3] About $2.1 billion of insurance company benefits was paid out under group contracts. Thus, $4.4 billion, or about 85 per cent of the $5.2 billion of benefits was paid by these organizations to persons covered under group plans. As will be seen later in this chapter, there are many factors that account for the dominance of the group insurance method of covering health losses.

DISTRIBUTION OF COVERAGE

Estimates of the relative importance of each type of health insurance indicate that more benefits are paid under hospital expense contracts than under any other type of contract. The plans underwritten by all types of private insurers have been classified as follows:

TYPE OF CONTRACT	PER CENT OF TOTAL BENEFITS		PER CENT INCREASE IN NUMBERS COVERED 1952 TO 1959
	1952	1959	
Hospital expense..............	51	56	40
Loss of income...............	23	16	13
Surgical expense ⎫			63
Regular medical expense ⎬.......	26	28	130
Major medical expense ⎭			3,100
Total.....................	100	100	

Source: Health Insurance Data 1960 (New York: Health Insurance Institute), pp. 11 and 39.

Hospital expense coverage, although showing a 40 per cent increase in the number of individuals covered, accounted for only a modest increase in its share of total benefits over the period 1952–1959. Major medical expense insurance coverage enjoyed the greatest gain in numbers covered, showing an astounding increase of 3,100 per cent from a mere 689,000 individuals covered in 1952 to 21,850,000 in 1959.

[3] *Source Book of Health Insurance Data 1960* (New York: Health Insurance Institute, 1960), p. 37.

In a study, based on a sample of 2,000 families in 1957, it was revealed that only 27 per cent of the group were totally uninsured for health losses.[4] The remaining 73 per cent had coverage distributed as follows:

Type of Contract	Per Cent of All Families
Hospital only	5
Some combination of hospital, surgical, and regular medical	29
Major medical and any combination of hospital, surgical, and medical	18
Loss of income only	1
Loss of income and any combination of hospital, surgical, medical, and major medical	20
Major medical only, or covered, but kind unknown	**
	73

**Less than .5 per cent.

This study, based on actual interviews with consuming units, supports the conclusion that most families have more than one type of health insurance. A combination of medical, surgical, and hospital insurance is the most widely used type. Loss of income insurance is used by only 20 per cent of all families, generally in conjunction with other types of coverage.

In a survey of attitudes toward health insurance, the study shows that 29 per cent of all families interviewed either thought that the loss of income peril was not important or that it was less important than other health perils. These findings sharply contradict the actual facts as documented in Chapter 19, where it was shown that loss of income was by far the most important health loss. For hospital bills, 81 per cent of the families believed that these were very important, more important than any other health loss. Only 62 per cent thought that doctor bills were very important and only 56 per cent considered drugs and medicines very important. Yet Table 19–4, page 514, shows that total private expenditures for physicians' services exceeded those for hospital expenses by a considerable margin, and that the total outlay for medicines equaled that for total hospital bills. The survey indicated that 75 per cent of all insured families felt that their protection was "about right," and of those who wanted more coverage, only 20 per cent wanted more income loss coverage.[5]

---

[4] *A Profile of the Health Insurance Public* (New York: Health Insurance Institute, 1959), p. 13.
[5] *Ibid.,* p. 21.

Experience with insurance claims among the 2,000 families surveyed provide some indication of why health insurance has shown such an increase in public acceptance and recognition since World War II. Of the group, 69 per cent had submitted a claim under their policies at some time, 38 per cent within the past year. Only 31 per cent had never had a claim. Among those with hospital coverage, 57 per cent had submitted a claim, and 80 per cent of those with a complete package of coverage (loss of income and any combination of hospital, surgical, medical, and major medical) had submitted a claim.

As a group, the families were apparently satisfied with the method by which the claims were paid, even though coverage was by no means complete, since only slightly more than one half of the claimants had their entire bill covered. Only 12 per cent of the families indicated that they received less than they expected, primarily because they did not understand their contracts or because the bill was higher than they expected.

It is significant that 14 per cent of the families reporting claims had bills exceeding $500, and that of these bills, only 38 per cent was fully compensated by insurance. Yet, for bills of $100 or less, incurred by 32 per cent of all families, some 65 per cent received payment for all or most of the bill.[6] These data suggest that the health-insuring public as a whole is apparently purchasing contracts that provide full coverage of small bills but inadequate coverage of large bills. This practice, of course, violates the basic insurance buying principles that were developed in Chapter 4.

COMMON PROVISIONS OF INDIVIDUAL HEALTH INSURANCE CONTRACTS

Because the form of individual health insurance contracts is not standardized, it is impracticable to discuss any one given type of policy. Rather, an analysis of the major types of contractual provisions typically found in these contracts will be given.

Persons covered

Health insurance may cover only the applicant, or it may cover both the applicant and certain named dependents. Since the health failure of dependents is often as severe, if not more severe, in its financial impact as the health loss of the breadwinner, coverage on dependents is consid-

---

[6] *Ibid.*, pp. 27–28.

ered extremely important. Loss of income coverage, of course, is not written for dependents, but all other types of health contracts generally permit the insured to cover his dependents. Sometimes, however, dependents are covered under different schedules of benefits or the dependents may be subject to certain limitations not imposed on the breadwinner.

Defining the peril

All individual health insurance contracts define, both specifically and by exclusions, what perils are intended to be covered. Two general forms may be found—those insuring accidents and those insuring both illness and accident.

Accident only contracts. *Accident only* contracts generally offer quite limited coverage. It is not uncommon to find accidents narrowly defined to include only those injuries caused by *accidental means*. If this wording is used, something abnormal, unusual, and unexpected must have occurred immediately prior to the injury if the insured is to be considered as covered. Some examples of the implications of the accidental means clause were given in Chapter 21 in connection with the discussion of the double indemnity clause in life insurance. Accident only policies are commonly issued as travel accident contracts, vacation policies, etc.

Illness and accident contracts. Since over 90 per cent of all physical disabilities may be traced to illness rather than to accident, it is not surprising that the greatest demand in health insurance contracts is for the *illness and accident* contract. However, even though a contract covers illness and accident, it will usually narrow the meaning of illness or accident in certain ways. For example, disabilities or expense caused by mental disease, tuberculosis, childbirth or pregnancy, dental treatment, intentionally self-inflicted injuries or attempted suicide, whether sane or insane, pre-existing illnesses, cosmetic surgery (unless required after an accident), injuries recoverable through workmen's compensation, war injuries or aviation accidents, may be excluded. The main reason for these exclusions is that either recovery can be made from other sources, or that the claim is not insurable because to include it would raise the cost of the contract beyond the means of the average purchaser.

Defining losses

All individual health insurance contracts are extremely careful to define just what type of health loss is intended to be covered. If hospital expenses are to be insured, the contract will set the limit of these expenses as so much per day, for so many days, or subject to a maximum amount. Blue Cross contracts usually set no daily maximum, since the room and board agreement is on a service basis; but they may specify dollar limits on certain hospital services, such as laboratory fees, X-rays, blood plasma, and special nursing.

If the policy offers medical or surgical coverage, it will contain specific limitations on the extent to which doctor bills will be paid. An "operation" is defined as certain surgical procedures, such as cutting, suturing, treatment of fracture, taping, giving injection treatment, electrocauterization, and artificial pneumothorax. If two surgical procedures are performed in one operation, the policy is limited to indemnification for the more serious of the two.

Recurring losses. The policy must define when one loss ends and when another begins. For example, suppose the maximum hospital expense benefit period is 90 days and the insured is hospitalized for 60 days. He is discharged and five days later must re-enter the hospital because of a relapse. Has a new loss begun, entitling him to 90 additional days' benefits, or is the second loss a resumption of the old, with only 30 additional days of indemnification payable? Under a *recurrent disability clause,* the contract will specify that the second re-entry must either be from an entirely new set of causes, or that some period, such as one to six months, must have elapsed between hospitalizations, in order for the second period of disability to be considered a new period of entitlement. This definition is also important in ascertaining the application of a deductible or a waiting-period provision. In group contracts this provision is quite liberal in that the test is "Did the insured return to work?" If he did, and is later hospitalized, a new period of entitlement begins.

In order to specify what losses are to be paid, the contract will generally provide definitions of eligible hospitals. A hospital may be defined as an institution operated pursuant to the law for the care and treatment of sick and injured persons, with organized facilities for major surgery and 24-hour nursing service. Bed confinement to a private clinic during the course of one day is thus probably not a day of hospital confinement. Likewise, nursing homes, sanitariums, rest homes, and similar institutions are not "hospitals."

In addition, the policy covers only bills of "legally qualified physicians." Professional fees of optometrists, clinical psychologists, etc., may not be covered.

Disability income. In loss of income policies, two classes of disabilities are usually recognized—total and partial.

Total disability. For a disability to be considered *total,* a contract may specify that a fairly liberal definition applies for the first one or two years, and thereafter a much stricter definition applies. For example, the contract may state that during the first 24 months of disability, the insured must be able to perform none of the duties of his *regular* occupation. Thereafter, he must be able to perform none of the duties of *any* occupation. Sometimes the contract will reflect court decisions and further define what is meant by *any* occupation. Thus, one contract states:

Total disability means:

1. For the purpose of determining the commencement of total disability and thereafter for the first 24 months that the Monthly Income Benefit may be payable during any continuous period of such disability, total disability means only such complete incapacity of the Insured that he is able to perform none of the duties of his occupation, business or employment, and
2. for the remainder of any such period of continuous disability, total disability means only such complete incapacity of the Insured that he is able to perform none of the duties of any occupation, business, or employment; provided, however, that in no event shall total disability exist for any purpose of this policy during any period in which the insured is engaged in his or any occupation, business or employment for remuneration or profit.

Partial disability. *Partial disability* refers to the continuous inability of the insured, because of accidental bodily injury, to engage in one or more of the important duties of his occupation. For example, an insured has a loss of income policy that pays lifetime benefits of $200 each month in the event of disability by accident and for 10 years in the event of disability by illness. He suffers a heart attack and is unable to work for six months, after which he goes back to work but in another capacity requiring less strenuous activity and at a much lower salary. Assuming that the contract has no waiting period, the insured will recover only six months' indemnity. Because he is not disabled with regard to *any* occupation, he may not continue to draw disability income, even though he is in a much lower income level. On the other hand, if the only job the insured could get is selling pencils on the street, in all likelihood he may continue to draw his disability income because the contract does not require him to work in a position for which he is not reasonably fitted by education, training, or experience.

In order to reduce controversies over whether or not a disability is really permanent, the contract states that the disability will be *presumed* permanent after the lapse of a given time period. The waiting period may sometimes vary according to the wishes of the insured at the time the contract is issued. For example, a reduced premium may be granted if the insured specifies a waiting period longer than the ordinary time period. Sometimes the indemnity is retroactive to the date the disability began. However, disability income riders on life insurance policies stipulate a four or six months' waiting period which is usually not retroactive. This means that the insured will not collect for the initial period of his disability, even if the disability exceeds the waiting period.

Partial disability provisions are uncommon in sickness policies because of the difficulty in determining what constitutes partial disability and because of considerable probability of abuse. Sickness is such a personal matter that it would be difficult to refute a claim by the insured that he "did not feel well enough to work a full day." In accident provisions a partial disability clause may provide indemnity of one half of the benefits for total disability, for a limited period only, if the insured is unable to perform "an important daily duty pertaining to his occupation." Since disabilities such as these are comparatively rare, the benefit does not cost much, although it is obviously potentially subject to abuse.

Occasionally commercial health policies further restrict the concept of loss to exclude those disabilities for which the insured is not confined to his house. Put in as a strict test of what constitutes a sufficiently serious disability, the *house confinement clauses* are rare in modern policies.

Sometimes a disability policy contains what is known as an *aggregate clause,* which places an upper limit of total liability on the amount of income benefits payable. Thus, a policy might promise a weekly income benefit of $25, but the aggregate limit might be $500. Obviously such a limit places a 20-week maximum for total disability during the income period, a factor which might escape the notice of the purchaser unless he reads his contract carefully.

Deductibles and elimination periods

Health insurance policies present serious problems to underwriters because of the difficulties in controlling both moral and morale hazards.[7] It is often difficult to determine whether or not the loss has actually occurred, because illness is a subjective matter that does not always lend itself to definite medical diagnosis. The same disease may cause severe illness in one person but may not even disable the next. There are no standard charges for medical care, especially for physicians' costs, since the fees are commonly adjusted according to the patient's ability to pay

---

[7] See Chapter 1 for definitions and examples of these hazards.

rather than according to the nature of the illness. For these reasons underwriters must not only place definite maximum limitations on losses payable, but also generally require the insured to bear a portion of his own loss in the form of a deductible of some type.

Deductibles in health insurance are of two general types: (1) dollar or percentage deductibles from the amount of the loss, and (2) waiting periods or elimination periods. As an example of a contract containing both dollar and percentage deductibles, we shall consider the major medical contract.

Major medical contract. One of the distinguishing features of the major medical contract, which has enjoyed a rapid growth since its introduction after World War II, is the large limitation of loss which characterizes it and the absence of limitations on expenses within this maximum. The policy may be written with a maximum of $10,000 or $15,000 for any one disability. There is no limitation as to how much of this amount may be accounted for by doctor bills, hospital bills, private nursing, medicines, and other expenses stemming from a single physical disability, so long as the expenses are reasonable and necessary. The policy contains exclusions for certain types of care, but theoretically, if an item is not excluded, the entire bill could consist of, say, doctors' fees and be eligible for payment if it were a reasonable charge.

To control the losses payable under major medical contracts, it is common to provide a large dollar deductible, such as $300 to $750. The dollar deductible is used to eliminate claims which are presumably covered by other health policies or are assumed by the insured himself. It is the intent of the major medical contract to cover only catastrophic expenses which the ordinary person cannot assume. To prevent the insured from incurring extravagant medical expenses once the dollar deductible amount has been expended, the contract agrees to pay for only a certain proportion of the expenses over the deductible, commonly 75 or 80 per cent. This provision is known as a *coinsurance deductible.* Since the insured is required to share the cost of every medical bill, he is thus less inclined to incur unnecessary medical expenses.

Suppose the insured is in a severe automobile accident and requires specialized medical care over a period of two years for such things as skin grafts, cosmetic surgery, and artificial limbs. The cost of physicians' services, private nursing, and special hospitalization might easily reach $8,500. Under the $10,000 major medical policy with a $500 deductible and an 80 per cent coinsurance clause, the insured would recover 80 per cent of all amounts over the deductible, or $6,400. He himself must bear

$2,100 of the costs. Without the deductible, and the coinsurance clause there would be an inevitable tendency for both the patient and the doctor to be less conservative in the expenditure of amounts needed to purchase the required medical services. In all good conscience the doctor might be able to justify a larger fee if he knows it is covered by insurance. The patient might well order a more costly type of hospital service than he otherwise would.[8]

Elimination periods. A contract may contain two types of waiting periods. There may be a waiting period after the contract is in force before any benefits are payable for certain perils. This is often called an *elimination period.* For example, the contract may specify that no benefits will be payable during the first month, or first three months, of the contract for physical conditions or illnesses which the insured had at the time the policy went into effect. This provision permits a policy to be issued even if the insured is ill at the time he applies for coverage. After the elimination period has elapsed, full coverage is provided.

A second type of waiting-period clause, found in loss of income policies, specifies that no benefits will be paid until the disability, once it has occurred, has lasted a certain length of time. The waiting period of this clause, mentioned on page 604, may vary from one week to three or four months, at the option of the insured. If the insured feels that in the event of illness or accident his employer will continue his salary, say for one month, he may select a waiting period of one month and thus effect considerable savings in his premium. It is common to require a minimum of a 7-day waiting period to eliminate small claims which are uneconomical to insure. For example, one large insurer quotes rates for loss of income policies as follows: for each $100 monthly indemnity, for two-year sickness-lifetime accident coverage, male, age 25, and 7-day waiting period for sickness only, $60.44 annually. For the same policy, but with a 30-day waiting period for sickness only, the rate is $50.44 annually, a savings of about 16 per cent. If the insured is willing to accept a 90-day waiting period for sickness, the rate decreases to $44.91, a reduction of only about 10 per cent. For waiting periods longer than 90 days, the rate is reduced only a very small amount, reflecting the considerable likelihood that most sicknesses are of shorter duration than 90 days.

---

[8] Indeed, such a tendency has been well documented in the Anderson-Feldman study, cited earlier (O. W. Anderson and J. J. Feldman, *Family Medical Costs and Voluntary Health Insurance: A Nationwide Survey*). The average expenditures for medical care tend to increase with ability to pay, as evidenced both by insurance status and income level. The average annual gross expenditures among the 2,600 families surveyed was $207. The average insured family, however, spent $237, as opposed to the $154 spent by uninsured families. For the income class $3,500–$4,999, the average family spent $207, while those families earning $7,500 a year and over spent $353, on the average.

Cancellation and renewability

Unlike a life insurance contract, the health insurance contract is sometimes cancelable by the insured or the insurer during the policy term. Also, unlike most life insurance policies, the health insurance contract may not be renewable unless the insurer is agreeable. It is important to observe the difference between cancelability and renewability. A health insurance policy may not be cancelable within the policy term, but the insurer can cancel it at time of renewal if the insured's experience has been bad; or the insurer may renew the policy subject to exclusions for certain diseases on which the insured may have had a claim.

Guaranteed renewable provision. The safest type of health insurance contract is one which is both noncancelable and guaranteed renewable. In this case the *insured* has the option as to whether or not he will renew, and may, if he wishes, renew it indefinitely, or until he reaches a certain maximum age, usually 64. The importance of renewability from the viewpoint of the insured should be emphasized. Suppose "A" has a disability income contract which is noncancelable within the policy period but is renewable "at the option of the company only." He carries this policy for 15 years against the time when a serious disability could cripple him. "A" has a slight stroke, makes a claim for disability, and recovers income payments for six weeks. At the end of the year the insurer has the privilege of failing to renew this policy or renewing it subject to an exclusion for all future claims arising out of "diseases of the nervous system." If the insured retains his coverage at all, he probably retains it without coverage on the very difficulty which is most likely to cause him future disabilities. The insurer may, of course, be generous and renew as before, but this means that other policyholders are being asked to bear claims not contemplated when the original rates were formulated. Certainly the insured cannot assume such generosity. The obvious solution is to purchase noncancelable, guaranteed renewable coverage if possible. If the risk of physical disability is worth insuring at all, it is worth insuring on a permanent basis if such a contract is available and can be afforded.

For example, one large insurer quotes rates for loss of income policies as shown in the table on the opposite page. These policies are for an income of $10 per month with one-week waiting period for both sickness and accident, two-year sickness-lifetime accident coverage, male, class 1 occupational status. Thus, the insured pays about 20 per cent more for the noncancelable policy than he does for the cancelable policy, but undoubtedly the advantages of the noncancelable policy outweigh its extra

Renewal Provision	Annual Premium Per $10 Monthly Income
Cancelable..	$3.80
Guaranteed renewable, but with the premium subject to change upon renewal...	3.98
Noncancelable, and guaranteed renewable at the same rate.....	4.59

cost, providing the insured is qualified for this type of policy. Oftentimes underwriting requirements for noncancelable health insurance are considerably stricter than for other types.

A word of caution is necessary at this point in interpreting "guaranteed renewable." Some insurers issue a contract which is called guaranteed renewable, but the *rate* is subject to change. The insurer may charge whatever rate it deems correct for the age group and class of risk concerned. Thus, this form has the disadvantage that while the insured knows that he can always maintain his insurance, he does not know at what premium, and there is always the possibility that the premium may become prohibitive.

As shown above, a fixed-premium, noncancelable, and guaranteed renewable policy costs more money than a cancelable commercial policy or one which does not guarantee the premium rate at which it is renewable. The main reason for this is that reserves must be accumulated to meet the higher morbidity costs which characterize older age groups, just as a higher rate is charged for a permanent life insurance contract. The premium will depend not only on the age of the insured when the contract is issued, but also upon the occupation of the insured, the period during which income is guaranteed (if it is an income policy), and the character of the medical or hospital benefits.

If a policy is guaranteed renewable at a fixed premium, there are certain other clauses that are generally included. These are: (1) waiver of premium clause, and (2) incontestability clause. The *waiver of premium clause* is generally included because it would be incongruous as well as difficult for the insured to be receiving benefits and yet be required to maintain premiums on his contract. The *incontestability clause* has a purpose in health insurance similar to its purpose in life insurance, but the clause is worded in such a way that its effect on underwriting is not so strict. This clause is analyzed on pages 616 and 617.

Not guaranteed renewable provision. If a policy is not guaranteed renewable, the renewal clause states that the coverage terminates at the expiration of the period for which premiums have been paid, unless within some stated period prior to the expiration of the policy, ranging from 5 to 30 days, the insurer has mailed a notice of intention not to renew. If this notice is not sent, the insured may renew the contract for another year. Such policies never have a policy period beyond one year.

Most health insurance policies state that if the insured fails to remit the premium, he generally has a grace period of 30 or 31 days in which to pay during which coverage remains in force. The typical health insurance contract contains a reinstatement clause under which the policy may be reinstated after it has lapsed simply by acceptance of the premium by the agent. In such cases the policy does not cover illness for the first 10 days after reinstatement, although it will cover accidents. If the applicant is in poor health when he reapplies for his policy, the agent does not have authority to accept the premium unless he requires an application for reinstatement and gives a conditional receipt for the premium. The effect of this requirement is that the policy is not reinstated unless officials in the insurer's home office approve it. The reinstatement clause provides that if these officials fail to act on the application within 45 days, the policy is automatically reinstated. The intent of the reinstatement clause is to give the insured an opportunity to put his coverage back in force with protection against unreasonable action by the insurer to prevent effective reinstatement or to cast doubt as to the validity of such reinstatement.

Incontestability

Most health insurance contracts contain an incontestable clause which is sometimes found under the heading "Time Limit on Certain Defenses." This clause is as follows:

> *Time Limit on Certain Defenses*—(a) After two years from the date of issue of this policy no misstatements, except fraudulent misstatements, made by the applicant in the application for such policy shall be used to void the policy or to deny a claim for loss incurred or disability (as defined) commencing after the expiration of such two year period.
>
> (b) No claim for loss incurred or disability (as defined) commencing after two years from the date of issue of this policy shall be reduced or denied on the ground that a disease or physical condition had existed prior to the effective date of coverage under this policy unless, effective on the date of loss, such diseases or physical condition was excluded from coverage by name or specific description.

It will be seen that *fraudulent misstatements,* but not other misstatements, can be used to void the policy. In no event can misstatements about a pre-existing disease or physical condition be used to deny or reduce benefits unless such condition is specifically excluded from coverage. It will be recalled that in life insurance, *no* misstatements can be used as a defense by the insurer against paying the claim once the period of incontestability clause has expired. Suppose the applicant is asked whether he has ever had a claim under another health insurance policy within a period of five years and he says "no." Three years later upon recovering a claim, the insurer discovers that the insured had made several claims under other policies, and had this information been known, the contract would never have been issued. The insurer denies liability and the question arises as to whether the insured's false answer is a fraudulent misstatement. In all likelihood it would be so considered, if it could be shown that the statement was made deliberately to deceive the insurer, and that the latter relied on this statement to its detriment. Therefore, the insurer could deny liability for any claim and could cancel the contract, even though the two-year period had passed. This applies no matter whether the policy was guaranteed renewable or not. In a life insurance policy the insurer undoubtedly would have to honor the claim even though the insured's misstatement was held to be fraudulent.

Indemnity clauses

The health insurance policy generally contains no clause that strictly limits the amount that can be collected by an insured in the event that he has more than one policy covering the same loss, *if* they are issued on a valued basis. It is common for the policy to exclude benefits for expenses recoverable under workmen's compensation or for services rendered in a governmental hospital. But if the insured has two private hospitalization policies, there is nothing to prevent him from "making money" on a hospitalization for which he collects twice or more. The insured is generally required to reveal the existence of other health insurance policies when he makes application for coverage, and thus the underwriter has some check on this type of moral hazard.[9]

On income loss policies it is the usual procedure to include some sort of restriction on the indemnity payable to the insured in case the total coverage exceeds all or some proportion of his average past earnings. A typical clause provides that if at the time the insured makes a claim, he has other policies which also pay a disability income, and the total disability income benefits exceed his average earnings in some time

---

[9] It is becoming more common to insert an "other insurance" clause in health insurance contracts. This clause limits the total indemnity payable in case of other insurance covering the same loss.

period, the amount payable will be reduced. The amount payable is obtained by taking that proportion of the disability income promised which the actual average income bears to the total disability income insurance payable. For example, assume that an insured has a policy with Company S paying $300 each month and one in Company T paying $200 each month. Both policies contain the average earning clause. At the time of his disability, his average income over the past two years is only $400 each month. He would collect only ⅘ x $300, or $240 each month from company S, and ⅘ x $200 or $160 each month from Company T. In this way at least the insured does not collect *more* than his actual average income. If he were permitted to collect more, there would be even less inducement for the insured to overcome his illness and return to work. As a matter of fact, a considerable moral hazard can exist in the field of income loss coverage because not all contracts contain the average earnings clause. In the example above, if Company T's policy did not contain the clause, it would pay the full $200 and the insured would be recovering $440 each month, tax free, whereas before he had earned $400 which was subject to taxes and other deductions.

When disability income insurance was in its early development in the period 1910–1930, competition within the industry led to loose underwriting standards. Guaranteed renewable contracts were issued somewhat indiscriminately and at inadequate premiums. When the depression of the 1930's struck, many insureds found themselves worth more disabled than they were worth physically fit. Loss claims soared and due to excessive claims, at least one insurer went into bankruptcy. Other insurers with aggregate limitations in their contracts, or with only a small amount of guaranteed renewable contract business, survived the losses. Many insurers withdrew from the guaranteed renewable income loss business entirely and have re-entered the field only recently, since about 1950. Because most workers are covered by workmen's compensation and by social security for income loss, and because many private income loss contracts contain no average earnings clause, or none with exclusions for social insurance income, a potential moral hazard might still exist in this area. Insurers rely on careful underwriting methods to control potential moral hazards.

Change of occupation

One of the obvious advantages (to the insurer) of health insurance contracts which are renewable at the option of the company only is the opportunity to reunderwrite the policy annually. Under some conditions, however, the insurer is unwilling to wait until the end of the policy term to adjust benefits or premiums in the policy. In income loss contracts it is common to provide, under a *change of occupation clause,* that if the insured changes his occupation during the policy period to an occupation more hazardous than he had when he took out the policy, "the company will pay only such portion of the indemnities provided in this policy as the premium paid would have purchased at the rates and within the limits fixed by the company for such more hazardous occupation." Thus, if the insured were a clerk when he applied for coverage but shortly thereafter entered the tree surgery field, the contractual benefits would be altered by the operation of the change of occupation clause. Undoubtedly, tree surgery occupations fall into a more hazardous class than those of the clerical field. If the rates for the occupational class in which tree surgery falls are twice as high as those for the clerical field, the monthly income under the policy will be halved.

If the insured enters an occupation which is *less* hazardous than the one he had at the date of the policy inception, the insurer agrees to return the difference in premium applicable to the two occupational classifications.

Misstatement of age

For reasons similar to the situation in life insurance, the loss of income health contract provides that if the insured has misstated his age, the benefits are reduced to that level which would have been purchased by the premium actually paid had the true age been given. Such a clause is particularly important in contracts that provide lifetime income benefits. If the insured misstates his age, this misrepresentation, even if it is discovered after the period of incontestability, alters the promised benefits but does not deny the insured all benefits.

GROUP HEALTH INSURANCE

As was indicated before, far more people are covered under group insurance than are covered under individual contracts.

In the private insurance sphere the two major insurers of group contracts are Blue Cross–Blue Shield associations and insurance companies, with the latter covering about 30 per cent more individuals than the former. In the public sphere are various social insurance programs which are discussed in Chapter 24.

Some of the basic reasons for the growth of private group health insurance plans are:

1. Group insurance is available at lower cost than individual contracts.

2. Group contracts usually provide more generous benefits than individual contracts.

3. Group contracts have been actively promoted by organized groups such as labor unions and hospital associations.

4. Group insurance has received much publicity as a result of various social insurance programs and legislative discussions about socialized medicine.

Cost advantages of group health insurance

The sources of savings in group health insurance stem from the same factor as in group life insurance.

Freedom from adverse selection. Group health contracts enjoy relative freedom from adverse selection because the covered group exists for some reason other than to obtain insurance. In view of the high moral and morale hazards which characterize this field, the element of adverse selection in individual policies is especially severe, requiring higher relative premiums than in group insurance. There is a general requirement that at least 75 per cent of a covered group must enroll in a contributory plan, in the realization that if 75 per cent subscribe, a sufficient spread of risk is obtained. Furthermore, benefit levels must be determined by some method over which the employee has no control, such as according to income level or job status. In this way, the poorer risks cannot select larger limits of coverage. Since most insured groups are working groups, the health level in group insurance will usually be higher than that of the average individual contract policyholder. Statistics of group underwriters reveal that losses are indeed fewer under group plans than among individual policyholders.

Lower administrative costs. Administrative costs in group health insurance plans are lower than those for individual policyholders. Employers frequently perform the premium collection function by withholding from each employee's pay check his contribution to the plan. As this process involves only one more entry on payroll records, it is relatively economical to perform, and therefore saves considerable expense over the system whereby the insurer must send out premium notices to individuals, handle thousands of small checks, and credit individual policy records. In group insurance the insurer receives one premium check periodically from the employer. Costs such as those involved in lapses of individual policies are nonexistent. Employers also generally screen claims, help the employee fill out his form properly, answer employee questions, and perform other duties of this nature which would otherwise absorb the attention of a sizable claims staff employed by the insurer. The fact that the employer usually has a vested interest in getting the employee back to work is a further check on unreal or exaggerated claims or on unduly prolonged disabilities.

Lower acquisition costs. Acquisition costs are generally much lower for group insurance than for individual insurance. An individual salesman must be paid a substantial share of the first annual premium in order to compensate him for his time in selling the policy. A group representative of the insurer and a small staff may in a week's time sell and install a plan involving thousands of dollars of annual premium. Naturally the percentage acquisition cost will be a small fraction of the total cost of individual selling.

Exemption from taxes and economy in purchase of services. Some group plans, being nonprofit in nature, are exempt from taxes, and may obtain medical and hospital services at wholesale prices. This advantage characterizes Blue Cross, community sponsored, industrial sponsored, group clinic, and other plans. To a lesser extent this advantage also characterizes mutual insurer organizations which pay some taxes, but at a lower level than that paid by stock insurers. Hospital associations such as Blue Cross do not compensate the individual insured for expenses, but instead purchase services directly from hospitals and thereby obtain a lower price than is obtained by an individual patient.

Tax advantage for employee. The federal government, in effect, subsidizes group health insurance by granting a tax exemption to the individual employee in a group plan for the value of health insurance paid for by his employer. Since the employer often contributes half or more of the total cost, there is a substantial advantage in arranging group coverage over individual coverage. For example, suppose that an employer pays $100 a year on behalf of an employee and his family in a group health insurance plan. The employee pays no income taxes on this $100. If, however, the employer were to drop the plan and increase the employee's salary, he would have to pay the employee at least $125 in order to provide him with the same benefit, after taxes, as before.

Group contracts v. individual contracts

The contractual provisions of group insurance are in many respects similar to those of individual contracts. There are, however, certain differences which reflect the fact that the group contract is a contract between the employer and the insurer, with individual employees being third party beneficiaries, as in group life insurance. There is a master contract, which spells out such matters as when the employee may be covered; who is eligible for coverage; termination of coverage; benefit schedules; cancellation, renewal, and premium provisions; and other necessary details.

In some respects the provisions of the group contract that affect the employee are more favorable than under individual contracts, but less flexibility is permitted. For example, the group contract, as far as the individual employee is concerned, is guaranteed renewable and noncancelable. As long as the employee remains in the group, his coverage cannot be changed unless the entire group contract is changed or abandoned. Of course, there is an element of inflexibility attached to a group contract in that the provisions cannot be tailored to meet one person's exact needs. Furthermore, if the employee changes jobs, he may find that his new employer does not have a group policy. Except in unusual circumstances the employee does not have the option of converting his group coverage to an individual contract, as he does in group life insurance.[10] However, no matter how poor his state of health, he may continue his protection as long as the master contract is in force and as long as he is a member of the group.

Another liberalization concerns the definition of disability, which is expressed in terms of whether or not the employee can perform any and every duty pertaining to *his* occupation. If the employee is too ill to report for work, he is probably considered disabled. Under individual policies it must generally be shown that the employee is unable to perform a job for which he is reasonably fitted by training and education. The liberal definition of disability in the group contract admittedly is a result of the fact that the benefit period for income loss is not long—usually less than six months.

A third advantage of a group contract is the tendency on the part of the insurer to be very liberal in claims settlement. The insurer has to consider that an entire plan involving a large annual premium may be lost by a miserly claims policy. The employee thus receives the benefit of

---

[10] Blue Cross offers an individual contract, but it is not the same as the group policy coverage.

any doubt when he has a claim. For example, most contracts cover non-occupational claims and exclude coverage on occupational injuries which are compensable under workmen's compensation laws. If there is some doubt as to whether a given accident is job connected, the insurer will usually pay the claim under the group policy and, if necessary, later recover the amounts paid from those who were actually obligated to pay the claim.

In spite of its advantages, group health insurance is not a complete solution to the problem of obtaining insurance protection against health losses. Group insurance does not replace individual coverage but supplements it. For example, benefit levels under group insurance are often quite limited and require supplementation from other sources. Income loss contracts in particular are usually limited to short periods and do not at all meet the problem of long-term disability. Hospitalization policies usually do not meet the entire burden, particularly if the illness is long lived or falls under one of the excluded categories, such as mental illness. If an employee falls ill and is no longer able to work, he and his dependents must be dropped from the group and coverage for future disabilities is lost. Adequate health insurance for retired workers is not yet available on a group basis, except in isolated instances. Finally, by no means do all employers have group disability insurance, and the group contract is not available to just any group formed for the purpose of obtaining coverage.

MAJOR PROBLEMS IN HEALTH INSURANCE

While all types of insurance have their problems and "growing pains," perhaps no field has been subject to so much criticism and controversy as the health insurance field. There is no universal agreement as to what this rapidly expanding field shall be called, some refer to it as "accident and sickness"; some, "accident and health"; and others as simply, "health," the term adopted in this text and by the Committee on Health Insurance Terminology of the American Risk and Insurance Association.[11] Dissatisfaction with the general health of the nation has caused some officials to push for a general plan of compulsory health insurance similar to Great Britain's plan of socialized medicine. Among private agencies competing for health insurance business, several issues have arisen, which will be briefly analyzed on pages 624–628 as an illustration of the major problems in the field. These issues revolve around the gen-

---

[11] Formerly the American Association of University Teachers of Insurance.

eral problem as to how best to meet, through insurance, the problem of economic loss through health failure. More specifically, the issues center on how best to provide health insurance for everyone needing it, at the lowest cost consistent with adequate coverage, and without the wastes associated with excessive moral and morale hazards. Most of the issues discussed here are interrelated, as will be recognized.

Problem 1

What can be done to prevent the existence of insurance from causing a rise in medical costs that otherwise would not take place? As we have seen, there is a tendency for doctors to charge more when the ability to pay, as evidenced by insurance or income level, increases. There may also be a tendency for hospitalization costs to rise because, through insurance, the ability of patients to pay for hospital services is enlarged. This comes about because hospital associations such as Blue Cross are more or less controlled by the hospitals themselves. It becomes easier to incur higher costs and to pass these costs on because the insurer is in the position of determining both the costs and how much the insured shall pay. This is not to criticize doctors or hospital managements for inefficiency and conspiracy to raise medical charges, but rather to point out that there are few, if any, built-in checks to ever-rising medical costs. In a similar way, Blue Shield plans are controlled by physicians. In fields of insurance such as property, those who remedy the loss are subject to competitive pricing and differ from those organizations, the insurance companies, that pay the bills. In health insurance it is usually not feasible for the insured to shop around for the lowest cost service, nor for the insured to require bids and to accept the lowest bid for medical services.

Insurance organizations have combated this tendency by placing limitations of recovery in their contracts and by the use of deductibles, as we have seen. However, this is no actual solution since the burden is only transferred to the insured and there is little hope that the insured himself can somehow reduce his bills substantially. The first step in any real progress toward solution of the problem must come through the action of physicians to agree on some system of pricing their services in a predictable manner so that their costs can be successfully met through insurance. Further progress must come through increased cooperation between insurers, insureds, hospital administrators, physicians, and others to seek methods of increasing the efficiency of group health insurance plans, and of controlling the costs of medical care, and the administrative and acquisition costs of insurance.

Problem 2

Closely related to the preceding problem is that of controlling the overutilization of hospital and medical services by the insured himself. As one physician from a famous clinic stated,[12]

> Patients often demand that they be hospitalized, although a physician knows well that it is unnecessary. . . . Lest I appear too virtuous I should point out that if I were engaged in individual private practice and if a patient of long standing presented himself requesting hospitalization and if I did not hospitalize this patient another physician down the hall certainly would, then the stresses on my integrity might be greater.

There is an unfortunate tendency for individuals to feel that they have not received any value from their health insurance policy unless they have been ill and collected a claim from the insurer. Pressure is applied on physicians to yield to this desire. Ridiculous as such an attitude may appear to an impartial observer, it nevertheless is an important obstacle in solving the problem of overutilization. It leads to the exaggeration of insurance claims and a consequent increase in premiums. Furthermore, insurers have little ability to withstand overutilization as long as physicians certify that the care is needed and that there is no satisfactory substitute for it.

On the other side of this question is the fact that what may appear to be overutilization to some is certainly not so to others. A patient may have a pain that could be a symptom of a very serious condition requiring extensive medical examinations and hospitalization to diagnose. The pain could also be an indication of an entirely different and nonserious condition. Should the physician decide not to risk the patient's health and hospitalize him, or should he suggest that the patient "wait a few days" to see what happens? If the physician is conservative, he may be charged with contributing to the problem of overutilization, and if he is not, he may be charged with malpractice. Clearly there is no simple solution to this problem.

Problem 3

How can health insurance be made generally more adequate? As we have seen, the provisions of health insurance contracts are somewhat

---

[12] Haddon M. Carryer, "Health Insurance at the Mayo Clinic" (Mimeographed speech delivered at a forum of the Health Insurance Association of America, November 16, 1959).

restrictive because of the underwriting problems involved. A relatively small part of the total medical costs are being met through insurance (see Table 19–4, page 514). While there is no doubt that insurance is not an appropriate method of paying for 100 per cent of all medical bills, there is also no doubt that it can be expanded much more than it has been and that provisions can gradually be liberalized so that more illnesses can be covered, larger limits of liability can be provided, more classes of people can be made eligible for insurance, income benefit periods can be lengthened, and claims settlement can be treated less technically.

For example, only since 1950 have the benefits of health insurance been made available, still on an experimental basis, to individuals past the age of 65. An illustration of this is a plan introduced in 1957 by the Continental Casualty Company. This plan is made available without a medical examination on a modified guaranteed renewable basis to all those past age 65.[13] The element of adverse selection is generally controlled by limiting the enrollment period. The plan is announced through national newspaper advertisements which explain the contractual details and each year set a final subscription date about a week after the ads appear. The plan is generally reopened each year for new enrollment for a limited period. As yet, the benefits of the plan are limited to 31 days of hospital confinement for $10 each day, $100 indemnity for hospital extras, and a $200 surgical schedule. Pre-existing illnesses are excluded, as is hospitalization in governmental hospitals. The policy is guaranteed renewable at the same premium unless all premiums in a given geographical area are raised. While the policy is not a "cure all," it represents the beginning of an attempt on the part of private industry to provide coverage for aged people.

As another example, the Teachers Insurance and Annuity Association (T.I.A.A.) has introduced a group loss of income policy on a long-term basis. The plan is integrated with pension plans for employees of colleges and universities. It provides disability income up to $500 each month until age 65 for an employee who is disabled through sickness or accident so as to be unable to work. At age 65 the pension plan takes over the income payment responsibility. As yet, long-term disability plans such as this one are relatively rare. Social security amendments have provided for disability income payments for workers, but the amount of the benefit is conservative and represents only a "floor of protection." Much remains to be done in this area.

---

[13] The Mutual Benefit Insurance Company of Omaha claims to be the first to enter nationally the market for health insurance on aged people.

Problem 4

How can the problem of overinsurance in the field of health insurance be solved? Strange as it may appear, following a discussion of the inadequacy of health insurance benefits, there is such a problem and it is one of the important causes of inadequacy of benefits. Overinsurance has two forms: (1) insuring the "first dollar" of claims instead of the "last dollar," and (2) purchasing multiple policies in the hope of "making money" out of an illness or an accident. When a person insures the "first dollar" of benefits, he is using insurance premiums in an uneconomical manner, as was discussed in Chapters 3 and 4. This practice is especially uneconomical if small, frequent claims are likely. Funds that could be used to pay for the severe and catastrophic losses are being used to pay for the small losses which could be more economically paid by the individual himself. Thus, the demand for major medical policies has been outstripped many times by contracts which promise to pay the entire bill and which contain no deductibles.

Purchasing multiple policies in order to profit from an illness or an accident may be done consciously or unconsciously. It may result from too much sales pressure, for example. Desire on the part of underwriters to obtain more business on the books or to introduce new insurance contracts, may contribute to the lowering of underwriting standards. Advertisements stating that "this policy pays you its benefits in addition to any other insurance you may have" are common in the field. In some states, clauses similar to the pro rata liability clause in fire insurance contracts are not permitted in health insurance, thus making it more difficult to control the problem of overinsurance by this method.

Overinsurance is a serious problem for many reasons. Not only does it lead to excessive premiums for health insurance and to a reduction of funds for more adequate health insurance coverage, but it also leads to excessive medical costs. For example, if a physician knows that a patient has five insurance policies each paying $100 for a certain operation, it is likely that a bill which might have been $100 will be doubled or tripled. Overinsurance leads to public ill will since, if overinsurance becomes common, the general policyholder realizes that through his premium payment, certain individuals are receiving payments that are essentially unfair to the insured group as a whole. Overinsurance may easily threaten the solvency of the insurer, especially if a severe depression were to occur. Excessive disability income coverage on many individuals can result in a deluge of claims if a depression reduces employment opportunities. Even the loss ratios in hospitalization and medical expense insurance tend to mount in depression periods.

A case history of an overinsured individual was related as follows: [14]

> A professional man, age 58, without question, had been work-
> ing extremely hard and had become tired. His situation became
> more critical with the development of hypertension and complete
> exhaustion. He kept his office going for a year during which time he
> received $800 a month overhead insurance. In addition, he had
> $1,200 a month for ten years or to age 65 and an additional $1,200
> a month for five years. Another feature of this claim which we
> rarely consider was the presence of a life insurance program with
> waiver of premium worth $6,500 a year. Roughly, this gentleman's
> disability and the above program meant $45,000 a year for the first
> year, going down slowly to age 65 when a well-organized retirement
> program starts paying off. In addition, he had a substantial un-
> earned income. Who was surprised when at the end of a year, he
> closed his office for keeps because of disability? While this claim
> may have been perfectly legitimate, I suggest to you that his heavy
> insurance program and our current tax structure made it much
> easier for him to decide not to go back to work. If he had much less
> insurance, there would have been more incentive and economic
> pressures that would have helped him to decide that he should try to
> resume his professional activities again.

SUMMARY

1. Health insurance, as a private approach to the problem of disability and
   loss of income through illness and accidents, has shown a more rapid
   rate of growth than almost any other line of insurance since World
   War II.

2. Measured by the benefits paid, insurance against hospitalization expense
   is larger than any other single type of health insurance, constituting over
   half of all benefits paid in 1959. Benefits under loss of income, surgical,
   and medical expense insurance contracts followed in that order. Studies
   reveal that approximately three fourths of all families have some type of
   health insurance, but that only one fourth of the total health losses are
   paid through the medium of insurance. Chief among the reasons for this
   are the relative newness of coverage, the difficulty of underwriting health
   losses, and the high cost of medical care.

3. Contractual provisions of private health insurance contracts, both group
   and individual, are complex and relatively little understood. There is
   often a wide discrepancy between insurance meaning and the meaning
   commonly attributed to insurance terms by the layman. Assiduous reading of policy provisions is an absolute prerequisite to an understanding
   of what the benefits are, the limitations of benefits, definition of the peril
   and the loss, operation of deductibles, and other important matters.

---

[14] Francis W. Evans, "Overinsurance Dangers" (Multilithed report of forum of
Health Insurance Association of America, November 17, 1959).

4. One of the major difficulties with an individual health insurance contract, from the viewpoint of the insured, stems from the fact that the insurer generally reserves the right to reunderwrite the policy annually, to raise the premium, to eliminate coverage on certain named perils, or to cancel the contract altogether. The only sure protection against this is to purchase noncancelable and guaranteed renewable coverage, at a substantially higher premium. Until the nature of morbidity statistics improves, major advances in offering a level-premium lifetime contract in the field of health insurance, such as exists in life insurance, will likely be slow in coming.

5. Deductibles and waiting periods of various types are a necessary adjunct to keeping the costs of health insurance within the reach of most insureds. These deductibles serve the purpose of eliminating small claims, which are costly to administer, as well as placing restrictions on large claims, which are at least partially within the control of the insured.

6. Insurers are only gradually using contractual provisions which prevent the insured from collecting more than his actual medical expenses or loss of income. Prevention of overinsurance and overutilization of health insurance benefit rights are major underwriting problems.

7. Because of several major factors, chiefly less cost and easier administration, group coverages have been very popular in the field of health insurance. Group plans cover about 70 per cent of all those who have health insurance protection.

8. One of the basic unsolved problems in the field of health insurance is how to prevent the existence of insurance from causing an uncontrollable rise in the cost of the peril against which it is directed. Until this problem and other related problems are solved, it will be difficult to accomplish such objectives as raising the level of adequacy of benefits, extending benefits to more classes of insureds, reducing various deductibles, and simplifying complex terminology now deemed necessary to limit coverage in various ways.

QUESTIONS FOR REVIEW AND DISCUSSION

1. A writer stated, "Even with strict limits on the amount of insurance and strict underwriting control in general, it seems that disability benefits for life cannot be promised for two reasons."
   (a) What is referred to by "underwriting control"? Give examples.
   (b) Suggest two possible reasons as to why the author felt that disability income benefits for life cannot be promised.

2. A critic of health insurance stated, "The principal adverse criticisms one hears or deduces . . . of commercial accident and health insurance . . . may be reduced to four; it does not meet adequately the disability hazard of the average man; it treats covered disability much too technically—that is, with too many restrictions and phrased in language too complex for the average man to understand; it costs too much; it is not

dependable. This is a formidable battery; as we shall see, it is the more so because the solutions are in considerable part mutually exclusive."

(a) Evaluate these criticisms, indicating what you think the author meant by each.

(b) In what way would a solution to these problems be "mutually exclusive"? Explain.

3. The opinion has been expressed concerning the need for longer disability income contracts, ". . . even more alarming is the assurance that 'today things are different.' For this new circle of insured persons, insurers generally dispense with medical selection and inspection reports; they leave out the average earnings clause and otherwise underwrite very much as they do cancellable risks. . . . It does not follow that a limited sickness benefit for the new clientele will be an adequate control when jobs are scarce and wages are down." Do you agree? Why or why not?

4. James has three loss of income policies with promised monthly indemnities as follows: Company X, $300 each month; Company Y, $100 each month; and Company Z, $200 each month. James happens to be an engineer and at the time he became totally disabled from a fall from a work platform, he was earning $500 each month. Company X's policy contains an average earnings clause, but the other two policies do not.

(a) As long as James is disabled, how much may be collected from each insurer? Show your calculations.

(b) Is this sound insurance economics? Why?

5. The text states, "Because most workers are covered by workmen's compensation and by social security for income loss, and because many private income loss contracts contain no average earnings clause, or none with exclusions for social insurance income, a potential moral hazard might still exist in this area."

(a) Explain why the conclusion follows in the statement given.

(b) Does the average earnings clause have a purpose similar to the coinsurance clause in fire insurance? Why? If not to what fire insurance clause is it similar? Explain.

6. A major medical policy contained the following clause:

If the company terminates this policy by refusal to renew for reasons other than nonpayment of premium, such termination shall not reduce or end such liability as the company would have had under the policy had such termination not occurred, in respect to any loss resulting from injuries occurring or sickness contracted while this policy is in force, provided such loss occurs within 90 days after such termination of this policy or during a period of continuous compensable loss or losses, which period commences during such 90 days.

(a) Explain the meaning of the above clause, with examples.

(b) Suggest possible reasons for including this clause in a major medical policy. Would you expect to find it in a guaranteed renewable major policy? Why or why not?

7. The number of people covered under major medical insurance policies expanded from zero to 22 million people in the period 1950–1959. By the end of the year 1959, the number of people so covered was 30 per cent higher than the year before. What is meant by major medical insurance and what reasons probably accounted for this rapid growth?

* Questions 8 through 11 are based on the study, *A Profile of the Health Insuring Public,* published by the Health Insurance Institute in 1959.

8. In the survey as to suggestions for improvement in health insurance, it was found that the most common suggestion was that more information should be provided; the second most common idea was to provide more benefits; and the third most common suggestion was to reduce costs. Among those families without insurance, however, one of these suggestions was made twice as frequently as for families which were insured. Which suggestion would you think it would be? Why?

9. Among the favorable attitudes toward health insurance, it was found that half of the individuals surveyed thought that it provided "a means of budgeting and prevents savings depletion." This was mentioned twice as frequently as the next most common attitude, "gives security and saves worry." Which of the two attitudes expressed above is more closely in line with sound principles of insurance buying? Why?

10. Among families expressing suggestions for improving health insurance, the more frequently mentioned suggestions applying to insurance companies indicated a desire for changes in cancellation rules, improvement in claim service, and more information. What is probably meant by the reference to "changes in cancellation rules?" Explain, with reference to policy provisions.

11. Among families surveyed who had health insurance and later dropped it, 36 per cent said they could not afford to keep it, 31 per cent reported they lost their coverage under group insurance when they changed employment, 15 per cent said that a claim was not paid satisfactorily, 7 per cent said the contract had been misrepresented, and 5 per cent said the benefits did not seem worth the premiums.
    (a) Since probably half of the reasons for dropping can be traced to the unwillingness or the inability of individuals to pay the premiums, what arguments would you, as a premium payer, advance to justify your expenditure for health insurance?
    (b) Do the findings support the idea that individual health insurance policies are of little importance in view of the dominance of group contracts? Why?

12. In general, individuals covered for hospital expenses recover a larger proportion of their health bills if they are hospitalized than do individuals covered for regular or major medical expenses. Basic trends also indicate that more patients are being hospitalized, but that the duration of their stay is being greatly shortened through improved postoperative treatment, early ambulation, use of antibiotic drugs, etc.

(a) With reference to policy provisions, indicate why it is more likely that a hospitalized insured would recover a larger portion of his bill than a nonhospitalized patient, assuming insurance exists for both patients.

(b) Is there any connection between the existence of insurance and the fact that more and more patients are being hospitalized? Discuss.

13. It is estimated that about 20 per cent of the patients in a hospital are very ill and need intensive medical care, such as constant nursing, oxygen, fluids, and blood transfusions. About 60 per cent require much less help than this, and 20 per cent need very little help, being able to walk to a hospital restaurant to eat meals, to give themselves personal care, etc. What are the implications of these facts for the cost of health insurance?

14. Concerning insurance reports which are required in support of claims, a physician stated, "A cost accounting appraisal . . . indicates that it takes a physician 6 minutes to dictate a report and a secretary 13 minutes to type it, which, along with other factors, makes the cost of a report just under $5. . . . It costs almost as much to process a claim for $10 as it does to process a claim for $500. We are receiving an increasing number of requests for medical reports . . . for benefits in the range from $5 to $25." What vital fact about health insurance buying principles does this statement illustrate?

15. A writer stated, "Overinsurance is the carrying of insurance for speculative purposes rather than for the indemnification against loss."

(a) Do you agree that this definition coincides with that given in the text? If you agree, give any qualifications you would make. If not, explain.

(b) Compare *overinsurance* with *overutilization*.

16. An insurance company claims adjuster in health insurance stated, "The overinsured case usually follows a pattern which includes frequent periods of hospitalization and often confinement for check-ups of comparatively minor chronic conditions, routine physical examinations, etc. All periods of hospitalization are extended. . . . We sometimes wonder why a man must go to the hospital on Friday for a surgical operation on Monday . . . proration clauses should be worked out in the medical-hospital coverages. While I don't recommend it, if the companies can't cope with this problem on their individual initiative, it may be necessary to work with the supervisory authorities toward a solution."

(a) Suggest reasons for the pattern observed in the overinsured case.

(b) Explain what is meant by the statement about the use of proration clauses. Does such a clause help prevent overinsurance?

(c) What type of regulatory solutions might be directed against the problem?

17. An insurance company executive stated, "In 1957 some 43 per cent of the people over 65 had some form of voluntary health insurance. By the end of 1959 about 60 per cent will be covered and it is hoped that about

80 per cent will be voluntarily insured by 1965. . . . By 1970 there will be some 19 million people 65 years of age and over and these men and women will represent almost 10 per cent of the population."

(a) Contrast health insurance and life insurance needs for the over-65 age group.

(b) Which type of health insurance is needed most by those past 65? least? Why?

(c) What major weakness exists in the private insurance plans that are available for aged people?

18. (a) What are the major factors accounting for the dominance of group health insurance over individual forms?

(b) Which of these factors are likely to become more important as time goes on?

19. Is there a close correspondence between health losses (see Table 19–4, page 514) and the relative emphasis on the various types of health insurance? Why or why not?

20. An insured, a laborer, has a life insurance policy on which is attached a loss-of-income rider that pays $10 a month in case the insured becomes totally and permanently disabled. Because of diabetes, the insured made a claim for total disability. His physician stated that the diabetes was fairly well controlled and that the insured could do "light work." The insurer refused payment. In your opinion should the insured be considered sufficiently disabled so as to receive benefits? Why?

21. A surgeon suffered an infection in his fingers and hands and had to cease his practice. He made claim for disability benefits under the health insurance provisions of his life insurance policy but was denied benefits. In the resulting trial the insurer brought evidence that the insured frequently washed automobiles, using a hose and rags, and that he drove the cars. Furthermore, it was shown that the insured had made no effort to enter a gainful occupation. Should disability income benefits be paid in this case? Why or why not?

22. In an application for hospitalization insurance, the insured stated that he did not have any other hospital insurance, when in actuality he had a number of similar policies that provided about $44 a day if he should become hospitalized. The insurer, in denying a claim under the contract, stated that if the answer had been truthful, the company would not have issued its policy. A trial court held the answer to be false, but not material to the risk since it did not contribute to the event which matured the claim and the insurer appealed to a higher court. Decide the results of this case, with reasons.

23. "C," an insured, has a major medical policy with a $10,000 limit, $300 deductible, and 75 per cent coinsurance. He has a covered claim amounting to $14,000 plus lost wages of $7,000. The benefit clause reads: "The Company will pay benefits equal to 75 per cent of the covered expenses in excess of the deductible amount which are incurred on behalf of a covered person as a result of an accident or sickness."

"C" claims 75 per cent of $13,700, or $10,275, but the agent states he cannot recover more than 75 per cent of $9,700 or $7,275.

(a) Who is right? Why?

(b) What does this example illustrate with regard to the possible abuse of major medical contracts? Explain.

24. A certain newspaper advertises a health insurance policy that will pay $25 a week in the event of disability for certain accidents. There is a lump-sum benefit of $1,000 in case of accidental death by certain causes. The annual premium is $1.50. What further questions would you have before purchasing this policy? Why?

25. A certain policy is advertised as noncancellable, but when it is examined, bold type across the front states "This policy is renewable at the option of the company only." Are these two provisions inconsistent?

26. Differentiate between a waiting period and an elimination period in a health insurance policy. What purpose is served by these clauses?

27. An insured applied for and was issued a life insurance policy with a waiver-of-premium rider under which all premiums would be waived if the insured should become totally and permanently disabled. The insured failed to disclose that he had consulted an eye specialist four months prior to issuance of the policy. It developed that the eye specialist had diagnosed an incurable condition which ultimately led to blindness. The insurer attempted to cancel the waiver-of-premium rider, on the grounds of material misrepresentation, after the period of incontestability under the policy had expired. The insured contended that he was totally disabled and that he did not realize that his illness was severe at the time he applied for the policy. How should this case be decided (a) under the incontestability clause of the life insurance policy and (b) under the incontestability clause of the health insurance policy? Explain your reasoning in each case.

28. Why, in a group health insurance contract, is there the requirement that an employee's benefit level be determined by some factor such as income level, job status, or length of service? Explain.

29. "In some respects the provisions affecting the employee in group insurance are more favorable than under individual contracts, but less flexibility is permitted." Explain this statement.

30. An underwriter of health insurance, commenting on major medical insurance, stated "Our salesmen have told the policyholder we will pay 80 per cent of anything, so when we pay other than what is billed, we disturb the employer, the claimant, and the doctor. . . . A few doctors mistakenly believe that a contract for a fee between the doctor and his patient is binding on the insurance company." To what provisions in the major medical policy was this underwriter referring? Explain.

31. So-called "comprehensive" medical plans often involve a primary cover, such as Blue Cross and Blue Shield, on top of which is superimposed a major medical plan. In this way the employee obtains truly catastrophic coverage as well as first-dollar coverage. In such plans it is common to

require what is called a "corridor deductible" of say $100, which must be borne by the employee before any major medical benefits are payable. Discuss the justification for the corridor deductible.

32. The following suggestions have been put forth as possible methods to control the tendency for costs under major medical insurance to rise to prohibitive levels:
    (a) Require a higher coinsurance deductible for insureds with higher income levels.
    (b) Exclude payment for costs covered under other policies or from other sources.
    (c) Require a subrogation clause.
    (d) Limit psychiatric care to, say, 50 visits per year, with 50 per cent coinsurance applying.
    (e) Place an extra deductible on drugs.

    State what you believe is the purpose of each of these proposals and evaluate its probable effectiveness.

33. The Federal Employees Health Benefits Act of 1959 provides that the federal government will contribute up to certain amounts on behalf of government employees under one of four optional plans: (1) Blue Cross–Blue Shield, (2) insurance company sponsored plans, (3) employee organization sponsored and administered plans, and (4) comprehensive medical plans offered by medical groups such as the Health Insurance Plan of New York or the Kaiser Foundation on the West Coast. The health insurance industry appointed a committee to draft tentative provisions of an over-all comprehensive plan to be made available to those employees who select an insurance sponsored arrangement. Two plans, whose major features are those given below, were put forth:

	Plan 1	*Plan 2*
Deductible amount	$50	$50
Indemnity for hospital expense not subject to deductible	$250	$2,000
Coinsurance	25%	20%
Lifetime maximum benefit	$10,000	$30,000
Annual amount subject to reinstatement on lifetime maximum	$500	$1,000
Options on leaving the group	May convert to individual policy within 31 days. If confined to hospital, benefits are continued for 91 days or until prior release	
Optional maternity benefit	$150	$150
Deductible for out-of-hospital drug expense, each calendar year	$30	$30

    (a) Explain with an illustration how the "lifetime maximum benefit" provisions should operate. Are such restrictions likely to prove an undue hardship in many cases?

(b) What difference does it make whether the deductible amount is $50 per calendar year or $50 per illness? Explain.

(c) What difference would it make if the various deductibles were to apply only to the primary insured, or to each member of his family?

(d) Should the coinsurance be higher or lower as maximum benefits increase? Why?

(e) Suggest possible reasons why the Congress of the United States elected to have various private insuring groups compete for the business of insuring federal employees rather than have a central organization such as the Social Security Administration underwrite the whole plan.

34. At a 1960 meeting of health insurance underwriters, Mr. V. J. Skutt stated that annual benefits paid to the American public under group health insurance increased from $957 million to over $5 billion in the decade of the 1950's. Furthermore, the rate of increase in numbers of people covered in this period, 66 million to 127 million, was $4\frac{1}{2}$ times the rate of increase in population. By 1960 more than 7 out of every 10 people with health insurance were included under group coverages. Yet, "it is seriously suggested in Washington that only the National Government can provide and properly administer health insurance. . . . Can any thinking American believe that it will help the stability and security of our nation to load upon its government the myriad of offices, records, equipment, paperwork, and thousands upon thousands of additional employees necessary to substitute a government health insurance program for our voluntary system?"

(a) To what extent do you believe that the threat of governmental action in the field of health insurance brought about the rapid growth of private coverage?

(b) Point out some of the differences between health insurance and other centralized governmental social insurance programs (social security old-age and survivors insurance) which militate against socializing the field of health insurance.

35. In Senate hearings on possible amendments to the Social Security law in 1960, it was brought out that people over 65 years of age have two or three times as much chronic illness as the rest of the population and must stay in the hospital twice as long as other people. They use drugs and medicines steadily, rather than occasionally, and, generally, spend 90 per cent more than other people on health. However, of the expected 17 or 18 million aged people in the population in 1965, only about 9 million are expected to have some insurance, much of it inadequate. Two million persons will be eligible for welfare, leaving six or seven million uninsured for medical bills.

(a) In your opinion, to what degree is private health insurance, in its present form, a potential solution to the problem of the six or seven million uninsured aged people? Explain.

(b) In your opinion, should the federal government subsidize wholly or partially the insurance protection for health losses of aged people?

Social

Insurance

So far in this text we have been concerned primarily with private approaches to the problem of economic insecurity. Public agencies also concern themselves with the problems of premature death, health loss, old-age dependency, and unemployment, the four major perils which threaten personal financial security. Public bodies use several methods to handle these problems, but we shall be concerned in this chapter with the insurance method. Social insurance may be said to include all insurance plans either operated by or financed by governmental agencies, or operated by private agencies under close control and supervision of the government.

We have defined insurance as an economic institution which reduces risk both to society and to individuals by combining under one management a large group of objects so situated that aggregate losses to which it is subject become predictable within narrow limits. There is the implicit assumption that the insurance management accumulates an advance fund for payment of these losses. Not all governmental plans to meet personal security problems fall within this definition, and those which do, do so somewhat imperfectly. For example, a state home for the poor or a school for the blind may be aimed at meeting a personal problem of financial security, but there is no actuarial calculation of the probability of loss and no advance accumulation of funds to meet the contingency of blindness or old-age dependency. The state simply meets these costs, as they occur, out of general tax revenues. On the other hand, a state plan to finance unemployment benefits by charging each employer a premium, which bears some relationship to the risk involved, does generally fall within the definition of a social insurance scheme. However, there are certain important distinctions that characterize social insurance plans as opposed to private insurance. These are developed below. The types of social insurance to be analyzed in this chapter include: (1) Old-age, survivors, and disability insurance (OASDI), (2) Workmen's compensation insurance, (3) Unemployment insurance, and (4) Temporary disability insurance.

It is not claimed that these represent all the types of insurance which might conceivably be classified as *social*. For example, life insurance offered to veterans under various federally sponsored agencies or by state agencies, compulsory automobile insurance, federal crop insurance, federal guarantees of credit, and the aid to dependent children, aged individuals, and indigent persons provided under social security legislation could be considered social insurance. However, the four plans listed above constitute the most generally accepted list of social coverages.

THEORY OF SOCIAL INSURANCE

Basic purposes

As a generalization, it can be argued that social insurance plans tend to be introduced whenever a social problem exists which requires governmental action for solution and where the insurance method is deemed most appropriate as a solution. A social problem is a social condition or set of circumstances that society as a whole finds repugnant or otherwise undesirable, and for which the solution is generally beyond the control of the individual. Examples are the problems of crime, poverty, unemployment, mental disease, ill health, dependency of children or aged persons; economic privation of a certain class, such as agricultural workers, drug addicts, industrial accident victims, and divorcees and their families. Insurance is not an appropriate method of solution for many of these problems since the peril is not accidental, fortuitous, or predictable. In other instances insurance is perhaps feasible, but due to the catastrophic nature of the event (as in unemployment), private insurers cannot undertake the underwriting task because of lack of financial capacity. This means that if the insurance method is to be used as a solution for certain problems, governmental agencies must either administer or finance the insurance plan.

The justification for social insurance, then, lies in the fact that some insurance tasks either cannot or are not accomplished by private insurers without assistance from a government. These tasks concern social problems which are deemed too important to ignore. The economic problems involved in social insurance are such that governmental action is necessary to solve legal difficulties, to supplement financing, to introduce compulsion, to give organization, or to supply other ingredients in a successful insurance formula.

It is only natural that in an increasingly industrialized society the economic and social problems requiring some centralized attention tend to multiply. The greater the level of density of population, dependence on money income, international tensions, dependence on mass production, and similar factors, the more complex all social and economic problems tend to become.

The United States, slow to get started in the field of social insurance,[1] has developed the field rapidly since the passage of federal social security legislation in 1935. As revealed in Table 24–1, the premium income of all governmental insurers is already about one third of the level of the premium income from all private insurers. From another viewpoint, the importance of social insurance can be seen by the fact that in 1959 there were 13.5 million OASDI beneficiaries, and 1.1 million unemployment insurance beneficiaries.[2] Approximately seven out of every ten aged individuals are receiving benefits under OASDI.

Table 24–1 records the growth of the major social insurance programs in the United States. Public employee retirement plans and OASDI account for about two thirds of the total benefit payments, while unemployment, workmen's compensation, and nonoccupational disability insurance account for the remaining one third.

Total welfare expenditures, as shown in Table 24–1, amounted to about $43.7 billion in the period 1957–58. Social insurance expenditures have constituted a growing portion of total welfare payments over the years, until in the 1957–58 period they were over one third of the total. The growth of these programs has caused concern among those who fear that the United States is fast becoming a welfare state to the exclusion of free enterprise.

Data in Table 24–1 show that while welfare expenditures are indeed significant, they have not risen as a proportion of total governmental budgets, but have tended to decline somewhat. Total welfare expenditures have in the post-World War II period constituted approximately 10 per cent of the total gross national product. Social insurance

---

[1] For example, Germany passed the first modern workmen's compensation statute in 1884 under the sponsorship of Von Bismarck. It was reviewed as a method of counteracting the growing strength of the Socialist Party in Germany. England followed suit in 1897. It is interesting that today in the United States many observers look upon social insurance legislation as the forerunner, not a counter-measure, to socialism. Most western nations of the world have adopted various forms of social insurance, many of which are more complete than those forms existing in the United States. For an excellent summary of the national social insurance legislation in the following countries, see *International Survey of Social Security* (International Labour Office, Geneva, 1950): Argentine Republic, Australia, Austria, Belgium, Bolivia, Brazil, Bulgaria, Canada, Chile, Columbia, Cuba, Czechoslovakia, Denmark, Dominican Republic, Equador, Egypt, Finland, France, Greece, Guatemala, Haiti, Hungary, Iceland, India, Iran, New Zealand, Norway, Panama, Peru, Poland, Portugal, El Salvador, Sweden, Switzerland, Turkey, Union of South Africa, United Kingdom, United States, Uruguay, and Venezuela.

[2] "Social Security in Review," *Social Security Bulletin* (December, 1959), pp. 1–2. Latest data are published monthly.

Table 24-1

EXPENDITURES FOR SOCIAL INSURANCE AND PUBLIC WELFARE, SELECTED FISCAL YEARS, 1934-1958

(Billions of Dollars)

	Total Welfare [1]	Expenditures As a Per Cent of Total Budget		Total Social Insurance [2]	Per Cent Insurance to Total Welfare [3]	OASDI	Public Employee Retirement	Unemployment [4]	Non-occupational Disability [5]	Workmen's Compensation
		Federal	State							
1934-35	$14.1	47.9	54.0	$ .383	2.7	$ ...	$ .210	$ ...	$ ...	$ .174
1939-40	18.3	36.1	61.2	1.214	6.8	.281	.255	.552	...	.245
1944-45	14.2	3.6	62.6	1.363	9.5	.267	.383	.162	.005	.398
1949-50	28.8	24.4	64.3	4.764	16.5	.784	.743	2.082	.072	.628
1954-55	34.2	20.2	57.8	9.879	29.0	4.436	1.379	2.114	.219	.943
1955-56	36.7	21.5	56.6	10.639	29.0	5.485	1.577	1.621	.233	1.008
1956-57	39.1	22.0	55.4	12.462	31.8	6.666	1.785	1.842	.268	1.084
1957-58	43.7	24.6	58.0	15.975	36.7	8.221	2.032	3.312	.303	1.148

[1] Total welfare payments are made up of expenditures in social insurance, education, health and welfare, veterans affairs, public housing, and public assistance, which are not shown here separately but are available in the source cited for this table.

[2] Totals do not add across because they include railroad insurance programs which are omitted in the table.

[3] Ratio of column four to column one.

[4] Includes unemployment compensation for federal employees and payments under the Veterans' Readjustment Assistance Act of 1952, but excludes railroad unemployment compensation, which amounted to another $16 million in 1957-58.

[5] Includes expenditures by private insurers, state funds, self-insurers, and estimated costs of state administration.

Source: Ida C. Merriam, "Social Welfare Expenditures, 1957-58," *Social Security Bulletin* (October, 1959), pp. 4-9.

outlays accounted for 3.6 per cent of gross national product in 1957. It may be argued, too, that under social insurance the nation is provided with a formal system of meeting certain costs. Without insurance these costs would still have to be met. Presumably the certainty of benefits outweighs the cost of the administration of the insurance.

Thus, social insurance has a basic purpose of providing a certain degree of economic security to members of a society against risks which are beyond the control of either the individual or a group of private individuals organized for mutual protection by a private insurance company. Neither private agencies nor the individual were able to meet successfully the various problems leading to old-age dependency or unemployment. In an industrialized economy these problems are essentially beyond the power of any individual to solve. It is no longer accepted reasoning, for example, that an individual is solely to blame for his unemployment and should bear the entire cost himself. It is also recognized that it may be beyond the power of the individual to provide completely for his own old age because of the nature of the economy in which he earns his living.

Social insurance has the further purpose of helping to stabilize the economy in various ways and to maintain a full employment level. Unemployment insurance benefits, for example, have a recognized stabilizing effect in periods of recession. If an employee without savings loses his job, he does not have to go on relief roles immediately, but perhaps may only find it necessary to reduce his standard of living temporarily until a new job is found. If a community's main source of employment is cut off, the blow to business activity is thus softened, although in the long run, a new source of employment must be found to replace that which was lost.

Social insurance v. private insurance

An understanding of social insurance coverages can be facilitated by an appreciation of the basic differences between these and privately sponsored insurance devices.

Compulsion. Most social insurance plans are characterized by an element of compulsion. This is not true, however, of private insurance. Because social insurance plans are designed to solve some social problem it is necessary that everyone involved be required to cooperate. Thus, if an employer qualifies under the law, he and his employees must pay social security taxes, and his employees must be covered by workmen's compensation or unemployment insurance. All must be treated equally.

Set level of benefits. In social insurance plans little, if any choice, is usually given as to what level of benefits may be provided. Thus, even if he so desires, an employee cannot purchase either more or less unemployment insurance than is offered under the plan. All persons covered under the plan are subject to the same benefit schedules, which may vary according to the amount of the average wage, length of service, or job status. In private insurance, of course, one may usually buy any amount of coverage he wishes.

Floor of protection concept. A basic principle of social insurance in a system of private enterprise is that it aims to provide a *minimum level* of economic security against perils which may interrupt income. This principle, known as the *floor of protection concept,* is not always strictly observed, but it is still a fundamental theme of social insurance coverages in the United States. In workmen's compensation insurance, for example, an injured worker is usually given complete medical care; but under most state laws he receives less than half of his former income during the time he is disabled. Under the 1961 provisions of social security, a worker may not receive, upon retirement, more than $127 per month, or if he has a dependent spouse, not more than $190.50 per month. He is expected to have made other arrangements through private insurance plans if he wants a more adequate level of benefits than that provided under social security. The purpose of social insurance plans is to give all qualified persons a certain minimum protection with the idea that more adequate protection can and should be provided through individual initiative. The incentive to help oneself, a vital element of the free enterprise system, is thus preserved.

Subsidy concept. All insurance devices have an element of subsidy in that the losses of the unfortunate few are shared with the fortunate many who escape loss. In private insurance, however, a basic principle is that each insured group, as a unit, shares its own losses and thus pays a premium which is closely related to the losses of the group. In social insurance it is anticipated that an insured group may not pay its own way but will be subsidized either by other insured groups or by the taxpayers generally. Thus, when retirement benefits were introduced into social security legislation, many individuals who worked only a minimum of one and one-half years were able to draw a lifetime pension which had a value far in excess of the premiums paid by them and their employers. The younger workers, of course, were subsidizing the old, and still are.

Most social insurance plans have access to general tax revenues if the contributions from covered workers are inadequate.

Unpredictability of loss. For several reasons the cost of benefits under social insurance cannot usually be predicted with great accuracy. Therefore, the cost of social insurance is unstable. For example, in a general depression unemployment may rise to unusual heights, causing tremendous outlays in unemployment benefits which may threaten the solvency of the unemployment compensation fund. Old-age benefits under social security depend on such unpredictable matters as future fertility rates in the population; the general level of employment opportunities for the aged; the proportion of widows who will elect to work rather than receive benefits at age 62; and the average wage level of the worker over his earning years.

Attaching conditions to the right to receive payments is not a feature of private insurance, as it is in social insurance. In a life insurance contract, the worker may elect to use cash values at retirement to purchase a life annuity of a definite promised amount, regardless of what his employment status is, or whether he meets a "retirement test." In a private loss-of-income contract, a worker receives a definite benefit if he is disabled; but in workmen's compensation his benefit may depend on what his average earnings were, how many dependents he has, or whether he is permitted to bring legal action against a third party who was the cause of his loss.

Because of these uncertainties it is difficult for a private insurer to know in advance what his costs are likely to be, except within broad ranges. Without governmental participation in the plan, particularly in instances such as unemployment insurance which is subject to the catastrophic hazard, a private insurer cannot operate safely.

One might argue that it is wrong to attach conditions upon recovery in social insurance under the theory that one should "receive benefits as a matter of right." However, an insured worker has no particular inalienable right except the right given him by the social insurance law under which he is protected. His right can and probably should be conditional. To have it otherwise would mean that some would be receiving payments not really needed, and either costs would rise or others would be deprived of income which is their sole source of support. One of the basic advantages of social insurance is this very flexibility which permits those most in need to receive a greater relative share of income payments than others whose economic status is such that they do not require as much.

One of the basic requirements of an insurable peril is that the losses be sufficiently predictable so as to permit the calculation of a premium. Where this condition is not met, a private insurer is greatly handicapped and social insurance is the only solution if the insurance device is to be employed. Those who oppose social insurance in principle as unnecessary governmental interference into what should be a private matter often ignore the fact that private insurers simply cannot handle certain problems which are social in nature and which must be handled, if they are to be handled at all, by some social insurance scheme. This is not to say that there are no areas in which social insurance legislation has been employed where private solutions are possible; but, in general, the public has not invaded an area for social insurance coverage unless private insurance has failed to do the job.

Attachment to labor force. While it is not a necessary principle of social insurance, most social insurance plans cover only groups that are or have been attached to the labor force. Private insurance contracts, of course, are issued to individuals regardless of their employment status. The basic reason for this feature of social insurance is that nearly all governmental insurance plans are directed at the personal risk, at those perils which interrupt income, for example, unemployment, old age, premature death, and loss of health.

The requirement of attachment to the labor force has been a subject of frequent criticism by those who want a greater expansion of social insurance. Among the questions asked are: What about the family man who is unemployed but is not eligible for unemployment insurance benefits because he has not worked long enough, or has not worked in covered employment? What about the unemployed person who is injured while looking for a job and is not eligible for workmen's compensation because he was not employed at the time and hence did not receive a work-inflicted injury? These represent problem areas which so far have not been answered by social insurance, but may be handled by other means, either private or public in nature.

OLD AGE, SURVIVORS, AND DISABILITY INSURANCE

Background and development

The Old Age, Survivors and Disability Insurance program (OASDI) is the only large plan of social insurance which is both federally financed and administered.[3]

---

[3] Unemployment insurance is federally financed, in part, but is state administered. Workmen's compensation and temporary disability insurance are both state financed and administered plans.

OASDI is one of the four basic parts of the Social Security Act originally passed in 1935. The other three programs are: (1) grant-in-aid plan to states for assistance to the needy aged, the blind, the totally and permanently disabled, and to dependent children, (2) grant-in-aid plan to states for services provided for maternal and child welfare, and (3) grant-in-aid plan to states for administration of state unemployment compensation funds. The first two grant-in-aid plans mentioned are usually referred to as *public welfare* plans and the third, as simply the *unemployment insurance program*.

The various public welfare plans will not be discussed in this text because it is felt that they are not true examples of social insurance. Applicants for public welfare receive benefits for which they pay no premiums, and must demonstrate that they have no other means of support. There is no compulsion to apply for benefits, *i.e.,* the program is voluntary in nature. Recipients of social insurance benefits, on the other hand, pay premiums which are related to the level of benefits, under plans which are compulsory, and benefits are paid regardless of the need of the individual. Welfare programs are financed by states out of general tax revenues with the help of federal subsidies. No advance accumulation of funds is made as is the case in true insurance plans.

State welfare plans were the forerunners of the federal OASDI plan. Recognizing that state homes for the poor were unsatisfactory, Arizona passed a state pension law in 1914 providing a maximum of $15 per month. This law was declared unconstitutional and by 1930 only 10 state laws had been passed. Under the impetus of the depression, the movement for pensions grew and by the time of the passage of the Social Security Act in 1935, 30 laws were in effect. However, because of requirements for long periods of residence, low average pensions (about $15 per month), and inability of states to raise the necessary money for financing, these plans were considered unsatisfactory and federal assistance was deemed necessary.[4]

An interesting side light of the pension movement was the Townsend Plan, a crusade developed by Francis Townsend, a retired physician who reportedly lost all his savings in the 1929 stock market crash. Under this plan $200 would be given each month to each person over 60 who agreed to retire and spend promptly all funds received. The argument was that this plan would not only remove unneeded laborers from the employment force, but would also stimulate business to the point that economic recovery would be quickly attained. Thus, an early connection was seen between social insurance and general economic policy. While

---

[4] Domenico Gagliardo, *American Social Insurance* (New York: Harper & Brothers, 1955), pages 49–52.

the Townsend plan had many fallacies, it stimulated the pension movement which finally culminated in the Social Security Act.

OASDI has been changed considerably over the years. The original 1935 act provided only retirement benefits for workers who had contributed to the plan for sufficient periods to entitle them to an insured status. There were cash refunds to survivors when the wage earner died and to living workers aged 65 who had not been in covered employment long enough to qualify for benefits. In 1939 the act was amended to bring in benefits for survivors of covered workers. This marked the first of a series of changes which has been proceeding ever since. The law has been amended in almost every session of Congress,[5] and these amendments have accomplished several liberalizations. First, they have gradually brought under coverage almost every type of employment, so that about nine out of every ten workers must now contribute to some type of social insurance retirement plan, whether it be one sponsored by a state government or some federal agency. Amendments have liberalized eligibility requirements, and have served to increase the dollar level of benefits to correspond to changes in price levels. New types of coverages (e.g., disability income benefits were first added in 1956) have been added. Details of financial arrangements have been altered, although the basic plan of financing has not changed.

OASDI benefits

While the level and type of benefits have changed frequently under OASDI, it is instructive to examine the main features of current benefit provisions as a basic for understanding the law itself. Benefits are of three major types—1) retirement, 2) disability, and 3) survivors. These will be examined in that order. The discussion below is based on the act, as amended in 1961.

1) Retirement benefits. The basis on which all OASDI benefits are paid is the primary insurance amount of an insured worker. The monthly benefit, based on the worker's average monthly wage, is subject to a minimum of $40 and a maximum of $127. (The actual benefit is determined from the statutory table.) The formula used in calculating the monthly benefit gives about three times as much weight to the first

---

[5] See Robert J. Myers, "Old-Age, Survivors, and Disability Insurance Provisions: Summary of Legislation, 1935–1958," *Social Security Bulletin* (January, 1959), for an excellent summary of the details of these changes through 1958. See W. S. Cohen and W. L. Mitchell, "Social Security Amendments of 1961: Summary and Legislative History," *Social Security Bulletin* (September, 1961), for changes through 1961. See current issues of the *Bulletin* for the most authoritative reports on current changes in social security legislation.

$110 of average monthly wages as it does to the remaining earnings. Thus, the low-income earner is treated more favorably than the high-income earner.

The average monthly wage of an insured individual is computed by determining the total of his wages paid in, and self-employment income credited to, his "benefit computation years." The benefit computation years are determined by deciding the *number* of years to be included in the computation and *which* of the years will be used. After the number of years to be used has been determined, the five lowest years of earnings are deleted. The total received during the remaining years is then divided by the number of months elapsed during those years.[6] In computing the average monthly wage of an individual, the amount of wages and self-employment income to be taken into account is limited to the amount specified by the law in effect at the time the wages and income were paid. For example, after 1958 the amount of wages and self-employment income to be taken into account is limited to $4,800 a year.

A simple illustration of the calculation of the primary insurance amount will clarify the rules above. Suppose that Jones reached age 65 in 1961 and qualified for benefits under his social security coverage. Jones had already received $4,800 in wages for 1961 at the time of his retirement and had received the maximum taxable wages each year since 1950 as follows:

$3,600 each year during 1951, 1952, 1953, and 1954,
$4,200 each year during 1955, 1956, 1957, and 1958,
$4,800 each year during 1959 and 1960.

Under the 1961 amendments, it is first necessary to determine the number of elapsed years after 1950 and before the first year after 1960 in which Jones qualified for benefits and had reached retirement age. In Jones' case the number of elapsed years is ten. This number of elapsed years is then reduced by five to a total of the five highest years as the benefit computation years. Thus, Jones' computation base years are 1957 through 1961 and his average monthly wage is computed as follows:

1957—$ 4,200
1958—   4,200
1959—   4,800
1960—   4,800
1961—   4,800
Total $22,800 ÷ 60 = $380, average monthly wage.

---

[6] The 1960 Amendments retained the former method of computing the average monthly wage for those who cannot qualify under the new method because they became entitled to old-age benefits or died before 1961.

By reference to the statutory table of primary insurance amounts and maximum family benefits, it is determined that the amount of Jones' primary insurance benefit is $123.

If Jones has a dependent wife, or a child under age 18, his benefit is increased by one half for each such dependent, subject to a family maximum.[7] Jones must be 62 before he is eligible for retirement, and his wife, too, may draw her benefit when she is 62 or over. If Jones is 62 and his wife is 60, his retirement benefit is $98.40, until his wife becomes eligible for benefits at age 62. Under the current regulations, the permanent benefit is reduced if the insured elects to receive it at age 62 rather than at age 65.[8]

Retirement test.   Before Jones may receive his retirement benefit, he must meet a "retirement test." This test is expressed in terms of income earned in any employment or from self-employment after age 65. Basically, this is the way the retirement test works. Jones is permitted to earn income up to $1,200 each year and receive all benefits for the year. If his earnings exceed this exempt amount, his benefits are reduced. Jones will have $1 in benefits withheld for each $2 that he earns from $1,200 up to $1,700. For every $1 that his earnings exceed $1,700, $1 of benefits will be withheld. However, no deductions may be imposed for months in which Jones neither earns over $100 in wages nor renders substantial services in self-employment.

For example, if Jones earns $450 a month for five months and does nothing for the rest of the year, he has earned $2,250; but he will lose only five retirement benefit checks. If he is also self-employed during the year and has no net earnings from self-employment, total benefits of $800, or six full months plus $62 in the seventh month, will be withheld.[9] This additional deduction would be imposed since, presumably, Jones was rendering substantial services in self-employment and therefore was not "retired." When Jones reaches age 72, the monthly benefits are paid to him regardless of how much he earns.

---

[7] Under the 1958 Amendments, the maximum family benefit is the lowest of the following three amounts: (a) $254, (b) 1.5 times the primary benefit, or (c) 80 per cent of the average monthly wage.

[8] There is a permanent reduction of 8⅓ per cent for each year under 65. Thus, if the dependent's wife elects to receive benefits at age 62 (assuming her husband is 65 or over) she receives 75 per cent of the amount to which she would have been entitled at age 65. Her pension is thus 37½ per cent rather than 50 per cent of her husband's primary benefit. A widow's benefit is not reduced at age 62.

[9] Calculated as follows: Earnings $2,250 minus $1,200 exemption equals $1,050 "excess" earnings. Of this $1,050, Jones "loses" one half of the first $500 and all of the remaining $550, or $800. Since in the seventh month he was not retired and since he has so far "lost" only $738 ($123 × 6), he is subject to an additional deduction of $62 from his check during the seventh month. If he earns nothing else during the year, even though self-employed, he would receive all of his remaining benefit checks. The example assumes that Jones retired at age 65 and has a primary benefit amount of $123.

Over the years the retirement test has been repeatedly liberalized. The original 1935 act permitted no earnings from covered employment, but the 1939 amendments raised the amount of earnings to $14.99, the 1950 amendments to $50, and the 1952 amendments to $75. The 1954 amendments switched the retirement test from a monthly basis to an annual basis, and included all earnings whether from an occupation covered by the social security law or not. A person was permitted earnings of $1,200 each year without loss of benefits. For each $80 (or fraction thereof) in excess of $1,200, one month's benefit was withheld, except that no deduction may have been imposed for any month in which the beneficiary neither earned wages of more than $100 nor rendered substantial services in self-employment. Now the test applies to all employment, covered or not, but does not apply to income received from other pensions, investment income, or any other income received from sources other than active employment. The worker will not lose his OASDI benefits because he has investment income of any amount, the theory being that the income test is not a "needs" test but a retirement test. This preserves the basic theory of social insurance as being a true insurance plan under which benefits are received automatically, in contrast to a welfare program where a retired person must be a pauper to receive benefits.

2) Disability benefits. In 1956 Congress amended the Social Security Act to provide disability income to an insured worker who became disabled between the ages of 50 and 64. Dependents of the disabled worker became eligible for benefits in 1958. In 1960, Congress amended the act to provide for the payment of disability benefits to workers regardless of age and to their eligible dependents. The disability income is equal to the individual's primary insurance amount, and the benefits are increased if the worker has dependents. The dependents each receive one half of the primary benefit, subject to a family maximum.

In order to prove disability there must be medical evidence that the insured is unable to engage in substantial gainful activity. There is a waiting period of six months, and the impairment must be such that it is expected to continue indefinitely. Thus, an illness that is disabling for a period longer than six months, but which is not expected to be long, continued, and indefinite in duration, is not compensable under the law. This illustrates the fact that social insurance does not replace private insurance, but merely supplements it. A disability which is fully compensable under a commercial disability income policy may not be compensable at all under OASDI, because of a different definition of disability, or a different standard of claims adjustment.

3) Survivors benefits. OASDI provides for substantial amounts of "life insurance" under the survivors provisions. Subject to certain conditions, dependents of a deceased worker may receive benefits as follows:

Who are eligible	*Amount of benefit*	*Duration of benefit*
Widow, at or over age 62	82.5% of her deceased husband's primary insurance amount	For life, or until time of remarriage.
Mother, with child entitled to a child's benefits	75% of her deceased husband's primary insurance amount	Until youngest child is 18 or prior remarriage. Benefit continues after age 18 if child is disabled.
Child	75% of the parent's primary insurance amount	Until reaching age 18, prior remarriage or adoption. Benefits continue after age 18 if child is disabled.
Widower, if husband was dependent on the wife; dependent father age 65 or over; or mother, age 62 or over	82.5% of deceased's primary insurance amount. If two parents qualify, the maximum allowance is 150 per cent.	For life, or until time of remarriage in the case of a widower.
Any survivor [10]	Lump sum of three times the primary insurance amount, subject to $255 maximum	

The value of the life insurance benefits provided under OASDI, while it cannot be determined with certainty because of the conditional nature of these benefits, is seen to be substantial. In fact, Social Security Administration estimates placed the total value of benefits as of January 1, 1957, as follows: widow's, $98 billion; mother's, $81 billion; child's, $229 billion; and lump sum, $17 billion, for a total of $425 billion. This compares to an estimated $458 billion of insurance in force for all private insurers in 1957. These amounts represent the present value of all future benefits, based on a three per cent interest assumption, under OASDI. It is indeed remarkable that the amount of life insurance in force under OASDI is approximately equal to the combined coverage in private insurers. It may be observed, however, that even with nearly

---

[10] Widow, widower, or anyone paying burial expenses (as reimbursement).

$900 billion of life insurance in force, this still represented less than three times the national income in 1957. It would be conservative to say that the market for life insurance is certainly not exhausted by the addition of social insurance. Rather, it becomes possible for more people to develop through private insurers a really adequate program of life insurance coverage for their dependents by considering OASDI as a base upon which to build.

Insured status

The benefit provisions discussed above apply only if the worker is either "fully insured" or "currently insured" under the law. A worker becomes "fully insured" upon meeting certain tests, and once this status is reached, he and his dependents are entitled to certain benefits. If a deceased worker fails to meet the test of being fully insured but meets the test of being currently insured, monthly benefits may be payable to his minor children and to his widow for as long as she has minor children in her care.

A person becomes *fully insured* if he meets either of two tests:

1. he has worked in covered employment for 40 quarters (10 years), or

2. subject to a minimum of six calendar quarters, the person has worked in covered employment at least one fourth the number of calendar quarters elapsing from his starting date until the time he attains retirement age, becomes disabled or dies, whichever occurs first.

Generally, a worker is credited with a quarter of coverage if he is paid at least $50 in any calendar quarter. (Different tests apply to self-employed persons and to agricultural laborers.) Thus, if a worker's starting date is January 1, 1962, he becomes fully insured under OASDI if he works continuously in covered employment for at least one and one-half years and continues to work in at least one fourth of the elapsed quarters until his death or retirement. Once he has worked 10 years he is fully insured no matter how much longer he works. It should be observed that being "insured" has nothing to do with the calculation of benefits. Insured status is simply a prerequisite to being eligible for *any* benefits.

A worker is *currently insured* if he has worked in covered employment at least six of the last 13 quarters including the quarter in which he dies or in which he becomes entitled to benefits. Thus, a worker could enter the covered labor market 30 years after his starting date, work for six quarters, and if he dies he is currently insured and has certain rights under the law. A summary of the insured status requirements for different types of benefits under the 1961 amendments is given in the following table:

BENEFICIARY CATEGORY	INSURED STATUS REQUIRE-MENT FOR WORKER
Retired worker (62 or over)................................	Fully
Disabled worker (any age under 65).........................	Fully and for disability determination *
Dependents of retired or disabled worker:	
Wife (62 or over)..	Fully
Husband (62 or over).....................................	Fully and currently
Child (under 18, or any age if disabled)....................	Fully
Survivors of worker:	
Widow (62 or over)......................................	Fully
Widow or dependent divorced wife, at any age, if caring for child entitled to benefits................................	Fully or currently
Widower (62 or over)....................................	Fully and currently
Parent (62 or over)......................................	Fully
Child (under 18, or any age if disabled)...................	Fully or currently
Lump-sum payment beneficiary...........................	Fully or currently

* A disabled worker must not only be fully insured but also must meet additional requirements specified for disability determination. These requirements are that he shall have worked 20 quarters (five years) in the preceding 40 quarters, including the quarter of his disability.

In the preceding example, the young widow and children of the worker who worked six quarters in covered employment just before his death would receive benefits under the law, since a currently insured status is all that is required. If the widow had not had children, however, the deceased worker would have had to be fully insured. A retired worker need only have fully insured status for his widow to be eligible for benefits upon his death, but a widower cannot receive benefits unless his spouse was both fully and currently insured.

Financing the OASDI program

OASDI is financed by a tax on both the employee and the employer in equal amount. At first, an employee paid a one per cent tax on the first $3,000 of annual income earned in covered employment, but this base has been gradually increased until the 1958 amendments raised it to $4,800. The tax rate on covered wages has also been raised so that in 1962 it is $3\frac{1}{8}$ per cent for both the employee and the employer. Under the Social Security Act as amended in 1961, the following rates of tax are imposed on employers and employees for OASDI benefits:

It is seen that a worker and his employer may pay an average of, say, eight per cent of wages up to $4,800, or $384 a year, for a monthly

Years	Employment Tax on Wages		Tax on Self-Employment Income
	Employers	Employers	
1962	3⅛%	3⅛%	4.7%
1963–1965	3⅝	3⅝	5.4
1966–1967	4⅛	4⅛	6.2
1968 and after	4⅝	4⅝	6.9

pension of $127 when the worker reaches age 65. The annual premium for a private annuity of this amount would be approximately $635 if the worker is age 35. If the worker has a wife, his OASDI pension increases by 50 per cent, but there are no added taxes to pay. How is it possible for the government to offer such a bargain? Is the plan actuarially sound?

The actuarial soundness of the OASDI program has been analyzed by the Advisory Council on Social Security Financing, appointed by Congress to study the matter. The Council reported that the present rate of contributions is sufficient for both short-range and long-range costs, based on the best estimates available. Specifically, the Council concluded that the program is in close actuarial balance since the level-premium cost of OASDI is 8.27 per cent of payroll, based on intermediate cost estimates, as compared to the level-premium equivalent of the contributions of 8.02 per cent. The level-premium cost of the disability insurance part of the program is .49 per cent of payroll, compared to a .5 per cent contribution rate.[11]

This standard of actuarial solvency is of course not the same as for a private life insurance company, which must have on hand at all times reserves to meet all future obligations even if future premium payments are entirely cut off. The OASDI has trust funds of about $23.2 billion (September, 1961) which are intended to meet only short-term contingencies, not all future promised pensions. The Advisory Council concluded that it would be inappropriate to require a "full reserve" by private pension standards, since the social insurance plan can reasonably be expected to continue indefinitely. Furthermore, if Congress wishes to change benefits or if future fluctuations in employment reduced or increased collections, the plan would be in continual trouble under full-

---

[11] "Financing Old-Age, Survivors, and Disability Insurance: Report of the Advisory Council on Social Security Financing," *Social Security Bulletin* (February, 1959), pp. 3–4. Because the 1960 amendments permitted workers below age 50 to draw disability benefits, the actuarial cost of these benefits is currently a little higher than .5 per cent of payroll. See *Actuarial Cost Estimates and Summary of Provisions of OASDI As Modified by Social Security Amendments of 1960.* September, 1960. (U.S.G. P.O., 1960) p. 17.

reserve methods because the reserve would constantly tend to be either "too large" or "too small."

It may now be seen why OASDI appears to be such a bargain as compared with private pensions. The premium for the private pension must be large enough to permit the insurer to accumulate a full reserve. The private insurer must pay the pension under definite contractual agreements and must collect a given premium. In social insurance neither of these variables is fixed. The income of the social insurer may increase or decrease, and not all workers will be paid a pension even if they have contributed all of their lives. For example, a worker may have paid taxes all his life and die at age 64 with no dependents. He is paid little or nothing under OASDI, with his contributions and those of his employer going to the benefit of others. A widow may remarry, thus cutting off her social insurance benefits. A retired worker may continue to work part time so that he fails to meet the retirement test, and thus lose his benefits, even though he paid taxes all his life. Because of these and other factors, the promised benefits under OASDI appear large in relation to private plans. However, as noted, there are good reasons why this is true, and it is not because the plan is actuarially unsound, unless one wants to argue about the definition of actuarial unsoundness. Rather, the above result follows from the basic nature of a social insurance plan under which individual benefits are not necessarily closely related to the amount of individual premiums paid.

WORKMEN'S COMPENSATION INSURANCE

Development

Workmen's compensation was the first type of social insurance legislation adopted in the United States. It is unique in several respects. It is the only type of social insurance underwritten primarily by commercial insurers with only very general supervision by governmental units. It is also unique since in about half of the states it is not strictly compulsory. Furthermore, the standard workmen's compensation policy combines two types of insurance in one—employer's common law liability and workmen's disability benefits for injured employees who suffer on-the-job injuries or occupational diseases. Thus, workmen's compensation insurance represents a merging of private and social insurance. It represents one of the first examples of a phenomenon that has become common in advanced industrial societies dedicated to free enterprise—that of governmental regulation and participation when an unregulated system tends to create a social problem.

The social problem which gave rise to workmen's compensation was that of uncompensated victims of industrial accidents. In the latter half of the 1800's, it became evident that the system of employer's common law liability for injuries to workmen resulted in many hardships. First, the development of mass-production techniques and its accompanying factory system increased the number of job injuries to significant levels. Second, an injured employee seeking redress had no alternative except to sue his employer for damages at common law for presumed employer negligence. Third, such suits, if they were successful at all, resulted in awards which were inadequate, long delayed, and uncertain.

It is probable that the real beginnings of unrest which culminated in workmen's compensation legislation rested with a famous early court decision, the English case of Priestley v. Fowler.[12] Prior to this decision an employee had been in the same legal position as a member of the public in bringing an action against his employer for negligence. This decision placed the employee in an even worse relative position than before by establishing the employer defense which has become known as the fellow servant rule.[13] This rule held that if the employee were injured by a fellow workman, the employer was not to blame. Without blame, he could not be required to pay any damages to the injured workman. Other defenses, the contributory negligence and the assumption of risk defense discussed previously, were also available to the employer and had the effect of shifting the risk of occupational injuries substantially on the shoulders of the employee who was generally unable to bear it.[14] In the years subsequent to the Priestley v. Fowler decision, legislation and court decisions tended to weaken or eliminate the effect of the common law defenses, but it was generally agreed that what was needed was a system of paying for medical and income losses resulting from occupational injuries, a system which did not require an employee to file suit against his employer and which did not rest on the doctrine of employer or employee fault. The first United States laws to accomplish this worthwhile purpose were not passed, however, until after 1900.

Basic structure of compensation

The first workmen's compensation legislation attempting to embody the principle of liability without fault was declared unconstitutional on the grounds that it was wrong and inconsistent with the common law that

---

[12] 3 M. & W. 1, 1837.

[13] See Chapter 14 for a discussion of employer's liability and his common law defenses.

[14] For an excellent discussion of the inadequacies, both logical and practical, of employer's liability system, see Domenico Gagliardo, *op. cit.,* Chapter 15.

anyone, employers included, could be held liable for something for which they were not to blame.[15] These constitutional objections were finally overcome, but as a result of the uncertainty which they brought, about half the states enacted compensation laws which were elective to the employer. This is the reason why workmen's compensation is not strictly compulsory. It is true that an employer who rejects coverage under a law which is elective generally loses his three common law defenses, a factor which makes it somewhat easier for a successful employee lawsuit. This gives the employer a strong incentive to purchase coverage. In the remaining states, workmen's compensation insurance is compulsory and employee suits are generally prohibited (except under certain conditions).[16] The employee is expected to take as his sole remedy the benefits provided for him under a schedule embodied in the law.

Insurance methods

There are three different methods by which an employer can provide the coverage required by law for his employees:

1) Purchase a workmen's compensation and employer's liability policy from a private commercial insurer.
2) Purchase insurance through a state fund set up for this purpose.
3) Self-insure.

All states except Louisiana require selection of one of these methods by employers subject to the law.

1) Private insurance. The standard workmen's compensation and employer's liability policy has two major insuring agreements. These are: (1) Coverage A to pay all claims required under the workmen's compensation law in the state where the injury occurred, including occupational disease benefits, penalties assessable to the employer under the law, and other obligations, and (2) Coverage B to defend all employee suits against the employer and pay any judgments resulting from these suits. Coverage B is separate and distinct from Coverage A. While it is not anticipated that there will be many employee suits, such claims are surprisingly frequent because methods are constantly being found to bring

---

[15] For example, see *Ives* v. *South Buffalo Railway Co.* 201 NY (2) 71 (1911) in which New York's first workmen's compensation law was held unconstitutional as a deprivation of liberty and property without due process of law. Maryland is credited with the first law, passed in 1902, which was declared unconstitutional two years later.

[16] An example of when an employee can sue his employer who is covered under workmen's compensation arises when the employer deliberately injures an employee, when an employer fails to pay his compensation insurance premiums, or when an employer violates certain provisions of the compensation statute.

an action against the employer in spite of the intention of the statutes to discourage such suits. Under Coverage B there is a basic limit of liability per accident of $25,000, an amount which may be increased by appropriate endorsement. Coverage B is similar to that given in general liability policies. There is no specific limitation for Coverage A; any limits are outlined by the state compensation law.

Third and fourth coverages, known as the all states and voluntary compensation endorsements, are available with the standard workmen's compensation and employer's liability policy. Under the *all states endorsement,* an employer may provide coverage automatically for unexpected situations when an employee may be sent into a state in which the employer does not normally operate and when, through the operation of that state's law, an employee becomes entitled to coverage. The employer is thus insured even if he has not listed that state as one in which he is operating.

Under the *voluntary compensation endorsement,* coverage is provided for the situation in which there is no applicable compensation statute and the employer desires to offer the employee the coverage that might have otherwise been applicable had the employee been under some governing statute. For example, suppose the employer has elected not to be covered under a workmen's compensation statute, or is employing workers who are not required to be covered under the applicable law. Through the voluntary compensation endorsement, the injured employee may be offered the same schedule of benefits as he would have received had he been insured under the compensation act, on a voluntary basis. If he accepts the compensation so offered, he must sign a release that absolves the employer from any common law liability he might have had for the injury.

While the private insurance method involves a contract between the employer and the insurer, the insurer deals directly with the employee and is primarily responsible to him for benefits. Thus, even if the employer goes out of business, the injured employee's security is not jeopardized.

2) *State fund.* In 11 states [17] an employer has his choice of using a private insurer or a state fund as the insurer of workmen's compensa-

---

[17] Arizona, California, Colorado, Idaho, Maryland, Michigan, Montana, New York, Oklahoma, Pennsylvania, and Utah.

tion. In seven states [18] the employer does not have his choice, but must insure, if at all, in an exclusive state fund. Five of the compulsory state funds were established during the period 1913–1915 when compensation laws were new and the success of private insurers in handling the business was uncertain. Most of the Canadian provinces established exclusive state funds.

3) Self-insurance. In all but six states, under specified conditions an employer is permitted to self-insure the workmen's compensation coverage.[19] Self-insurance is generally not permitted in Canada. Self-insurers must generally be large concerns with adequate diversification of risks in order to qualify under the law.

Evaluation of insurance methods. Data from the Social Security Administration covering the period 1939–1957 reveal the following trends in total losses paid under each of the insuring methods above: Losses paid by private insurers increased from 52 to 62 per cent of the total; losses paid by state funds decreased from 29 to 25 per cent of the total; and losses paid by qualified self-insurers decreased from 19 to 12 per cent of the total. Apparently employers are gradually favoring the selection of private insurers over other methods.[20] Some of the major reasons for these trends appear to be:

1. Private insurers offer the employer an opportunity to insure in one contract all the liability he is likely to have for damages arising out of work-connected injuries, whether these damages stem from employee suits, statutory benefit requirements, or other sources.
2. Private insurers offer more certainty in handling out-of-state risks. Most compensation laws are extraterritorial and there are many complexities to consider in making sure of coverage if the employer has widespread interests. Most state funds do not automatically cover such risks.

---

[18] Nevada, North Dakota, Ohio, Oregon, Washington, West Virginia, and Wyoming. In Nevada, Oregon, and West Virginia, the laws are elective so that if an employer stays out of the act, he may either purchase voluntary compensation from a private insurer; he may noninsure; or he may purchase employer's liability insurance for protection against possible employee suits. In Oregon, for example, only employers in hazardous industries are required to make an election. If such an employer elects to come under the act, he must purchase coverage from the state fund, but he is not *required* to take insurance under the act, or to make any other arrangements if he does not wish to do so. Of course, he will lose his common law defenses in any employee action in such a case. An employer in a nonhazardous industry (as defined) is not required to make an election to stay in or out of the fund.

[19] Nevada, North Dakota, Oregon, Texas, Washington, and Wyoming.

[20] For an excellent discussion of these issues, see Ashley St. Clair, "The Case for Private Insurance of Workmen's Compensation," and Jacob Clayman, "In Defense of State Workmen's Compensation Funds," in *Rocky Mountain Law Review,* Vol. XXXI, No. 4 (June, 1959).

3. While the expenses of state funds, at least exclusive state funds, are somewhat lower than those of private insurers, this difference is not so great as rough comparisons often lead one to believe. After adjustment for differences in the quantity and the quality of services rendered, many would argue that the supposed cost advantage of exclusive state funds is of insufficient size to warrant giving up the convenience and certainty involved in the private contract, including the ready availability of agents who provide services not usually supplied by the state fund.

4. Self-insurance has the handicap that it is necessary for the insured to "enter into the insurance business," which is essentially unrelated to insured's main operations. Contributions to a self-insurance fund are not tax deductible, a factor which may add materially to the cost and the risk involved in self-insurance.

5. Experience rating and retrospective rate plans (to be discussed in Chapter 26) enable the large firm to use a private insurer's facilities in transferring as much of or as little of the risk as is desired, at a very modest cost.

Major legal features of state laws

The provisions of workmen's compensation laws are subject to constant change, but a basic pattern exists even though details of the provisions may vary with each meeting of the state legislature.[21] We shall make comments on those features necessary for general understanding of the coverage provided by these laws as of 1960.

Employments covered. One of the shortcomings of compensation laws is that they do not cover all workers.[22] For example, farm labor, domestic labor, and often public employees are excluded. Employers with just a few employees are excluded even under compulsory laws,[23] and under elective laws there is no guarantee that the employee will be covered. One result of this unfortunate condition is that liability suits are necessary if an excluded worker is to recover anything, even though a basic purpose of compensation legislation was to eliminate this condition

---

[21] The Chamber of Commerce of the United States prepares periodically an "Analysis of Workmen's Compensation Laws" outlining the details of the law in each state. The study dated January, 1960, forms the basis of the discussion here.

[22] A study by A. M. Skolnik of the Social Security Administration revealed that in 1956, 7 states covered less than 60 per cent of their workers; 14 states between 60–70 per cent; 16 states between 70–80 per cent; 7 states between 80–90 per cent; and only 5 states greater than 90 per cent. See A. M. Skolnik, "Trends in Workmen's Compensation: Coverage, Benefits, and Costs." *Social Security Bulletin* (August, 1958), p. 7.

[23] In the following states with compulsory type laws, the given number of employees are excluded: Employers in Mississippi with fewer than eight; employers in Virginia with fewer than seven; employers in Arkansas and New Hampshire with fewer than five; employers in New York, Massachusetts, and Rhode Island with fewer than four; employers in Wisconsin, Ohio, Arizona, Delaware, and Michigan with fewer than three; and employers in Oklahoma with fewer than two.

as a prerequisite for employee recoveries. It is the small employer who is excluded from compensation laws and who is most likely to be the object of such suits. His smallness often could mean that either (1) a successful suit will bankrupt him, or (2) if he is more or less judgment proof, the injured workman will recover nothing. Neither of these alternatives is at all desirable.

Income provisions. Compensation laws recognize four types of disability for which income benefits may be paid. These are permanent and temporary total disability, and permanent and temporary partial disability. The laws generally limit payments by specifying the maximum duration of benefits, the maximum aggregate amount payable, and the maximum weekly amount payable.

For permanent total disability benefits, about half the states permit lifetime payments to the injured workman if he is unable to perform the duties of any suitable occupation. In the remaining states a typical limitation is between 400 and 500 weeks of payments, and there is also usually a limitation on the aggregate amount payable. Of the 26 states giving lifetime benefits, 20 have no aggregate maximum. There is a common limitation that income benefits cannot exceed about two thirds of the worker's average weekly wage, or some dollar amount, usually ranging between $40 and $50 per week. A few states make extra allowances for dependents.[24] Because average weekly wages have risen faster than legislative adjustments, the limiting factor is usually the dollar maximum, and it is estimated that workmen's compensation typically restores less than one half of a worker's wage.

Weekly benefits for temporary total disability are usually the same as for permanent total disability, except that often there is a lower maximum aggregate limitation and a lower time duration applicable to such payments.

In addition to income benefits, most workmen's compensation laws specify that lump sums may be paid to a worker as *liquidating damages* for a disability, such as the loss of a leg or an eye, that is permanent but which does not totally incapacitate the worker. The worker may usually draw income benefits during the time that his permanent partial disability prevents him from doing anything, and then he may receive a lump sum which varies with the seriousness of the injury. There is little consistency

---

[24] All states except Oregon also specify a waiting period of between three and seven days. Arizona, Utah, Massachusetts, North Dakota, Vermont, Nevada, Illinois, Wyoming, Idaho, Montana, Oregon, Washington, and Michigan provide dependent allowances.

among the states on the size of permanent partial disability benefits. For example, in Hawaii, a worker receives $8,437 for loss of a *thumb,* while in Massachusetts he receives only $3,500 for loss of an *arm* at the shoulder. In Ohio a worker would receive $9,800 for loss of a *leg* at the hip, which is less than a worker would receive for loss of a *foot* in such states as Arizona ($22,000), Washington, D. C. ($11,070), Wisconsin ($10,-000), and California ($10,500). Furthermore, the laws give no recognition to the relative seriousness of the injury. For example, the loss of an eye to one worker might not prevent him from returning to his old job as before, but would force another worker into a totally different job at lower pay. Yet, each worker would receive the same settlement. The only solution, if any, to the gross inconsistencies in permanent partial benefit schedules seems to be the adoption of a uniform national scale of benefits by all states.

Survivor benefits.   In case of fatal injuries, the widow and children of the worker are entitled to income benefits, subject to various limitations. Thirty states place a maximum duration of between 300 and 500 weeks on such income payments. The remaining states do not specify time limitations. The maximum benefits to the widow alone are generally less than they would have been to the disabled worker, but if the widow has children, these benefits are comparable to what the worker would have received for permanent total disability.

Medical benefits.   Most but not all workmen's compensation laws provide relatively complete medical services to an injured workman. About 60 per cent of the states have some type of limitation on medical benefits, expressed either as a time limitation or as a dollar limitation, or both, and 40 per cent have no statutory limitations on medical benefits. A few states have limitations which appear to be quite low. Colorado, for example, limits costs to $1,500 and the period must not exceed six months. Georgia limits medical benefits to $1,500. Most states which have medical limitations, however, provide that extensions either in time or amount may be granted where circumstances warrant.

Benefits for rehabilitation, both physical and occupational, are provided by only 23 states, and it is generally recognized that the quantity and the quality of these services are subject to wide variation. The general area of rehabilitation of the injured worker is one which needs much closer attention than it has received in the past. Examples of the potential saving in medical costs, community aid, and in the resultant lowering of compensation premiums made possible through rehabilitation demonstrate that from an economic standpoint alone, the effort is extremely worthwhile. For example, a study in New York of 40 patients who were referred to a community rehabilitation service showed that the state fund saved an average of $4,250 in compensation costs per case.[25]

In most states benefits are provided for occupational *diseases* as well as accidents, but the disease must be identified as one whose *proximate* cause was the worker's employment. Thus, benefits would not be paid for disability caused by pneumonia, unless it could be shown that long hours of exposure to the elements were necessitated by working conditions, and that these conditions resulted in the disease for which compensation is claimed. Common compensable diseases are silicosis, radiation sickness, and gas poisoning. Many borderline situations arise in which it must be determined if working conditions brought on such things as a heart attack, loss of hearing, or failing eyesight. In Massachusetts, for example, lobar pneumonia and death caused by inhaling smoke and water while fighting fire at the employer's direction were held compensable, but pneumonia caused by falling in a swamp while wandering during an attack of amnesia was held not compensable.[26] The court allowed compensation for eye injury from years of inadequate lighting conditions, but disallowed blindness allegedly caused by exposure to naphthalene while unloading a boat.[27] The court allowed a claim for tuberculosis caused by inhalation of dust which aggravated a pre-existing latent tubercular condition, but disallowed a claim for tuberculosis where evidence was not clear as to the onset of the condition during employment.[28]

Costs. The subject of rate-making in workmen's compensation will be considered in Chapter 26. In a typical year, premiums average about one per cent of the covered payroll. For individual employers the premium ranges widely, depending on the hazards attached to the employer's particular line of business. The rate for clerical help, for example, may be .1 per cent of payroll, and that for metal bridge painters, 24.5 per cent. This rate will also vary by geographical area. Then, too, costs depend on the type of insurer chosen, type of rating plan used, and other factors.

[25] W. Scott Allan, *Rehabilitation, A Community Challenge* (New York: John Wiley & Sons, Inc., 1958) p. 169. This book presents an excellent critique of nationwide rehabilitation efforts.

[26] Cases reported in *Workmen's Compensation Law of the State of Massachusetts, 1959* (New York: Association of Casualty and Surety Companies, 1959) pp. 19–21.

[27] *Ibid.*

[28] *Ibid.*

Value to workers. It is difficult to evaluate in monetary terms the value of workmen's compensation coverage to the worker, but estimates of average claim costs may tend to throw some light on the subject. In 1954, for example, the average payment nationally for a death resulting from a job-connected injury was $9,207. The average payment for permanent total disability was $16,758; for permanent partial disability, $5,010; for a minor permanent partial disability, $986; and for a temporary total disability, $247.[29] These amounts covered all types of payments—medical, lump sum, income, and survivor's benefits.

UNEMPLOYMENT INSURANCE

The unemployment problem and insurance

The problem of unemployment is perhaps the most serious single economic problem faced by modern industrial societies under the free enterprise system. The economic reasons for unemployment in a capitalistic society and the proposed solutions have occupied the attention of economists for many centuries. In the United States a typical peacetime year finds from three to five per cent of the civilian labor force unemployed at any one time, and during depression years this figure is often much higher, reaching nearly 25 per cent in 1933. The problem is considered so serious that, in the Full Employment Act of 1946, Congress expressed its intention to do whatever possible to prevent unemployment.

While it will not be our purpose here to analyze the causes of unemployment or to propose solutions, it is important to distinguish the major types of unemployment and to indicate which of these types are subject to partial solution by the insurance method. Unemployment has been classed as temporary or permanent, voluntary or involuntary, total or partial, seasonal or cyclical, technological, frictional, personal, and in many other ways. The type of unemployment which has been found to be susceptible to partial solution by the insurance method is essentially *short-term, involuntary* unemployment.

Long-term unemployment, which may be due to such factors as economic depression, technological changes which make a worker's skills obsolete, and permanent ill health, is considered too serious to be handled by insurance, primarily because long-term unemployment is subject to a severe catastrophic peril. Depression causes concurrent loss to a majority of the exposure units. Extended periods of such claims would bankrupt any insurer, perhaps even the government.

---

[29] Skolnik, *op. cit.,* p. 9.

Voluntary unemployment arises because the worker has decided that he wishes to remove himself from the labor force for his own reasons. He may wish to rest and live from savings, to attend school, to take a vacation, or he may simply be too discouraged to seek employment because he can find none that suits him. His reason for not working lies within matters more or less subject to his own control and it is easy to see that insurance against this type of unemployment is not feasible. Such unemployment does not meet the fundamental requirement that a peril must be accidental or fortuitous. Sometimes it is difficult to determine whether a worker is actually involuntarily unemployed. Thus, one of the tests used in unemployment insurance legislation is that the worker shall give evidence that he is continuing to seek work but is unable to locate any for which he is qualified by experience and training.

Unemployment insurance is designed, therefore, to alleviate certain types of unemployment, but not all unemployment. Unemployment problems are more serious for some industries than for others, for some occupations than for others, for certain age and racial groups than for others, but unemployment insurance makes no distinction between them. In keeping with the basic purpose of a social coverage, unemployment insurance tends to offer only a floor of protection for everyone, leaving the remaining areas of coverage to be handled by private solutions. To do otherwise might tend to reduce initiative, to remove incentive for personal saving, to cause unwarranted work stoppages, to discourage efforts on the part of private industry to stabilize employment, and to have other undesirable economic side effects.

Formal unemployment insurance plans were practically unknown in the United States before passage of the Social Security Act in 1935. One state, Wisconsin, had an unemployment insurance law which went into effect in 1934. Drafters of the Social Security Act wished to encourage each state to pass and administer its own act and to do this an ingenious device, called the tax offset, was employed. A federal law imposed a tax of three per cent on wages of employers (as defined), but the employer was allowed to credit up to 90 per cent of this tax for amounts payable to the state in which he operated under a state unemployment insurance law which met certain minimum standards. All the state had to do was to enact a suitable law and the employer could avoid 90 per cent of his federal tax. Ten per cent of the tax went for federal administration of the system. All states have now passed unemployment compensation statutes.

On the international scene, a survey by the International Labor Organization [30] revealed that more than a score of nations have adopted plans for payment of benefits and allowances for involuntary unemployment.[31] The main features of these plans are similar to laws in the United States. Most of the laws are compulsory. Many apply to all types of labor and do not exclude agriculture, as is done in the United States. The majority of laws state that the applicants for benefits must be capable of and available for work, and there is usually a waiting period before benefits begin. In some countries benefits are a flat amount, but usually benefits are expressed as some percentage of a worker's wage. All laws are aimed at short-term unemployment, but in some countries there is no specific limit on the duration of payments. In Great Britain allowances may usually extend to 30 weeks, and in some cases up to one year. It is interesting to observe that in no nation do private commercial insurers handle unemployment insurance. In some countries trade union-employer groups operate with semi-independent status, but in all cases there is close supervision by central authorities.

The main features of state unemployment laws are given below.[32]

Employment covered

The state unemployment insurance laws of all states, conforming to federal requirements, cover firms employing four or more workers. Twenty state laws cover employers with one or more workers. Most states also specify that the worker must have been with the employer for some minimum period, often 20 weeks, before the employer must pay a tax on the worker's wages. The laws do not cover all types of employments. Among employments usually (but not always) excluded are railroad workers (covered under a separate federal law), agricultural labor, domestic service in private homes or in fraternity and sorority houses, service rendered by a child under 21 for a parent, employees of nonprofit organizations, state and local government employees (although many states provide some form of coverage for their own workers), maritime workers, and self-employed persons. In most states, employers may elect, on a voluntary basis, coverage of services which are excluded from the

---

[30] International Labor Office, Action Against Unemployment (Geneva: International Labor Office, 1950), Chapter III.

[31] These include Austria, Belgium, Bulgaria, Czechoslovakia, Denmark, Finland, France, Greece, Italy, Luxembourg, Netherlands, Norway, Poland, Portugal, Sweden, Switzerland, United Kingdom, Ireland, Uruguay, Australia, New Zealand, Union of South Africa, Canada, and the United States.

[32] For a detailed treatment of the specific provisions of state laws, see *Comparison of State Unemployment Insurance Laws,* United States Department of Labor, published periodically.

definition of employment under their laws. The effect of these exclusions is that about one half of the total unemployment is insured.[33]

Benefits

The various states have developed somewhat complicated and diverse formulas for defining the benefits under their unemployment insurance acts. There is general agreement on the main features, but in any one state it is necessary to examine the law in order to determine what rights an insured worker may have.

In most states the worker must have worked for some minimum period during a base year, as defined, or have earned some minimum amount of wages, or both. Most states also require some waiting period, usually one week of total or partial unemployment, before benefit payments begin. The amount of benefit is some fraction of the wages earned during the base year or during some part of the base year. The base year is usually defined as the year preceding the date that the claim is filed, with some lag ranging from a week to six months. Once a claim is filed and the weekly income payments begin, a "benefit year" commences and payments typically continue for a period not to exceed 26 weeks. However, a few states have extended this period to as many as 39 weeks. The benefit formula is so arranged that if a worker was fully employed during his base period he may, subject to a minimum and maximum amount, expect to receive benefits equal to about one half of his normal wage. If he did not earn anything during his base year, he receives nothing. If he was employed only part time or earned very little, his benefits are reduced accordingly, subject to a minimum weekly amount ranging from $5 to $17, but averaging about $10–$15 per week. As of 1960, the maximum weekly benefits ranged from $26–$70, with a typical figure lying between $30–$40 per week. The average weekly benefit amount in December, 1960, was $32.87. In a number of the states the amount of the benefit is enlarged if the worker has dependents. The average weekly benefit of claimants in those states in December, 1960, was $48.45. State laws usually permit some unemployment benefits if the worker is not totally unemployed but is able to earn something, say through odd jobs, which is less than his usual wage. In most states the amount of the benefit is his regular benefit less actual earnings. If actual earnings are less than some allowances, say one half or one third the weekly benefit, there is no reduction in payment. The effect of these provisions is to reduce the

---

[33] See current issues of *Labor Market and Employment Security* for up-to-date data on insured employment.

temptation for a worker to cease all attempts at earning something for fear of losing his unemployment check.

Most states have provisions which may result in the reduction of benefits if the unemployment compensation fund is nearing exhaustion. In over half of the states the administrative agency must notify the governor and the legislature if it is believed that the fund will be inadequate to pay the statutory benefits. The legislature may then raise taxes or permit benefits to be reduced as it may deem fit. In other states if the fund falls below a specified level, the administrative agency may be empowered to do such things as reduce the maximum benefit, reduce the duration of benefits, increase the waiting period, change qualifying requirements, or some combination of these acts.

Eligibility requirements

In order to receive benefits, an unemployed worker must usually demonstrate not only that he is unemployed but also that he is actively seeking work, that he is able and willing to work, that he is not out of work because he voluntarily quit his job without good cause or was discharged for misconduct, and that he has not refused suitable work or is disqualified for other causes. The enforcement of these conditions is different in each state, not only because of legal provisions but also because the administrative agency may choose to enforce them differently.

Ability to work.   All states require that a claimant be able to work if work is offered. Except in a few states, physical illness would therefore cause a worker to be ineligible for benefits. A worker can usually satisfy the ability-to-work requirement by registering for work at a public employment office. Only four states have enacted special legislation to care for workers who are unemployed and unable to work because of physical disability. (See discussion on page 671.)

Available for work.   While each state law specifies that the worker must be available for work, if offered, as a condition for drawing benefits, the enforcement of these provisions varies widely. In nine states the law says that the worker need only be available for suitable or usual work or work for which the applicant is reasonably fitted by training and experience. In other states it is suspected that administrative officials enforce the available-for-work provisions with some latitude. Oftentimes the law may make an exception of certain types of workers; thus, in Connecticut and New Hampshire, workmen are not required to be available for work between the hours of one a.m. and six a.m.; in Alaska a worker does not lose his benefit check because he is out hunting or fishing for survival (and hence not available), providing no suitable work is offered him.

Disqualification. The unemployment insurance laws of all states have provisions under which a worker may be disqualified for benefits. Having been disqualified, the worker loses his benefit for some specified number of weeks or for the duration of his unemployment, or suffers a reduction in his benefit, depending on the nature of the disqualification. Certain penalties may or may not be attached to leaving work voluntarily without "good cause" (as determined in each jurisdiction); different penalties may be attached for being discharged for "minor" misconduct; and still other types of penalties apply for "gross" misconduct. Refusing suitable work is grounds for disqualification. "Suitability" is defined either by specific provision in the law or by administrative rulings.

Under certain conditions in many states, workers unemployed because of a labor dispute with their employer are disqualified for benefits. A labor dispute is defined under the laws in different ways. Nine states, for example, exclude lockouts from these provisions on the grounds that a worker should not be denied benefits because his employer refused to permit him to enter the premises. A few states do not deny benefits to workers who are unemployed because a labor dispute has closed a plant when the dispute does not involve them directly. There are many similar escape clauses which permit benefits to be paid to certain classes of workers during strikes.

Many state laws have special provisions directed at certain groups in the labor force. For example, unemployment insurance benefits cannot usually be paid to women who quit because they are pregnant. Students who leave employment in order to attend school full time usually cannot draw benefits because they have voluntarily withdrawn themselves from the labor force. However, in many states special provisions apply. For example, Indiana will consider as "available for work" students attending night school or part-time school and who are unemployed.

Claimants are disqualified for fraudulent misrepresentations in order to obtain benefits and, furthermore, must repay the amounts paid to them as a result of such misrepresentations. Usually the recipient is allowed to make restitution in cash or have the overpayments offset against future benefits to which he may be entitled. Only four states (California, Minnesota, Tennessee, and Virginia) provide punishment under criminal statutes for this offense.

A final reason for disqualification stems from the fact that the claimant may be receiving certain types of income during a period of unemployment. For example, receipt of workmen's compensation payments, old-age insurance benefits, employer's pension, wages in lieu of dismissal notice, dismissal payments, and supplemental unemployment benefits are among the types of income which in some states disqualify a worker for unemployment insurance benefits. Only four states (Indiana, North Carolina, Ohio, and Virginia) do not permit a worker to receive supplemental unemployment benefits made payable under various versions of guaranteed annual wage plans.

Financing

Many interesting problems arise in connection with the financing of unemployment compensation systems. These problems, the chief ones of which are summarized below, illustrate some of the complexities of social insurance and the resulting difficulties that would face a private insurer if this type of coverage were offered commercially. Analysis of these problems reveals why the unemployment peril is considered essentially uninsurable by private concerns. For example, in deciding such matters as how to vary tax rates to maintain solvency of the fund, treating all employers consistently with regard to contribution rates, and deciding the conditions under which employees shall be eligible for benefits are all questions with serious political and economic overtones. For a private agency to handle the administration of such a system would involve it in many arguments with organizations such as labor unions, employer groups, and legislatures. Even if these relationships could be satisfactorily worked out, the offering of unemployment insurance would subject the assets of the insurer to serious depletion in the event that a general economic depression were to cause mass unemployment. If private insurers withdrew from the field in such an event, there would be pressure for the establishment of a state fund. Anticipating these difficulties, the Social Security Act caused state funds to be set up initially.

Source of revenue. The employer's standard rate of contribution is 2.7 per cent of the first $3,000 paid each employee during the calendar year (plus .8 per cent to the federal government under the 1961 amendments to the Social Security Act). In several states, the amount of annual wage taxable is greater than $3,000.[34] Usually, however, because of his

---

[34] In 1962, the employer paid taxes on the first $3,600 of wages in Delaware, Hawaii, Massachusetts, Nevada, and Rhode Island; on the first $3,800 in California and Oregon; and on the first $7,200 in Alaska.

experience rating, the employer's contribution rate is much lower than 2.7 per cent.[35] Except in Alabama, Alaska, and New Jersey no tax is paid directly by the employee himself, since the states generally prefer to collect the revenues from the employer. The federal government bears the cost of administration, although the states perform the actual task of carrying out the provisions of the law.

Criticisms of unemployment insurance

How well does unemployment insurance work? Labor groups criticize it because of the tight administrative standards which, it is claimed, are unduly restrictive. Management groups complain that the taxes are too high, benefits are too loosely administered, and financing is unstable. While no attempt will be made to resolve the various issues raised by these criticisms, a listing of the major arguments surrounding the operation of the unemployment compensation system may be helpful in pointing out the main areas which deserve further study.[36]

1. Are benefit levels adequate? As of December, 1960, the average weekly payment under unemployment insurance was $32.87, with the average benefits among the various states ranging from about $30 to $40. It is doubtful if these benefits represent the proportion of wage restoration that the original framers of the legislation had in mind, since an average payment of $33 would represent only about 30 per cent of average weekly wages.

2. As yet only about 75 per cent of total civilian wages and salaries are covered by unemployment insurance, representing a little over half of the total number of workers. Essentially only urban workers are covered and there is some question that it is only these groups which are deserving of coverage.

3. The experience rating system, which will be analyzed in Chapter 26, is subject to many criticisms.

4. Since the unemployment insurance program is state controlled, many inequities arise because the worker is treated differently in each state, even though the conditions preceding his unemployment may have been identical. In some states he receives allowances for dependents, while in others, nothing. In some states he

---

[35] In all states except Alaska, employers may reduce their unemployment tax through experience rating. This topic is elaborated in Chapter 26.

[36] There have been many studies of unemployment compensation systems, both on a state and a national level. One useful survey was published by the Bureau of Employment Security, *A Digest of the Survey of Unemployment Compensation Beneficiaries in Pittsburgh, Pennsylvania* (United States Department of Labor, 1955), which analyzed the adequacy of benefit payments. Turnbull, Cheit, and Williams, *op. cit.*, present a good summary in Chapters 7 and 14 of the major economic issues surrounding unemployment insurance.

may be disqualified for benefits because the administrative agency might decide that he did not leave his job for "good cause," while in another state the same situation might be interpreted much more liberally. It has been suggested that a federal program would help to eliminate many of these difficulties and, in addition, would help equalize the tax burden among states. Under present conditions, employers in states with unstable employment due to the nature of their industry are penalized in relation to competing employers in other states.

5. A glaring weakness in most unemployment insurance laws is that no provision is made for a worker who is unemployed because of physical disability. Such a worker is not able or available to work and is therefore usually disqualified. He generally has no protection under OASDI unless his disability is expected to be permanent. Unless his disability was caused by accident, he receives nothing under workmen's compensation. A description of the laws in the states which partially remedy this defect is given below.

TEMPORARY DISABILITY LAWS

Temporary disability laws, sometimes called nonoccupational disability laws, grew out of the fact that unemployment compensation statutes usually deny benefits to employees who are not able and available for work; in other words, the statutes cover only *healthy* unemployed persons. Six states—Idaho, Maryland, Vermont, Tennessee, Nevada, and Montana—amended their unemployment insurance laws so that an unemployed worker would not be denied benefits simply because he became disabled. Four states went further than this and passed separate temporary disability laws under which an employee could draw income benefits if he became disabled, regardless of whether he was employed or unemployed at the time his disability began. In two of these states, California and Rhode Island, there is a program of benefits that covers the worker no matter what his status was at the time of disability. In two other states, New York and New Jersey, there is a differentiation between workers who were employed and those who were unemployed when they became disabled, with a somewhat less generous treatment being accorded the latter group.

It is significant that temporary disability laws provide for benefits regardless of whether the disability is caused by illness or accident. Since workmen's compensation is intended to cover most job-connected injuries and occupational illnesses, temporary disability laws may be properly described as essentially *nonoccupational;* although, in a strict sense of the word, this distinction is not always made. In Rhode Island, for example, a worker may receive *both* workmen's compensation and temporary disability benefits under certain conditions, not to exceed 85 per cent of his weekly wages or $58 per week, whichever is smaller.

In California, Rhode Island, and New Jersey, temporary disability laws were generally patterned after unemployment laws and provide very similar benefits. The laws are administered by the employment security agency, since it was thought that this was the logical agency to perform this function. The financing of the laws in these states comes from employee contributions that formerly were made to unemployment insurance funds.

In New York, the last state to pass a temporary disability law (1949), it was felt that payment of disability income was more logically a function of the state workmen's compensation board, which was more experienced in the problems of disability insurance than an employment security agency. Furthermore, in New York, separate financing was necessary since employees made no contribution to unemployment insurance. New York also departed from procedures followed in other states in that while a competing state fund was established, it was put on equal footing with private competing insurers. In Rhode Island no private insurer is allowed to compete for this business, and in California and New Jersey private insurers are allowed to compete only if they can offer the employer a plan which is in all respects equal to the state plan and, in at least one respect, superior to it.

The major features of temporary disability laws are compared in Table 24–2. To be eligible for benefits, a worker must generally show that he is unable to perform his regular or customary work because of his physical or mental disability. Disabilities due to pregnancy and intentional self-inflicted injuries are excluded. The employee's contribution is generally considered the main source of financing, although the employer contributes to some extent. A claimant must have been attached to the labor force at one time or another, earning some minimum amount of wages, in order to qualify. The amount of the benefit is low, conforming to the floor of protection concept, and the duration is limited generally to not over 26 weeks. In general, if a worker is disqualified for unemployment benefits, he will also be disqualified for disability benefits. The benefit formulas are similar to those for unemployment insurance, except in New York. The laws are all compulsory except that individuals who depend on prayer or spiritual means for healing may "elect out" of the coverage.

Table 24–2

A COMPARISON OF TEMPORARY DISABILITY LAWS

	Rhode Island	California	New Jersey	New York
Date established..............	1942	1946	1948	1949
Contributions:				
Employee..................	1% of first $3,600 of wages	1% of first $3,600 of wages	.5% of first $3,600 of wages	.5% of first $60 of weekly wages
Employer..................	...	...	.25% subject to experience rating	All additional costs
Weekly benefits...............	$10–$36 ($\frac{1}{26}$ of highquarter wages in the base period plus $2 per dependent under 16, up to $8.)	$20–$65, depending on base period earnings plus $12 per day in hospital	$10–$35 ($\frac{2}{3}$ of first $45 and $\frac{2}{5}$ of remaining average weekly wage of prior eight weeks)	$20–$50 ($\frac{1}{2}$ of average weekly wage in prior eight weeks)
Duration of benefits.........	7–26 weeks	26 weeks, disability income; 20 days for hospital benefit	13–26 weeks	20 weeks
Waiting period..............	7 consecutive days	7 consecutive days	7 consecutive days	7 consecutive days
Type of insurer.............	Monopolistic state fund	State fund competing with private insurers, or self-insurer	State fund competing with private insurers, or self-insurer	State fund competing with private insurers, or self-insurer
By whom administered........	Unemployment Compensation Board	Unemployment Compensation Board	Unemployment Compensation Board	Workmen's Compensation Board

Source: Drawn from *Comparison of State Unemployment Insurance Laws* (United States Department of Labor, 1958), pp. 129–141.

In conclusion, it appears that temporary disability legislation is aimed at a real need, one which may be filled by either public or private insurance methods. Unlike unemployment insurance, however, there seems to be no real reason why private insurers could not handle this particular need without assistance since the peril is fully insurable and there are no insurmountable administrative problems. The growth of private insurance plans has probably been a factor in the failure of any further successful action by states to follow the example of those four states which have adopted temporary disability laws. It is also likely that extensive discussion of these laws in many state legislatures has stimulated private insurers to promote appropriate disability income policies.

SUMMARY

1. Social insurance, which is defined to include all insurance plans either operated by or financed by governmental agencies, is to be distinguished from public assistance plans under which governments make gratuitous payments to individuals in need and who have no resources of their own. The chief types of social insurance are: (a) old age, survivors, and disability insurance (OASDI), (b) workmen's compensation insurance, (c) unemployment insurance, and (d) temporary disability insurance.

2. Social insurance is generally introduced when it is impossible or impractical for private insurers to solve a social problem which lends itself to solution by the insurance method. The volume of social insurance in the United States has grown from a negligible amount in 1935, when the Social Security Act was passed, to a point where, 25 years later in 1960, expenditures equal about four per cent of gross national product. Trends suggest that the insurance method is gaining fast as the preferred way to meet social problems that cause an interruption of income and therefore threaten personal financial security.

3. The basic distinctions between social and private insurance are that social insurance, in contrast to private contracts: (a) is compulsory, (b) does not allow individual choice in selecting the amount of benefit, (c) provides only a floor of protection, a minimum level of benefit, (d) is subsidized by groups other than the insured group, (e) has a total cost which is basically unpredictable, and (f) covers only individuals who have been attached to the labor force and meet certain minimum requirements.

4. Measured by benefit payments, OASDI and public retirement plans are three times as large as unemployment insurance, and about seven times as large as workmen's compensation and temporary disability insurance combined. OASDI, which is operated by the federal government, provides three basic types of income payments to qualified beneficiaries: (a) retirement income to the worker and his dependents, (b) income to dependents in case of the worker's death, and (c) income to the worker

and his dependents in case of permanent disability. The size of these benefits depends on the amount of earnings and the length of time the worker has contributed taxes.

5. In common with all plans of social insurance, OASDI benefits are conditional on many factors. One of the basic reasons why the size of the promised pension can be so large in relation to the total taxes paid is that a certain proportion of those who pay taxes will not qualify for benefits. For example, many persons will not actually retire, and thus will not collect pensions. Many will die with no dependents, and their contributions will be made available to others.

6. In 1956, disability benefits were introduced under OASDI. Even though at present they are a relatively small part of the total benefits, they represent the first attempt to meet the problem of long-term disability through social insurance and will undoubtedly become more important as time goes on and as qualification standards for benefits are liberalized.

7. The oldest example of social insurance in the United States is workmen's compensation insurance. It is the only type of social insurance in which private insurers, under governmental requirements, underwrite a major share of the total volume. Under the workmen's compensation contract, the employer is protected not only for his liability under a state compensation act, but in addition, for his common law liability to workers for negligence.

8. The basic purpose of workmen's compensation insurance is to replace the negligence system as a method of meeting the costs of occupational injuries. In this task the compensation system has only partially succeeded because: (a) not all employments are covered, (b) not all employers in covered employment are required to come under the laws, (c) benefit levels are such that they restore on the average only about half of a worker's wage lost through disability, and (d) more ways are being found to bring legal action against employers for damages under employer's liability.

9. All states now have workmen's compensation laws, under which benefits include lifetime payments if necessary for permanent disabilities, income benefits for dependents, death benefits, lump-sum benefits for permanent partial disabilities, and medical and rehabilitation benefits.

10. Unemployment insurance was designed to relieve only certain types of losses, namely those arising from short-term, involuntary unemployment. Long-term, voluntary unemployment is not covered, since the standard length of coverage is about six months. Unemployment insurance, administered by the states, had its origin in 1935 with passage of the Social Security Act. All states have these acts, which must meet certain minimum federal standards.

11. Benefits under unemployment insurance depend on the amount of wages an employee is able to accumulate during a given base period. Benefits generally may not continue longer than six months and restore up to one half of the worker's wages during his benefit period. The worker must be

able to and available for work at all times. Refusing suitable work, as defined, is a cause for stopping his payments.

12. Among the weaknesses of unemployment insurance is the fact that under most laws a worker who is physically unable to return to work cannot qualify for unemployment benefits because he is not able to accept employment. To overcome this weakness, four states have passed temporary disability laws under which a worker may draw certain benefits, regardless of whether he was employed or unemployed at the time he became disabled.

13. In the four states that have passed temporary disability laws—California, Rhode Island, New Jersey, and New York—a worker may usually draw benefits if he would generally be qualified for unemployment benefits had he not been disabled, regardless of whether it was an accident or illness which disabled him, and regardless of whether this disability was suffered on or off the job.

QUESTIONS FOR REVIEW AND DISCUSSION

1. (a) Distinguish between social *welfare* plans and social *insurance* plans.
   (b) Which, if either, of these types of plans is inclusive of the other?

2. In general, a social problem must exist before a social insurance plan is introduced, but not all social problems lead to social insurance.
   (a) Do you agree? Explain your concept of a social problem.
   (b) Could a situation be considered a social problem in one society, but not in another?

3. If a social problem is subject to solution by the insurance method, why have not private insurers supplied the insurance facilities to meet certain problems? In other words, why has it been necessary for governmental insurers to step in?

4. (a) Is the United States the only major country to "go in for social insurance" on a large scale?
   (b) Has the United States been a leader in the field of social insurance? Why or why not?

5. Account for the pattern of expenditures under unemployment insurance observed in Table 24–1 as contrasted to the steady growth in expenditures under other social insurance plans.

6. What evidence (see Table 24–1) do you find for the position that (a) welfare expenditures are increasing at an alarming rate and should be curtailed, and (b) welfare expenditures, particularly social insurance expenditures, are not an unreasonable burden and could be expanded without undue difficulty?

7. It has been said that there is a "double subsidy" in social insurance plans. Explain.

8. In your opinion, has the floor of protection principle in social insurance been violated? Explain.

9. It has been argued that it is not fair for some workers to receive OASDI benefits and for others who have paid in an equal amount of taxes to be denied benefits because they failed to meet the retirement test. Rather, it is claimed, all should be paid "as a matter of right." Analyze this argument and state what results would follow if the situations were "corrected."

10. Those who have urged the adoption of socialized medicine point out that a system of national compulsory health insurance would not provide coverage for everyone needing it, but would meet only some part of the need for coverage. Referring to the six basic differences between social insurance and private insurance outlined in the text, draw a conclusion as to the correctness or incorrectness of this position.

11. The Advisory Council on Social Security Financing stated, "The financing of this (OASDI) program is the largest financial trusteeship in history. It involves in varying degree the personal security of practically all Americans—not only those who have retired or are nearing retirement age but those just starting to work, those who are children today, and the generations of the future."
    (a) Is the OASDI financing sound, in view of the fact that its reserves are admittedly not "full" as compared with the reserves required of life insurers? Why?
    (b) What aspects other than the size of the reserve are important in determining the ability of the plan to provide for generations of the future? Discuss.

12. Suppose Congress passed a law which said that the OASDI trust fund should be increased immediately to meet the standards of actuarial solvency required of a private insurer. Assess the economic implications of such a law for the coming year.

13. An author stated, "The use of the word 'insurance' in connection with the OASDI program is frequently criticized, especially by those having to do with the insurance business and its specific guarantees. . . . Under OASDI . . . neither premiums nor benefits are guaranteed. Congress can change either at will. . . . Some pay relatively little as compared with the value of their benefits . . . while others pay relatively much more."
    (a) Give examples from the provisions of OASDI which illustrate the correctness or incorrectness of the comments about lack of guarantees.
    (b) Should the word insurance be used in OASDI? If your criterion is that of the existence or nonexistence of guarantees, can you think of some features of private insurance which are not guaranteed? Give an example.

14. A speaker declared concerning OASDI, "To see how little we are paying for current benefits as compared with their value, consider the following example. A person has been in covered employment since 1937 and has always earned enough to pay the maximum employee taxes. The total

OASDI taxes paid by him and his employer up to the end of 1958 amount to $2,010. If at that time he should have retired at age 65 with a wife of the same age, their total old-age benefit would have been $175 a month. This benefit (including the widow's survivor benefit) has a single-sum value at age 65 of about $23,300, based on a mortality table used by the Social Security Administration and three per cent interest, or more than 11 times the total taxes paid. How is such a result possible? . . . The answer is that the future generation will do it by paying more than their benefits will be worth." Do you agree? Why, or why not?

15. Suppose Smith dies while he is fully insured and leaves a widow with six children under 18. The family is entitled to maximum benefits of $254 each month.
    (a) How long will they receive this benefit?
    (b) What conditions could operate to reduce or stop the benefits?

16. Brown has retired at age 65 under OASDI, but he becomes restless after one year and opens a real estate office. Prior to the time he opened this office, he and his wife were receiving $150 each month from OASDI. He operated this business for seven months, but it was unsuccessful. Although he devoted full time to the business, he made only one sale, clearing $500 in the fourth month. The next year Brown rented a resort property and operated it for three months during the summer, earning $3,000. The rest of that year he did nothing. How many social security pension checks did Brown lose (a) during the year he engaged in the real estate business? (b) during the year he operated the resort? Explain why in each case. (c) Is the OASDI retirement test "fair"? Discuss.

17. Life insurance agents sometimes object that their sales are hampered by the fact that individuals feel their life insurance needs are fully cared for by OASDI. Do you think this fear has any justification? Discuss.

18. How is it determined under OASDI whether or not a worker is considered as having been attached to the labor force to an extent sufficient to entitle him to coverage? Explain.

19. In what respects is workmen's compensation insurance unique as a type of social insurance?

20. (a) Why was the Priestly v. Fowler decision an important landmark in the development of workmen's compensation insurance?
    (b) Without this decision do you feel that compensation insurance would have developed along the same lines that it did?

21. (a) Why is the loss of the three common law defenses a strong stimulus for the employer to purchase workmen's compensation insurance?
    (b) Does this loss mean that any employee lawsuit is practically certain to be successful? Why?

22. The state of California has made workmen's compensation insurance compulsory for all farm workers. Formerly there was an elective coverage for employees of farm operators whose payroll for the year was $500 or

more, and voluntary coverage for others. Is California's legislative action typical? Why or why not?

23. A writer declared that there are several services rendered by an agent in workmen's compensation which are worth as much as, if not more than, the remuneration he receives from the sale of the workmen's compensation policy. One proof of this is the fact that in several states where an exclusive state fund operates, separate agencies called service bureaus exist which are retained by employers to perform certain services made necessary by workmen's compensation insurance. Thus, in 1946 there were approximately 25 such bureaus in Ohio, and 6 in Washington. In West Virginia, coal mine operators paid an estimated 12 per cent or more of their workmen's compensation premiums for additional services. Make a list of the services presumably performed for the employer by the agent in connection with workmen's compensation insurance.

24. In the period 1948–56, published ratios of expenses to premiums earned in workmen's compensation insurance for stock and mutual insurers were 35.8 per cent and 24.0 per cent, respectively (based on national experience of companies operating in New York). During the same period the comparable figure for 18 state funds was 9 per cent.
    (a) Suggest explanations for the substantial differences noted.
    (b) Is it likely that most of the difference is a result of greater efficiency of one type of insurer?
    (c) Are some insurers performing needless and unwanted services? Explain.

25. In 1956 only 13 states provided maximum weekly income benefits in workmen's compensation which were in excess of 50 per cent of the average weekly wage in the state. Yet in the United States, only five states specified an *intention* (through legal provisions) of restoring less than 60 per cent of a worker's wage.
    (a) Account for the failure of most laws to meet their benefit objectives.
    (b) Find out what the average weekly wage is for your state and compare it with the maximum weekly benefit in your state's workmen's compensation law for permanent total disability. Is your state above or below the average of benefit levels in surrounding states?

26. Assume that the disability period for an average case of temporary total disability resulting from occupational injury is 18 days. It can be seen that because of a one-week waiting period under a typical workmen's compensation law, a worker might collect only $75 in income benefits for his disability, assuming he collected a typical maximum benefit. Estimate what proportion of an average worker's wage loss is restored.

27. An employer in a state with an exclusive workmen's compensation fund elects not to come under his state's law. The law prohibits purchase of private workmen's compensation insurance and the employer does not wish to noninsure the risk. What alternatives, if any, to insuring in the state fund are available to him?

28. "A" and "B," who work for the same company, a national concern, are both involved in employment which results in their complete loss of hearing. "A," who works in Arizona, receives $33,000 as a workmen's compensation award, while "B," who works in Nebraska, receives only $3,700. How is such a result possible?

29. Studies have shown that an injured workman who suffers a permanent partial disability, such as the loss of an eye, often has a difficult time being rehired, even though he is physically rehabilitated. Suggest one reason for this which flows out of the workmen's compensation system.

30. A writer stated ". . . the positive achievements of unemployment compensation have been of high value. The billions of dollars that have been channeled into the hands of workers' families with a high propensity to consume have been of prime importance in keeping standards of living relatively high, as well as in sustaining business activity. This in turn has reacted favorably on the level of employment and on the unemployment compensation funds themselves."
    (a) Explain how unemployment compensation payments might help solve the problem of fund depletion.
    (b) Do you agree with the author's reasoning? Why?

31. Why is unemployment insurance generally considered too perilous to write for a private insurer?

32. One of the dangers of unemployment insurance is that it will fail to provide incentives for the employee to return to work. What measures have been taken to combat this tendency?

33. It is estimated that only about half of the civilian labor force is at any one time covered under unemployment insurance laws. Indicate some of the factors which account for the exclusion of so many workers from coverage.

34. Technically, unemployment insurance is financed by a federal tax of $3\frac{1}{2}$ per cent on certain payrolls. Yet, state unemployment insurance laws are passed and state agencies administer them. How is the operation of state laws financed?

35. In December, 1959, it was reported that 1,545,000 individuals received unemployment insurance checks in the United States and 122,500 exhausted their benefits. What factors affect the exhaustion rate at any one time?

36. In the first quarter of 1959, the United States Department of Labor reported the following data on disqualifications per 1,000 unemployment insurance claims: 35 were refused benefits because they quit voluntarily, 13.2 for misconduct, and 6.5 for not being able or available for work. For claimants already receiving benefits, the number of individuals disqualified for refusing suitable work averaged .5 per 1,000. Can it be concluded from these data that the disqualification provisions of unemployment insurance laws are actually not very restrictive? Why, or why not?

37. An author stated, concerning unemployment insurance tax rates, "Calculations for 1955 indicate that the average contribution rate for fifty-one states and territories was 1.2 per cent . . . a result probably has been to keep the benefit structure lower than it would otherwise have been."
    (a) Suggest possible reasons for this conclusion.
    (b) Do you agree? If so, would you also agree that experience rating be eliminated?

38. A survey made by the International Labor Office indicated that in 1949 unemployment was a problem in most of the major countries of the world. As a percentage of the labor force, unemployment ranged from .6 per cent in Norway and .8 per cent in Australia to 15 per cent in Italy. Unemployment in the United States was 5.3 per cent at that time.
    (a) What type of unemployment probably accounted for the figure in each country?
    (b) Is unemployment insurance a likely solution to all types of unemployment? Explain.

39. A writer stated, "From a national and international viewpoint, unemployment represents a waste of productive resources. From the human standpoint . . . unemployment means something more personal and catastrophic. It marks a complete stoppage of his regular income, and unless there is a substitute for this, will usually mean a drastic reduction in his standard of living and that of all persons dependent upon him. . . . It can seriously impair the morale of the worker by making him feel that society no longer has need of his services. . . . There is a need for social measures which will deal with the personal economic problem of each individual worker who loses his job. . . . So long as unemployment continues to exist, modern civilized nations must accept responsibility for plans which ease the impact of unemployment on those who produce its goods and services."
    (a) Contrast the philosophy embodied in the quoted statement with the laissez faire philosophy on which capitalism was founded.
    (b) Is unemployment insurance "out of place" in a modern capitalistic society, or is it consistent with the goals of modern society?

40. One problem arising out of experience rating is that an employer has an incentive to challenge an employee's claim for benefits in case of doubt about the employee's eligibility. This follows because the employer's account is charged with all claims arising out of former employees and the effect may be to increase his future contribution rate.
    (a) Under what conditions might an employee not be eligible for benefits? Explain.
    (b) Do you think the problem referred to above is a serious one? Why?

41. A study covering the recessions of 1945–1946 and 1948–1950 indicated that unemployment payments covered 12.1 per cent and 20.2 per cent of the total income loss respectively. What conclusions can you draw from these figures about the efficacy of unemployment insurance in stabilizing the economy? Why?

42. In California private insurers offering temporary disability coverage under the state's unemployment compensation disability law have two major complaints: (1) They are forced to offer a plan that is superior to that of the competing state fund for no increase in premium, and (2) They are subject to premium taxes and other taxes not payable by the state fund. Yet, private insurers have successfully gained a foothold in this business, having covered 12 per cent of the employers and 48 per cent of total taxable wages by the end of 1957. Suggest possible reasons why private insurers have been able to underwrite this business successfully in the face of the disadvantages noted.

43. For all state temporary disability insurance programs combined, private insurers underwrite plans involving about two thirds of all taxable wages, and 45 per cent of all employers. State funds underwrite the remaining business. Suggest reasons for the type of distribution noted.

44. In California the average weekly benefit for plans underwritten by the state fund in temporary disability insurance was $34.09 in 1957, while the average weekly benefit under private plans was $40.39. State probable reasons for the higher benefit noted for private plans.

45. In a study to determine whether claims for temporary disability insurance ran parallel to unemployment, it was found in two recession periods during 1950–1958 that when unemployment claims increased, the rate for extended disability payments actually fell, and vice versa. Suggest possible reasons (a) why the hypothesis arises that these two variables should be positively correlated, and (b) why the negative correlation is found.

46. A critic stated, "One may question . . . whether temporary disability insurance legislation of the current type does make optimum use of our resources." Presumably if funds now devoted to temporary disability insurance were directed at the health problem in some different manner, a greater social utility would result. Suggest alternative ways in which these funds could be used to solve the health problem and, in your opinion, would result in higher social utility.

Government Regulation of Insurance

It has been stated that the general purpose of government is to defend the public good and to champion the cause of the weak. In carrying out these objectives, government has always laid down rules governing the conduct of business, and insurance is no exception. In the case of insurance, however, special attention has been given by the government and as a result, the insurance industry has benefited immensely. Some of the reasons for this will be clarified in this chapter.

WHY INSURANCE IS REGULATED

There are special social characteristics of insurance which set it apart from tangible-goods industries and which account for the special interest in regulation noted above. First, insurance is a "commodity" which people pay for in advance and whose benefits are reaped in the future, sometimes in the far distant future, often by someone entirely different from the insured and who is not present to protect himself when the contract is made. Second, insurance is effected by a complex agreement which few laymen understand and by which the initiating party could achieve a great and unfair advantage if disposed to do so. Third, insurance costs are unknown at the time the premium is agreed upon and there exists a temptation for unregulated insurers to charge too little or to charge too much. Charging too little results, in the long run, in removing the very security which the insured thought he was purchasing, and charging too much results in unwarranted profits to the insurer.

Future performance

The first factor mentioned above, that of future performance, raises the question of the need for regulation in many ways. First, the insured is, in effect, serving as a trustee of policyholders' funds. The management of other people's money, particularly when it has grown to be one of the largest industries in the nation, immediately suggests itself as a likely candidate for regulation because of temptation by the unscrupulous to use these funds for their own ends instead of for the ends of those to whom the funds belong. Second, the fact that one party to the contract (the insurer) receives his payment currently but the ultimate performance is contingent upon the occurrence of some event which may not happen for many years raises the question of how the insured can obtain a guarantee that the insurer's performance will be forthcoming, and how justice can be obtained in case of failure by the insurer. How different this insurance transaction is from that in which a suit of clothing is purchased. The buyer can examine the merchandise, try on the suit, have it tailored to his specifications, and make payment after everything is found to be satisfactory. Both the buyer and the seller are on equal footing, and, in a free market, neither particularly needs protection from the other. No elaborate system of guarantees or police protection is indicated to see that the transaction is fair to both sides.

Complexity

We have learned from prior chapters that the insurance contract is not a particularly simple instrument. There are many instances in which even if the laymen understands the implications of every legal clause in a contract, his rights are vitally affected by the operation of certain legal principles or industry customs to which no reference exists in the written contract. The legal battles which have been fought over the interpretation of the contractual wording of a policy bear mute testimony to the proposition that grave misunderstandings can arise over the meaning of provisions even after the best legal minds have attempted to make the intent of the insurer clear. If such misunderstandings can arise when they are unintended, it is easy to see that in the absence of any restraint, an insurer would find no difficulty in framing a contract which looks appealing on the surface but under which it is possible for the insurer to avoid any payment at all.[1]

Unknown costs

The price which the insurer must charge for his service must be set far in advance of the actual performance of this service. The cost of this service depends on many unknown factors, such as the random fluctuations in loss frequency and unexpected changes in the cost of

---

[1] See Chapter 9 for a discussion of the insurance contract.

repairing property. If an insurer is seeking to increase his business, he may consciously or unconsciously underestimate future costs in order to justify a lower premium and thus attract customers. If large losses develop, he may be unable to respond and the security which was contracted for will have vanished. If, on the other hand, the insurer refuses to accept business except at a very high premium, consciously or unconsciously overestimating future costs, those who pay may be overcharged, and those who cannot pay will go without a vital service. Inability to obtain insurance may even prevent potential insureds from engaging in business because of inability to obtain credit or offer surety.

We have observed in Chapter 2 that very large numbers of exposure units are sometimes required before an insurer can reduce his risk to tolerable limits. It is seldom that one insurer can obtain sufficient numbers of exposures to develop reliable rates in all the classifications in which he must quote. Hence, rate-making organizations are set up on an industry-wide basis to collect loss data and promulgate rates, to the end of reducing the probability of making serious mistakes in quoting the price of insurance. This necessarily involves cooperation among insurers and without regulation there might be a strong temptation to set rates arbitrarily high. It is easy to see that some outside control over pricing in insurance is desirable for both insured and insurer.

In summary, we may say that insurance is regulated because, through experience, it has been found that some governmental supervision is necessary to protect both the best interests of the public and the best interests of the insurance companies. Insurance is a social device and as such cannot escape the public eye. Its position of financial importance and its position of public trust exert such a far-reaching influence on the smooth operation of the economy that governmental supervision is a practical necessity.

THE BACKGROUND OF REGULATION

Before 1850

Insurance traditionally has been regulated by the separate states. In each state there is an insurance department and an insurance commissioner or superintendent who has several specific duties, which are outlined later in the chapter. This was not always so. Prior to 1850, insurance was operated as a private business with no more regulation than any other business enterprise. There was a lack of any financial guarantee that losses would be paid when due; little control was exercised over the investment of funds collected as premiums; and, in general, the doctrine of caveat emptor was the rule.

An early fighter to correct abuses in insurance was Elizur Wright, who became the first insurance commissioner of Massachusetts in 1855. Wright, who was a professor of mathematics, early became interested in the mathematics of life insurance. At that time life insurance rates were not based on sound statistics. History reveals, for example, that of 300 life insurance companies formed in England in the early 1800's, over 80 per cent failed, partly because of fraud, but largely because of inadequate knowledge of actuarial concepts by their organizers. Accordingly, Wright developed his own tables of reserves which became the legal requirements for all life insurers in Massachusetts. In this way, each insurer had to prove that it could honor all obligations as they fell due in the future. Wright attacked other abuses in insurance. On a trip to England in 1844 he reported:

> What I saw at that sublime center of trade (The Royal Exchange) was a sale of several old policies on very aged men to speculators . . . to be kept up by them by paying their annual premiums to the company till the decease. This was done, I was told, because the company made it a rule *"never to buy their own policies."* A poor rule it seemed to me! I had seen slave auctions at home. I should not like to have a policy on my life in the hands of a man with the slightest pecuniary motive to wish me dead.[2]

It was a result of Wright's persuasion that nonforfeiture legislation put an end to the speculative sale of life insurance policies, and guaranteed that the life insurer would always be available and willing to buy back its own policies at predetermined prices.

A picture of the atmosphere in the insurance world existing about 1850 in the United States was graphically portrayed by one historian in describing the difficulties besetting a rash of companies which failed in this period:

> In 1850 . . . there was no State regulation to fix or enforce standards of solvency; neither was there . . . any voice of such absolute authority among the informed critics that it could pronounce the need and not let public opinion and competition right any wrongs which could be shown to exist. . . . Although many of these new companies were certainly embarked upon programs of

---

[2] P. G. Wright and E. Q. Wright, *Elizur Wright, The Father of Life Insurance* (Chicago: 1937), p. 3.

low rates, high dividends, or poor investment plans, if not actually upon all three at once, it is equally true that practically every one of their more notable and more successful competitors was also involved at one time or another in practices grossly and obviously unsound. . . .[3]

An example of one of the unsound practices of the day was that of issuing life insurance and accepting premium notes instead of cash, with the promise that the large dividends being paid could be used to liquidate the notes. Six companies, for example, professed in advertising to be paying dividends at the rate of 40 per cent of the premium, but failed to reveal that dividends were not paid every year.[4] Not only were policyholders misled, but insurers also sometimes found themselves without sufficient cash to pay operating expenses.

Early regulation

As a result of the early abuses of insurance, with their resulting ill effects on the consuming public and upon the insurers alike, the need for regulation became apparent. Although many states by 1850 had passed statutes affecting insurance, no state established special enforcement agencies until 1850, when New Hampshire appointed an insurance commissioner. Massachusetts, California, Connecticut, Indiana, Missouri, New York, and Vermont followed this example shortly afterward, and by 1871 nearly all states has some type of control or supervisory bodies.

In 1868 an important United States Supreme Court decision, Paul v. Virginia,[5] established the right of states to regulate insurance by holding that insurance was *not commerce,* but was in the nature of a personal contract between two local parties. Since insurance was held not to be commerce, the federal government would have no direct regulatory power through its right to govern interstate commerce as given under the commerce clause of the Constitution. This decision was upheld repeatedly until reversed by the famous decision in 1944, the South-Eastern Underwriters Association case.

In 1871, three years after the Paul v. Virginia decision, an organization which has had far-reaching effect on regulation was formed. This was the National Association of Insurance Commissioners, a group of state insurance commissioners through whose efforts a considerable

---

[3] J. O. Stalson, *Marketing Life Insurance—Its History in America* (Cambridge: Harvard University Press, 1942), pp. 222–224.
[4] *Ibid.,* pp. 340–341.
[5] 8 Wall. 168, 183 (1868).

measure of uniformity in regulation has been achieved. One of its first tasks was to introduce some uniformity into regulations governing the type of reports which insurance companies were required to make. Another task was to agree on a system of exchange of information as to the solvency of insurers, so that an insurer did not have to prove solvency to the satisfaction of each state in which it operated. Still another job was to agree on uniform systems for valuation of legal reserves of life insurers.

The nature of the tasks facing the National Association of Insurance Commissioners is indicative of the regulatory problems of the day and the difficulties encountered by separate state regulation of a business which even then was essentially interstate in nature. Considerable hardship was imposed by the separate, and sometimes inconsistent, insurance laws to which insurers were subject. There were many, Elizur Wright among them, who opposed state regulation and urged federal regulation. The Paul v. Virginia case, however, pretty much decided the matter and as a result, state regulation developed a strong foothold.

Insurance investigations of 1906 and 1910

Two investigations in New York State which had considerable impact upon the later development of the insurance industry were symptomatic of the early struggles of the states to bring an end to abuses in insurance management. These were the Armstrong investigation of 1906 (life insurance) and the Merritt Committee investigation of 1910 (property and liability insurance).

The Armstrong investigation. The Armstrong investigation revealed many instances of the failure of regulatory bodies to prevent excessive failures of life insurers, or to prevent such abuses as extravagant and inefficient operation of life insurance management, and practices which defeated the rights of policyholders. As a result, New York passed a new insurance code which was widely imitated by other states. This code was much more strict than had formerly been the case. It imposed limitations on the powers of officers, on the size of agent's commissions, and on the investment of policyholders' funds in common stocks. Nepotism, rebates of premium, and political activities of directors to gain favors, were among the corrupt practices prohibited.

Because of a strong recommendation by Charles Evans Hughes, chief counsel of the committee, many life insurers, including those companies which have since become among the nation's largest, were converted from stock companies into mutual companies in the years immediately following the Armstrong investigation. It is generally agreed that the effect of the Armstrong investigation was to place life insurers on a much sounder basis and to lay the groundwork for a rapid growth of business which has resulted in part from increased consumer confidence in the integrity of life insurers generally.

The Merritt Committee investigation. The Merritt Committee investigation was in many ways more restricted than the Armstrong investigation since the former dealt primarily with the rate question. The investigation arose following public opposition to the rate-making practices of insurers, particularly in the field of fire insurance. In the period 1885 to 1912, some 23 states had passed laws forbidding cooperative rate-making by insurers. Known as *anticompact statutes,* these laws were directed at the prohibition of what seemed to be out-and-out price-fixing in restraint of trade. The philosophy of cooperative rate-making in insurance had long been an integral part of the insurance business because of the inability of one single insurer to develop loss statistics on a sufficiently broad basis to form a *credible* rate (See discussion of credibility in Chapter 26). With the passage of anticompact laws, many insurers avoided the effect of the prohibition by using the services of independent bureaus which issued advisory rates. However, in many cases unrestricted rate competition drove rates down below levels which were actuarially sound, causing inability of the insurers to pay losses when catastrophes struck. For example, in the 1906 San Francisco fire and earthquake, many insurers "went under" because of the twin influence of concentration of business in a single geographical area and inadequate reserves, which in turn resulted primarily from rates which were too low. On the one hand, the public objected to what seemed to be price-fixing in violation of anticompact laws, and on the other hand, they objected to competitive rate reductions which sometimes led to losses and even to failures of insurance companies.

The Merritt Committee [6] recognized the desirability of cooperative rate-making in creating a sound rate structure, but saw that some type of regulation of these activities would be necessary. Following the committee's report, the state of New York passed legislation recognizing and supervising company-sponsored fire-rating bureaus. Other states passed similar legislation. Texas assigned the function of rate-making, other than for marine and casualty insurance, to a state agency. In general, the

---

[6] Merritt Committee Report, New York Assembly Document 30 (1911).

pattern of state laws on this point is that of recognizing rating bureaus, but permitting an individual insurer to deviate from the rates promulgated by the bureau if satisfactory evidence is submitted that the rate charged is fair, adequate, and nondiscriminatory. These criteria are examined in more detail in Chapter 26. It is common for the law to require that all rates promulgated by a bureau or an independent insurer be filed with the state insurance commissioner for approval. The filing requirement, however, is not universal. Some states have eliminated filing (California, for example) because of the great practical difficulties experienced in enforcing the criteria of sound rate-making. Instead, periodic inspections of the rating systems are made to prevent abuses. Anticompact laws have been either repealed outright or generally replaced by other regulatory rate legislation.

The S.E.U.A. case

The controversy over rate-making practices raised by the Merritt Committee and by the Armstrong group arose again with a landmark decision handed down in 1944, the case of the South-Eastern Underwriters Association.[7] In the period 1912–1944 many states had attempted to achieve satisfactory regulation of rates, but few had succeeded, except perhaps in the area of fire and workmen's compensation insurance.[8]

The S.E.U.A. case overturned by a four to three vote of the court the Paul v. Virginia ruling that insurance was not commerce. The court held that insurance was "commerce" and that when conducted across state lines, it was interstate commerce. The impact of this decision was to make insurance subject to federal regulation, and, of course, to all federal laws regulating trade practices in interstate commerce. Laws which were to apply included the Sherman Anti-Trust Act, the Clayton Act, the Federal Trade Commission Act, and the Robinson-Patman Act, dealing with the control of business activities in restraint of trade, particularly price-fixing, unfair trade practices, false advertising, and the like. The S.E.U.A. case overruled many decisions formerly made by the Supreme Court that exempted the insurance industry from these statutes, and caused considerable excitement in the industry, as well as great uncertainty as to the future status of regulation.

---

[7] 322 U. S. 533.

[8] Fifteen states had no rate legislation at all. The best developed systems of regulation were those of New York, Texas, and Virginia. See discussion by I. S. Wekler and Donald Knowlton in *State Regulation of Insurance,* a statement submitted to the United States Senate Committee on the Judiciary, Subcommittee on Antitrust and Monopoly by the National Association of Insurance Commissioners, November, 1959.

The cause of the uncertainty was certainly not without foundation. The Sherman Act, passed in 1890, was the first American antimonopoly bill. It prohibited all combinations in restraint of trade. The Clayton and Federal Trade Commissions Acts, passed in 1914, prohibited certain business techniques, such as interlocking directorships, boycotts, acquisition of stock and assets of competitors, and all types of unfair trade practices. The Robinson-Patman Act, passed in 1936, prohibited price discrimination that could not be justified by cost savings and prohibited middlemen from receiving commissions without the rendering of services. Certain practices in the insurance industry would appear to be outlawed by these laws. The use of rating bureaus might be interpreted as collusive price-fixing in restraint of trade. Fleets of companies may be said to constitute interlocking directorates, and in some instances undoubtedly are effected by acquiring ownership of a former competitor. Brokers are legally agents of the insured, but are paid by the insurer; thus it would appear that their status is made uncertain by the applicability of the Robinson-Patman Act.

The S.E.U.A. decision arose out of the activities of a rate-making organization in Virginia, South Carolina, North Carolina, Georgia, Florida, and Alabama, known as the South-Eastern Underwriters Association. The court charged that:

> The member companies of the S.E.U.A. controlled 90 per cent of the fire insurance and "allied lines" sold by stock fire insurance companies in the six states. . . . The conspirators not only fixed premium rates and agents' commissions but employed boycotts together with other types of coercion and intimidation to force non-member insurance companies into the conspiracies, and to compel persons who needed insurance to buy only from S.E.U.A. members on S.E.U.A. terms. Companies not members of S.E.U.A. were cut off from the opportunity to reinsure their risks, and their services and facilities were disparaged; independent sales agencies who defiantly represented non-S.E.U.A. companies were punished by a withdrawal of the right to represent the members of S.E.U.A.; and persons needing insurance who purchased from non-S.E.U.A. companies were threatened with boycotts and withdrawal of all patronage. The two conspiracies were effectively policed by inspection and rating bureaus in five of the six states, together with local boards of insurance agents in certain cities of all six states.

Public law 15

The S.E.U.A. decision made it clear that some insurance associations had influence extending considerably beyond that of cooperative rate-making. Certainly it was not the intent of state regulatory laws that boycotts and coercion should be a result of permission to form cooperative rates. Yet, the complete abandonment of state regulation of insurance in favor of federal regulation was not desired by either the insurance industry nor state insurance commissioners. Accordingly, the National Association of Insurance Commissioners proposed a bill which later became known as the McCarran-Ferguson Act, or Public Law 15. This bill, which became law on March 9, 1945, declared that:

1. It was the intent of Congress that state regulation of insurance should continue, and that no state law relating to insurance should be affected by any federal law unless such law is directed specifically at the business of insurance.
2. The Sherman Act, Clayton Act, Robinson-Patman Act, and the Federal Trade Commission Act, shall, after a three-year delay, be fully applicable to insurance but only "to the extent that the individual states do not regulate insurance."
3. That part of the Sherman Act relating to boycotts, coercion, and intimidation shall henceforth remain fully applicable to insurance.

Except to the extent indicated by the provisions of Public Law 15, the insurance business continues to be regulated by the several states. It will be noted, however, that the law does *not* exempt the insurance business from federal regulation and in fact provides for a limited applicability of certain federal laws to insurance. As an example of the subsequent activity of the federal government in this regard, the Federal Trade Commission, in 1954, charged some 41 mail-order health insurance companies with false and misleading advertising. In denying the charges, many insurers claimed, among other things, that the FTC lacked jurisdiction (citing Public Law 15) because the states in which the insurers were doing business had laws governing advertising practices. However, the right of the FTC to regulate this matter was generally admitted, especially in states where inadequate laws or enforcement exist.

Following the passage of the McCarran-Ferguson Act, the National Association of Insurance Commissioners formed a model bill which was designed to accomplish at the state level what the Sherman, Clayton, FTC, and Robinson-Patman Acts accomplish as applied to business generally. This model bill, which was adopted in whole or in part by most states, contained many recommendations. In general, the philosophy of the legislation emerging from these recommendations is that rate-making cooperation is *neither required nor prohibited*, except to the extent necessary to meet the general requirement that rates be adequate, not excessive, and nondiscriminatory. Machinery is provided whereby an insurer may file a *lower* or "deviated" rate upon showing that the rate meets these requirements. Membership in a rate-making organization is not required.[9] Rating bureaus are carefully regulated and provision is made that the rights of subscribers and minority members shall be protected. Competition is encouraged. The philosophy of freedom of independent action pervades the statutes. This philosophy has been carried out to a much greater degree in some states than in others. In California, for example, the law expressly prohibits any agreement by insurers to use a certain rate, and no rate filings by any insurers are required. Prior approval by the insurance commissioner for use of a given rate is not required. Idaho, Missouri, and Montana are other states which, in the case of casualty lines, require no rate filing. These are the exceptions, however, and most states have attempted to strike a balance between the extremes of no rate regulation and the unduly restrictive regulatory measures such as existed in the South-Eastern Underwriters Association.

In summary, the regulatory philosophy has undergone great swings, starting with one which encouraged unrestrictive competition (before 1910), especially in rate-making, to one which discouraged any competition in rate-making (1910–1944), back toward the direction of encouraging more competition (1944 to date). It remains to be seen how far the present trend will continue before it turns back, if indeed it ever turns back.

COMPETITION IN INSURANCE

The question arises, in what ways does competition make itself felt in the field of insurance? Can competition exist in an industry subject to such extensive regulation as the insurance industry? The answer is that a great deal of evidence can be marshalled to show that much competition exists in insurance in spite of rating bureaus and governmental regulation, or perhaps, because of it.

There are at least three ways in which an insurer may compete for business. It may 1) offer lower rates for the product, 2) provide better contracts or more flexible underwriting conditions, and 3) offer greater service.

---

[9] In some states where a state agency makes rates, this philosophy obviously does does not apply. In Louisiana a state agency specifies maximum casualty insurance rates. In Massachusetts a state agency specifies automobile rates, and in Texas, the Board of Insurance Commissioners specifies maximum fire and workmen's compensation rates. In other states, there is a requirement of membership in a rating organization, such as in the case in California, Indiana, Minnesota, New Jersey, and Wisconsin for workmen's compensation insurance; in North Carolina for compensation and automobile insurance; and in Virginia for automobile insurance.

1) Lower rates for the product

The existence of price competition in insurance, in spite of the use of rating bureaus to gather loss data and promulgate uniform rates, is evidenced by the fact that in one study of 24 states, about 25 per cent of all fire and extended coverage insurance was written with premium rates lower than bureau rates, *i.e.*, on a deviated rate basis.[10] In automobile insurance, as another example, four large rate-deviating insurers increased their premium volume over five times, compared to a growth in total automobile insurance premium volume of less than two times, during the ten year period 1948–1958.[11]

2) Better contracts or more flexible underwriting conditions

In the area of coverage, it might appear that little real competition can exist, because of the use of relatively uniform contracts. This, however, is misleading. The standard fire policy, for example, serves as the universal base of the fire insurance contract, but countless varieties of arrangements are possible in adopting this policy to the individual requirements of an insured through the use of the form and various endorsements. Competition in fitting the contract in this manner is endless. In the field of multiple-line contracts, an insurer has an opportunity to offer broader coverage in competition with those insurers who do not offer such coverage. An insurer may change its underwriting requirements to accommodate an insured whose agent requests it.

3) Greater service

In the area of service, competition exerts itself through efforts of an insurer to offer superior claim-settlement procedures, better agency representation, loss-prevention service, and the like. In the field of workmen's compensation, two insurers (Liberty Mutual and Employers Mutual of Wisconsin), for example, have created a national reputation for themselves by stressing their rehabilitation services for the benefit of injured workmen. "Bureau" companies stress the advantages that their insureds have in being served by independent agents.

In these and other ways, vigorous competition exists among insurers to secure business and to expand their share of the market. The consuming public has undoubtedly benefited a great deal from the various types of competition to which the insurance industry has been subject.

---

[10] Wikler and Knowlton, *op. cit.*, p. 100.
[11] Allstate, Nationwide, State Farm, and Government Employees.

FEDERAL V. STATE REGULATION

For many years the argument as to whether federal regulation would be superior to the present system of state regulation of the insurance industry has been of considerable concern to parties both within and without the insurance business. As we have seen, it appears that state regulation is still secure. However, federal regulation is a continuing possibility, since the S.E.U.A. case opened the door, a door which was not entirely closed by Public Law 15. The chief arguments for federal regulation, many of which amount to criticisms of state control, are:

1. State regulation is not uniform, and in spite of certain accomplishments toward this end by the National Association of Insurance Commissioners, is not likely to become so. Insurers are subjected to different requirements in each state, a result which is expensive and raises the cost of insurance more than need be. For example, an insurer doing business nationally must file different financial reports, adhere to 50 different sets of laws, maintain facilities in all jurisdictions regardless of economical considerations, and otherwise be subjected to overlapping and duplicating requirements.

2. State regulation is relatively ineffective. It is not a suitable mechanism to regulate or control the activities of an insurer which is nationwide in its operation. For example, if a given state prohibits a certain activity as being dangerous or unlawful, this of course does not affect the operation in another state, and so the objectionable practice continues elsewhere. If the particular practice is really dangerous, its continuation may affect the insurer's operation in the particular state, even though the practice is not carried on in that state. After all if, for instance, an insurer charges a rate which is "unreasonably low" and threatens its solvency, eliminating this low rate in one state to the exclusion of other states may have little effect. If the company becomes insolvent as a result of this low rate in other states, policyholders in the first state may be hurt just as surely as if the practice were not prohibited at all.

   This complaint gave rise in the state of New York to a law known as the Appleton Rule, whereby an insurer admitted to do business in New York must adhere to New York's requirements not only in New York, but in *all other states* where the insurer is doing business.[12] Thus, if New York prohibits an insurer from issuing a certain type of policy in that state, the insurer, as a condition of continued operation there, would have to forego its right to issue the policy in any other state where it

---

[12] The Appleton Rule has been upheld by the courts. See *Firemen's Insurance Co. of Newark, N. J. v. Beha*, 30 F. 2d 539 (1928).

is doing business. The Appleton Rule had the effect of greatly extending the influence of New York's insurance underwriting requirements in other states because of the great size of the insurance market and the desire of insurers to operate there. However, many insurers do not operate in New York and are not subject to the Appleton Rule.

3. Federal regulation should be more competent than state regulation. Many ill-advised statutes have been enacted by various states which presumably would be avoided under federal control because of the greater political insulation from local pressures enjoyed by national legislators. For example, an early law in Texas, known as the Robertson Law, required that all life insurers operating in Texas invest three fourths of their premium collections within the geographical bounds of Texas. Many life insurers withdrew from Texas altogether as a result of this requirement, although they later returned when Texas became too important a market to ignore. Such a law probably could not have been passed at the federal level.

Federal legislators are full-time representatives, whereas state legislators usually work only part time. Federal legislators would therefore, it is argued, have more time to devote to the specialized problems of the insurance industry and could give them more thorough attention. The result should be a higher quality of administration and regulation. With state regulation, insurers generally must support a lobby in each state to protect their interests, whereas with federal regulation only one lobby would be required. This would result in a considerable savings in expenses. Furthermore, better salaries could be paid to national insurance administrators and more adequate staffs provided. This would raise efficiency and greatly reduce professional staff turnover. In many states, the salaries of insurance commissioners are very low and the turnover is high,[13] since, with each new political administration, a new commissioner is appointed. Staffs are often inadequate and the quality of supervision necessarily suffers.

Another aspect of this factor is that state regulation often results in excessive influence on legislation overly favorable to the insurance companies. It has been argued that the insurance department in such a case is likely to be excessively dependent on insurance companies for advice and help in carrying out the supervisory tasks, perhaps to the long run detriment of the insuring public.

---

[13] In 1958, for example, salaries of insurance commissioners were below $8,000 annually in 10 states. A typical salary was in the $10,000–$12,000 range, a low salary indeed compared with the salary of an executive with comparable status in private industry.

Opposing these arguments, are those who favor continued state regulation. In general, state insurance commissioners and representatives of the insurance industry, particularly those representatives engaged in the marketing of insurance, are opposed to federal regulation. The major arguments in favor of state regulation are:

1. State supervision and regulation of insurance is reasonably satisfactory and there is therefore no overpowering reason why federal regulation should be necessary. Certainly the burden of proof that a change is necessary should fall upon those who seek the change, and such proof is yet to be forthcoming.

2. Most of the arguments of those who favor federal control rest upon dubious claims of inefficiency and upon unproved claims that federal control would necessarily be more efficient. There is reason to believe that federal control would actually be less efficient because of isolation from local conditions and inability to deal with these problems from afar.

3. While lack of uniformity is admitted, the really important needs for uniformity have been achieved, or are being achieved through the voluntary cooperation of state insurance commissioners. For example, duplicate financial and accounting examinations have been eliminated through an agreement to divide the work into various zones and to exchange the results of these examinations among the various states, thus enabling a much more thorough audit of an insurer's operations. Among the other efforts of the National Association of Insurance Commissioners in this respect are the development of uniform state fair trade practices, uniform unauthorized insurers service-in-process acts, uniform standards for valuation of securities, uniform standard provisions for health insurance contracts, uniform insurer liquidation procedures, uniform life insurance contract provisions, uniform multiple-line laws, uniform laws conforming to Public Law 15, and many others.

4. State regulation is much more flexible than federal regulation would be. State regulation can regulate to local needs. It encourages experimentation and new development in insurance procedures and contracts. This follows because a new proposal can be tried out in a given state without involving the entire country; if successful, adoption of the new development can be used elsewhere; if not successful, no particular harm has been done. Permission to try out new plans can be obtained locally and it is unnecessary to "go to Washington" for everything. Insurance is in a constant state of adjustment and change, and federal regulation might serve as a "straight jacket" to stifle new developments. As an example, three states are experimenting with compulsory automobile insurance, several states with "safe driver merit rating" plans, one state with a new system of classification

of residential fire risks. Such experimentation might well be discouraged under federal regulation.

5. Those who favor continued state regulation point out that if federal regulation were imposed, the result might be two systems of regulation instead of one. The operations of a very large number of insurance companies are confined entirely within the boundaries of a single state. Presumably the states would continue to regulate these activities as intrastate commerce. Hence, state insurance departments would have to continue their existence and the federal system would be superimposed on a state system, which would result in more wasteful overlapping, confusion, and duplication than now exist.

RESPONSIBILITIES OF THE INSURANCE DEPARTMENT

The specific nature of what aspects of insurance are regulated will now be investigated. We can classify the responsibilities of the insurance department in four different categories:

1) Enforcement of minimum standards of financial solvency.
2) Regulation of rates and expenses.
3) Control of business-acquisition practices.
4) Control over contractual provisions and their effect on the consumer.

1) Financial solvency

It is the primary responsibility of the insurance department to see that insurers operating within the boundaries of the state are financially responsible. In order to accomplish this task, the insurance commissioner enforces the state's laws regarding the admission of an insurer to do business, the formation of new insurers, and the liquidation of insurers who become insolvent. He must see that adequate reserves are maintained for each line of insurance written and that the investments of the insurer are sound and comply with the state requirements.

Minimum capital. To do business in a state an insurer must first be *licensed*. Licenses are granted according to the type of insurance business to be conducted. Different capital standards are applied to each type. Minimum financial standards are set forth in each state and they vary considerably from state to state and by type of insurer. The minimum capital and surplus standards for New York, as an example, are set forth in Table 25–1.

It will be noted from Table 25–1 that for some types of insurance greater financial requirements exist than for others. Thus, while only

Table 25–1

EXAMPLES OF MINIMUM CAPITAL AND SURPLUS REQUIREMENTS FOR STOCK AND MUTUAL INSURERS IN NEW YORK

Kind of Business	Stock Insurers		Mutual Insurers	
	Capital	Surplus	Initial Surplus	Minimum Surplus
Life insurer.........................	$ 300,000	$150,000	$ 150,000	$100,000
Annuities........................			50,000	50,000
Accident and health				
Excluding noncancelable.........	50,000		150,000	100,000
Including noncancelable..........	50,000		200,000	150,000
Boiler and machinery..............	50,000		50,000	
Burglary and theft insurer............	150,000		50,000	
Personal injury liability..............	250,000		250,000	
Fire insurer........................	250,000		150,000	
Ocean marine insurer................	250,000		500,000	
Multiple-line insurer				
On acquisition of multiple-line				
powers........................	1,800,000	900,000	1,925,000	
To be maintained.................	1,800,000		1,575,000	

Note: These requirements apply to each type of insurance separately. If an insurer writes more than one type, it must possess the capital requirements indicated for each type. Thus, a multiple-line insurer, writing fire, marine, and casualty lines, organized since 1940, must possess total capital and surplus of $3,550,000. Slightly lower requirements exist for insurers organized prior to 1940.
Source: *Examination of Insurance Companies,* New York Insurance Department, Vol. 2. 1953, pp. 74–77.

$50,000 of capital must be provided to write boiler and machinery insurance, five times this amount is necessary to write personal injury liability insurance. The reason for this difference lies, of course, in the much greater exposure to loss for liability insurers than for boiler and machinery insurers. In many states no distinction is made in capital requirements according to the type of insurance written, but a blanket amount is required for insurers writing any of a long list of contracts. In some states the combined amount of capital and surplus required is as low as $100,000.

Investments. The assets of an insurer may not be invested in just any type of securities. If no regulation were imposed on the investment of assets, it is clear that there would be little point in requiring the existence of so much capital as a condition of doing business. Accordingly, all states impose investment limitations. In general, the philosophy behind these limitations is to require that funds belonging to policyholders, funds which have been paid in as an advance payment of premiums, be invested conservatively in bonds, mortgages, and other fixed-income securities. The objective is to maintain safety and to give sufficient liquidity to enable insurers to pay claims when due, if necessary, by selling assets. Oftentimes the law will specify that each bond or mortgage meet certain minimum standards of asset protection, interest coverage, etc. The law also specifies the manner in which each asset is to be valued; bonds are valued on an amortized basis and stocks at cost or market, whichever is lower.

Furthermore, certain types of assets are not recognized or admitted for purposes of state regulation. Nonadmitted assets typically include office furniture, overdue balances from agents, and other assets not normally subject to liquidation for purposes of meeting obligations due policyholders.

In most states different standards of investments apply to life insurance companies than to property and liability insurers. Most states will not allow a life insurer to invest in equities such as common and preferred stocks, or real estate (other than a home office building) to any degree whatsoever. Part of the reason for these laws stems from the Armstrong investigation, referred to earlier. It was found that some insurers had been furnishing funds for speculative activities of officers and directors, who would frequently join with the insurer in a purchase of securities not for permanent holding, but for resale within a short period. Other abuses were also noted. The Committee concluded that investment in common stocks by life insurers was entirely inappropriate and that owning any common stock would be in conflict with the best interests of policyholders. Following the lead of New York, most states amended their laws to prohibit any investment in equities by life insurers.

In later years, however, (starting in 1940) New York relaxed this provision to the extent of permitting life insurers to invest in certain public housing projects, and in 1951 it permitted life insurers to invest up to three per cent of their assets in approved common stocks. To be eligible the common stocks had to have paid certain minimum cash dividends for at least 10 years immediately prior to purchase, could not be stocks of insurance companies, and had to be listed on an organized exchange. In addition, to prevent a life insurer from participating in the management of another corporation, it was required that the common stock so acquired could not exceed two per cent of the issuing corporation's total outstanding stock, nor one tenth of one per cent of the admitted assets or one third of the surplus of the insurer. The effect of these restrictions is to permit investments in reasonably safe common stocks which would not entail an undue amount of concentration of investments of the insurer and would not impose any serious risk on the policyholders, nor have the effect of leading the insurer into other lines of business. New York also permits a life insurer to invest up to two per cent of its assets in certain preferred stocks. All in all, life insurers in New York can invest in equities (common stock, preferred stock, and income-producing real estate) up to eight per cent of their assets. This situation is not generally true in other states, although the effect of these liberalizations is widespread due to the financial size and importance of insurers chartered in New York.

In property and liability insurance, an insurer is restricted to certain bonds, mortgages, and other fixed-income obligations to the extent of its minimum capital, surplus, and reserve requirements, but may generally invest its stockholders' surplus in qualified common stocks. It is not uncommon to find that the 50 per cent or more of the assets of a property insurance company are invested in common stocks. This follows because the portion of assets represented by stockholders' equity is much larger in stock property insurers than in life insurers, where policy reserves represent a large portion of total assets. The subject of reserves and their adequacy is explored in detail in Chapter 27.

Liquidation. The insurance commissioner is charged with the responsibility of liquidating an insolvent insurer. While the rate of insurance company failures is not particularly high, an equitable treatment of policyholders and other creditors is essential. As we have seen, some types of insurers subject their policyholders to additional assessments in the event of financial inability to pay claims, and the insurance commissioner must see that these obligations are paid. For example, from the period 1859–1957, some 67 life insurers chartered in New York ceased business for one reason or another. Most of these occurred prior to 1930 and of the 12 which ceased doing business after this time, four represented name changes, two were mergers, three were described as "involuntary liquidation," and three as being reinsured, *i.e.,* their liabilities assumed by other insurers.[14] Unfortunately, the extent and reasons for the failures of insurers and the problems attendant thereto have not been widely researched. It has been observed, however, that the failure rate tends to be higher in states with histories of minimum standards of solvency, such as Texas.

Security deposits. Most states require that each insurer licensed to do business within state boundaries make a deposit of securities with

---

[14] *New York Insurance Report, Vol. 1, Life Companies* (1958), pp. 264a–266a.

the insurance commissioner to guarantee that policyholders will be paid claims due them. These laws have been unpopular for several reasons. The size of the deposit is generally too small, in proportion to the volume of business carried on, to be of any real protection to the insured. The state should logically depend upon the quality of its examinations and other procedures to see that the insurer is solvent. The size of the deposit required generally bears little or no relationship to the size of required amounts of capital and surplus or reserves. It is common for one state to waive the requirement for insurers operating within its boundaries if other states do likewise for insurers chartered in that state. Thus, the security deposits may give little added protection to policyholders and constitute one additional complication of regulating the business.

2) Regulation of rates and expenses

Reference has already been made to the important role of rate and expense regulation in the history and development of insurance regulation. This is of such importance that it is reserved for further detailed analysis in Chapter 26. The relationship between rate regulation and financial solvency is intimate. If insurers are allowed to charge inadequate rates, insolvency becomes a real threat. If insurers charge excessive or discriminatory rates, complaints from the insuring public are forthcoming. It is the task of the insurance department to see that insurers steer a course between these extremes, not an easy job at best.

3) Business acquisition practices

A large part of the cost of insurance lies in the payments made to secure policyholders. In the early development of insurance, it was thought that insurance was of such obvious benefit to the public that it would not be necessary to pay an agent to persuade people to buy. It was soon discovered, however, that in order to get sufficient volumes of business to operate, selling effort was necessary. The agent has been a dominant figure in the insurance industry almost from the beginning, and for most consumers the agent is the only contact with the insurer. Since insurance is a complex business, it is vital that the agent be well trained and possess a requisite degree of business responsibility. To that end most states require any insurance representative to be licensed and, as a condition of licensing, to pass some sort of an examination covering insurance and the details of the state's law governing business-getting activities.

Most state licensing laws do not set standards of insurance knowledge at a rigorously high level in granting a license. Often the only preparation needed is the study of a book containing certain questions and answers, a selection of which appear on the examination. Some states require no examination at all, assuming that since the agent binds his principal, the insurers will use care in selecting qualified representatives. A few states require evidence that the applicant for an agent's or a broker's license has attended an approved training course. However, these measures have not succeeded in eliminating poorly qualified agents.

Part of the reason for the failure of insurers to insist upon higher standards is traceable to the fact that agents are generally paid on a commission basis and the insurer assumes that since nothing is paid out unless the agent produces business, the easiest way to obtain more business is to hire more agents. In such an atmosphere, of course, the insurer is not likely to insist that its agents be exceptionally well trained. Some insurers are gradually seeing the error of their ways and standards of licensing and training are steadily improving. It is being recognized that a poor agent may cost the insurer dearly in terms of public ill will and lawsuits, not to mention the cost of furnishing the agent with service, training materials, and the like.

Most state laws prohibit such practices as twisting, rebating, and misrepresentation in the sale of insurance. *Twisting* occurs when an agent persuades an insured to drop an existing insurance policy by *misrepresenting* the true facts for the purpose of obtaining an insured's business. *Rebating* occurs when an agent agrees to return part of his commission to an insured as an inducement to secure business. An agent's license can be revoked for any one of these offenses.

4) Regulation of the "product"

We have seen before that the provisions of many insurance contracts are determined by statute. In life insurance, the law requires the inclusion of such clauses as the grace period, incontestability, and non-forfeiture options. The standard fire policy or slightly modified version thereof is required in all states. The contract provisions of health and automobile insurance are governed by law in most states. Most states require a standard workmen's compensation policy. New policy forms must be approved in most states before they are offered to the public.

The insurance department of the state handles complaints of the insuring public which arise over the interpretation of policy provisions. As we have seen, misunderstandings often arise, even over provisions which are considered "standard." In 1957, for example, the insurance department in New York State processed 3,823 complaints involving loss settlements or policy provisions.[15] About half of these involved automobile insurance, and 476 involved accident and health insurance. It is interesting, but not surprising, that only half of these complaints were upheld, indicating the extent of misunderstanding by members of the insurance buying public as well as the considerable necessity of exerting some regulatory control over the insurance product.

MISCELLANEOUS INSURANCE LAWS

Service-in-process statutes

When a legal action is brought against an insurer, it is necessary to deliver a court summons to the insurer's representative. For insurers admitted to do business within a given state, the insurance commissioner is generally the individual who is authorized to receive such a summons, under what is called a *service-in-process statute.* Formerly a problem arose as to how best to service an insurer which did not operate within a given state. An insured may have obtained a policy by dealing with the insurer by mail, or he may have obtained a policy in one state but subsequently moved to another state wherein the insurer was not admitted to do business. Through the National Association of Insurance Commissioners, most states have now passed statutes known as the *unauthorized insurers service-of-process acts.* Under these statutes it is no longer necessary for an insured to resort to distant courts in order to bring suit on contracts written by such unauthorized insurers. It is only necessary for him to serve summons on the insurance commissioner or upon someone representing the out-of-state insurer.

Retaliatory laws

Most states have on their books laws requiring that if an insurer chartered in, say, state R, is subjected to some burden such as an increased tax or license fee on business it does in another state, T, then state R will automatically impose a like burden on all of state T's insurers which are operating in state R. Such laws are known as *retaliatory laws,* and about three fourths of all states have them. The effect of these laws is to discourage each state from passing any unusual taxes on foreign insurers operating within its borders for fear that the same burden

---

[15] *Ibid.,* p. 119a.

shall immediately apply to its own insurers operating in other states. Only those states without any domestic companies can ignore retaliatory laws and there is a tendency, therefore, for states with the most domestic insurers to have the lowest insurance taxes. The constitutionality of these laws has been attacked on the ground that they cause one state to surrender its taxing authority to another state, but it has been established that the laws are constitutional.[16]

Reciprocal laws

In contrast to a retaliatory law, a *reciprocal law* provides that if one state does something for another, that state shall do the same thing for the first. For example, it is common for state financial responsibility laws to provide that if under another state's laws an uninsured motorist would be disqualified from driving, this motorist shall also be prohibited from driving in the first state. Under uniform insurers liquidation acts, it is possible for a claimant of an insolvent insurer in another state to make a claim locally and have it honored, avoiding the necessity of traveling to the other state. In workmen's compensation insurance, if an employee is temporarily employed outside a state and if the other state will excuse the employer from complying with that state's compensation law, the first state will do likewise. In this way state legislation is made to work much more smoothly than it otherwise would.

Anticoercion laws

As an example of one of the effects of the S.E.U.A. case, *anticoercion statutes* have been passed in a number of states. These laws are aimed against the former practice of some lending agencies to require, as a condition of granting a loan, the placing of insurance with the agency. Thus, the purchaser of a home might be prevented from placing his property insurance with insurance agents and companies of his own choice. Such agents were effectively prevented from competing for business on property controlled by the lending agency, and the borrower had to pay insurance premiums which were not necessarily the lowest he could obtain elsewhere. Such tie-in practices were held to be in restraint of trade and illegal under one or more federal antimonopoly law.[17] As a result, anticoercion laws were passed in many states to prohibit specifically these practices.

---

[16] *American Indemnity Company* v. *Hobbs*, 328 U. S. 822 (1946).
[17] See *United States* v. *Investors Diversified Services*, Civil No. 3713, D.C. Minn. (June 30, 1954).

TAXATION OF INSURANCE

Insurance companies represent a relatively large source of revenue to states. It is estimated that the taxes and fees on insurers produce about one sixth of the total state revenues from major business taxes.[18] In 1958 it was revealed by one study that the total state taxes and fees from some 5,000 insurers in the United States amounted to $520 million, compared with only $20 million (3.9 per cent) spent by the state insurance departments to supervise insurance.[19]

In each state these revenues are raised mainly from a tax on gross premiums. Premium taxes vary from one to four per cent, with the most typical amount being two per cent, plus an additional one-fourth or one-half per cent for the support of the state fire marshall's office. Many states have, in addition, special taxes or assessments in connection with different lines of insurance, such as workmen's compensation.

Insurance companies are also subject to federal income taxation. Stock property insurers pay taxes on both underwriting and investment income at regular corporate rates. Mutual property insurers are treated separately. If a mutual or a reciprocal insurer has a net income of less than $75,000, it is exempt from taxation.[20] It is estimated that about three per cent of the total mutual premium volume is written by tax-exempt companies. For larger mutuals, the tax is the larger of one per cent of gross income (net premiums written less policyholder dividends, plus net investment income) or that tax which would be collected by applying regular corporate rates to investment income only, as defined.[21]

It has been claimed that mutual insurers receive unfairly favorable treatment as compared with stock insurers. While this seems to be implied by the outright tax exemption of certain mutuals, the subject is a complex one and no authoritative study exists which will decide the question one way or the other.

Life insurers are subject to a special formula for federal income taxation. While the details will not be explored at this point, it may be stated that life insurers pay taxes on that portion of net investment income which exceeds the amount necessary to maintain legal reserves, plus a portion of net underwriting gain. Until 1959 life insurers were exempt from taxes on underwriting profits and enjoyed a favorable for-

---

[18] George D. Haskell, "The Taxation of Property Insurance Companies," *Journal of Insurance* (Spring, 1959), Volume XXVI, No. 1, p. 31.
[19] *Journal of American Insurance* (March, 1960), pp. 16–17.
[20] Section 501 (15) Internal Revenue Code (1954).
[21] Sections 821, 822, 823 Internal Revenue Code (1954).

mula for the taxation of net investment income. The new federal taxation formula had the effect of approximately doubling the taxes levied on life insurers.[22]

SUMMARY

1. Insurance is regulated because of several characteristics which set it apart from tangible-goods industries. These include the complexity of insurance, its importance to the financial security of millions of people, the public nature of its many activities, and the necessity for some control over its pricing policies.

2. Insurance is regulated by states, but the federal government, by virtue of the 1944 decision in the case of the South-Eastern Underwriters Association, and Public Law 15, also has certain regulatory authority, chiefly in the area of competitive trade practices.

3. For many years a debate has existed over the relative merits of federal versus state regulation of insurance. In spite of some possible advantages of federal regulation, it appears unlikely that the present system of state rule will give way unless more convincing proof of the superiority of federal regulation is forthcoming.

4. The chief areas of regulation have to do mainly with rate supervision, standards of financial condition, business acquisition methods, and policy provisions. An insurer must be formally admitted to do business in a given state, must give evidence of its financial ability to meet all claims, and must subject almost every phase of its operations to the supervision of the insurance commissioner.

5. In general, regulation of insurance has had a beneficial effect upon the institution by maintaining public confidence, securing desirable uniformity, and preventing destructive practices arising from unrestricted competition within the industry.

QUESTIONS FOR REVIEW AND DISCUSSION

1. A writer stated: "The current probability estimate of long-run socialization of large segments of the insurance business must be placed quite high. Several segments of the business are now waging battles against acute threats of socialization."

---

[22] For an interesting treatment of the background of taxation of life insurers, see R. L. Hogg, "Federal Income Taxation of Life Insurance Companies," *Journal of Insurance* (Spring, 1959), Vol. XXVI, No. 1.

   (a) Which types of insurance is the author probably referring to? Why?

   (b) Indicate the chief characteristics of insurance which place it in "jeopardy of being socialized."

2. The advertising campaign of the National Association of Insurance Agents was started in 1959 to bolster the position of the independent agent in the distribution system for insurance. Among the statements made in this campaign were the following, "The direct writer captive agent . . . cannot share with us . . . the leverage which we can use on our companies . . . the independent agent is a friend at your side, someone to make sure you get prompt, fair payment." Discuss any connection you see between such statements and the regulation of insurance.

3. A United States Senator stated, "Insurance is not just another business. Its importance to our country cannot be measured by financial statistics alone. Insurance has been indispensable in the development of our government, for it is through insurance that our people can, on their own initiative, and through their own thrift, provide for their future security and protect themselves against the catastrophies of life. If this protection and security had not been available through private enterprise, the people would have demanded that government do the job and this would have brought about an establishment of a welfare state beyond any present conception." Is there any conflict between this view and those who favor more governmental regulation in insurance? If so, reconcile this statement with the view of those who favor the extension of governmental regulation and governmental participation in the insurance mechanism.

4. A regulatory official stated in a speech, "The character of competition within the insurance industry is not precisely the same as in other business. You sell for cash today a promise to fulfill your contractual obligations in the future, and competition must not be such as to destroy your ability to mature your future obligations . . . but we cannot allow the necessity of forbidding malignant competition to stand as an excuse for the elimination of all competition and we cannot in recognizing the right of the companies to act in concert permit them to form combinations, directly, or through bureaus, which are designed to coerce conformity, to the destruction of all individual corporate initiative." Give some examples of practices present or past within the insurance industry which illustrate (a) "malignant" competition and (b) coercive action which oppressed corporate initiative.

5. A widely quoted statement of a superintendent of insurance of the State of New York is, "In permitting combination through rating bureaus, it was not intended to destroy competition or to make rates uniform . . . absent a threat to insolvency, a company has the right to compete in the market not only as to rates but also methods of merchandising, regardless of whether they are novel or merely modifications or extensions of existing patterns." What state of affairs probably gave rise to the above attitude? Discuss.

6. A representative of an association of insurance agencies stated, "The very nature of our business requires the most rigid adherence to sound methods of operation and therefore there are few who will argue its need for regulation. . . ." Why is it concluded that insurance requires regulation when such an argument would usually be opposed in tangible-goods industries as an interference with the right of free enterprise? Comment.

7. A representative of a group of agents stated, "Because we are small, we do fear federal regulation; while it is difficult enough for the average insurance agent to participate in regulatory problems at the state level, it would be a virtual impossibility for most of us to take our problems to Washington. . . ." What relationship does this argument have to the general case against federal regulation of insurance? Do you agree with it? Explain.

8. Before the time when state regulation required nonforfeiture values in the life insurance contract, there were instances of companies doing whatever they could do to encourage lapsation of policies. Cases have been recorded where the insurer started a rumor of insolvency so as to start a panic among policyholders, which would result in their dropping their policies. Explain how lapsing of a life insurance policy could result in a profit to the insurer. Is this true today? Why?

9. A writer stated, "Virginia has an early history of insurance regulatory legislation dating back to the 1860's. . . . Virginia's laws have run the gamut from an absolute minimum in regulation to its present system of mandatory membership in a rating organization for fire, automobile liability, and automobile physical damage insurance. In 1898 Virginia enacted an anticompact statute. Within four years, it was repealed because it brought in its wake chaotic conditions, unreasonable competition, and discriminatory rates and practices. By such repeal the Virginia legislature, in effect, invited collaboration in rate-making through a voluntary rating organization."
   (a) Suggest reasons why the anticompact law brought "chaotic conditions," and why its repeal invited collaboration.
   (b) Contrast the present regulatory philosophy of Virginia with that of California. Which do you believe will work out best in the long run? Why?
   (c) What is the regulatory philosophy in your own state?

10. An insurance commission wrote the following opinion on a rate deviation case:

   All insurers do not operate in the same manner, and an insurer which by reason of its method of operation can operate at less cost should be permitted to pass on to the public such savings as a result therefrom in the form of lower rates. This is fair both to the company and to the public and it has been the policy of the Commission to permit those companies which have lower expense ratios than those

established for all companies to deviate from the rates fixed by the
Commission on the basis of such lower expenses.

Does the philosophy expressed above represent the philosophy which
existed generally between the period 1910 and 1944? Why or why not?

11. A writer stated, "In certain fields of insurance, such as fire and casualty,
the problems presented are controlled by, and may vary to a great extent
according to, the geography of the area. The habits and customs of people, the terrain and climate, the type of construction, the density of the
population and type of community activity, all have an important bearing
upon the problems inherent in insurance."
   (a) Give some examples of how the factors mentioned have an "important bearing upon the problems inherent in insurance."
   (b) What relationship does this statement have to the argument of state
versus federal regulation of insurance? Explain.

12. Commenting on New York's Appleton Rule, a writer stated, "A license
may be issued to a foreign insurer to do specified kinds of insurance business based upon financial requirements applicable to such insurance business. However, if the insurer did other kinds of insurance business outside
this State for which additional financial requirements are imposed by our
law, and such an insurer were not required to comply with those conditions, the purpose for which such financial requirements are imposed
would be defeated. It is obvious that an insurer cannot be divided into
compartments according to the state in which it does business, and therefore, it is important from the standpoint of supervision to evaluate the
obligations of a company wherever they are incurred."
   (a) What is the Appleton Rule?
   (b) Do you agree with the above statement? Under what conditions are
different financial requirements imposed for different kinds of insurance? Explain.
   (c) Is the Appleton Rule an argument for or against state regulation of
insurance? Why?

13. In the famous Armstrong report, the commission stated:
Investments in stocks should be prohibited. They are fundamentally
objectionable, as the corporation, instead of holding a secured obligation, acquires a proprietary interest in another business, with rights
subject to all indebtedness which may be created in the conduct of it,
and often direct liabilities as stockholders. This interest must be nour-
ished and supported. . . . If the stock holdings constitute a small
minority the investment is at the mercy of administrators chosen by
the majority stockholders. If the stock interest be a large one, it is
frequently found advisable to increase it until a substantial control is
effected, and the insurance corporation is not only engaged in a dif-
erent enterprise, but directly undertakes its management. Such relations afford ready opportunities to conceal irregular transactions and
to hide the malversation of funds.

(a) What answers to these objections would you raise today on the side of permitting life insurers to invest in common stocks? Discuss.

(b) If you were allowed to decide what percentage of assets a life insurer could invest in common stocks, what percentage would you choose? Defend your answer.

14. One of the practices outlawed as a result of the Armstrong investigation was known as the "tontine plan." Prior to 1910 it was common for life insurers to place all dividends in a special fund to be distributed to all survivors at the *end* of a specified period, say 20 years. Agents frequently made promises that the insured's dividends would amount to large sums, say $1,000 on a policy of $1,000 face amount. Dividends were not paid to anyone who dropped out. Suggest possible reasons why the tontine plan was frowned upon by the Armstrong committee.

15. States generally exercise control over the insurance "product." For example, most states require that in liability insurance contracts there be a provision that bankruptcy or insolvency of the insured shall not relieve the insurer of any of its obligations under the policy. Why should such a requirement be imposed on all insurers?

16. An insurance commissioner of a large state wrote, "The commissioner's position is not a particularly happy one today. He is . . . criticized for increases in rates, for a lack of insurance markets, for the insolvency of some companies, for maintaining too high a degree of uniformity in rates or coverage, or for being much too soft in the regulation of the industry. On the other hand, the commissioner is sometimes criticized by people in the insurance industry for a lack of uniformity and for regulating too severely . . . strangulation of the business instead of . . . regulation." In your opinion, is it the task of the insurance commissioner to deal with each of the questions listed above? If so, give an example of the type of activity falling under each category.

17. Justice William O. Douglas was quoted as follows on the subject of dual regulation, "Dual regulation—both by state and federal laws—may be logically permissible but practically unsound. Dual regulation may be inherently so disruptive of the policy of the federal law that the purpose of Congress to foreclose state action may be implied."

(a) Explain the meaning of this statement.

(b) From this comment do you think Justice Douglas is for or against federal regulation of insurance?

18. A tabulation in 1958 showed that on the average about 700 insurance companies are admitted to do business in each state. The number ranged from a low of 254 in Alaska to 1,838 in Texas. Considering that each insurer offers hundreds of different policies and policy forms to its customers, what is suggested concerning the regulatory tasks facing the typical insurance commissioner?

19. The chief counsel of the Congressional Committee investigating insurance is quoted as saying, "If the rating bureaus are unable to justify the broad grant of power over rates they now possess, the Subcommittee may wish to consider whether the public interest would be better served by a different system. Among the suggested possibilities is the system whereby each insurer sets its own rates but where all companies would belong to a statistical bureau. This agency would develop pure premium upon the combined loss experience of all carriers since practice has demonstrated that sound actuarial principles require the pooling of experience. No company would be permitted to charge a rate less than this pure premium. . . . If greater latitude for rate competition by this or any other system were thus allowed, the way would be open for minimizing the burdensome regulatory duty which now devolves upon the insurance commissioner . . . is there any reason to believe that honest competition would promote unsound insurance companies?"

    (a) If insurers all charged the same pure premium in a given line but "competed on expense items," would you conclude that the solvency of the insurer would therefore be protected? Why?

    (b) In your opinion, would it be safe to let competition regulate rate levels so as to free the insurance commissioner from this task, as the statement suggests?

20. (a) Why are interlocking directorates looked upon as an undesirable business practice?

    (b) Why are interlocking directorates an especially important practice in the insurance industry? Do you think that there is any special justification for them in insurance? Why?

21. (a) Suggest reasons why all states do not license insurance *brokers*.

    (b) What is the effect of the federal law that affects the operations of brokers?

    (c) Are insurance brokers regulated by this law?

22. It has been suggested that under federal regulation of insurance, local conditions could be handled through a system of district offices similar to that which exists in the case of the Federal Reserve System. Each of these offices could be given certain degrees of autonomy to adjust to localized conditions. In this way all the advantages of national uniformity could be achieved without any of the disadvantages of rigid supervision by distant authorities. Evaluate this plan, pointing out advantages and disadvantages.

23. In your opinion does real competition exist in the field of insurance? If so, give specific examples.

24. In New York a stock life insurer must possess total capital of $450,000 to begin business; in Illinois this requirement is only $150,000. What justification, if any, is there for the substantial differences noted?

25. In general, it is common for a state to prohibit an insurer from investing in the stock of another insurer beyond a certain extent. In New York, for

example, such investments may not exceed 35 per cent of the surplus to policyholders or 50 per cent of the surplus over liabilities and capital, whichever is greater. Suggest possible reasons for these restrictions.

26. A representative of one insurer contends that the state insurance commissioner should value a certain group of bonds at the insurer's "cost." The insurance examiner argues that these bonds have declined in market value and should be valued much lower than cost. Who is correct? Why?

27. In addition to meeting the organization requirements applicable to a stock insurer, a mutual insurer must meet such requirements as having a minimum number of applications for insurance, a minimum number of risks, and a minimum amount of premiums from these risks. For example, in New York, a mutual insurer desiring a license for personal injury liability insurance must have applications from at least 100 members for insurance on at least 500 separate risks, of which not more than five shall be risks of any one member, with an annual premium cost of at least $50,000 annually. If this is true, how is it practicable for a mutual insurer ever to get started?

28. You are approached by an insurance agent who promises to return 20 per cent of his commission to you if you will give him your business. Is this acceptable business practice? Comment.

29. Many professional insurance agents object strongly to the use of part-time agents and are generally in favor of much stricter licensing requirements than most states presently have. Why are part-time agents objected to more than full-time agents?

30. "A" buys an insurance policy from a mail-order insurer and following a loss is unable to secure payment. In fact, the insurer does not even answer "A's" letter in which the loss was reported. A local agent informs "A" that this particular insurer is not "admitted" in his state and has no representatives there. Is it necessary for "A" to go to the state in which this insurer is charactered in order to bring legal action? Why?

31. A legislator in your state urges that a good way to raise additional state revenue would be to increase the premium tax on all insurers operating within the state. What point should you investigate first, before recommending that this tax be passed? Why?

32. Differentiate between a retaliatory law and a reciprocal law.

33. You have applied to a mortgage company for a loan on your new home. The representative of the company indicates that your application will be approved if you agree to purchase fire insurance through him. You inform your insurance agent that although you would prefer to deal with him, he will have to forego this business because you need the loan. What action should the insurance agent take if he wants to retain your business? Why?

Problems in
Insurance Pricing

The cost of insurance is one of the most important factors in a sound analysis of risk, both from the viewpoint of the insured and the insurer. The insured wishes to understand why his premium is as high (or low) as it is and the insurer wishes to set his premium so that it will be high enough to cover all future costs, yet low enough to meet competition. Both the insured and the insurer are interested in a rate that is fair so that each insured group is charged its proper share of the total loss and expense burdens, no more or no less. This chapter attempts to throw light on how some of these problems in insurance pricing may be analyzed.

MAKE-UP OF THE PREMIUM

The insurance *rate* is the total number of dollars charged per unit of exposure. The insurance *premium* is the product of the insurance rate and the number of units of exposure. Thus, in life insurance, if the rate is $20 per $1,000 of face amount for ordinary life issued at age 30, the premium will be $200 for a $10,000 policy. In the discussion to follow, we shall be primarily interested in the insurance *rate*.

The insurance rate may be split into two parts: that portion intended to cover the pure loss cost per unit of exposure (or pure premium) and that portion, called *loading*, intended to cover the sales expense, overhead, and profit of the insurer. In automobile collision insurance, for example, the pure loss cost might be $30 per low-priced "standard car," plus $10 for loss adjustment and claims costs, bringing the pure premium to $40. The loading is usually expressed as a percentage of the final premium (gross premium) and might be 40 per cent of the final premium. The loading is composed of selling agents' commissions, taxes, underwriting expenses, administrative overhead, and expected profit. The insured's premium therefore includes allowances for two main types of expenditures—those expenditures returned

714

to the insured group as a whole for loss and loss adjustment expenses, and those expenditures necessary for the insurance service.

The relative size of loading in insurance premiums often surprises the uninitiated. The first reaction is "Why must the expenses of distribution be as much as 40 per cent of the total premium?" There is the feeling that somehow the insured group is not getting any value from the expenditures for administration in connection with the insurance plan, whereas it "gets back" that part of the premium devoted to payment of pure losses. There are several answers to this, including the following:

1. The insured usually is getting more "direct" value than the statistics reveal. For example, the expenses for loss-prevention efforts, the costs of paying a claim, and even the expenses later returned to the insured as a dividend are often buried in general expenses, thus making them appear greater than they are.
2. It is a mistake to assume that the insured is getting no benefit from general insurer administration, for without these expenses there could be no insurance mechanism. The costs of administering and distributing insurance are no more, for example, than the costs of marketing many of the tangible commodities we consume each day.
3. In a free economy, unnecessary expenses may be expected to be eliminated by a process of squeezing out the marginal producer through the effects of competition. As we have seen, governmental regulation in insurance is an additional factor which prevents expenses from exceeding reasonable bounds.

CRITERIA FOR SOUND RATE-MAKING

As a frame of reference, any plan of rate-making should incorporate certain basic essentials, some of which are laid down by state regulation, and most of which are not mutually exclusive. The rate:

1) Should be adequate to meet loss burdens, not excessive.
2) Should allocate cost burden among insureds on a "fair" basis.
3) Should be revised reasonably often so as to reflect as current a degree of loss experience as is feasible.
4) Should encourage loss-prevention efforts among insureds, if possible.

While these criteria seem simple enough upon casual review, they raise many difficult problems in their application. Some of these problems, many of which will probably never be completely solved either by insurers or by regulatory authorities, are described on pages 716–718.

1) Adequacy of the rate

If a rate is to be "adequate" and yet "not excessive," how wide a margin for error should these limits impose? From one standpoint, an underwriter may reason that to have an adequate premium he must collect an amount sufficient for all unknown contingencies, while another underwriter may have a much different view of the size of these possible contingencies. This problem arises from the fact that the insurance rate must be set *before* all the costs are known. In many lines of business the entrepreneur may ascertain all or nearly all his costs before he sets a price. If he cannot determine his costs, he usually will insist that the contract of sale be subject to later adjustment to reflect the actual costs, or he will insist on a "cost plus" type of contract. In insurance, however, a definite estimate must often be made in advance with no possibility of a later renegotiation if the estimate of loss was incorrect. Frequently an estimate is inaccurate because the underwriter uses past experience to estimate the future, while the insurance contract may involve a substantial future period during which the original conditions on which rates were based change drastically. It is easy to see that opinions as to the future of insurance costs can vary widely.

The problem of preventing rates from becoming excessive has been the subject of much legislation, as we have seen in Chapter 25. Anti-compact laws were generally abandoned because of the recognition that cooperation in rate-making (pooling of loss data) is an essential part of sound rating, and that unrestricted competition often leads to rates that are too low for the long-run solvency of the insurance fund. Having rates too low is just as undesirable, if not worse, as having them too high. Above all, the insured is seeking assurance that his losses will be paid if and when they occur.

2) Fair allocation of cost burden

Just how far should the underwriter go in developing a rate that completely reflects the true quality of the individual hazard, thus making the rate "fair"? Theoretically, it might be argued that, for life insurance purposes, there should be an attempt to set individual premiums on the basis of occupation, income, marital status, automobile accident record, years during which cigarettes have been smoked, and longevity of parents. In practice, none of these factors affect the premium individually, since age and sex are the sole discriminants. If the criteria as to fairness are carried to an extreme, it might be said that each person should receive a slightly different rate to reflect his own unique nature. This, of course, would be impossible to administer and would make the rate-making task hopelessly complex. However, a decision must be made just where to draw the line and as to what criteria of fairness should be used.

Another class of problems arising out of the criterion of "fairness" deals with the determination of the exposure unit to which the rate is applied. Automobile rates, for example, apply to the individual car; workmen's compensation rates, to each $100 of payroll; fire insurance rates, to each $100 of building value; and life insurance rates, to each $1,000 of policy amount on an insured life. Consider workmen's compensation insurance. There are two employers in the same rating class, one paying 300 men $4 per hour, on the average, and the other paying 400 men $3 per hour, on the average. Assuming that each has an hourly payroll of $1,200, each would pay the same workmen's compensation premiums, but the first employer has an exposure of 300 men, while the second has 400 men. Should each employer pay the same premium? It could be argued persuasively that the first employer, aside from having fewer workers exposed to accident, probably hires a better class of men who might have fewer accidents than the more poorly paid workers. However, experience suggests that there is no feasible base on which to charge workmen's compensation premiums other than payroll. Similar problems exist for other types of insurance.

3) Frequent revision to reflect loss experience

Insurance rates are generally revised slowly. Oftentimes it is many years before rates can be altered to reflect higher or lower costs. Consider automobile insurance, for example. Suppose it is desired to collect all loss experience data for a given year, X. Since policies are issued continuously throughout year X and have a one-year term, the rate-maker must wait until the *end* of year X plus one before he can start to collect loss data. It may take him an additional six months to gather and interpret all data and obtain approval for a rate change. The new rate he promulgates for the coming year is, on the average, one year and three months old (one half of the period dating from the beginning of year X to the time X plus one and one half). The lag is much greater for policies issued for terms longer than one year. In life insurance new mortality tables are adopted only after periods of several years and any errors in rate-making assumptions must be corrected, if at all, through changes in dividend schedules. Because of the lags noted, certain allowances are made by the rate-maker for observable trends. Errors in these allow-ances necessarily affect the criteria, adequacy and reasonableness, dis-cussed on pages 715–717. However, if a method could be found to in-corporate loss data into the rate structure immediately as the losses are experienced, it would probably be undesirable to do so since insurance is a commodity which does not lend itself to daily changes in price, as may be true of wholesale quotations of foodstuffs, for example. Again, some reasonable compromise between the extremes of immediate adjustment and prolonged delay must be found, even at the expense of some un-certainty and error in future rates.

4) Encouragement of loss-prevention efforts

While ideally the insurance rate should encourage loss prevention on the part of the insured, it is difficult to achieve this objective. This may be understood when it is recalled that most insurable perils occur out-side the control of the insured. In some lines of insurance, such as fire, rate credits are given for measures which tend to reduce the severity of losses once the peril occurs, but there is great difficulty in defending the size of these credits, since any decision as to how much a safety device is worth in reducing losses is largely an arbitrary judgment. This problem is usually handled by some form of merit rating, to be discussed below.

RATE-MAKING METHODS

One of the most difficult problems in insurance lies in the problem of developing rate-making methods that meet the criteria analyzed previously. As we shall see, the methods employed very often can meet these criteria only imperfectly, and underwriting judgment, unsupported by statistical evidence, often plays a major role in rate-making. Even when statistical evidence is available, judgment plays a major role in rate-making in the interpretation of the statistical data, leading perhaps to rates which ap-pear entirely arbitrary. Actuarial formulas themselves represent judg-ments as to which data will be weighed and how much weight will be accorded each type. Mathematics plays an important role in seeing that rate-making has a degree of consistency so that all members of an insured group who fall into predetermined categories are treated alike. However, as will be demonstrated, the calculation of an insurance rate is in no sense absolute or completely "scientific" in nature. As in most areas of the social sciences, the scientific method in insurance makes its greatest contribution in narrowing the area within which executive judgment must operate.

The basic approaches in rate-making are:

1) The manual, or class rating (pure), method.
2) Individual, or merit rating, method.
3) Some combination of the first two methods.

1) Manual, or class rating (pure), method

In the first basic approach, the *manual,* or *class rating, method,* the procedure is to set rates that apply uniformly to each exposure unit falling within some predetermined class or group. These groups are usually set up in such a manner that loss data may be collected and organized in some logical fashion. Everyone falling within a given class is charged the same rate. Any differences in hazard attributable to individual risks are considered unmeasurable or relatively small.

The major areas of insurance that emphasize use of the manual rate-making method are life, workmen's compensation, liability, automobile, surety, health, and residential fire. For example, in life insurance the central classifications are by age and sex. Loss data are collected for each person by age and sex, and rates are promulgated on the same basis. In workmen's compensation insurance, a national rate-making body collects loss experience data of more than 600 industrial groups, and these data are broken down territorially by state. In automobile insurance, the loss data are broken down territorially, by type of automobile, by age of driver, and by major use of the automobile. In each case it is necessary only to find the appropriate page in a manual to find out what the insurance rate is to be, from which the term manual rate-making is derived.

Pure premium. The central technique in manual rate-making is the *pure premium method.* This involves collecting all loss data falling into each class which is to be rated, dividing by the number of exposure units, and arriving at a pure premium. For automobile insurance, as an example, suppose the pure premium in collision insurance ($50 deductible) for low-priced passenger cars in five counties of state Y, class 1A drivers (no male operator less than 25 years of age, and car not used in business nor to drive to and from work) is $30 for a certain time period. This means that *on the average* the insurer had to pay $30 per car for collision losses falling into the classification named. The rate-maker must then allow for loading. Since loading is usually expressed as a percentage of the final gross premium, the pure premium is divided by one minus the loading percentage. If in the case above, loading is 40 per cent of the final premium, the final premium is found by dividing $30 by .60, thereby obtaining a figure of $50. The reader may verify that the insurer will have sufficient funds to meet expected future losses by subtracting .40 × $50 from $50 and arriving at $30, the pure loss cost. Although in practice more refined methods than this are used, this simple formula is the basis of rate-making by the pure premium method.

Loss ratio method. In some cases it may be impractical to employ the pure premium method in developing a rate because of the existence of too many classifications and subclassifications in the manual. In other words, there may be so many categories involved that losses on only a small number of exposures occur in a given time period. This small exposure may be deemed insufficient on which to base decisions from a statistical point of view.[1] As a consequence, the new rate is developed by comparing the *actual* loss ratios, A, of combined groups with the *expected* loss ratios, E, and using the formula $\frac{A}{E} =$ Per cent change indicated. For example, suppose that the actual loss ratio is .70 while only .60 was expected when the old rate was promulgated. In this example, $A = .70$, $E = .60$, and the formula yields $\frac{.7}{.6}$. The new rate would be $\frac{7}{6}$ times the old, or nearly 17 per cent higher. The loss ratio method is actually a rate-*revision* method rather than a rate-*making* method.

Before we can analyze the individual or merit rating method of rate-making, it is necessary to pause and define the concept, credible rate.

Credibility. A concept of basic importance in insurance rate-making is credibility. In general terms, *credibility* refers to the degree to which the rate-maker can rely on the accuracy of loss experience observed in any given area. For example, assume that the rate-maker is faced with the task of revising a rate for a certain type of policy issued by his company in a given geographical area. There are 50 policies outstanding and the loss ratio on these policies indicates that losses have been considerably higher than anticipated. Should future rates be based

---

[1] See the following discussion on credibility.

on the experience of these 50 policies, or is there a considerable likelihood that the last year under consideration produced higher than average losses only by random chance? In other words, the rate-maker wishes to know the extent to which the experience is "believable." He wishes to know how many policies there would have to be before the loss experience observed should be given 100, 90, 80, 50, or 10 per cent weight in preparing the rate revisions.

The answers to these questions are of obvious importance not only to the insured but also to the insurer. If upon the next renewal the rate-maker raised the insurance premium of everyone who had suffered a loss, the purpose of loss-spreading, which is inherent in the insurance mechanism, would be largely lost. If each small group were "required to pay for its own losses," it is clear that the idea of risk transfer would not be achieved. It would not do to raise the fire rates of a small community which had a disastrous fire in one year, because the experience for such a small class, particularly in only one year, is certainly not credible. Yet, the insurer, in the interest of fairness, must make reasonable classifications of insureds and perils and charge an appropriate rate for large groups falling within these classifications. It is not "fair" for one group to subsidize another group, if each group is large enough to develop loss experience that is reasonably credible.

The statistical basis for the determination of what constitutes a credible number lies in the fact that losses in insurance are deemed to occur as independent random events and are more or less normally distributed. This means that we can determine the number of "trials" in a sample necessary to produce, with some predetermined degree of accuracy, a loss ratio which falls within some stated error range of the expected loss ratio. For example, it can be determined mathematically under assumptions of the normal distribution that if the probability of a temporary disability per year in a given territory is .06, and it is desired to find what number of employees must be considered before a pure premium can be developed which is within .006 of the expected loss frequency of .06 (*i.e.,* within 10 per cent of expected loss frequency), the rate-maker must observe the loss experience of about 18,800 employees in order to know with 90 per cent probability that his loss experience will be as he has assumed.[2]

---

[2] Based on the formula given in Chapter 2, $N = S^2/4e^2$, where $S = 1.645$ (1.645 standard deviations on either side of the mean of a normal distribution include 90 per cent of the area under the curve, so the results have a 90 per cent confidence interval) and e, the standard of accuracy, is .006.

If the rate-maker observes fewer experiences than this, he may not assign full weight to the pure premium so developed.

In general, the smaller the probability of loss, the greater is the number of exposure units needed to develop a "dependable" pure premium. In fact, the number of exposures necessary for credibility varies inversely with square of the degree of accuracy required and with the square of the probability of loss. This follows because the degree of accuracy required varies directly with the probability of loss. Thus, the smaller the probability of loss, the smaller is the absolute value of the degree of accuracy which will be required. (If the probability of loss is .30, a degree of accuracy of .03 may be required; but if the probability of loss is .03, the same relative degree of accuracy is now .003.) Therefore, if the degree of accuracy is fixed, the number of exposures necessary for credibility varies inversely with the square of the probability of loss. Hence, if the probability of loss in one territory is one half that of another territory, four times as much exposure is required for the same degree of credibility.[3] An intuitive understanding of why this is true may be obtained by considering what would happen if the insurer for workmen's compensation were to base its premium for fatal accidents on an exposure of 1,000 employees, each with an average wage of $4,000. The pure premium might be .0006 × $4,000,000 or $2,400. One fatal accident costing, say, $5,000 would be more than double the expected loss. On the other hand, with $40,000,000 of payroll exposure, one fatal accident more than was expected would not affect the pure premium nearly so much.

The rate-maker generally develops a scale of credibility running from zero to 100 per cent. Zero credibility means that the number of exposures is too small to warrant any consideration in rate revision, while 100 per cent credibility means that the group being rated is large enough to be virtually self-rating. For example, assume that the observed loss ratio is .70 as compared with an expected loss ratio of .60, as in the above example, producing a rate increase of 17 per cent. However, the number of exposures on which the .70 loss ratio was calculated was of such size that only 60 per cent credibility can be attached to it. This means that rates would be increased only .6 × 17, or 10.2 per cent instead of 17 per cent.

As another example, slightly more complicated, in the field of fire insurance, consider the data in Table 26–1 dealing with one analyst's

<hr>

[3] One of the first casualty actuaries believed to apply mathematical techniques similar to the ones illustrated here and in Chapter 2 was Albert H. Mowbray, in "A New Criterion of Adequacy of Exposure," *Proceedings, Casualty Actuarial Society,* Vol. LV, pp. 263–273.

Table 26–1

CREDIBILITY IN FIRE INSURANCE

Credibility Percentage	Dwellings (Millions of Dollars)	Mercantile Contents (Millions of Dollars)	Manufacturing (Millions of Dollars)
10	$ .19	$ 1.55	$ 5.8
20	.28	2.24	8.4
30	.39	3.13	11.8
40	.54	4.32	16.2
50	.75	5.98	22.5
60	1.01	8.47	31.8
70	1.43	11.45	43.0
80	1.62	12.95	48.7
90	1.80	14.44	54.2
100	2.00	15.94	59.9

Source: R. L. Hurley, "A Credibility Framework for Gauging Fire Classification Experience," *Proceedings of the Casualty Actuarial Society* (1954), p. 170.

view of a possible credibility framework. According to Table 26–1, it requires consideration of a sufficient number of buildings to develop earned premiums of $2 million in dwellings, nearly $16 million in mercantile contents, and $60 million in manufacturing facilities before 100 per cent credibility can be attached to the loss experience developed from each class. The differences can be explained in terms of homogeneity of the risk. Thus, in dwellings, which are fairly uniform in value and are not usually subject to simultaneous destruction nor to catastrophic losses, only one eighth as much exposure is required as is true of mercantile contents. In the latter field there is not as much uniformity and very large values are often exposed in a single location. The standard (admittedly arbitrary) for 100 per cent credibility in this instance is that in 97 per cent of all cases, the observed loss ratio will not vary from the true loss ratio by more than 10 per cent.[4]

2) Individual, or merit rating, method

The *individual,* or *merit rating, method* differs from the manual rating method in that ways are developed to recognize the individual features of a specific risk and to give this risk a rate which more or less reflects its particular hazard. A variety of merit rating plans are used to give recognition to the fact that some *groups* of insureds, and some individual insureds have loss records which are sufficiently credible to warrant reductions (or increases) in their rate from that of the general class to which they belong.

---

[4] For a mathematical analysis of credibility procedures, see A. L. Bailey, "Credibility Procedures—LaPlace's Generalization of Bayes' Rule and the Combination of Collateral Knowledge with Observed Data," PCAS, Vol. XXXVII (1950), pp. 7–23.

Special rating classes. One very generally used device is for the underwriter to set up *special rating classes* to which discounts from the manual rate are made, either beforehand in the form of a direct *deviation,* as it is called, or as a dividend payable at the end of the period. Presumably, only those insureds meeting certain requirements are eligible for the special rate. Sometimes insurers restrict their business in such a manner that the entire policyholder group is meant to be a risk superior to that of the general public and therefore qualifies for a lower rate than that charged by insurers dealing with all types of risks. For example, some direct writing companies, such as factory mutuals, severely restrict the classes of risk they underwrite and, if warranted, pay substantial dividends as a reward for loss-prevention efforts. In the field of life insurance, mutual insurers pay dividends that differ in amount according to the type of policy. Life insurers also grant rate deviations for special classes of insured groups known as "preferred risks," and charge extra premiums on other groups called "substandard risks." Automobile insurers have experimented with this method by distinguishing among applicants on the basis of their automobile accident and traffic violation records. In workmen's compensation, certain groups are entitled to a premium discount which varies according to the size of the annual premium.

Schedule rating. Another widely used plan of individual rating is called *schedule rating.* The best example of this is in the field of commercial fire insurance, where each individual building is considered separately and a rate established for it. The physical features of the structure are analyzed for factors that presumably affect the probability of loss, and credits in the rate are given for good features. These credits are in the form of a listing, or a schedule. In effect, the insured is rewarded in advance for features which it is hoped will yield a lower loss cost for all similar structures as a group. Schedule rating is also used in burglary insurance, with the insured being given credits in his rate for loss-prevention devices such as burglar alarms and burglar proof safes.

Experience rating. A third way in which an individual risk may receive special consideration by the rate-maker is through *experience rating.* Experience rating is permitted in cases where the hazards affecting the insured's operation are sufficiently *within his control* so that it is reasonable to expect him to be able to reduce his losses through special effort. If this is done, he is permitted a lower insurance rate for the coming period. The experience rating plan applies to insureds with a relatively large exposure so that the experience which is developed has some chance to be credible. Thus, experience rating formulas generally apply to business firms with large and diversified types of operations and where the loss ratio is at least partially within the control of the insured. Unlike schedule rating, which grants a discount for safe features, experience rating requires that the insured *prove* his ability to keep loss ratios down before being qualified for a loss reduction. Most experience rating formulas also impose a rate *increase* in case the loss ratios become higher than expected. Experience rating plans are used in workmen's compensation, general liability, group health, unemployment, and other lines of insurance. Examples of these plans are analyzed below.

Retrospective rating. A final way in which attention is given to the problem of recognizing individual differences in risk is through *retrospective rating*. In contrast to experience rating under which rate adjustments apply only to the future period, retrospective rating permits an adjustment in rates for the period just ended. The premium is determined, in whole or in part, by the actual record of losses suffered by the insured during the policy year. The contract is renegotiated, so to speak, after all the facts have been determined. The employer becomes a partial self-insurer, but he uses the commercial insurer to limit his losses.

3) Combination method

In many lines of insurance a *combination* of the two methods—manual and merit rating—is used in different degrees. In other words, the rate-maker may develop a manual rate and then proceed to set up a system whereby individual members of a group may qualify for reductions from the manual rate, if certain requirements are met, or be subjected to rates higher than the manual rate under certain conditions.

EXAMPLES OF MERIT RATING PLANS

To appreciate some of the problems in individual risk rating, or merit rating, five examples of merit rating plans will be presented:

1) The "safe driver" plan in automobile insurance.
2) Experience rating in workmen's compensation.
3) Experience rating in unemployment insurance.
4) Retrospective rating in workmen's compensation.
5) Schedule rating in fire insurance on commercial property.

1) The safe driver plan

In the field of automobile insurance it is common to hear the complaint, "I've been driving for 30 years and have never had an accident; yet, I pay the same rate as the man who has had a series of accidents. It isn't fair." In the past this argument has been answered by the observation that the driving experience of one person simply is not credible. No matter how safe the past driving record, a person could have a series of accidents the very next year. Furthermore, since over 90 per cent of all motorists are "safe drivers," a plan to recognize accident-free records would necessarily mean reducing the rates of most of the insured group. To do this it would necessitate an increase in the initial rate so that sufficient funds would be available to pay losses. Thus, the rates would have to be raised so that a "discount" could be granted.

However, in the field of automobile insurance, various merit rating plans have proved successful. Such plans have been used in England for many years. Actuaries in Sweden and Canada have reported success with the plans. A few insurers in the United States attempted merit rating plans in 1929 but dropped them shortly thereafter during the depression of the 1930's. Since 1952 New York and North Carolina have used a "demerit plan" which penalizes unsafe drivers. In 1959, following a study in California that associated claims frequency with traffic law violations, several insurance companies in certain states initiated what has become known as the *safe driver plan.*[5]

In the state of Texas, the safe driver plan is mandatory for all private passenger automobiles insured under the family automobile policy. A three-year experience record is compiled and for each accident, as defined, points are charged against the driver, the number depending upon the nature of the accident. Discounts of 20 per cent from the manual premium are permitted for drivers who have accumulated less than a specified number of points during the three-year period. For poor drivers, extra charges ranging from 20 to 100 per cent are added to the renewal premium, according to a schedule of accident points tallied against them.

The safe driver plans actually represent an alteration in automobile rating classifications. Instead of rating classes being developed exclusively on the basis of territory, age of driver, distance traveled to and from work, and other factors, drivers are also classified according to their driving records. Loss experience data can presumably be gathered by this new classification, and discounts from the basic rate can be calculated

---

[5] By June, 1961, 36 states and the District of Columbia had adopted safe driver plans.

with some assurance. Thus, a basic objection to safe driving plans, namely, that the experience of an individual driver is not credible, is overcome. The rate is based on a group of drivers with differing degrees of safe driving records.

Although it is too early to assess the degree of success of these new safe driver plans, it remains to be seen whether drivers who are subject to a substantial rate increase will continue to purchase insurance, in spite of financial responsibility laws.[6] If the poor drivers with accident and traffic conviction records tend to drop out of the insured group, the remaining drivers may obtain certain savings in the automobile insurance premium, but this may be obtained at the expense of an increase in the number of uncompensated victims of uninsured motorists.

Safe driver plans have the laudable objective of rewarding loss-prevention efforts as measured by actual accomplishments rather than by classification factors that are supposed to distinguish safe and unsafe drivers. Thus, the plans help meet two of the important criteria of rate-making: making a proper distinction between types of risk, and rewarding loss prevention. There are several practical difficulties in these plans, however, such as the difficulty in obtaining accurate information about a driver's traffic violations or accident record, inequities in the penalty scale, arguments over assessing points against the driver in a given accident, and the general administrative burden of handling the plan. Unless the plan is kept very simple, it is likely that drivers will not understand it, and the cost of administering the plan may exceed its value.

2) Experience rating in workmen's compensation

Experience rating plans are widely used in workmen's compensation insurance. The general theory is that an employer has some control over his loss ratio and is entitled to a credit for a good loss-prevention record, or, on the other hand, should pay a higher rate if his loss record is poorer than the average.

In the experience rating plan adopted by private insurers and administered by the National Council on Compensation Insurance, a national rate-making agency, each employer must have some minimum premium which would be payable if standard manual rates were charged. In Massachusetts, for example, the minimum premium is $500. The details of the plan are quite involved, but the general procedure is to determine for each occupational class some "expected" loss ratio against

---

[6] This, of course, will not be a factor in states with compulsory automobile insurance. Safe driver plans may become a factor in spreading the use of compulsory insurance.

which is compared the insured's actual loss ratio. If the actual loss ratio is 90 per cent of the expected loss ratio, the insured's rate for the coming year is 90 per cent of the manual rate. If the actual loss ratio is 130 per cent of the expected loss ratio, the insured must pay at 130 per cent of the manual rate during the coming year.

Under experience rating plans not all losses suffered by an insured are counted. The plan involves a stabilizing factor so that unusually large losses cannot operate to increase unreasonably the small employer's rate. However, for the large employer, large losses receive increasing weight so that if in Massachusetts, for example, an employer's standard premium is $380,000 or more, all losses are considered, no matter how large. The effect is that the very large employer is more or less self-rating, while the medium-size and small employers, in those years following a period of low losses, receive a credit which is not as large as it would be if they were self-rating. In those years following a period of high losses, the medium-size and small employers pay a penalty which is not as large as it would be if they were self-rating. Over a period of years if the loss experience in a given category of industry is consistently bad, the manual rate and expected losses for that class will be adjusted so that in any given period a certain rating class of risks will tend to bear its total loss burden. But experience rating deals with rate adjustments for individual insureds within a given class on a year-to-year basis.

Experience rating in workmen's compensation has the advantage that it gives employers an incentive to do whatever is within their control to prevent accidents, a very desirable objective of any rating system. It rewards the safety efforts of employers by the test of "what effect did it have," not "what effect should it have had," as is the practice in fire insurance. Employers may spend a great deal of money on safety efforts, but if these efforts fail, no rate credit will be forthcoming.

3) Experience rating in unemployment insurance

Under the general theory that an employer can control the rate of employment in his firm, all states, except Alaska, have laws which provide that if the employer has a favorable record of losses, his unemployment insurance tax may be reduced. An employer's rate can be reduced to zero in some states, but in most states it cannot fall below .1 per cent of covered payrolls. On the other hand, this rate cannot be increased above 2.7 per cent except in 18 states, and in no case can the tax be raised beyond the 4.5 per cent level.[7]

---

[7] *Comparison of State Unemployment Insurance Laws as of January 1, 1960* (United States Department of Labor, 1960), p. 22.

Although there are many different formulas of experience rating in use, each formula has the basic purpose of providing an incentive to the employer to stabilize his employment and to allocate the cost of unemployment as nearly as feasible to those who are considered mainly responsible for it. In about half the states an employer must have three or more years of experience with unemployment claims before he is eligible for a reduction from the standard 2.7 per cent rate. In the remaining states the law may permit a reduction based on as little as one year's experience for a new employer. If during this period unemployment insurance benefits paid to workers who were laid off were less than the contributions paid in, a "reserve" is established for the employer's account. If the ratio of this reserve to his total payroll falls below a certain point, the employer is entitled to a reduced tax rate for the future. For example, in Ohio, excerpts from the most favorable experience rating schedule as of January 1, 1960, reveal the following:

RESERVE RATIO	CONTRIBUTION RATE
Minus balance	2.7%
.5	2.0%
2.5	1.6%
5.0	1.0%
7.0	.6%
Above 10	.1%

Thus, in Ohio, if an employer has a reserve balance even as small as .5 per cent of his payroll during the time he has paid unemployment taxes, his rate for the coming period is 2 per cent. If his total contributions exceeded benefits paid to former employees by 10 per cent, his rate is only .1 per cent. This type of experience rating formula, known as the *reserve ratio* type, is used in 33 states. In Ohio, the reserve ratio is the ratio of total reserves accumulated in all past years to the average payroll of the preceding three years. Because of experience rating, unemployment taxes in the past have averaged about 1.2 per cent of the covered payroll.[8]

Most state laws contain provisions which seek to excuse the employer from penalties in his experience rating for conditions over which he has little or no control. Thus, it is common to find that there is a maximum limit which can be placed on the amount charged any one employer, where more than one employer has hired a worker during his base period. Oftentimes, no employer is charged for certain types of un-

---

[8] See *Labor Market and Economic Security* for current estimates of this figure.

employment benefits paid, such as those paid when the period of employment was of short duration.

Experience rating permits an individual employer to earn lower unemployment compensation taxes, but it is possible that a state may find itself in an embarrassing position if the combined tax collections are insufficient to meet all claims. For this reason, a majority of the states provide that the total fund must be of a certain size before *any* employer is entitled to an experience rate. In 17 states the fund must be equal to some percentage of total payrolls (as defined) in that state before any experience rate can be permitted.

Administrative arrangements have been worked out so that a worker may file a claim in a state other than that in which he has been employed. Thus, the worker may collect benefits in the new state, but the former state is "charged" with his claim and must reimburse the state of new residence. In this way, labor mobility is not reduced and employers in the new state are not required to bear the burden of a new worker's unemployment benefit payments.

Weaknesses of experience rating in unemployment insurance. Experience rating in unemployment compensation insurance has been criticized on several grounds. The main element of the criticism is that the fundamental basis of experience rating is invalid for this type of insurance. Experience rating presupposes that the insured, particularly if he is a large employer, can to a large extent control his own losses. Through experience rating the insured is given a financial incentive to take measures to accomplish this end. In unemployment insurance, however, an employer frequently is subject to market forces over which he has no control and therefore cannot help the unemployment situation except in certain cases. For example, he has some control over technological changes within the plant or malfunctions in production scheduling which cause unemployment. On the other hand, he has little control over the buying habits of his customers.

Another criticism is that experience rating has a destabilizing effect on unemployment. This is caused by the fact that the employer's contributions increase during depression times when he can least afford them, and decrease during good times when he can most afford to lay aside funds for future obligations. Experience rating is therefore said to impose penalties on an employer for conditions over which he has no control, and to reward him for reducing unemployment when individually he had little to do with the economic recovery which gave rise to lowered unemployment.

4) Retrospective rating in workmen's compensation

In workmen's compensation insurance, experience rating is applied automatically, but retrospective rating is entirely a voluntary agreement between the insured and the insurer. If the employer's payroll is such that a standard premium of $1,000 or more is entailed, it is considered that the firm is large enough to develop experience that is partially credible. (A *standard premium* is defined as what the employer would have paid at manual rates after adjustment for experience rating, but before any adjustment for retrospective rating.) In practice, an employer likely to use retrospective rating would generally be considerably larger than this, since a standard premium of only $1,000 means that the payroll approximates $100,000 and the number of employees is therefore only about 25 (assuming an average wage of $4,000 a year). Even one accident could easily cause a loss in excess of $1,000. This might cause a very substantial increase in the employer's retrospective premium, depending on the nature of the plan he selects.

There are various plans of retrospective rating and the employer must make a choice among them. Assuming that the employer is large enough and that both parties are agreeable to retrospective rating, which plan should the employer use? Essentially this question reduces to one of how much risk the employer is willing to assume, *i.e.,* how great a loss he is willing to accept, if his experience turns out to be bad, in return for a reduced premium if his experience is good.

The basic retrospective rating formula may be given by the expression: [9]

$$R = [BP + (L)(LCF)]TM,$$

where R = Retrospective premium payable for the year in question.

        BP = A basic premium (in dollars) designed to cover fixed costs of the insurer in handling the business.

        L = Losses (in dollars) actually suffered by the employer.

    LCF = Loss conversion factor, a multiplying factor designed to cover the variable costs of the insurer (such as claim adjustment expenses).

    TM = Tax multiplier, a factor designed to reflect the premium tax levied by the state on the insurer's business.

---

[9] There are other elements in retrospective rating formulas such as adjustments for individual loss limitations, but for simplicity, they will be ignored in the present discussion.

The formula tells the rate-maker to take the amount of the insured's losses in a given year, multiply it by some percentage (LCF), add the result to a basic premium, and multiply this result by another factor (TM). The basic premium declines as the size of the employer increases, and differs with the type of plan used. The loss conversion factor is a constant percentage, as is the tax multiplier, regardless of the size of the employer. The formula is subject to the operation of certain minimums and maximums, both of which decline as the size of the employer increases, except for the plan in which the maximum amount paid by the employer is the standard premium.

The operation of the formula is such that the larger the employer, the less risk there is associated with the use of retrospective rating (the maximum and minimum premium declines). Yet, a relatively small employer who is accepted for retrospective rating has an opportunity to lower his premium if he can keep his losses within bounds, and still obtain protection against paying more than he would in the absence of the retrospective plan.

To illustrate the operation of retrospective rating, consider the case of employer Jones, whose standard premium is $10,000. Two of the choices open to him in retrospective rating are charted in Figure 26–1.

Figure 26–1

OPERATION OF A RETROSPECTIVE RATING FORMULA

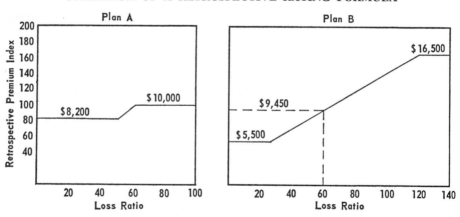

It is assumed that the employer has a payroll such that his standard premium is $10,000. A standard premium is that which the insured would have paid in the absence of a retrospective rating plan. "Loss ratio" represents the ratio of actual losses suffered to the standard premium. "Retrospective premium index" is the ratio of the employer's finally determined retrospective premium to the standard premium. This index is converted to dollars and shown on the graph for an employer with a $10,000 standard premium.

If Jones takes Plan A, his premium is guaranteed never to exceed $10,-000, but on the other hand, he has the opportunity to reduce his premium modestly to $8,200, which is the minimum for an employer of his size. For example, if Jones has losses of only $5,000, his retrospective premium would be calculated according to the formula, as follows: [10]

$$R = [\$2,800 + (\$5,000)(1.14)]1.026 = \$8,721$$

Since the retrospective premium is higher than the minimum of $8,200 but lower than the maximum of $10,000, Jones's workmen's compensation premium for the year is $8,721. If Jones has losses less than $4,600, he receives no further credit on his premium, due to the operation of the minimum. On the other hand, if his losses are approximately $6,000 or more, Jones pays the maximum premium of $10,000.[11]

One might wonder why every employer would not seek to use Plan A. It would seem that he would have nothing to lose and yet would have a possibility of gain. The answer is that not every employer may be acceptable to the insurer for retrospective rating, particularly if the employer pays little attention to safety procedures. Furthermore, the employer may wish the opportunity of reducing his premium by a greater amount than is possible through Plan A.

Under Plan B, Jones may reduce his premium to as low as $5,500, but his maximum possible premium now rises to $16,500, 165 per cent of his standard premium. Under Plan B, Jones trades the possibility of additional premium savings for the possibility of larger losses. Figure 26–1 shows what Jones's retrospective premium would be for any loss ratio under the two plans. For example, if Jones has a loss ratio of 60 per cent (*i.e.*, $6,000 in compensation losses during the year) he will pay a total premium of $9,450 under Plan B, which is less than he would have paid under Plan A with the same loss ratio. This is due to the fact that the basic premium is less under Plan B than under Plan A for an employer of Jones's size. Actually, the majority of the total premium volume in workmen's compensation which is subject to retrospective rating is under another plan (Plan D) which permits greater flexibility in selecting the precise limits of liability which the insured may wish to assume. Thus, the insured may select the maximum and the minimum loss ratio which he wishes to assume and may also incorporate within the plan not only his workmen's compensation exposure but also his general liability exposure subject to certain limits.

---

[10] The LCF of 1.14; the TM of 1.026; the minimum premium, $8,200; and the basic premium, $2,800; are those applying to employers of this size class in Massachusetts in 1960.

[11] The student should verify to himself that this is true by substituting each figure in the basic retrospective rating formula.

Financial results of retrospective rating. An employer might not know the results of a retrospective rating plan until several years after the expiration of the policy year, as it may take a long time to reach a final determination of the actual amount of the loss that a given job injury has caused. Furthermore, the retrospective rating plan may be written to encompass a three-year period, a factor which delays the final result even further. Nevertheless, statistics over the past years suggest that an employer may expect to pay, on the average, about 80 per cent of what he would have paid under a standard premium plan.[12] This result does not seem to vary materially no matter which type of retrospective rating plan is being used.

5) Schedule rating in fire insurance on commercial property

Fire insurance rating systems employ two basic methods: (1) schedule rating for commercial buildings, and (2) manual rating for dwellings. Schedule rating is discussed below; manual rating is treated in the following section, "Rate-Making in Other Lines of Insurance."

The main objective of schedule rating in the fire insurance field is to provide an incentive for loss prevention on the part of the insured and to achieve fairness by recognizing basic differences in fire hazards among insured property. It would obviously be unfair to assign a farm building the same rate as a building directly across from a fire station, or to give a small retail store building the same rate as a factory building. Therefore, a rather elaborate method has been developed to provide for equity in fire insurance rating.

It is not practical to reward the owner of a "safe" building by the techniques of experience or retrospective rating. Losses occur so infrequently that an insurer would be in a position of granting a very large "discount" annually to almost every insured. If a loss did occur, the insured's premium for the year in question would certainly be increased, but it is inconceivable that it could be increased enough to compensate for all the years during which very low premiums were paid. An important purpose of retrospective and experience rating is to reward the insured for careful, continuous attention to loss prevention, an effort that is especially productive when losses occur frequently, as they do in workmen's compensation and unemployment insurance. This condition does not fit fire insurance. Therefore, a system of rewarding the insured for

---

[12] Based on data supplied by the National Council of Compensation Insurance, for three-year plans beginning in 1953. There were 476 accounts with standard premiums of $51,554,176, on which the retrospective premium was $41,099,131, or 79.7 per cent. The data represented experience for insureds with both stock and nonstock insurers.

adopting safety features which are judged to reduce the fire hazard has been adopted. Since every commercial building is unique in this respect, rating organizations are set up in each state to inspect and "rate" each building. Through mutual agreement, most insurers adhere to the rate so promulgated.

Details on fire insurance rating methods vary from state to state. There are, however, two basic systems of rate-making for commercial buildings—the Dean analytic system,[13] and the Universal Mercantile Schedule (UMS). Under each system an arbitrary (basic) rate is assigned to a building of a certain type. Each building to be rated is subjected to a *schedule* of debits and credits from this arbitrary rate to determine the existence or absence of certain safety features. Hence, the term "schedule" arises. Under the Dean system, the debits are made in dollar amounts and credits are made in terms of percentages, while the UMS employs only dollar amounts. The debits and credits are more or less arbitrary and are not changed frequently. For example, a schedule may add five per cent to the basic premium for the absence of fire extinguishers, or certain fire walls in the building. Credits of 20 per cent or more may be allowed for an approved sprinkler system. The amount of charge or credit is not based on statistics but on engineering judgment as to how much a particular feature affects the probability of loss. The basic premiums or starting points are also more or less arbitrary. As its starting point, the Dean system might use a one-story brick building of average construction in a city with relatively poor fire protection. (Other tables used in the Dean system might employ a different starting point.) A basic rate of $1 per $100 may be assigned. This arbitrary rate is assumed to cover the unanalyzed hazards facing the building. The debits and credits to the basic rate are then computed and are intended to reflect those hazards which can be analyzed. Since the rate for such a building is assumed to be high, most of the schedule changes grant credits, according to how much better than this is the building being rated. Under the UMS, the starting point is a much higher class building and therefore there are more frequent uses of charges against the basic rate.

The basic rate and the debits and credits in both systems are affected by four major underwriting factors: 1) the fire protection class of the city of location, 2) the type of construction, 3) the class of occupancy of the building, and 4) the degree to which the building is exposed to losses originating *outside* the building confines.

---

[13] Named after its originator, A. F. Dean, who introduced it in 1901.

1) Fire protection class. The National Board of Fire Under-writers has established 10 classes of cities of more than 25,000 population, according to such factors as water supply, fire department, fire alarm systems, building laws, policy protection, and structural conditions in the city. A Class 10 city is one with very little fire protection and a Class 1 city has fewer than 500 deficiency points. Basic rates might vary from $1 per $100 of building value in Class 10 cities to about $.50 per $100 for Class 1 cities, depending on the height of the structure and its occupancy. Thus, a Class 2 city might receive fire rates approximately five per cent lower than a Class 3 city. Such a system obviously provides a loss-prevention incentive for the community as a whole.

2) Type of construction. There are four basic types of construction recognized in fire insurance rating: A, B, C, and D. A Class A building is one with walls, floors, and roof of masonry or concrete, and with all load walls supported by an independent steel frame. A Class B structure is similar to Class A except that interior walls and floors are not constructed of masonry or concrete. Class C is similar to Class B except that it does not meet all the specific requirements of Class B. For example, a Class C structure may have a frame structure on the roof, or it may have one or more exterior walls of hollow tile. Class D buildings are generally frame structures and include most private residences.

3) Class of occupancy. Occupancy is an important factor in schedule rating, since some tenants of commercial buildings, such as hat shops, lumberyards, and explosive manufacturers, obviously present a more serious fire hazard than hardware stores or grocery stores. Consideration is given to susceptibility of stock to loss, speed with which fire may spread, and other factors.

4) Exposure to losses outside the building. Exposure to other structures will affect the fire insurance rate on commercial buildings. For example, charges are made when other buildings are located too close to the building being rated.

Even though the main objectives of the fire insurance schedule rating systems may be to give incentives for loss prevention and to achieve fairness in rating by recognizing various types of fire hazards, the correctness of the systems cannot be defended statistically since the rating formulas are largely a matter of underwriting judgment.

One may ask, "Why are fire insurance rates not based on statistics, gathered for each type of building, to justify the rate charged?" The answer lies in the fact that because commercial structures are so different with respect to each of the four basic rating factors, it would be extremely difficult to gather credible data for each factor. In the entire country there may be a dozen Class B buildings, with a certain type of occupant, subject to a certain type of exposure, in a certain protection district, with the same set of fire protective devices. Since fires are relatively infrequent, many years must pass before a sufficient record of losses could be accumulated to lend credence to a rate so charged. By the time sufficient losses would have been recorded, the management, protection class, exposure, and even type of construction may have changed so much that an entirely different classification would have to be made. The rate-maker cannot wait for all this to happen, but must develop some type of rate presently, according to the best methods open to him. In other words, the rate-maker faced with exposures that are not homogeneous in nature would have to separate his exposures into so many groups that sufficient loss experience to develop a credible rate would be impossible to obtain for each group.

RATE-MAKING IN OTHER LINES OF INSURANCE

Fire insurance on residences

Manual rating on residences is justified on the grounds that the exposure units are fairly homogeneous in character and it is neither necessary nor practical to make an inspection of each building for particular fire hazards. Manual classifications are therefore made with the following rating factors: type of roof, nearness to fire hydrants, and type of fire protection district in which the residence is located. Generally, the rate for contents, both in residential and in commercial property, is higher than the rate applicable to the building because of their greater susceptibility to loss. This follows because total losses are relatively rare and oftentimes a majority of the damage is done to the contents instead of to the building itself.

Multiple-line rate-making

As we have seen earlier, a multiple-line policy, one covering many different types of perils under one contract, is mainly distinguished from other property liability contracts in that a separate rate is devised for a given class of insureds which is *indivisible*. In other words, the rate is not made up by adding together the separate rates applicable to each different peril, such as fire, windstorm, or explosion, but is promulgated on some other basis, generally according to payroll or sales. A year-end audit determines the final premium. Under this approach, known as *composite rating,* a single rate is promulgated for an entire group of exposures regardless of the location, type, special hazards in given areas, or other underwriting factors. Loss data are collected on an entirely different basis than the usual underwriting factors. Special rating organizations have been organized to collect loss data and to promulgate rates for the multiple-line contracts. Usually these plans involve experience rating.

In certain multiple-line contracts, such as homeowners policies, indivisible rates are made up for contracts which cover both liability and physical damage perils. Rate-making in multiple-line contracts generally is in an experimental stage and there is little agreement upon the methods which should ultimately be adopted.

Marine insurance

In marine insurance, both inland and ocean, underwriting judgment plays an even greater role than in commercial and residential insurance because of the great diversity of exposures. For example, because of changed conditions of weather, cargo, political conditions, nationality of the vessel, and other factors, the rate quoted for a given ocean voyage might be different for each trip. Two identical ships might be assigned a different rate depending on the type of operation in which each is engaged. In inland marine insurance, a given contractor's rate for an equipment floater will depend on the type of equipment used, record of losses, conditions under which the work is being done, etc. Past statistics are of little help in formulating insurance rates for such diverse exposures. The underwriter must exercise his best judgment as to the value of the risk and act accordingly.

Rate-making in life insurance

In life insurance the pure premium method is the basis of what is essentially manual rate-making. As has been seen, the pure premium is derived from tables of mortality which tell within narrow limits what the death costs will be. There are two basic factors that affect the pure premium—the costs of mortality and the interest rates earned by the insurer of funds deposited with it. These funds arise because of the practice of requiring payment in advance for life insurance protection, and because of the practice of issuing policies on a *level premium* basis. We shall see precisely how these two factors affect the calculation of the pure premium. Once the pure or net premium has been determined, a loading formula is applied and the final gross premium to the policyholder is determined. The following discussion will deal first with the calculation of the *pure* premium.

Net single premium.   The *net single premium* is the amount the insurer must collect in advance to meet all the claims arising during the policy period. To illustrate the general method of calculating the net single premium, we shall assume that a given insurer wishes to determine the premium for a one-year term insurance contract with a face amount of $1,000 for a group of entrants, age 20. Reference to the CSO 1958 table of mortality reveals that the probability of death at age 20 is .00179. This means that out of 100,000 persons living at the beginning of the year, 179 will die during the year. The rate-maker in life insurance makes two assumptions in calculating the necessary premium:

1. All premiums will be collected at the *beginning* of the year and hence it will be possible to earn interest on the advance payment for a full year.

2. Death claims are not paid until the *end* of the year in question. In practice, of course, death claims are paid whenever death occurs. Thus, the assumptions of the rate-maker are inaccurate, for on the average, one half of a year's interest will be lost on the sums so paid. However, an adjustment for this loss of interest is made in the loading formula, to be discussed later in the chapter.

Calculation of the premium under these assumptions is simplified since the insurer knows that if a $1,000 policy is issued to each of the 100,000 entrants, death claims of $179,000 will be payable at the end of the year. The problem then is one of *discounting* this sum for one year at some assumed rate of interest. Thus, if the insurer is to guarantee earnings of 2.5 per cent, $.9756 must be on hand now in order to have $1 at the end of one year.[14] Therefore, to find the present value of $179,-000 at the end of one year, this amount is multiplied by .9756, obtaining $174,632. The proportionate share of this obligation attaching to each entrant is $174,632/100,000, or $1.75. If each entrant pays $1.75, the insurer will have sufficient funds on hand to pay for death costs under the policy. The $1.75 is known as the *net single premium*.

The net single premium for a $1,000 term policy of, say, three years is calculated in a similar manner, except that the calculation is carried out over a three-year period instead of one. The following tabulation illustrates the method.

---

[14] The present value of $1 at the end of one year at rate of interest *i* may be found by using the formula $\frac{1}{1+i}$. The reader may easily verify this by multiplying the result $.9756 by 1.025, obtaining $1. To find the present value of $1 at the end of *n* years at rate of interest *i*, the general formula is $\frac{1}{(1+i)^n}$. Fortunately, tables are available which make arithmetic calculations for these amounts unnecessary.

NUMBER ASSUMED TO BE LIVING AT		NUMBER DYING	AMOUNT OF DEATH CLAIMS	PRESENT VALUE OF $1 AT $2\frac{1}{2}\%$ INTEREST	PRESENT VALUE OF DEATH CLAIM
Age 20	100,000	179	$179,000	.9756	$174,632
21	99,821	183	183,000	.9518	174,179
22	99,638	186	186,000	.9286	172,720
				Total	$521,531

$$\frac{\$521,531}{100,000} = \$5.22, \text{ Net single premium}$$

It will be observed that each person must pay *in advance* the sum of $5.22 for three years of protection.

While the above calculation is, of course, a very simple one, it serves to illustrate the basic method of premium calculation in life insurance. The net single premium for a whole life policy, for example, is figured in exactly the same manner as the example above, except that the calculations are made for each year from the starting age to the "end of the mortality table," instead of only for three years.

As another example, the net single premium for a 20-year endowment policy is developed in a manner similar to that above, but with two modifications: (1) the above calculations are carried out for each age from the starting age until the end of 20 years, and (2) provision is made for payment of the face amount of the policy, $1,000, to each person who survives the 20-year period. Thus, if out of the original 100,000 individuals entering the insured group, 90,000 are expected to be alive at the end of 20 years, the present value of $90 million payable in 20 years, or roughly $54 million must be collected in advance in order to meet this obligation. This amounts to $540 per person. Adding this to the amount needed per person for death claims gives the net single premium for the endowment policy.

Net level premium. It would be impractical to attempt to collect a net *single* premium from each member of an insured group. Few people would have the necessary funds for an advance payment of all future obligations. Therefore, actuaries must calculate an *annual* premium. At first consideration, it might be assumed that the annual premium would be found by dividing the net single premium by the number of years in the premium paying period. Such a calculation would produce a net annual premium of $1.74 (5.22/3) in the preceding example for a three-year term policy. However, such a calculation would be erroneous for two reasons: (1) Since the insurer will not have the entire amount of the net single premium on hand at the beginning of the period, it will not earn the amount of interest assumed in the calculation of the net single premium, and (2) The individuals who die will, of course, not be able to make their annual premium payments. In calculating the net single premium, it is assumed that each member of the insured group will contribute his share of total claims *at the beginning* of the policy period.

Actuaries find the net level premium by dividing the net single premium by an amount known technically as the *present value of an annuity due,* which provides for an appropriate adjustment of the two factors described above. The present value of an annuity due of $1 a year for three years is the present value of a series of payments of $1 each year, the first payment due immediately, adjusted for the probability of survival each year. The calculation may be shown as follows:

AGE	PRESENT VALUE OF $1, FIRST PAYMENT DUE IMMEDIATELY, AT $2\frac{1}{2}\%$ INTEREST	NUMBER OF ENTRANT GROUP STILL LIVING	DISCOUNTED VALUE OF EACH "PAYMENT"
20	$1.00	100,000	$100,000
21	.9756	99,821	97,385
22	.9518	99,638	94,835
		Total	$292,220

$$\frac{\$292,220}{100,000} = \$2.92, \text{ Value per entrant}$$

The present value of an annuity due may be interpreted as follows: What is the present value of a promise of a large group of people to pay a sum of $1 each year for three years? Since the first payment is due immediately (corresponding to the fact that life insurance premiums are collected in advance), its present value is $1. The second payment is due one year from now. If everyone lived to pay his share, the present value of the second payment would be $.9756. Since not everyone will live, however, the $.9756 must be reduced to reflect this fact. The amount is therefore reduced by a factor which specifies how many may be expected to live to pay their share (*i.e.,* the amount is multiplied by the probability of survival of the original group of entrants). This process is continued, and we find that the present value of the promise is $2.92. If this sum is divided into the present value of the total death claims (*i.e.,* the net single premium), the insurer knows how much he must collect annually from a specified group of insureds in order to have a sum which will enable him to pay all obligations. The net level premium for the three-year term policy is thus, $\dfrac{\$5.22}{\$2.92} = \$1.78$, which is of course, greater than the

quantity $\dfrac{\$5.22}{3} = \$1.74$, determined by a simple division of the net single premium by the premium paying period.

Gross annual premium. The net level premium for life insurance represents the "pure premium," which is unadjusted for the expenses of doing business. The pure premium is actually the contribution that each insured makes to the aggregate insurance fund each year for the payment of both death and living benefits. Various formulas are used to "load" the pure premiums to allow for the necessary expenses of the insurer. In general, an attempt is made to separate all costs into two categories: (1) fixed overhead cost per policy, representing a portion of those costs which continue regardless of the volume of business being conducted, and (2) variable cost per policy, reflecting those expenses made necessary by issuance of a particular contract. Variable costs are further subdivided into those which depend primarily on the amount of the premium per policy and those which depend on other factors, such as face amount, type of contract, and special underwriting considerations.

Examples of fixed overhead loading would be the proration of expenses such as home office clerical costs, executive salaries, rent, and other expenses which continue at the same rate regardless of current business volume. Each policy may be assigned a flat dollar amount as its pro rata share of these costs.

Examples of variable costs depending on the amount of premium per policy include agent's commissions, premium taxes, and loss of interest due to the fact that premiums are not always collected in full at the beginning of a policy year, but may be collected in installments. Acquisition costs are large by comparison with the annual premium, often amounting to more than the annual premium. To eliminate an extra charge in the first year, these costs are usually spread out over the premium paying period. A further loading factor must be added to offset the fact that due to lapses, a certain portion of these costs will not be collected.

Examples of variable costs depending on factors other than premium size, include the following:

1. The physician's medical examination fee.
2. Loss of interest due to the fact that death claims are paid immediately rather than at the end of the policy year.

3. Higher mortality costs resulting from the fact that certain types of contracts, especially those with a large term element, have an element of adverse selection. (Thus, those with term policies who suffer poor health are more likely to convert them to permanent contracts than those whose health remains sound.)
4. Additional costs of service since certain contracts require more service than others, *e.g.*, industrial insurance policies in which premiums are collected at the insured's residence.
5. Contingency costs. Life insurance contracts are written for long periods and are predicated on forecasts of mortality, interest, and loading factors, all of which may vary from those values on which the contract is based. Therefore, each contract is loaded to provide a margin for these fluctuations. In participating policies, any excess amounts are returned to the policyholders in the form of dividends.

Loading formulas which reflect these elements in the premium may sometimes be quite complicated in practice. Furthermore, there is little uniformity in specific methods of loading. For competitive reasons, a nonparticipating insurer must calculate its loading costs more carefully than a participating insurer, since there is no possibility for the former to return any excess collections through dividends. An insurer that is expanding its business rapidly will have a greater loading cost than one which is more or less "holding its own." These factors should be taken into consideration in any comparison of expense factors between different insurers. (See Chapter 6.)

Effect of other factors. In the discussion above, it was assumed that age is the only factor taken into consideration in determining the life insurance rate. In recent years, however, many insurers have taken into consideration other factors such as sex, policy amount, and general health status, in calculating their life insurance rates. For example, while it has been long known that women outlive men on an average of five or six years, still only a few insurers grant women a lower life insurance rate, although they universally charge them a higher rate for annuities. Among insurers granting a lower rate to women, the typical practice is to charge women the rate that applies to a man age three years younger.

As mentioned in Chapter 20, many insurers now offer "specials" at lower rates than standard, reflecting a variety of cost-reducing factors achieved through savings inherent in issuing larger policy amounts, by reduction of agent's commissions, or by inserting less liberal settlement options. The rates on these "specials" are usually accounted for in the loading formulas.

Most life insurers will accept an applicant with a medical or physical handicap at a "substandard" (higher) rate, depending on the nature of the handicap. Extra premiums for substandard physical risks are promulgated largely on the basis of underwriting judgment, supported by some statistical evidence on the longevity of these classes.

Soundness of life insurance rate-making. Life insurance rate-making is based to a large degree on statistical procedures and is quite "scientific" in nature, more scientific than the rate-making for many other types of insurance. However, once a life insurance premium is promulgated for a given insured, it is guaranteed to remain fixed during his life. In the case of whole life policies, the insurer must guarantee the same rate for a period which may range up to 100 years (in case of a policy issued on an infant). Under settlement options, the obligations of the insurer under a single contract may exceed this period. Therefore, it is common for life insurers to charge premiums that are loaded for contingencies and which may turn out to be excessive. For example, the mortality table itself contains a built-in "safety factor" since the actual death rates are overstated by a certain amount. Insurers guarantee only a minimum rate of interest which is almost invariably much lower than the amount they expect to earn on investments. If death rates are lower than those anticipated and if earnings are greater than those expected, the insurer has charged more than necessary. In the case of mutual insurers, dividends represent the return of the excessive premiums and may be looked upon as a method of achieving necessary adjustments in the premium rate as costs vary over the years. Stock insurers who issue non-participating policies attempt to meet the competition of mutuals by issuing a rate which is lower than the mutual rate by approximately the amount of the anticipated dividend.

Life insurance rate-making gives no specific recognition to the criterion of loss prevention, other than perhaps the suicide clause, since it is assumed that each insured already has a strong incentive to continue his life and no further stimulus is required. Of course, life insurers themselves are among the strongest supporters of campaigns to reduce death claims and to maintain health standards.

SUMMARY

1. The insurance premium is designed to cover two general types of costs: (a) the costs of loss claims under the contract, and (b) the costs of ad-

ministering the insurance mechanism. The former cost is usually referred to as the pure or net premium, while the total charge is called the gross premium.

2. Criteria for sound rate-making specify that a rate should be adequate, but not excessive, and should distinguish risks fairly according to the degree of hazard. These criteria are usually specified in state regulations, but there is no general agreement on just how the criteria shall be applied to each type of insurance. Additional criteria for sound rate-making are that rates should be kept current and they should, if possible, encourage loss-prevention efforts by the insured.

3. Rate-making in insurance is far from an exact science. Although statistics form the basis of many rate-making methods, in other instances it appears that the rates are more or less arbitrarily or subjectively determined. In all cases, underwriting judgment plays an important part in determining the final rate.

4. There are two basic types of rates: the manual or class rate, and the individual or merit rate. For the manual rate, it is assumed that homogeneous classes of insureds can be distinguished and each risk in the group is charged the same premium, representing its fair share of the total losses. For the merit rate, it is assumed that individual risks are sufficiently different that recognition can be given to particular hazards attaching to each risk.

5. A concept of great importance in rate-making is credibility, the degree to which the observed loss experience can be relied upon in formulating or revising a rate. Merit rating plans are based on this concept, which in turn rests upon the basic assumptions of the law of large numbers.

6. Individual or merit rating plans are of four general types: (a) those where special recognition is given to particular *subclasses* of insureds beforehand in the form of manual rate deviations or afterward in the form of dividends for meritorious loss experience. An individual insured is entitled to the special rate only if he meets certain qualifications not met by the general class to which he belongs. (b) those plans using *schedule* rating, where the particular hazards of an insured's operation are recognized by special charges or credits from some base rate. (c) those plans involving *experience* rating. (d) those plans involving *retrospective* rating.

7. Experience rating affects the individual rate of an insured *after* his actual loss experience in a given period has been analyzed. The revisions, if any, affect his *future* premium rate. Retrospective rating allows the insured to determine his premium, in whole or in part, for the period under consideration; *i.e.,* the final premium for a period is determined by the loss experience of that period. Both of these plans have in common the objectives of achieving a rate that is fair, adequate, not excessive, and flexible, and of rewarding for loss-prevention efforts. Unfortunately, the plans cannot be applied to all insured groups, but only to those meeting the general qualification that the losses are relatively frequent, the num-

ber of exposure units is sufficient to achieve some degree of credibility, and the insured has some control over his losses, such as in workmen's compensation and unemployment insurance.

8. Rate-making in fire insurance for commercial buildings is perhaps the best known example of schedule rating. The particular fire hazards of each structure are analyzed and a listing, or a schedule, of charges and credits is applied to an arbitrarily determined base rate. There is little or no statistical basis for the particular schedule of charges or credits used, and so it is a mute question of whether fire insurance rates on commercial property are really "fair." The schedule system does give a financial incentive for adoption of loss-prevention measures, and the criteria of adequacy and reasonableness of the rate can be met by adjustments in the general level of premiums collected.

9. Rate-making in life insurance is among the more "scientific" applications of rate-making in insurance. A pure premium is determined by reference to a table of mortality and a consideration of minimum assumed interest rates. The gross premium is determined by application of somewhat refined loading formulas that represent the costs of doing business. Since life insurers usually earn more than the minimum interest rate and since mortality tables are conservative and are revised only periodically, the life insurance rate is made to meet the criteria of adequacy and reasonableness by means of dividends, in the case of mutual insurers, and by competition, in the case of nondividend-paying insurers.

QUESTIONS FOR REVIEW AND DISCUSSION

1. (a) What is the main distinction between a *rate* and a *premium?*
   (b) In this connection, why is reference usually made to a retrospective *premium* rather than to a retrospective *rate?*

2. Judgment in insurance rate-making enters in at least two major respects. It is common to mention the role of judgment in arriving at rates on new coverages or unique exposures where no adequate statistics are present. What is the second way in which judgment affects rate-making? Discuss.

3. A certain insurer announced a plan under which automobile liability insurance would become guaranteed renewable for a period of five years assuming certain conditions were met. (It is the usual practice for an insurer to reserve the right to cancel automobile insurance upon 10 days' notice.) The renewal rate is not guaranteed, but may be altered to reflect changed costs. Reasoning from the practices of insurers who typically grant noncancelable insurance in other lines (for example, life insurance) estimate the logical effect which this new provision may have on the rate for the contract. Suggest reasons for introduction of this new provision and why the practice is not widespread.

4. A witness at a Senate hearing on insurance stated, "An insurance rate is the price charged for insurance. The price should bring enough money into the insurer's pockets so that the insurer will be able to pay claims

when and as claims are made. That principle is the law and the prophet; all else is commentary. Everything else . . . must take second place to this elementary point that if the insurer does not get enough money to pay claims as they mature, then he is not an insurer but a fraud."

(a) Which of the criteria for sound rate-making is this person emphasizing?

(b) Do you agree that this criterion is of greater importance than any other?

(c) What fundamental characteristic of insurance rate-making differentiates it from pricing in other lines? Does this characteristic explain the emphasis in the above comments? How?

5. Many insureds cannot see why the administration of the insurance mechanism should be so expensive. We have seen that in some cases a group of insureds will form their own insurance company in order to reduce the cost coverage, particularly their expenses. This is the basic motivation for the reciprocal form of organization. Even in this form of organization, however, the attorney-in-fact is usually paid a management fee of approximately 35 per cent of the premiums. What other characteristics of a reciprocal suggest that the savings achieved are not so large as many believe? (See Chapter 5 for a discussion of reciprocals.)

6. An actuary stated, "A dependable pure premium is one for which the probability is high (at least equal to an assigned value), that is, does not differ from the absolute (true) pure premium by more than an arbitrary limit which may be selected in view of the other factors referred to."

(a) Explain, with an example, the meaning of this statement.

(b) The following represents a table of credibility for automobile liability rate revisions. Assume that, based on 510 claims in a given territory during the previous year, an insurer has experienced losses of $500,-000 on a premium volume of $933,334. His rates were based, however, on an expected loss ratio of 50 per cent. By how much will the rate-maker increase rates in the coming year?

NUMBER OF CLAIMS	CREDIBILITY
0– 10	0
11– 42	.10
43– 97	.20
98–172	.30
173–270	.40
271–389	.50
390–530	.60
531–693	.70
694–877	.80
878–1083	.90
1084 and over	1.00

(c) How would your answer be changed if the loss experience had been based on 785 claims? on 1,100 claims?

(d) How do you account for the fact that when the number of exposures increased from 510 to 785, an increase of 55 per cent, the credibility attached to this increased exposure rose from .6 to .8, or only 25 per cent?

7. In the field of credit insurance a critic charged that under the experience rating system used, if an insured has a large loss in a given year, his premium is immediately increased in the following year. The result is that he "pays for his own losses" in the higher premiums that are charged. The conclusion is reached, therefore, that if an insured must pay for his own losses in any event, the insurance contract is of little value, except perhaps as a device to smooth out fluctuations in bad debt loss experience. Criticize the above conclusions.

8. "Z" notices in the paper a report that national fire losses are 10 per cent above the previous year's level. He asks your advice as to whether he can expect fire insurance rates to rise correspondingly in his area on a commercial building he owns. What would you tell him?

9. A financial publication reported, "For most people, insurance is second only to the car itself among the costs of owning an automobile. . . . Yet the cost of auto liability insurance, which has been climbing steadily . . . seems sure to go higher still . . . and many motorists will find it increasingly difficult to buy insurance at all . . . for 1957 underwriting losses probably will total some $300 million. . . . The size of the coming rate increases will vary widely from area to area."

(a) What factors are likely to be dominant explanations of the increase in automobile rates?

(b) What general method of rate-making is used in automobile insurance, as suggested by the reference to area differences?

10. In a press release an executive of a large insurer stated, "Labor leaders and a few members of the legislature have stated that insurance companies receive annually $70 million in workmen's compensation premiums in Massachusetts and pay only $31 million to injured workers. These statements are misleading and an explanation is offered to correct them." The attached exhibit of explanation, covering the calendar year ending June 30, 1959, was as follows:

Earned standard premium	$67,942,657	
Less: Premium discounts	4,008,616	
New premium collected	63,934,041	
Less: Dividends	5,082,103	
Net cost to policyholders	58,851,938	100%
Less: Losses and loss-adjustment expense	46,428,064	78.9
Taxes on premiums	1,471,299	2.5
Commissions	4,505,872	7.6
Balance for expenses	6,446,703	11.0
Less: Company expenses	7,593,407	12.9
Net underwriting loss	$ 1,146,704	1.9

(a) What was the apparent implication of the labor leaders whose statement was quoted? Does the exhibit support this view?

(b) How could the data have been presented to make the insurer's loss look smaller? The return to workers smaller? Would such a presentation be as legitimate as the one given? Why?

(c) Does the exhibit support, in your opinion, a case for higher workmen's compensation rates in the state? Lower rates? Why?

(d) In view of the losses reported, how could the insurers afford to pay dividends?

11. Why is cooperation among insurers regarding certain rate-making procedures looked upon as desirable and even essential when there are strict prohibitions against collusion in price-fixing among sellers of tangible commodities? Explain.

12. Following the San Francisco earthquake of 1906, many insurers failed to liquidate all their claims and went into insolvency. Suggest a fundamental rule of rate-making which may have been violated by those insurers.

13. It has been suggested that the practice of rating automobiles on the basis of the number of exposed vehicles introduces an element of unfairness into automobile rating structures. The claim is that one car may be driven by several drivers and another car may be driven only by one driver. Yet both cars would be assigned the same rate, other things being equal. In your opinion is there any justification in this argument? Comment.

14. In life insurance rate-making, a critic stated, "Life insurance has deliberately been made complicated, confusing and unintelligible so that you pay blindly, faithfully, and uncomplainingly whatever excess premiums you may have signed up for. . . . Assuming the 1955 rate of actual earnings is 3.51 per cent, the companies which used 2.5 per cent in calculating reserves are picking up net earnings of 1 per cent on each and every dollar entrusted to them." Criticize this argument, considering the case of both mutual and stock insurers.

15. You are given certain data (simplified) below:

Age	Number Living	Number Dying	Present Value of $1 at 2 Per Cent	
			Year	Factor
25	1,000	10	1	.98
26	990	12	2	.96
27	878	13	3	.94

(a) Calculate the net single premium for a two-year term insurance policy of $1,000 issued at age 25.

(b) Calculate the net level premium for the same policy.

(c) What premium will the insured actually pay?

(d) Why cannot the net level premium for the policy be properly computed by dividing the net single premium by two? Explain.

16. State what modifications you would make in the calculations in Problem 15 if the problem were to find the answer for (a) a whole life policy, and (b) a 30-year endowment policy.

17. Using the following fictitious data, calculate the net single premium and the net level premium at age 110, at 3 per cent interest, for a face amount of $1,000 for: (a) an ordinary life policy, (b) a three-year pay whole life policy, and (c) a two-year endowment policy. (d) Does your answer suggest why life insurance is seldom purchased by the aged?

AGE	NUMBER LIVING	NUMBER DYING	NUMBER OF YEARS	DISCOUNT FACTOR
110	50	10	1	.97
111	40	10	2	.94
112	30	10	3	.92
113	20	15	4	.88
114	5	15	5	.85
115	0	...	...	...

18. In life insurance the probability of death per 1,000 persons born was such that 25 per cent of the group would die by age 5 in 1850, by age 25 in 1901, by age 48 in 1930, and by age 63 in 1959. This remarkable decline in mortality over the last 110 years has not been accompanied by proportionate decreases in life insurance premiums. For example, an advertisement by Mutual Life of New York in the *Boston Daily Advertiser* dated February 28, 1843, quoted insurance rates "for life" for a person age 35 as $27.60 annually. Seven-year term insurance for age 35 was quoted at $15.30 and one-year term insurance at $13.60. Today term insurance rates are about one half those levels, and ordinary life rates only four fifths of those quoted. Suggest possible reasons why rates are not even lower today in spite of the great decline in mortality rates.

19. An insurer initiated a merit rating plan in automobile insurance in 1953 with the following schedule of discounts:

		LOSS RATIO, EACH GROUP 1955–1958
New applicants pay	Basic rate	74
After 1 claim-free year	5% discount	59
" 2 " " "	10% "	53
" 3 " " "	15% "	44
" 4 " " "	20% "	43
" 5 " " "	25% "	36

After the plan had been in effect for a few years, the loss ratios for each class were found to be as shown in the third column above. If an insured had an accident, he was moved back to the beginning and had to pay the basic rate again. Each successive year without an accident reduced the renewal rate by five per cent to a maximum of 25 per cent off the base rate. The plan did not apply to medical payments or to comprehensive coverage.

(a) In your opinion does the experience of this insurer demonstrate that a merit rating plan reduces the loss frequency? Why or why not?

(b) Observing that the loss ratio of the group with five claim-free years is one half that of a new applicant group, suggest probable reasons why the discount is not correspondingly large.

(c) What advantage does this plan have over the safe driver plan used in several states?

20. Concerning unemployment insurance a writer stated, "Experience rating may in part tend to be self-defeating. Employers, in attempting to secure more favorable tax rates, are likely to engage in a variety of practices (some ethically defensible, others not so) that may increase employment stability for a small core of employees, but which will greatly increase the instability for another group." Explain how this might be possible.

21. What is the basic distinction between experience rating and retrospective rating? What is the basic similarity?

22. Employer "X" and his insurer agree to retrospective rating for the workmen's compensation risk, but "X" is undecided as to which of the two plans, A or B, is better. "X's" standard premium would be $10,000 if no plan were selected. "X" is inclined to believe that due to an unusually effective effort of his safety engineer in operating a loss-prevention campaign in his plant, his loss record will be very low. Advise "X," pointing out the advantages and disadvantages of your recommendation.

23. It has been argued that retrospective rating eliminates the need for self-insurance in the lines of insurance where it is used. Do you agree? Why?

24. (a) What are the chief factors affecting the fire insurance rate in commercial structures?

(b) Are the rating systems that reflect these factors based on statistics? Why or why not?

25. A representative of a rate-making organization stated, "Competition for business, inadequate rates, refined classification systems, merit rating plans, variation in policy forms, increases in the number of assigned risks, inadequate premiums for assigned risks, politics in the automobile field and a near breakdown of cooperative rate-making are all interrelated. . . . . The experience base for rate-making becomes less reliable as variations in policy forms increase. Combination of experience becomes more and more difficult and less and less meaningful as classification systems multiply. . . . With the trend toward independent filings, optional bureau programs . . . stability in the automobile rate field becomes more and more difficult."

   (a) In what way are the factors mentioned in the first sentence of this statement interrelated? Explain.

   (b) Explain the reasons behind the author's conclusions that stability in automobile rate-making is becoming more and more difficult.

26. An actuary stated that rate-makers should give more weight to the frequent occurrence of small losses rather than to the less frequent occurrence of larger losses, even though in both cases the total amount of the loss is the same. Why should this be true? Explain.

27. A few insurers still issue what are known as perpetual fire insurance policies, whereby one "single premium" covers a building for its entire life. For example, to cover a $20,000 house, a premium of $800 might be charged. If the insured wishes to cancel the policy, his entire deposit is returned.

   (a) In what respect is such a policy similar to single premium life insurance? Dissimilar?

   (b) Would you expect this type of rate-making system to be popular? Why or why not?

28. In California the law defines an "excessive" and "inadequate" insurance rate as follows:

> "No rate shall be held to be excessive unless (1) such rate is unreasonably high for the insurance provided *and* (2) a reasonable degree of competition does not exist in the area with respect to the classification to which such rate is applicable.
>
> "No rate shall be held to be inadequate unless (1) such rate is unreasonably low for the insurance provided *and* (2) the continued use of such rate endangers the solvency of the insurer using the same, *or* unless (3) such a rate is unreasonably low for the insurance provided and the use of such rate by the insurer using same has, or if continued will have, the effect of destroying competition or creating a monopoly."

   (a) With respect to the definition of an excessive rate, suggest a condition which might lead to the existence of a rate for insurance in California which is higher than that which would be obtained in states which do not have this definition of "excessive."

   (b) With respect to the definition of an inadequate rate, suggest a condition under which the rate for insurance might be lower in California than that which would be permitted in other states with different criteria for inadequacy.

29. In announcing a new policy of life insurance to be issued to any person under 97 (premium rate, $363.33 issued at age 90, and $771.87 issued at age 96) the president of the company was quoted as saying, "We've smashed the age barriers. . . . We feel there is a proper premium rate which will make almost every person insurable, regardless of health or occupation." Do you anticipate that many insurers will follow the example set above? Why or why not?

Reserves and the

Financial Statement

There are several features of financial statements of insurance companies which require special interpretation and explanation. Of special importance are the reserves, or liabilities, of insurers. These reserves may be calculated in several different ways and the final result depends on what methods are used and the particular problems involved. The size of the estimates for reserves is a vital element in assessing the degree of financial security given to the insured. Also, an understanding of how the reserves are developed is necessary before an intelligent judgment can be made as to the "net worth" of the insurer, from the viewpoint of the investor or insurer management. The relative size of reserves is a reflection of the adequacy or inadequacy of past rate-making practices, and so a careful analysis of how reserves are developed throws light on this question.

In Chapter 6 we discussed a general approach to the analysis of financial statements of insurers, under the assumption that the amounts on a financial statement could be accepted as given. As we shall see, this assumption is not always justified and the results of our financial statement analysis must sometimes be modified.

THE BALANCE SHEET

The balance sheet of an insurance company has a purpose similar to the balance sheet of any other corporation, namely to reveal a picture of the financial standing of the corporation at a given point in time. This balance sheet shows what the chief assets are and who owns them, the liabilities, and the net worth. As we have observed in Chapters 6 and 25, the assets of an insurance corporation are made up primarily of marketable stocks and bonds, the composition and nature of which are carefully regulated by law. The liabilities of an insurer are somewhat different than the typical liabilities found on the balance sheet of an industrial corporation. First, there is seldom any long-term debt on an insurer's balance sheet. The reason for this is that there is seldom any reason to float a long-term debt since the insurer has no great need for tangible assets. Second, most of the liabilities are estimated and appear as "reserves" instead of "accounts payable" as is true on the balance sheet of an industrial corporation. It will become clear later why insurers show their liabilities in this manner.

We shall devote our major attention to the nature of an insurer's liabilities and its net worth. Table 27–1 shows the balance sheets of two

Table 27–1

BALANCE SHEETS OF TWO PROPERTY LIABILITY INSURERS

	Insurer A * (Millions of Dollars)	Insurer B † (Millions of Dollars)
Assets:		
Bonds (amortized value).....................	$ 5.5	$11.8
Stocks......................................	6.4	8.2
Cash, premium balances, etc.................	1.8	3.6
	$13.7	$23.6
Liabilities and surplus:		
Loss reserve.............................	.9	10.2
Unearned premium reserve..................	6.7	6.4
Miscellaneous liabilities....................	.4	.5
Total liabilities...........................	$ 8.0	$17.1
Paid-up capital.............................	1.0	1.0
Policyholders' surplus......................	4.7	5.5
	$13.7	$23.6

* Insurer A is a stock company writing primarily fire and extended coverage insurance.
† Insurer B is a stock company writing no fire insurance, but distributing its business among workmen's compensation, automobile and general liability insurance, and boiler and machinery insurance.

small stock insurers: Insurer A, writing primarily fire and allied lines, and Insurer B, whose business is largely workmen's compensation and liability insurance. What is the capital structure of these insurers, and what accounts for the differences observed? By *capital structure* is meant the composition of liabilities and net worth, that is, in what manner the corporation has raised its funds. A corporation's liabilities may be looked upon as a description of the manner and extent to which creditors of various types have loaned money to the firm. Liabilities, then, are a source of funds, in the same manner that stockholders' contributions, capital, and surplus are a source of funds for the insurance firm.

Insurer A's capital structure may be described as follows: creditors have furnished $8 million of the firm's assets, and stockholders, the balance of $5.7 million. For each dollar of assets contributed by stockholders, creditors (who are policyholders) have furnished $1.40. In Insurer B, for each dollar of assets contributed by stockholders, the policyholders have contributed approximately $2.60. The question arises, what accounts for these relationships? What set of conditions operated to create these particular results? What are the financial problems involved? What are the various factors affecting an insurer's surplus? Is it desirable for an insurer to have as large a surplus as possible? These and other questions are discussed below.

Capital and surplus

The capital of the insurance firm is represented by two items, capital stock and surplus. *Capital stock* represents the value of the original contributions of stockholders, and *surplus* represents a combination of both the original paid-in capital and the accumulated profits. On the balance sheet of an insurer, the surplus is commonly called "policyholders' surplus" instead of stockholders' surplus, which it really is. The surplus, representing the claims of stockholders on existing assets, is a cushion against the decline in value of assets for the protection of creditors, which in the case of an insurance company, are policyholders.

Types of reserves

The reserve is the major type of liability on the balance sheet of an insurer. Oftentimes a reserve is referred to as though it were a fund of some sort, out of which policyholders or others can be paid. Of course, the reserve is not a fund, but is a name describing the ownership of assets.

The two main types of reserves are loss reserves and unearned premium reserves. The *loss reserve* is set up to estimate losses, loss adjustment expenses, and other related items. Since oftentimes the exact losses are not known at the time the balance sheet is prepared, the insurer sets up a "reserve" or an estimate designed to approximate the eventual liability which the insurer has or will have. The *unearned premium reserve,* on the other hand, arises because policyholders pay for insurance in advance. These collections, which are returnable to the policyholder in whole or in part in the event of cancellation of the contract, must be closely accounted for and give rise to the liability to policyholders, which is called the unearned premium reserve.

In Table 27–1, the loss reserves are relatively small for Insurer A but relatively large for Insurer B. The unearned premium reserve is by far the most important liability of Insurer A, and is an important liability of Insurer B. One of the reasons for this lies in the nature of business done by each insurer. In Insurer A, when a fire or a windstorm strikes, the loss can usually be quickly determined and paid. Therefore, there is little need to carry a large reserve to earmark assets for the payment of future claims. Perhaps the chief need for a loss reserve is to estimate the liabilities on losses which have occurred but are unpaid because the loss happened just before the insurer prepared its balance sheet.

On the other hand, the unearned premium reserve is generally large in a fire insurer because of the practice of writing business for a three- or a five-year term. The advance premium is relatively large and a reserve must be set up showing this liability to policyholders, who, as we have seen, have a right to cancel their insurance and obtain a return of premium if desired.

In Insurer B the situation is reversed. Loss reserves are relatively large because in liability and workmen's compensation insurance, it is usually impossible to determine the extent of loss immediately following an accident which gives rise to the claim. A liability suit may be "hanging fire" for months or even years. In workmen's compensation the insurer may be required to set aside a large fund to pay a lifetime pension to an injured workman. On the other hand, unearned premium reserves are considerably lower than loss reserves because in casualty lines it is not common for the policyholder to pay premiums for more than one year in advance. Sometimes premiums are not paid in advance at all, but are paid monthly, or six months in advance. In workmen's compensation insurance, it is common to require a relatively small deposit premium, with the final premium liability determined by audit of the insured's payroll at the end of the year. For these reasons, the unearned premium reserve in Insurer B is smaller than the loss reserve.

PROBLEMS ARISING FROM THE UNEARNED PREMIUM RESERVE

It would appear entirely equitable to require an insurer to set up a liability for advance premium payments by its policyholders in the form of an unearned premium reserve. However, there are many important financial problems caused by the manner in which this is done. To obtain an insight into these problems, let us take a simple series of accounting transactions to illustrate how the unearned premium reserve arises, and the financial effects of these transactions.

Transaction 1

On January 1 the ABC Insurance Company is authorized under its state law to begin business as an underwriter of fire and allied lines. Its initial capital is $100,000 and its "surplus" is $50,000. The $150,000 capital and surplus was obtained by selling 1,000 shares of $100 par value common stock at $150. The reason for selling stock "at a premium" will become apparent later. Ignoring any investment in office equipment, organization expenses, and the like, the balance sheet at the start of business would appear as:

ABC INSURANCE COMPANY
BALANCE SHEET
JANUARY 1, 19—

ASSETS		LIABILITIES AND SURPLUS	
Cash......................	$150,000	Capital stock...............	$100,000
		Surplus....................	50,000
		Reserves....................	–0–
Total assets...............	$150,000	Total liabilities & surplus.....	$150,000

Transaction 2

During the first month of business, local agents submit 400 three-year term fire insurance policies on residences for a total premium of $30,000. This $30,000 represents advance payment by policyholders for fire insurance protection during the coming three-year period. The law requires the insurer to set up a reserve for unearned premiums, representing the liability to policyholders. Before any expenses are paid, the balance sheet appears as follows:

ABC INSURANCE COMPANY
BALANCE SHEET
JANUARY 31, 19—

ASSETS		LIABILITIES AND SURPLUS	
Cash...........................	$150,000	Unearned premium reserve........	$ 30,000
Cash collections................	30,000	Capital stock....................	100,000
		Surplus.........................	50,000
Total assets....................	$180,000	Total liabilities & surplus........	$180,000

Transaction 3

Insurance companies, in contrast to most other business firms, are required to keep their accounts on a cash basis, instead of on an accrual basis. In other words, all the expenses in connection with issuing a policy are written off at the time the advance premium is collected instead of being pro rated over the life of the policy. The expenses in the case on the preceding page might be as follows:

Agents' commissions (25 per cent) ......$ 7,500
Premium taxes (2.5 per cent) 750
Miscellaneous (15 per cent) 4,500
     Total (42.5 per cent) $12,750

After paying these expenses, the balance sheet appears as:

ABC Insurance Company
Balance Sheet
February 1, 19—

Assets		Liabilities and Surplus	
Cash.............................$167,250		Unearned premium reserve........$ 30,000	
		Capital stock.................... 100,000	
		Surplus......................... 37,250	
Total assets $167,250		Total liabilities & surplus.........$167,250	

Payment of the expenses reduced cash and surplus by $12,750. None of this amount may be paid from the assets represented by the unearned premium reserve. In other words, our new insurer must have a surplus to begin with or it would not be allowed to write any business. (This explains why the initial stock was sold at a premium of $50 per share.) This fact is of vital importance in understanding the balance sheet of an insurer and cannot be overemphasized. The amount of the surplus determines the ability of the insurer to expand its business and, in effect, is a measure of its *underwriting capacity.*

The unearned premium reserve is sometimes called the *reinsurance reserve.* This name arises because if our insurer had decided to go out of business as of February 1 and to request some other insurer to assume the liabilities in connection with the fire insurance on the books, the reinsurer would demand a payment about equal to the unearned premium reserve, less an allowance for the expenses already paid. On the assumption that the $12,750 of first-year expenses represents approximately 95 per cent of all expenses which will be paid under the policies during their three-year life, the reinsurer knows that if it collects about $18,750, it will have enough funds to pay any remaining expenses which might be incurred, plus expected losses and profits, as follows:

Remaining expenses (5 per cent) ......$ 1,500
Expected losses (52.5 per cent) 15,750
Profit (5 per cent) 1,500
                                        $18,750

The implication of all this is that because of the cash basis of accounting, there is a hidden "equity" in the unearned premium reserve, represented approximately by the advance payment of expenses on insurance premiums. This "equity" is normally recovered as the policies run their term. In the case on page 758, the amount "borrowed" from surplus to pay these expenses was $12,750. We saw that a reinsurer might be willing to assume all the liabilities under the policies for a payment of $18,750. This leaves $11,250 for the ABC company and, in effect, allows it to recover all but $1,500 of its outlay in putting the business on the books. This sum, $11,250, actually belongs to the insurer's stockholders, thus explaining the use of the term "equity in the unearned premium reserve."

For fire insurers the equity in the increase in the unearned premium reserve from year to year is often approximated at 40 per cent. For various lines of property liability insurance, this estimate varies, depending on the size of the advance premium payment and upon the advance expenses. The larger the advance premium payment and expense allowance, the larger the equity in the unearned premium reserve. A figure of 35 per cent is often used to estimate this equity for property liability insurers.

Recovery of the equity in the unearned premium reserve

The equity in the unearned premium reserve may be recovered through reinsurance, as explained above. More usually, however, it is returned to surplus gradually as the policies run their term. Continuing with the preceding case a bit further, assume that one year has passed and the ABC Insurance Company submits a balance sheet as of December 31. Assume also that no other insurance business has been transacted, and that losses have been exactly as planned for in the premium structure, 52.5 per cent, or $5,250. (The premiums for the first year would be $10,000 since the $30,000 represented three-year term policies). Assume that no further expenses have been incurred. The cash account is reduced by $5,250, the loss payments. Since one third of the time has elapsed, the insurer is permitted to reduce the unearned premium reserve by one third of its initial amount; that is, the insurer is allowed to recognize one third of its advance collections as being earned. Thus, $10,000 is transferred from the unearned premium reserve to surplus. Surplus, in turn, is reduced by $5,250, representing the loss payments. The balance sheet would then appear as shown at the top of the following page.

ABC Insurance Company
Balance Sheet
December 31, 19— (end of first year)

Assets		Liabilities and Surplus	
Cash............................	$162,000	Unearned premium reserve........	$ 20,000
		Capital stock....................	100,000
		Surplus.........................	42,000
Total assets....................	$162,000	Total liabilities & surplus........	$162,000

By comparing the December 31 balance sheet with that of February 1, one can observe that there has been only one change in the cash account, that of reducing it by the amount of the loss payments. The unearned premium reserve is two thirds of its former level and the surplus *has increased* by the net difference between the reduction in the unearned premium reserve and the loss payments. Part of the equity in the unearned premium reserve has been "recovered."

What happens now to the company's financial position during the second year of operation? For simplification, let us assume that no further insurance is sold and again the losses are exactly as planned. The identical change that we noted above occurs. Cash is reduced by $5,250, and surplus is increased by $10,000 minus $5,250, or $4,750. The same thing happens again in the third year. At the end of the third year, the unearned premium reserve has been completely eliminated because the insurer has no further liability, the contracts having run their full term. The balance sheet then appears:

ABC Insurance Company
Balance Sheet
December 31, 19— (end of third year)

Assets		Liabilities and Surplus	
Cash............................	$151,500	Unearned premium reserve........	–0–
		Capital.........................	$100,000
		Surplus.........................	51,500
Total assets....................	$151,500	Total liabilities & surplus........	$151,500

We may summarize the results of the insurer's operations in the three years as follows:

Premiums collected $30,000
Less:
      Losses (52.5 per cent) $15,750
      Expenses (42.5 per cent) [1] 12,750   28,500
Profit (5 per cent) .... $ 1,500

[1] Assuming that there were no further general expenses incurred.

As we expect, the insurer's balance sheet at the end of the period, under the simplified assumptions made, ends with cash and surplus increased by a net amount of $1,500, the planned profit. In the meantime, however, surplus has fallen as low as $37,250. Without an initial surplus, the insurer would never have been able to accept the business offered it by its agents, since under legal requirements it would have started out with a deficit and would have been legally insolvent. This result stems from the cash basis of accounting. The cash basis of accounting, in turn, stems from the desire of public regulatory authorities to provide protection for the advance premiums of the insuring public.

We are in a position now to appreciate the reason why a rapidly growing young insurance company often has the appearance of losing money, in comparison to the older, more mature company. Observe, for example, the results of the first year of the ABC Insurance Company. At the end of the first year on December 31, the income statement would be reported to the insurance commissioner as follows:

Premiums written		$30,000
Increase in the unearned premium reserve		20,000
Premiums earned		$10,000
Less: Losses	$ 5,250	
Expenses	12,750	18,000
Statutory underwriting loss		$ 8,000

Although the insurer has had exactly the experience which was anticipated in the rating structure, it shows a "loss" because of the way of keeping books required by law. Hence, the underwriting results reported to the insurance commissioner are known as a *statutory* underwriting profit or loss to distinguish them from the real underwriting results. To obtain the actual underwriting results, the statutory underwriting loss must be adjusted by adding back the equity in the net increase of the unearned premium reserve in the first year of $20,000. In the case above, this equity amounted to 42.5 per cent of $20,000 or $8,500. Thus, the real underwriting results produce a profit of $500, which is five per cent of earned premiums, as expected.

Once an insurer reaches a point where its business is stabilized (it no longer is increasing its new premium writings), the recoveries from unearned premium reserves of past business will offset new requirements imposed by new business. The statutory underwriting profit will, assuming that loss experience has been as predicted, be equal to the anticipated underwriting profit. There will be no net increase in the unearned premium reserve and hence no necessity of adjusting profit for this factor. By similar reasoning, it follows that if an insurer is reducing its premium volume and hence its unearned premium volume by some absolute amount, it will show a statutory underwriting profit which is *greater* than its true underwriting profit in the period under consideration.

Unless the above considerations are understood, it is likely that the analyst would interpret the financial results of an insurer in exactly the opposite manner that he should. He would suppose that the new rapidly growing insurer is destined for bankruptcy because of statutory underwriting losses, and would erroneously conclude that the insurer which had reduced its business and had a rising statutory underwriting profit is the "healthier" of the two.

Financial effects of the unearned premium reserve

The important financial conclusion to draw from the analysis above is that because the unearned premium reserve is redundant, an artificial restriction on insurance underwriting capacity is introduced. The unearned premium reserve is redundant for several reasons, two of the most obvious of which are: (1) Not all the amounts required to be set aside are actually paid out irrevocably. Agents' commissions on the unearned part of a premium must be returned if a policy is canceled. Thus, if an insurer collects $100 in advance premiums and pays an agent $25 and the policy is canceled by the insurer after the contract has run half its course, the agent must return $12.50 of this amount. This sum becomes available to the insurer to be returned to the policyholder. (2) If the insured cancels his policy, he does not receive a full pro rata return, but a short-rate return. In the case above, the insured who canceled after the contract had run half its term would receive not $50, but closer to $40 in return of premium. Yet the unearned premium reserve requirement would be $50. Thus, in extremely few cases would the entire premium reserve be necessary if all policyholders canceled their policies and demanded a return of premium.

Because of the necessity of drawing on surplus to meet unearned premium reserve requirements and because the size of surplus is not an unlimited quantity, there is an artificial restriction on the ability of the insurer to accept new business, that is, on the insurance underwriting capacity. This is particularly true of the small and growing insurer. It is precisely among such insurers that new equity funds might be attracted into the insurance field. With the limitation on growth imposed by unearned premium reserve requirements, the anticipated profit to potential investors in insurance is necessarily limited too. As a result, there has been a problem of attracting sufficient new equity capital to insurance in the market. Another result is that underwriting tends to become unduly strict during certain periods.

Evidence of the limitation of capacity is seen in the ability of alien insurers, such Lloyds of London, to write substantial volumes of business which is considered "too risky" for American underwriters. Another evidence of this phenomenon is the attractiveness of self-insurance to certain large firms, who are unable to obtain commercial insurance on terms sufficiently liberal. Other evidence is the difficulty in securing insurance on certain types of risks, such as nuclear hazards, foreign operations, and earthquakes and floods. It has been urged that at least some relief could be obtained from lack of insurance capacity by allowing property and liability insurers to maintain reserves on an accrual basis instead of on a cash basis, as is done in life insurance. So far nothing has come from these arguments. Another cause of the lack of underwriting capacity stems from the somewhat dismal record of profits in the stock insurance industry. This point will be examined later in the chapter.

Calculation of unearned premium reserves

In actual practice, an insurer does not keep separate records of required unearned premium reserves on every policy written, but uses some sort of an averaging process to obtain a reasonable estimate. Under the half-year method, for example, it is assumed that business is written evenly throughout the year and that therefore on the average, the unearned premium reserve will equal six months' premiums. The insurer would accordingly set up in the unearned premium reserve one half of all one-year premiums, one fourth of all two-year premiums, and one sixth of all three-year premiums. This method is permitted by most states. For its own guidance, however, an insurer generally uses a more exact semimonthly method, whereby at the end of the year $1/24$ of the gross premium of all one-year policies written in January is placed in the unearned premium reserves, $23/24$ having been considered earned. For one-year policies written in February, $3/24$ of the gross premium is set aside, $21/24$ having been considered earned, etc.

In recent years it has become very common for insurers to allow payment of an advance premium on the installment plan. For example, the insured may pay a full annual premium the first year and for successive four years, 78 per cent of the annual premium. The amount which should be set up as the unearned premium reserve depends on the amount which is returnable to the insured in case of cancellation prior to the expiration of the policy term.

LOSS RESERVES

There is little argument as to how the unearned premium reserve is determined, and, assuming that assets are valued properly, there is little argument as to the adequacy of these reserves. As we have seen, they are undoubtedly redundant. The situation is somewhat different for *loss* reserves, however, because an element of judgment necessarily enters into the decision as to how much shall be set aside for the payment of claims against the company up to and including the date of the balance sheet. It should be recognized that a loss reserve is an *estimate* of a liability, and not an exact statement. If the exact liability were known, but unpaid, it probably would not be called a "reserve," but simply something like "accrued claims payable."

Estimating loss reserves

Two basic types of problems in estimating loss reserves are: (1) that of estimating the amount of reserves which should be set up on claims known to have occurred, but where the amount of the claim is uncertain, and (2) that of estimating the amount of reserves on claims not known to have occurred, but which past experience indicates most probably have occurred. For example, a claim might have occurred on December 28, but notice of the accident has not reached the insurer at the time it estimates its reserves for the balance sheet as of December 31.

There are several methods of estimating reserves. For claims known to have occurred, very often the underwriter makes an individual estimate of the final loss for each case. This method, known as the *individual case estimate,* is widely used and forms the basis for many loss reserves. Where the average amount of the claim is small, or not subject to much variation, the underwriter may assign an *average value* to each claim notice received. When the amount of the claim is dependent on such factors as length of life, probability of remarriage, or average duration of total disability, tables are consulted which are similar in nature to life insurance mortality tables. This method is called the *tabular value* basis of estimating claims.

For certain lines of insurance, such as workmen's compensation and liability, the loss reserve is estimated on a *formula* basis set up by statute. In New York, for example, the law in workmen's compensation requires an insurer to set up 65 per cent of the *earned* premium as a loss reserve, (60 per cent in liability insurance) less any losses and expenses paid at the date of the annual statement. This reserve must be maintained for three years. The law provides that if the insurer's individual case estimates of reserves exceed the amount required by the 65 per cent formula, the individual estimates will become the required reserve. For long-term claims (those running three years or longer), the law requires that the loss reserve shall be the estimated present value, at 3.5 per cent interest, of all future payments.

In general, past experience is the guide for setting up loss reserves on incurred, but not reported, claims. If in the last five years it were discovered that following the appearance of the annual statement a certain number of claims were ultimately reported which occurred in the prior period, it would be assumed that this experience will be repeated, and the number of claims to be expected would be assigned some average value and a reserve set up on this basis.

Adequacy of loss reserves

It is difficult to assess the adequacy of loss reserves in a given insurer except by the test of past results. There are no reliable "rules of thumb" which can be used to make comparisons among various insurers because of the important differences in operating conditions giving rise to different reserves. While the composition of coverages written by an insurer is primarily responsible for the relative size of its reserves, there are other factors which should be considered, namely: 1) territory of operation, 2) age of the insurer, and 3) rate of growth.[2]

1) Territory of operation. The territory of operation affects the size of reserves because losses vary by territory. Several examples will make this clear. In one territory the law may, as we have seen, provide far larger benefits for workmen's compensation than in other territories. An insurer operating in the high-benefit territory must set up larger estimates for losses than an insurer operating in a low-benefit territory. In the field of fire insurance, certain areas may be subject to more severe wind losses than others, and hence larger reserves must be set up in these areas. In some areas courts may have a tendency to be more liberal with personal injury awards than in other areas. Insurers must behave accordingly.

2) Age of the insurer. The age of the insurer is an important factor in assessing the size of loss reserves. An insurer which has been in business for many years has had an opportunity to obtain a diversified num-

---

[2] There are undoubtedly many other factors which affect reserves. For example, some insurers set up contingency reserves for large losses. Reinsurance arrangements also affect the size of reserves, as will the proportion of claims going to court.

ber of risks with the high expectation that losses will follow a predictable pattern. This follows because through its broad underwriting experience, the insurer has greater knowledge of the various hazards to which it is exposed and will have had an opportunity, through reinsurance or more careful selection, to protect itself against the unusual loss. A new company has much less grounds on which to base its estimates of reserves. Therefore, the loss reserves of the new insurer may not be at all typical of what might be found if the company had been in business for a longer period.

3) *Rate of growth.* The faster an insurer is gaining in premium volume, the more rapid, generally speaking, will be the rate of growth of its loss reserves (as well as its unearned premium reserves.) The size of loss reserves is often larger than normal because of the uncertainties involved in accepting new insureds. An insurer which has stabilized or has a slow rate of growth has loss reserves based on known experience with old risks. There is a likelihood that its loss reserves will be relatively smaller because it has had an opportunity to weed out the bad risks and is not taking on new ones.

For example, assume that there are two insurers of the same size and writing the same line of business, but one has larger loss reserves than the other. Can it be concluded that the one insurer is "stronger" than the other? Not at all. Both of the insurers may be writing workmen's compensation, but this business may be written in different territories. Due to differences in benefit scales in the different territories, one insurer's reserves may be larger than the other but still inadequate considering the type of law under which it is operating. One insurer may be rapidly growing and the other declining in premium volume. One may be an old, established insurer writing business in a market in which it has accumulated much experience, while the other may have just ventured into a new market in which it has little experience.

About the only way to determine the adequacy of loss reserves is to check the loss reserves by each type of insurance and to make comparisons in subsequent periods to see if the actual loss payments are fairly close to the reserves used to estimate them. If an insurer consistently underestimates its future liabilities, the analyst will have to conclude that this insurer's reserves tend to be inadequate. It is obvious that such an insurer is also overestimating its underwriting profits and portrays a false picture to the insurance buying public, the financial analyst, and the state regulator.

Unfortunately, it is not generally feasible for the typical insurance analyst to use this method of testing the adequacy of loss reserves because published financial statements are seldom so detailed that it is possible to see what the loss reserves are *by line of insurance*. However, such information is available in the statement supplied to the insurance commissioner of the state in which the insurer operates, and is available if one will take the trouble to secure it. The usual attitude is, "This is what we pay the insurance commissioner for." Most interested parties are content to observe the published statements of underwriting profits over a period of years to obtain an indirect check of the ultimate quality of underwriting results of any given insurer.

Implications for financial analysis

We are now in a position to appreciate better the difficulties and dangers of conventional balance sheet analysis in assessing the relative strength of two insurers, in a manner outlined in Chapter 6. For example, in Table 27–1 on page 754, the ratio of net worth to liabilities for Insurer A is $5.7/8$, or 71 per cent, and for Insurer B, $6.5/17.1$, or 38 per cent. Does this mean that Insurer A is a stronger company than Insurer B, because of the greater relative protection for its policyholders against possible declines in the value of assets? On the surface it would so appear. However, the truth of this conclusion must rest upon an analysis of the accuracy of the loss reserves, especially in Insurer B, which will yield facts as to the nature of the claims giving rise to the loss reserves shown, will indicate whether the reserves are conservative or not, etc. We must also recognize that Insurer B has about 50 per cent of its assets invested in bonds, while Insurer A has only 40 per cent so invested. Hence, there is an element of safety in Insurer B, which offsets in part the lower ratio of net worth to liabilities. Until more facts are known, there is little we can say as to the relative financial strength of these two insurers, which are operating in entirely different lines of business, have different financial problems, may be operating in entirely different territories, and may be subject to different philosophies of underwriting.

Determination of profit

The amount of profit shown on the insurer's income statement depends vitally upon the adequacy of its reserve liabilities, more particularly its loss reserves. An adjustment must be made to reflect the equity in the unearned premium reserves. It can be appreciated that the profit shown in a single year is somewhat unreliable as an indicator of the true profits since only over a period of time can it be determined whether or not the loss reserves have been adequate. Some insurers publish income statements on the basis of *policy year* statistics rather than *calendar year* statistics in order to overcome this difficulty. Under policy year statistics, all losses attributable to the policies issued in a given year are accumulated and charged back to the premiums collected on those policies. Obviously it will be two or more years before complete policy year data are available, and by that time the analyst may have little use for them. Therefore, calendar year data are normally used and estimates must be made, on the basis of past experience, as to the reliability of the loss estimates.

Assuming that all reserves are fairly and adequately estimated, it is possible to obtain an estimate of the final net profit of a property and liability insurance company by considering two major sources of "gain"— underwriting profit and investment profit. As pointed out above, the statutory underwriting profit must be adjusted for the equity in the unearned premium reserve, if any. For an insurer of fire and allied lines, this is done by adding to the statutory underwriting profit or loss, approximately 40 per cent of the *increase* in the unearned premium reserve during the prior period. As noted above, a figure of 35 per cent is often used for an underwriter of liability, compensation, automobile, and other casualty lines.

In most property insurers, investment income resulting from dividends, interest, and capital gains has been a source of profit which is at least as important as underwriting profits. According to a tabulation made by Best, the investment income from dividends and interest exceeded net underwriting profits for a large group of stock insurers in every year but five between the years 1920–1959. When total investment results (investment income plus profit or loss from sales of securities) were considered, the investment gain exceeded the profits from underwriting in all but eight years during this period.[3]

The total earnings of stock fire and casualty insurers have not been impressive. In the period 1945–1959, for example, the total earnings, both investment and underwriting, have been negative in five of the years, between zero and four per cent of the earned premiums in six years, and above four per cent in four years.[4] This has resulted in spite of the intent

---

[3] *Best's Fire and Casualty Aggregates and Averages* (1960), p. 24.
[4] *Ibid.*

of the National Association of Insurance Commissioners, stated both in 1921 and again in 1948, that a "fair" underwriting profit to insurers is five per cent of earned premiums. Not only has underwriting profit failed generally to equal this allowance in the rate-making formula, but total profit has also not equaled this return.

Perhaps profit may be more logically measured by relating it to assets invested instead of to earnings. Total earnings on net worth, after adjustment for the equity in the unearned premium reserve, for 50 leading stock fire and casualty insurance companies, were only 3.5 per cent in 1958 and 5.3 per cent in 1959.[5] These results are similar to those of an earlier but more elaborate study covering the period 1941–1950 based on data for a large group of stock fire insurers reported by Best. This study showed that the ratio of return on average equity was 4.11 per cent.[6]

The conservative profits reported by stock insurers in the property insurance field have had serious financial consequences in the financial management of insurers. It has been difficult for many insurers to build up their surplus and consequently their underwriting capacity, in spite of the almost universal practice of restricting all dividend payments to some portion of investment profits alone. The management of insurance companies has been reluctant to enter the capital market to sell new common stock, perhaps because of the relatively low value that investors place on the holdings in insurance companies as a group. For example, the average price placed on the common stock of 52 insurers showed that investors were willing to pay an average of only 71 per cent of the net worth for insurer shares.[7] Practically all the growth in insurance capacity has had to be financed by retained earnings.

The implication of these data is that, in spite of rate regulation, insurers as a group have been unable to maintain their premium rates at a sufficient level to produce long-run profits of more than a nominal amount. Consequently, they have been unable to expand their underwriting capacity. By comparison with other industries such as banks or public utilities, where the element of risk is theoretically as low, the profits of insurers have been properly termed "inadequate." [8]

---

[5] Robert Chaut, "The Fire-Casualty Insurance Industry, Aggregates—Fifty Major Companies" (New York: Kidder, Peabody & Co., 1960, Mimeographed).

[6] Robert A. Hedges and Neil Helbing, Urbana (mimeo), 1952, reported in Hearings, Subcommittee on Antitrust and Monopoly, Committee on the Judiciary, U. S. Senate, 86th Congress, on the Insurance Industry, Part 2 (Washington, D. C., USGPO, 1960) p. 1114.

[7] Chaut, *op. cit.,* p. 7.

[8] See testimony of Robert Hedges on this point in the source cited above.

RESERVES IN LIFE INSURANCE

In a life insurance company the reserve liabilities are of much greater size than in property insurance because of the practice of issuing life insurance contracts on a level-premium basis for long periods of years. As we have seen, this results in the collection by an insurer of amounts in excess of current mortality costs. These reserves are held in trust for the insured until such time as the policy matures or is terminated, when the fund is returned to the insured. Thus, the reserve in life insurance may be looked upon as an unearned premium reserve, although its official name is simply "policy reserve," of which there are many different classes.

Loss reserves are not of great financial size in a life insurer because of the speed with which all losses are paid when due and because there is no difficulty in determining, as a usual thing, the amount of the loss. There is no uncertainty as to whether or not death has occurred nor, since life insurance is a valued contract, the amount of the indemnity. Hence, at the date of the balance sheet the loss reserve is of minimal size, representing the few claims that are outstanding which have not been paid for some reason.

Determination of reserves

The policy reserve must be large enough so that if the insurer ceased doing business, it would have sufficient funds on hand to pay all claims on existing life insurance contracts outstanding. The reserve in life insurance may be looked upon in two ways, retrospectively and prospectively. *Retrospectively,* the reserve is the excess of accumulated net premiums over outlays. More precisely, it represents the sum of all net premiums collected by the insurer, plus guaranteed interest assumed by the contracts, less tabular death claims. The reserve deals with *total* funds, not the funds assigned to an individual policy. We speak, therefore, of *aggregate* reserves, not individual reserves. Furthermore, the reserve calculation is based on net premiums, not the gross premium. Also, the amount of the reserve is determined by certain authorized assumptions as to mortality and interest, and not in terms of actual results. In other words, the reserve is expressed as a legal requirement, and hence is a *legal reserve.* This expression is used in describing an insurer as a *legal reserve life insurance company.* The insurer must have actual assets equal to its required legal reserves, or it is said to be insolvent. Normally, the actuarial assumptions involved in making up rates are so conservative that the insurer will have no difficulty in meeting these legal requirements. In other words, the insurer will guarantee a lower rate of interest than it actually earns and will use a mortality table that overstates actual mortality by some extent. If the company earns more interest than it guarantees or has fewer death claims than is assumed, the excess earnings are returned, in a mutual company, to its policyholders.

Looked upon *prospectively,* the reserve in life insurance represents the amount an insurer must have on hand now in order to meet all future claims. More precisely, the prospective reserve must be equal to the

Figure 27–1

RESERVE = *PV* FUTURE BENEFITS − *PV* FUTURE PREMIUMS

THE RESERVE LOOKED UPON PROSPECTIVELY

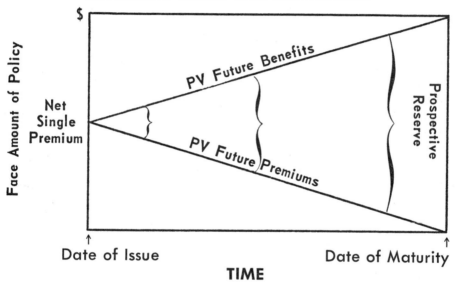

present value of future benefits, less the present value of future premiums to be collected. It will be recognized that when a life insurance policy is first issued, the present value of future premiums *equals* the present value of future benefits. Indeed, this is the way the net single premium is calculated (see Chapter 26). However, as time goes on, the present value of future benefits rises because the time is nearer when claims must be paid, and the present value of future premiums declines since fewer premiums remain to be paid. Hence, the insurer must have a reserve equal to this difference. Schematically this result is seen in Figure 27–1.

In Figure 27–1 it will be seen that at the date of maturity of any contract, the reserve must equal the face amount of the policy. At the date of issue, the present value of future benefits equals the present value of future premiums, but a difference begins to appear immediately and gradually widens until the policy matures. The reserve is, of course, the same no matter whether it is looked upon retrospectively or prospectively. In general, it is easier to see the true nature of a reserve by looking at it prospectively.

Factors affecting the size of the reserve

The reserve in life insurance is affected by several important factors, the most significant of which are the: 1) interest assumed, 2) mortality rate assumed, and 3) reserve basis.

1) Interest assumed. The higher the interest assumed, the lower the amount of the reserve and *vice versa.* The truth of this relationship can be seen by going back to the basic formula, Reserve = Present Value of Future Benefits — Present Value of Future Premiums. The higher the interest, the less is the present value of future premiums. Remember that the present value of future premiums represents the present worth to the insurer of a stream of income to come to it in the future. This quantity may be looked upon as a sum of money, which at the interest rate assumed, will produce, together with liquidation of principal, the promised income. The greater the interest to be earned, the less this sum has to be. Hence, the higher the interest, the lower is the present value of future premiums.

Increasing the interest rate also lowers the present value of the future benefits but by a greater amount than it reduces the present value of future premiums. This is true because of the workings of compound interest. Thus, a higher interest rate always produces a lower reserve and *vice versa.*

2) Mortality rate assumed. The greater the rate of mortality assumed, the greater must be the reserve. It is not the *level* of mortality at each age that matters, but the rate of change in mortality from year to year. If the rate of mortality were constant, as is the rate of loss (as a general rule) in property insurance, there would be no necessity for a reserve. Of course, the higher the *level* of mortality, the higher the premium must be. But if there were no change from year to year in the rate of loss, there would be no necessity to accumulate a fund for the payment of "excess" rates of loss in later years. The steeper the rate of change in loss from year to year, the more that must be accumulated to meet these future liabilities.

3) Reserve basis. The reserve *basis* in life insurance deals with the question of whether the reserve is to be valued on a "net level premium" basis, or on some "modified reserve basis." The problem in life insurance is similar to that which exists in property insurance. First-year expenses are heavy, often exceeding the first-year premium. Unless some arrangement is made to prevent heavy first-year expenses, they will constitute a drain on surplus, as we explored earlier in the analysis of the unearned premium reserve for property insurers. In life insurance if an insurer keeps its reserves on a net level premium basis, all the first-year expenses are charged off against surplus (to the extent necessary) and a full reserve is set up the first year. Of course, this is the most conservative way of stating a reserve liability. Large insurers with generous surpluses often use this basis of valuing their reserves.

For a new or a small insurer with a relatively small surplus, it would be very difficult for substantial growth to take place if the reserve liabilities had to be maintained on a full net level premium basis. Hence, under most state laws a modified reserve valuation method is permitted. The most common of these bases is known as the Commissioners' Standard Valuation method. Under this method the policies are divided into two classes: (1) those for which the premium is less than that of a 20-pay life policy issued at the same age for a like amount, and (2) those where the premium exceeds this amount.

For the first group of policies, the insurer may use the method known as the *full preliminary term* method of valuation. Under this method the law allows the insurer to view the policy as though the first year of the policy period were represented by a term insurance contract, and the remaining years as a whole life contract for one year less than usual. Thus, a 30-pay life policy would be viewed as a combined one-year term policy plus a 29-pay life policy. Since the term policy has no reserve requirement, there would be no reserve liability during the first year and the entire first-year premium would be available for payment of the heavy first-year expenses. The reserve liability for later years builds up at a slightly higher rate than would be true if the insurer used the full net level premium reserve method.

For the second group of policies, those whose premium exceeds that of a 20-pay life policy, use of the full preliminary term method would leave an inordinate amount of the first-year premium for expenses. Since this might constitute an inducement for management to make reckless and competitive expenditures to acquire new business, the law states that for policies falling into this classification, a partial reserve is required the first year. We shall not go into the details of how this reserve is calculated, since the formula becomes quite complicated; but the intent is to require that by the end of the policy term, the reserve should equal the amount which would be available under the net level premium reserve basis.

The modified reserve basis is a slightly less conservative method of calculating reserves than the full net level premium basis. However, use of the modified reserve basis is actually more logical in many ways than the more conservative net level premium basis, since it permits the insurer to recognize that the payment of acquisition expenses in the first year is a nonrecurring expense and should not have to be written off all at once. To do so understates the true earnings of the life insurer in that year. It should be noted that if the insurer wishes to use more conservative assumptions than those dictated by the Commissioners' Standard Valuation method, it may do so. For example, in most states the CSV method permits the use of a 3½ per cent interest assumption. If the insurer wishes to use a lower interest rate, thus increasing its required reserves, it may do so. Also, the insurer may (and frequently does) put aside voluntary reserves for various types of contingencies, such as a reserve for dividends and a reserve for group life contingencies. In most states there is a limitation on the size of the voluntary reserves, usually 10 per cent of the legal reserves, to prevent an unreasonable accumulation of funds and to encourage a quicker return of redundant premium collections to policyholders.

Nonforfeiture values

Calculation of the cash values and other nonforfeiture values on a life insurance contract is entirely separate from the calculation of a reserve. In determining a schedule of cash values, the insurer considers not only mortality and interest, but also expenses. These assumptions may be different from those used in calculating the reserve, although the law specifies some minimum basis for calculation. The nonforfeiture values are a matter of contract between the insurer and the insured and cannot be changed, although the reserve basis of the contract can be changed at any time.

The standard nonforfeiture valuation legislation (also known as the Guertin laws) places a limitation of 40 per cent of the "adjusted" premium (or four per cent of the face amount of the policy) as the maximum allowable expense. The adjusted premium differs from the net premium in that it includes the initial first-year expenses on the contract.

The calculation is such that the insurer recovers the heavy first-year expenses during the premium paying period of the policy. If the policy lapses before these expenses are recovered, the insurer loses that much money. To offset this loss, additional loading is charged on all policies in the same way that a department store includes a charge in the mark up for anticipated mark downs on certain goods.

Effect of life reserve methods on surplus

The liabilities of a life insurer, as expressed by the various reserves, are generally overstated, but probably not to the same extent as is true of the unearned premium reserve in property and liability insurers. This is due to the practice, at least in large insurers, of using full net level premium reserves. There are several other features, however, which have the effect of overstating the reserve liabilities in a life insurer. These are:

1. The use of a mortality table which overstates the actual mortality experience.
2. Assuming in reserve calculations a much lower rate of interest than is being earned.
3. Use of voluntary reserves to offset possible future increases in costs. The effect of this is to raise premiums above the level actually required, thus giving mutual insurers a considerable "safety margin." Dividends to policyholders vary according to the actual results achieved by the insurer.

In a mutual insurer, under which form a substantial majority of all life insurance is written, reserve practices affect the amount of dividends which can be ultimately paid. However, redundancy in reserves is not too important a problem in mutuals. It probably makes little difference, in affecting safety, how the various liability and surplus items on the balance sheet are arranged, since the policyholders have contributed all of the capital employed. In stock insurers, however, the redundancy in reserves means that the surplus is understated and since surplus is the source of ultimate dividends to stockholders and represents accumulated profits, the matter is of greater importance. Furthermore, if a stock company is going to compete with a mutual insurer on a net cost basis, it must make somewhat less conservative assumptions in reserve calculations and attempt to predicate its premiums on actual experience as to mortality, interest, and expenses. However, since the relative size of surplus is small in life insurance (approximating eight per cent of the total capital), a stock insurer cannot afford to take chances in estimating reserves which may turn out to be too low. It must steer a middle, and often somewhat more precarious, course than a mutual in this regard. Many stock companies have adopted the practice of issuing participating policies to be on an equal footing with mutuals.

Surplus also tends to be understated in an insurance company because of the accounting conventions that have been adopted in the valuation of assets. For example, an insurer will have certain assets, such as furniture and fixtures, which are not shown on the balance sheet because they are "non-admitted" under state regulatory conditions. The item "premium balances" (accounts due from agents after a certain span of time) is also in this category, even though in the normal course of business the premium balances will either be collected or the liabilities on business which they represent will be canceled. An insurance company may be very prone to understate the true value of its home office or real estate, particularly that real estate which has been acquired by foreclosure. To the extent that an insurer actually has valuable assets which it has not shown or has undervalued, its surplus, the balancing item on a balance sheet, is also understated.

The net effect of overstating the liabilities and understating the assets may make it appear that the insurer is financially weaker than it actually is. In any given case, of course, the true facts must be investigated by the analyst. Unfortunately, the true facts are often difficult to determine, even by an examination of the insurer's annual report, which may not even give such elemental information as the reserve valuation basis, whether it is full net level premium reserve or some modified reserve basis. In many cases only direct inquiry from the home office officials will produce the desired financial information necessary to make a thorough analysis.

SUMMARY

1. Analysis of the reserve practices of an insurance company shows that how an insurer estimates its liabilities is very important in understanding many financial problems in insurance. The relative security of the insured, the adequacy of rate-making, and the value of an insurance company from the viewpoint of an investor are among the important questions affected by reserve valuation methods.

2. Two major reserves on the balance sheet of an insurer are unearned premium reserves (which in a life insurer are called policy reserves), and loss reserves. Unearned premium reserves represent the liability of the insurer for advance premium payments made by the insured, while loss reserves represent estimates of the amount of losses and loss expenses attributable to losses that the insurer has incurred. Loss reserves are gen-

erally relatively large in property and liability insurers, while unearned premium reserves are dominant in fire and allied line insurers and in life insurers.

3. The accounting requirements in connection with the unearned premium reserve cause several financial problems for the property and liability insurer, chief among which are the drain on surplus for an expanding insurer and the resulting limitations on its potential growth. Insurance capacity is reduced and underwriting standards are tightened as a consequence. Recognition of these accounting requirements is vital in an interpretation of the financial statements of property and liability insurers.

4. In interpreting the loss reserves of an insurer, attention must be given to the type of insurance written, the territory of operation, the trend of premium growth, and the age and experience of the insurer in a given line of business. The only feasible way to determine the adequacy of loss reserves is to make a statistical comparison of reserves which are set up in each line of insurance with losses which develop on these reserves.

5. Policy reserves (unearned premium reserves) in life insurance are by far the most important liability on the balance sheet of a life insurer. Loss reserves are minimal. Policy reserves are large because of the practice of issuing life insurance on a net level premium basis over a long period of years, which causes a collection of premiums in considerable excess over current outlays for mortality.

6. Policy reserves must be at such a level that if the insurer ceased doing business, all existing obligations on outstanding contracts could be met. Looked upon prospectively, the reserve is defined as the present value of future claims less the present value of future premiums to be collected. Looked upon retrospectively, the reserve represents the net difference between premiums collected, plus interest, and death claims assumed to have occurred. Both views of the reserve produce identical results.

7. Policy reserves are generally considered to be redundant in life insurance because of the practice of assuming a lower rate of interest than is actually earned and of using a mortality table which overstates the actual rate of mortality. The policy reserves are also overstated in insurers that employ the net level premium method of reserve valuation. This fact causes gross premiums to be higher than actually required in mutual insurers and results in a safety factor for this type of insurer. Dividends to policyholders equalize the difference between stock companies and mutuals.

QUESTIONS FOR REVIEW AND DISCUSSION

1. An insurance firm writes $100,000 of new premiums in a certain year on fire insurance policies with a term of two years.
   (a) How much liability should be shown in the unearned premium reserve at the end of the first year, assuming that the business is written evenly throughout the year? Explain.
   (b) What would the unearned premium reserve be if the policies had been for a five-year term?

2. Why is a new insurer likely to show a statutory underwriting loss for the first few years after it begins business, even though its underwriting experience may be considered "profitable"? Explain.

3. The chief auditor of the New York State Insurance Department wrote as follows: "Theoretically, the unearned premium reserve in the fire and casualty statement is the amount that will discharge all obligations of the company that can possibly occur in the unexpired terms of all policies in force as of the statement date. Actually, it is greater, since it is computed on the premium charged, which is gross as to commissions, and, therefore, represents a liability carried by the company in excess of the actual amount necessary to discharge all obligations that may be incurred during the periods the policies have yet to run."

   (a) Is it true that the unearned premium reserve represents an amount which will discharge all obligations of the company that can *possibly* occur on the unexpired policies in force? Explain.

   (b) Do you agree that the unearned premium reserve is excessive?

   (c) What financial problems are introduced by the requirement that the unearned premium reserve be excessive?

4. Given below is an abbreviated set of financial statements for the Actual Fire and Casualty Company, for the two years, (1) and (2).

BALANCE SHEET, DECEMBER 31
(000,000's OMITTED)

	(2)	(1)
Admitted Assets:		
Bonds	$5.6	$5.3
Stocks	.8	.9
Real estate	.4	.4
Cash	.3	.3
Premium balances	.3	.6
Other	.6	.1
	$8.0	$7.6
Liabilities:		
Loss and expense reserve	$2.3	$2.0
Unearned premium reserve	2.6	2.2
Other	.1	.3
Total liabilities	$5.0	$4.5
Paid-up capital	1.0	1.0
Net surplus	2.0	2.1
Total liabilities & surplus	$8.0	$7.6

INCOME STATEMENT
FOR YEAR ENDED DECEMBER 31
(000,000's OMITTED)

	(2)	(1)
Premiums written	$5.4	$4.7
Premiums earned	5.0	4.6
Expenses (35%)	1.9	1.6
Losses	3.3	2.8
Underwriting profit (statutory)	−.2	.2
Investment profit	.1	.1
Total	$ .1	$ .3

DISTRIBUTION OF PREMIUM WRITINGS
IN YEAR (2):

Fire and allied lines	$ .1
Auto liability	2.2
Auto physical damage	2.0
Miscellaneous	1.1
Total premiums written	$5.4

   (a) In your opinion, what is a more accurate estimate of year (2) underwriting results than the one shown above? Explain.

   (b) In your opinion, what is the true net worth of this company? Explain.

   (c) Explain the difference between premiums written and premiums earned. What is the probable reason why the difference between these two quantities was greater in year (2) than in year (1)?

(d) Comment on the investments of the company. Would you say they are more or less conservative than need be? Why?

(e) If you did not know the distribution of premium writings of this insurer, what evidence is there that it is not primarily a fire insurer?

5. In establishing loss reserves, how can an insurer set up a reserve for losses which have been incurred, but are unreported at the time the statement is prepared?

6. A state insurance department auditor stated, "If during a period of mounting claim costs on certain casualty lines, a company's reserves on them did not reflect the trend, a question as to the adequacy of its claim reserves would arise. If on a line of business on which past experience was credible the company's reserve seemed unreasonable when compared with previous statement figures, the liability carried would be questioned." Judging from these criteria employed by an insurance examiner, would you say that an audited statement of reserve liabilities can be relied upon? Why?

7. In a period of rapidly increasing auto liability losses, one insurer showed practically no increase in loss reserves, while a second insurer indicated a rather substantial increase. Yet both insurers had nearly the same premium volume and the same amount of paid losses in the given year. Can it be properly concluded that the second insurer is more conservative than the first? Explain.

8. A witness testifying before a congressional hearing on regulation and rate-making in the insurance industry stated, "The industry needs a better measure of its future liabilities and a more useful and accurate treatment of its income statements in any event, but if a better measure of future liabilities can be found, one which is not tied directly to the rate level, as the unearned premium reserve is . . . then fire and casualty insurers' solvency can be watched and preserved while the rates charged to the customers are left free to fluctuate . . . according to individual companies' needs, opportunities, and markets."

(a) In what sense is the unearned premium reserve tied to the rate level?

(b) Will it be generally true that a company with low rates will have a relative advantage, surplus-wise, over a company with high rates, because of unearned premium reserve requirements? Why? If so, does this mean that the unearned premium reserve requirements result in rates higher than those which would otherwise exist?

(c) Suggest some way of estimating an insurer's liability to policyholders other than the method currently used and represented by the unearned premium reserve.

9. In a study covering the period 1941–1950, it was determined that the average rate of return (after taxes) on stockholders' equity in a large group of property insurance companies was slightly over 4 per cent. This compares with an average return of 7 or 8 per cent for electric utilities, and nearly 15 per cent for a cross section of manufacturing corporations. What implications does the relatively low rate of return in insurance have for the future expansion of underwriting capacity? Would you say these data are representative? Why?

10. (a) Why are life insurance companies often identified as "legal reserve life insurers"?
    (b) What aspects of life insurer reserves are subject to law?
11. The formula for the prospective reserve in life insurance is calculated as the present value of future benefits less the present value of future premiums. After a policy has been in force for a few years, why is it that the present value of future benefits exceeds the present value of future premiums, thus necessitating a reserve?
12. Why is it that the "reserve" on an individual ordinary life policy increases continually until at maturity it is equal to the face amount, whereas the *aggregate* reserve of the insurer for all ordinary life policies declines, until at maturity of all policies it is exhausted? (See Figure 27–1.)
13. It may be said that the life insurance reserve for any particular policy year is obtained by adding the net level premium for that year to the terminal reserve of the preceding year, increasing this sum by the minimum rate of interest guaranteed by the insurer, and deducting the cost of insurance for the current year. What method of calculating the reserve is thus described?
14. (a) Calculate the required reserve on a 20-payment life policy issued at age 30 for a level premium of $27.04 by the time the insured is age 45. The present value of future claims at age 45 is $551.37. The present value of one dollar due from all survivors age 45 for five years is $4.68. What reserve calculation method is illustrated here?
    (b) How would you proceed in calculating the $551.37?
15. Explain why the higher the interest assumed, the lower is the required reserve in life insurance.
16. A life insurance agent stated, "When the new (1958) mortality table was adopted, premium rates, and hence the reserve requirements, went down." Is this statement wholly true, wholly false, or partly true and partly false?
17. It has been stated that life insurers are permitted to reduce their reserve requirements by the amount of the heavy first-year expenses involved in putting a policy on the books, but a property insurer is not so permitted. Is this true, and if so, can you think of some reason for it?
18. In calculating life insurance policy reserves, which is the more conservative, the net level premium method or the Commissioners' Standard Valuation method? Why?
19. (a) What is the preliminary term method of valuation?
    (b) In what way is this method related to the Commissioners' Standard Valuation method?
20. A writer stated, ". . . in most life insurance companies there is probably some understatement of surplus as a result of valuing assets low and liabilities high . . . this relation probably varies considerably from company to company."
    (a) Suggest specific ways in which liabilities might be overstated and asset values understated in a life insurance company.
    (b) How should this information be considered in judging the relative safety of a given insurer? Explain.

APPENDIX A

Explanation of Best's Ratings of
Property and Liability Insurers *

Companies and associations are assigned two ratings: a "Policyholders' Rating" and a "Financial Rating." If an insurer is not rated, it may be for one of the following reasons: (1) necessary information was refused, or furnished too late for use, (2) a company disputes the application of the rating system, or disputes the construction of items appearing in the annual statements, (3) the insurer writes primarily life insurance, or (4) four years' operating experience is not available.

GENERAL POLICYHOLDERS' RATINGS

Six policyholders' rating classifications are used, namely, "A+" and "A" (Excellent), "B+" (Very Good), "B" (Good), "C+" (Fairly Good), and "C" (Fair), to reflect Best's opinion of the relative position of each institution in comparison with others, based upon averages within the insurance industry.

The highest rating classification (Excellent) is subdivided by use of two symbols, "A+" and "A." Companies classified as (Excellent) are considered to be outstanding on a comparative basis, whether rated "A" or "A+." Only nominal variances from industry standards generally exist among "A" companies, with the most common difference being in underwriting results. For other rating graduations the variances, or median points, widen at each level.

Five main factors enter into policyholders' ratings: 1) quality of underwriting, 2) economy of management, 3) adequacy of reserves for undischarged liabilities of all kinds, 4) adequacy of resources to absorb unusual shock, and 5) soundness of investments.

---

* Source: *Best's Insurance Reports, 1960,* pp. xvii–xviii.

1) Quality of underwriting

A comparison of incurred losses and claim adjustment expenses with premiums earned is made. Premiums earned reflect the increase or decrease of the equity in the unearned premiums, an important underwriting factor. Expenses incurred are compared with premiums written. This procedure gives an underwriting profit or loss ratio which takes into account the increase or decrease of the equity in unearned premium reserve.

The amount of the underwriting profit or loss so calculated is then compared with the earned premiums, as a measure of the underwriting ability of the management. The underwriting profit or loss is also compared with the net safety factor, for the reason that the same amount of profit or loss might be of negligible importance to one company having large net resources but of great importance to one having small net resources.

2) Economy of management

This factor is measured by the ratio of expenses incurred (excluding claim expenses, which are added to losses) to premiums written.

3) Adequacy of reserves

Unearned premiums are calculated in accordance with laws so clear and uniform that there is little or no possibility for honest error, and this item is accepted as it appears in the statements, except in those infrequent instances where the customary formula is not used by the insurer under review. The reserves for pending loss claims are set up on a formula basis in connection with liability and workmen's compensation business. On most other lines, loss reserves represent the opinion of the management of the ultimate cost of each pending claim. Various schedules comparing the final cost of claims with the reserves originally set up against them are available, and are very carefully analyzed. If these data indicate that the claim reserves set up in the current statement are inadequate (even though they may be in accord with statutory provisions), such an apparent deficiency is considered in testing the adequacy of the surplus to policyholders. Similarly, if reserves are more than adequate, any indicated equity in such reserves is taken into account.

4) Adequacy of net resources

Surplus is a safety factor used to absorb increases above normal in loss and expense requirements. An insurance company may be doing too great a volume of business in proportion to its net resources, just as any other kind of business may be overextended; and this is a very dangerous practice which is prejudicial to the safety of policyholders. This question does not hinge wholly upon the volume of premiums written; a company which has a high average profit may safely write a larger volume of business in proportion to net resources than another which operates with less favorable results. Again, some companies operate on a basis which requires the setting up of little or no unearned premium liability, as, to illustrate, companies writing only accident and health business on the weekly or monthly premium plan. Such companies have only their capital and surplus to absorb the shocks of unfavorable operating results, while other companies collecting premiums in advance, and setting up the statutory unearned premium liability, have an equity in that item which can be realized if an emergency makes necessary the reinsurance of the business. The character of assets and the maintenance of proper claim reserves are of great importance. These and many other variations, including diversification and spread of underwriting commitments, are taken into account in measuring the adequacy of net resources.

5) Soundness of investments

Best's rating as to investments is based upon the elements of soundness, diversification, and liquidity. The standards used are not arbitrary, but, as in other sections of the rating schedule, are based primarily upon current averages of all companies. It is possible for an insurance company to show an apparently adequate safety factor—that is, excess of assets and equities over present and potential liabilities—and yet be in an unsafe position so far as policyholders are concerned. Assets, to illustrate, may be of such character that they cannot readily be converted into cash for the purpose of either reinsuring the business and liquidating other liabilities or of meeting any unusual demand for cash, such as might arise through an abnormal loss ratio or because of an increase in the cost of liquidating claims now pending over the amount of the reserves set up against them. Various other matters of importance are considered, particularly where some condition exists which is dangerous to policyholders.

Effect of size of insurer

A small insurer can be just as safe as a large insurer. Many small insurers writing specialized lines are carefully and efficiently managed, and are sound in proportion to liabilities assumed. The policy of a small specialty fire insurance company which writes only moderate lines and conscientiously avoids writing in any congested area more than it could afford to pay in the event of a conflagration or a catastrophe may be more desirable than that of a much larger concern operating in less conservative lines.

FINANCIAL RATINGS

The financial rating indicates Best's estimate of the net safety factor of each company and is based upon the surplus to policyholders, plus equities, and less indicated shortages in reserves, if any. Policyholders' surplus is the sum of capital and surplus funds in stock companies, and surplus funds as regards mutual companies, Lloyds organizations, and reciprocal exchanges, including guaranty or permanent funds, if any; contingent resources are not considered.

Ratings of foreign companies are based upon their home office balance sheets which include the assets and liabilities of the United States branches.

Foreign companies keep in trust, for the exclusive benefit of U. S. Branch policyholders and creditors as required by law, funds to cover all liabilities and statutory deposit requirements. Furthermore, all assets, whether trusteed or not, are subject to withdrawal only with the consent of the State Insurance Department of qualified entry. In addition to resources in this country, all of a company's free funds, capital and surplus, are liable for losses wherever incurred.

To prevent confusion of these ratings with the general policyholders' ratings, the financial ratings in all cases consist of at least two letters. The letters used to indicate net safety factors are as follows:

Financial Rating	Net Safety Factor
AAAAA	$25,000,000 or more
AAAA+	20,000,000 to $25,000,000
AAAA	15,000,000 to 20,000,000
AAA+	12,500,000 to 15,000,000
AAA	10,000,000 to 12,500,000
AA+	7,500,000 to 10,000,000
AA	5,000,000 to 7,500,000
BBBB+	3,750,000 to 5,000,000
BBBB	2,500,000 to 3,750,000
BBB+	1,500,000 to 2,500,000
BBB	1,000,000 to 1,500,000
BB+	750,000 to 1,000,000
BB	500,000 to 750,000
CCC	250,000 to 500,000
CC	250,000 or less

APPENDIX B

Bibliography

Part I The Nature of Risk and Risk Bearing

Books:

American Management Association. *The Changing Picture in Corporate Insurance,* Insurance Series No. 114. New York: American Management Association, 1957.

――――. *Corporate Insurance Buying: Guides to Improved Efficiency,* Insurance Series No. 102. New York: American Management Association, 1954.

――――. *Corporate Risks Management: Current Problems and Perspectives.* New York: American Management Association, 1956.

――――. *A Critical Look at the Insurance Buyer's Role,* Insurance Series No. 100. New York: American Management Association, 1953.

――――. *A Critical Scrutiny of Corporate Insurance Buying,* Insurance Series No. 111. New York: American Management Association, 1955.

――――. *Factors in Reducing Insurance Costs,* Insurance Series No. 117. New York: American Management Association, 1957.

――――. *Hazards and Insurance Requirements of Atomic Energy,* Insurance Series No. 117. New York: American Management Association, 1958.

――――. *Meeting New Needs in Insurance Management,* Insurance Series No. 115. New York: American Management Association, 1957.

――――. *New Factors in Corporate Insurance Planning,* Insurance Series No. 104. New York: American Management Association, 1954.

――――. *Operating Guides for the Corporate Insurance Buyer,* Insurance Series No. 98. New York: American Management Association, 1953.

――――. *Problem Areas in Corporate Insurance Planning,* Insurance Series No. 113. New York: American Management Association, 1956.

――――. *Significant Trends in Corporate Insurance,* Insurance Series No. 103. New York: American Management Association, 1954.

――――. *What's New in Risk Management?* Insurance Series No. 27. New York: American Management Association, 1959.

Hardy, C. O. *Risk and Risk-Bearing.* Chicago: University of Chicago Press, 1931.

Harper, Floyd S. and George A. Parks. *Elementary Mathematics of Life Insurance.* New York: Life Office Management Association, 1955.

785

Knight, Frank H. *Risk, Uncertainty and Profit.* Boston: Houghton Mifflin Company, 1921.

Kulp, C. A. *Casualty Insurance.* New York: The Ronald Press Company, 1956.

La Place. *Essai Philosophique sur les Probabilities.* Translated by F. W. Truscott and F. L. Emory. New York: Dover, 1951

McCormick, Roy C. *Coverages Applicable,* Eighth Edition. Indianapolis: Rough Notes Company, 1956.

Mielke, R. G. *Insurance Surveys: Business-Personal; A Guide for Selling and Making Manufacturing, Mercantile, and Personal Risk Insurance Surveys,* Fourth Edition. Indianapolis: Rough Notes Company, 1959.

Pfeffer, Irving. *Insurance and Economic Theory.* Homewood, Ill.: Richard D. Irwin, Inc., 1956.

———. *The Nature and Significance of Insurance Principles.* Philadelphia: The Society of Chartered Property and Casualty Underwriters, 1958.

Shackle, G. L. S. *Decision, Order, and Time in Human Affairs.* Cambridge, England: University Press, 1961.

Snider, H. W. *Readings in Property and Casualty Insurance.* Homewood, Ill.: Richard D. Irwin, Inc., 1959.

Werbel, B. G. *General Insurance Guide.* New York: Werbel Publishing Company, 1954, and supplements.

Willett, A. H. *Economic Theory of Risk and Insurance.* Philadelphia: University of Pennsylvania Press, 1951.

Zoffer, H. J. *Corporate Risk Analysis.* Pittsburgh: Bureau of Business Research, University of Pittsburgh, 1957.

Periodicals:

Babbitt, Robert M., Jr. "The Place of Self-Insurance in the Business," *The Annals of the Society of Chartered Property and Casualty Underwriters,* Vol. XI (No. 3, February, 1959).

Belth, Joseph M. "The Cost of Life Insurance to the Policyowner—A Single Year Attained Age System," *The Journal of Insurance,* Vol. XXVIII (No. 4, December, 1961).

Berridge, William A. "Economic Research as an Aid to Management Planning: A Case Study of One Life Insurance Company," *The Journal of Insurance,* Vol. XXIV (No. 3, December, 1957).

Bickley, John H. "The Nature of Business Risk," *The Journal of Insurance,* Vol. XXV (No. 4, February, 1959).

———. "Public Utility Stability and Risk," *The Journal of Insurance,* Vol. XXVI (No. 2, Summer, 1959).

Blanchard, Ralph H. "Risk as a Special Subject Study," *The Journal of Insurance,* Vol. XXVI (No. 1, Spring, 1959).

Clark, J. B. "Insurance and Business Profit," *The Quarterly, Journal of Economics,* Vol. VII (pp. 40–54, October, 1892).

Friedman, M., and L. J. Savage. "The Utility Analysis of Choices Involving Risk," *Journal of Political Economy,* Vol. LVI (1948).

Greene, Mark R. "Marketing Research as an Aid to Insurance Management," *The Journal of Insurance,* Vol. XXIV (No. 3, December, 1957).

———. "Applications of Mathematics to Insurance and Risk Management," *The Journal of Insurance,* Vol. XXVIII (No. 1, March, 1961).

Hawley, F. B. "The Risk Theory of Profit," *The Quarterly, Journal of Economics,* Vol. VII (pp. 459–79, July, 1893).

Houston, David B. "Risk Theory," *The Journal of Insurance,* Vol. XXVII (No. 1, March, 1960).

Latane, Henry A. "Individual Risk Preference in Portfolio Selection," *The Journal of Finance,* Vol. XV (No. 1, March, 1960).

Loman, H. J. "Credit Insurance," *Encyclopedia of the Social Sciences,* Vol. IV (Second Edition). New York: The MacMillan Company, 1948.

McCauley, J. L. "Credit Insurance," *The Insurance Law Journal,* October, 1956.

Morrison, Robert M. "Atomic Energy—A Problem for Insurance," *The Annals of the Society of Chartered Property and Casualty Underwriters,* Vol. VIII (No. 1, February, 1956).

Pither, Allan L. "The Position of the Insurance Carriers," *The Annals of the Society of Chartered Property and Casualty Underwriters,* Vol. XI (No. 1, February, 1959).

Rennie, Robert. "The Measurement of Risk," *The Journal of Insurance,* Vol. XXVIII (No. 1, March, 1960).

Rodda, William H. "Self Insurance and Large Deductibles," *The Annals of the Society of Chartered Property and Casualty Underwriters,* Vol. XI (No. 1, February, 1959).

Seldow, Leona. "Inter-Relationship of Economics and Insurance," *The Annals of the Society of Chartered Property and Casualty Underwriters,* Vol. XI (No. 1, February, 1959).

Snider, Dr. H. Wayne. "The Risk Manager," *Best's Insurance News,* Fire and Casualty Edition, Vol. LVI (No. 9, January, 1956).

Snyder, Arthur. "Economics and Insurance," *Best's Insurance News,* Fire and Casualty Edition, Vol. LVII (No. 1, May, 1956).

Strain, Robert W. "The Impact of Increased Life Insurance Purchases on the Consumption Function," *The Journal of Insurance,* Vol. XXV (No. 4, February, 1959).

Theobald, Henry E. "Self Insurance from the Buyer's Viewpoint," *The Annals of the Society of Chartered Property and Casualty Underwriters,* Vol. XI (No. 1, February, 1959).

Torrance, Charles M. "Gross Flows of Funds through Savings and Loan Associations," *The Journal of Finance,* Vol. XV (No. 2, May, 1960).

Williams, C. Arthur, Jr. "Game-Theory and Insurance Consumption," *The Journal of Insurance,* Vol. XXVII (No. 4, December, 1960).

Williams, Walter. "A Comment on Insurance and the Consumption Function," *The Journal of Insurance,* Vol. XXVII (No. 2, June, 1960).

Willis, J. Brooke. "Gross Flows of Funds through Mutual Savings Banks," *The Journal of Finance,* Vol. XV (No. 2, May, 1960).

Wright, Kenneth M. "Gross Flows of Funds through Life Insurance Companies," *The Journal of Finance,* Vol. XV (No. 2, May, 1960).

Part II   The Insurance Institution

Books:

Best, A. M. *Fire and Casualty Aggregates and Averages.* New York: A. M. Best Company, annually.

Best, A. M. *Insurance Reports.* New York: A. M. Best Company, annually.

Bickley, J. S. *Trends and Problems in the Distribution of Property-Liability Insurance.* Columbus: Bureau of Business Research, College of Commerce, Ohio State University, 1956.

Blair, B. Franklin. *Interpreting Life Insurance Company Annual Reports.* Philadelphia: The American College of Life Underwriters, 1958.

Controllers' Congress, National Retail Dry Goods Association. *Expense Saving Ideas.* New York: National Retail Dry Goods Association, 1959.

————. *Insurance Manual for Departmentized Stores.* New York: National Retail Dry Goods Association, 1955.

Federal Crop Insurance Corporation. *Report of the Manager.* Washington, D. C.: U. S. Government Printing Office, annually.

Gibbs, D. E. W. *Lloyds of London: A Study in Individualism.* New York: St. Martin's Press, 1957.

Kenney, Roger. *Fundamentals of Fire and Casualty Strength.* Dedham, Mass.: Roger Kenney, 1957.

Krogh, Harold C., and Frank P. Dobyns. *The Local Insurance Agency in Kansas.* Lawrence, Kans.: Bureau of Business Research, School of Business, University of Kansas, 1957.

Kulp, C. A. *Casualty Insurance.* New York: The Ronald Press Company, 1956.

Maclean, J. B. *Life Insurance.* New York: McGraw-Hill Book Company, Inc., 1957.

McGill, Dan M. *Life Insurance Sales Management.* Homewood, Ill.: Richard D. Irwin, Inc., 1957.

Michelbacher, G. F., and others. *Multiple-line Insurance.* New York: McGraw-Hill Book Company, Inc., 1957.

National Association of Insurance Commissioners. *Proceedings of Annual Meeting.* National Association of Insurance Commissioners, annually.

New York Insurance Department. *Examination of Insurance Companies,* Volumes 1, 2, 4. Albany: New York Insurance Department, 1954.

Reed, P. B. *Fire Insurance Underwriting.* New York: McGraw-Hill Book Company, Inc., 1940.

Rees, Fred H. *Claims Philosophy and Practice.* Philadelphia: The Spectator, 1947.

Scharf, Robert. *Beware of the Three-Legged Ostrich: A Study in Best Investments.* Atlanta: Consumer Economics, Inc., 1956.

Thompson, Kenneth. *Reinsurance.* Philadelphia: The Spectator, 1951.

Periodicals:

Editorial. "Operating Expenses—Stock, Mutual," *Best's Insurance News,* Fire and Casualty Edition, Vol. LVIII (No. 8, December, 1957).

Hayes, Douglas A. "Evaluating the Investment Management Record of Fire Insurance Companies," *The Analysts Journal,* Vol. XIV (No. 4, August, 1958).

Hedges, Bob A. "Evaluation of Property Insurance Companies' Expense Ratios," *The Journal of Insurance,* Vol. XXV (No. 4, February, 1959).

Heins, Dr. Richard M. "Extension of Group Marketing Principles to Property and Casualty Insurance," *The Annals of the Society of Chartered Property and Casualty Underwriters,* Vol. X (No. 1, January, 1958).

Huebner, S. S. "Future Patterns of Life Insurance Distribution—An Educator's View," *The Journal of Insurance,* Vol. XXIV (No. 3, December, 1957).

Icks, Robert J. "American Agency System," *Best's Insurance News,* Fire and Casualty Edition, Vol. LIX (No. 1, May, 1958).

Kenney, Roger. "Critique of the American Agency System," *The Journal of Insurance,* Vol. XXV (No. 1, July, 1958).

Rennie, Robert A. "Management's Approach to Alternative Methods of Insurance Distribution," *The Journal of Insurance,* Vol. XXIV (No. 3, December, 1957).

Schwentker, F. J. "The Life Insurance Agency System," *The Journal of Insurance,* Vol. XXV (No. 1, July, 1958).

Weghorn, John C. "The American Agency System," *Best's Insurance News,* Fire and Casualty Edition, Vol. LVI (No. 3, July, 1955).

Zimmerman, C. J. "Future Patterns of Life Insurance Distribution—A Company View," *The Journal of Insurance,* Vol. XXIV (No. 3, December, 1957).

Part III   Fundamentals of Insurance Contracts

Books:

Angell, Frank J. *Insurance Principles and Practices.* New York: The Ronald Press Company, 1959.

Freedman, Warren. *Richards on the Law of Insurance.* New York: Baker, Voorhis & Company, 1952.

Goldstein, Herman B. *Cases on Insurance,* Second Edition. Chicago: John Marshall Law School, 1959.

Horn, Harold M., and D. Bruce Mansfield. *The Life Insurance Contract.* New York: Life Office Management Association, 1948.

Mehr, Robert I., and Emerson Cammack. *Principles of Insurance,* Revised Edition. Homewood, Ill.: Richard D. Irwin, Inc., 1957.

Patterson, Edwin Wilhite. *Cases and Materials on the Law of Insurance,* Third Edition. Brooklyn: Foundation Press, 1955.

———. *Essentials of Insurance Law.* New York: McGraw-Hill Book Company, Inc., 1957.

Smith, Chester Howard. *Smith's Review of Insurance for Law School and State Bar Examinations.* St. Paul: West Publishing Company, 1958.

Vance, William R. *Handbook on the Law of Insurance,* Third Edition, edited by Buist M. Anderson. St. Paul: West Publishing Company, 1951.

Periodicals:

Clark, Howard B. "Attractive Nuisance," *Best's Insurance News,* Fire and Casualty Edition, Vol. LVII (No. 5, September, 1956).

Friedman, Milton. "Landlords, Tenants and Fires," *Best's Insurance News,* Fire and Casualty Edition, Vol. LIX (No. 2, June, 1958).

Part IV   Major Property and Liability Insurance Contracts

Books:

Ackerman, S. B. *Insurance.* New York: The Ronald Press Company, 1939.

American Insurance Association. *Studies of Floods and Flood Damage 1952–1955.* New York: American Insurance Association, 1956.

Angell, F. J. *Insurance Principles and Practices.* New York: The Ronald Press Company, 1959.

Association of Casualty and Surety Companies. *Statutes Affecting Liability Insurance.* New York: Association of Casualty and Surety Companies, 1957.

Backman, Jules. *Surety Rate-Making, A Study of the Economics of Suretyship.* New York: The Surety Association of America, 1948.

Bardwell, Edward C., and Robert E. Schultz. *Property Insurance.* New York: Rinehart and Company, 1959.

Crist, G. W. *Corporate Suretyship,* Second Edition. New York: McGraw-Hill Book Company, Inc., 1950.

Elliott, Curtis M. *Property and Casualty Insurance.* New York: McGraw-Hill Book Company, Inc., 1960.

Huebner, S. S., and Kenneth Black, Jr. *Property Insurance,* Fourth Edition. New York: Appleton-Century-Crofts, 1957.

Klein, H. C. *Business Interruption Insurance.* Indianapolis: Rough Notes Company, 1957.

Institute of Oregon Underwriters. *Comprehensive Liability Insurance.* Eugene, Ore.: Association of Insurance Agents and Bureau of Business Research, School of Business Administration, University of Oregon, 1957.

The Insurance Industry. Hearings Before the Subcommittee on Antitrust and Monopoly of the Committee on the Judiciary, United States Senate, 85th Congress, Second Session, Pursuant to S. Res. 231, Part 1, *Aviation Insurance.* Washington, D. C.: U. S. Government Printing Office, 1959.

Lincoln, Walter O. *Building Construction as Applied to Fire Insurance.* Philadelphia: The Spectator, 1949.

Lucas, Julian. *The Standard Fire Insurance Policy of the State of New York.* New York: Davis Dorland & Company, 1943.

Mackall, L. E. *The Principles of Surety Underwriting,* Sixth Edition. Philadelphia: The Spectator, 1951.

Magee, John H. *General Insurance,* Sixth Edition. Homewood, Ill.: Richard D. Irwin, Inc., 1961.

————. *Property Insurance.* Homewood, Ill.: Richard D. Irwin, Inc., 1955.

McGill, Dan M. *All Lines Insurance.* Homewood, Ill.: Richard D. Irwin, Inc., 1960.

Mehr, Robert I., and Emerson Cammack. *Principles of Insurance,* Third Edition. Homewood, Ill.: Richard D. Irwin, Inc., 1961.

Michelbacher, G. F., and others. *Multiple-line Insurance.* New York: McGraw-Hill Book Company, Inc., 1957.

Montesani, Frank. *Report of Examinations of Credit Insurance Writing Companies.* New York: New York State Insurance Department, 1945.

Mowbray, A. H., and Ralph H. Blanchard. *Insurance, Its Theory and Practice in the U. S.,* Fifth Edition. New York: McGraw-Hill Book Company, Inc., 1961.

Participation by Small Business in Foreign Exports. Hearings before a subcommittee of the Committee on Banking and Currency, U. S. Senate, 80th Congress, First Session on S. 414. Washington, D. C.: U. S. Government Printing Office, 1947.

Pierce, John Eugene. *Development of Comprehensive Insurance for the Household.* Homewood, Ill.: Richard D. Irwin, Inc., 1958.

Ratcliffe, D. T. *General Liability Insurance Handbook.* Philadelphia: McCombs & Co., 1954.

Reed, P. B. *Fire Insurance Underwriting.* New York: McGraw-Hill Book Company, Inc., 1940.

Riegel, R., and J. S. Miller. *Insurance Principles and Practices,* Fourth Edition. Englewood Cliffs, N. J.: Prentice-Hall, Inc., 1959.

Rodda, W. H. *Fire and Property Insurance.* Englewood Cliffs, N. J.: Prentice-Hall, Inc., 1958.

————. *Inland Marine and Transportation Insurance,* Second Edition. Englewood Cliffs, N. J.: Prentice-Hall, Inc., 1958.

Shenkman, E. M. *Insurance Against Credit Risks.* London: P. S. King & Son, Ltd., 1935.

Snider, H. W. *Readings In Property and Casualty Insurance.* Homewood, Illinois: Richard D. Irwin, Inc., 1959.

Spell, R. V. *Public Liability Hazards.* Indianapolis: Rough Notes, 1955.

Trapp, J. T. *Credit Insurance: A Factor in Bank Lending.* Baltimore: American Credit Indemnity Company, 1953.

Werbel, L. G. *Multiple Peril Firms and Policies* (formerly *General Insurance Guide*). West Hempstead, N. Y.: Insurance Educational Publications, 1957, and supplements.

Winter, W. D. *Marine Insurance.* New York: McGraw-Hill Book Company, Inc., 1952.

Zoffer, H. Jerome. *The History of Automobile Liability Insurance Rating.* Pittsburgh: University of Pittsburgh Press, 1959.

Periodicals:

Bonnasse, P. "L'assurance-credit a l'Exportation," *Revue Generale des Assurances Terrestres.* Paris: 1949.

Clarke, George W. "Loss Logic—Business Interruption Claims," *Best's Insurance News,* Fire and Casualty Edition, Vol. LIX (No. 4, August, 1958).

Harger, Kenneth H. "Real Estate Leases," *Best's Insurance News,* Fire and Casualty Edition, Vol. LVIII (No. 5, September, 1957).

Hirst, B. B. "Forest Fire Insurance," *Insurance News,* Vol. XLIV (No. 10, October, 1956).

Hollis, Stanley E. "Foreign Credit Insurance and its Ramifications," *Exporters' Digest,* issue, 1953.

Howard, William M. "Perpetual Fire Insurance," *The Journal of Finance,* Vol. XIII (No. 1, March, 1958).

Johnstone, Q. "Title Insurance," *Yale Law Journal,* Vol. 66 (pp. 492–524, F. 1957).

Mason, Charles. "Charitable Immunity," *Best's Insurance News,* Fire and Casualty Edition, Vol. LVIII (No. 6, October, 1957).

McCauley, J. L. "Credit Insurance: Its History and Functions," in *Examination of Insurance Companies,* Vol. 4. New York: New York Insurance Department, 1955.

National Underwriter Company. "Multiple Insurance" and "Dwellings," *Fire, Casualty, and Surety Bulletins,* published continuously as a loose-leaf service. Cincinnati: National Underwriter Company.

Patrick, A. N. "The Insurance of Trade Credits," *The Journal of the Chartered Insurance Institute,* London: 1947.

Rodda, William H. "Multiple Line Headaches," *Best's Insurance News,* Fire and Casualty Edition, Vol. LVIII (No. 9, January, 1958).

St. Louis Chapter, Society of Chartered Property and Casualty Underwriters. "The Private Car Owner's Liability to His Passenger," *The Annals of the Society of Chartered Property and Casualty Underwriters,* Vol. VIII (No. 1, February, 1956).

Wiederkehr, E. J. "Product Liability Insurance," *Casualty and Surety Journal,* Vol. XIX (No. 3, May, 1958).

Part V   Life and Health Insurance

Books:

Advisory Council on Social Security Financing. *Financing Old-Age, Survivors, and Disability Insurance.* Washington, D. C.: U. S. Government Printing Office, 1959.

Allan, W. Scott. *Rehabilitation, a Community Challenge.* New York: John Wiley & Sons, Inc., 1958.

Anderson, Odin W. *Voluntary Health Insurance in Two Cities.* Cambridge, Mass.: Harvard University Press, 1957.

———— and Jacob J. Feldman. *Family Medical Costs and Voluntary Health Insurance: A Nationwide Survey.* New York: McGraw-Hill Book Company, Inc., 1956.

Association of Teachers of Preventive Medicine, Committee on Medical Care Teaching. *Readings on Medical Care.* Durham, N. C.: University of North Carolina Press, 1958.

Bankers Trust Company. *A Study of Industrial Retirement Plans.* New York: Bankers Trust Company, 1960.

Black, Kenneth, Jr. *Group Annuities.* Homewood, Ill.: Richard D. Irwin, Inc., 1955.

Chapman, F. P. *The Standard Nonforfeiture and Valuation Legislation.* Philadelphia: American College of Life Underwriters, 1949.

Collins, S. D. *Long-Time Trends in Illness and Medical Care.* U. S. Department of Health, Education and Welfare, Public Health Service, Public Health Monograph No. 43. Washington, D. C.: U. S. Government Printing Office, 1957.

Dickerson, O. D. *Health Insurance.* Homewood, Ill.: Richard D. Irwin, Inc., 1959.

————. *Long Term Guaranteed Renewable Disability Insurance.* Philadelphia: University of Pennsylvania Press, 1955.

Dover, Victor. *A Handbook to Marine Insurance; Being a Text-Book of the History, Law, and Practice of an Integral Part of Commerce for the Business of Man and the Student.* London: H. F. & G. Witherby, 1957.

Dublin, Louis I., Alfred J. Lotka, and Mortimer Spiegelman. *Length of Life,* Revised Edition. New York: The Ronald Press Co., 1949.

Falk, I. S., Margaret C. Klim, and Nathan Sinai. *The Incidence of Illness and the Receipt and Costs of Medical Care Among Representative Families: Experiences in Twelve Consecutive Months During 1928–1931.* Committee on the Costs of Medical Care, Report No. 26. Chicago: University of Chicago Press, 1933.

Faulkner, Edwin J. *Health Insurance.* New York: McGraw-Hill Book Company, Inc., 1960.

Fessler, Max E. *Hail Insurance on Kansas Wheat.* Lawrence, Kans.: Bureau of Business Research, School of Business, University of Kansas, 1958.

Flitcraft, Inc. *Flitcraft Compend.* New York: Flitcraft, Inc., annually.

————. Settlement Options. New York: Flitcraft, Inc., annually.

Follmann, J. F., Jr. *Voluntary Health Insurance and Medical Care.* New York: Health Insurance Association of America, 1958.

Gagliardo, D. *American Social Insurance,* Revised Edition. New York: Harper & Brothers, 1955.

Garbarino, Joseph W. *Health Plans and Collective Bargaining.* Berkeley: University of California Press, 1960.

Greene, Dorothy Kittner. *Digest of One Hundred Selected Health and Insurance Plans Under Collective Bargaining, Early 1958.* U. S. Department of Labor, Bureau of Labor Statistics. Washington, D. C.: U. S. Government Printing Office, 1958.

Greenough, William C. *Pensions, Meeting Price Level Changes.* Homewood, Ill.: Richard D. Irwin, Inc., 1955.

————, and Francis P. King. *Your Retirement Security—the New Oasi and Retirement Plans.* New York: American Association of University Professors, 1954.

————. *Retirement and Insurance Plans in American Colleges.* New York: Columbia University Press, 1959.

Gregg, Davis W. *Group Life Insurance,* Revised Edition. Homewood, Ill.: Richard D. Irwin, Inc., 1957.

————. *Life and Health Insurance Handbook.* Homewood, Ill.: Richard D. Irwin, Inc., 1959.

Harper, F. S., and G. A. Parke. *Elementary Mathematics of Life Insurance.* New York: Life Office Management Association, 1955.

Haber, William, and Wilbur Cohen, Jr. *Social Security Programs, Problems and Policies.* Homewood, Ill.: Richard D. Irwin, Inc., 1960.

Hamilton, James A., and Dorrance C. Bronson. *Pensions.* New York: McGraw-Hill Book Company, Inc., 1958.

Health and Medical Care in New York City. Commonwealth Fund. Cambridge: Harvard University Press, 1957.

Heinrich, H. W. *Industrial Accident Prevention,* Fourth Edition. New York: McGraw-Hill Book Company, Inc., 1959.

Herrick, Kenneth W. *Total Disability Provisions in Life Insurance Contracts.* Homewood, Ill.: Richard D. Irwin, Inc., 1956.

Horne, H. M., and D. B. Mansfield. *The Life Insurance Contract.* New York: Life Office Management Association, 1938.

Huebner, S. S. *The Economics of Life Insurance.* New York: Appleton-Century-Crofts, Inc., 1959.

————, and Kenneth Black, Jr. *Life Insurance.* New York: Appleton-Century-Crofts, Inc., 1958.

Ilse, Louise Wolters. *Group Insurance and Employee Retirement Plans.* New York: Prentice-Hall, Inc., 1953.

Jacobson, James B. *An Analysis of Group Creditors Insurance.* Newark, N. J.: Prudential Insurance Company of America, 1955.

Kip, Richard de Raismes. *Fraternal Life Insurance in America*. Tallahassee, Fla.: Florida State University Press, 1953.

Larson, R. E., and E. A. Gaumnitz. *Life Insurance Mathematics*. New York: John Wiley & Sons, Inc., 1951.

LeVita, M. H. *An Arithmetic of Life Insurance*. New York: Life Management Association, 1936.

Life Insurance Fact Book. New York: Institute of Life Insurance, annually.

Lynch, David. *The Concentration of Economic Power*. New York: Columbia University Press, 1946.

Maclean, J. B. *Life Insurance*. New York: McGraw-Hill Book Company, Inc., 1961.

McCahan, D., ed. *Accident and Sickness Insurance*. Homewood, Ill.: Richard D. Irwin, Inc., 1954.

———. *Life Insurance Trends at Mid-Century*. Philadelphia: University of Pennsylvania Press, 1950.

———, and others. *The Beneficiary in Life Insurance*. Philadelphia: University of Pennsylvania Press, 1948.

McGill, Dan M. *Fundamentals of Private Pensions*. Homewood, Ill.: Richard D. Irwin, Inc., 1955.

———. *The Beneficiary in Life Insurance*. Homewood, Ill.: Richard D. Irwin, Inc., 1956.

———. *Life Insurance*. Homewood, Ill.: Richard D. Irwin, Inc., 1959.

Mehr, Robert I., and Robert W. Osler. *Modern Life Insurance*. New York: The Macmillan Company, 1961.

———, and Hugh G. Wales. *Business Life Insurance and Its Economic Applications*. Urbana, Ill.: University of Illinois Press, 1950.

Menge, Walter O., and James W. Glover. *An Introduction to the Mathematics of Life Insurance*. New York: The Macmillan Company, 1935.

Osborn, Grant M. *Compulsory Temporary Disability Insurance in the United States*. The S. S. Huebner Foundation of Insurance Education. Homewood, Ill.: Richard D. Irwin, Inc., 1958.

Osler, Robert W. *Guide to Accident and Sickness Insurance*, Revised Edition. Indianapolis: The Rough Notes Company, 1959.

Pickrell, Jesse F. *Group Health Insurance*, Revised Edition. The S. S. Huebner Foundation for Insurance Education. Homewood, Ill.: Richard D. Irwin, Inc., 1961.

Porterfield, James T. *Life Insurance Stocks as Investments*. Stanford, Calif.: Graduate School of Business, Stanford University, 1956.

President's Commission on the Health Needs of the Nation. *Building America's Health*, Vol. 2. Washington, D. C.: U. S. Government Printing Office, 1952.

A Profile of the Health Insurance Public. New York: Health Insurance Institute, 1959.

Rauch, Raymond C. *The Problem of the Uninsured Motorist in Oregon*. Eugene, Oregon: Bureau of Business Research, University of Oregon, 1959.

Redeker, Harry S. *Life Insurance Settlement Options*. Boston: Little, Brown, & Co., 1957.

Reid, Charles K., II. *Fundamentals of Government Life Insurance and Related Benefits*, Revised Edition. Philadelphia: The American College of Life Underwriters, 1959.

Schultz, Robert E. *Life Insurance Housing Projects.* Homewood, Ill. Richard D. Irwin, Inc., 1956.

Serbein, Oscar N. *Paying for Medical Care in the United States.* New York: Columbia University Press, 1953.

Snider, H. W. *Life Insurance Investment in Commercial Real Estate.* Homewood, Ill.: Richard D. Irwin, Inc., 1956.

Somers, H. M., and A. R. Somers. *Workmen's Compensation.* New York: John Wiley & Sons, Inc., 1954.

Spiegelman, Mortimer. *Ensuring Medical Care for the Aged.* The Pension Research Council. Homewood, Ill.: Richard D. Irwin, Inc., 1960.

―――. *Significant Mortality and Morbidity Trends in the United States Since 1900,* Revised Edition. Philadelphia: The American College of Life Underwriters, 1956.

S. S. Huebner Foundation for Insurance Education. *Pensions: Problems and Trends.* Homewood, Ill.: Richard D. Irwin, Inc., 1955.

Stalson, J. Owen. *Marketing Life Insurance.* Cambridge, Mass.: Harvard University Press, 1942.

Stephenson, Gilbert T. *Estates and Trusts,* Revised Edition. New York: Appleton-Century-Crofts, Inc., 1955.

Steiner, Peter O., and Robert Dorfman. *The Economic Status of the Aged.* Berkeley: University of California Press, 1957.

Turnbull, John G., Jr., C. Arthur Williams, and Earl F. Cheit. *Economic and Social Security.* New York: The Ronald Press Company, 1957.

Unemployment Compensation. Hearings before the Committee on Ways and Means, House of Representatives, 86th Congress, First Session, on the Subject of Proposed Amendments to the Federal Laws on Unemployment. Washington, D. C.: U. S. Government Printing Office, 1959.

U. S. Department of Health, Education, and Welfare, Public Health Service. *Health Statistics from the United States National Health Survey,* Series B-1. Washington, D. C.: U. S. Government Printing Office, 1958.

―――, Division of Public Health Methods. *The National Health Survey, 1935–1936: Significance, Scope, and Method of Nationwide Family Canvass of Sickness in Relation to Its Social and Economic Setting.* Washington, D. C.: U. S. Government Printing Office, 1938.

U. S. Department of Labor, Bureau of Employment Security. *Comparison of State Unemployment Insurance Law* as of January 1, 1958. Washington, D. C.: U. S. Government Printing Office, 1958.

U. S. Internal Cooperation Administration. *Investment Guaranty Handbook; U. S. Government Guaranties Available for New American Investments Abroad under the Investment Guaranty Program.* Washington, D. C.: U. S. Government Printing Office, 1957.

Wheeler, Walter J., and Thomas L. Todd. *Safeguarding Life Insurance Proceeds.* New York: McGraw-Hill Book Company, Inc., 1940.

White, Edwin H. *Business Insurance.* Englewood Cliffs, N. J.: Prentice-Hall, Inc., 1956.

―――. *Fundamentals of Federal Income, Estate and Gift Taxes,* Fifth Edition. Indianapolis: Research & Review Service of America, Inc., 1959.

Welfare and Pension Plans Investigation. Report of the Committee on Labor and Public Welfare, United States Senate, 84th Congress, Second Session; together with Supplemental Views of Mr. Allott and a Statement by Mr. Neely; pursuant to S. Res. 225 as amended and S. Res. 40 as amended, Washington, D. C.: U. S. Government Printing Office, 1956.

Williams, C. A. *Price Discrimination in Property and Liability Insurance.* Studies in Economics and Business No. 19. Minneapolis: University of Minnesota Press, 1959.

Periodicals:

Bickley, John S. "The Nature and Methodology of the Insurance Survey Course," Proceedings of the 18th Annual Meeting, *Journal of the American Association of University Teachers of Insurance,* Vol. XXI (No. 1, March, 1954).

Chastain, James J. "The A, B, C's of Life Insurance Rate and Reserve Computation," *The Journal of Insurance,* Vol. XXVII (No. 4, December, 1960).

Conway, Richard D. "Effect of Income Tax on Insurance Buying," *The Annals of the Society of Chartered Property and Casualty Underwriters,* Vol. IX (No. 1, June, 1957).

Flemming, Arthur S. "Social Insurance: A Prospective View," *The Journal of Insurance,* 27 1 (March, 1960).

Greene, Mark R. "Federal Income Taxes and the Variable Annuitant," *The Journal of Insurance,* Vol. XXV (No. 4, February, 1959).

————. "Life Insurance Buying in Inflation," Proceedings of the 18th Annual Meeting, *Journal of the American Association of University Teachers of Insurance,* Vol. XXI (No. 1, March, 1954).

Greenough, William C. "Variable Annuities through CREF," *The Journal of Insurance,* Vol. XXVII (No. 1, March, 1960).

Holran, Virginia T., and Albert Hermalin. "Who Owns Life Insurance and What Do People Think about It?" *Best's Insurance News,* Life Edition, Vol. LVI (No. 11, March, 1956).

Johnson, George E. "The Market for Equity Annuities," *The Journal of Insurance,* Vol. XXV (No. 4, February, 1959).

Loewy, Harris. "Net Cash Moneyflows through Life Insurance Companies," *The Journal of Finance,* Vol. XI (No. 4, December, 1956).

McCracken, Paul W. "Are Variable Annuities the Answer to Inflation?" *The Journal of Finance,* Vol. XI (No. 2, May, 1956).

Mehr, Robert I. "The Variable Annuity," *The Journal of Finance,* Vol. XIII (No. 3, September, 1958).

O'Connor, James C. "All-Line Insurance," *The Journal of Insurance,* Vol. XXVI (No. 1, Spring, 1959).

Patterson, E. W. "Insurable Interest in Life, *Columbia Law Review,* Vol. 18, p. 381.

Peterson, Charles A. "Credit Life Insurance," *Best's Insurance News,* Life Edition, Vol. LVIII (No. 9, January, 1958).

Scharf, Robert. "Investment Dilemmas," *Best's Insurance News,* Life Edition, Vol. LIII (No. 11, March, 1958).

Sternhill, C. M. "The New Standard Ordinary Mortality Table," *Transactions of Actuarial Society of America,* March, 1957.

Weiss, Edward H. "How Much is Your Life Worth?" *Best's Insurance News,* Life Edition, Vol. LVII (No. 8, December, 1956).

Part VI   Government Regulation of Insurance

Books:

Government Insurance in the United States. New York: Association of Casualty and Surety Companies, Department of Research, 1950.

Gregg, Davis W., and Dan M. McGill. *World Insurance Trends.* Proceedings of the First International Insurance Conference. Philadelphia: University of Pennsylvania Press, 1957.

The Insurance Industry, Part 1, Aviation Insurance. Hearings before the Subcommittee on Antitrust and Monopoly of the Committee on the Judiciary, United States Senate, 85th Congress, Second Session, Pursuant to S. Res. 231, Washington, D. C.: U. S. Government Printing Office, 1959.

The Insurance Industry, Part 3, Ocean Marine, Rating and State Rate Regulation. Hearings before the Subcommittee on Antitrust and Monopoly of the Committee on the Judiciary, United States Senate, 86th Congress, First Session, Pursuant to S. Res. 57. Washington, D. C.: U. S. Government Printing Office, 1960.

The Insurance Industry, Aviation, Ocean Marine, and State Regulation. Report of the Committee on the Judiciary, United States Senate; together with Individual Views Made by Its Subcommittee on Antitrust and Monopoly; 86th Congress, Pursuant to S. Res. 238. Washington, D. C.: U. S. Government Printing Office, 1960.

Kimball, S. L. *Insurance and Public Policy.* Madison, Wisconsin: University of Wisconsin Press, 1960.

Life Insurance Company Income Tax Act of 1959. Report together with Supplemental Views of the Committee on Finance, United States Senate, to accompany H.R. 4245, A Bill Relating to the Taxation of the Income of Life Insurance Companies. Washington, D. C.: U. S. Government Printing Office, 1959.

Michelbacher, G. F., and others. *Multiple Line Insurance.* New York: McGraw-Hill Book Company, Inc., 1957.

New York Insurance Department. *Examination of Insurance Companies.* Albany: New York Insurance Department, 1954, Vols. I, II, III, IV, V.

Taxation of Income of Life Insurance Companies. Hearings before the subcommittee on Internal Revenue Taxation of the Committee on Ways and Means, House of Representatives, 85th Congress, Second Session. Washington, D. C.: U. S. Government Printing Office, 1958.

Temporary National Economic Committee. *Investigation of Concentration of Economic Power,* Monograph No. 28, Study of Legal Reserve Life Insurance Companies. Washington, D. C.: U. S. Government Printing Office, 1941.

Williams, C. A. *Price Discrimination in Property and Liability Insurance.* Studies in Economics and Business No. 19. Minneapolis: University of Minnesota Press, 1959.

Periodicals:

Davis, S. C. "Insurance Company Investment Portfolio," *Annals of Chartered Property and Casualty Underwriters,* Vol. XI (No. 1, February, 1959).

Faust, J. Edward. "Automobile Bodily Injury Liability Rate-Making on a Prospective Basis," *Proceedings of the Casualty Actuarial Society,* Vols. XLIV, LXXXI, and LXXXII (1957).

Hamilton, John S., Jr. "Antitrust Decisions," *Best's Insurance News,* Fire and Casualty Edition, Vol. LIX (No. 9, January, 1958).

Hansen, Victor R. "Insurance and the Antitrust Laws," *The Journal of Insurance,* Vol. XXVI (No. 1, Spring, 1959).

Haskell, George D. "Taxation of Property and Casualty Insurance Companies," *The Journal of Insurance,* Vol. XXVI (No. 1, Spring, 1959).

Hurley, Robert L. "A Credibility Framework for Gauging Fire Classification Experience," *Proceedings of the Casualty Actuarial Society,* Vols. XLI, LXXV, and LXXVI (1954).

Kelly, A. B. "How Factory Mutual Rates are Established," *National Insurance Buyer,* November, 1957.

Lent, George E. "A More Permanent Formula for the Taxation of Life Insurance," *The Journal of Insurance,* Vol. XXVII (No. 4, December, 1960).

Marshall, Ralph M. "Workmen's Compensation Insurance Ratemaking," *Proceedings of the Casualty Actuarial Society,* Vols. XLI, LXXV, and LXXVI (1954).

Otteson, Paul M. "Group Accident and Health Therapeutic Benefits–Measurement of Loss Costs for Rate Making Purposes," *Proceedings of the Casualty Actuarial Society,* Vols. XLI, LXXV, and LXXVI (1954).

Stern, Philipp K. "Current Rate Making Procedures for Automobile Liability Insurance," *Proceedings of the Casualty Actuarial Society,* Vols. XLIII, LXXIX, and LXXX (1956).

Williams, Ira Jewell. "Should Insurance Be Taxed?" *Best's Insurance News,* Life Edition, Vol. LVIII (No. 6, October, 1957).

INDEX